# Lawyering Skills and the Lega

*Lawyering Skills and the Legal Process* bridges the gap between academic and practical law for students undertaking skills-based and clinical legal education courses at university. It emphasises the extent to which lawyering is a dynamic process, shaped by a range of legal, business and ethical considerations, and encourages students to develop a critical and reflective approach to their own learning which is designed to help them to manage this dynamic environment.

The student's oral and written communication, group working, problem solving and conflict resolution skills are developed in a range of legal contexts: client interviewing, drafting, managing cases, legal negotiation and advocacy. The book is designed specifically to help students to:

- Practise and develop skills that will be essential in a range of occupations.
- Develop a deeper understanding of the English legal process and the lawyer's role in that process.
- Enhance their understanding of the relationship between legal skills and ethics.
- Understand how they learn and how they can make their learning more effective.

This book provides a stimulating, accessible and challenging approach to understanding the problems and uncertainties of practising law that goes beyond the standard approaches to lawyers' skills.

CAROLINE MAUGHAN is Principal Lecturer in Law at the Law Faculty, University of the West of England. She currently teaches lawyers' skills to undergraduates and Bar students.

JULIAN WEBB is Professor of Law, School of Law, University of Westminster. He teaches lawyers' skills, philosophy of law and dispute resolution.

# The Law in Context Series

Editors: William Twining (University College London) and
Christopher McCrudden (Lincoln College, Oxford)

Since 1970 the Law in Context series has been in the forefront of the movement to broaden the study of law. It has been a vehicle for the publication of innovative scholarly books that treat law and legal phenomena critically in their social, political, and economic contexts from a variety of perspectives. The series particularly aims to publish scholarly legal writing that brings fresh perspectives to bear on new and existing areas of law taught in universities. A contextual approach involves treating legal subjects broadly, using materials from other social sciences, and from any other discipline that helps to explain the operation in practice of the subject under discussion. It is hoped that this orientation is at once more stimulating and more realistic than the bare exposition of legal rules. The series includes original books that have a different emphasis from traditional legal text-books, while maintaining the same high standards of scholarship. They are written primarily for undergraduate and graduate students of law and of other disciplines, but most also appeal to a wider readership. In the past, most books in the series have focused on English law, but recent publications include books on European law, globalisation, transnational legal processes, and comparative law.

## Books in the series

Anderson, Schum & Twining: *Analysis of Evidence*
Ashworth: *Sentencing and Criminal Justice*
Barton & Douglas: *Law and Parenthood*
Bell: *French Legal Cultures*
Bercusson: *European Labour Law*
Birkinshaw: *European Public Law*
Birkinshaw: *Freedom of Information: The Law, the Practice and the Ideal*
Cane: *Atiyah's Accidents, Compensation and the Law*
Clarke & Kohler: *Property Law: Commentary and Materials*
Collins: *The Law of Contract*
Davies: *Perspectives on Labour Law*
de Sousa Santos: *Toward a New Legal Common Sense*
Diduck: *Law's Families*
Elworthy & Holder: *Environmental Protection: Text and Materials*
Fortin: *Children's Rights and the Developing Law*
Glover-Thomas: *Reconstructing Mental Health Law and Policy*
Gobert & Punch: *Rethinking Corporate Crime*
Harlow & Rawlings: *Law and Administration: Text and Materials*
Harris: *An Introduction to Law*
Harris: *Remedies in Contract and Tort*
Harvey: *Seeking Asylum in the UK: Problems and Prospects*

# Lawyering Skills and the Legal Process

Second edition

**Caroline Maughan**
*University of the West of England*

*and*

**Julian Webb**
*University of Westminster*

CAMBRIDGE
UNIVERSITY PRESS

CAMBRIDGE UNIVERSITY PRESS
Cambridge, New York, Melbourne, Madrid, Cape Town, Singapore, São Paulo

Cambridge University Press
The Edinburgh Building, Cambridge CB2 2RU, UK

Published in the United States of America by Cambridge University Press, New York

www.cambridge.org
Information on this title: www.cambridge.org/9780521619509

First published 1995
This edition published by Cambridge University Press 2005
Reprinted 2006

Printed in the United Kingdom at the University Press, Cambridge

*A catalogue record for this book is available from the British Library*

ISBN-13 978-0-521-61950-9 paperback
ISBN-10 0-521-61950-5 paperback

# Contents

# Preface to the second edition

This book provides a bridge between academic and practical law. Its purpose is to introduce you to a set of highly transferable oral and written communication, group working, problem-solving and conflict resolution skills, and to develop them in a range of lawyering contexts: client interviewing, drafting, managing cases, legal negotiation and advocacy. The aims of this exercise are not to turn you, the reader, into a ready-formed legal practitioner, but:

- to help you develop a range of skills and attributes that will be useful to you in a variety of occupational settings;
- to enable you to experience and reflect critically on the problems and uncertainties of 'real' law, from the perspective of both lawyers and their clients;
- to enhance your understanding of the interplay between legal knowledge, skills and values in the lawyering process;
- to encourage and empower you to understand your own learning processes and to reflect critically upon them.

It is this dual emphasis on understanding lawyers' skills 'in context' – whereby our understanding is shaped by the contributions of socio-legal research into what lawyers do – and on reflection and critique which we believe distinguishes our 'academic' approach from the more functional emphasis of the vocational courses. At the same time we share with the vocational courses (and any undergraduate skills-based course for that matter) a belief that learning has to be grounded in *doing*. Skills are not acquired passively, but actively by experimentation and practice. Please do not skip the Introduction which follows, where we talk extensively about the learning approach we take and our expectations of you, the reader.

The materials in this book are based on well over a decade of teaching skills to law undergraduates at a number of universities. We have written the book primarily for students in England and Wales on law degree programmes possessing stand-alone skills and clinical modules. We were delighted that the first edition was also used outside this jurisdiction, and on some professional courses where students have been encouraged to think beyond the technical aspects of skills acquisition.

Much has changed in the nine years since we wrote our first Preface. Skill-based learning is far more established in our law schools today than it was in 1995, and the 'employability' of graduates has moved up the political and educational agendas. In terms of scholarship too, the volume of research into the legal profession and practice in the UK has grown significantly. Accordingly, every chapter has been updated to take account of both new research on lawyers and lawyering, and (where necessary) the extensive changes to both civil and criminal practice since the first edition. In addition to the inevitable updating and polishing, we have made other substantial changes. This edition contains an entirely new chapter (Chapter 4) on working and studying in groups – skills that are increasingly recognised to be of both pedagogic and practical importance. Chapter 6, on the ethical dimension, has been substantially re-written around a single case study, and revised to take account of the development since the mid-1990s of a whole new domestic literature on lawyers' ethics. Chapters 8 (drafting) and 9 (negotiation) have both been revised to take account of changes following the Woolf reforms, and the chapter on advocacy has been expanded into two. The first of these (Chapter 10) is now exclusively on case preparation and management in an adversarial context, and incorporates much of the material on legal problem-solving that appeared in chapter three of the first edition, while the other (Chapter 11) focuses on the courtroom skills of the advocate. Teachers in particular might also like to note that, in addition to our statement of learning objectives, each chapter now commences with a brief statement of the QAA Benchmark Skills that are supported by the materials and exercises in that chapter. We hope you find these helpful in terms of your curriculum design and development. This edition is also supported by a website which contains additional materials that we believe will be useful to both teachers and students – again we say more about this in the Introduction which follows.

Inevitably we have accrued numerous debts and obligations in the process of writing and revising this text. Our greatest debt is to Mike Maughan, who has made an incalculable contribution to our own learning and development over the years. We are particularly grateful to Professor William Twining for his advice and support, and his commitment to bringing the second edition 'home' to the *Law in Context* series. Our thanks are also due to Ron Tocknell for his excellent illustrations, and Moira Bailey for sharing her insights into values-based training, and for being both a 'guinea pig' and friendly critic for much of the new material in Chapters 6, 9 and 11. Thanks, too, to Sue Heenan, Caroline's current teaching partner at UWE. More generally, we would like to acknowledge numerous friends, colleagues and students at UWE, Westminster and elsewhere, who, knowingly or otherwise, have contributed to this book in its various manifestations. Last, but by no means least, we owe a special 'thank you' to Mike and Moira respectively for their love and support during the very protracted gestation of this edition.

Finally, to anyone reading this book: we welcome your feedback and evaluation. Whether teacher, student or practitioner, we would be pleased to hear about your experiences in using this book, and any suggestions you have for ways in which we could improve it.

Caroline Maughan
Julian Webb
*August 2004*

# Table of Statutes

## Statutes

## Statutory Instruments

## Foreign Legislation

# Table of Cases

## Cases

# Introduction

This book has a single underlying theme: that being a skilled lawyer means much more than acquiring the capacity to manipulate legal rules. It means having the ability to deal with people and their problems as a competent, ethical and socially responsible lawyer.[1] This in turn requires that skills are developed in a reflective and critical environment, through a combination of what we call 'skills' and 'process' learning.

The main skills we explore are the classic lawyering or 'DRAIN' skills – Drafting (and its underlying writing skills), Research (which we widen into a concept we call problem-solving), Advocacy, Interviewing and Negotiation. You will be expected to develop those skills by practising, by analysing your practice, and then practising some more. At this level we hope you will gain some real insights into the 'what' and the 'how' of law in action.

The 'process' dimension takes us more deeply into the 'why' of lawyering. We shall ask you to draw on your experiences of the course and to reflect on our discussions of the practice of law, together with psychological, sociological, linguistic and management research which sheds light on what really happens in the law office and the courtroom. Through this, we hope you will be able to stand back from the skills and think about lawyering as something that is socially and culturally constructed. The lawyer plays an important role as a 'gatekeeper to legal institutions and facilitator of a wide range of personal and economic transactions'.[2] How we choose to play that role, and with what consequences for ourselves and our clients are two of the most central questions about law in society. It seems extraordinary to us that legal education frequently fails to address either of them in any depth, if at all. We hope that thinking about the lawyer's role will help you determine how you will deploy the skills at your disposal.

---

1. Cf. G. S. Laser, 'Educating for Professional Competence in the Twenty-First Century: Educational Reform at Chicago–Kent College of Law' (1993) 68 *Chicago–Kent Law Review* 243. We discuss this notion of lawyering further in Chapter 1.
2. W. Felstiner, R. Abel and A. Sarat, 'The Emergence and Transformation of Disputes: Naming, Blaming, Claiming' (1981) 15 *Law and Society Review* 631 at 645; also J. McCahery and S. Picciotto, 'Creative Lawyering and Business Regulation' in Y. Dezalay and D. Sugarman, *Professional Competition and Professional Power: Lawyers, Accountants and the Social Construction of Markets*, Routledge, London and New York, 1995, p. 238 at pp. 240–1.

## The aims of this book

These are:

- To encourage you to develop:
    (1) a range of practical legal skills:
        - client interviewing and counselling;
        - ethical decision-making;
        - writing and drafting;
        - negotiating;
        - case preparation and management;
        - advocacy.
    (2) a range of general intellectual and interpersonal skills:
        - oral communication;
        - written communication;
        - team working;
        - problem-solving;
        - reflection and conceptualisation;
        - self-assessment;
        - peer evaluation.
- To increase your capacity for independent and reflective learning.
- To encourage a critical awareness of:
    - the impact of legal procedures on the lawyer and other participants in the legal process;
    - the importance of a client-centred approach to legal practice;
    - the ethical responsibilities of lawyers;
    - the value conflicts and uncertainties that arise in legal practice.

## How to use this book

WARNING: this book is not just another textbook! You cannot learn skills only by reading; skills development requires doing, and this book is designed to make you do.

Tutors can use it either as a course workbook, or as a flexible resource from which to select and adapt materials. We developed most of its content in the context of an LLB option called 'Legal Process' that we launched at the University of the West of England in 1990. This is a skills-based programme constructed around simulated case studies in the civil and criminal law. The materials are team-taught in a series of three-hour workshops, running across a full academic year. Not everything in the book is taught every year. To work through all these materials in this way would certainly take more than one academic year! With some care it is possible to pick and choose materials rather than follow everything to the letter. Many of the exercises can be undertaken by students working outside formal class contact time. The materials can also be adapted for delivery as a single semester module, or as a series of discrete skills modules (e.g. on interviewing, trial advocacy, etc). Julian has used the interviewing, writing, drafting, negotiation and ethics chapters selectively to deliver a weekly two-hour workshop to second year LLB students at Westminster since 1999. Unlike Legal Process, this is an assessed core module delivered (currently) to in excess of 300 students annually.

Tutors should also note that there is an accompanying website,[3] which replaces the short *Teachers' Guide* that we published to accompany the first edition. The website provides additional guidance for tutors on our experiential method (we also say more about that in the following sections of this introduction); additional guidance and materials for running exercises in this book,[4] and some other exercises and materials we have not included in this volume.

Teachers might also like to note that there are three exercises which require the use of questionnaire materials from outside the book. Exercise 2.8 relies on the learning styles questionnaire which is produced as part of Honey and Mumford's *Manual of Learning Styles*. We have been advised that users of the 1992 edition of the *Manual* can freely copy the questionnaire for training purposes. Later versions require you to purchase a user licence. We find the 1992 version is quite adequate for our purposes. Exercise 4.6 asks students to complete the Belbin questionnaire on team roles which can be found in R. Belbin, *Team Roles at Work* (1993), along with the necessary scoresheet. Exercise 9.2 relies on a questionnaire published in Johnson and Johnson's *Joining Together* (2003), pp. 385–7. The original is rather longer and more detailed then we really need, so we adapt it for our own purposes. There are two other exercises – 4.3 and 4.9 – for which you will need extra materials from Johnson and Johnson, pp. 83–5 and 579–81.

## Structure and rationale

We have deliberately adopted a fairly standardised structure for each chapter, which reflects our overall design of the text as a skills workbook. The format is as follows.

### Introductory material

Each chapter begins with a brief summary of its contents. This is followed by a list of learning objectives and of relevant Law Benchmark Statements. The intention of these features is to maximise the transparency of our objectives, and make clear what tutors and students can expect from each chapter. The Benchmark Statements[5] are an addition since the first edition. These Statements were intro-duced by the (UK) Quality Assurance Agency to provide a broad specification of

---

3. At www.cambridge.org/9780521619509.
4. Most materials for the exercises are incorporated into the text, however, in some cases (which we identify in the text) we want students to discover the purpose of the exercise for themselves, or have other reasons for maintaining a greater element of surprise. Providing instructions in the text would give the game away, so we have put all the materials on the website.
5. See www.qaa.ac.uk/crntwork/benchmark/law.pdf.

the skills that a law graduate can be expected to acquire in the course of a qualifying law degree. The Benchmarks are designed as outcome statements: that is, as generic behavioural indicators of what a student should be able to do by the end of the degree, and as such they do not add greatly to the more detailed learning objectives we have identified for each chapter. Nevertheless, we have included them here primarily to assist teachers in curriculum planning and design. It will be apparent from the range of Benchmark specifications included that a well-designed lawyers' skills module can help satisfy a significant part of these Benchmark requirements. In each chapter we have only emphasised those Benchmark skills that are a significant feature of that chapter. In so doing we have deliberately not laboured the extent to which some Benchmarks are supported to some degree by every chapter – notably the capacity to reflect on one's own learning (see Key Skill 5: Autonomy and ability to learn) and the ability to work in groups (see Key Skill 7: Other key skills).

**Information and exercises**

The substance of each chapter is organised to achieve three main goals:

1.  to enable students to learn experientially from exercises and activities;
2.  to provide a necessary minimum of skills and process knowledge;
3.  to encourage discussion and reflection.

So far as possible we have structured the materials to encourage you – the students – to think about skills and process issues for yourselves – usually by engaging in an activity and discussion which encourages you to engage with the issues from personal experience. This approach, of course, runs counter to much of the conventional way of learning, not just on law degrees, but on most academic programmes.

To help students (and perhaps tutors too) to adapt to this style of learning, Chapters 1 and 2 set out the learning theories this book is built around. Our experience as teachers tells us that students are much better equipped to learn experientially once they have a basic grasp of how they learn.[6] If you intend to follow our programme, rather than just use this as a secondary resource book, we strongly recommend that these chapters are covered first. Apart from that, we leave issues of coverage to you.

## Consolidation and further reflection

At the end of every chapter there is a sequence of exercises designed to consolidate learning based on that chapter:

(a)  Concept check: this exercise enables students to assess whether they have understood the information in the chapter.

---

6.  See further C. Maughan and J. Webb, 'Taking Reflection Seriously: How Was It for Us?' in J. Webb and C. Maughan (eds.), *Teaching Lawyers' Skills*, Butterworths, London, 1996.

(b)  Review: this allows students to reflect on and discuss important issues covered in the chapter. Tutors may prefer students to do these exercises after doing some further reading.

(c)  Further skills building exercises, where appropriate.

(d)  Learning points: in Chapters 1, 7, and 9, we have introduced an additional exercise to help students focus on their own needs and abilities in specific skills situations, and to explore how they will adapt certain theoretical constructs for their own use.

**A note on footnotes**

We thought long and hard before adopting footnotes. They are unusual in (English) skills books, particularly in the quantity we have. In the end we felt that they were necessary given our intention to put legal skills 'in context', and would be less distracting than endnotes or Harvard referencing. We have not distinguished in footnotes between materials tutors might need to follow up more than students, or vice versa. The further reading section at the end of each chapter is designed more with students in mind.

## How to learn from this book

We base our learning methodology on the experiential learning cycle devised by David Kolb and the methods of reflective practice developed by Donald Schön (see Chapter 2). Learning is based around a large number of practical exercises. By doing these exercises students observe and analyse their own behaviour, thoughts and feelings and those of their fellow students. This process of reflection enables them to identify what worked well, what did not, and why. They can then experiment with new forms of behaviour at the next opportunity.

This methodology will be unfamiliar to some law teachers,[7] and probably to many law students. It may therefore involve you in a re-appraisal of your attitudes to learning and your perceptions of tutor and student roles in the learning process. We therefore think it will be helpful if we address a number of issues involved in this type of learning.

### Do I have to join in?

**To students:**

Yes, this is essential! Because you are 'learning by doing', you will take a much more active role in class than you may be used to. You will participate actively

---

7. Some accessible discussion of learning methodologies can be found in the following collections: K. Raaheim, J. Wankowski and J. Radford, *Helping Students to Learn*, SRHE/Open University Press, Milton Keynes, 1991; N. Gold, K. Mackie and W. Twining (eds.), *Learning Lawyers' Skills*, Butterworths, London, 1988; M. Le Brun and R. Johnstone, *The Quiet (R)evolution: Improving Student Learning in Law*, Law Book Co, Sydney, 1995; J. Webb and C. Maughan (eds.), *Teaching Lawyers' Skills*, Butterworths, London, 1996; H. Brayne, N. Duncan and R. Grimes, *Clinical Legal Education: Active Learning in your Law School*, Blackstone Press, London, 1998; R. Burridge, K. Hinett, A. Paliwala and T. Varnava, *Effective Learning and Teaching in Law*, Kogan Page, London, 2002.

in the practical exercises, often by role playing. You will give and receive feedback both on your own performances and the performances of other members of the class. Your tutor may video exercises to help you review your performance.

Active learning also means taking responsibility for your learning. This book and your tutor provide much of the learning content, but you are in charge of the process. This means you will analyse your behaviour, thoughts and feelings, experiment actively to change your behaviour, and challenge your personal values and attitudes. We strongly advise that you record your learning process in your own personal learning diary, which (we suggest) need not be read by your tutor unless you think that would help you to learn.

**To tutors:**
If you are new to skills teaching, the process will be as much a challenge for you as it is for the students. Active learning for students does not mean that teachers can become passive! Preparing, structuring and running skills workshops can be exhausting. At times we ask you to role play, so you will have to learn the role and then act it out. While groups are doing practical exercises, you will probably want to circulate and listen in, to check that your students have got the hang of what they are supposed to be doing. You will also want to note down points to raise in the feedback sessions. You will find you spend a great deal of time summarising on boards, flipcharts and overhead transparencies, sticking flipchart pages on walls, or providing the materials for your groups to do all these things. And don't forget the video! This is an incomparable part of feedback. When we first set up the course we used to spend probably too much time trying to review videos in class. We still use them for demonstration purposes, but have found that it is far more effective to let the students take the videos of their performance away with them for either individual or small group analysis.

Keeping to time can be a major problem. It is important to devote plenty of time to feedback, so as to enable students to reflect on and conceptualise their experiences in the workshops. You may set aside what you think is sufficient time, but find you exceed it, because you do not want to cut off valuable feedback. This still happens to us. We have yet to find any easy solution which does not involve us imposing a strict, and sometimes quite arbitrary, time limit.

Will my tutor tell me everything?

No, definitely not!

**To students:**
Taking more control over your learning means that your relationship with your tutor may be different from the one you are used to. Your tutor's job is to set up conditions and situations in which you can experiment and improve your skills.

Your tutor will want to become redundant as soon as possible, by enabling you to evaluate for yourselves the success or otherwise of your performance.

You will spend a good deal of your time working in groups. This method of working may be new to you. It involves a number of skills. You will have to work out how to allocate responsibility for tasks within the group, and find ways of handling any problems which arise between members of your team. Group work is dealt with in detail in Chapter 4.

**To tutors:**

We can all find it difficult to break long-established habits of didacticism. However, telling students how to perform the skill will not enable them to learn it. Similarly, feedback should not consist of the tutor telling the student how they should have performed. To develop the skill of critical self-assessment, students need to evaluate their own performance before anyone else does it for them. After all, they are the people who are going to have to deal with the problem next time, not you.

How do I reflect on and evaluate my experiences?

Through feedback and your learning diary.

**1 Feedback**

We think feedback has two functions: (a) it should encourage the performer to reflect on their performance; (b) it should support that reflection and reinforce good practice.

(a)  We suggest the following feedback sequence should always be used:
   (i) Start with the student who has performed the exercise. So, for example, in a practice client interview, the 'lawyer' feeds back first.
   (ii) The 'client' responds with views on her feelings and perception on the process.
   (iii) Anyone else actively involved in the exercise.
   (iv) Observers (the student's group or the whole class).
   (v) The tutor.

   If you are to encourage reflection you need to start by questioning the performer on their behaviour, and their thoughts and feelings about the performance. We start feedback by using a very general, open, question to get a response from the performer. We then use the performer's responses to focus on specifics. By your questioning you should try to get the performer to recognise their own strengths and weaknesses, without you telling them. Don't give them advice at this stage. For example:

OBSERVER: How do you think the interview went?

LAWYER: OK. I didn't do as well as I hoped: he seemed a rather difficult client.

OBSERVER: What made him 'difficult'? Was there anything in particular which gave you that feeling?

LAWYER: I don't think I established a rapport with him.

OBSERVER: So what could you have done to improve rapport?

LAWYER: Perhaps if I'd made fewer notes, and looked at him more, responded a little more openly, that would have helped.

(b)   If you are going to give advice then address specific aspects of performance rather than just giving a general 'I think Jo could have summarised the facts better'. What aspects of recapping could be improved upon, and how? Be prepared to share experiences in this kind of feedback.[8]

Remember, whether you are asking questions, or giving advice, or reflecting on your performance: feedback needs to be focused, constructive and honest. Performers and observers should try and avoid feedback that sinks to the level of banality. Observers should not offer destructive or 'negative' feedback. It can damage a performer's confidence, and encourages them to be defensive, rather than open, about their practice.

## 2  The learning diary or portfolio log

The UWE course uses learning diaries or 'journals' as the primary means of recording reflection. The Westminster variant adopts portfolio-based assessment.[9]

*To students:*

You should make an entry in your learning diary or log after you have had a few hours to think about your behaviour, thoughts and feelings during the exercise and the feedback session immediately afterwards. Wherever possible, however, you should make contemporaneous notes about your performance, your feelings and the feedback you gave and received. Use these to help construct your learning diary or log entries. Try and avoid writing up entries purely from memory – it can be misleading.

*To tutors:*

If you adopt our original methodology learning diaries play an important part. We recognise that there is a long-standing debate over whether tutors should even review, never mind assess, student diaries. For what it is worth, our position is that review is useful, but should be a consensual aspect of the course rather than a formal requirement.[10] The student diaries are personal and may include much confidential material. We suggest you don't include them in your assessment of students for that reason. There is also a problem of determining what you would be assessing: the student's performance, their reflection and evaluation of it, or their ability to write an experiential learning diary?

---

8.  Good practice in giving feedback is set out in Chapter 4, at p. 103.

9.  See also J. Webb, 'Portfolio-based learning and assessment in law' at www.ukcle.ac.uk/resources/portfolios.html.

10.  These issues are less significant with the model developed at Westminster. Log sheets are assessed as part of the portfolio.

You may also find it useful to keep a diary to record your own learning, particularly if you are not experienced skills tutors. We have found it both a salutary experience, and a hard discipline to maintain.

## Will I enjoy it?

We certainly hope so. Here are some comments from two LLB students at the end of the first term's work:

(1)  I love the style of teaching that has been adopted. As well as allowing you to meet new people I feel that group work enables you to learn more. It allows you to talk about your ideas with other members of the class and also hear their ideas, some of which you may not have thought of. The relaxed and friendly atmosphere makes you want to listen and understand. Even though I am aware of the importance of the theory we are being taught . . . It is beneficial to put this theory into practice through doing role plays and writing letters . . . I have gained detailed knowledge of the learning process and self assessment. Previously I never really thought about how I acted in a particular situation and whether my performance would affect future conduct.

(2)  . . . the three hours do fly past. It has become a real motivator for me. I struggled last year with my subjects and was nervous about my final year. This teaching format has taught me more about my ability to cope, and me as a person, and has given me more confidence.

Our own experience is that learning skills can be stressful, frustrating, infuriating . . . and more fun than you ever thought studying could be – but only if you are prepared to get involved and make it work!

Figure 1.1. Law graduation – The Descent into the swamp

# 1

# Descent into the swamp

In this chapter we explore the concepts of professionalism, legal professional knowledge and the art of lawyering. To resolve the problems of uncertainty, uniqueness and value conflict which are the reality of legal practice (the 'swamp'), legal practitioners use their artistry: a combination of tacit knowledge, technical knowledge of the law, and practical skills. The aim of this book is to help you to develop your artistry before you hit the swamp.

## Objectives

To:

- Identify and discuss the separation of theory and practice in traditional legal education.
- Examine and evaluate notions of professionalism and professional knowledge as they relate to the legal profession.
- Examine the nature of 'artistry' in legal practice and its use in non-routine problem solving.
- Consider, in a preliminary fashion, the lawyer's social responsibility.
- Enable you to discover and reflect on concepts and principles introduced in this chapter.

## Supports benchmark statements

Students should demonstrate:

1. Knowledge:
   - knowledge of a substantial range of major concepts, values, principles and rules of [the English legal] system.
2. Application and problem-solving:
   - a basic ability to apply their knowledge to a situation of limited complexity in order to provide arguable conclusions for concrete problems (actual or hypothetical).

3.  Analysis, etc:
    - a basic ability to recognise and rank items and issues in terms of relevance and importance.
    - a basic ability to make a critical judgement of the merits of particular arguments.
    - a basic ability to present and make a reasoned choice between alternative solutions.

## A dinosaur snack?

In the first *Jurassic Park* movie, a lawyer is shown abandoning two children threatened by a tyrannosaurus rex. He attempts to hide from the creature in a toilet, but the dinosaur demolishes the hut housing the toilet, picks up the terrified lawyer from his seat of shame, tosses him about playfully and eats him. The audience response to this, in our experience, ranged from gruesome satisfaction to downright delight. He got what he deserved.

Of course, we can only speculate why Spielberg picked on a lawyer, but it is tempting to suggest that he knew there would be little sympathy for his target. In short, lawyers today are not held in high regard. Although surveys have yet to indicate that the lawyer's image has plumbed the depths explored by the archetypal used-car salesman, there is enough to suggest that the perception of lawyers (reflected in the plethora of anti-lawyer jokes) as 'dishonest, arrogant, greedy, venal, amoral, ruthless buckets of toxic slime'[1] is closer to the mark than we might wish. What has happened to give this conventionally high status profession its dubious image, and what has it got to do with the subject of this book?

The late Donald Schön points us towards a possible answer. In *Educating the Reflective Practitioner*,[2] Schön offers this proposition: that within the last thirty years we have come to face a public crisis of confidence in professional knowledge, which has challenged the legitimacy and status of professions in general, and has led to a similar crisis of confidence in professional education. Schön was writing about professionalism and professional education in the US, but sociologists and educationalists in Britain and Europe have also observed a decline in public trust of experts and expert knowledge,[3] and a growing sense of uncertainty around the nature and function of 'professional' education.[4] In fact, the idea of crisis seems to pervade much of the modern literature on professions.[5]

In some ways this is strangely counter-intuitive because, at least in the highly developed, post-industrial, societies of the world, this is very much the age of the

---

1.  J. D. Gordon III, 'How Not to Succeed in Law School' (1991) 100 *Yale Law Journal* 1679 at p. 1680.
2.  Jossey-Bass, San Francisco 1987.
3.  A. Giddens, *The Consequences of Modernity*, Polity Press, Cambridge, 1990; U. Beck, *Risk Society: Towards a New Modernity*, Sage, London, 1992.
4.  R. Barnett, *The Limits of Competence: Knowledge, Higher Education and Society*, Open University Press, Buckingham, 1994; M. Eraut, *Developing Professional Knowledge and Competence*, Falmer Press, London, 1994.
5.  W. S. Sullivan, *Work and Integrity: The Crisis and Promise of Professionalism in Modern America*, New York, 1995; A. A. Paterson, 'Professionalism and the Legal Services Market' (1996) 3 *International Journal of the Legal Profession* 137; H. M. Kritzer, 'The Professions are Dead, Long Live the Professions: Legal Practice in a Postprofessional World' (1999) 33 *Law and Society Review* 713.

professional. More and more occupations define themselves as professional in an environment where 70 per cent of economic activity is geared to the production of services, and only 30 per cent to the old 'core' economic activities of manufacturing, farming and mining.[6] The professionalisation of society has thus been such that it is tempting to suggest 'we are all professionals now'. The paradox is that this is occurring in the face of what Kritzer has called a 'postprofessional'[7] economic and political context, where, as the historian Harold Perkin puts it, the 'safety net [of professional society] has gone, blown away by the random winds of the free market'.[8] The question is, how has this affected lawyers as a specific social group? And what does this have to do with legal professional knowledge? The dialogue in the following exercise is designed to introduce you to the debate:

### EXERCISE 1.1  Is legal professionalism in crisis?

Imagine this question has been set as a topic for a seminar discussion. The dialogue which follows represents the opening part of the seminar.

TIGER (THE TUTOR): OK, so how did you get on?

MARIA: I found it quite hard to get to grips with this question until I had thought quite a lot about what a profession is.

DAVID: Yeh, me too; I didn't really get the point of all this theory of professions stuff we had to read – you know, what professions are and what they do – until I discussed it with Jonny and we sussed out that maybe that's where this crisis thing begins. Isn't it about professionals not being what they ought to be anymore – well-trained, ethical people committed to serving the public?[9]

JONNY: But the theory shows up the self-serving side of professionalism too, like the way professions use their specialist knowledge, their need for training, their status, to create conditions for what Abel calls 'social closure' – in effect the ability to create and control their own markets.[10] A lot of the Thatcherite attack on professions in the 1980s was about limiting their monopoly power,

---

6. See H. Perkin, *The Third Revolution: Professional Elites in the Modern World*, Routledge, London, 1996.

7. Kritzer, (1999) 33 *Law and Society Review* 713 at p. 715: 'we are moving into a period in which the role of professions such as law and medicine as they are known in the Anglo-American world is radically changing and may be in sharp decline … [T]he changes wrought by postprofessionalism will not mean the extinction of professions, but rather a wholesale reshaping of this turn-of-the-millenium institution …'

8. H. Perkin, 'Crisis in the professions: ambiguities, origins and current problems', *Exploring Professional Values for the 21st Century: Briefing Paper 3*, Royal Society of Arts, London (not dated), p. 4.

9. David is describing elements of what sociologists would call a 'functionalist' account of professions. According to this model, professions are characterised by their skills and expertise, developed through specialist education and training, the autonomy they have over their own work, their commitment to a service ethic and high ethical standards in general, their collegiality as a professional group, and their collective self-regulation, usually through the disciplinary powers of their professional association.

10. This is the other dominant model of theorising about professions – Weberian market control theory. The classic general statement of the theory is M. S. Larson, *The Rise of Professionalism: A Sociological Analysis*, University of California Press, Berkeley, CA, 1977. Its primary exponent in respect of the Anglo-American legal professions is Richard Abel – see his *The Legal Profession*

and you can still see echoes of that in the system.[11] Look at the continuing complaints about the earnings of 'fat cat' lawyers, also the Office of Fair Trading's ongoing review of professional practices which may be anti-competitive.[12]

WAYNE: Maybe you're right Jonny, but I still don't get *why* government and public opinion turned against the professions, and particularly lawyers.

JONNY: Well, I'm not sure lawyers have ever been all that popular.[13] We think we're helping people and they think we're making a living out of someone else's misfortune, like running court cases where the only real winners financially seem to be the lawyers!

MARIA: Sure, but something fundamental does seem to have changed, to do with the role of the state and of lawyers themselves in the marketplace. As I understand it, a lot of the present crisis revolves around this interplay of state and market.[14] Even sixty-odd years ago, the state played little part in legal services. Then we had the development of legal aid, and now we have a  situation where, what with the return to a more non-interventionist notion of the state, using tools like conditional fees and Legal Services Commission contracts, the state is reducing its role in the legal services market. Legal aid firms are now working in a shrinking and some say increasingly de-professionalised market.

At the same time the specialist corporate legal sector has grown massively since the 1970s, creating a large and powerful group of lawyers whose interests are in many ways opposed to those of the legal aid and traditional high street firms, and whose future is very much governed by their ability to meet the commercial needs of their clients.[15]

TIGER: OK Maria, that's all very good, hold it there for a moment. Who can see where this is going: Paula?

PAULA: I reckon a lot of it is about control and the loss of control. Lawyers are technically self-regulating, which is an issue for government if it is putting a lot of public money, basically, into the hands of private businesses – which is what

in *England and Wales*, Blackwell, Oxford, 1988 (see pp. 8–21 for the statement of market control theory to which Jonny refers here) and 'The Politics of Professionalism: The Transformation of English Lawyers at the End of the Twentieth Century' (1999) *Legal Ethics* 131. The analysis is more thoroughly updated in Abel's latest book, *English Lawyers Between Market and State: The Politics of Professionalism*, Oxford University Press, Oxford, 2003.

11. See, e.g., M. Burrage, 'Mrs Thatcher Against the 'Little Republics': Ideology, Precedents and Reactions' in T. Halliday and L. Karpik (eds.), *Lawyers and the Rise of Western Political Liberalism*, Clarendon Press, Oxford, 1997.

12. Office of Fair Trading, *Competition in Professions: A Report by the Director-General of Fair Trading*, March 2001, and *Competition in Professions: Progress Statement*, April 2002.

13. See, e.g., the literary references to lawyers in D. Luban, 'Introduction' in Luban (ed.), *The Ethics of Lawyers*, Dartmouth, Aldershot, 1994.

14. See particularly G. Hanlon, *Lawyers, the State and the Market: Professionalism Revisited*, Macmillan, London, 1999.

15. On the rise of the City (and so-called 'global') law firms, see generally R. Lee, 'From Profession to Business – The Rise and Rise of the City Law Firm (1992) 19 *Journal of Law and Society* 31; J. Flood, 'Megalawyering in the Global Order – The Cultural, Social and Economic Transformation of Global Legal Practice' (1996) 3 *International Journal of the Legal Profession* 169. See also Hanlon, *Lawyers, the State and the Market*.

law firms are. The state's strategy, until recently at least, has been to put pressure on the profession to keep its house in order, rather than try to regulate it more directly.[16] At the same time it imposes controls on the areas of legal work it's financing, by creating a kind of market for publicly funded legal services.[17]

TANNI: And while all this is going on, the rise in corporate lawyering is creating a very different kind of legal services delivery from the traditional high street approach. Corporate lawyers are having to become far more business-like, more client-driven and competitive – as they are competing far more for the big international contracts, both with other lawyers and with other professions, like accountants, who are providing overlapping services.[18] The result is that the profession is becoming more and more fragmented into different sectors and different styles and types of service delivery.[19] Some solicitors even seem to be questioning the idea that they can continue to be one profession,[20] and that will undermine the principle of collegiality and maybe risk splitting whatever powerbase the profession has.

JONNY: Ironically, too, in the process of holding on to clients, corporate lawyers may also be losing control, in a different sort of way. They could be losing some of the sense of autonomy that goes with the idea of being a professional ...

THIERRY: OK, but being client-centred[21] is an important issue for all sectors of the profession, and for consumers and the regulators too. And I think this issue shows that it's not just about politics and control – there is a real quality of service thing mixed in with all this. It's not just 'look what a hard time the government's giving us'. Lawyers are often very quick to argue they're business people, yet a lot of them don't seem to be very good at the kinds of things businesses see as essential: good customer service and client relations! Just look

---

16. For further detail on professional regulation, see Chapter 6.

17. See, e.g., G. Bevan, 'Quasi-Markets for Legal Aid' in W. Bartlett, J. Roberts and J. Le Grand (eds.), *A Revolution in Social Policy*, Policy Press, Bristol, 1998; R. Moorhead, 'Legal Aid in the Eye of a Storm: Rationing, Contracting and a New Institutionalism' (1998) 25 *Journal of Law and Society* 365.

18. See G. Hanlon, 'A Fragmenting Profession – Lawyers, the Market and Significant Others' (1997) 60 *Modern Law Review* 798, and on lawyers and accountants generally, Y. Dezalay and D. Sugarman (eds.) *Professional Competition and Professional Power: Lawyers, Accountants and the Social Construction of Markets*, Routledge, London, 1995.

19. This sense of fracturing is becoming a common theme in the literature on the professional restructuring of law. The issue is not the traditional separation between solicitors and barristers, but the 'segmentation' around the corporate/private client 'hemispheres'; see, e.g., J. Heinz and E. Laumann, *Chicago Lawyers – The Social Structure of the Bar*, Russell Sage Foundation/ American Bar Foundation, New York, 1982, where segmentation was first discussed as a concept and Hanlon, (1997) *Modern Law Review* 798 for a discussion in the English context. Increasingly, research is also acknowledging the gender segmentation of professional work – see H. Sommerlad, 'Women Solicitors in a Fractured Profession: Intersections of Gender and Professionalism in England and Wales' (2002) 9 *International Journal of the Legal Profession* 213 (discussing the culture of corporatisation in law firms and how it serves to marginalise women).

20. As one City solicitor put it, 'Why do ... firms like [this] subscribe to the same trade union [meaning the Law Society] as a man above a betting shop in Billericay High Street?' – in T. Goriely and T. Williams, *The Impact of the New Training Scheme: Report on a Qualitative Study*, Law Society, London, 1996, p. 122.

21. But consider whether Thierry makes a bit of a jump here equating client-directed practices and client-centred practice. We discuss client-centred practice more extensively in Chapter 5.

at the data on complaints and client care, especially for solicitors. The problem has been there for years, and – I know this is a generalisation – it seems like the profession as a whole doesn't want to know.[22] Even now, after the Law Society had thrown millions at sorting out its complaints mechanisms, the Legal Services Ombudsman said: 'it is self-evident from the performance statistics that ... [professional] initiatives have largely failed to keep pace with consumer expectations or to reverse the decline in public confidence in lawyers.'[23] And it's now got to the point where it looks pretty certain there will be some kind of new 'super-regulator' overseeing the legal services market.[24]

MARIA: And even the top corporate law firms may not be getting it all right. I found a piece in *The Lawyer* from a couple of years back where in-house lawyers for some of the big corporations said they were concerned whether the big global law firms had the ability to deliver the quality of service of some of their more 'local' competitors.[25]

JONNY: So, what it all means is: we've got government, the regulators, clients and consumers all on the legal profession's case, and, as the gap widens between the corporate and private client sectors, which are like the 'haves' and 'have-nots' of the legal world, the profession itself seems to be fragmenting into different interest groups. I can see that might well count as a bit of a crisis!

MUTTHIA: But that isn't all of it, is it?

TIGER: Go on ...

MUTTHIA: Well, there's the impact of all this change on the lawyers themselves, isn't there? It seems there's not a lot of fun in being a lawyer any more. A lot of small firms have had a really hard time of it. They were hit by the hikes in indemnity contributions,[26] then the Law Society needed to get more funds from the profession to pour into its Complaints Service, plus they have had to

22. The Law Society reported receiving 14,880 complaints in 2002 (approximately one complaint for every six solicitors), as against 10,585 in 2001; the Bar Council received 743 complaints (one for every 18 barristers) in 2003, as against 829 in 2001: *Taking up the Challenge: Office of the Legal Services Ombudsman Annual Report, 2002/2003*, OLSO, Manchester, p. 30. For research into 'client care' (note that this is a technical term of art, based on the conduct rules contained in Practice Rule 15 of the Solicitors' Practice Rules 1990), see R. James and M. Seneviratne, 'Solicitors and Client Complaints (1996) 6(3) *Consumer Policy Review* 101; C. Christensen, S. Day and J. Worthington, 'Learned Profession? The Stuff of Sherry Talk: the Response to Practice Rule 15' (1999) 6 *International Journal of the Legal Profession* 27.
23. See *OLSO 2002/2003*, p. 5. Ironically, perhaps, the latest OLSO Report, *In Whose Interest? Annual Report for the Legal Services Ombudsman 2003/2004*, OLSO, Manchester, p. 32, noted that complaints handling at the Law Society 'finally appears to be showing signs of appreciable improvement'.
24. As a consequence of the ongoing Clementi Review of regulation of the legal services market, which is due to report in December 2004. See further Chapter 6.
25. See C. Smith and J. Clothier, 'The World is Not Enough', *The Lawyer*, 17 January 2000, pp. 16–19.
26. Until September 2000 solicitors were obliged to pay for cover for professional negligence through the Solicitors Indemnity Fund. The Fund had run into difficulties after its failure to obtain reinsurance cover in 1991, this left the Fund entirely dependent on the profession to cover the cost of claims until the Law Society introduced new Indemnity Rules in 2000, allowing solicitors to buy (cheaper) indemnity insurance in the marketplace (see M. Davies, 'Whither Mutuality? A Recent History of Solicitors' Professional Indemnity Insurance' (1998) 5 *International Journal of the Legal Profession* 29 at p. 47).

cope with the decline in the real value of legal aid funding, all these things have hit some of them really hard. I know I could be over-generalising here, but there seems to be evidence that this is having a real impact on the workloads and morale of many working in that area.[27] A lot of small firms seem to have either shut up shop, moved away from publicly-funded legal work, or merged in order to get enough critical mass to produce the amount of work necessary to be profitable.[28] The pressures seem to be pretty enormous. There's quite a lot of concern now about stress, and people with drug and alcohol dependency problems in the profession – and that really surprised me ...[29]

PAULA: Me too, Mutthia; if I was you I'd forget about law and go back to playing cricket! Seriously though, I was kind of surprised by these issues and evidence of discontent in the big firms – though like you said it's hard to get an idea of how big or small the overall problem is, as, obviously, people aren't going to be particularly open about it all.[30] I mean, I'd heard all the war stories about having to work 72 hours solid to close a deal, and you think, yes, that's got to be tough, but it's not the whole story, and it's part of the price for the good salary and, I suppose, the glamour of being part of this kind of big deal-making culture. But clearly it's not enough for everyone and there seems to be

---

27. See H. Sommerlad, 'The Implementation of Quality Initiatives and New Public Management in the Legal Aid Sector in England & Wales: Bureaucratisation, Stratification and Surveillance' (1999) 6 *International Journal of the Legal Profession* 311; '"I've Lost the Plot": An Everyday Story of the "Political" Legal Aid Lawyer' (2001) 28 *Journal of Law and Society* 335.

28. Mutthia does not point to any supporting evidence. Is he right? Can you find any statistical evidence of what has been happening to the legal aid and small firm sector?

29. See, e.g., A. Burnyeat, 'Drink problem rises' *The Lawyer*, 20 September 1994, and *The Times*, 22 January 2000 (noting that alcohol-related deaths in the legal profession are twice the national average); 'Putting the stress on support', *The Lawyer* 16 June 1998; J. Wilson, 'Young city lawyers pay price for salary rise' *The Guardian (G2)*, 7 August 2000; P. Thomas, 'Law's Faustian bargain' *The Times*, 5 September 2000. The issue of stress also comes up a number of times in A. Boon and A. Whyte, *Legal Education as Vocational Preparation? Perspectives of Newly Qualified Solicitors*, UKCLE, Warwick, 2003, pp. 62–5. One of their solicitor respondents comments as follows (p. 62):

> 'I think people need some type of appreciation that it is going to be stressful but I don't think you could ever teach anyone [about] the pressures of work. I think it's just a shock to the system from being at college ... Exams; you think they're stressful but they're not really. I found like mid twenty-five-ish it was just awful and I just thought "what am I doing, why am I doing this job?" ... ask any of the people who know me, "what have you done for the last seven years?" And I would say, "I've worked". You know, that has been my life and it has taken up a lot of my life and I think the older I'm getting, the more resentful of using my own time I become. I think you've got to be very prepared to work long hard hours and, like I said, I've got friends who work in the commercial side, people who work in the City, you know, quite a broad spectrum of people within the profession and I think the general consensus is we can't believe how hard we work and I think in London at the moment, if your firms aren't as prosperous as they used to be and you know one of my friends in particular worked in a firm where they've laid people off and you've got to keep on working hard. Now, he said he feels under as much pressure now as he did years ago.'

> Nevertheless, data from the Law Society Cohort Study in 1999 indicated that, overall, 70 per cent of new solicitors were satisfied with the balance between their work and family life, though only a quarter of those in City practice actually felt their job *improved* their quality of life, far fewer than in high street firms – see A. Boon, L. Duff and M. Shiner, 'Career Paths and Choices in a Highly Differentiated Profession: The Position of Newly Qualified Solicitors' (2001) 64 *Modern Law Review* 563 at pp. 579–80, 588.

30. Though note the references cited in n. 21 and n. 23 above.

more stuff in the legal press about the work not being satisfying, and about firms becoming 'law factories', where lawyers are pressured to produce profits through high billable hours.[31] I've read that firms are getting worried about how to keep hold of their people, other than by paying them so much they can't afford to leave![32] I don't know, it's got me wondering, well maybe it isn't quite so glamorous after all.

TIGER: OK, now this is something a number of writers have touched on when they talk about lawyering today as lacking a sense of 'meaningful work'.[33] Now, sure, we can say there is maybe a touch of naivity here. It may suggest a golden age of lawyering that never was, but I think there's value in developing a link between this idea and something else we've touched on in the discussion today. That probably sounds a bit obtuse, but can anyone see what I have in mind?

WAYNE: Simon describes 'meaningful work' as work that is an expression of ourselves and of our relationship with others.[34] I've been struggling with that, feeling more than a bit sceptical I suppose, and struggling to see why it should be so important. But I think I'm on to something ... and maybe it has to do with what you're talking about ...

TIGER: Yes? ...

WAYNE: It seems to me now that Simon uses meaningful work to try to redefine what it means to be a lawyer. Being a lawyer isn't just about what we know and what we do, it is about *who we are for ourselves*. And a lot of that comes, surely, from our relationships – with other lawyers, clients, friends, whatever. From what we've been saying today, a lot of what is shifting – what we've called the crisis of professionalism – is to do with these relationships. There's the loss of public respect, and the fragmentation of the professional community, that must have some impact on collegiality. The law factory image, too, goes with a culture where there is a lot less loyalty around the professional relationships. Clients, particularly in the corporate sector, are a lot more demanding, and perhaps less loyal – if they don't get what they want, they'll find another lawyer who's prepared to give it to them. There's less

31. See R. G. Lee, '"Up or Out" – Means or Ends? Staff Retention in Large Law Firms' in P. Thomas (ed.), *Discriminating Lawyers*, Cavendish, London, 2000. A number of pundits have pointed to the famous leaked memo out of Clifford Chance US LLP (formerly Rogers & Wells before its merger with the London-based Clifford Chance ) as evidence of embedded cultural problems in the legal world. The New York associates' concerns included: a culture of high billable hours which encouraged 'padding of hours, inefficient work, repetition of tasks and other problems', favouritism in assigning work, and poor communications and working relations with partners. See J. Ashworth, 'Clifford Chance Denies Young Lawyers' Charges' *The Financial Times*, 29 October 2002. Clifford Chance were quick to deny that any other parts of the organisation were implicated, and it has been noted that there was already some history of poor relations in Rogers and Wells before the merger: see R. Lennon, 'The Memo Heard Round the World' *American Lawyer*, 3 December 2002.

32. See, e.g., Lee, *ibid*. Also D. Jordon, 'Clark makes assistant retention a priority' *The Lawyer*, 29 January 2001.

33. W. H. Simon, *The Practice of Justice: A Theory of Lawyers' Ethics*, Harvard University Press, Cambridge, MA, 1998, p. 112. See also D. B. Wilkins, 'Practical Wisdom for Practicing Lawyers: Separating Ideals from Ideology in Legal Ethics' (1994) 108 *Harvard Law Review* 458 at p. 475.

34. *Ibid*.

loyalty within firms too; lawyering's no longer a job for life. Lawyers do get fired or made redundant, and something we haven't mentioned so far, they will leave to move on to other firms too, in a way that wasn't common forty or fifty years ago. I suppose, being a lawyer has become just another job, and I think the traditional professional ideal had it as something more than that …

TANNI: Can I say something here? I think Wayne's on to something, but maybe the old notion of professionalism is partly at fault too. Perhaps lawyers have been too focused on the idea that what they sell is expertise, whereas what they're really selling is a relationship. But …, and maybe this is part of the problem, none of our training is really about that. I'm in my final year at law school and no-one's ever really talked to me about 'professionalism' before,[35] let alone what it really means to be a lawyer …

Now consider the following:

(a)   Summarise the arguments put forward by the participants for the idea that there is a crisis of (legal) professionalism.

(b)   Do you agree with them, or do you think the case for 'crisis' has been overstated by the participants? If you disagree, provide evidence countering those arguments you disagree with.

This exercise was to get you to think about whether the legal profession is in crisis and, if so, what that crisis involves. But what about Schön's assertion that there is a crisis in professional knowledge? Knowledge is self-evidently an important part of what it means to be a 'professional' – we have already seen that the functionalists saw it as part of what defines a profession. However, it is even more fundamental than that. It is axiomatic that our work as professionals is dependent on mastery of a body of knowledge. The nature of that knowledge, the status which mastery of it confers upon us, and the way we make use of it in our day-to-day work are therefore all vitally important. So let's begin by analysing what exactly this 'knowledge' consists of.

EXERCISE 1.2   **Redefining knowledge**

Imagine you are watching a highly competent advocate cross-examining a witness in the Crown Court.

(a)   List the skills and characteristics she is displaying.
       No doubt your list will include a number of items in addition to excellent knowledge of the relevant law.

(b)   Now consider which items on your list, in your view:
       (i)   you can learn from books;
       (ii)  you can learn on the law degree;

---

35.  A recent study by Amanda Fancourt for the UK Centre for Legal Education notes that one of the two major criticisms made of trainee solicitors by firms was that they lacked an 'appropriate professional attitude' and awareness of office life – 'Hitting the Ground Running? Does the Legal Practice Course Adequately Prepare Students for the Training Contract?', forthcoming).

*(iii)  you can learn on the Legal Practice, or Bar Vocational course; and*

*(iv)  which items cannot be taught at all.*

## Where the action isn't

This exercise should have helped you discover and define other kinds of knowledge the lawyer needs for successful practice besides technical knowledge of the law. Yet it is this that forms the bulk of most law school curricula. Wesley-Smith points out the dangers of relying on 'knowing the law' as preparation for legal practice:

> Mere acquisition of legal knowledge in law school is of little value to a practitioner because that knowledge (a) can only be a tiny part of the whole (b) can be understood only superficially (c) is easily forgotten or only partially or inaccurately remembered (d) is rarely needed in practice in the form in which it is learned (e) is likely to be quickly outmoded and thus dangerous to rely on and (f) is of little use where new problems arise to be solved.[36]

According to this view, therefore, legal knowledge is of little use in professional problem-solving. Is this true?

EXERCISE 1.3  **What's the problem?**

Here is a 'problem' question from a first year Contract Law course. Read it and answer the questions that follow.

Webb Ltd writes to Maughan Ltd: 'We are in the market for 70,000 Flibber bricks at not more than 30p per brick, inclusive of delivery, which must be within 28 days of contract date. Agreement to be on our standard terms.'

On 1 April Maughan Ltd, which has never dealt with Webb Ltd before, writes back: 'We have bricks – our price 28p.'

Webb Ltd receives Maughan's note on 2 April and replies, 'Please send bricks', with an accompanying order form which contains their usual terms of business, including the period of delivery as specified in their original letter.

Maughan Ltd sends a confirmation of order form on 5 April which has their usual terms of business on the back. One of these clauses gives Maughan the right unilaterally to change the date of delivery. This letter is unread and filed.

Advise Webb Ltd on their legal position in the following alternative circumstances:

36.  P. Wesley-Smith, 'Neither a Trade Nor a Solemn Jugglery: Law as Liberal Education' in R. Wacks (ed.), *The Future of Legal Education and the Legal Profession in Hong Kong*, 1989, cited in J. Macfarlane, 'Look Before You Leap: Knowledge and Learning in Legal Skills Education' (1992) 19 *Journal of Law and Society* 293 at p. 299.

(a)     On 10 May Maughan Ltd delivers the required number of bricks and Webb accepts them but then decides to sue for the lateness of delivery.

(b)     On 10 May Maughan delivers the required number of bricks but Webb refuses to accept them.

(c)     The facts are as in (b) above, but the two companies have contracted many times before.

1.     *What are the legal issues you need to determine for your client? (Be brief!)*
2.     *Once you have 'solved the problem', will your client go away satisfied? Why/why not?*
3.     *What else might the client want to know?*
4.     *What things do you need to know about your client in order to represent his interests adequately?*
5.     *Put yourself:*
       *(a) in the judge's position;*
       *(b) in your client's position.*
       *Would your advice differ? If so, how?*

If this were an examination question you would do well to concentrate on Question 1 and ignore the others. In professional practice, however, *all* the questions are relevant.

This is not to say that the knowledge of principles and rules learned at university is without value. It forms part of what is known as the *social knowledge* of the legal profession. That is to say, it represents the body of knowledge that a lawyer needs to share with other members of her profession. It is valuable because it enables the law student or novice practitioner to sort things into categories. *Ah yes! This is a battle of the forms problem: has a contract been made at all, and if so, on whose terms?*

It marks a starting point for the professional to get to grips with any case she takes on. (If this starting point has eluded you because you have forgotten your contract law, please re-read the Wesley-Smith quotation on p. 20.)

The danger lies in the assumption that many academic and practising lawyers make, that this social knowledge plus a few 'bolt-on' skills, such as client interviewing and negotiation, is all that needs to be learned. The exercise that you have just done should have demonstrated to you that each case you deal with has an element of routine law about it, but also has aspects which are unique, and which are not taught in the traditional law syllabus, and are not to be found on the library shelves.

## Where the action is

Schön has referred to this social knowledge learned at university as the 'high ground' but maintains that the real practice of any profession takes place 'in the swamp'. By this he means that the everyday cases that come before a practitioner, such as that in Exercise 1.3, have an element of the routine about them, but are never as clear-cut as a law school problem might lead us to believe. What are your client's best interests in the situation? How can you assist her to identify and articulate them?

What kind of timescale is involved? How much will it all cost? Are you getting the whole story? None of these 'swampy' factors is broached by the law school problem, nor are they susceptible to a technical, high ground solution. Nevertheless, all of them, and many others, are relevant in every case you undertake.

Karl Mackie, too, makes this point when he argues that in professional practice knowledge of the rules is only one of a number of factors involved in making a 'legal' judgment:

> ... in many other cases, possibly a majority, such a simple analysis is misleading in that it fails to acknowledge the often problematic nature of law, of the behavioural alternatives available within the terms of the law, and the problems of proof, evidence and enforcement in the application of legal rules to behaviour. Legal rules are generally abstract 'essence' statements which are designed to apply to a range of diverse fact-situations by way of prohibition or of mandatory guidance. The problematic nature of legal rules is particularly clear in modern regulatory controls over detailed business practices, although it is also at the heart of the common law. Thus, unfair dismissals are in most instances assessed in terms of whether the company acted 'reasonably' 'in all the circumstances'; what does this standard on its own really tell anyone about guiding behaviour in practice? Similarly ambiguous criteria can be found in many other areas of law from negligence to health and safety legislation or rules regarding certain exclusion clauses in consumer contracts. Added to this core element of obscurity in many legal provisions is the uncertain nature of factual evidence and the interpretation of that evidence in court – what facts are available to support the evidence for one's interpretation of the legal rule? Can they be used in court? What evidence will be put forward by the other party? Will particular aspects of the situation carry special weight with the judicial forum? Will an issue be presented adequately by counsel? And so on. Finally, the enforcement of a law may be erratic, uncertain or unlikely.[37]

Here Mackie is describing the kinds of issues that lawyers have to make decisions about in order to get a conflict resolved, hopefully in their client's favour. Stephen Nathanson introduces us to a different, less controversial, lower profile lawyer role: the 'conflict blocker'. The most important decisions this lawyer must make when drafting, say, a contract, will or separation agreement will involve minimising the risk of any future conflict:

> What is critical is whether or not a conflict might arise and whether or not the other side can maintain a credible position arguing their case. The lawyer's task is to create a

37. K. Mackie, *Lawyers in Business*, Macmillan, London and Basingstoke, 1989, pp. 95–6. Stephen Nathanson draws a distinction between *law school thinking* in which students, like appeal court judges, focus on legal issues and how to resolve them, and *lawyer thinking*, focusing on clients' legal problems. 'In its most elemental form, law school thinking calls for issue-spotting. The law student's basic strategy for learning law in this environment is first, to memorise as many legal issues as possible and secondly, to practise spotting them in old examination papers. Learning to think in this way will probably improve performance in law school, but does not do enough to train students to be competent lawyers.' S Nathanson, *What Lawyers Do: A Problem Solving Approach to Legal Practice*, Sweet and Maxwell, London, 1997, p. 54.

list of these potential conflicts and to use various documents and procedures to block them ...

Legal conflicts are costly – not only in time and money but in the amount of human misery they can cause. Clients who are sophisticated and understand the unhappiness that legal conflict brings appreciate this type of legal work. They like agreements and documents that are 'airtight', that have no 'loopholes' and that stand the 'test of time'. The conflict-blocker is not a law-warrior. He or she is a law-maker, legislating private agreements and documents for and between people who need control over, and clarity in, their lives ...

The role played by conflict-blocking lawyers is one of the least understood and most neglected in law schools. Law schools spend much of their time on sources of law such as judgments and legislation, but the one source that probably produces more law than any other is overlooked. That source is conflict-blocking lawyers who are engaged in the enterprise of law-making. This, of course, is not the law-making that goes on in legislatures or the courts, although it is related to these sources. This is the vast enterprise of law-making that goes on every day in lawyers' offices and in the legal departments of thousands of firms: the creation of private law accomplished through the negotiation and drafting of agreements and transactions that govern legal relations between people. [38]

On the high ground your legal judgment is further circumscribed in the sense that the law school academics decide on the nature and constraints of the problem being attempted. These are usually carefully thought out to raise specific points of legal principle for you to grapple with. In the swampy lowlands, on the other hand, you are the one who will have to define the problem for yourself and for your client. How many aspiring lawyers are taught to do that?

[T]he problems of real world practice do not present themselves to practitioners as well-formed structures. Indeed, they tend not to present themselves as problems at all but as messy, indeterminate situations.[39]

Consider, for example, this comment by Laurence Lee, the solicitor defending eleven-year-old Jon Venables in the James Bulger murder:

I knew I would have to try to get to the bottom of what went on. I developed a plan. I would go and visit him every week at the home where he was being kept and took along a computer game ... That's the only way I could ever really take instructions from him ... It doesn't appear in any textbook, this sort of situation.[40]

The indeterminacy here was not 'legal', but situational. It was not a question of knowing and applying the law, but far more fundamentally, of working out how to get through to the client in the first place.

---

38. *Ibid.*, pp. 59, 61.
39. D. Schön, *Educating the Reflective Practitioner*, Jossey-Bass, San Francisco, 1987, p. 4.
40. *The Guardian*, 25 November 1993, p. 2. Jon Venables and Robert Thompson were convicted of the murder of two-year-old James Bulger in 1993. At the time of the murder, they were both ten.

Schön argues that the high ground problems, although of interest technically, are unimportant to the individual and society at large. The problems of greatest human concern lie in the swamp:

> The practitioner must choose. Shall he remain on the high ground where he can solve relatively unimportant problems according to prevailing standards of rigor, or shall he descend to the swamp of important problems and non-rigorous inquiry?[41]

Some, however, might argue that Schön undervalues high ground technical competence. Without it, would the novice practitioner be able to distinguish what is and what is not routine and unimportant?

## The skills of lawyering

How, then, do professionals deal with the indeterminate zone that is the swamp? What other kinds of knowledge besides 'knowing' the law do they use?

Go back now to the list of skills needed for advocacy which you made in Exercise 1.2. Here are some which you might have identified:

COMMUNICATION SKILLS
- listening;
- putting questions which the witness (and the jury) understand;
- speaking clearly;
- using body language appropriate to the jury, judge, witness;
- conveying to the jury your response to a witness's answers through selective summarising, tone of voice, follow-up questions.

ORGANISATIONAL SKILLS
- case preparation and management.

COGNITIVE SKILLS
- assessing a situation;
- reacting quickly and appropriately (thinking on one's feet);
- sorting out the important/relevant from the unimportant/irrelevant ('seeing the wood from the trees').

This practical kind of knowledge is *knowing how*, rather than *knowing what*. It is not learned from books or lectures, but acquired through experience. No manual, for example, could ever teach you to drive. Reading a book does not put you into the position where you have to process as much data as you need to process when you drive. You need to experience the whole act of driving in order to learn how to do it and to improve. This is normally achieved with the aid of an instructor who talks you through performance of the various activities until you are able to carry them out without consciously thinking about them. It is not surprising that this takes time when you consider the amount of data that a driver has to process when driving. He not only has to operate the mechanical functions of the car, but also has

41. Schön, *Educating the Reflective Practitioner*, p. 4.

to be aware of and respond to the changing environment in which he is driving and at the same time remember and act according to the rules of the road.

## Knowing in action

The ability to perform activities automatically, without having consciously to think about what you are doing is known as *tacit*, or *personal* knowledge. Schön calls it *knowing in action*. When you perform the skill you observe a set of rules, but because you do not know what the rules are, you are unable to state them explicitly:

> If I know how to ride a bicycle or how to swim, this does not mean that I can tell how I manage to keep my balance on a bicycle or keep afloat when swimming. I may not have the slightest idea of how I do this or even an entirely wrong or grossly imperfect idea of it, and yet go on cycling or swimming merrily. Nor can it be said that I know how to ride a bicycle or swim and yet do not know how to co-ordinate the complex pattern of muscular acts by which I do my cycling or swimming. I both know how to carry out these performances as a whole and also know how to carry out the elementary acts which constitute them, though I cannot tell what these acts are. This is due to the fact that I am only subsidiarily aware of these things, and our subsidiary awareness of a thing may not suffice to make it identifiable.[42]

Let's take this concept of knowing in action a little further.

EXERCISE 1.4 **When you were a child** ...

All human beings possess the capacity for language. All learn to speak, unless they are prevented from doing so by malfunctioning organs of hearing or speech, or extreme social deprivation. Consider the following questions:

(a)   *How old were you when you began to speak?*
(b)   *Did someone give you lists of rules to use to help you to speak?*
(c)   *Did you have formal lessons in the language?*
(d)   *What kind of knowledge did you use (and still do use) to enable you to produce speech?*

As a young child you had the ability to produce utterances spontaneously which you had never heard before, using rules you had not only never been taught, but the existence of which you were unaware. This creative, dynamic power of humans to produce language is probably the most vivid illustration of tacit knowledge in operation because it demonstrates the innate capacity we all have to make and develop rules and theories. You will hear young children make grammatical mistakes in their speech, such as 'He *goed*' for he *went*, or 'I *brang*' for I *brought*. They are experimenting with the past tense rules of English. In the first example the child assumes that *goed* follows the normal rule: add *-ed* to the verb to form the past tense, as in *look-ed*, *walk-ed*. In the second example she is clearly aware there are

42. M. Polanyi, *Knowing and Being*, Routledge & Kegan Paul, London, 1969, pp. 141–2.

exceptions to this rule, but applies the incorrect one, assuming perhaps that *bring* is like *sing*, which has past tense *sang*. The child is very unlikely to have heard these forms from adults, so cannot be said to be copying what she's heard.

## The art of lawyering

The kind of improvisation illustrated above is what lawyers do when confronted by the uncertain and unique situations of practice. They search through their repertoire of knowledge and experience, and select, adapt or invent strategies which they try out in the situation. The way the professional integrates her legal knowledge, practical know-how and tacit knowledge to produce competent performance of her tasks forms what Schön calls 'the *art* of practice'. What do we mean by this?

The art of practice reflects a capacity for holistic learning. Artistry is built upon your technical knowledge of law and procedure, your experience of practice and your ability, intuitively, to respond effectively to a new situation. It is not just standardised, textbook, knowledge. Just as you go on to be your own driver, driving quite differently from when you took your test, the professional develops her own highly personalised legal artistry.[43]

The word 'artistry' is potentially misleading, because it can suggest that only some people are capable of developing it; the 'brilliant' advocate, the charismatic politician, the talent shown by David Beckham curling a 35-yard pass with pinpoint accuracy to the foot of Wayne Rooney. The example of language learning above should dispel this suggestion. Everyone is capable of developing artistry. It is merely an extension of what we all do already in the swamp of everyday life: we use our *knowing in action* to make perceptions, decisions and judgments spontaneously in unpredictable situations. For example, think of the ways in which parents have to alter their responses to their children's behaviour as the children grow up.

Laser illustrates how the lawyer uses her artistry in situations of uncertainty:

> The ways in which the lawyer frames to herself each separate uncertainty in the case and the way in which she balances all of the uncertainties in framing the overall problem or problems of the case to herself are also functions of her artistry. There is artistry in strategising, given the uncertainty of a client's or adversary's case. The lawyer must decide whether the client should admit the weaknesses in her case as a preemptive strike or ignore them in the hope that the other party will not identify them. The lawyer must decide whether to resolve a particular factual uncertainty with or without the aid of discovery. If she chooses discovery, she must implement a

---

43. In their research on the skills needed by trainee solicitors, Kim Economides and Jeff Smallcombe provide us with a good example of developing artistry. They identify a composite problem-solving skill which they term 'break-in'. This is the ability to 'get inside' a new subject or problem. It involves the capacity to absorb information quickly and to interpret it accurately and efficiently. Clearly, it is not the kind of skill that is 'taught' in academic training, nor is it one that all trainees in their research had developed, either at all or to the same degree. This suggests that it is an art: a more developed kind of performance than mere technical competence. See K. Economides and J. Smallcombe, *Preparatory Skills Training for Trainee Solicitors*, Research Study No 7, Law Society, London, 1991, p. 23.

discovery plan deciding which discovery devices she should use, and in what order. With a legal uncertainty, such as the likelihood of prevailing on a motion for summary judgment, deciding whether to bring the motion and how to present the issue to the client are also functions of the lawyer's artistry.

There is often much uncertainty in deciding whether to settle or go to trial; some law firms bring in a different team of lawyers to negotiate, for fear that their litigators would resolve the uncertainty in favor of going to trial for the unacceptable reason that litigators like to try cases. There is artistry in evaluating the uncertainty present at trial – for example whether the case is being well received by the judge and jury. Finally, there is artistry in considering the uncertainties of an appeal. The art of lawyering in the face of uncertainty involves the way in which the lawyer selects and formulates the issues, organises them, and chooses the strategy for the case.[44]

The quote from Laser focuses on a particular aspect of artistry: the need to make practical decisions for which the law school leaves you relatively unprepared. This, however, is only one kind of 'swamp' problem anticipated by Schön. A solution may be difficult to determine because a problem forces you – the lawyer – to confront some kind of moral or ethical dilemma. To be a competent practitioner thus requires not only practical artistry, but the ability to develop your own sense of ethics and social responsibility, and to make decisions consistent with those values. This is the issue we now turn to.

## The values of lawyering

### EXERCISE 1.5  High ideals

Would you like to help the less fortunate?
Would you like to see liberty and justice for all?
Do you want to vindicate the rights of the oppressed?
If so you should join the Peace Corps. The last thing you should do is attend law school.[45]

*In your groups, discuss which professional values you think are fundamental to legal practice.*

If you agree with James D. Gordon III that promoting justice, equality and morality is the lawyer's social responsibility, you might have listed:

● Striving to ensure that legal services are available to those who cannot afford to pay for them.
● Striving to rid the profession of discrimination on the basis of gender, race, age, sexual orientation, disability.
● Striving to ensure that legal institutions do justice.

---

44. G. Laser 'Educating for Professional Competence in the Twenty-First Century: Educational Reform at Chicago-Kent College of Law' (1992) 68 *Chicago-Kent Law Review* 243 at pp. 253–4.
45. 'How Not to Succeed in Law School' at p. 1679.

Other possibilities are:

- Achieving and maintaining high standards of competence in your dealings with clients.
- Improving the profession. This might entail assisting with the preparation and training of new lawyers.
- The pursuit of financial goals, to underpin the other fundamental values of ensuring a high quality legal service.
- Maintaining the status of the profession in society.

When you have reflected on and discussed these issues, move on to the following exercise.

EXERCISE 1.6 **Swampy situations?**

In small groups, imagine you are discussing the following cases with colleagues in practice. What decisions would you make in each case?

(a)  You are members of a small environmental law department in a firm of solicitors. A major chemicals company approaches you to take on its environmental casework. You know that the company has a poor environmental record, and anticipate that it will enlist you not only to defend it in court, but also to advise on pollution control avoidance. At the same time, the company has indicated that if you take on the job, it would be willing to transfer all its other external legal work to your firm. This would give a major boost to your department, and greatly increase its status in the firm (and possibly your own prospects of a partnership).
   *1. Would you take on the client?*
   *2. Why/why not?*

(b)  You are an expert in housing law at the Bar. A client and his family are referred to you after they have been evicted from their home by the local council. The details of the case reveal that the ground for the eviction is the family's persistent racial harassment of their next-door neighbours. They do not deny the harassment, but their solicitor thinks the council may have breached certain procedural requirements in evicting her clients, thereby possibly making the eviction illegal.
   *1. Would you take the case?*
   *2. Why/why not?*

We are now back in the swamp. You may find that, when working in a professional environment, notions of social responsibility, personal values and interpretations of the professional code of conduct are in conflict. Even if it's not an internal conflict for you,[46] your superiors or your colleagues may take a different ethical stance on the problem, and these differences may need to be resolved. In the second situation, you might feel that professional ethics (the cab rank rule) require that you take the case, and the reasons for this may well accord with your notion of professional/social responsibility. In one or both of the above situations, however,

---

46. We discuss this in more detail in Chapters 2 and 6.

you – or your colleagues – may find it *morally* unacceptable to act for the clients. Has law school prepared you for this kind of dilemma?

Similarly, what if your objection is not moral, but simply a profound dislike of the client? Technical knowledge alone won't help you here. Again, as with all the unique and unpredictable messes of the swamp, the practitioner needs to use her artistry to resolve such dilemmas.

## Learning the art of lawyering

Traditionally, lawyers have acquired the basic values of legal practice and the art of lawyering after graduating, in the swamp of legal practice. It is knowledge picked up as they go along, gained largely from their own experience and that of fellow professionals. Whether they develop artistry or not is therefore a matter of chance; unfortunately, not all develop it to the same degree.

It is this hit and miss process that has led many to believe that artistry cannot be taught. However, if legal education treats the 'high ground' as isolated from the swampy lowlands, then it is hardly surprising that the novice practitioner flounders. The social knowledge acquired in law school in no way equips her to practise competently.[47] Moreover, the belief that it does must retard the development of artistry, which as we have seen is a holistic learning process, involving the combining of various kinds of knowledge and experience.

The purpose of this book is to provide a framework in which you can begin to develop artistry *before* you enter the swamp. We attempt to put in place a setting in which you can become what Schön calls *reflective practitioners*. You will encounter problems and perform tasks which, as far as possible, simulate the swampy lowlands of practice, containing elements of uniqueness, uncertainty and value conflict. This chapter introduces you to the current context in which lawyers work, in particular, notions of professionalism and professional knowledge which we would like you to keep in mind and re-evaluate from time to time as you work through the book.

EXERCISE 1.7  **Crisis? What crisis?**

We hope our analysis so far of the nature of legal knowledge gives you a clearer picture of what – in Tanni's words – it really means to be a lawyer, and the range of different types of 'knowledge' needed for competent practice. Are we now in a position to justify Schon's assertion of a crisis in professional knowledge? And can we discover any link between such a crisis – if there is one – and the crisis in professionalism we discussed earlier?

---

47. Some teachers of law argue that this is not its purpose, but that might come as a bit of a surprise to some of their students.

Please read the three extracts below, then discuss the questions which follow in groups of four or five.

1.  H. W. ARTHURS, 'A LOT OF KNOWLEDGE IS A DANGEROUS THING: WILL THE LEGAL PROFESSION SURVIVE THE KNOWLEDGE EXPLOSION? (1995) 18 *Dalhousie Law Journal* 295, pp. 296–7, 308–9:

John Willis, one of the wisest men I ever met, spent one of his lives reincarnated as a legal practitioner in Nova Scotia. He coined a motto for his law firm: 'We know everything; we do anything; we stop at nothing.' 'We know everything': vintage Willisonian irony that, and characteristically to the point. Practising lawyers are indeed licensed to 'do anything', a privilege which, given the logic of professionalism, necessarily implies a claim to 'know everything'. To know what? To know real estate and criminal law, company and municipal law, income tax and the Charter; to know how to advocate, negotiate, strategize and draft; to know about advising large banks and small businesses, quarrelling spouses and nervous testators, governments and protest groups.

And more yet. We are supposed to know about the mechanics of legislation and adjudication. We are supposed to be ethicists capable of working out difficult moral dilemmas – our own and those of our clients. We are supposed to be fluent in the epistemology and semiotics of law, so that we can continue to decipher its mysteries as they are handed down in monthly tablets from the Supreme Court of Canada. And – not finally, but finally enough – we are supposed not only to know all these things at any given moment, but to keep our knowledge current over careers which might last thirty or forty years or more.

. . . Central to the very notion of a profession is the existence of a common body of knowledge which binds its members together, and which defines the profession's relationship to clients, to the state, and to other groups in society. In the case of the legal profession, belief in the existence of such a common body of knowledge is reflected in our continued adherence to a single model of education and training, a single practise credential, a single code of professional ethics, a single standard of competence . . . a single repertoire of professional regulatory strategies.

But with the growth of knowledge and the diversification of knowledge, that common core has ceased to exist. The desire to know, the need to know, the resources to know have divided us into subprofessions clustered around different bodies of knowledge. Furthermore, these subprofessions are increasingly defined by the non-lawyer collaborators with whom they work, and the particular clienteles they serve. As a consequence, the notion of a single unified legal profession is becoming increasingly less plausible.

2.  A. BOON AND A. WHYTE, *LEGAL EDUCATION AS VOCATIONAL PREPARATION? PERSPECTIVES OF NEWLY QUALIFIED SOLICITORS*, UK CENTRE FOR LEGAL EDUCATION, WARWICK, 2003, p. 55; published at www.ukcle.ac.uk/research/boon.rtf.

The career paths of participants in this study often took unexpected twists and turns. This may have made earlier specialisation irrelevant and is an argument for a focus [in legal education] on more general and transferable knowledge and skills. For one participant, for example, legal education had:

*... no relevance to what I'm doing at the moment, and little or none to what I've done since I finished my training contract. The reason for this though is because of my career path. I did my training contract in a twenty partner commercial firm, where the LPC training was useful. And then I had a year in a high street firm where, again, it was useful. But since then I had four years doing professional indemnity work for defendants, and the LPC concentrates really on claimant work, and there's little or nothing, I think, on defendants. And I haven't done any professional negligence, either in my degree or in the LPC, so it was all on the job training. And now I'm working in house for the Financial Services Authority doing insurance regulation work, and again there was nothing, so it's all on the job training.*

Similarly, for another:

*I'm sort of working in-house for (a regional television company) ... so I've changed really from doing more high street or commercial litigation to doing media and entertainment which is, obviously, totally different and also working in-house which is also a difference so ... university education and then the LPC ... didn't cover any direct relevant law which would be of use for me in my work today because, obviously at that time, I didn't anticipate I'd be doing this.*

The unpredictability of the kind of work an entrant to the profession might eventually do may be an argument for breadth in the formal stages, with the detail of specialist areas being left until later. This, however, may be unrealistic for, as a participant observed, the training contract is an unreliable means of acquiring relevant training:

*... I think certain firms, maybe the small to medium sized ones, which are the ones that I've had experience of, don't have as formalised a training structure as perhaps they should ... that can leave you bereft sometimes of the more practical elements of the job, of doing it day to day ... I started at one firm, did my training contract then moved to the other ... I'm not sure comparatively but I do think this is a profession where you ... have to be really very positive and dynamic about the kind of things you want to learn. It's not laid on, or you're not put through a prescribed route. It's very 'open plan' and that's great if you have a good idea of what you want to do and you're proactive about looking at courses, going to see the Head of Training and saying, look I want to go on this, this and this because I think this will be useful.*

Therefore, to shift more responsibility for specialisation training into the training contract would require an even higher level of monitoring:

*... the training contract part needs to be more regulated because, you know, I was given a training contract and I think you have to register with the Law Society or whatever but in practice nobody would have any idea what I was doing and I could be there doing nothing for two years and someone would sign the form at the end and I would be qualified as a solicitor.*

Increasing specialisation in legal practice creates a tension between the demand for higher-level skills and knowledge and the length of legal education. Much of the substantive knowledge learned will be irrelevant. This puts a premium on the skills and attributes developed in the process of legal education and training.

3. A. Boon, 'History is Past Politics: A Critique of The Legal Skills Movement in England and Wales', (1998) 25 *Journal of Law & Society* 151 at p. 166.

The rationale for the introduction of the LPC also had an ethical foundation related, as it was, to a perceived discipline problem in the profession. The place of values remains a gap in the present model, particularly because undergraduate legal education is not value neutral. It supports the values of objective enquiry and detached judgment and desensitizes students to value issues. Certain values, engagement in the client's cause, a commitment to service, or a commitment to developing the ethical orientation of the profession are all understated in legal socialization. The often cited aim of legal education, adopted by traditionalists and radicals alike, is to encourage students to 'think like lawyers'. For both camps the emphasis must, perforce, reflect how lawyers do think rather than how they could think. It is perhaps not surprising that new members of the profession are unlikely to regard its collective honour as important. Dominated by the pursuit of technical competence, we have done nothing to cause them to think otherwise.

Technical competence is only one dimension of professional responsibility. The inherent problem of atomism, and hence of the vocational stage, is that the importance of exploring values is denied . . . . Skills training emphasized the instructor's choice of values and therefore gave students no basis for reflective choices about who they are becoming as lawyers or about what lawyers as individuals can or ought to contribute to their profession or to a just and stable society. In fact atomistic approaches risk rendering the skills curriculum a series of empty technical exercises leading to the replication of existing professional failings.

In your groups, discuss:

(a)    What are the main components of legal knowledge?
(b)    What evidence is there that legal knowledge is 'falling apart'?
(c)    How, if at all, does the possible crisis around legal knowledge contribute to any crisis in professionalism?

EXERCISE 1.8  Concepts[48]

In this chapter we have discussed a number of concepts. We list the main ones below. The procedure for learning these concepts is as follows:

1.    *Divide into pairs.*
2.    *Each pair is to:*
       (a)  *define each concept, noting the page on which it is discussed, and*
       (b)  *make sure that both members of the pair understand the meaning of each concept.*

48. This exercise is taken from D. W. Johnson and F. P. Johnson, *Joining Together*, Allyn & Bacon, Boston, 8th edn, 2003.

3.    *Combine into groups of four. Compare the answers of the two pairs. If there is disagreement, look up the concept and clarify it until all agree on the definition and understand it.*

| | |
|---|---|
| high ground | swamp |
| knowing in action | holistic learning |
| social knowledge | personal/tacit knowledge |
| legal artistry | reflective practitioner |

EXERCISE **1.9** **Review questions**

1.    *How do you think the skill of problem solving differs from the art of problem solving?*
2.    *In the light of the discussion so far, how would you define legal professional competence?*
       *(a)  Divide into pairs.*
       *(b)  Draw up a list of the competences you think a lawyer in practice should have.*
       *(c)  Compare your list with the list in the Report of the Lord Chancellor's Advisory Committee on Legal Education and Conduct.*[49]
       *(d)  Is there anything you would add to your list or ACLEC's list? If so, what?*

EXERCISE **1.10** **Learning points**

In this chapter we have tried to get you thinking about the philosophy behind this book. *What, if anything, have you learned from this discussion:*

*(a)    About legal education generally?*
*(b)    About your legal education?*
*(c)    About yourself?*

If it helps, first make a brief summary of the discussion.

## Further reading

*Legal Education and Professional Development – An Educational Continuum* (The MacCrate Report), American Bar Association, Chicago, 1992.
D. Schön, *Educating the Reflective Practitioner*, Jossey-Bass, San Francisco, 1987, ch. 1.
C. Stanley 'Training for the Hierarchy? Reflections on the British Experience of Legal Education' (1989) 22 *Law Teacher* 78.
J. Macfarlane, 'Look Before You Leap: Knowledge and Learning in Legal Skills Education' (1992) 19 *Journal of Law and Society* 293.
C. Menkel-Meadow, 'Narrowing the Gap by Narrowing the Field: What's Missing from the MacCrate Report – Of Skills, Legal Science and Being a Human Being' (1994) 69 *Washington Law Review* 593.
W. Twining, *Blackstone's Tower: The English Law School*, Sweet & Maxwell, London, 1994.

49. *First Report on Legal Education and Training*, ACLEC, London, 1996.

# 2

## Learning to live in the swamp

This chapter introduces you to the concept of experiential learning. This demands that you take charge of your own learning and practise critical self-assessment. We will ask you to record your learning in a personal journal and to make an assessment of your preferred learning style. Experiential learning processes enable you to develop a flexible repertoire of responses and techniques which you will continuously refine through new experiences and reflection. This is how you acquire artistry.

## Objectives

To:

- Examine Schön's concept of reflection.
- Outline behaviourist and cognitive learning theories.
- Explain the principles and techniques of experiential learning.
- Enable you to discover and apply these principles and techniques.
- Examine the concept of discrepant reasoning.
- Discuss and assess techniques for self-assessment, in particular the learning diary and learning styles questionnaire.

## Supports benchmark statements

Students should demonstrate an ability:

4.  Analysis, etc.:
    - to recognise and rank items and issues in terms of relevance and importance;
    - to bring together information and materials from a variety of different sources;
    - to produce a synthesis of relevant issues in relation to a topic;
    - to make a critical judgment of the merits of particular arguments;
    - to present and make a reasoned choice between alternative solutions;
5.  Autonomy and ability to learn
    - to act independently in planning and undertaking tasks;
    - to reflect on their own learning and to seek and make use of feedback;

6.  Other key skills:
    ● to work in groups as a participant who contributes effectively to the group's task.

## What is reflection?

In Chapter 1 we made the following points:

● All aspiring lawyers can learn the art of lawyering.
● It is a form of holistic learning.
● It integrates *knowing* and *doing*.
● 'High ground' learning separates knowing and doing.
● 'High ground' learning alone will not enable competent practice.
● Artistry means using your *knowing in action*.

However, in the examples we gave – swimming, riding a bike, producing speech – it was clear that it is not possible to describe the processes involved in the performance of these skills because we are not aware of what is going on. Likewise, ask an experienced advocate why she put a particular question in cross-examination, and she may find it difficult to give you a rational explanation. 'Intuition', or 'Just a hunch', she might reply. Our *knowing in action* is spontaneous, and we rely on it to get us through the routine tasks of the day, which for an experienced advocate will include cross-examining a witness in court.

"ACTUALLY, NOW YOU MENTION IT... THAT'S A DAMN GOOD QUESTION"

Figure 2.1. The reflective chicken!

But what happens when we are faced with a situation which is not routine?

EXERCISE 2.1 **To smoke or not to smoke?**

Students divide into pairs. One plays the role of the Boss (Jane/John). One plays the role of the Smoker (Paul/Pauline).

Allow the players 15–20 minutes to prepare their roles. The interview should last 10–15 minutes. Each pair then feeds back to the group.

**Feedback**

(a)   Ask both role players:
    (i)   *What was the outcome? Did the interview go as you had planned? Did you get what you wanted? If not, why not?*
    (ii)   *What were the key stages in the interview? How were you feeling at each key stage? What was going through your mind?*

(b)   Ask the boss:
    (i)   *Where, if at all, did you find it difficult to go on/lose control of the interview?*
    (ii)   *How did you feel when this happened? How did you handle it?*

The process of reflection you have just gone through in this exercise should have brought your tacit knowledge to the surface and articulated it. What you were doing in the situation was what we all do in unpredictable situations: frame the problem, and improvise to find a solution – during the action, on the spot. Donald Schön calls this type of analysis *Reflection in Action*. Reflection after the event, in this case during feedback, he calls *Reflection on Action*. In both situations you hold a 'reflective conversation' with yourself, a kind of internal dialogue.

Let's try this in a 'legal' situation.

EXERCISE 2.2 **An unexpected visit**

**Background**
A student plays the role of the lawyer, Jo(e) Evans. The tutor plays the role of the client, Mr/Ms Cross.

The interview takes place in the firm's reception area and should last 10–15 minutes. Allow the players 10 minutes to prepare their roles.

**Feedback**

(a)   *As the lawyer, describe your thoughts and feelings at the following points in the scenario:*
    (i)   *When the receptionist asks you to come down.*
    (ii)   *When the abuse is hurled at you.*

To show you more clearly how the process of reflection can work, here is one possible reflective conversation on Exercise 2.2:

*Problem framing:*    Oh no! Something's wrong, and no one's here to deal with it. I'm going to have to. Can I stall?

| | |
|---|---|
| *Reflection:* | What can I do? I haven't been in this situation before. I could get the file and look through it. That might help me spot the problem and give me time to get my thoughts together. |
| *Problem framing:* | (*file not found*) I'll have to see them. See what the problem is. Here goes. Try not to look stupid. Try to keep cool and be helpful. |
| *Problem framing:* | They're having a go at me. Why? I hate them. It's not my fault. |
| *Reflection:* | I feel really upset. But it's not me, there must be a reason. Nobody behaves like this without a reason, surely. Stay calm and polite. Find out the reason. |
| *Problem framing:* | Ah! Now it's getting through. They've got a genuine worry, but I still don't know what to do about it. I can't solve their problem, because I don't know their case. I can't give them a more general idea of what might happen, because I don't know this area of law. |
| | Why won't they stop shouting at me? I don't like it. What can I do about it? How dare they behave like this? |
| | It's uncivilised. I want to be rude back. That would be a way of getting rid of them. It worked that time when that gang of idiots kept pestering us in the pub. |
| *Reflection:* | I've got to calm things down and give them some sort of answer. Obviously I can't deal with it. |
| *Problem framing:* | The best thing would be to get hold of Mary Carmichael. I can't do that off my own bat. I'll go and see one of the senior partners. They'll have to do it. |

(b)    On reflection, are you happy with the way you dealt with the situation?

(c)    If the situation were to be repeated, what might you do differently?

## Experiential learning and the learning cycle

By the time you have answered (c) above, you have gone through several processes of reflection and experimentation which enable you to use your tacit knowledge to solve a problem. Reflection *in* action allows you to improvise on the spot. Reflection *on* action provides you with a description of the process, which you will then add to your repertoire for use in the future.

Although the term 'reflective practitioner' was coined by Schön, the notion that reflection is an essential part of personal and professional development has a long history in educational theory.

Modern theories about learning fall into two broad categories, with several variants or developments of each. The first group of theories comes under the general title of *behaviourism*. Broadly, this approach says that learning takes place by the learner responding to external stimuli, and altering behaviour according to the type of reinforcement that the stimulus provides. Burning your hand in a fire, for example, would lead you to alter your behaviour so that you avoided contact between fire and your body. This kind of stimulus is known as *negative reinforcement*. There also exists the notion of *positive reinforcement*. This is where a certain kind of behaviour elicits a reward which encourages the learner to emulate that behaviour in order to get more of the reward.[1]

The second approach is the cognitive[2] one which says that human beings not only respond to their environment but actively seek out experience from their surroundings in order to make sense of the world around them. This making sense takes the form of the learner formulating and memorising rules of how to respond, and how to behave autonomously. Child language acquisition, which we discussed in Chapter 1, is a good example. This approach stresses the importance of the personal, subjective interpretation of your past experience, so that your learning is dependent on the integration of experience with reflection, of theory with practice.

Johnson and Johnson use the term *action theories* to denote the rules made in this way:

> All humans need to become competent in taking action and simultaneously reflecting on their action to learn from it. Integrating thought with action requires that we plan our behaviour, engage in it, and then reflect on how effective we were. When we learn a pattern of behavior that effectively deals with a recurrent situation, we tend to repeat it over and over until it functions automatically. Such habitual behavioral patterns are based on theories of action. An action theory is a theory about what actions are needed to achieve a desired consequence in a given situation. All theories have an 'if ... then ...' form. An action theory states that in a given situation if we do x, then y will result. Our theories of action are normative. They state what we ought to do if we wish to achieve certain results. Examples of action theories can be found in almost everything we do. If we smile and say 'hello', then others will return our smile and greeting. If we apologize, then the other person will excuse us. If we steal, then we will be punished. If a person shoves us, then we should shove back. All our behavior is based on theories that connect our actions with certain consequences.
>
> In essence we build an action theory. As our behavior becomes habitual and automatic our action theories become tacit (we are not able to put them into words). When our behavior becomes ineffective, we become aware of our action theories and modify them.

1. A brief and basic explanation of the theories of Pavlov and Skinner can be found in D. Rollinson, *Organisational Behaviour and Analysis: An Integrated Approach*, Pearson Education, Harlow, 2002, pp. 175–81. More detailed description and analysis of behaviourism can be found in J. Medcof and J. Roth (eds.), *Approaches to Psychology*, Open University Press, Milton Keynes, 1979.
2. No single theorist has dominated the field of cognition in the way that Pavlov and Skinner have tended to dominate behaviourism. Indeed there is a multiplicity of cognitive approaches. We emphasise here the *social* and *developmental* aspects of cognition. For a fuller discussion see Medcof and Roth, *Approaches to Psychology*.

As children we are taught action theories by parents and other socializing agents. As we grow older we learn how to modify our action theories and develop new ones. We learn to try and anticipate what actions will lead to what consequences, to try out and experiment with new behaviors, to experience the consequences, and then to reflect on our experiences to determine whether our action theory is valid or needs modification.[3]

The authors go on to define the cognitive-based theory of *experiential learning:*

*Experiential learning* may be defined as generating an action theory from your own experiences and then continually modifying it to improve your effectiveness. The purpose of experiential learning is to affect the learner in three ways: (1) the learner's cognitive structures are altered, (2) the learner's attitudes are modified, and (3) the learner's repertoire of behavioral skills is expanded. These three elements are interconnected and change as a whole, not as separate parts.[4]

The experiential approach is characterised by a model of learning known as the *learning cycle:*[5]

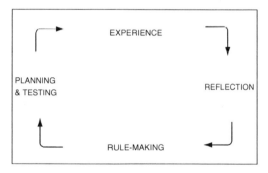

Figure 2.2. Learning cycle.

Learning is a sequential four-stage process:

| | |
|---|---|
| *Experience* | You experience an event, or problem. It unsettles you, excites you, perplexes you. |
| *Reflection* | In order to make sense of it, you examine and analyse both the experience and your feelings and attitudes towards it. |
| *Rule-making* | Out of this reflection come new meaning and perspectives, new ideas about how things work. You formulate rules (action theories) about what constitutes appropriate behaviour in similar situations. |

3. D. W. Johnson and F. P. Johnson, *Joining Together: Group Theory and Group Skills,* Allyn & Bacon, Boston, 8th edn, 2003, pp. 48–9.
4. *Ibid.*, p. 50.
5. See D. A. Kolb, *Experiential Learning: Experience as the Source of Learning and Development,* Prentice Hall, New Jersey, 1984.

*Planning and*    These rules provide the basis for experimentation. At the next
*testing*    opportunity you modify your behaviour, in order to test
whether your new action theories will give you the outcome
you would prefer.

These action theories then become the basis of future behaviour, and so the cycle
begins again. When an appropriate event next occurs, you put your plan
into action and continue through the cycle, refining your behaviour and revising
your action theories in the light of your reflection, until you are satisfied (see
Figure 2.3).

The notion of the learning cycle is a very powerful one, because it suggests that
pursuit of knowledge for its own sake is insufficient for learning, as is a merely
leisurely appraisal of your strengths and weaknesses. Learning and self-development
will only take place if there is a challenging, stringent assessment of your own
behaviour, thoughts and feelings.

Moreover, experience alone does not constitute learning, because it will not
generate any action theories. As Aldous Huxley said: ' . . . experience is not what
happens to a man; it is what a man does with what happens to him.'[6]

Those of you who drive can probably think of other drivers you have encountered on the road (or narrowly missed) who have not had 20 years' driving
experience, but one year's experience 20 times over. Unless we analyse it, we may
fail to understand our own behaviour and its impact.

## Discrepant reasoning

### EXERCISE 2.3  The discrepant solicitor?[7]

Alex, a solicitor, has been working for a large city firm for ten years. Bridget is
her principal. Alex has recently been performing well below standard, not for
the first time. She has a reputation for 'sloppy' client care: she is late with
correspondence, and a couple of clients have complained about arrogance. Also,
over the last quarter, she has been submitting fewer billable hours than the firm
would expect. Bridget has been assigned to talk to Alex, in order to help her
improve performance. Bridget's view is that the firm wants to keep Alex in the job,
but that this is the final warning. If there is no improvement, unpleasant but
appropriate action will have to be taken.

6. *Texts and Pretexts* (1932), in T. Augarde (ed.), *Oxford Dictionary of Modern Quotations*, Oxford
   University Press, Oxford, 1991, p. 109.
7. Adapted from C. Argyris, *Reasoning, Learning and Action*, Jossey-Bass, San Francisco 1989,
   pp. 28–9, and D. Schön, *Educating the Reflective Practitioner*, Jossey-Bass, San Francisco, 1987,
   pp. 260–1.

The following is a transcript of some of the things Bridget said to Alex. These statements represent the whole range of meaning that Bridget communicated to Alex.

'Alex, your performance is not up to standard and, what's more, you seem to be carrying a chip on your shoulder. It seems to me that this has affected your performance in a number of ways. I have heard words like "sloppy", "uncommitted", "disinterested" used by others in describing your recent performance. Our people cannot have those characteristics.

Let's discuss your feelings about your performance, Alex. I know that you want to talk about the injustices you feel have been perpetrated against you in the past. The problem is that I am not familiar with the specifics of those problems. I don't want to spend a lot of time discussing things that happened several years ago. Nothing constructive will come of it. It's behind us. I want to talk about you today, and about your future in the firm.'

(a)   *Write an analysis and critique of the way Bridget dealt with the problem.*

(b)   *What recommendations would you give to Bridget to make her performance more effective?*
      You are a colleague of Bridget's. Imagine that Bridget comes to you and asks: 'How well do you think I dealt with Alex?' What would you tell her? You are to assume that Bridget's purpose in coming to you is to learn.

(c)   *You have 10 minutes' preparation time. Make a note of what you will say to Bridget. Note down any thoughts or feelings which, for whatever reason, you will not communicate to her.*

(d)   *In pairs, take turns at role playing the conversation between Bridget and her colleague.*

(e)   *Feed back to each other and the group.*

Self-development is not just a question of formulating new rules or action theories to shape future behaviour. It also involves modifying or even eliminating old ideas and attitudes which have outlived their usefulness. This is not easy, since many of our attitudes and beliefs stem from our cultural backgrounds and our value systems as well as our past experience. They are deeply ingrained and powerful. They may therefore continue to shape our behaviour even though we are prepared to accept and try out new ideas.

Argyris and Schön[8] describe two kinds of action theories:

- *Espoused theories*, which are what we say we believe in. In other words, we use these to justify our behaviour. Here is a familiar scenario: 'the tutors are always telling us how important it is in exams to answer the question rather than write all we know about the subject. I ignore that at my peril, because if I write all I know about the subject, I'll lose marks for irrelevance.'

- *Theories-in-use*, which are implicit in what we actually do, and so are usually tacit. They often conflict with our espoused theory. If we take our example further, the speaker, going against her espoused theory, writes everything she knows about the

---

8. *Theory in Practice: Increasing Professional Effectiveness*, Jossey-Bass, San Francisco, 1974, and *Organisational Learning*, Addison-Wesley, Reading, Mass., 1978.

subject in the exam. She may be unaware of this, or if she realises she has done so, cannot explain her behaviour.

### EXERCISE 2.4  Write all I know about . . .

*In your groups, consider which values and assumptions you think underpin this particular theory-in-use.*

In your reflective conversations, then, you deconstruct your theories-in-use to learn about and challenge the values and assumptions that shape your behaviour, and other people's. Argyris and Schön call this *double loop* learning. On the other hand, failure to confront the validity or otherwise of your theories-in-use restricts your learning to *single loop;* you are defensive about your actions and this closes your mind to new ideas and change. As Argyris says:

> Individuals or organisations who achieve their intentions or correct an error without reexamining their underlying values may be said to be single loop learning.[9]

Furthermore:

> We strive to organise our individual and organisational lives by decomposing them into single loop problems because these are easier to solve and to monitor.[10]

As we saw in Chapter 1, the swamp is crawling with double loop issues. Imagine, for example, that a client goes to see a solicitor about a divorce. She wants to take her husband 'to the cleaner's' and stop him seeing the children. This particular lawyer, on the basis of his experience and reflection, firmly believes that disputes like this have better outcomes if resolved through mediation. This is his espoused theory. His client, on the other hand, is adopting an adversarial position. The lawyer's suggestion that she consider mediation therefore falls on deaf ears. She is looking for confrontation.

How is the lawyer going to resolve the conflict between his espoused theory and what the client wants him to do?

If the lawyer decides to go along with the client's wishes, how might he justify going against his espoused theory?

His internal conversation might go something like this: 'Let's look at this coolly, objectively and rationally. The client isn't interested in a mutually acceptable compromise. This is a win-lose situation. My duty is to do what the client wants. My own feelings about it are immaterial. Moreover, if I insist too strongly on getting my own way, she'll probably get herself another lawyer and the firm will lose the business. Anyway, who knows, she's probably right about her situation. A fight may well be the best thing in this instance.'

---

9. C. Argyris, *Reasoning, Learning and Action*, Jossey-Bass, San Francisco, 1989, pp. xi–xii.
10. *Ibid.*, p. xii.

## Distancing and disconnectedness

Studies done by Argyris and Schön[11] give us information on how discrepant reasoning works. They distinguish two reasoning processes: *distancing* and *disconnectedness*.

DISTANCING means that, consciously or unconsciously, we find reasons not to follow our espoused theory. In our example, the lawyer uses three typical ways of distancing himself from responsibility for following his espoused theory:

1.  He objectifies the issue: 'Let's look at this objectively and rationally … My own feelings are immaterial.'

    Although his espoused theory is based on his experience, reflection and personal value system about acceptable outcomes, he is trying to persuade himself that there is an objective reality about the situation which can be arrived at through a depersonalised reasoning process.

2.  He claims to follow a 'greater good' argument by saying that there are commercial imperatives which overshadow his personal beliefs and preferences: '… she'll probably get herself another lawyer and the firm will lose the business.'

3.  He seeks refuge in the safety of professional ethics. In denying the validity of his own feelings about the matter he is falling back on the principle that a lawyer has a duty to do what the client wishes, provided that this is not illegal or unethical: '… My duty is to do what the client wants.'

This use of the norms and values of a group or organisation to which we belong, in order to avoid following our espoused theory, is common in the distancing process.

Alternatively, we may make a deliberate decision not to follow our espoused theory: 'My career is more important to me than rocking the boat'; or 'I've got such a heavy caseload that I haven't got the time or energy to justify recommending mediation to the client or justifying it to the senior partner.'

DISCONNECTEDNESS occurs where you are unsure or unconfident about your own reasoning processes. In our example the lawyer's final remark in his internal conversation appeared to doubt the universal validity of his espoused theory: '… she's probably right about her situation'. Often a person's disconnectedness may arise from their unwillingness to challenge the norms and values of a group, membership of which is valued by the individual.[12] This is particularly likely to be the case with members of a profession like law which has powerful socialisation processes. The traditions, ethics and prestige of the profession all combine to discourage individuals from challenging its norms and values. The long-standing resistance of many barristers and judges to fusion in the legal professions is a good example.

---

11. See above, Exercise 2.3, note 7.
12. K. Lewin, *Resolving Social Conflicts: Selected Papers on Group Dynamics* (1948), cited in Johnson and Johnson, *Joining Together: Group Theory and Group Skills*, pp. 36–42.

You may also find it difficult or impossible to reason in a frame-breaking way because you are not sure what theory you espouse: 'I'm not altogether happy with this system, but it's been operating for 20 years, so there must be some good in it.' Or you might keep changing your mind about it: 'Normally I would say we should stick to the rule, but in this case I'm prepared to make an exception.'

We fall prey to these processes of distancing and disconnectedness fairly frequently. We are not usually aware that they are happening because they are such automatic responses to difficult or threatening situations. Moreover, we would argue that the notion of 'espoused theory' is essentially technical–rational in that it assumes we have access to our innermost reasoning processes and can articulate them. This is certainly not the case; some processes are more deeply embedded in our unconscious than others and uncovering these may be impossible. Where we can identify and analyse such processes, we may begin to develop the art of double looping. However, it is problematic to assume that we can always convert unconscious into conscious reasoning.

## Summary

To summarise the discussion on experiential learning so far:

---

- Having experiences does not constitute learning.
- Learning is a cyclical process which continues through life.
- The process involves double looping: questioning not only your behaviour, but your values and attitudes too.
- You need to train yourself to recognise when you are distancing or disconnecting yourself from your espoused theories.

---

## The learning diary

### EXERCISE 2.5  Re-cycling

*Either:*

(a)  *think back to your reflective conversation in Exercise 2.1; or*
(b)  *reflect on some other event/problem/dilemma which is on your mind.*

*Then write your reflective conversation in circle form.*
(Figure 2.3 below might help you.)

From the discussions and feedback on these exercises you will doubtless have noticed that some reflections, action theories and feelings may be shared by a number of the group. You will find that the process of sharing in group work and group feedback and discussion will assist your own learning process.

However, you will also have discovered much that is personal to you. Your learning circle for Exercise 2.5, for example, will be quite different from those of your fellow students. The purpose of Exercise 2.5 is to introduce you to the device of the

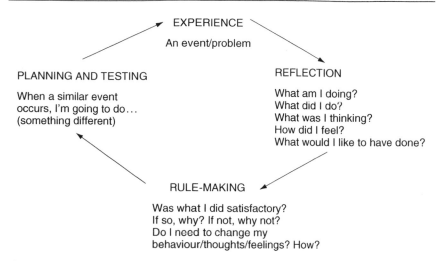

Figure 2.3. Detailed learning cycle.

learning diary, or personal learning log, where you record your reflective conversations with yourself and, if helpful, those with others. This is, of course, your reflection-on-action, and you need to record it as soon as possible after the event.

To guide you into the habit of keeping a log, Honey and Mumford recommend a simple procedure for carrying out steps 2, 3 and 4 of the circle.[13] We summarise it as follows:

1.  *Reviewing the experience*    Start by thinking back over the experience and selecting a part of it that was significant for you. Write a detailed account of what happened. Don't at this stage put any effort into deciding what you learned.
2.  *Concluding from the experience*    List the conclusions you have reached as a result of the experience. These are your personal learning points. Don't limit the number and don't worry about the practicality or quality of the points.
3.  *Planning the next steps*    Decide which learning points you want to use in the future and work out an action plan which covers:
    (a)  what you are going to do;
    (b)  when you are going to do it.

Spell out your action plan as precisely as possible so that:
    (a)  you are clear what you have to do: and
    (b)  it is realistic.

Not only is it essential to get into the recording habit quickly, it is also important to keep in mind its purpose. Remember, careful analysis of your behaviour and attitudes during an event won't enable learning to take place. You need to complete the cycle. This means bringing your action theories to the surface where possible,

13.  P. Honey and A. Mumford, *Using Your Learning Styles*, Honey, Maidenhead, 1986, p. 26.

recognising discrepant reasoning, and experimenting with and modifying your behaviour, thoughts and attitudes. Several circuits will probably be needed before you can do all this. The process is perhaps more accurately described as a spiral in which you continue to refine your action theories in the light of novel experiences.

It is also important to remember that in some instances reflection takes time. It may take several days, weeks or even months before you can make sense of an experience completely.

To give you ideas on the sort of material that is usefully entered in learning logs, here is an example.

### Experience

Today was my assessed negotiation on the civil case.

Up until the day before there really was little to negotiate on, as we had all been caught short over the time. There was much more to do than we appreciated. We were at a pre-action stage but our client did not want to go to court. It was quite interesting thinking about all this later in the week, as on Wednesday morning the settlement between Michael Jackson and a young boy was announced with both sides maintaining their positions. This is what I had wanted to achieve: a settlement with no admission of liability.

My strategy was to avoid an in-depth discussion on liability. I assumed that the other side would readily admit fault and was taken by surprise by how strongly Andy argued about this.

I did plan to start by denying liability but then to concede this quite readily in return for the same from Andy and then discuss quantum.

I was well prepared for this, as we felt the sum they wanted was realistic and quite near to our own estimation. I had looked at comparators in Kemp & Kemp and was quite happy that the amount we both had in mind was reasonable. How could we go wrong? Easily! I did not foresee what happened and found myself unable to steer the conversation round to what I wanted to discuss. Andy took the lead.

### Reflection

I should not have made any assumptions. We were both extremely (unbelievably) nervous and I wonder if that was why Andy talked and talked? Did nerves make him seem adversarial?

I had to interrupt him as I was feeling increasingly lost and uncomfortable. I remember thinking: he hasn't heard the sound of my voice yet! I almost felt superfluous as I couldn't respond at all. He was listing things outside my agenda. This wasn't what I wanted.

If I had been discussing this with Andy as myself, a student, I would probably have admitted that the evidence was inconclusive and going to court would be an expensive gamble, so how much would be reasonable? I should have done this.

I wish I had decided that if the negotiation didn't move my way, after say 10 minutes, then I should have simply changed the tone completely and effectively stopped the messing about and asked about quantum, simply and directly.

We wasted so much time on the evidence that I felt threatened, in that Andy really wanted to hammer home the question of fault. I wasn't brave enough to leave it to one side. It was difficult to counteract his pugnaciousness. I didn't know how to. It's obvious that much comes with experience. Why was I afraid?

I could have regained the initiative and softened the tone if I had done this. We were suspicious of each other. The atmosphere was not open and trusting. Despite myself I was drawn into a stereotypical confrontation.

## Rule-making

I was well prepared on the facts and quantum but my strategy failed. I should not have assumed anything and should been willing to change my plan as the negotiation went on.

I was unable to isolate the real issue and my opening position was not the best. I was in a reactive position and failed to diffuse the atmosphere.

## Planning and testing

I must not be put off by a negotiator who appears competitive. Although I felt totally flattened I could have turned the discussion by being honest and not reacting to this style in a defensive manner. After all, if a fight was what he wanted then no strategy of mine would achieve a fair settlement or any settlement at all.

Next time I would either interject sooner, or allow the negotiator to run out of steam, ignore (more or less) what was said and start again. I played the game this time. I must not allow myself to be intimidated and must try to stay calm and relaxed.

It was fascinating that Andy also said he felt trapped into a situation he didn't want to be in. It was almost as if we were both in a corner and too proud to come out.

I would certainly handle a negotiation differently and remember that this means agreement – a problem solved! I must re-read the manual on this.

EXERCISE 2.6  **More re-cycling**

The following diary entry was made after a workshop on fact analysis. This took place in the second week of a Legal Skills and Process course, when the students had just started to work together in small groups.

*In your groups, consider these questions:*

1.   *What is the event or problem which concerns this author?*
2.   *Under which heading is this problem identified?*
3.   *Is the section headed 'Rule-making' relevant to the author's reflections on the problem?*
4.   *What does the author plan to do at the next opportunity?*
5.   *If you were recording this event, what would you do that is different? Why?*

**Experience**
We were asked to construct a plausible diagram of an inadequately described road
traffic accident as a group effort.

**Rule-making**
A group task which demonstrated that without a clear common view of the goal
much effort is wasted in negotiation. It also demonstrated that without adequate
information it is impossible to choose between alternative or multiple scenarios,
except by the exercise of assumptions/prejudices which are necessarily
idiosyncratic and not always consciously recognised.

**Reflection**
No surprises or enlightenment here but a good opportunity for challenging
one's own abilities and self-image. The necessity of working in a group highlights
my own lack of patience and a need for restraint when dealing with others. I must
accent the positive aspects of each group member and praise their efforts. Survival
in the profession, especially during articles, will depend upon co-operation and
mutual respect; I must take advantage of the opportunity to practise 'social
interaction' and accord each member the respect they feel they deserve.

I can easily mess this up! J (my partner) describes me as having the 'personality
of a bulldozer' and I must resist the temptation to push the group in the direction
I have chosen. I must practise encouraging and motivating them as individuals
through skilled negotiating rather than bullying tactics.

**Action**
Speak softly and leave the big stick behind. Learn to value others and their
contributions. Learn to trust others to perform their tasks while giving them what
help they ask for.
*Do not dominate, do inspire.*

We should point out that your learning diary, like all diaries, is confidential.
We do not make a habit of analysing your entries in public or asking other students
to do so. However, you might find it helpful to discuss an entry with a tutor or
another group member if you are not sure that your recording method is enabling
you to learn. The purpose of Exercise 2.6 is to show you there are more and less
effective ways of recording and to give you an idea of the possible pitfalls.

## Student/teacher roles and relationships

By now some of you may be wondering what you have let yourselves in for,
choosing a course where it appears you are required to 'let it all hang out', often
in public. And you haven't even had a go at client interviewing yet. What is going
on? Is all this 'touchy feely' stuff really necessary?

EXERCISE 2.7  **Re-learning**

You should now be in a position to reflect on the experiential learning method as we have used it so far in this book.

*What comparisons can you make between this method and the more usual method you have experienced in your legal studies? To help stimulate your thoughts, here are some pertinent questions:*

(a)    *Is learning active or passive?*
(b)    *What is the relationship between teacher and student?*
(c)    *Who controls the learning process?*
(d)    *What is assessed?*

This type of learning is very different from what most of you are used to. In your law studies the content is usually determined by your tutors and delivered in a formal way, through lectures and seminars. The emphasis is normally on the *outcome* of the teaching provided, i.e. you are assessed by 'answers' given in assignments and exams. Formal instruction of this kind is so familiar that most of us are comfortable with it. We know what is expected of both teacher and students.

Experiential learning, however, is more concerned with the *process* of learning: hence its emphasis on the analysis of behaviour, thoughts and feelings. It is not only important to practise performing the skill, it is just as important to know what you are feeling when doing it. This can be quite discomfiting, even threatening, for some of us at first, because we naturally feel inhibited in front of people we don't know very well.

It would be so easy if we could pick up skills by sitting there quietly, absorbing information and saying nothing, while the teacher or fellow-students do the talking and make fools of themselves role-playing. Or perhaps we could 'mug up' from a textbook like this one and miss a workshop or two. However, as we have said, you learn a skill by doing it. This means practising and experimenting actively. Others will observe and perhaps comment on your mistakes. Losing some of your self-esteem can be painful.

Furthermore, your tutor is not the expert in control that you are used to, with more or less right answers that you can depend on. Much of what your law lecturer tells you will be new information. In skills-based learning, however, she will be helping you develop and transfer skills you already have to a different context. For example, you may know nothing about the Companies Acts at the start of your company law course. However, all of you know how to ask questions, and spend a good deal of your time asking questions. What you probably won't yet know is how to use your questioning skills effectively in client interviewing, legal negotiation and advocacy.

The skills tutor's task is to design situations in which reflective practice can take place. In this sense she has control of the content, like the law lecturer. However, much of the rest is left up to you. This can be disconcerting at first. We won't give you a set of rules on how to conduct a negotiation, for example. We can help you develop guidelines on how to structure a negotiation, but the context is so unpredictable and open-ended that your guidelines could inhibit your reflection in action if you suddenly find yourself in the swamp.

Likewise, we won't tell you afterwards how you should have conducted the negotiation. This is the subject of your reflection, where you discover what works for you and make your own rules through your own learning cycle. You are therefore in control of your learning, whereas our task is to provide the opportunity for you to test, reflect and share your experience with us and the group. This is more valuable than going through the process on your own.

## What kind of learner am I?

What formal courses do not take into account is that people have a variety of learning styles. We are all able to use different strategies at different times in the process of learning. Some of you will consider yourselves good at exams, for example, while others will be happier talking in seminars. Most of us have one or two preferred styles, and find difficulty in adapting to ways of learning we find uncomfortable.

Honey and Mumford[14] have identified four styles:

- Activist;
- Pragmatist;
- Reflector;
- Theorist.

Any attempt at self-development must begin with a self-assessment. This should take the form not only of an assessment of needs in relation to *what* should be learnt, but must also take into account *how* it should be learnt in the light of what you know about your own learning style and your other personal strengths and weaknesses.

EXERCISE 2.8  **The learning styles questionnaire**

(a)    *Complete Honey and Mumford's questionnaire and plot your answers on the graph provided.*

(b)    *Read Honey and Mumford's Learning Styles – General Descriptions.[15] How accurately do you think the questionnaire results describe your learning style preferences?*

(c)    *Exchange your results with a friend and discuss the extent to which your self-assessment corresponds with their assessment of your learning style preferences.*

(d)    *What do you think are the strengths and weaknesses of each style?*

14. P. Honey and A. Mumford, *The Manual of Learning Styles*, Honey, Maidenhead, 1992. David Kolb also describes four learning styles: diverger, converger, assimilator, accommodator: *Experimental Learning*, pp. 61–98.

15. See Honey and Mumford, *The Manual of Learning Styles*.

(e)    *Which type(s) of learner(s) learn(s) most or least from the following learning activities?*
  – *taking part in games and role-playing exercises;*
  – *listening to lectures;*
  – *working in groups;*
  – *working alone;*
  – *activities emphasising feelings and emotions;*
  – *lots of examples to illustrate how things are done;*
  – *open-ended exercises, such as client interviewing;*
  – *preparing answers to questions for a seminar;*
  – *preparing a number of drafts for an essay;*
  – *being offered systems, theories, checklists;*
  – *being 'pitchforked' into an activity with no apparent purpose;*
  – *practising techniques and getting feedback;*
  – *giving a seminar presentation;*
  – *brainstorming.*

(f)    *Do you think that your legal education is geared towards a particular learning style?*

Exercise 2.8 should have helped you not only to identify your own habits, likes and dislikes and the reasons for them, but also to draw some more general conclusions:

(a)    the four learning styles correspond to points on the learning circle;
(b)    we tend to prefer a style we are familiar with;
(c)    no one learning style is better than any other;
(d)    some types of learning involve activities appropriate to more than one style;
(e)    other types of learning are heavily dominated by one type of activity, so that only those learners with the corresponding style will benefit from it.

Identifying learning preferences may not resolve all our learning problems, but should at least encourage reflection. Most of our students have found it helpful to discover *why* they don't enjoy, or learn from, particular learning activities.

Moreover, the questionnaire can provide the starting-point for you to aim to become an all-round learner, so that all four styles are within your repertoire. If you are a Theorist/Reflector, for example, you now know you will need to develop Activist/Pragmatist styles to help you come to terms with experiential learning techniques.

Look again at the questionnaire items you crossed. These are pointers to what you will need to think about. For instance, if you crossed Question 15: 'I take care over the interpretation of data available to me and avoid jumping to conclusions', you will probably conclude that this is not an advantageous position to adopt when collecting and analysing the facts of your client's industrial accident!

It might help to divide your crossed items into strong and less strong disagreements:

●    this is me most of the time;
●    this is me in some situations, not in others, etc.

Do you tend to jump to conclusions when answering a problem question in an exam as well? Are you prone to making value judgments? If so, what kind, and in what situations?

Careful reflection and analysis will help you develop strategies for improving on your weak points, and pinpoint opportunities for trying them out: at the next seminar on problem analysis, for example. There is plenty of material for your learning diary here.

EXERCISE 2.9  **Concepts**

In this chapter we have discussed a number of concepts. We list the main ones below. The procedure for learning these concepts is as follows:

1.   *Divide into pairs.*
2.   *Each pair is to:*
     *(a) define each concept, noting the page on which it is defined and discussed, and*
     *(b) make sure that both members of the pair understand the meaning of each concept.*
3.   *Combine into groups of four. Compare the answers of the two pairs. If there is disagreement, look up the concept and clarify it until all agree on the definition and understand it.*

| | |
|---|---|
| *reflection in action* | *reflection on action* |
| *tacit knowledge* | *action theory* |
| *espoused theory* | *theory-in-use* |
| *discrepant reasoning* | |
| *double loop learning* | *single loop learning* |

EXERCISE 2.10  **Review questions**

**1. Formal and informal learning**
*In your groups, consider:*

(a)   *What do the following scenarios have in common?*
      *– a child falling off a bike;*
      *– an employee receiving instruction on how to work new equipment;*
      *– a law student listening to a lecture;*
      *– a pupil barrister watching a judge sum up to the jury;*
      *– a young football fan watching a match for the first time.*[16]
(b)   *What don't they have in common?*

16.  Adapted from L. Mullins, *Management and Organisational Behaviour*, Pitman, London 1993, p. 115.

(c)    *What are the main features of*
    (i)  *formal, and*
    (ii) *informal learning?*
(d)    *It is said that learning is a social process. What does this mean?*
(e)    *What are attitudes, and what purpose do they serve?*

## 2. Experiential learning
*Divide into pairs. Each member of the pair should:*

(a)    *briefly describe the characteristics of experiential learning, and then*
(b)    *explain these to her partner, so that she understands them. Illustrate with examples if it will help.*

## 3. There's a hole in my bucket
*In your groups, discuss this statement:*

> *Trainers too often assume that learners are empty buckets waiting to be filled up by the training method the trainer favours. The fact that the buckets are different sizes, and/or leak and/or are upside down is conveniently overlooked.*[17]

## 4. When did you last double loop?

(a)    *Think back to the last time you analysed a legal problem in a seminar. Did you use single or double loop thinking processes?*
(b)    *Do you think judges should use double loop thinking when deciding cases? If so, why? If not, why not?*

## 5. What have you learnt from this chapter that is new to you?

## Further reading

J. Webb, C. Maughan, M. Maughan, M. Keppel-Palmer and A. Boon, *Lawyers' Skills* (Legal Practice Course Guide), OUP, Oxford, 2004, ch. 11.

P. Honey and A. Mumford, *Using Your Learning Styles*, Honey, Maidenhead, 1986.

P. Honey, and A. Mumford, *The Manual of Learning Styles*, Honey, Maidenhead, 1992.

D. Schön, *Educating the Reflective Practitioner*, Jossey-Bass, San Francisco, 1987, Chapters 2, 10.

17.  Honey and Mumford, *The Manual of Learning Styles*, p. 1.

# 3

## Law talk and lay talk: lawyers as communicators

The primary purposes of this chapter are to examine why communication skills have become such an important issue for professional practice; to explore the nature of communication processes; to consider ways in which various communication problems arise, and hence to identify opportunities for increasing communicative effectiveness.

## Objectives

To:

- Increase your awareness of the part played by communication skills in legal education and practice.
- Enable you to obtain greater technical understanding of the communication process.
- Encourage you to experiment with a number of communication processes, and reflect on those processes.
- Enable you to articulate your own principles for effective communication.
- Enable you to reflect critically on the nature and role of communication skills in legal practice.

## Supports benchmark statements

Demonstrates a basic ability

4. Analysis, etc:
   - to bring together information and materials from a variety of different sources;
   - to produce a synthesis of relevant issues in relation to a topic;
   - to make a critical judgement of the merits of particular arguments;
   - to present and make a reasoned choice between alternative solutions;
5. Autonomy and ability to learn:
   - to act independently in planning and undertaking tasks;
   - to reflect on their own learning and to seek and make use of feedback;

6.   Communication and literacy
   ● to present knowledge or an argument in a way which is comprehensible to others
     and which is directed at their concerns.


## Lawyers need to talk!

Our ability to communicate in language rather than just signs is perhaps the most
distinctive feature of human evolution, and central to our ability to order and
make sense of our world. To say that communication skills are important to all of
us is therefore an incredibly trite understatement.

The importance of communication skills for the lawyer should be equally
obvious, but, until quite recently, this aspect was neglected by legal education
and training. The academic image of the lawyer is of someone poring over text-
books and law reports, or perhaps arguing some fine point of principle before the
Court of Appeal or House of Lords. The need to communicate actions and ideas to
people, other than through the very rarefied medium of appellate argument,
does not figure highly in the traditional model. Indeed, though legal education
offers plenty of practice in certain, structured, kinds of writing – notably essay
writing – oral skills and the other dimensions of writing skill are frequently taken
for granted (at least at the academic stage). The reality of lawyering is usually very
different.[1]

Lawyers talk to clients; they negotiate and do deals with other lawyers; they
mediate and arbitrate; they act as advocates before courts and tribunals. Of course,
written communication is also important in most lawyering processes: letters have
to be written; statements of case and other documents drafted. But initial impressions are made, and outcomes often determined, by spoken language. As we shall
see, however, communication – both written and spoken – is more problematic
than we think. Even in the most general of circumstances, communication can be
disrupted by distractions, distortions and misperceptions.

To provide a foundation for your communication skills, we address four key
issues in this chapter:

1.   Why communication skills matter.
2.   How the communication process operates.
3.   The barriers and bridges to effective communication.
4.   The importance of effective intercultural communication.

1. For research emphasising the primacy of orality, see J. Morrison and P. Leith, *The Barristers'*
   *World*, Open UP, Milton Keynes, 1993. In legal theory, the concern with (oral) communication is
   particularly apparent in the hermeneutic and rhetorical concerns of Critical Legal Theory – see,
   e.g., B. de S. Santos, 'The Postmodern Transition' in A. Sarat and T. R. Kearns, *The Fate of Law*,
   Michigan UP, Ann Arbor, 1991.

## Why communication skills matter

Let's begin with something you are all familiar with.

EXERCISE 3.1 **What makes a good teacher?**

In this exercise we want you to think about your experiences in education – either in university or if you prefer, at school or college. It is unlikely that you will have uniformly good impressions of all the teaching you have received, so:

(a)   *What, from your experience, are the characteristics of a good teacher? Make a note of the main skills and attributes you would expect of a good teacher.*

(b)   *Consider how many of those features are aspects of communication skills.*

(c)   *Now, by analogy, identify the communication skills you would expect a lawyer to display.*

We would guess that most of the skills and attributes you have discussed will have at least a communicative dimension. For teachers and lawyers, being knowledgeable about the area is not enough – most of us have come across the problem of the teacher who 'knows his stuff, but can't put it across' to understand why that is the case. The ability to explain a problem, to recognise where and how comprehension problems will arise, to give meaningful feedback (orally and in writing) all depend on communication. Even intangibles like 'enthusiasm' are conveyed, at least in part, by the way teachers communicate. And we shall see that most, if not all, of these attributes are relevant to lawyers as well.

However, the weight of evidence points to the conclusion that lawyers are not effective communicators. As long ago as 1979 the Benson Commission commented that:

> We consider that more should be done to emphasise the importance of gaining the client's confidence and establishing a sound professional relationship with him ... To establish good communications with another person is a professional skill which must be, and is, learnt by many others besides lawyers.[2]

In a representative sample survey conducted for the Law Society in 1988, about a third of the people surveyed thought of solicitors as easy to talk to, and even fewer – only a quarter – described them as easy to understand. As the researchers note, this placed solicitors about on a par with bank managers in terms of perceived approachability. That just about says it all! Even among those respondents who had used solicitors, only a third described them as easy to understand, though 45 per cent said that they were easy to talk to.[3]

2. *Royal Commission on Legal Services, Final Report*, vol I, Cmnd. 7648, HMSO, London, 1979, para. 22.31.

3. J. Jenkins, E. Skordaki and C. Willis, *Public Use and Perception of Solicitors' Services*, Research Study No. 1, The Law Society, London, 1989, pp. 9–10.

Given the centrality of communication skills to most legal tasks, a statistic which suggests that one out of every two clients is likely to have had communication problems with their lawyer is rather alarming. It certainly suggests that communication difficulties form part of the crisis of confidence in the professions.

So, why are lawyers poor communicators? The causes are bound to be quite complex, but it might be helpful to try and identify at least some of the factors if we are to improve the situation for ourselves.

EXERCISE 3.2 **The problems with 'law talk'**

*Stop reading at this point and write down no more than three general reasons why lawyers might be poor communicators. Then compare your list with the comments that follow.*

We suggest that the following are key considerations.

### Differences between legal and everyday language

These differences are, of course, an underlying cause of our problems. They are most obvious at the semantic level. As lawyers we have a distinctive vocabulary which uses words from outside of the general language, and words which are part of the general language, but which have radically different meanings in legal and general usage – like the term 'consideration', for example.[4] There are also a number of more subtle, but equally fundamental, differences in the grammatical and discourse[5] features of legal language which also serve to restrict its comprehensibility, especially in written as opposed to spoken communications.[6] In legal writing the differences include unusual word order in sentences, *nominalisations* (i.e. the use of nouns created from verbs), repetition of whole phrases and sentences, etc. Take, for example, the following extract from a consumer contract:

> . . . and to consent to immediate execution upon any such judgment and that any execution that may be issued on any such judgment be immediately levied upon and satisfied out of any personal property of the undersigned . . . and to waive all right of the undersigned . . . to have personal property last taken and levied upon to satisfy any such execution.[7]

---

4. This point is developed more fully by J. A. Holland and J. S. Webb, *Learning Legal Rules*, OUP, Oxford, 5th edn, 2003, pp. 90–8.
5. For present purposes we use 'discourse' simply to mean the use of language in a 'succession of related sentences, as in a conversation or text': S. Pinker, *The Language Instinct*, Penguin, Harmondsworth, 1994, p. 475.
6. We discuss written communication in greater depth in Chapters 7 and 8
7. Cited in V. Charrow, J. Crandall and R. Charrow, 'Characteristics and Functions of Legal Language' in R. Kittredge and J. Lehrberger (eds.), *Sublanguage: Studies of Language in Restricted Semantic Domains*, de Gruyter, Berlin, 1982, p. 175 at p. 178.

It is too easy to say that the problem is just one of language, however. The *real* problem is the apparent incapacity of lawyers to overcome the communication barriers that these linguistic differences create. We cannot assume we are effective translators between legal and everyday English, but of course that does not make it any the less our *responsibility* to ensure we are understood.

### The professionalising process

This in itself is a substantial part of the problem. We spend three (or more) years in law school where the emphasis is on thinking – and sounding – like a lawyer. Julius Getman,[8] for example, has stressed the way law school introduces us to, and expects us to use, a variety of rhetorical styles, which he terms 'professional', 'critical' and 'scholarly' voices, while 'human voice' – 'language that uses ordinary concepts and familiar situations without professional ornamentation'[9] – becomes lost and undervalued. How is this so?

During this period most of our 'law talk' is directed at other lawyers: students and teachers who are themselves immersed in the legal language. This is an obvious feature of classroom interaction where, crucially, the law is normally presented and discussed on the assumption that the participants have command of a shared legal language. But, as research has shown, the closed nature of law talk can also spill over into, and be reinforced by, less formal interaction among lawyers. The law school and its members are often socially and spatially self-contained.[10] Many law faculties have their own buildings and separate library facilities; law teachers and students frequently emphasise the importance of their identity and distinctiveness as 'lawyers'. Law students themselves may structure a significant part of their social lives separately from other students – the success of many student law societies is a testament to this.

There is a tendency, therefore, for lawyers to emerge as a race apart from the rest of the institution. However, once qualified, the shift to a practice environment involves a radical change in communicative context. Much of our law talk must now be directed to lay clients who do not share our common legal language.

### Difficulties in identifying and resolving communication problems in practice

We need to recognise that the ability to communicate is the classic tacit skill. This has two implications: first, we tend to assume that we all communicate more or less effectively with each other on a day-to-day basis. Furthermore, having qualified, we tend to assume that we are pretty clever, articulate, human beings, and therefore

---

8. 'Voices' (1988) 66 *Texas Law Review* 577.    9. *Ibid.*, p. 582.
10. S. Urmston Philips, 'The Language Socialization of Lawyers: Acquiring the "Cant"' in G. Spindler (ed.), *Doing the Ethnography of Schooling: Educational Anthropology in Action*, Waveland Press, Prospect Heights, II, 1988, pp. 176–209.

efficient communicators. Unfortunately, as a vast body of research into individual psychology and organisational behaviour has shown, this is not necessarily so.

Second, we rarely reflect on what or how we are communicating except when things go wrong (if then). If a communication failure is not identified at the time, there is no obvious reason to try and modify our behaviour. In the professional context, clients do not always articulate their dissatisfaction and, even if it is clear that the client is displeased, the cause – if it is poor communication – may not always be identified as such, even by the client. Sometimes communication failures may not emerge simply because the client does not come back.

The availability of advice and training once we are in the working environment tends to be variable in both quantity and quality. This will affect a firm's capacity both to identify poor communication, and to do anything about it.

### The lack of training in communication skills

There was a serious lack of training in this area until the last ten years or so. Fortunately, communication skills training is now firmly embedded into vocational training and available through continuing education courses, as well as in a growing number of undergraduate programmes.

What does this exercise tell us about our potential to be effective communicators? Well, we would suggest that it shows how necessary it is to start thinking more deeply about the communication process, and to question the linguistic assumptions which we tend to make as students (and teachers) of law. In this sense it may require us to unlearn some of the established practices of traditional legal education. Let's begin this process by going back to basics.

## How we communicate

When we communicate with someone we are actually putting into operation quite a complex process of social interaction, involving perception, articulation, response, etc. Psychologists have attempted to describe this communication process through the construction of communication models. Can you devise your own model?

EXERCISE 3.3 **Communication models**

*Illustrate, diagrammatically or pictorially, your view of what is happening in:*

(a)   *a conversation between two people; and*
(b)   *writing a letter to a friend (you are advised to try and describe each process separately).*

If possible, do this exercise in class, so that you can compare your different models. Then compare your own models with those devised by psychologists: see, for example, the models presented by Michael Argyle,[11] and by Hargie and Marshall,[12] which emphasise the dynamic nature of social interaction in rather different ways. *When you have done this, consider:*

(a)   *What differences, if any, exist between the two models of communication you have considered?*

(b)   *Are there particular aspects of the process which the formal models emphasise, but yours does not?*

(c)   *Do the formal models you have considered give a 'full' picture of the communication process or, in your view, do they miss anything important?*

We will leave you to work out the differences for yourselves, but do remember that the existence of such differences does not make either form of communication better or worse than the other. It simply tells us that each will serve some purposes better than others. This does mean that we have to be sensitive to what has to be conveyed through and achieved by each particular communication.

## Barriers and bridges to effective communication

Good communication is not just about the right choice of medium or message. There are many other aspects of the communication process which, if taken for granted, can destroy effective communication, but which equally, if used constructively, can increase our potential as communicators.

In this section we consider factors that are important in constructing bridges or barriers to effective communication. We cannot realistically hope to regulate all of them all of the time, but an awareness of their impact can help us to sustain the quality of interaction.

Underlying all of these factors is one basic problem. That is, of course, that creating a climate for good communication is rather more difficult than we generally realise. We can begin to see why via a further exercise.

EXERCISE 3.4   **A Martian description**[13]

For this exercise you need two participants:

A.   (your tutor) plays the Martian visitor,
B.   You, the helpful Earthling.

Participants should sit back-to-back, so that there is no possibility of eye contact.

---

11. *The Psychology of Interpersonal Behaviour*, Penguin, Harmondsworth, 5th edn, 1994, p. 117.
12. O. Hargie, 'Interpersonal Communication: A Theoretical Framework' in O. Hargie (ed.), *The Handbook of Communication Skills*, Routledge, London, 1997, pp. 30–2.
13. Loosely adapted from P. Bergman, A. Sherr and R. Burridge, 'Games Law Teachers Play' (1986) 20 *Law Teacher* 21 at pp. 25–6.

A friendly Martian is visiting the planet Earth and is eager to find out more about the daily lives of its people. You (participant B) are in radio contact only with the Martian. Your Martian friend speaks basic English reasonably fluently, but has only a rudimentary understanding of the language, and may not fully comprehend the meaning behind many words. S/he (i.e. participant A) will ask you to describe a typical day in your life, and, during the course of your description, may ask you to explain or clarify words/activities s/he does not understand.

After running this exercise, the group should:

(a)   ask the participants to describe the communication problems they confronted, and to explain how those problems made them feel; then

(b)   reflect on the implications this exercise has for lawyer–client communication.

The kind of problems you are likely to identify in this exercise reflect a number of generic difficulties which we shall now explore in more detail in the following five sections.

## The effect of non-verbal cues

The Martian exercise was made more difficult by the lack of face-to-face conversation. This cut out any reliance on things like facial expression or hand gestures, which can greatly facilitate communication. These are both examples of *non-verbal communication* (NVC). NVC is simply a global term that is used to describe ways of conveying meaning other than by words.

NVC is extremely important to the communication process. Birdwhistell, for example, has estimated that the verbal component of face-to-face conversation accounts for only 35 per cent of the total 'message' while 65 per cent of the average communication is non-verbal.[14] In part this reflects the fact that NVC is 'multi-channelled'[15] – i.e. it can be transmitted and received by visual, auditory, tactile or olfactory means. It is not restricted to the auditory channel of verbal communication, nor to the visual channel of written communication. By recognising the interplay between verbal and non-verbal communication we can begin to appreciate just how much we communicate with *all* our senses, not just the obvious ones.

Research also suggests that the verbal and non-verbal components of a message are used to convey different things: the verbal element mainly conveys information, while NVC more often conveys mood, feelings and attitudes.

In this section we shall focus on two key aspects of NVC. The least commonly known of these is properly called *prosody*, or sometimes *paralanguage*. This term describes the non-verbal vocalisations we all use to express things. Sighs are thus a form of prosody, as are all the other grunts and snorts we use to express our

14. R. L. Birdwhistell, *Kinesis and Context*, Allen Lane, London, 1971.
15. T. Singelis, 'Nonverbal Communication in Intercultural Interactions' in R. W. Brislin and T. Yoshida (eds.), *Improving Intercultural Interactions*, Sage Publ., Thousand Oaks, Calif., 1994, p. 268 at p. 275.

feelings – for example, the sorts of things that appear in comics as 'Erm' or 'AAARGH!!' Other more subtle modifications, such as changes in pitch, stress and intonation, or rhythm, and pauses in speech are also aspects of prosody. As an example, try saying the following statements out loud, first as a command:

*You're not going out there!*

then as a question:

*You're not going out there?*

In this example you can hear how prosody serves the same function as punctuation in written communication.

The more widely known form of NVC is, of course, *body language*. An awful lot of academic material has been produced about the importance and meaning of body language; some of this, often in a very partial and misleading form, has found its way into general folklore. It is particularly dangerous. Much was written on the meaning of body language in the 1970s and early 1980s which lacked rigour. Do remember that the meaning of body language is largely dependent on the specific context, culture and status of the actors; it must be viewed as part of the whole communication process – both verbal and non-verbal – and meanings cannot safely be reduced to the checklist approach favoured by some textbooks.

What is important is to try and ensure that your own body language does not serve as a possible barrier to communication. It means, as a minimum, that you need to raise your own awareness of the kinds of signals we send out. The next two exercises are intended to help in this process.

EXERCISE 3.5 **The lights are on ...**

This exercise is in two stages. For the first phase, you need to divide into pairs. Then follow your tutor's instructions.

Now, for the second phase, divide into groups of three. Then, again, follow your tutor's instructions.

*Feed back from this exercise before moving on to Exercise 3.6.*

EXERCISE 3.6 **Body talk**[16]

This exercise works with pairs or groups of three. If you are working in a threesome, one person should act as observer for each 'experimental' part of the exercise. In our own workshops, we like to get two pairs/threes working on each set of exercises independently, and then reporting their findings to the group as a whole. We have laid out the exercise in a way that encourages you to work through the first three

16. Adapted from S. Habeshaw and D. Steeds, *53 Interesting Communication Exercises for Science Students*, Technical and Educational Services, Bristol, 1987, pp. 25–9.

phases of the learning cycle. Some of the exercises may only serve to remind you of some fairly basic precepts of social behaviour, so we have not automatically included a final testing phase to close the circle. If you feel it is helpful to do that for yourselves, then you should go ahead and do so. To help you we have given some indication with the first exercise of the kind of things that ought to go under each heading. With each category you might also like to think of its relevance or significance for legal practice.

## Proximity

(a)   Experience: Carry on a brief conversation with a partner:
    (i)   standing too close for comfort;
    (ii)   standing too far apart for comfort;
(b)   Reflection: (Describe your feelings. Why did you feel like that?)
(c)   Rule-making: (What appear to be the rules about physical distance between people in our society?)

## Posture

(a)   Experience: Practise:
    (i)   tense and relaxed postures;
    (ii)   welcoming and rejecting postures.
    Without identifying your choice of posture verbally, get your partner to describe what they see/feel.
(b)   Reflection:
(c)   Rule-making:

## Orientation

(a)   Experience:
    (i)   Compare the orientation of students and teacher(s) in the room. What do you see?
    (ii)   Choose an appropriate moment for one member of the pair/team to turn their back on the rest of the group. Wait for comments.
(b)   Reflection:
(c)   Rule-making:

## Physical appearance

(a)   Experience:
    (i)   Think back to your first impressions of someone else in the group. Do you think your first impressions were right?
    (ii)   Describe somebody you know well. What elements of the description are most important to you?
    (iii)   Contrast the sets of characteristics you have used.
(b)   Reflection:
(c)   Rule-making:

**Hand/head movement**

(a)   *Experience: Look around the room; what can you infer from:*
   (i) *hand movements (especially hand to head or face);*
   (ii) *position and movement of heads.*
(b)   *Reflection:*
(c)   *Rule-making:*

One of the things this exercise (indirectly) emphasises is the potential for the communicative context to be manipulated, and for non-verbal communication to be used to convey very powerful messages about the speakers. While you might wish to question the ethics of some such practices, note that lawyers are becoming increasingly conscious of the importance NVC can have in presenting a person in a particular light. This is illustrated in the following extract, which shows how video-taped evidence enabled counsel in one major American lawsuit to use witnesses' NVC to reinforce their theory of the case. The issue in *Pennzoil v Texaco* was whether Texaco had fraudulently induced a third company, Getty Oil Company, to break a binding merger contract with Pennzoil. This required the Pennzoil lawyers, Terrell and Jeffers, to establish that Texaco management had *actual knowledge* of Pennzoil's deal with Getty. As is commonly the case with American fraud trials, the issues of fact were to be determined by a jury, from a bewildering array of evidence – lengthy depositions and extremely dense and unexciting corporate communications ...

Of the 63 depositions spanning 15,000 pages of transcript during the 'discovery' phase of the case, 15 had been video-taped by Jeffers and Terrell to assure the jury got a first-hand look at 'the flavour of these people'. Besides permitting Pennzoil to introduce exhibits, the video depositions also enabled it to retell the story of the Getty Oil war – a story intended to depict Petersen [Getty Oil's chairman] and his people as double dealers.

Gordon Boisi, the investment banker who solicited Texaco's bid to defeat [Getty's] deal with Pennzoil, fluttered his eyelids, sniffed and chuckled at the lawyers' questions and held forth in the gobbledygook of the takeover game. When asked in the video-tape whether he would be testifying as a live witness at the trial, Boisi replied, 'If my schedule allowed' – not the kind of answer that impresses jurors who by that time had given up nearly a month of their lives to the case. And when he was asked in the video whether he had come and gone during Gordon [Getty]'s absence from the 'back door' board meeting, he swallowed before answering, 'I guess that occurred'.

Bart Winokur, the outside counsel for Getty Oil who had entered the Getty Oil board meeting in Houston in Gordon's absence, gave intelligent and straightforward responses but appeared a little shifty. He fidgeted in his seat. His eyes darted around the room. His voice at times adopted a somewhat sassy tone ... There was something just a little unconvincing about Winokur; while he testified that it was not his practice to take notes during meetings, he was holding a pen in one hand.

Sid Petersen, an executive whose career had been scuttled just as it was reaching its peak, came off as smug and defensive, tossing his head, folding his arms across his chest, heaving sighs. When he was asked a question about [Pennzoil chairman, Hugh] Liedtke's agreement to honour his golden parachute, Petersen snapped, 'I don't give a damn what Mr Liedtke approved. He had nothing to say about it. *I* had a contract.'[17]

## Environmental factors

Communication can be influenced by a huge range of environmental or situational factors. These are commonly lumped together under the term 'noise' which rather graphically describes the distracting effect that such extraneous factors can have on communication. 'Noise' in this sense will include obvious factors such as interruptions, the comfort of our physical environment, the layout of a room or office, or the impact of *real* noise (a pneumatic drill outside the office window!), etc.

Subtler elements, like the absence of face-to-face communication (as in the Martian exercise), or whether or not we are on 'home territory' will also influence the quality of communication.

Note that these are all factors which tend to be more or less controllable, which means we almost always have some capacity to improve the environment within which we communicate.

## Personal factors

Personal factors may also create considerable disruption to effective communication by, for example, creating misunderstandings or by generating a sense of social distance between lawyer and client. Examples of personal factors which can influence communication include:

**Appearance**
Whatever the rights and wrongs of this, clients tend to expect their lawyers to look like their image of the typical lawyer. Going against that expectation is risky. Too casual an appearance will raise questions about your professionalism; equally, in some contexts, dress that is too 'slick' or expensive will emphasise the social distance between you and your client.

**Credibility**
Your effectiveness as a communicator depends in part on your credibility. This will be enhanced by evidence of reliability, consistency and trustworthiness on your part. It will be damaged by your failure to respond promptly, or appropriately, to

17. From T. Petzinger Jr, *Oil & Honor: The Texaco–Pennzoil Wars*, 1987, cited in K. Roberts and D. Hunt, *Organizational Behaviour*, PWS–Kent Publ., Boston, Mass., 1991, p. 242. The jury found in Pennzoil's favour and ordered Texaco to pay the extraordinary sum of $10.53 million to Pennzoil for the loss of access to Getty's oil reserves.

other communications; by poor quality work and by inconsistent advice and decision-making.

### Expertise

Generally individuals who are perceived to have expertise on the topic in question are thought to be more credible and effective as communicators. As research by Avrom Sherr[18] into lawyers' interviewing skill casts some doubt on clients' capacity to rate the communicative competence of their lawyers, the emphasis here appears to be very much on *perceptions* of expertise rather than the reality. Perhaps it doesn't matter so much what you know, so long as you sound convincing!

### Sincerity

Insincerity can often become apparent through a lack of congruence between verbal and non-verbal communication. The lawyer who makes all the appropriately sympathetic noises when interviewing, but manages to look totally uninterested in the whole business is not going to convince.

### Stereotyping

This is a device we all use to some degree to form impressions about people. Our stereotypes will commonly provide some basis for our opinions of others as good, bad, friendly, reserved, honest or dishonest, etc.[19] Such stereotypes can then influence the messages we send out to or about those individuals. Since stereotypes are often based on characteristics like gender, race, disability, body size, or language,[20] they can be potentially prejudicial, if not downright discriminatory. The dangers are obvious: beware of acting on stereotypical information.

For the client in particular, such personal failures can be alienating, contributing to a sense that the lawyer is not interested in her problem.

One other particular personal factor than can influence communication is *emotion*. How we react to certain people or situations has a tremendous impact on our social interaction. At one level this is obvious: our mood, level of stress, etc, all affect the way we react, and are things that we seek, consciously or intuitively, to display or suppress according to the nature of particular situations. But our concern with emotion goes deeper than that. Once you start to think about it, it is also fairly obvious that connections exist between a person's emotional state, their behaviour and their 'cognition' or thought processes. For example, think how

18. 'The Value of Experience in Legal Competence' (2000) 7(2) *International Journal of the Legal Profession* 95.
19. Cf., in the legal context, R. Bull, 'The Influence of Stereotypes on Person Identification' in D. P. Farrington, K. Hawkins and S. Lloyd-Bostock (eds.), *Psychology, Law and Legal Processes*, Macmillan/SSRC, London and Basingstoke, 1979, p. 184.
20. For example, the concept of *standard language ideology*, i.e. that there is only one 'proper' way to speak English, serves as a classic form of social stereotyping – see generally E. B. Ryan and H. Giles (eds.), *Attitudes towards language variation: Social and applied contexts*, Edward Arnold, London, 1982. Cf. Chapter 7 below.

extremes of emotion, like fear or anger, can interfere with our capacity to 'think straight.'[21]

As professionals, often dealing with people in stressful situations, we need therefore to develop ways of coping with both our own emotions and those of others, particularly our clients. The emotional dimension of the lawyer's work cannot simply be ignored.[22]

## Cultural factors

It can be argued that the very fact you are a trained lawyer presents a culture gap between you and your clients. This gap is created by the same training and professionalisation processes we talked about at the beginning of this chapter. These can have a number of effects on your communication. We have identified three main issues here.

First there is the matter of what Getman terms *voice*: the use of conventional professional or scholarly voice has a number of effects on lawyers' discourse.

It encourages the use of more complex sentences than we tend to use in informal speech situations. Examples of what we mean include the obvious, like legalistic (or pseudo-legalistic) phraseology (e.g. 'Now, Mr Smith, can you tell me what you were doing on the night in question?'). It also covers the adoption of unusual grammar, such as the use of the passive in question construction (e.g. 'Who was chased by the policeman?' rather than 'Who did the policeman chase?'). We know that people are far more likely to make mistakes in answering passive than active questions.[23] Even if the grammar you are using does not make you harder to understand (neither of the examples here are difficult), it can emphasise difference or social distance.

It also encourages you to fall into the trap of using 'jargon' or technical terms of art where that is unnecessary. Clients do not usually need to know that they might have an action under s.2 of the Unfair Contract Terms Act; nor are comments like 'We need to ask for further and better particulars' likely to leave them much the wiser about the progress of their case. The same problem does not, of course, arise in communications with other lawyers, where technical language can actually facilitate communication by acting as a kind of shorthand. Other lawyers will generally understand references to 'TWOC-ing', 'disclosure', etc.

Next there is *linguistic ability*. Distinct from the problems of officialese, you will have to face the fact that your use of language may be different from some, perhaps even most, of your clients. This may be apparent in the respective breadth of your

21. This commonsense notion is supported by psychological research: see D. Meichenbaum and L. Butler, 'Cognitive Ethology: Assessing the Streams of Cognition and Emotion' in K. Blankstein et al (eds.), *Advances in the Study of Communication and Affect*, Vol 6, Plenum Press, New York, 1980.
22. We return to this theme in Chapter 5.
23. See, e.g., P. Wright, 'Is Legal Jargon a Restrictive Practice?' in S. Lloyd-Bostock (ed.), *Psychology in Legal Contexts: Applications and Limitations*, Macmillan/SSRC, London and Basingstoke, 1981, p. 121 at p. 123.

vocabularies; the fluency of your speech; the range of sentence structures you use. This may not only serve to heighten apparent social difference, but may serve to emphasise the powerlessness of a particular client – even if the client comprehends the language you are using, she may be unable to use it effectively to converse with you or to exercise her rights against another.

Lastly, legal practice also involves a number of *'translation' problems*. This does not simply mean that lawyers confuse by jargon, though that may be part of it. Rather, it means that, in talking about problems, lawyer and client are essentially on different wavelengths, focusing on different objects in their discourse. This is because law serves as a *meta-language* – a mechanism, as Mulholland puts it, for 'declaring in words what is happening in words'[24] – a different language for describing what has already been described.

In part, translation is a necessary feature of legal work. As Maureen Cain has pointed out, the discrepancy between legal and everyday discourse goes beyond mystification. The lawyer has first to translate the client's ordinary-language problem into an object that has some legal identity. So, a problem relating to the joint ownership of a house can only be resolved once it is clear to the lawyer whether the property is held on a joint tenancy or tenancy in common. As Cain explains:

> . . . [t]he house which in everyday discourse the wife and husband regard as 'theirs' turn[s] out in legal discourse to be capable of being theirs in many different ways . . . if the legal discourse had exactly paralleled the everyday discourse it would not have been possible to achieve a solution in one but not the other . . . [25]

Further translation is then required for the lawyer to convert the objective in legal discourse (e.g. transfer of ownership from joint tenancy to tenancy in common) into the outcome desired by the client (e.g. the ability to dispose of the share in the property by will). As Cain concludes: '[a]bility to translate is the specific skill of lawyers, and . . . their definitive practice.'[26] For lawyers it is this ability to move between discourses[27] that has to become tacit, yet, perhaps for the reasons we have already discussed, this frequently does not happen.

Moreover, there are at least two particular problems that can arise during the translation process. To understand how each of these problems arise, we need to

---

24. *The Language of Negotiation: A Handbook of Practical Strategies for Improving Communication*, Routledge, London and New York, 1991, p. 78; see also M. Cain, 'The General Practice Lawyer and the Client: Towards a Radical Conception' in R. Dingwall and P. Lewis (eds.) *The Sociology of the Professions: Lawyers, Doctors and Others*, Macmillan, London and Basingstoke, 1983, p. 106 at p. 111.
25. Cain, 'The General Practice Lawyer and the Client' p. 117.     26. *Ibid.*, p. 118.
27. However, lawyers are extremely adept at this kind of code switching when it suits their purposes; research by W. O'Barr and his colleagues shows that trial lawyers use a range of language varieties in court, including formal legal language, standard English, colloquial English, and the local dialect: *Linguistic Evidence: Language, Power and Strategy in the Courtroom*, Academic Press, San Diego, 1982, p. 25.

understand a bit about how communication works. This takes us first into what is technically termed the 'pragmatics' of communication, and then into the structure of what are called 'communication episodes'.

At one level, communication tends to build on certain shared expectations. As Pinker puts it:

> ... listeners tacitly expect speakers to be informative, truthful, relevant, clear, unambiguous, brief and orderly. These expectations help to winnow out the inappropriate readings of an ambiguous sentence, to piece together fractured utterances, to excuse slips of the tongue ... and to fill in the missing steps of an argument.[28]

If communicative action is based on these assumptions of good faith, then failure to meet the expectations created by the communication will clearly be damaging to the relationship between the communicators. To give an extreme example, if Caroline tells a student 'no one has ever failed Julian's Welfare Law course' the student might be less than pleased to discover, on starting the course, that no one had failed because the course had not run before. While one cannot say strictly that Caroline's statement is untrue, the reasonable expectation created by that speech act is that the course *has* run and no one has failed.

However, we also have the capacity to break these good faith rules *without* destroying understanding. In certain situations we deliberately use what is *not* said to convey covert layers of information. Stephen Pinker provides a good example with the following letter of recommendation:

> Dear Professor Pinker,
>
>     I am very pleased to be able to recommend Irving Smith to you. Mr Smith is a model student. He dresses well and is extremely polite. I have known Mr Smith for three years now, and in every way I have found him to be most co-operative ...[29]

This is the sort of reference that is guaranteed not to secure you a job. The letter contains no information relevant to the employer's needs. The covert message sent out by this breach of expectation is: 'this is not the person for you.' The necessity for the disguise is understood on both sides. One does not lightly engage in the breach of trust implicit in writing a reference that actually says, in Pinker's memorable phrase: 'Stay away from Smith, he's dumb as a tree.'[30] So long as these conventions are understood, there is no failure of communication. So much for the theory, now back to the problems.

Our first problem is that the complexity of the translation process can lead to a mismatch in lawyer and client expectations. In essence, we get problems of incomplete translation, where the implications of a lawyer's statement do not

---

28. *The Language Instinct*, Penguin, Harmondsworth, 1994, p. 228. Note that such shared expectations are likely to be absent in intercultural communication; see below.
29. *Ibid.*, p. 229.   30. *Ibid.*

'connect' in lay terms, because the 'what-goes-without-saying' for a lawyer needs to be said for a lay person to appreciate it. We cannot break the good faith rules here, because there is not the shared understanding necessary to convey the covert message. Mismatched expectations about legal costs and how they are to be met are a perennial favourite in this context.[31]

Now, to return to the theory again, we said that we also need to consider how communications are constructed as stories or 'episodes'.

We tend to communicate events and feelings by organising them into particular narrative, story, structures. These psychologists call *communication episodes.*[32] Communication episodes display the following 'ERAC' (Events – Response – Actions – Consequences) features:

● Stories are initiated by something happening or something being said: *Events.*
● A character in the story will have a psychological *Response* to those events.
● The character will use that response to construct goals which are reflected in later *Action.*
● These actions will then have certain *Consequences.*

For example: Laurel and Hardy go to a nightclub. Laurel's girlfriend Fay meets them there. Fay really fancies Hardy and spends most of the evening dancing with him. Laurel is jealous; he sits glowering at the bar and gets more drunk as the night goes on. He finally snaps and 'glasses' Hardy in the face. Hardy is taken off to hospital.

This short story conforms to all the characteristics of an episode. The initiating event is Hardy and Fay dancing. Laurel responds by getting more and more jealous. Laurel's jealousy apparently leads to more and more drink and then to the moment of violence (action) and Hardy's injury and hospitalisation (consequences). The causal links between the ERAC stages ensure that it rings true. Theory suggests that even complex narratives correspond to this structure, because they contain sets of embedded episodes – stories within the story.

So, let's apply this particular bit of theory to law as well. First, as we will argue further in Chapter 10, lawyers need to understand how stories are constructed so as to reconstruct and use them in a way that makes sense to the audience – for example, the jury in your client's trial. Research suggests that we are not always effective as professional storytellers. Second, at an ideological level, the translation process this involves can significantly change the nature and even the 'ownership' of the client's story. This is a difficult idea, so let us try and explain.

---

31. See, e.g., G. Davis, *Partisans and Mediators: The Resolution of Divorce Disputes*, Clarendon Press, Oxford, 1988.
32. D. E. Rumelhart, 'Understanding and summarizing brief stories' in D. La Berge and S. Samuels (eds.), *Basic Processes in Reading: Perception and Comprehension*, Lawrence Erlbaum Associates, Hillsdale, NJ; T. Winograd and F. Flores, *Understanding Computers and Cognition*, Ablex, Norwood, NJ, 1986.

In traditional practice,[33] a point will come in a case where the lawyers take possession of the client's story and translate it from a lay into a legal narrative. In translating it for a legal audience, the lawyers will frequently change aspects of the communication episode on which it is based. This may be because the client's version of the story does not seem to fit the legal argument in the way the lawyers want, or it may be that the parts of the story that are of the greatest social relevance to the client are not of great legal significance. This, it is argued, has a number of disempowering consequences for the client. If this sounds overly dramatic, consider the case of Sara Thornton. In 1990 she was convicted of the murder of her alcoholic husband, Malcolm, after stabbing him as he lay on her sofa in a drunken stupor. As is so often the case, the evidence was contradictory and confusing. Thornton had a long history of violence against Sara and her ten-year-old daughter Louise. When drunk he gave way to violent and possessive rages. But Sara too had a reputation for a violent temper and a history suggesting mental instability.

One of the problems which emerged in Sara's trial appears to have been a problem of incomplete translation. Thornton's defence had decided to develop a theme of diminished responsibility. Given that the law of provocation did not provide a defence[34] where the killing was premeditated (as was arguably the case here), the defence, perhaps understandably, chose not to follow that line. Yet Thornton's testimony in court was far more consistent with a 'lay' theme of provocation (i.e. provocation in response to a long period of abuse, rather than a single incident), than with either of the 'legal' defences of provocation or diminished responsibility. The result was that the story did not fit the legal frame. While the lay version provided the necessary causal links between the ERAC features (husband's long term violence (E) – created a 'pressure cooker' response (R) – pressure finally 'blew' with the stabbing (A) – husband died (C)), the legal version did not. For whatever reason, it looks suspiciously as if her lawyers had failed to carry their client with them in their translation of the case from one of 'lay' provocation to 'legal' diminished responsibility.

We shall return to the issues of client narrative and empowerment in Chapter 5.

## Inter-cultural factors

In court, witnesses are not allowed to decide how to tell their stories. During examination-in-chief the examiner takes control of the narrative away from the storyteller with a strict question-answer format which moves from requests for

---

33. From an ethic of care perspective, ownership of the narrative is recognised as a participation issue. As a lawyer you need to be open to the needs of the client, even if this means that your strategy becomes focused on how you lose the case, rather than whether you win.
34. The definition of provocation has substantially altered since the House of Lords decision in R v Smith [2001] 1 AC 146, which permits characteristics of the defendant to be taken into account when assessing the degree of provocation and the ability to exercise self-control. This whole area of provocation is currently under discussion; see Law Commission Consultation Paper 173, *Partial Defences to Murder*, 2003.

brief narrative towards more controlling or coercive questions: for example, 'Did you hear the defendant shout those words?' (Yes or No?) or 'Did you see who was bending over the victim, the defendant or her friend Chris?' (Allows only two options). The trial lawyer's task is to steer the witness's testimony in very specific directions in order to obtain persuasive evidence to support the client's case, hence the need for rigid control.[35]

This style of controlling narrative is problematic for witnesses not accustomed to it. For example, Aboriginals testifying in Australian courts, unfamiliar with the question-answer format, tend to say 'yes' to questions (or 'no' to negative questions) regardless of whether they agree the answer is 'yes' (or 'no'). They may respond in the same way if they don't understand the question. This style is known as *gratuitous concurrence*.[36] It is consistent with the emphasis on maintaining surface harmony and dealing with conflict 'behind the scenes' in Aboriginal culture. 'Yes' may mean something like 'I know I have to cooperate with your lengthy questioning, and I hope that this answer will help bring the questioning to an end' – or it may signal agreement to the proposition in the question.

Diana Eades has found that gratuitous concurrence is significant when investigating poor communication and misunderstanding between Aboriginal and non-Aboriginal speakers of English in court hearings, police interviews and client interviews. The concurrence is likely to increase with repeated and pressured questioning, especially over a lengthy period of time. In one study she analysed a trial held in Brisbane in 1995 in which three young teenage Aboriginal boys had accused six police officers of unlawfully depriving them of their liberty. Her aim was to show how the defence lawyers took advantage of this tendency to use gratuitous concurrence in their cross-examination of the boys.

> The much-quoted evidence classic . . . claims that cross-examination 'is beyond any doubt the greatest legal engine invented for the discovery of truth'. But this 'greatest legal engine' for the discovery of truth is based on a fundamental legal assumption that repeated questioning is the way to test the consistency of a witness' story. Elsewhere . . . I have pointed out that this cultural assumption is not necessarily shared with Aboriginal societies.[37]

The defence's central purpose was to cast doubt on the prosecution claim that the police had forced the boys into their car. If they succeeded in showing that the boys got in voluntarily, then clearly the prosecution would fail. The questioning therefore sought to undermine the credibility of the boys by showing they were

---

35. See P. M. Tiersma, *Legal Language*, University of Chicago Press, Chicago, 1999, p. 159.
36. See K. Liberman, 'Understanding Aborigines in Australian Courts of Law', 40 *Human Organisation* 1981, pp. 247–55.
37. 'Evidence Given in Unequivocal Terms: Gaining Consent of Aboriginal Young People in Court' in J. Cotterill (ed.), *Language in the Legal Process*, Palgrave Macmillan, Basingstoke, 2002, pp. 162–79. The magistrates accepted the defence's argument that the boys were criminals with 'no regard for the community'; in Eades' words, the boys gave up their liberty voluntarily 'while the police took them for a ride, both literally and metaphorically'.

unreliable in some way or that their stories were contradictory and inconsistent. The extract below reveals the aggressive style of one member of the defence team (text in capital letters indicates shouting):

1.  DC1: And you *knew* when you spoke to these six police in the Valley that you didn't have to go anywhere with them if you didn't want to, didn't you?
2.  W: No.
3.  DC1: You *knew* that Mr Coley I'd suggest to you, PLEASE DO NOT LIE. YOU KNEW THAT YOU DIDN'T HAVE TO GO ANYWHERE if you didn't want to, didn't you? DIDN'T YOU? DIDN'T YOU, MR COLEY?
4.  W: Yep.
5.  DC1: WHY DID YOU JUST LIE TO ME? WHY DID YOU JUST SAY 'NO' MR COLEY? YOU WANT ME TO SUGGEST A REASON TO YOU MR COLEY? THE REASON WAS THIS, THAT YOU WANTED THE COURT TO *BELIEVE* THAT YOU THOUGHT YOU HAD TO *GO* WITH THE POLICE, ISN'T THAT SO?
6.  W: Yep.
7.  DC1: AND YOU *LIED* TO THE COURT, TRYING TO, TO YOU *LIED* TO THE COURT TRYING TO PUT ONE OVER THE COURT, DIDN'T YOU?
8.  W: No.
9.  DC1: THAT WAS YOUR REASON, MR COLEY WASN'T IT? WASN'T IT? MR COLEY?
10. W: Yep.
11. DC1: YES. BECAUSE YOU WANTED THE *COURT* TO *THINK* THAT *YOU* DIDN'T KNOW THAT YOU COULD TELL THESE POLICE YOU WEREN'T GOING *ANY* WHERE WITH THEM. THAT WAS THE REASON WASN'T IT? WASN'T IT?
12. W: Yep.
13. DC1: Yes.

Although we can't know for sure what was in the witness's mind here, the harassment and shouting certainly suggest gratuitous concurrence as a possibility. The 'yep' answers in 4, 6, 10 and 12 seem to indicate that the witness recognises he will be harassed until he gives the answer the questioner wants; we can't confidently assume he intends to agree the answers are 'yes'. Note, too, the complex sentence in 11. There are four embedded clauses, likely to confuse many witnesses regardless of age, linguistic and cultural background.[38]

This example of miscommunication illustrates the extent to which cultural assumptions and shared expectations underpin the way we communicate. Common language, values and rules of behaviour form the basis on which members of a culture exchange meaning with one another in their daily lives.

---

38. The Aboriginal boys' ages may also have contributed to misunderstanding. When subjected to the question–answer interrogatory style in court, child witnesses may answer questions with the answer they think the questioner wants rather than the truth. (See K. J. Saywitz and S. Moan-Hardie 'Reducing the Potential for Distortion of Childhood Memories', (1994) 3 *Consciousness and Cognition* 408–25). However, if questioned in a way which helps them tell their version of events, their testimony may be as reliable as that of adults. (M. Zaragoza et al (eds.), *Memory and Testimony in the Child Witness*, Sage Publications, Thousand Oaks, Calif., 1995.)

What we have in common enables us to predict the responses to some of our messages because we take for granted a shared assumption that others see the world in the same way as we do. But people growing up in other cultures see things very differently. So how do people understand each other when they do not share a common cultural experience? And how are you going to handle cultural difference in legal practice?

The way we dealt with cultural difference in the past is nothing to write home about. Milton Bennett describes our initial 'flight or fight' response, inherited from our ancestors. We flee behind walls or to the suburbs to avoid it, or if we have to confront it, we fight. Further:

> Historically, if we were unsuccessful in avoiding different people, we tried to convert them. Political, economic and religious missionaries sought out opportunities to impose their own beliefs on others. The thinking seemed to be, 'If only people were more like us, then they would be all right to have around.' This assumption can still be seen in the notion of the 'melting pot' prevalent this century in the United States. It is difficult for many people to believe that any understanding at all is possible unless people have become similar to one another.
>
> When we could not avoid or convert people who were different from ourselves, we killed them. Examples of genocide are not so very far away from us, either in time or distance, and individual cases of hate crimes are tragically frequent. Of course, one doesn't need to physically terminate the existence of others to eliminate them. When we make their lives miserable in our organisations and neighborhoods, we also 'kill' them – they cannot flourish . . .[39]

Modern theories of communication in cross-cultural situations take cultural difference rather than similarity as their starting point to provide answers to a central question: how, in a pluralistic society, do we balance the need for common understanding with the need to preserve cultural diversity?

### Non-verbal behaviour

When we consider the impact of cultural difference in communication behaviour, NVC is one aspect that stands out because, as we noted earlier, most of the message is conveyed through this medium. Moreover, much of NVC is unconscious. For example, one unconscious NVC behaviour, thought to be universal, is 'eyebrow flashing':

> When people greet each other at a distance, wishing to show that they are ready to make social contact, they raise their eyebrows with a rapid movement, keeping them raised for about one-sixth of a second. The behaviour has been noted in many parts of the world, and is considered universal (though some cultures suppress it, e.g. the

39. M. J. Bennett, 'Intercultural Communication: A Current Perspective' in M. J. Bennett (ed.), *Basic Concepts in Intercultural Communication: Selected Readings*, Intercultural Press Inc, Yarmouth, Me., 1998.

Japanese, who consider it indecent). We are not usually aware that we use this signal, but it evokes a strong response in a greeting situation, and is often reciprocated. To receive an eyebrow flash from someone we do not know is uncomfortable, embarrassing, or even threatening.[40]

Have you ever noticed yourself or your friends eyebrow flashing?

An interesting distinction is that made by Edward Hall, describing 'high' and 'low' context cultures. A high-context communication is one in which 'most of the information is already in the person, while very little is in the coded, explicit, transmitted part of the message'. An example of a high context culture is Japanese. Speakers imply and infer meaning from relatively vague statements: the way something is said, who says it and to whom, where, at what time, and where it comes in relation to utterances said before or after it. Most of the message is conveyed through NVC – 'in the person'.

Low-context cultures (e.g. English-speaking) convey more of their message in verbal language: 'communication where the mass of information is vested in the explicit code.'[41] Non-verbal behaviour is seen as adding to, or commentary on the verbal message rather than a necessary part of it. However, even in low-context cultures NVC carries a significant percentage of the meaning, so it is vital to avoid interpreting a message solely in the context of one's own culture.[42]

Turn-taking in a group conversation gives rise to a variety of responses across cultures. English speakers cue turns using eye contact. The speaker ends her turn with her eyes in contact with the person she thinks will speak next. If she lowers her eyes instead, no one knows whose turn it is, and a confused babble might result. However, in some Asian cultures the speaker does not make eye contact with anyone at the end of her utterance, and participants are expected to stay silent for a short while before the next person speaks. In a group of 'eye-intensive' participants, an Asian who is not familiar with this cultural pattern may never get a turn. Some African-American, Middle Eastern and Mediterranean cultures use a 'relay-race' pattern. Whoever wants the next turn just starts talking. Both Asians and English-speaking cultures may interpret this as interrupting.

## Communicating our thought processes

Across cultures, differences in our thinking patterns will be reflected in different communication behaviour. North Europeans and US Americans (particularly men) apparently tend to use a linear, logical thinking style, moving through a series of linked steps to a conclusion. If a speaker or writer strays off line, a listener or reader may respond: 'I don't follow', or 'What point are you making?' or 'Stop going all round the houses and get to the point!' This is a culturally embedded,

40. D. Crystal, *The Cambridge Encyclopedia of Language*, Cambridge University Press, Cambridge, 2nd edn, 1997, p. 406.
41. *Ibid.*, p. 61.    42. In the literature this is known as 'ethnocentric interpretation'.

Western style of rational, clear, critical thinking we are expected to learn and use in our education system. However, Milton Bennett tells us about a quite different style:

> An example of a contrasting style occurred in a group of international and US American students. I had asked a question about early dating practices, and the Americans all answered with fairly concise statements that made some explicit connection to the question. When a Nigerian in the group replied, however, he began by describing the path through his village, the tree at the end of the path, the storyteller that performed under the tree, and the beginning of a story the storyteller once told. When, in response to the obvious discomfort of the Americans in the group, I asked the Nigerian what he was doing, he said, 'I'm answering the question.' The American students protested at that, so I asked, 'How are you answering the question?' He replied, 'I'm telling you everything you need to know to understand the point.' 'Good,' said one of the Americans. 'Then if we're just patient, you will eventually tell us the point.' 'Oh no,' replied the Nigerian. 'Once I tell you everything you need to know to understand the point, you will just know what the point is!'

What this student was describing is a circular, or contextual discussion style. It is favoured not only by many Africans but also typically by people of Latin, Arab, and Asian cultures. And in the United States, the more circular style is commonly used by African Americans, Asian Americans, Native Americans, Hispanic Americans, and others. Even among European Americans, a contextual approach is more typical of women than of men. The only natural cultural base for the linear style is Northern European and European American males. That doesn't make the style bad, of course, but it does mean that other, more prevalent styles need to be considered as viable alternatives. To some extent, this issue has been addressed in the context of gender differences, and it is getting increasing attention in the context of multicultural classrooms.[43]

When people who favour a contextual approach generate an ethnocentric interpretation of the linear style, they may see it as simple or arrogant: simple because it lacks the richness of detail necessary to establish context, and arrogant because the speaker is deciding what particular points you should hear and then what point you should draw from them! On the other hand, proponents of a linear style are likely to interpret the circular style as vague, evasive and illogical.[44]

EXERCISE 3.7  **Straight to the point or circumlocution?**

In small groups, discuss possible strengths and limits of each style. Think of examples where one might be preferred to the other.

---

43. On gender differences, see, e.g., M. Field Belenky et al, *Women's Ways of Knowing: the Development of Self, Voice, and Mind*, Harper Collins, New York, 1997.
44. Bennett, 'Intercultural Communication', pp. 20–1.

## Values and assumptions

Something fundamental to Western culture is the 'self versus society' assumption – that society is the enemy of the individual because it imposes demands which conflict with the individual's desire for self-realisation. This idea is strange to many Asian and African cultures which view the self as existing only in relation to others; it is your position in a social network that determines who you are. Responsibilities to the group supersede the pursuit of personal rights. Cultures like Japanese that typically value interdependence in groups more highly may therefore regard some manifestations of individualism as unnecessarily selfish. On the other hand, Americans, who typically favour individual rights and the 'pursuit of happiness', may consider some forms of collectivism to be unnecessarily conformist.

The belief in collectivism may help to explain the value put on fixed, hierarchical relationships in Eastern cultures. This is discussed by the American sociolinguist Deborah Tannen. She identifies a mode of communication in Western public discourse she refers to as the 'argument culture': the 'tendency to view everything through the template of a battle metaphor, and to glorify conflict and aggression':

> It is a tendency in Western culture in general, and in Britain and the United States in particular, that has a long history and a deep, thick, and far-ranging root system. It has served us well in many ways but in recent years has become so exaggerated that it is getting in the way of solving our problems. Our spirits are corroded by living in an atmosphere of unrelenting contention.[45]

Socialised as we are into the common law adversarial system, we can easily recognise where Tannen is coming from! In contrast, Eastern cultures value harmony as a method of diffusing conflict. Asian cultures such as Japanese, Chinese, Vietnamese and Thai are strictly hierarchical. Power relations are fixed; this ensures inclusion in the group, which in turn increases intimacy. British and Americans may think it odd that harmony is dependent on hierarchical relationships, because hierarchy suggests the reverse: 'them and us', whereas we tend to associate harmonious relationships with those we conduct on a more equal footing. Tannen illustrates how a 'harmony' culture might express disagreement. She refers to a scandal in Japan in 1992 when the former prime minister was accused of engaging organised crime to stop a public campaign of harassment against him by an opposition political party. The campaign depicted the prime minister as 'a great leader with integrity and honor matched by no other'. Weird. What kind of harassment is this? you'd be forgiven for thinking. Tannen explains with reference to the contrasting American and Japanese customs of giving praise:

> It is common for Americans to offer extravagant praise both publicly (in award and recognition ceremonies) and privately (with expressions like 'Great!', 'Good job!' and 'Terrific!'). Self-evidently good as this may seem to Americans (we tend to assume that

45. D. Tannen, *The Argument Culture: Changing the Way we Argue*, Virago, New York, 1998, p. 5.

praise is a natural motivator – and my own research suggests that it is), Japanese tend to regard such displays as inappropriate and embarrassing ... The minimal human unit in Japan is not the individual but the group, so praising someone who is close to you in your personal or professional life comes off sounding like praising yourself – in other words, boasting ...

Because Japanese are not expected to pile on praise, when they do so, it is interpreted as sarcasm. Also, since everyone knows that criticism will not be expressed directly, they are attuned to indirect means of expressing it. An example ... is a comment like 'What a healthy, well-built young girl you are!' – said to a child who is obviously overweight. In this spirit, making exalting comments about a public figure leads everyone to conclude that the opposite is true. That is the logic by which piling on inflated praise can amount to a harassment campaign that the Japanese press dubbed *homegoroshi*, to 'kill with praise.' The opposition party tried to praise their opponent to death.[46]

Of course, this is not to suggest that Asian cultures don't have ways of expressing aggression and conflict. There are ritualised customs that allow people to let off steam without engaging in physical violence. For example, it has been observed in a part of Papua New Guinea that women 'angered by husbands, relatives, or fellow villagers, can erupt in a *kros*, shouting insults and obscenities loudly enough to be heard by all around'.

Villagers stop what they are doing to listen or get closer. The screaming woman stays near or (preferably) inside her house and often waits until the offender is at some distance or even gone from the village. Were she to venture from the house or engage the offender in direct dialogue, she would risk escalation to actual violence. Though there is a ritual aspect to the display ... It is provoked by genuine anger.[47]

In Asian societies the value placed on harmony, interdependence and the perception of individuals as part of a social network and hierarchy is reflected in the assumption that disputes are often better settled by involving third party intermediaries. In Britain and America, on the other hand, disputes are expected to be resolved by the individuals themselves – 'this is just between us'. Others are unlikely to be invited to help unless we fail to sort it out ourselves. And if the matter gets as far as court, the matter proceeds on a 'win–lose' basis.

Intercultural communication, like lawyer-lay person communication, requires us to recognise that since 'objective' reality doesn't exist, we must take into account the 'clash of differing realities'. To build understanding across cultures and across diverse social groups in our own culture we need to apprehend 'essentially alien experience'.[48] This involves expanding our worldview to acknowledge, understand and respect the behaviour and values of other cultures and social groups we come into contact with as lawyers.

46. *Ibid.*, pp. 220–1.    47. *Ibid.*, p. 222.    48. Bennett, 'Intercultural Communication', p. 15.

EXERCISE 3.8 **Concepts**

After working through this chapter, see if you can come up with your own definitions of the following technical terms. The procedure for learning these concepts is as follows:

*Divide into pairs. Each pair is to:*

(a)  *define each concept, noting the page(s) on which it is discussed, and*
(b)  *make sure that you both understand the meaning of each concept.*
(c)  *Combine into groups of four. Compare the answers of the two pairs. If there is disagreement, look up the concept and clarify it. Make sure you are all agreed on the definition and understand it.*

| | | |
|---|---|---|
| *body language* | *meta-language* | *prosody* |
| *cognition* | *NVC* | *ERAC* |
| *communication* | *translation* | *turn-taking* |
| *gratuitous concurrence* | | |

EXERCISE 3.9 **Jury instructions: clarity or confusion?**[49]

In most US states there are standard instructions drafted by a committee of lawyers and judges, often taken directly from the text of a statute or judicial decision. The instructions are read to the jury by the judge. Below is an extract taken from the 1994/5 O.J. Simpson trial in Los Angeles, instructing the jury on how to evaluate the evidence.

*In small groups:*

(a)  *Identify the features in the text which you think make it difficult to understand.*
(b)  *Trial lawyers are sufficiently motivated to communicate very clearly with the jury in the earlier stages of trial. Can you think of any reasons why the profession doesn't speak clearly to them at this very important stage – before they retire to consider their verdict?*

Discrepancies in a witness testimony, or between his or her testimony and that of others, if there were any, do not necessarily mean that the witness should be discredited. Failure of recollection is a common experience and innocent misrecollection is not uncommon. It is also a fact that two persons witnessing an incident or transaction often will see or hear it differently. Whether a discrepancy pertains to a fact of importance or only to a trivial detail should be considered in weighing its significance.[50]

---

49. We discuss the language of jury instructions further in Chapter 8.
50. Trial transcript vol. 229 at 47136/6, 22 September 1995. See Tiersma, *Legal Language* 1999.

EXERCISE 3.10  **Testing the evidence or badgering the witness?**

In April 2002 two teenage brothers were acquitted of the murder of ten-year-old Damilola Taylor in Peckham, South London. Crucial eyewitness testimony was given by 'witness Bromley', aged twelve. Her evidence collapsed under cross-examination and it was thought that this probably led to the defendants' acquittal. After the trial, Chief Superintendent Tony Crofts, in charge of the murder investigation, expressed doubts about whether a 'fairly vulnerable person, in a very alien environment, who perhaps didn't understand quite what was going on, and where there were others in the court who didn't understand her', in short, a member of the 'underclass', could get a fair hearing. The extract below is taken from a radio interview with Bromley, talking about her several days of cross-examination:

> B: I didn't understand what was happening in court . . . It was very hard and upsetting. He didn't give me a chance to talk properly, like as soon as I'd given him the answer he wanted, he'd stop and then ask the next question . . . he stood there, yeah, and tried to twist my head so I'd come out with the wrong answer . . . so that sometimes I'd sit there, yeah, and I'd think I'm not answering you until I've figured out what you're talking about, so that I'd kind of figure it out, yeah, and then he'd ask me again, and at one point I had to ask the judge if he'd ask Mr Griffiths to give me some time to answer the questions, cos I can't come out with them straightaway.

Interviewer: So you got very confused.
B: And I was getting annoyed as well.[51]
*In small groups, discuss:*

(a)    *the factors that contribute to an unequal distribution of power between speakers in court, and in other legal contexts;*
(b)    *the professional responsibility of the trial lawyer in relation to vulnerable witnesses.*

## Further reading

M. Argyle, *The Psychology of Interpersonal Behaviour*, Penguin, Harmondsworth, 5th edn, 1994.

O. Hargie, *The Handbook of Communication Skills*, Routledge, London, 2nd edn, 1997.

J. G. Getman, 'Voices' (1988) 66 *Texas Law Review* 577.

J. Gibbons (ed.), *Language and the Law*, Longman, London and New York, 1994.

D. Tannen, *The Argument Culture: Changing the Way We Argue*, Virago, New York, 1998.

O. J. Simpson was a former football player who was accused of stabbing to death his ex-wife Nicola and her male companion. Note that English judges in their summing up work from a set of specimen directions to be read to a jury, similar to US pattern instructions. However, judges do not have to use the exact words. See Judicial Studies Board, *Crown Court Benchbook: Specimen Directions*, London, 1999.

51.  *It's my Story*, BBC Radio 4, 7 August 2003. See also the Damilola Taylor Murder Investigation Review: The Report of the Oversight Panel, December 2002, ch. 5: the Trial. http://www.met.police.uk/damilola/ (last accessed 27.10.03).

# 4

# You'll never work alone: group learning and group skills

> We are social beings who spend every day interacting in one group or another, indeed survival without co-operation is unimaginable. However, just because working in groups comes naturally does not mean that we always want to do it, or that we always do it well. In this chapter we introduce you to theories of group behaviour and discuss the qualities that enable people to work and learn together successfully in small groups. The exercises will allow you to test the theory in the learning groups you are involved in. Finally, we consider the role of group work in legal practice.

## Objectives

To:

- Gain an understanding of basic research and theory of group dynamics.
- Identify the essential characteristics of successful learning groups.
- Explore issues that affect the dynamics of small group work.
- Observe and reflect on your own group skills and behaviour, and the skills and behaviour of other group members.
- Consider the role of collaborative work in legal practice and issues that affect the dynamic of lawyer teamwork.

## Supports benchmark statements

Students should demonstrate an ability:

1. Application and problem-solving
   - To apply knowledge to a situation of limited complexity in order to provide arguable conclusions for concrete problems
2. Autonomy and ability to learn
   - To act independently in planning and undertaking tasks
3. Other key skills
   - To work in groups as participants who contribute effectively to the group's task.

## Stone age instincts

Evolution has determined that in order to survive, we must co-operate with our fellow humans. Why?

Physically, humans are slow and weak compared with our wild animal companions: only two legs, blunt teeth, no claws, no wings, and a poor sense of smell. In order to find food, and overcome dangerous predators, early humans learned to pool their knowledge and resources and hunt and protect themselves in groups. Modern man, *homo sapiens*, probably emerged around 200,000 years ago. By 45,000 years ago groups of *homo sapiens* hunter-gatherers were increasingly scattered across the world. These were working family communities, bound by kinship and regulated by informal contracts.[1]

Our genetic constitution has barely altered since then. We have the bodies and brains of Stone Age people who possess an instinct to live and work with other humans.

Of course, our survival instinct is essentially one of self-interest. Selfish gene theory, developed by Richard Dawkins and others, focuses on the role of genetic mutation as the basis of evolutionary change.[2] A gene which promotes its own survival and replication will spread at the expense of other genes. It is self-interested in that its principal ambition is its own evolutionary survival. However, it is only partly true to say that because our genes are selfish, so are our relationships with others. Although we compete with each other, fight over territory, quarrel over possessions and partners, co-operation and altruism can be as advantageous to our genes as competition. For example, a parent will risk injury or death in order to save a child. As Dawkins acknowledges, in the long term 'nice guys', counter-intuitive though it may seem, really do finish first.[3]

From the moment we are born to the moment we die we live, work and learn in groups. Can you imagine yourselves existing without your family or your friends? Almost every part of our lives depends entirely on co-operation and trust, and on taking risks that are dependent on trusting others. As Robert Winston says, 'with barely a second thought we risk flying in jumbo jets, even though we know nothing of aerodynamics and have never met the pilot'.[4] It is by belonging to groups that we develop and modify our ways of thinking and behaving. So why should lawyers be any different?

The nature of legal practice has changed substantially in recent years as firms have had to adapt to changes in their scale of operation, their clientele (and client expectations), and the various professional demands for improved quality and efficiency. Particularly in the larger corporate and commercial practices, such

1. N. Nicolson, *Managing the Human Animal*, Crown Publishers, New York, 2000, p. 21.
2. R. Dawkins, *The Selfish Gene*, OUP, Oxford, 1976, revised edn 1989.
3. *Ibid.* See also Robert Axelrod's ground-breaking book, *The Evolution of Co-operation*, Penguin Books, London, 1990. We discuss the importance of this work for negotiation theory in Chapter 9.
4. R. Winston, *Human Instinct*, Bantam Press, London, 2002, p. 264.

external pressures have led to the creation of new internal management structures and working practices:

> As the nature and focus of work has changed, commercial firms' traditional departments have been complemented by new speciality groups, sometimes within a department, but frequently drawing members from across the firm. Also, lawyers increasingly work as members of teams instead of as Lone Rangers, or at least that is an expressed aspiration.[5]

Even outside of this specialised context there is often a group dynamic to certain aspects of lawyers' work, particularly litigation, which is increasingly characterised as involving team work between solicitor (or solicitors), support staff and paralegals, barrister and client.[6] In Boon and Flood's study of lawyer attitudes following the abolition of the Bar's exclusive rights of audience in the higher courts, solicitor participants valued the opportunity to brief a barrister in line with a client's wishes, and the Bar stressed the importance of building and maintaining good working relationships with solicitors. Moreover, a City senior partner commented:

> We will often have barristers in the office working and going through documents on cases or coming along to a conference in the office, meeting with clients, talking through problems. So I think the Bar has become a lot less stuffy and much more co-operative and, in truth, good barristers have taken on board the idea that it is all – you know, you just become another, albeit very important, member of the team.[7]

But simply recognising that team working and team management skills play an important part in legal work is not enough. Despite our evolutionary tendency to co-operate, we are not all necessarily effective in teams. Some argue that this may be particularly true of lawyers who are often perceived to be instinctive (or are perhaps trained to be?) 'lone rangers', in Greenebaum's term, rather than team players. In a study in the early 1990s, Boon reported that many solicitors felt that the skills and attitudes necessary to good team work were missing or undervalued by the profession. As one of his respondents observed:

> Team management skills are important and something which many solicitors are not good at; it is not something that they are ever coached in or shown how they should go about it. It is also an area of human behaviour where the average lawyer thinks they are

---

5. F. H. Greenebaum, *Coping with a Turbulent Environment: Development of Law Firm Training Programs*, Legal Skills Working Papers, Institute of Advanced Legal Studies, London, 1991, p. 8.
6. See, e.g., E. H. Greenebaum, 'Law Firms and Clients as Groups: Loyalty, Rationality and Representation' (1988) 13 *Journal of the Legal Profession* 205.
7. A. Boon and J. Flood, 'Trials of Strength: the Reconfiguration of Litigation as a Contested Terrain' (1999) 33 *Law and Society Review* 595 at p. 605. However, none of the firms surveyed favoured barristers working 'in house' as advocates. One head of litigation commented: *Barristers are not very house trained. We have many years ago now taken a couple and it was a disaster on their side. They sort of operated as if they were still sole practitioners taking up pretty much any client that they wanted, to do whatever they wanted and it just does not really work.*' (p. 604).

doing alright; they do not need to be shown how to do it. They think it is second nature to them and it is not ... [8]

Like any skilled activity, group working is a learned behaviour and something we can – and should – develop in the context of legal work and training. That, of course, is where this chapter comes in. But as Boon observed, team work is not just about skills, it is about attitudes and values too – things that go to make up our sense of group *identity*.

### EXERCISE 4.1 Who am I?

*In pairs, discuss what groups you belong to.*

The way our family, friends and work colleagues perceive us and interact with us determines our personal identity, so defining the groups you belong to actually helps define you as an individual (for example: 'I'm a law student at the University of Westminster'; 'I'm Welsh'; 'I'm female'; 'I play football for the university'; 'I'm in seminar group 10', etc.). Furthermore, what you do as a solitary person during one day is probably very little indeed compared with what you do in the company of others. Nevertheless, it is all too easy to take for granted our vast knowledge and experience of working with others, and our need to do so. Perhaps this is because so much of what we do involves a number of unconscious processes and interactions. For example, going into a shop to buy some chocolate is a conscious decision, but the actual buying is 'played by ear', dependent on an embedded and unconscious series of interactions and rituals which are culturally determined: (smile ... 'hello' .... 'please' .... 'thank you', etc.).

On the whole, group and individual interests coincide in situations where pooling resources or subscribing to a shared goal help each of us achieve a personal goal we could not achieve alone. For example, in this country we co-operate with our fellow citizens by driving on the left and we trust we can rely on everyone else to do the same; it is certainly not in our self interest or anyone else's to do otherwise. For similar reasons, when in France we do as the French do, adapt our behaviour and drive on the right.

On the other hand there are situations where co-operation runs counter to our self interest. If you and a colleague both apply for the same job, it is unlikely the two of you will get together to prepare for your interviews! Conflict between group and individual interests may be the principal reason why co-operation fails, but our relationships with others can lack harmony for a number of reasons. Often it is to do with the distribution of power and responsibilities within groups. One group member may feel they have no say in decision-making, another may feel frustrated at having to make all the decisions because other members are not 'pulling their

---

8. A. Boon, 'Assessing Competence to Conduct Civil Litigation: Key Tasks and Skills' in A. Boon, A. Halpern and K. Mackie, *Skills for Legal Functions II: Representation and Advice*, Legal Skills Working Papers, Institute of Advanced Legal Studies, London, 1992, p. 43.

weight'. Alternatively, some group members may not feel committed to a group task they find boring or which has no clear purpose. So just because we are creatures designed to co-operate and work in groups does not necessarily mean we always want to do it, or that we always do it well.

Nigel Nicholson makes the point that certain structures, such as bureaucratic organisations, rulebooks or management hierarchies make us do the things that come naturally to us in an unnatural way and that this creates a tension.[9] This is because these structures reflect a rigid and formal surrounding culture imposed, as it were, on the community from outside. Do you remember the scenario we discussed in Chapter 2 in which Bridget had to tell Alex that her work was not up to scratch? This is difficult for Bridget to handle because their relationship is a formal, hierarchical one. Bridget knows that what she says may adversely affect Alex's future in the firm; she may feel unable to be as frank, open or affectionate with her as she could be with, say, a member of her own family or a close friend in this situation.

So to make sure group working works for us, we need to define those qualities that enable groups to work as far as possible in tune with our natural group instincts. As a starting point, let's now begin to analyse your knowledge and experience of working in groups a little more closely.

## Learning in groups: what is it good for?

*Come learn with me and we shall be exemplars of proficiency.*
*But if you yearn to be alone, then you must learn it on your own.* (Anon)

### EXERCISE 4.2  Groups I have known, groups I would like to know

1.  *In your studies, how often do you do the following with fellow students?*
    *(a) Discuss topics and assignment work.*
    *(b) Share resources (e.g. library research, IT resources, lecture or seminar notes).*
    *(c) Use their expertise as a learning resource (e.g. to get help with IT, difficult topics, etc.).*
2.  *What other informal learning activities do you do in company with one or more other people?*
3.  *For each of the activities below, would you prefer to work alone, with a friend, or in a small group? Give your reasons.*
    *– Preparing and delivering an oral presentation or moot.*
    *– Solving a legal problem (advise x).*
    *– Researching an aspect of the law of trusts.*
    *– Preparing and writing a piece of coursework.*
    *– Writing a letter to a client.*
    *– Drafting a contract.*

9. *Managing the Human Animal*, pp. 17, 18.

> – *Defending a client in the Crown Court.*
> – *Negotiating a settlement on behalf of a client.*
> – *Revising for an exam.*
> 4.   *For small group work:*
>   (a) *What are the most important personal qualities you would look for in your fellow group members? Why?*
>   (b) *What personal characteristics would you most want to avoid in your fellow group members? Why?*
>   (c) *What personal qualities can you offer the group to help it work effectively?*
> 5.   *In pairs, discuss your findings, then feed back to the whole group.*

Social scientists do not seem able to agree on what a group is. This should not surprise us, since groups vary in size, purpose, membership, motivation, etc. Below we present a list of characteristics most commentators would probably agree are essential for a group to work successfully:

---

## What is a successful group?

*Membership* – two or more individuals join together to achieve a goal they are unable to achieve by themselves.

*Common purpose* – members have a belief in shared aims and goals.

*Interdependence between members* – each member will succeed only if all members succeed: 'we sink or swim together'.

*Social organisation* – a group is a social unit with norms, roles, statuses, power and emotional relationships.

*Interaction* – members communicate with each other face-to-face and otherwise; the sense of 'group' exists even when members are not together.

*Mutual influence* – each member influences and is influenced by every other member.

*Collective consciousness* – members perceive themselves as belonging to a group.

*Cohesion* – all members are committed to the group and its aims.

*Mutual trust* – members feel comfortable and emotionally secure.

*Involvement* – all members participate and decisions are made by consensus.

---

Kurt Lewin noted that when individuals merge into a group, a new entity is created.[10] This produces synergy, that is, the collective output is greater than the sum of the individual contributions. Members are committed to the common

---

10.  K. Lewin, *A Dynamic Theory of Personality*, McGraw-Hill, New York, 1935. Lewin (1890–1947) is considered one of the most important twentieth-century psychologists. With his associates and students he formulated a number of theories and research programmes in the area of group dynamics – the scientific study of group behaviour.

purpose of maximising their own and each other's success. Effective working groups are therefore extremely powerful instruments for learning and getting things done.

> If you ask people what is characteristic of the best groups they have ever been members of, the same traits keep being mentioned: small, informal, egalitarian, inspired by shared goals, the knowledge that what they do is recognised and valued. They report that the group does its work in a spirit of energised sharing, with much constructive self-examination. Individual members seem to know exactly what their distinctive contribution is, but at the same time they have a feeling of 'losing' their egos in the group. The group takes on a life of its own.[11]

## Group theory and research

Research on co-operation has been influenced by three general theoretical perspectives. The most influential of these is *social interdependence theory*, based on the work of Kurt Lewin, Morton Deutsch and others. The essential group characteristic is the interdependence among members, created by the group's common goals. Group members encourage and influence each other's efforts towards goal achievement, and each individual's outcomes are affected by the actions of all the others.

*Behaviourism*[12] focuses on the impact of group reinforcers and rewards on behaviour; actions which are rewarded will tend to be repeated. Theories of social learning derive from the behaviourist idea and reward group members for behaviours that contribute to the achievement of group goals.

*Cognitive development theory* is based on the work of Piaget, Vygotsky and others. Piaget's model of cognitive development works like this: when your ideas or views are challenged by people with different views or conclusions, you become uncertain about the correctness of your views and lose confidence in the strength of your intellectual position. (Piaget describes this state as 'cognitive disequilibrium'.) To resolve the uncertainty you search for new information and experiences and a more adequate reasoning process. This process of reviewing and modifying the way you think expands your perspectives and frameworks of understanding. Vygotsky's work is based on the premise that knowledge is social, constructed from cooperative efforts to learn, understand and solve problems.[13]

Research reviews conducted by Johnson and Johnson over the last 100 years, together with their own 35 years of research programmes,[14] provide strong

11. Nicholson, *Managing the Human Animal*, p. 56.
12. See Chapter 2, pp. 37–8 for a brief explanation of behaviourist and cognitive learning theories.
13. See D. W. Johnson and F. P. Johnson, *Joining Together: Group Theory and Group Skills*, Allyn & Bacon, Boston, 8th edn, 2003, p. 93 and p. 103: 'Most efforts to achieve are a personal but social process that requires individuals to cooperate and to construct shared understandings and knowledge. Both competitive and individualistic structures, by isolating individuals from each other, tend to depress achievement and productivity.'
14. See D. W. Johnson and R. T. Johnson, *Co-operation and Competition: Theory and Research*, Interaction Book Co., Edina, MN, 1989, and *Joining Together*, pp. 99–103.

empirical evidence of the cognitive, social and affective benefits of cooperative learning. The research suggests that group learning typically produces higher achievement, more positive relationships and greater psychological health than competitive or individualistic learning.[15]

Let's look at each of these claims in a little more detail:

## Higher achievement

Working in groups, Johnson and Johnson argue, can promote individual intellectual development in a number of ways:

### Improved reasoning and understanding

When you collaborate on a task or a project you are in effect learning material to 'teach' it to others rather than learning it for your own purposes. Conceptualising and organising this material to present to others involves more advanced reasoning strategies than those you need for your own understanding. Explaining, summarising and elaborating on your knowledge so that others can grasp it involves you having to consolidate and strengthen *your* understanding of it. Furthermore, establishing meaning and understanding through the process of conveying it in this way helps you to store and retain the information in your long-term memory.

### Creative thinking

Working with others will introduce you to novel ideas, perspectives and ways of thinking which will not only expand your knowledge but also stimulate and develop your capacity to think critically and creatively. It involves the ability to hold your own and other people's perspectives in mind simultaneously.

### Peer review

Group work involves giving and receiving feedback on members' thoughts and ideas. Subjecting members' reasoning processes to critical examination in this manner allows ideas to be explored and critically examined, understanding to be checked and deepened. By monitoring the cognitive activities of the group members in this way, individual intellectual development is enhanced.

---

15. In a *competitive* learning situation, people work against each other to achieve a goal which only one or a few can achieve. You seek an outcome which benefits you personally, but puts the other group members at a disadvantage. An *individualistic* learning situation is one in which you work alone to accomplish goals unrelated to those of others. Each individual perceives that she can achieve her goal regardless of whether other individuals achieve or do not achieve theirs. In both situations the social interdependence and interpersonal exchange necessary for effective collaboration are missing. See D. W. Johnson and R. T. Johnson, 'Encouraging Thinking Through Constructive Controversy' in N. Davidson and T. Worsham (eds.), *Enhancing Thinking Through Cooperative Learning*, Teachers' College Press, New York, 1992.

**Constructive controversy**

When members interact there are sure to be disagreements about ideas, values, opinions, information, etc. If the group has created a positive relationship of equality, openness and mutual trust, such conflicts can be managed constructively in ways which enrich everybody's learning, as described above.

## More positive relationships

The studies analysed by Johnson and Johnson suggest that co-operative work promotes considerably more liking among individuals than competitive or individualistic work.

> An extension of social interdependence theory is **social judgment theory**, which focuses on relationships among diverse individuals. The social judgments individuals make about each other increase or decrease the liking they feel towards each other. Such social judgments are the result of either a process of acceptance or rejection. The process of **acceptance** is based on the individuals promoting mutual goal accomplishment as a result of their perceived positive interdependence. The promotive interaction tends to result in frequent, accurate, and open communication; accurate understanding of each other's perspective; inducibility; differentiated, dynamic and realistic views of each other; high self-esteem; success and productivity; and expectations for positive and productive future interaction. The process of **rejection** results from oppositional or no interaction based on perceptions of negative or no interdependence. Both lead to no or inaccurate communication; egocentrism; resistance to influence; monopolistic, stereotyped and static views of others; low self-esteem; failure; and expectations of distasteful and unpleasant interaction with others. The processes of acceptance and rejection are self-perpetuating. Any part of the process tends to elicit all the other parts of the process.[16]

Members are more likely to commit to the group and its tasks if the goals are clear, if the goals are ones they want to achieve and if it is clear how the goals can be achieved. However, for positive relationships to evolve, power within the group needs to be distributed equally and shared. If decisions are always made by one or the same group members, if there is little discussion because participation is unequal or disagreement suppressed, the group will not develop as a cohesive unit. We consider the use of power in group relationships in more detail on p. 101.

## Psychological health

Studies suggest that working in groups encourages emotional security, well-adjusted social relations, strong personal identity, ability to cope with adversity, social competencies and basic trust and optimism about people.

> Personal ego strength, self-confidence, independence, and autonomy are all promoted by being involved in cooperative efforts. Individualistic attitudes tend to be related to a

16. *Joining Together*, p. 104.

number of indices of psychological pathology, such as emotional immaturity, social maladjustment, delinquency, self-alienation, and self-rejection. Competitiveness is related to a mixture of healthy and unhealthy characteristics. Whereas inappropriate competitive and individualistic attitudes and efforts alienate individuals from others, healthy and therapeutic growth depends on increasing individuals' understanding of how to cooperate more effectively with others. Cooperative experiences are not a luxury. They are absolutely necessary for healthy development . . .

. . . An important aspect of psychological health is social competence. **Social skills and competencies tend to increase more in cooperative than in competitive or individualistic situations.**[17] Working together to get the job done increases students' abilities to provide leadership, build and maintain trust, communicate effectively, and manage conflicts constructively.[18]

EXERCISE **4.3 Broken squares**[19]

The exercise illustrates how goals are defined by members of a group. Each group will complete a task involving a puzzle.

(a)   *Form groups of five: three participants and two observers.*
(b)   *Your tutor will give each observer a set of instructions, and each participant an instruction sheet and an envelope containing pieces of the puzzle. Do not open your envelope until the tutor gives you the signal.*
(c)   *Each group solves the puzzle, making a note of the time taken to solve it.*
(d)   *Pair off with another group. Share and discuss your instructions and experiences.*
(e)   *Each group records its conclusions about the differences between working in a cooperatively-orientated and a competitively-orientated problem solving group.*
(f)   *Feed back to the whole group.*

The benefits for learning derived from collaborative working are confirmed by our own experience as facilitators over many years. On the whole we find that small group work provides a supportive environment for learning which caters for students with different learning styles. It can also give you the chance to involve yourself in a variety of tasks not usually built in to the more formal settings of lectures and seminars, like group presentations, casework and project work. And students who do not feel confident enough in front of a tutor to express their opinions, test their understanding of a complex topic, or experiment with new ideas, find that they can do these things in the company of a group of peers who are open with and supportive of each other.

In summary, working in a small group can enable you to:

- Get to know other students.
- Identify common areas of ignorance.

17. See *Co-operation and Competition.*   18. *Joining Together*, pp. 106–7.
19. See *ibid.*, pp. 83–5.

- Learn to evaluate your own and others' work (through the process of giving and receiving feedback).
- Deepen your understanding by having to explain/clarify/summarise your knowledge for peers.
- Test your own understandings with peers.
- Share expertise, study methods, ideas, concerns.
- Generate ideas (creative thinking).
- Take risks in an atmosphere of trust and confidentiality.
- Develop negotiation skills.
- Learn to give and receive feedback.
- Give and receive support.
- Develop self-confidence and increase motivation.
- Work through experiences and misunderstandings.
- Produce synergy.
- Learn to become less dependent on tutors and take more control over your own learning. Sounds brilliant, you might think – but it just doesn't accord with *my* experience. Why might this be?

## Barriers to effective group learning

EXERCISE 4.4 **What am I like in a group?**

*Please answer the following questions as honestly as you can by ticking the appropriate box.*

| When Working in a Group: | Yes | Sometimes | No |
|---|---|---|---|
| 1. I prefer to divide up the tasks | ☐ | ☐ | ☐ |
| 2. I prefer to work on a joint task | ☐ | ☐ | ☐ |
| 3. I give the task 100% | ☐ | ☐ | ☐ |
| 4. I work reliably to deadlines | ☐ | ☐ | ☐ |
| 5. I seek help from others when I have problems | ☐ | ☐ | ☐ |
| 6. I manage my time and workload well | ☐ | ☐ | ☐ |
| 7. I am willing to help out a colleague who is having difficulties | ☐ | ☐ | ☐ |
| 8. I prefer to work alone on my part of the task | ☐ | ☐ | ☐ |
| 9. I feel under pressure producing work for the group | ☐ | ☐ | ☐ |
| 10. I resent sharing the fruits of my efforts with others who don't work oo diligently | ☐ | ☐ | ☐ |
| 11. I listen to others | ☐ | ☐ | ☐ |

| | | | |
|---|---|---|---|
| 12. | I evaluate the suggestions of others | ☐ ☐ ☐ |
| 13. | I make suggestions to the others | ☐ ☐ ☐ |
| 14. | I challenge the views of others | ☐ ☐ ☐ |
| 15. | I raise and discuss problems about the task | ☐ ☐ ☐ |
| 16. | I come up with ideas when the group is flagging | ☐ ☐ ☐ |
| 17. | I easily lose interest if things aren't going well | ☐ ☐ ☐ |
| 18. | I push for my ideas to be accepted | ☐ ☐ ☐ |
| 19. | I put obstacles in the way of things I don't agree with | ☐ ☐ ☐ |
| 20. | I think consensus is better than getting your own way | ☐ ☐ ☐ |
| 21. | I find explaining things to others helps my understanding | ☐ ☐ ☐ |
| 22. | I find working with others improves my self-confidence | ☐ ☐ ☐ |
| 23. | I develop the ability to explain complex ideas | ☐ ☐ ☐ |
| 24. | I express my feelings openly | ☐ ☐ ☐ |
| 25. | I develop the ability to confront group conflict | ☐ ☐ ☐ |
| 26. | I willingly accept feedback from others | ☐ ☐ ☐ |
| 27. | I prefer to learn from the teachers, not from my peers | ☐ ☐ ☐ |
| 28. | I learn more when I express my thoughts to others | ☐ ☐ ☐ |
| 29. | I learn more when I disagree with another member | ☐ ☐ ☐ |
| 30. | I'm good at organising others | ☐ ☐ ☐ |

If you have between 16 and 22 'yes' ticks, you have a positive attitude to co-operative work and gain benefit from it. On the other hand, those of you who score low on 'yes' may have had negative experiences. Students may not enjoy group work for a variety of reasons. It may be a new and unfamiliar learning experience which you do not feel properly prepared for. Alternatively, you may not value it highly because the 'culture' of your institution values a more traditional lecture/ seminar teaching approach, with individual assessment weighted in favour of exams. Or you may think that group work obstructs your intellectual progress, particularly if one or more members are not pulling their weight. You may think that by taking responsibility for the performance of colleagues and letting colleagues assume responsibility for your work that you no longer have sufficient control of your learning. Some students prefer to work alone so that they remain 'in control' of the task. You can work at your own pace at times that suit you, with your own personal level of commitment. Finally, some of you may feel 'freer' sitting in a lecture!

Dislike of group work frequently stems from negative experiences of group relationships, for example in situations where 'personality' issues impede progress and enjoyment, or where a group member feels the others are taking advantage. Brayne, Duncan and Grimes report the following entry from a student log:

> *This was not a good day! . . . When I got to the lecture I realised most of the other groups had got together during the week and prepared a formal speech and some had even typed them. I gave my group my piece of paper with my ideas on and asked for theirs. They had not written anything down so no one could present all our arguments. On deciding who should represent, after realising none of us wanted to do it, I reluctantly agreed but felt angered and embarrassed that our contribution rested solely on my meagre efforts . . . I am angry with my group and I think they know but if it means this won't happen again then that's fine by me.*[20]

This occurred at an early stage of the group's development, when each member is seeking to establish an identity within the group and in relation to the other members.[21] The others picked up the student's concerns:

> *R said she would present it, which was fine until the time actually came for her to present it and she felt like fainting. We all rallied round her. K took her place and A and I comforted her . . . She insisted on leaving though.*
>
> *After she left and during a break, the rest of my group sat down and had a good talk. We were shocked at what had happened to R. We had known she wasn't eager to present but we didn't know the extent of how she felt.*

The group managed to work through these early difficulties. Seven weeks later, R recorded:

> *The group definitely interacted on a better level today. I must admit I have tried to make an effort to get on with one member with whom I don't altogether see eye to eye. In fact once my attitude changed, so did theirs although I don't think we will ever be 'best buddies.' I have thought about this situation and believe it is quite a valuable experience in that there may be times in the future that I may have to work with someone with whom I am incompatible but obviously I will have to resolve the situation or be miserable and inefficient.*[22]

Newly formed groups will create effective working relationships if each individual is sensitive to the feelings of the other group members and recognises that anything he says or does will have an effect on everybody else. Once trust is established it becomes easier to be open and honest with one another about negative feelings and frustrations. Handled insensitively, however, such honesty can seriously damage the working relationship. Brayne et al report the following example:

> *Last Monday when we all met we discussed the problem of certain group members not pulling their weight, not showing up for meetings, interviews etc. D and I made it*

---

20  H. Brayne, N. Duncan and R. Grimes, *Clinical Legal Education. Active Learning in Your Law School*, Blackstone, London, 1998, p. 203.

21. This is known as the 'storming' stage; see p. 97.

22. Brayne et al, *Clinical Legal Education*, p. 204.

*clear that we were not happy about it, and I think it cleared the air a lot. We decided to make a 'fresh start' and since then things have been a lot better.*

Fortunately, the peer pressure had the desired effect, as the reluctant participant himself recorded:

*Having missed the Thursday meeting with R, I did make it to the group meeting on Monday evening. However, what awaited me was quite a shock. Although perhaps I hadn't really been working at 100 per cent effort, I didn't think I was being totally slack. Nevertheless the group thought this to be the case. They said that I had missed several meetings and was not committed enough to the case. Maybe I had been a bit lazy, but I was still quite surprised at the ferocity of their attack.*

*However, in retrospect it was just the 'kick up the backside' that I needed. It made me realise the group had been carrying me and I hadn't been pulling my weight lately. I also realised that I couldn't get by just inputting into the group stupid wisecracks and jokes, that I would actually have to do some real work, not only for myself and to get a good mark but more importantly so I didn't let the group down.*[23]

## Group dynamics

For a group to work well, you want a mixture of people with different strengths which complement each other. A group full of 'activists' is unlikely to get the job done; you need one or two participants who are prepared to take on the hard graft. Understanding how people behave in groups will help you – and your tutors – gain insight into how to make your group work harmonious and constructive.

EXERCISE **4.5  Fishbowl**

(a)    *Ask your tutor to leave the room for 20 minutes.*
(b)    *The whole group divides into two to form a fishbowl: an inner and an outer circle of participants.*
(c)    *The group in the inner circle discusses the following questions:*
     (i) *When we are working with the tutor, in what ways does s/he exercise authority?*
     (ii) *What are our feelings about this?*
     (iii) *What can we learn from this about ourselves?*
(d)    *Meanwhile the outer circle makes notes on the following questions:*
     (i) *What is happening in the inner group without a tutor?*
     (ii) *How is authority assumed?*
     (iii) *Who takes initiatives?*
     (iv) *Is there any 'pecking order' in contributions?*
(e)    *When the tutor returns, the outer group explains what they observed. The inner group remains silent.*

23. *Ibid.*, pp. 205–6.

*(f)   The whole group reassembles and engages in open discussion with the tutor.[24]*

This exercise illustrates how a group's character is determined by the role or roles each participant plays in interactions with the other participants. We tend not to take much notice of the roles people play, say, in our family or groups of friends, when relationships are positive and harmonious – the group is functioning with unity of purpose. It is only when something disturbs the harmony and frustrates the group purpose that we may consciously think about how a particular participant is behaving.

### EXERCISE 4.6   **What are your preferred team roles?**

*(a)   Your tutor will give you a questionnaire and a scoresheet.[25] Working individually, complete the questionnaire and add up your score.*

*(b)   In your groups, compare your results. Does your perception of your preferred role(s) accord with your colleagues' perception of you?*

*(c)   Feed back to the whole group.*

A number of roles need to be performed if a group is to function successfully. Belbin has identified nine key roles that are present in an effective group (See Figure 4.1). Group members have more and less preferred roles, and switch roles unconsciously. A strong preference for one role often brings with it what Belbin refers to as 'allowable weaknesses' as well as factors which contribute to group effectiveness.

### EXERCISE 4.7   **Roles in my group**

Use the table in figure 4.1 to discuss which members of your group fit which role: for example: who is/is not a Resource Investigator, Team worker, and so on. Are you satisfied that you have a range of roles in your group?

## Setting ground rules

There are rules of behaviour implicit in all social situations which facilitate co-operation and help us to avoid conflict: 'you shouldn't swear in front of tutors (or at them)'; 'you mustn't be rude to a judge', and so on. For the same reasons, newly formed working groups need to establish a set of 'ground rules' to enable the group to function effectively. These may be agreed explicitly, or may evolve informally out of the participants' interaction. Procedures for agreeing deadlines, for contacting other group members, for keeping a record of meetings, for dealing with non-attenders should all be formulated early on. Any other matters the group feels strongly about should be included, such as ensuring group discussions are confidential, or banning smoking in meetings.

24. Adapted from D. Jaques, *Learning in Groups*, Kogan Page, London, 2000, p. 18.
25. R. M. Belbin, *Team Roles at Work*, Butterworth-Heineman, London, 1993.

| Role | Contribution | Allowable weaknesses |
| --- | --- | --- |
| Implementer | Disciplined, reliable, conservative, efficient, turns ideas into action | Somewhat inflexible, slow to respond to new possibilities |
| Completer | Painstaking, conscientious, anxious, looks for errors, delivers on time | Inclined to worry unduly, reluctant to delegate, can be nit-picker |
| Specialist | Single-minded, self-sharing, dedicated, supplies scarce knowledge and skills | Contributes on narrow front, dwells on technicalities |
| Plant | Creative, imaginative, unorthodox, solves difficult problems | Ignores details, often poor communicator |
| Resource investigator | Extrovert, enthusiastic, explores opportunities, develops contacts | Over-optimistic, loses interest early |
| Co-ordinator | Mature, confident, good chairperson, clarifies goals, promotes decision making | Can be manipulative, prone to delegate personal work |
| Shaper | Challenging, dynamic, thrives on pressure | Can provoke others, hurts people's feelings |
| Monitor-evaluator | Sober, strategic and discerning. Sees all options, judges accurately | Lacks drive and ability to inspire others. Overly critical |
| Team worker | Co-operative, mild, perceptive and diplomatic. Listens. Averts friction | Indecisive in crises, can be easily influenced |

Figure 4.1. Roles in groups table

## How groups grow

People who work with groups, in almost any capacity, come to recognise that any well-functioning unit of individuals always has a developmental history. At its inception the unit is a chaotic, loosely organized aggregate with a tendency toward being highly dependent on external direction. What happens to a chaotic, disorganized collection of people that makes it a coordinated, interdependent unit has been of interest and often of vital concern to those who work directly with people in almost every walk of life. Leaders in the military, industry, government, education, and religion have been and remain particularly concerned with understanding those factors and events that produce effective groups and those that result in unsatisfactory ones. Until the present century most of what was understood about the functioning of small groups was based on trial and error, intuition, and a kind of folk wisdom. The purpose was primarily controlling human behaviour through a 'disciplined subservience to leadership rather than improving the ability of group members to work together cooperatively and creatively' (Knowles and Knowles, 1965, p. 15).[26]

During the last 100 years, research in social science and psychology has provided us with a wealth of information on the stages of group development. Probably the most well-known theory was formulated by Tuckman in 1965. His model has four general stages. In order to work effectively, groups must pass through each stage in turn:

1. FORMING. At this first stage the group is essentially a collection of individuals, particularly if they don't know each other. Group members concentrate on getting to know each other rather than thinking about the task. Interaction is cautious, tentative, polite; individuals are 'feeling each other out' and trying to create an impression.

2. STORMING. This is the stage of interpersonal conflict. There may be disagreements about ground rules and allocation of tasks:

   ... individuals make bids for territory and position in the group, and as these personal agendas and goals surface, a degree of interpersonal hostility and conflict emerge as people compete to get their ideas adopted. This is often a highly uncomfortable stage for everybody concerned. Sometimes the bonds and alliances made in the first stage are broken, and new ones are formed. Although it seldom seems so at the time, this stage has a highly positive function, because before convergence can take place, it is usually necessary for polarised views to come out in the open, and unless this happens, differences can remain beneath the surface as unresolved problems. This stage is vital if the group is eventually to fuse into one that can effectively accomplish its task, and if it is not skilfully handled, the group can fragment into cliques and cabals that carry on the battle afterwards.[27]

3. NORMING. Conflict subsides and cooperation emerges. Members begin to focus on the group task and work out their methods of operation, along with ground rules for interacting with one another.

4. PERFORMING. The group is now ready to focus on the task and get some work done. As long as the previous three stages are successfully negotiated, at the fourth stage task and interpersonal aspects of group work come together and support each other. Creating a sense of belonging, generating trust and openness, sustaining interest and enthusiasm are aspects which underpin and facilitate the effective performance of the task; successful performance in turn increases trust and enthusiasm. 'The group acquires a distinct sense of itself as a culture.'[28]

26. R. B. Winston, W. C. Bonney, T. K. Miller and J. C. Dagley, *Promoting Student Development Through Intentionally Structured Groups*, Jossey-Bass, San Francisco, 1988, p. 53.
27. D. Rollinson, *Organisational Behaviour and Analysis*, Pearson Education, Harlow, 2nd edn, 2002, p. 327.
28. Jaques, *Learning in Groups*, p. 34.

For groups to grow, therefore, attention has to be paid to individual and team needs before task needs are attended to. Graham Gibbs summarises the position in the table below:[29]

*Relative influence of individual, team and task needs on team members' behaviour at different stages of team development*

| Stage of team development | Individual needs | Team needs | Task needs |
| --- | --- | --- | --- |
| Forming | high | medium | low |
| Storming | high | high | low |
| Norming | medium | high | medium |
| Performing | medium | medium | high |

### EXERCISE 4.8  What's going wrong? Tackling problems

If your firm is encountering problems you think are impeding progress on your casework , have a look at this exercise. Each member of your firm should work through it separately, ticking the items which describe what is happening in your firm. Then check with the others to see if you have ticked the same things. This should help the group identify problems and you can then discuss what to do about them.

- *We don't listen to each other.*
- *We get bogged down in argument instead of moving on.*
- *We keep interrupting each other.*
- *We just push our own views instead of encouraging and developing others' ideas.*
- *We allow dominant members to dominate.*
- *Some of us don't turn up.*
- *Some of us don't contribute.*
- *We don't compromise enough.*
- *We concentrate on making impressions rather than getting the job done.*
- *We don't have clear tasks or objectives.*
- *Nothing gets decided.*
- *We aren't clear about what has been decided.*
- *We don't make it clear who is to take action on decisions.*
- *We put each other down.*
- *We don't recognise that others have feelings about what is happening in the team.*
- *What else is going wrong?*[30]

29. *Learning in Teams: A Student Manual*, Oxford Centre for Staff Development, Oxford, 1994, p. 18.
30. Adapted from G. Gibbs, *Learning in Teams: A Student Guide*, Oxford Centre for Staff Development , 1994, p. 11.

*In your discussion you might find it useful to check:*

(a)    *What stage of development do you think the group has reached?*
(b)    *Are there any unresolved problems you need to bring into the open?*
(c)    *Have you established ground rules you are all agreed upon?*
(d)    *Are there any steps you need to take to develop as a group?*

A final thought for this section: do you think you could have managed your casework more effectively working alone? This brings us back to the issue of collaboration in legal practice.

## The dynamics of lawyer teamwork

Groucho Marx to a group of lawyers:

> *How do you get along at the office? Do you trust each other? Or does each have a separate safe for his money?*[31]

Of course, lawyers do not work in teams just for the sake of it. Group work in practice exists because it adds other people's skills and expertise to the individual's ability to solve the problem at hand. Co-operation may also be economically efficient. However, the kind of work that lawyers do as individuals can cause problems for a team:

> Perhaps the most salient characteristic of a lawyer's task is its ambiguity. Lawyers use a complex body of technical knowledge and skills to exercise judgment for clients regarding the interpretation and application of human norms and values by institutions. This interpretation rests on ambiguities about central values and has a fluid and uncertain outcome. If the task involves litigation, it is also intense and adversarial, often with an all-or-nothing outcome. To work effectively, then, lawyers must make continuous, multiple judgments about highly ambiguous situations . . .
>
> In litigation the ability to grasp the essentials of a situation and anticipate the relevant future possibilities encompasses a series of complex management decisions vitally tied to language and context. Lawyers must decide which facts to gather, retain, and use, and, equally important, which facts to ignore. They must assess the significance of legal precedents for a particular case and choose the best presentation of legal and factual arguments to key decision makers. Perhaps most important, they must decide what the case is worth in order to allocate available resources. Few of these decisions are clear cut. Just as important as a lawyer's decision about one of these matters is his decision about the amount of time to invest in any particular issue. One of the most uncertain aspects of litigation is the relative value of a particular strategic

31. Quoted in M. Twitchell, 'The Ethical Dilemmas of Lawyers in Teams', (1988) 72 *Minnesota Law Review* 697. Twitchell suggests that the very idea of a team of lawyers arouses suspicion in the popular mind. As the joke goes, if a group of lions is a pride, a group of lawyers is a conspiracy. This myth is based on fear – not that lawyers can't work together, but that they are too powerful when they do.

action. Much of a litigator's work will not affect the suit's outcome, but he is never sure which detail will turn out to be crucial. This all-or-nothing aspect of litigation puts great pressure on a lawyer trying to serve a client competently and efficiently.[32]

Moreover, the group dynamic itself can be a source of uncertainty. In law firms, as in other types of business, there is often an added organisational dimension to decision-making processes. In the working environment you are not a free agent. This lack of control is, in legal practice, often disguised by the apparent independence of the individual practitioner. You have your own cases, often your own support staff. You appear to be in control but you are not. Organisational choices are not necessarily determined by individual preferences and actions, but by a complex interaction of internal and external events and personalities. These changing contexts of organisational decision-making can lead to outcomes which are not really intended, or desired, by the individual decision-maker. To put it bluntly, in practice your choices will be influenced by factors like your status in the firm, and the commercial imperatives of that firm; the relative needs and statuses of your clients; the influence of different personalities and power dimensions in the firm's management – and so on. A lawyer can become caught between two constituencies, his superior in the firm and his client, with the result that he is forced to engage in sometimes quite difficult negotiations of status and power across his professional relationships.

Effective team working can undoubtedly reduce the stress of working in situations of uncertainty and fluidity. However, working ineffectively in a group may increase stress and inhibit the group's ability to work to capacity. For example, how is multiple decision-making to be allocated among team members? How is the task to be divided up? How will the work be monitored? How will information be communicated to all the members? And how will differences of interpretation about ethical issues, duties to client and the court – problematic in themselves – be resolved? Finally, isn't there a danger that the client will get lost in the 'pile of lawyers working on her case?' As Twitchell points out, complex decisions 'usually made by a single professional must now be made by a number of people, working within a model based on professional autonomy yet committed to a group goal'.[33]

The conflict between the need for autonomy and the obligation to share responsibility is one area of potential difficulty for lawyer teams. Are there any others you can identify? Try the following exercise:

### EXERCISE 4.9  Powerful conspiracies or lost causes?

(a)   To what extent could you describe the relationships set out below as 'teams'? Give reasons.

---

32. Twitchell, *ibid.* at pp. 710–11. We discuss uncertainty and ambiguity in lawyers' work at various points in this book; see particularly Chapters 1 and 6.
33. *Ibid.* at pp. 726 and 716.

(b)   *Read Johnson and Johnsons' seven Guidelines for the creation of effective groups.*[34] *Use the guidelines to help you identify aspects of these relationships which might (i) promote or (ii) inhibit efficient and successful teamwork.*

1.   *A solicitor briefs counsel to represent a client at Crown Court trial.*
2.   *Amos and Andy are two partners in a small firm of twenty lawyers. The two have worked together for ten years, handling all the firm's medical negligence litigation. Amos is a typical 'activist' – impulsive, impatient with detail, but grasps ideas quickly. Andy is cautious and precise in every detail.*
3.   *A number of lawyers from different firms become involved in a complex class action against a multinational drugs company.*
4.   *Lawyers working in a City firm which has been instructed to handle all the legal work for a large company.*

No doubt one thing you will have noted is that information is not all shared equally. Some members of the group will know more about the case than others.[35] In the larger teams only one or two members, in co-ordinating roles, are likely to have the whole picture. The efficacy of any team will thus depend on the quality of communication within the group. This will turn not only on the quality of co-ordination, and the establishment of appropriate procedures for communication within the group, but also on the abilities of each group member to send and receive messages.

One-way communication is common in group situations, and particularly those which are organised around an authoritarian hierarchy, so that messages tend to be conveyed down the hierarchy, rather than communicated direct.

Earlier in the chapter we pointed out that although co-operation is a natural human instinct, tensions arise when people work together in artificially created formal structures, particularly in those organised hierarchically. The unequal distribution of power within a group, along with the pressure to conform to group identity and culture, are built into the institutional structure of law practice. Even though there may be compelling arguments for establishing a non-hierarchical, shared decision-making process in law firms,[36] in reality hierarchy does exist and probably always will.[37] And this is the structure that newly qualified lawyers are most likely to encounter. The power relationship between a new lawyer and her

---

34. *Joining Together*, pp. 579–81.
35. A highly prized skill in lawyer teamwork is knowing exactly what needs to be passed on to another team member, and what does not.
36. See e.g. S. Bryant, 'Collaboration in Law Practice: A Satisfying and Productive Process for a Diverse Profession' (1993) 17 *Vermont Law Review* 159.
37. In terms of law firm organisation both centralised and distributed management systems appear to exist – see, e.g., the discussions in Greenebaum, *Coping With a Turbulent Environment: Development of Law Firm Training Programs*, p. 9.

supervising principal, for example, brings a certain pressure to conform which will determine her conduct.[38]

Of course, similar power imbalances may occur in law school. Catherine O'Grady describes an experiment conducted at the San Diego Law Clinic by Steven Hartwell:

> ... clinic students were invited to participate in a special Saturday morning clinic where they were told that they would individually interview and advise litigants in small claims court. The 'client', actually one of Hartwell's colleagues, asked each student for the same advice; how to best present her side of a rent dispute at an upcoming hearing. Hartwell told his students that he was available in an adjoining office and that the students could consult with him before giving the client advice. He told each of the twenty-four students who sought his advice the same thing: that they should instruct the client to lie under oath and say that she paid the rent. If a student asked for clarification, he 'uniformly responded, "You asked for my advice and my advice is that, if your client wants to win her case, then you must tell her to perjure herself."' Hartwell and his colleague expected the exercise to test the moral reasoning of the students and cause them to 'experience the pull between loyalty to authority ... and prescribed ethical conduct.' They predicted that most or all students would reject Hartwell's unethical advice and refuse to tell the client to commit perjury. To their surprise and distress, twenty-three of the twenty-four students succumbed to the teacher's authority and advised the client to perjure herself. [39]

The lawyer relationships we have been looking at in exercise 4.9 are probably best described as co-operative working arrangements rather than collaborative group work with consensual decision-making.[40] However, collaborative working clearly occurs among peers, even if the practice is organised hierarchically. When groups work collaboratively leadership and power tend to be negotiated rather than centralised. A collaborative group climate encourages equal participation by all group members. However, this can be difficult to achieve in the law school context, where there is still a strong emphasis on individual effort. Indeed, it is not unusual for us to think of our peers as competitors as much as colleagues. Competitiveness is very much a two-edged sword in this kind of environment. As Chris Argyris notes in one of his case studies, competitiveness can become linked with cohesiveness within a group.[41] Members of the group get a competitive 'spark' by trying to outdo the others. Ironically, in such an organisation, the more successful

---

38. There is evidence that suggests new lawyers see themselves not as professionals but as employees. See C. G. O'Grady, 'Preparing Students for the Profession: Clinical Education, Collaborative Pedagogy, and the Realities of Practice for the New Lawyer' (1998) 4 *Clinical Law Review* 485 at p. 503; and see Exercise 4.12 (the 'Kodak case').

39. *Ibid.*, pp. 519–20. Cf. the famous Milgram studies on obedience to authority: S. Milgram, *Obedience to Authority*, Harper & Row, New York, 1974.

40. We distinguish co-operation from collaboration. Collaboration is essentially joint decision-making; co-operation is division of labour where individuals and sub-groups are responsible for solving problems they have been allocated to work on.

41. *Reasoning, Learning, and Action*, Jossey-Bass, San Francisco, 1989, p. 308.

group members are in relying on their own resources rather than on the help of others, the more valued they feel. Nevertheless, competitiveness may create defensive forms of practice (e.g. a reluctance to share knowledge, or to admit to problems) and levels of non-communication that become counter-productive. Competition can be highly destructive both by limiting the group's capacity to define or reach its goals, and on a more personal level, where it can have a corrosive effect on working relationships.

Our experience of running a course which is heavily dependent on team-working is that it is probably the thing the groups think about least when starting out and end up worrying about most. This is a mistake. It is vital to plan and to share out team tasks. It is equally important that you make arrangements for meetings, etc., early on in any practical work you do, because once casework gets under way, you may have less time than you would like to reflect on group dynamics and effectiveness.

When you are setting or reviewing your ground rules, think about communication structures within your group. Are all members completely open with each other? A classic form of distancing which arises, especially within competitive environments, is what Argyris terms 'discounting'.[42] This is where members of the group attempt to maintain cohesiveness by disregarding the negative aspects of a member's actions or statements: 'She's just letting off steam' or 'If you ignore the whingeing, he actually has some good ideas.' Such discounting does not help the organisation unless both the discounting and the behaviour which creates it are discussable. Double loop learning means being able to reflect on distancing and blocking behaviours and then trying to change those behaviours: that is a prerequisite to progress.

## Feedback

It follows that group work depends crucially upon good quality (positive) feedback between members. The hardest environment to work in is one where there is no feedback on progress or performance. A lack of feedback will reduce self-esteem, motivation and participation. However, there are 'rules' on giving feedback; we summarise these below:

### The rules of feedback

1. **Comment on things the individual did well, as well as areas for improvement**. Negative feedback is counterproductive because it leaves people feeling inadequate, even humiliated. If you praise aspects of someone's performance, they are more likely to work positively to improve it.

42. *Ibid.*, pp. 308–9, 446.

2.  **Comment on observed behaviour** – what you saw someone do, not what you think they were thinking or intending. 'Your voice became much louder when the client complained about . . . ' rather than 'you were very aggressive'.
3.  **Offer a description of what you saw** – not a judgment: 'The client looked a bit worried when you raised your voice' , rather than 'it was a bad idea to raise your voice'.
4.  **Ask questions rather than make statements** – 'how else might you have reacted when the client complained?', rather than 'you should have . . .'. This allows the individual to think about the issues and reach their own conclusions.
5.  **Relate all your feedback to specific items of behaviour; don't waffle on about general feelings or impressions** – so that the person can learn from it and do it again: 'it was a really good idea to sit him down with a cup of tea' rather than 'there was a really nice atmosphere'.
6.  **Before offering feedback, think about its value for the recipient** – if there is no value, keep your mouth shut!

EXERCISE 4.10 **Concepts**

After working through this chapter, see if you can come up with your own definitions of the following technical terms. The procedure for learning these concepts is as follows:

1.  *Divide into pairs.*
2.  *Each pair is to:*
    *(a) define each concept, noting the page(s) on which it is discussed, and*
    *(b) make sure that you both understand the meaning of each concept.*
3.  *Combine into groups of four. Compare the answers of the two pairs. If there is disagreement, look up the concept and clarify it. Make sure you are all agreed on the definition and understand it.*

| | |
|---|---|
| Synergy | positive interdependence |
| Cognitive disequilibrium | constructive controversy |
| Forming | storming |
| Group dynamics | norming |
| Discounting | performing |

EXERCISE 4.11 **Tag wrestling**

1.  *Preparation*
    - *Divide into two teams, A and B.*
    - *Team A brainstorms the following proposition:*
      **We believe group work to be a beneficial learning experience.**

- *Team B brainstorms the following proposition:*
  **We believe group work to be a pointless exercise and a distraction.**
- *Teams brainstorm their topics (out of earshot of each other) for 20 minutes.*
- *Each team appoints one member to make a one-minute opening statement supporting their proposition. The statement must be made without interruption.*

2. *The Game. The opening speakers sit on chairs facing each other and make their statements.*

   *After the two opening statements, you may do any of the following:*
   (a) *the two opening speakers can pick up each other's points and argue;*
   (b) *an opening speaker can tag another member of the team to take their place on the chair;*
   (c) *another member of the team who is keen to have a go can tag and replace the speaker.*

3. *Review.*
   (a) *How did it feel to take part in this activity?*
   (b) *Name three things you enjoyed about the experience.*
   (c) *Name three things you did not enjoy.*
   (d) *When you were brainstorming, did you identify a leader? Any reluctant participants? How would you identify yourself?*

EXERCISE 4.12 **Guilt by association?**

Consider this account of a new lawyer's conduct while working with a senior member of his firm:

> During the deposition of a defendant's key expert witness, a senior defense lawyer told plaintiff's counsel that certain documents previously written by the expert witness and requested by both the court and the plaintiff had been inadvertently destroyed. An associate on the defense team, who had been primarily responsible for the defense's discovery and document work, heard the senior lawyer make this statement and knew it to be untrue. The documents in question were damaging to the defense because they indicated that the expert witness's initial position on the case was equivocal. The associate whispered to the senior lawyer that the documents had not been destroyed and were in fact back at their law firm. The senior lawyer, however, ignored the associate and eventually signed an affidavit attesting to the documents' destruction. Upon returning to the law firm, the associate located the documents and stored them away in a locked closet. The associate told the senior lawyer what he had done and then never discussed the incident again with anyone. Later in the litigation, through cross-examination of the expert witness at trial, the existence of the documents was dramatically revealed. The trial judge expressed shock that the lawyers had lied and had failed to disclose the documents. The jury was left with the impression that the defendant was hiding key evidence, which may have contributed to the jury's verdict in favor of the plaintiff. The law firm representing the defendant responded to the senior partner's lie and the associate's cover-up by

expelling the senior partner from firm partnership and cutting short the associate's future with the firm.[43]

*In your groups, discuss reasons why the associate might have decided to act as he did.*

## Reflective exercise: What is your current group skill level?[44]

Answer the questions below, describing yourself as accurately as you can:

- *How do you see yourself as a group member? What is your style of working within a group?*
- *What are your strengths in group working? How do they fit into the way you see yourself as a group member?*
- *What situations within groups do you have trouble with, and why? How do you feel when faced with them? How do you handle them? How would you like to handle them?*
- *Which group skills do you want to acquire or improve? What changes would you like to make in your present group behaviour?*

. . . And in your reflective log, consider:
*How well is your firm working as a unit?*

## Further reading

D. W. Johnson and F. P. Johnson, *Joining Together: Group Theory and Group Skills*, Allyn & Bacon, 2003.

G. Gibbs, *Learning in Teams: A Student Guide, and A Student Manual*, Oxford Centre for Staff Development, Oxford, 1994.

M. Twitchell, 'The Ethical Dilemmas of Lawyers in Teams' (1988) 72 *Minnesota Law Review* 697.

43. The 'Kodak case' (*Berkey Photo v Eastman Kodak Co* (1978)), as described in O'Grady, (1998) 4 *Clinical Law Review* 485 at p. 506; also Twitchell, (1988) 72 *Minnesota Law Review* 697 at pp. 743–6.
44. Based on Johnson and Johnson, *Joining Together*, p. 44.

# 5

# Interviewing: building the relationship and gaining participation

Client interviewing is probably the single most important context in which lawyers apply their oral communication skills yet, historically, lawyers have shown relatively little aptitude for it. In this chapter we enable you to identify and practise the skills of interviewing and counselling a client and provide a practical framework (WASP) through which you can develop your competence. The chapter also addresses research into and theories of lawyer–client interaction and uses these as a reflective tool for assessing practice. We conclude by offering a prospective model of client-centred lawyering building on notions of 'empathy' and 'community participation'.

## Objectives

To:

- Provide an understanding of the aims and objectives of the initial client interview.
- Explore critically the relevant assumptions underlying the lawyer–client relationship.
- Encourage you to develop an empathic understanding of that relationship.
- Examine and practise techniques of questioning, listening, advising and counselling in the context of lawyer–client interviewing.
- Identify the basic steps necessary to take a case beyond the initial interview.
- Explore the potential for greater client participation in the lawyer–client relationship.

## Supports benchmark statements

Students should demonstrate a basic ability

2. Application and problem-solving
   - to apply knowledge to a situation of limited complexity in order to provide arguable conclusions for concrete problems
3. Sources and research
   - to identify accurately the issue(s) which require researching

4.   Autonomy and ability to learn
   - to act independently in planning and undertaking tasks in areas of law already studied
   - to reflect on their own learning and to seek and make use of feedback
5.   Communication and literacy
   - to understand and use the English language proficiently in relation to legal matters
   - to present knowledge or an argument in a way which is comprehensible to others and which is directed at their concerns.

## The functions of the lawyer–client interview

Imagine your client is about to walk through the door in the next five minutes.

EXERCISE 5.1 **The objectives of interviewing**

*Make a note of what your main objectives will be when interviewing that client. Don't worry for now what the subject matter is – just think about what you need to achieve in general terms.*

Assuming it is a first interview, the key objectives are fairly easy to identify: you obviously want various categories of information. You need to know why your client is here – either what has happened to her or what she wants to achieve that needs the services of a lawyer. You need enough basic information about her situation to open a file and to advise her about possible costs. You will also probably have noted the need to give some advice or indication of future action on your part. That, after all, is what clients generally go to lawyers for. Even though you may not be able to give the client an answer to all their problems at this stage, it would be an unusual meeting which ended without some advice or information being imparted by the lawyer.

Those are, if you like, the 'macro' functions of client interviewing, but there are other important functions implicit in the processes of lawyer–client interaction. We would like you to read the following extract, and then we will use it to reflect on the process it describes:

> Mrs Celeste came to the legal aid office early Monday morning. By 8:00 am a line, two and three across, had formed in front of a small wooden table in the centre of the waiting room. A woman standing behind the table gave instructions in English and Spanish. The line grew throughout the morning.
>
> When the woman called out her number, Mrs Celeste stood up and walked to the door of the main office ... she entered a small room with doorways on three sides, plexiglass windows, and a large desk against the wall. In the adjacent space, a telephone switchboard rang. Mrs Celeste sat down in a chair next to the desk. When she started to tell the woman about the food stamps, the woman interrupted: 'Please just answer the questions. If you don't understand, you can see the lawyer for help.'

'What is your full name?' the woman asked, looking down at a case card. 'And your address? Telephone number? Age? Are you married? Hispanic? Do you need an interpreter? Are you here alone or with a group? Employed? Have you ever been here before? Whom were you referred by? Are you a citizen of the United States? What is your monthly rent? How many live in the apartment? Do you have any wages or income? What about welfare? SSI? Disability? Unemployment? Food stamps? Do you have any bank accounts, automobiles, assets or real property?'

Mrs Celeste answered questions for five or ten minutes. When she tried to expand her answers, the woman interrupted. After several interruptions, Mrs Celeste learned to keep her answers short. Once her case card was fully marked, the boxes checked, lines filled, and statistics compiled, Mrs Celeste was told to return to the waiting room. Two hours later she was called again.

'Good morning. My name is Tony Alfieri. I am a welfare lawyer here. Before we begin, let me explain how our office works. Every Monday morning we see about thirty or forty people with welfare problems. Although we would like to help everyone, we just don't have enough lawyers to go around. So in the afternoon, all the lawyers sit down and make hard choices about who we can and cannot help. That is an office decision. It is not my decision alone. *Do you understand?*

At this moment, I cannot tell you whether our office will be able to help you. That decision will be made later. In the event we cannot help you, we will make every effort to refer you to another legal aid office or give you enough advice so that you can help yourself. With legal advice from us many people are able to help themselves. *Do you understand?*

The first thing I'd like to do is check the information on your case card to make sure it is correct. That will save us time later. Let's begin with your name and address. Do you live in an apartment or a house? How long have you lived there . . . ?'[1]

EXERCISE 5.2 **The other side . . .**

*Pretend that you are Mrs Celeste. Describe in a letter to a friend, what you felt about your experiences at the legal aid office.*

(You may assume, if it helps, that the office has now agreed to help you in your case, which concerns the federal government's decision to reduce your food stamps (a kind of welfare payment) because you are in receipt of foster care payments.)

*Read some of your group's letters out loud, or exchange letters with other members of the group. What, in summary, are the feelings and reactions that you ascribe to Mrs Celeste?*

You might like to contrast what you have written with the comments of an English solicitor's client:

The first one I went to – I was very distressed at the time – I think he just took my name, address and age and noted how long I'd been married. He was totally

1. A. V. Alfieri, 'Reconstructive Poverty Law Practice: Learning Lessons of Client Narrative' (1991) 100 *Yale Law Journal* 2107 at pp. 2112–13.

disinterested. He didn't want to know. It felt as though I was talking to a brick wall. There was no offer of help, no 'come back and see me next week'. I just walked out of that office and burst into tears. I thought 'well, who the hell can I go to?' and that's when I phoned up the clerk to the justices … I just didn't know where to turn.[2]

What more do these clients' experiences tell you about the functions of the lawyer–client interview?

The point is an obvious, but nonetheless vital, one. The interview is not solely for information gathering. Being a lawyer is not just about dealing with the legal problem, it is about responding appropriately to the person as well. A lawyer–client interview is centrally concerned with developing and sustaining the relationship between lawyer and client, which, although it is a professional relationship, is also ultimately a *personal* one.

So, taking these elements together, we can suggest that the functions of the interview are essentially:

- to establish the interpersonal dimensions of the lawyer–client relationship;
- to identify the issues and obtain sufficient detailed information to advance the matter;
- to determine the client's objectives, and, so far as possible, advise accordingly;
- to prepare the way for further action on behalf of the client.

We can translate these aims into a broad structure for the interviewing process. A number of such models have been developed by writers in this field.[3] You may well find it helpful to use these models as your competence – and confidence – as an interviewer increases. However, we take the view that they over-complicate the process for novice interviewers. Our own students have said that such models leave them feeling a bit overwhelmed by the number of things they feel they have to remember to do.

We take the view that it is better to start off relatively unstructured; to identify your weaknesses through the process of reflection, and try to improve your skills gradually, concentrating on one major aspect at a time. If you try to do it all at once, you are far more likely to come unstuck.

We suggest you start by using a relatively simple model of the stages of an interview to guide you, like **WASP**:

- **W**elcome.
- **A**cquire information.
- **S**upply information and advice.
- **P**art.

We will use this as the basic framework for the rest of the chapter, once we have dealt with two preliminary issues.

2. Taken from National Consumer Council, *Making Good Solicitors: The Place of Communication Skills in their Training*, NCC, London, 1989, p. 3.
3. Notably Avrom Sherr's '13 tasks' in *Client Care for Lawyers*, Sweet and Maxwell, London, 2nd edn, 1999, pp. 8–10; also D. Binder, P. Bergman and S. Price, *Legal Interviewing and Counseling*, West Publ., St Paul, Minn., 1991.

## Assumptions about the relationship

First we need to consider the assumptions we bring to the lawyer–client relationship. The key suppositions, we suggest, are about control and participation.

In his research Avrom Sherr[4] asked a sample of practising solicitors and their clients who they felt was in charge during an interview that had just taken place. The responses he obtained were as follows:

| 'WHO'S IN CHARGE?' | LAWYER RESPONSE | CLIENT RESPONSE |
| --- | --- | --- |
| Client | 2% | 2% |
| Lawyer–Client equally | 33% | 51.4% |
| Lawyer | 59.5% | 38.5% |

Are you surprised by those figures, or do they suggest the sort of response you would expect? Is there anything that bothers you about the responses?

The finding that the vast majority of lawyers and clients agreed that the client was not in control might be pretty much as we would expect. But the fact that more clients than lawyers thought they had joint charge of the interview is interesting. Of course, these data reflect a particular experience. We should not automatically assume they tell us who the various parties thought *ought* to be in charge. However, they may still indicate that there is at least some confusion between lawyers and clients as to where control over the relationship actually lies. The potential for misunderstanding and dissatisfaction is obvious.

But what exactly do we mean by 'in charge', and what should the relationship be? Consider the following exercise.

EXERCISE 5.3 **Who's in charge here?**

One view of the professional role is to describe it as follows:

> Professionals, in contrast to members of other occupations, claim and are often accorded complete autonomy in their work. Since they are presumed to be the only judges of how good their work is, no layman or other outsider can make any judgment of what they can do. If their activities are unsuccessful, only another professional can say whether this was due to incompetence or to the inevitable workings of nature or society by which even the most competent practitioner would have been stymied. This image of the professional justifies his demand for

---

4. 'The Value of Experience in Legal Competence' (2000) 7 *International Journal of the Legal Profession* 102–3.

complete autonomy and his demand that the client give up his own judgment and responsibility, leaving everything in the hands of the professional.[5]

*(a)   Do you agree/disagree with this view?*
*(b)   Why?*

Now consider the following example of lawyer autonomy, as expressed by an American attorney interviewed by Rosenthal:

> Theoretically, it's unethical not to report accurately negotiations with an insurer to the client. But you can't, and no lawyer does. You tell him about it in such a way that he is prepared to be satisfied. Say the other side offers $5,000. You tell the client that they offered $3,000. He'll say, 'That's no good'. You agree and say, casually, that you will try and get $4,500 out of them which would be fine. He's still not so happy, but reluctantly agrees. Two days later you call him back with the 'good news' that you got him more than he expected, $5,000. Now the client is prepared to be happy. You know what is a good settlement and what he should take. If it is necessary to lie and cheat him to get him to accept what's good for him you do it.[6]

*(c)   Would you consider it appropriate for any other professional – e.g. a doctor – to be selective in the information she gives the client/patient?*
*(d)   Solicitors (but not barristers, or Health Service doctors) have a contractual relationship with their clients. Should that make any difference?*
*(e)   Can you think of any other relationship where one individual presumes, without the other's explicit consent, to decide what is best for that other?*
*(f)   How did you feel when a partner, parent or guardian last told you that you had to accept what was best for you?*

Before finally leaving this exercise you might find it helpful to reflect on Rosenthal's riposte to the traditional view of professionalism:

> Pressures, especially economic ones, often work against the lawyer's providing disinterested service to his client in making a personal injury claim. In many cases the lawyer's financial interest lies in an early discounted settlement while the client's interest lies in waiting out the insurer. The traditional ideal of professional service assists the lawyer in managing the claim so as to make it appear that no conflict of interest with the client exists. Lawyers do not disclose potential sources of conflict and the traditional model inhibits those active client requests for information that could expose issues of conflict, by making such requests appear to be mistrustful client behaviour. Although the norms of

5. H. S. Becker, *Education for the Professions*, National Society for the Study of Education, Chicago, 1962, pp. 38–9.
6. D. E. Rosenthal, *Lawyer and Client: Who's in Charge?*, Transaction Books, New Brunswick, NJ, revised edn, 1977, p. 111. We are not aware of any systematic research on this issue in England, but our own conversations with practitioners have suggested that similar 'cooling out' practices are sometimes adopted by solicitors in this country.

professional responsibility invite client participation, most lawyers believe that a lawyer–client relationship in which client collaboration is to be encouraged by extensive disclosure of critical issues would be inappropriate.[7]

Since the early 1970s, when Rosenthal completed his study, there have been growing calls for more 'participatory' or client-centred approaches to lawyering, to the extent that this has, particularly in terms of skills training, become very much the new orthodoxy.[8] Participatory approaches, it is claimed:[9]

- reduce the potential for conflicts of interest between lawyer and client;
- increase client satisfaction with the lawyer's work (this may be particularly important as a way of encouraging clients to become 'repeat players'[10] – i.e. to use you regularly for their legal work);
- enable clients to do better, in terms of case outcome, than non-participating clients.

In addition, it might also be argued that a participatory approach underpins any attempts to engage in 'empowering' professional practice. By this we mean:

> ... a process by which individuals, groups and/or communities become able to take control of their circumstances and achieve their goals, thereby being able to work towards maximising the quality of their lives.[11]

The main practical implications of the participatory model are that it requires:

- an increase in information exchange between lawyer and client, to facilitate a process of 'informed consent' by the client;[12]

7. *Ibid.*, p. 115. Rosenthal's research suggests that contingency fee arrangements account for much of this pressure. Given debates over conditional and contingent fee systems in England, it is perhaps worth noting that later research in America suggests that, while there is a correlation between the choice of hourly or contingent fee and the amount of effort the lawyer puts into the case, the relationship is probably more complex than Rosenthal suggests: see the discussion in H. Kritzer, W. Felstiner, A. Sarat and D. Trubek, 'The Impact of Fee Arrangement on Lawyer Effort' (1985) 19 *Law and Society Review* 251. There are differences between the US contingent fee and the conditional fee system in England which make it impossible to apply the US findings by simple analogy to the UK. See, however, S. Yarrow and P. Abrams, 'Conditional Fees: The Challenge to Ethics' [1998] *Legal Ethics* 192.

8. See, e.g., Binder, Bergman and Price, *Legal Interviewing and Counseling;* A. H. Sherr, 'Lawyers and Clients: The First Meeting' (1986) 49 *Modern Law Review* 323; M. Spiegel, 'Lawyering and Client Decision-making: Informed Consent and the Legal Profession' (1979) 128 *University of Pennsylvania Law Review* 41.

9. See, e.g., Rosenthal, *Lawyer and Client*, seriatim.

10. This term is taken from Marc Galanter's seminal article on how the legal process favours those who use it most frequently – 'Why the "Haves" Come Out Ahead: Speculation on the Limits of Legal Change' (1974) 9 *Law and Society Review* 95.

11. R. Adams, *Self-Help, Social Work and Empowerment*, Macmillan, London and Basingstoke 1990, p. 43. The notion of 'empowerment' has, since the late 1980s, become an important concept in many areas of professional practice. In the UK, it has developed extensively in a number of areas of health and welfare practice, and in management contexts. Similar trends are apparent in the US, and parallel notions are emerging in the literature on radical legal practice – though not necessarily under the label of empowerment; it would seem, for example, implicit in the ethic of care. We develop the issue further in the final section of this chapter.

12. Spiegel, (1979) 128 *University of Pennsylvania Law Review* 41 (cf. also Chapter 4, above).

- an emphasis on being accessible to the client and responsive to her needs;[13]
- a sensitivity to the human, rather than just the legal, dimensions of the client's problems.

We will work through the implications of this participatory approach for each of the WASP stages.

## Setting the scene: preparing for the interview

Often you will have very little information about your client and her problem before she walks through the door. Consequently, you may think there is little you need to do to prepare for an interview. Well, that is not entirely true.

### Consider your information needs

As we shall see shortly, information gathering is an important part of the first interview. But what you need to remember is that you have two kinds of information needs: one is, obviously, to obtain enough information on the problem to give initial advice and (if necessary) to begin further information gathering, research, letter writing, or whatever action is appropriate to further the matter. The other information need is your own and your firm's: you must obtain enough basic information on the client and her circumstances to open a file on the matter. Your aim, in terms of good information management, is for the file to be sufficiently clear and complete for another lawyer to be able to pick it up in your absence and find out precisely what the issues are and what has been done to date. The initial interview is the first step to creating that resource.

So let's begin by thinking about the kinds of information you need to obtain.

EXERCISE 5.4 **You get what you ask for**

This is quite a simple exercise to get you thinking about your information needs as a legal adviser; you can either note items down individually or brainstorm this in small groups.

*Assume your client has been in a road traffic accident.*

1.  *Consider:*
    *(a) Who might have knowledge of the accident that could be relevant to your client's case?*
    *(b) What kind of information might they have?*
    *(c) Is there anything else you need to know about your client so you can effectively work with her and prepare her claim?*
2.  *Look at the ideas and information you have gathered. Are there common categories or sets of information that you can identify?*
3.  *Use those categories you have identified to construct a checklist of the kinds of general information you might want to obtain from a client at the initial interview.*

---

13. Rosenthal, *Lawyer and Client*, p. 27.

Of course, the range of information sources available to you in practice is potentially vast, depending on the circumstances. Nevertheless, your initial, and some continuing, information needs are likely to be met from among the following:

(a)   Obviously your client – who is likely to be your first and often most important source of factual information. You will need her contact details; information about the accident, her injuries (if any) and where she was treated; her employment (if any) and whether she has taken time off work; whether she is or has been in receipt of any benefits, whether she has suffered any other losses; whether she was insured in respect of any losses or injury.

(b)   Other participants in the matter who may be potential witnesses – both lay participants (such as 'eye-' or 'ear' witnesses) and those who are professionally involved (police officers, paramedics, perhaps doctors and surgeons if the situation warranted it etc.);

(c)   The other party – perpetrator or victim? Either way, you need to know who they are, what they may have said at the time, and whether they have been in communication with your client.

(d)   Other lawyers – has the other party contacted a lawyer? Is that why your client has come to see you? If so, does she have a letter from them? Has your client sought initial advice from anyone else – another solicitor or a Law Centre or Citizens Advice Bureau?

(e)   You might have thought about 'experts' too; these are particularly important in personal injury or professional negligence, but also in some kinds of non-contentious, work. Many will not be involved in the forensic aspects of the case unless you instruct them at a later stage (e.g. medical experts). Some may have been involved already: claims investigators; scene of crime investigators, etc.

(f)   Physical evidence – you may be able to obtain access to many different kinds of documentary and real evidence: photographs, videos, police reports, potential witness statements, medical reports, site visits, and so on. Effective management and use of this material will be a critical part of any case management strategy.[14]

If you try to break this down into information categories that would assist you in an initial interview, you will hopefully get something that looks a bit like this:[15]

**Seven information categories**
*Personal information*
Name, address, phone numbers, family ties, work, age, nationality, income and health may all be relevant – though not necessarily in all cases.

*Other parties*
Basic personal details; solicitor instructed (if any); connection with the client (if any).

---

14.  See further Chapter 10.
15.  Based on Avrom Sherr's seven information categories in 'Lawyers and Clients: The First Meeting' (1986) 49 *Modern Law Review* 323.

*Witnesses (if relevant)*
Basic personal details (though often the client will not know these, so the solicitor must follow them up at a later date); witness to what and for whom? Connections with the client.

*Events*
Dates; times; place(s); people involved; the cause and course of events; people affected; property affected; incident which precipitated the visit to the solicitor.

*What the client wants*
Identify the main problem; desired outcome; difficulties in achieving outcome; people to be affected by outcome.

*Previous advice and assistance*
Anyone else consulted? Details of consultant; the advice given; action taken by consultant and by client; effects of any action taken. (In Sherr's research this and the next category were the areas least often addressed by trainee solicitors when interviewing.)

*Existing legal proceedings*
Nature of the proceedings; parties; stage of process; past/future hearing dates.

The point of this exercise is that these seven information categories are relatively standard to all basic forms of litigation, and a number of them will apply to most kinds of non-contentious work too. Consequently, you can use this as a template for devising your own basic interviewing checklist. Checklists can serve as a useful memory tool in interviews, but two words of warning. First, don't try to make them too detailed or use them as a substitute for thinking about the problem. Clients' problems are not standardised; most checklists are! Secondly, once you are in the interview, be aware also that it will not create a great impression with the client if you are simply reading questions off a sheet, writing notes and ticking boxes. Make sure your attention is on the client, not your checklist.

Some areas of work require their own very specialised checklists, reflecting the information needs of those fields. Many firms have created their own, and some practitioner books will also have specimen checklists available.

## Planning the physical environment

Assume now you are about to meet a new client for the first time. What do you think is the right environment, and what will you do to create it?

As always there are a number of aspects you might have stressed here. As we saw in the previous chapter, getting the physical environment right is obviously important. You should think about the following as a matter of course:

- Arrange to prevent interruptions from a secretary, colleagues, or incoming phone calls.[16]
- Present an organised and uncluttered appearance – which will boost your client's confidence.
- What about seating arrangements? Staring at your client directly across a desk can be intimidating, though it may help your own confidence in the early days. Experiment with various seating arrangements[17] to find one that is efficient and that you feel comfortable with.[18]

Many of these problems are reduced in firms with larger premises, by the routine use of interview and conference rooms for meeting clients. These provide a more controlled, appropriate environment away from the lawyer's normal workspace. Seating arrangements are relatively flexible. Issues of clutter, or concerns about unauthorised persons gaining sight of confidential material are thus simply avoided. Incidentally, it also means that firms can use their office space more efficiently. Your dreams of being an associate with your own office and a big desk are increasingly likely to turn into the reality of a workspace in an open-plan office! But for now, back to the realities of the WASP model.

## Welcoming: establishing a relationship in the interview

Other aspects of what Boon has called 'personal presentation' are also important in creating a client-centred environment. One of the litigators he interviewed in his research summed it up like this:

> ... the critical point, when you are first meeting a client, is to be open in your demeanour and approach; you are there to receive information that they want to impart about their problem ... you have to elicit the right level of information. It is a combination of trying to put the client at ease so that they feel they are going to get the help they are looking for, plus displaying that you understand the area in which they are working or in which the problem lies so that they have confidence in what you are doing ... It is important to try and achieve a rapport with the client so that they feel at ease and feel as if they can work with you ... [19]

There are many practical ways of building rapport. Opening the interview in a manner that is appropriate is an important part of this process. Have a go at the next exercise.

16. If this seems too obvious to be worth stating, it should be noted that in Sherr's latest study of 143 initial interviews, interruptions were recorded in over a quarter of them: (2000) 7 *International Journal of the Legal Profession* 102 at pp. 122–3.
17. See, e.g., the suggestions in H. Twist, *Effective Interviewing*, Blackstone Press, London, 1992, p. 42.
18. Though ultimately, in practice, your working environment may limit your flexibility to some degree – e.g. whether you actually have the physical space to ever interview away from your desk
19. A. Boon, 'Assessing Competence to Conduct Civil Litigation. Key Tasks and Skills' in A. Boon, A. Halpern and K. Mackie, *Skills for Legal Functions II: Representation and Advice*, Legal Skills Working Papers, Institute of Advanced Legal Studies, London, 1992, p. 9 at pp. 36–7.

EXERCISE 5.5  **Meet, greet and seat**

Pair up with a colleague; one of you agrees to be the lawyer, the other the client. The client may use a fictitious persona and problem that s/he has invented for the purpose. Your tutor will give the lawyer nothing more than the client's name, and a very general idea of the problem (e.g. road traffic accident, etc.). Now:

(a)   *Practice the welcoming phase of the interview, up to and including the point where the lawyer begins to elicit information about the problem.*

(b)   *Reflect together on the appropriateness of the lawyer's welcome: what worked well? What worked less well?*

(c)   *Try to consolidate the ideas in (b) into a set of written guidelines for opening an interview.*

(d)   *Compare your guidelines with those of other pairs. What do you find?*

(e)   *Lawyer and client should choose another case from the Appendix and switch roles. The aim of this is to test your consolidation in stages (c) and (d).*

Some of the points you have identified may seem very basic, even obvious, but our own experience has shown that it is often the most basic and taken for granted steps that people forget! Did the lawyers remember the social graces? For example, did they stand up to greet the clients, or did they greet them at the office door, or reception area? Did the lawyers introduce themselves by name? What did they do to 'break the ice'? Offer you refreshments? Engage in 'small talk'? Both? Neither? How did the lawyers open the questioning? Did they ask about the client's personal details, or did they ask about what had happened, or for some more particular piece of information? The questions you ask at this point can make a great deal of difference to the way the rest of the interview proceeds, as we shall see in the next section.

There are a number of other factors which may have occurred to you. Three which commonly arise are the issues of note-taking, of discussing costs, and of 'territory'.

## Note-taking

This is often one of the hardest tasks to get right.[20] It is extremely important that you obtain a good record of the events leading up to the interview, and of your client's relevant personal details, but it needs to be sensitively done. Excessive note-taking, especially in the first phase of the interview, breaks eye-contact and can become generally quite distracting for the client. Can you think how you might structure the interview to overcome this problem?

We suggest you listen first, then make notes as you start to probe for information. At the other extreme, do not attempt to rely purely on a note written up from memory after the interview. You will not retain detail that may well prove critical

---

20. Cf. Sherr (1986) 49 *Modern Law Review* 323 at pp. 329–30.

later on.[21] It does not do a lot for your credibility if you have to keep going back to clients to find out things they have already told you.

### Discussing costs

The appropriate moment for discussing costs might also need to be considered.[22] Costs are inevitably a matter of concern for clients, and an area, relative to other aspects of client care, where practitioners' performance is quite poor. A study by Neville Harris for the National Consumer Council in 1993 showed that over 25 per cent of the fee-paying clients surveyed received no information on costs until they received their bill.[23] The same study asked whether the adviser had checked that clients who had received information on fees or legal aid understood it. Forty-nine per cent of respondents in that category said that the lawyer had not asked if they understood.[24] Moreover, less than half the clients who told the lawyer they did not understand the costs felt that their adviser tried hard to explain it more clearly.[25]

The best approach, we suggest, is to be very matter of fact about costs. Ultimately, a lawyer is a person providing a service for a fee, and it is usually as well to recognise this and address the issue of cost sooner rather than later. Clients are well aware that services have to be paid for, even before they get the bill! Equally, if a client is entitled to legal aid, it is in the client's interests to ascertain that this is so. Having said that, there is no absolutely 'right' time to discuss fees. You must use your own judgment to pick the moment. But never assume that, because the client does not mention the fees, she is not interested in – or worried by – how much it will all cost. You should also be aware that the Law Society's code of conduct specifies the information solicitors should give clients about their charges.[26]

### Territory

So far, we have tended to assume that client interviewing takes place on your own home territory all the time, but this is not the case. Both in commercial and criminal work, you may find yourself working on someone else's territory, be it a witness's or the client's or, in the case of criminal work, at the police station. This shift of territory can make subtle but important differences to how you perceive others, and how they perceive you. Relationships can be shaped, at least partly, by

---

21. On note-taking techniques specifically, see Twist, *Effective Interviewing*, pp. 42–5.
22. On some academic courses, you may find you are instructed to ignore the question of costs because it can distract you from the interpersonal or skills elements of the exercise.
23. 'Do Solicitors Care for their Clients?' (1994) 10 *Civil Justice Quarterly* 359 at p. 365.
24. *Ibid.*, pp. 366–7.
25. *Ibid.*, p. 367.
26. See Practice Rule 15 of the Solicitors Practice Rules 1990. Details of this are contained in the *Law Society's Guide to the Professional Conduct of Solicitors*, available on-line at www.guide-on-line.lawsociety.org.uk. The nature and status of the *Guide* is discussed further in Chapter 6.

territorial considerations, which will affect the power balance between the various people involved.

In police station work, for example, the solicitor's role undergoes some important changes. Not only is the solicitor in the station to get instructions from a client detained in custody, she is often there to protect that client's interests in a very real way – by sitting in on police interrogations of that client. As Sanders and Young have pointed out,[27] the solicitor is in a difficult position. On the one hand, the adversarial nature of the process means that solicitors might be expected to act positively as advocates of their client's cause. On the other hand, for regular defence solicitors, the police station is very much part of the workplace, and while this may mean that they are more likely to feel comfortable in (or at least familiar with) the surroundings; it also means that they have a vested interest in not upsetting the police by their tactics. As one solicitor interviewed by David Dixon has put it:

> You've got to do the best for your client, but you've still got to live with the system many years on. So ... most solicitors do their best for their clients, but they also ... won't generally upset the police.[28]

It seems to us that, fundamentally, there is a contradiction between those objectives. You cannot have it all ways all the time. How do you handle those situations where, arguably, the *only* way of doing your best for a client involves upsetting the police? This is an interesting question that goes beyond technique and centres, again, on the ethics and duties of the lawyer:

> The proper role of the defence lawyer is not, as some would have it, merely that of an observer. If that were the case, the lawyer could be replaced by a video camera. Neither is it to maintain some kind of balance between police and suspect – it is unlikely that the defence will ever have the powers and resources to match those of the police. Nor is the defence lawyer's function merely, as the Court of Appeal has sometimes implied, that of provider of legal information. Rather, as Code C now states, 'the solicitor's only role in the police station is to protect and advance the legal rights of his client'. In our adversarial system, in which the police actively pursue the interests of the prosecution, the defence lawyer must actively pursue the interests of the suspect or defendant. To the extent that she or he does not do so, the lawyer will, as the Lord Chief Justice indicated in the case of *Paris*, be doing a disservice to the client, becoming in effect an arm of the prosecution.[29]

27. See *Criminal Justice*, Butterworths, London, 2nd edn, 2000, pp. 233–6.
28. 'Common Sense, Legal Advice and the Right to Silence' [1991] *Public Law* 233 at p. 239.
29. E. Cape with J. Luqmani, *Defending Suspects at Police Stations: The Practitioner's Guide to Advice and Representation*, Legal Action Group, London, 4th edn, 2003, p. 4; also the revised Code of Practice C under the Police and Criminal Evidence Act 1984 (1995) (latest version 2003), note 6D.

## Listening and questioning

The ability to listen and question effectively is obviously central to the interviewing process. Neither skill is as easy to acquire as we tend to think.

### Listening

The importance of listening is something we tend to overlook in much of our daily lives. Partly this is just habit: listening is simply part of our daily interaction and, unless something goes wrong, we function quite instinctively. Equally, for many of our normal activities we do not have to attend that closely to what is being said around us. We live and work surrounded by the talk of friends and colleagues, or by the radio or TV, etc., and switch in and out of 'listening mode' much as we choose. Even the lectures we listen to as students can often be taped for later consumption, or copied up from someone else or even, in some cases, read up in a textbook, if we find ourselves drifting off into a more interesting world . . .

In a professional context you do not really get that second chance. Failure to listen to the client's story will not only limit the accuracy of your information gathering and advice, but may damage your ability to build up a rapport and gain the client's confidence. Try the next exercise to see what we mean.

EXERCISE 5.6  **Is anybody there?**

(a)   *Divide into pairs: one speaker and one listener.*
(b)   *The speaker may choose any subject to talk about for two minutes (it's probably best to choose some interesting event or experience, rather than a technical topic).*

> Phase 1: The speaker should tell their story to the listener. The listener must remain completely passive: do not give any verbal or non-verbal encouragement to the speaker but, unlike Exercise 3.6, do not respond negatively to the story either.
>
> Phase 2: Repeat Phase 1, but this time with the listener responding normally to the story – i.e. using the verbal and non-verbal 'listening behaviour' you would normally adopt in such a situation. Listeners must remember two things, however:
>
> (i) You must not ask any direct questions of the speaker.
> (ii) You should try not to exaggerate your listening behaviour.

Now, in the same pairs:

(c)   *Discuss the different feelings/responses evoked in the speaker by the listener's behaviour in each of the above processes.*
(d)   *Make a list of the different types of verbal and non-verbal behaviour used by the listener in Phase 2.*

What this exercise identifies in a rather extreme way is some of the differences, and the links, between *active* and *passive* listening.[30]

Phase 1 illustrates neatly the extent to which we rely on some kind of positive feedback when talking to someone. Non-response can be as distracting as negative feedback. The dividing line between non-response and *passive listening* can be a relatively fine one, though it is a distinction that most of us manage to negotiate quite happily on a daily basis. Passive listening techniques include:

- *Constructive use of silence* We all know how uncomfortable silences can be when we are with people we do not know well. In interviewing, however, if carefully managed, silence can be helpful. Can you think of some ways in which you might use silence in an interview?
- *Using NVC to encourage further disclosure* In Phase 2 you will have almost certainly noted the ways in which the listener used NVC to show that they were listening – e.g. by smiling, nodding or using prosodic responses to encourage the speaker to continue.

Obviously, it would be a strange interview if you were just to sit there listening to the client's story, nodding and grunting occasionally! So what does active listening require?

Certainly it implies a particular kind of listening for content. Active listening involves attention not just to the words being used by the client, but the feelings and intentions underlying what the client is saying.

EXERCISE **5.7  Hyperactive?**

For this exercise follow your tutor's instructions.

Active listening also needs to be reflected back to the client. This can be achieved by a variety of verbal techniques. You can use *paraphrasing* to confirm your understanding of an event, and to help the client clarify their thoughts and feelings. Helena Twist gives the following example:

CLIENT: I was absolutely furious when she walked out. How was I supposed to manage? Looking after the kids, working long hours, how could I take care of them properly?

LAWYER: So, you were worried you wouldn't be able to manage your job and look after the children?[31]

---

30. These are not precise terms of art, and the boundaries between active and passive listening tend to be drawn differently by different writers on the field: cf. Sherr, *Client Care for Lawyers*, pp. 17–19 and Twist, *Effective Interviewing*, pp. 15–16. It does not much matter where you draw the line, so long as your use of the different techniques remains appropriate.
31. *Effective Interviewing*, p. 16.

Paraphrasing can also be developed as a reflective technique where you summarise not just what the client is saying but what they are feeling. Sometimes this is relatively easy, where the client makes feelings an explicit part of the story, thus:

CLIENT: I mean, I don't want to fight and I do want to fight, right? That's exactly what it comes down to.

LAWYER: Yeah, you're ambiguous.

CLIENT: Oh, boy, am I ever. And I have to live with it.[32]

But often you need to depend on other things to help identify feelings – the client's body language, the pace and modulation of their speech, for example; and it is these as much as the words that need to be reflected back. This can have empathic value and can serve as a basic form of what counsellors would call 'catalytic intervention'. We will develop ideas of empathy and intervention later in this chapter.

## Questioning

There are a number of basic question styles which can be used interchangeably during an interview to achieve different ends. In this section, we consider the kinds of questions you can use, and their effects.

*Open questions* are basic introductory questions which are intended to encourage the client to talk, while leaving the client to determine the parameters, e.g.

> *'You said you wanted to see me about a road accident you were involved in. Perhaps you could just tell me what happened?'*
> *'Is there anything else you think I ought to know?'*

These can sometimes yield a lot of information, particularly if the client is reasonably talkative, but they do not work well with all clients, or in all contexts. Sometimes a question (especially of the rather vague 'anything else' variety) can be so general that your client may feel unable to answer it because she has no idea of what you are after. Even with talkative clients, you will also need to use more precise, structured questioning to be sure of getting the information you should have. Structured questions fall into two broad categories: closed and probing questions.

As the term suggests, *closed questions* tend to be narrow, and designed to elicit a particular piece of information. The style of questioning is direct and encourages the client to give a fairly precise answer, and sometimes no more than a yes/no response:

> *'Did you see what he looked like?'*

The trick in interviewing is to try and get the right kind of balance and approach between open and closed questioning. Consider the following exercise.

---

32. Interview cited by A. Sarat and W. Felstiner, 'Law and Strategy in the Divorce Lawyer's Office' (1986) 20 *Law and Society Review* 93 at p. 123.

EXERCISE 5.8 **Me and Mrs Jones**

Here is an extract from a real client interview. Read the extract, then consider these questions.

*(a)    How effective was the lawyer's questioning?*
*(b)    What, if anything, might he have been done better?*

| | | |
|---|---|---|
| 1. Lawyer: | Come on in and sit down. | |
| 2. Client: | Thank you very much. | |
| 3. Lawyer: | Right now, Mrs Jones what can I do to try and help you? | |
| 4. Client: | Er, its a long story. | |
| 5. Lawyer: | All right, it's a matrimonial problem is it? | |
| 6. Client: | Yes it is. | |
| 7. Lawyer: | How long have you been married? | |
| 8. Client: | Nearly eight years. | |
| 9. Lawyer: | Have you any children? | |
| 10. Client: | Yes one, this is the problem, now um, as I say, I've been married for, I think it's eight years, I'm not divorced yet, by the way, because my husband committed adultery and you know all what's involved with that. | |
| 11. Lawyer: | Yes, yes. | |
| 12. Client: | Well the divorce just hasn't sort of been started, to my knowledge anyway. Now after we separated . . .[33] | |

Here the lawyer began with an open question (at no. 3), but that did not have the desired effect. The client did not get into her story, but rather gave the response noted at no. 4. The lawyer responded by going into a set of fairly formulaic closed questions, which were finally interrupted by the client beginning to tell her story (at no. 10). This was an example of the client taking over the initiative from the lawyer, and it cannot be guaranteed, in such a case, that the client will have the confidence to do this. We have both observed interviews where the interviewer has continued with closed questioning for ten to fifteen minutes before it becomes apparent what the client's real concern or objective is. With students especially, this behaviour is often associated with an almost slavish reliance on long, detailed checklists.[34] The effect on performance is dire. The interview becomes a form-filling exercise. There is virtually no eye contact between interviewer and interviewee, and no real opportunity for dialogue and the building of rapport.

---

33. Sherr, *Client Care for Lawyers*, p. 15.
34. We are not against the intelligent use of checklists, it is just that what we describe here is not very intelligent.

Such behaviour, so students frequently tell us, helps them feel in control of the interaction.[35] However, the effect is to convert the interview process from one of interaction into an interrogation. Many's the time we have observed client interviews with the feeling we were sitting in a police station! In an interrogation, the agenda is controlled by one participant, and the other does not participate willingly. In a free-flowing conversation, on the other hand, both participants want to communicate and do so openly. The closer to a conversation your interview is, the more likely you are to build rapport and get the information you need.[36]

Whether this behaviour reflects a lack of confidence on the part of the lawyer, or a fear that the client will just talk on endlessly about irrelevances is hard to say. If it is a fear of the latter, then that tends to be misplaced. Research indicates that clients rarely give information that is irrelevant (though, initially, it may appear irrelevant to the lawyer).[37] It has also been calculated that the average time clients take to tell their story is about seven minutes[38] – hardly an age, even by a lawyer's standards!

How might the lawyer in Exercise 5.8 have dealt with this situation, other than by closed questioning? See if you can think of a more effective way to get to the real issue (i.e. what emerged at no. 10).

In our view, the critical intervention is clearly no. 5. The client could well have been embarrassed or uncomfortable about the subject-matter, and was probably using her statement (at no. 4) as a gap filler as she composed herself, and thought about what she was going to say. The lawyer could have assisted her more effectively here by using some encouraging or enabling statement, rather than the closed question he chose. For example, something like 'Okay, that doesn't matter' or even 'All right, why don't you start from the beginning' would probably have had the desired effect. The moral is clear: do not use closed questions too soon; they may only serve to impose your own agenda on the interview.

A special form of closed question is the *leading question*. It is a question which is designed to elicit a specific response. For example, the question 'You saw the accident happen, didn't you?' clearly implies that you expect the answer 'Yes'. For that reason you should be very careful in using leading questions, particularly in respect of any matter which is contentious. If you have prompted your client's answer in respect of a contentious issue, you will need to look for verification of her version of events. We shall consider the role of leading questions again in the context of advocacy.

---

35. Some students – and, unfortunately, some tutors and skills manuals – refer to this as the need to 'control the client'. In our view this terminology, albeit inadvertently, discourages a client-centred approach to interviewing and conferencing. We prefer to discuss the issue in terms of 'managing the interview process'.
36. See C. Maughan and M. Maughan, 'Interviewing and Advising' in J. Webb et al, *LPC Guide: Lawyers' Skills*, Oxford University Press, Oxford, 2004, pp. 8–9.
37. Sherr, *Client Care for Lawyers*, p. 28.
38. We have been unable to track the source of this statement beyond the notes accompanying the LNTV (Legal Network Television) programme, *Solicitors as Communicators*. See programme notes for 16 September 1993, Programme 60, p. 3.

The other generic category of structured questions, we said, are *probing questions*. These serve to 'flesh out' the client's story by taking the client through the particular points which you consider necessary to develop.

You may find it helpful, as you develop an awareness of your own questioning style, to focus more specifically on the different kinds of probing question you can use, and to try and extend your repertoire of techniques. The following typology may prove helpful.

Interrogatory questions are the simplest form of probing question, hence:

'Why did you say that?'
'How long ago did this happen?'

These can be useful in moving the story along to a rather more specific level of analysis, while retaining some of the characteristics of open questions. Do bear in mind that the style of questioning is important here: too many interrogatory questions, or the wrong intonation, can make your client feel as if she is being cross-examined!

Keyword questions perform a rather more specific function, based upon your use of active listening skills. With this technique, you listen for words or ideas that seem sufficiently important for you to want the client to focus on them. You then repeat the keyword(s) to the client as part of a question. For example, imagine the following dialogue is part of an interview with the victim of a mugging, thus:

CLIENT: I wasn't really sure what was going on at first, but then he grabbed my arm and tore the bag out of my grip.
LAWYER: You say he grabbed your arm?
CLIENT: Yes, really hard, hard enough to leave bruises . . .

This is not just a good device for narrowing in on specific issues, but also provides the client with some reinforcement of their story. By mirroring the client's language, you can signal not only that you are listening closely to what is being said, but that you accept the importance of the client's own language and choice of narrative.

Reflective questions can be used to probe beyond the basic facts and to clarify a client's feelings or perception of a problem. As we have seen, questions form an important part of the active listening process. Reflective questions tend to be prefaced by terms such as 'How did you feel when . . .' or 'Did it seem to you that . . .' (though note that in the latter version there is a risk of leading your client). Reflective questions can not only clarify your client's position, they can also be an important way of testing your evaluation of the case, or of indicating some level of empathy with your client.

Hypothetical questions are really too well known to require much explanation. They take the form 'What if . . .', 'How would you feel if . . .' etc. Hypotheticals can be a useful vehicle for testing your theory of a case on a client, or for proposing a variety of solutions as part of your advice. However, they need to be used with a little caution, particularly if they might encourage a client to concoct a version of events which matches your hypothetical scenario.[39]

EXERCISE 5.9  **Tell me why**

(a)   *Form groups of three: two participants and one observer. Your tutor will give a different brief to each participant. The third person in the group will be given the observer briefing sheet.*

(b)   *Each participant should interview the other, using questions starting only with the words in their brief.*

  The aim is for the participants each to find out what the other did last weekend.

(c)   *At the end of the exercise, the whole group should consider:*

  (i)   *Who got the most information?*

  (ii)  *Why did they get more information than the other?*

  (iii) *Who had to work the hardest for information?*

  (iv)  *What do we learn from this exercise about questioning styles?*

## Pulling it all together

Listening and questioning are, clearly, closely interlinked skills and the quality of an interview will depend greatly on the way you deploy those skills. It is important to think about the following.

First, you must encourage the client to speak freely about the problem. Use open questions to start with and be prepared to listen and not cut in too early in the interview. Too much emphasis on closed questioning may result in you getting a very skewed version of the problem. Many of the skills books thus suggest you should think of the listening and questioning phase of the interview in terms of a funnel or 'T' in which you start with open questions and then probe. You should then summarise and check the information you have obtained. Sherr's research also suggests that lawyers who give their clients a chance to speak from the outset are less likely to have to go back over the factual issues in depth later in the interview, because the client has not 'had her say'.[40] However, you should always check over the key facts and events with the client before you attempt to give advice, for the obvious reason that this helps you avoid giving advice based on a misunderstanding of the situation.

One other key issue is when you take your client's personal details. Clearly, you need this kind of information for the file, and it may have further significance for the matter itself. While you need this information, it is not a good idea to get into a routine of automatically taking personal details at the outset of the interview. Certainly, a person who is highly agitated or upset about a situation is likely to be focused on talking about their problem from the moment they walk through the

39.  Aiding the client to concoct a defence etc will constitute a breach of the professional Codes of Conduct.
40.  *Client Care for Lawyers*, p. 43.

door. It is often a good idea to let them tell their story first, and then go back to get the details you need later. Be guided by your common sense and your awareness of the person's situation: what is the nature of the problem; does the client appear at all agitated or distressed?

In these welcoming and information gathering phases, the client should generally be allowed to lead the way. Your role is facilitative more than directive. As we shall see, the balance changes rather once you go into the next, advisory, phase of the interview, so let's sum up and try another interview before we move on –

PREPARE YOUR TERRITORY IN ADVANCE.
REMEMBER TO MEET, GREET AND SEAT YOUR CLIENT.
LET THE CLIENT DO THE TALKING.
SUPPORT THE CLIENT – USE ACTIVE LISTENING AND
   EMPATHIC QUESTIONING.
PROBE FOR DETAIL.
CHECK THE FACTS BEFORE ADVISING.

EXERCISE 5.10  **The client interview**

The aim of this exercise is to practise the information gathering phase only.

(a)    *Divide into the same pairs and same roles as for Exercise 5.9.*
(b)    *Conduct a lawyer–client interview only to the point where the lawyer is satisfied that s/he has acquired all the necessary information on the matter, and has checked the facts with the client. Do not give advice.*
(c)    *In your pairs, reflect and feedback in the normal way.*
(d)    *Don't forget to write up your experiences in your learning diary.*

## Advising and counselling

In this section we shall stress the interplay between two related lawyer roles. The first of these is fairly obvious. Our clients expect us to give them legal advice, and there are more or less effective ways of doing so. The second, counselling, role is perhaps less apparent, but no less central to a participatory approach.

### Lawyers as advisers

The advisory role is one where, conventionally, the balance of participation shifts. This phase is rather more lawyer-dominated – at least in so far as the lawyer, as adviser, needs to take a more active part than before.

What are the essentials of this phase?

EXERCISE 5.11  **Toast**

Divide into pairs: one lawyer and one client.

Your client is seeking advice on a relatively simple consumer problem. Neither lawyer nor client should assume that the client has any substantive knowledge of consumer law. The client has already told you (the lawyer) the basic problem, which can be summarised as follows:

The client's story

> Fed up with burnt toast in the mornings, I bought a top of the range toaster from a local department store. I have had it two weeks, and the mechanism has jammed, preventing the toast from popping up. I took the toaster back to the shop, and they say the mechanism could only have jammed in this fashion if the toaster had been dropped, or if some other excessive force was applied to the mechanism. There is no way either of these things have happened while I have had it, but the shop has refused to repair or replace the toaster, or to refund my money. They insist it is my fault and that the guarantee is therefore void.

The client's objectives

I want a new toaster or my money back.

(a)  *The lawyer's task:*
   (i)  *You have ten minutes in which to prepare your advice.*
   (ii)  *You then have a further ten minutes in which to advise your client and close the interview.*
(b)  *The client's task:*
   (i)  *In the ten minutes' preparation, make a note of what you consider to be the lawyer's objectives in advice-giving.*
   (ii)  *During the interview, be prepared to ask questions if the lawyer's advice seems uncertain or unclear to you in any way.*
(c)  *Reflection in pairs:*
   (i)  *Lawyers should consider their own performance – what worked, what did not work. Why/why not?*
   (ii)  *Lawyers – what problems arose which you did not anticipate at the outset? Why weren't they anticipated?*
   (iii)  *Clients – how accurately did the lawyer's reflection match your own experience? Did the lawyer meet the criteria on your list? Discuss with your lawyer the appropriateness of your criteria.*
   (iv)  *Discuss the outcomes of this exercise in the whole group, then compare your criteria with ours (below), and don't forget to reflect on and account for any differences you see!*
   (v)  *Make sure you draft an entry in your learning diary.*

Most obviously, you would expect the lawyer to give you some indication of your legal rights. It would not, of course, be sufficient to advise in the abstract, academic, sense. The lawyer would need to include some plan of action – i.e. an indication of the steps you, or the lawyer, would take to enforce your rights. Ideally, the lawyer might seek confirmation that you understand the advice and are happy with it, and should indicate whether, and if so when, you should have another meeting. So, in summary, good advice-giving involves four things:

- stating advice (so far as possible);
- devising and agreeing a plan of action;
- confirming client's understanding of advice and next steps;
- setting-up further contact (if necessary).

What does research tell us about the way lawyers approach this phase of the relationship? Sherr's research in the 1980s suggested that trainee solicitors were generally very poor at this phase, with, for example, 45 per cent of his sample failing adequately to give advice or to state a plan of action; 59 per cent failing to check for client understanding and agreement with that course of action; and 67 per cent failing to set up further contact.[41] In fact, Sherr found that this phase of the interview was the least well done of all. That might help you place your own performance in context! But what is it that makes advising so difficult? Let us use the four elements listed above to analyse this phase in more depth.

**Giving advice**

This is obviously central to the interview. It should also be something with which you are reasonably familiar from traditional academic study. But somehow that academic experience does not seem to help you a great deal. Why not? See if you can jot down three or four reasons.

Here are our own ideas.

First, you may never have had to use that book knowledge in action before. This has a number of consequences: (i) it means that by the time you come to do a live interview you may have forgotten most of the actual law; (ii) you will have to try and do a translation exercise to convert your academic knowledge into practical advice – this is quite complex because you have both to think through the legal consequences of the particular facts, and translate your advice into lay (rather than legal) language 'on the spot'.

Second, the 'law in action' that you need in order to give advice may be very different from the 'law in books' that you have encountered to date. The impact of procedural law, evidence, costs, and all sorts of other practical consequences, may make the academic law of more limited utility.

Third, as an extension of this second point, the client may not actually be helped by 'black-letter' legal advice. A variety of practical or 'non-legal' solutions may be far more appropriate than conventional legal action (we discuss this in more detail below). These may include referrals to other agencies, or advice on forms of self-help that might be available. Practitioners develop a network of such contacts through their own experience and through that of their colleagues. This takes time to develop, and can be difficult to replicate in a clinical context.

---

41. (1986) 49 *Modern Law Review* 323 at pp. 339–40. These findings, of course, pre-date the introduction of direct skills training on the Legal Practice Course.

You must be realistic about your own limitations. There are three key mistakes you must try and avoid in giving advice.

The most fundamental error you can make is to give advice that is clearly wrong in law. If you do not know the answer, you must find a way of explaining this to the client (without totally undermining your own position!) and build the need to clarify or confirm your advice into your action plan.

The next most critical mistake you can make is to give a client advice they do not understand, particularly if you expect them to act on it in some way. It is essential therefore to think about how you deliver your advice:

- Try to use language the client understands.
- Give the client some kind of structure, for example use the '3Ts'.[42]
- Confirm your advice with the client.

This last stage is crucial, but, in our experience, commonly forgotten. We shall return to it again.

The third, or perhaps equal second, major error is to give clients advice they do not want. By this we do not mean advice they do not want to hear – there will be times when you have to give bad news: that is part of the job. What we do mean is that you must take account of your client's objectives. This is the essence of participatory, client-centred, practice.[43] Yet there is a strong tendency among lawyers to 'talk past' their clients and focus on their own agendas for action, ignoring the central concerns of those clients.[44] As Sarat and Felstiner put it, cases proceed 'without the generation and ratification of a shared understanding of reality'.[45] This seems to us to indicate, at the least, a failure in the willingness of lawyers to negotiate outcomes with their clients. We should ensure that the client is adequately informed of the options, and given the opportunity to assess those options on her own terms.

### Devising and agreeing the action plan

There is no point in leaving the client with a blanket piece of advice which does not translate into a set of concrete tasks and expectations. A major cause of client concern is likely to be their ignorance of what the lawyer intends to do next. An action plan can include a whole variety of elements: your commitment to carry out

42. '3Ts':
   1. tell them what you are going tell them;
   2. tell them; then
   3. tell them what you have told them (i.e. check for understanding).
   Cf. Sherr's idea of 'advance organisers', *Client Care for Lawyers*, p. 74.
43. See Rosenthal, *Lawyer and Client*, p. 27.
44. See, e.g., S. Macaulay, 'Lawyers and Consumer Protection Laws' (1979) 14 *Law and Society Review* 115; A. Sarat and W. Felstiner, 'Law and Social Relations: Vocabularies of Motive in Lawyer–Client Interaction' (1988) 22 *Law and Society Review* 737. This view is not inconsistent with Sherr's finding that lawyers are generally competent at discovering the client's goals – the issue is, how the lawyer negotiates those goals subsequently: (2000) 7 *International Journal of the Legal Profession* 102.
45. (1988) 22 *Law and Society Review* 737 at p. 742.

some research, which will lead to fuller advice; an agreement to write a letter for the client, and/or a set of tasks for the client – e.g. to supply certain documents, or to contact some other person. It may even be no more than getting the client to reconsider her position in the light of your advice. Whatever it is, the critical point is that both lawyer and client have some shared knowledge of, and commitment to, future action.

### Confirming understanding and next steps

Within the structure of a participatory interview it is important that you get the client's informed consent to any next steps. The client should be aware (so far as you can advise) of the cost and other implications of alternative courses of action. To ensure this, it is important that you restate your advice in the context of the action plan – to show how the advice translates into alternatives for action, and to give the client a clear opportunity to ask questions and decide what they want to do. There is no reason why both lawyer and client should not make a note there and then about what has been agreed and what needs to be done, and by whom. In addition, your advice should always be confirmed in writing as part of your client care policy.[46]

### Setting up further contact

It would be a relatively unusual transaction that could be disposed of wholly within one meeting. Uncertainty about what is happening with their case, and when contact ought to be made, will only add to a client's other anxieties about the problem, and may reinforce any worries the client has about your competence. As Sherr notes:

> Research with clients in other fields shows that the immediate 'blush' of satisfaction at the end of a consultation begins to change during the few days afterwards. Clients tend to review in their minds what occurred during the consultation and may become more anxious than they were on leaving the professional's office. It therefore seems good policy to give the client something to look forward to in terms of the next contact.[47]

It may be that the immediate next steps can be conducted by post or phone, but the time scale should, so far as possible, still be made explicit during the first meeting.

## Lawyers as counsellors

> The traditional ideal of a lawyer is one of a person who is sharp, objective, takes charge, and wins arguments. The ideal of a counselor, as Carl Rogers puts it, is of someone who is accepting, understanding, and congruent. The two ideals are not entirely

---

46. See further the final section in this chapter, and Chapter 7 on writing.
47. *Client Care for Lawyers*, p. 76.

compatible. Lawyers suffer some difficulty in reconciling them. Maybe, as a result, we lawyers often function poorly with people. [48]

The essence of legal counselling is that you do not allow yourself to get into a mindset which sees a problem across the desk, not a person. The lawyer–client relationship is a working relationship. It is important in sustaining that relationship that the client feels that she is a special person – in the sense that the lawyer is able, visibly, to respond to her personality and perspective on the case. This does not necessarily require particular 'counselling' skills in a therapeutic sense. Sherr makes the point that 'counselling' in the legal context may indicate little more than presenting clients with the options and enabling them to choose.[49]

This may sound obvious good practice, or it may not. Either way it is not something that we should take for granted. Consider the following description of one highly committed and technically able lawyer:

> After watching Boz, you can easily come away with the impression that she sticks closely to technical legal issues to maintain control over both the boundaries of her relationship with a client and her overall workload. By sticking to technical issues, she can more readily draw the line between where she will help clients and where she wants nothing to do with them. 'Legal' and 'non-legal' become firm categories that play a particularly important function for Boz. Legal designates what the office does and what a lawyer should spend time doing. Non-legal designates everything else, all those things that Boz shouldn't be held responsible for not dealing with or handling badly . . .
>
> Boz's attitude can be as off-putting as her methods. During the Betty Bejarano interview, for example, she never seemed willing to acknowledge the legitimacy of Mrs Bejarano's problem or to credit her for taking steps to correct it herself. She missed virtually every opportunity to give Mrs Bejarano the sense that she had legitimately recognised a wrong that deserved to be righted and that trying to do something about it mattered a lot. She didn't expect anything more than a beaten down, resourceless, uncooperative client, and probably that's often all she ever ends up with. Its chilling to see that sort of behavior in someone who has dedicated herself to helping people.[50]

Would you agree with the author's conclusion after reading that description, or is 'Boz' just recognising what she does best and doing it? How far should lawyers get engaged in the 'non-legal' when advising a client? How would you begin to distinguish the 'legal' and 'non-legal'? You might like to compare your ideas with ours.

### The legal alternatives and their consequences

*Consider* – whether to proceed to trial/negotiate, arbitrate, abandon action, etc.; what time factors exist and what their potential impact on resolution of the dispute

---

48. T. L. Shaffer, 'Lawyers, Counselors, and Counselors at Law' (1975) 61 *American Bar Association Journal* 854 at p. 855.
49. (1986) 49 *Modern Law Review* 323 at p. 353.
50. G. Lopez *Rebellious Lawyering*, Westview Press, Boulder, CO, 1992, p. 110. The interview referred to is reproduced at pp. 103–9.

will be; the impact each alternative is likely to have on costs; the possibility of further litigation (e.g. any claims brought by the other side/third party; appeals). How well can your client handle the stresses and strains of each of these?

### The 'non-legal' alternatives and their consequences

*Consider* – scope for professional mediation or conciliation of disputes; forms of self-help that may be available without the (further) intervention of lawyers or other professionals; advice and assistance that may be obtained from a non-legal agency; note also the need to consider non-legal alternatives in conjunction with legal action.

Now consider what solutions you would offer in the following situation.

EXERCISE 5.12 **Home sweet home**

Imagine you are interviewing a client who is a single parent with a child at primary school. Your client is living in private rented accommodation – a first-floor flat she shared with her former partner until their relationship broke down, with considerable acrimony on both sides. She has a rent book, in her name, pays rent monthly and has to give a month's notice to leave. The rent is significantly below current market rates.

Her landlord is a friend of her 'ex'. He (the landlord) lives in the flat below, and has clearly taken sides against your client. He has sought without success to evict your client (the tenancy is protected) and is now engaged in harassing her. So far this has taken the following forms: playing loud music late into the night, leaving rubbish on the landing to impede her access to the flat, refusing to undertake such maintenance of the property as is required, and being generally aggressive and unpleasant. She wants your advice.

*Make a note of:*
*(a)   the possible legal courses of action your client has;*
*(b)   non-legal steps you might advise (if any);*
*(c)   relevant facts which may effect the utility of those courses of action.*

In brief, your answer would probably incorporate most of the following:

(a)   Private and local authority action in respect of noise pollution; the possibility of county court action for quiet enjoyment.

(b)   A lawyer might well offer advice and assistance in applying for alternative accommodation (e.g. either council or housing association).

(c)   If she takes legal action, she should be counselled as to the risk of on-going problems thereafter, but the practicalities of moving out would also need to be considered, e.g. in terms of the time it might take to get rehoused; whether re-housing would disrupt her child's schooling (would it involve changing schools, for example?) and its impact on her own work/social activities. The cost implications of both options would also need to be considered.

We take the view that, when thinking about consequences, you need always to consider the impact of any advice on the client's financial, social and psychological welfare. If you do not assess these, you are giving legal advice in a vacuum, and possibly doing more harm than good. As part of your advice you should give an assessment of risks inherent in any potential course of action. It is not sufficient simply to present a client with a range of alternatives, spell out the consequences of each and, in effect, say 'take your pick', without giving the client some assessment of the likely outcome of the case. As Binder et al suggest, there may be as many as five possible outcomes which you should seek to identify to your client; they term these:

(i)     the best possible;
(ii)    the best likely;
(iii)   the most probable;
(iv)    the worst likely;
(v)     the worst possible.

At a minimum, you should make sure your client is aware of and understands the middle three options; these will at least give her an idea of the range of likely results in her case.

Arguably, however, the approach we have outlined so far understates the extent to which even a limited understanding of counselling technique generally can have a positive influence on lawyer–client interaction.

Consider the following scenario.

EXERCISE 5.13  **Car trouble**

*The group should divide into pairs – a lawyer and a client. Your tutor will give each of you a brief. The aim of the interview is to counsel and advise only. The lawyers can assume that the following facts are known and agreed.*

Your client is Janet/John Jones, and s/he lives in Bristol.

About three months ago your client lent a car to a friend to use, as a favour. The car is a 1972 Volkswagen Beetle 'soft-top'; it is in extremely good condition for its age and is, now, becoming highly collectable. You are not sure of its current value, but the client has it insured for £2,500. Apart from its market value, your client has made it clear that the vehicle is of strong sentimental value.

The friend has now moved to Taunton, taking the car with him/her. Despite numerous verbal promises, the friend has not returned the car, and has not replied to a letter from your client (posted two weeks ago) asking for the immediate return of the vehicle.

Your client now wishes to resolve the problem and has made an appointment to discuss the options that are open to him/her.

(a)   *Role play the interview.*
(b)   *Feedback in the usual way.*

There are many different general theories and approaches to counselling. We propose to use one approach as a basis for what follows, which is John Heron's 'Six Category Intervention Analysis'.[51] This has the advantages of being a model that has been used in a variety of professional contexts, and also one that is consistent with our own approach to experiential learning.

Heron points out that a counsellor may adopt one of two roles, which he describes as *authoritative* and *facilitative*. In an authoritative mode, the counsellor takes a more dominant or assertive role, whereas in a facilitative mode, the counsellor plays a less obtrusive, enabling or empowering, role. The two approaches are not mutually exclusive. A counsellor may shift from authoritative to facilitative modes as dictated by the client's needs. In the lawyer–client context these styles of intervention may be used within the interview context to improve the quality of the interaction. Heron calls his six categories:

1. Prescriptive.
2. Informative.
3. Confrontational.
4. Cathartic.
5. Catalytic.
6. Supportive.

The first three are authoritative and the second three facilitative interventions. We shall now consider each of them in turn.

**Prescriptive**
The counsellor will actively give advice or attempt to direct the behaviour of the client. In professional counselling, the counsellor may take a judgmental or evaluative stance in this process. In the lawyer–client relationship, an evaluative stance is often an integral aspect of advice-giving; however, it is best to avoid being judgmental of the client's behaviour. Inevitably, perhaps, prescriptive interventions are widely used in the lawyer–client relationship.

**Informative**
The counsellor takes on a didactic role, imparting new knowledge or information to the client, usually in the hope that the client may then use that information constructively – so ultimately having a more facilitative effect.

**Confrontational**
A confronting intervention is intended to challenge directly the assumptions or behaviour of the client, e.g. by pointing out inconsistencies in the client's story, or by picking up on things which have not been said. Remember that confrontational

---

51. For an overview, see J. Heron, 'A Six Category Intervention Analysis' (1976) 4 *British Journal of Guidance and Counselling* 143. The model is more fully explored in Heron's *Helping the Client*, Sage, London, 1990.

does not equate with aggressive – the confronting must be carefully managed if you are not to lose the trust of your client.

### Cathartic

Here, the counsellor encourages the client to revive forgotten or repressed ideas about an earlier event which had a strong emotional impact. The aim of a cathartic intervention is to resolve some unconscious conflict in the client. Cathartic intervention needs to be very carefully managed and, as a technique, probably has little place in legal, as opposed to psychotherapeutic, counselling.

However, do remember that you will often be in a position where you are requiring a client to re-live an event that they have strong feelings about. Like genuinely cathartic intervention, this needs careful management. Be prepared to listen. Ask neutral questions which encourage the client to explain things literally – this can make a painful event easier to recount. Be sympathetic, but do not negate the client's feelings by saying things like 'cheer up' or 'never mind'; reflective statements showing an acceptance of the client's feelings (e.g. 'that must have been difficult for you?') are more empathic and can also encourage the client to continue her narrative – the same is true of a nod and a sympathetic smile! You should also try to avoid following such disclosures with uninvited prescription ('What you need to do is...').

In your professional careers you can confidently expect to be confronted with clients who are emotionally highly charged. Anger may be aimed at you directly, or you may be the target for displaced aggression. When confronted by such behaviour, you may feel wronged, defensive, intimidated even. You should try to avoid your own feelings being reflected in an inappropriate or defensive response to the client. This will only hinder the development (or recovery) of a good working relationship with the client. Distress is also very difficult to respond to. You may feel uncomfortable or embarrassed by a client breaking down in your office; or you may find it difficult to maintain professional detachment – in an extreme situation you may experience what Helena Twist calls 'emotional contagion'.[52] This is the situation where you have reached a high level of empathy with the client, to the extent that you are sharing some of the emotional charge with her.

EXERCISE 5.14 **Handling emotion**

*Divide into discussion groups of three or four people.*

(a)    *Each of you should then take a few minutes to describe a moment in your personal or professional lives when you had to manage the great anger or sadness of another. Talk about how you felt in that situation. What did you do to help that person? Did you attempt any interventions that were clearly counter-productive?*

52. *Effective Interviewing*, p. 85.

(b)    As a group, try to generalise from these experiences and produce some guidelines for dealing with emotion in a professional context.

### Catalytic

A catalytic intervention aims to encourage reflection and self-directed problem-solving in the client – e.g. by helping the client to identify the problem and potential resolutions. Listening is again a crucial element of catalytic interventions – a useful technique, as we have seen, is to listen for verbal cues which seem to carry particular significance for the speaker and feed those back to her.

### Supportive

In Heron's schema there are many forms of supportive intervention which are intended to show care and concern for the person or welfare of another.[53] Supportive interventions can have some applicability in the legal context, where they serve to confirm or validate the client's actions and worth. Never underestimate the importance of such support: many clients will be in your office precisely because they feel (at least) partly responsible for something going wrong. Supportive interventions affirm the worth of the client at a time when she may be at a 'low ebb'. Be careful that anything you do approve is not subsequently going to rebound and cause problems – qualified approval can be safer, but is obviously less affirmative of that person's worth!

A (fairly obvious) word of warning: to become a proficient counsellor requires specialised training. Practising law does not demand that level of proficiency and you should not seek to confuse your role with that of a professional counsellor. If a client needs specialist counselling, that is one course of action which you may recommend – do not try to usurp that role yourself.

Used carefully, however, we suggest that these techniques can serve a positive role in building and protecting the human dimensions of the lawyer– client relationship.

By way of conclusion, use the following exercise to build on what you have learnt, and to practise any counselling techniques you consider appropriate to the case.

EXERCISE 5.15  **Pressing problems**

*Again, the group should divide into pairs – a lawyer and a client. (Your tutor will give you the roles to prepare.)*

*Role play the advising and counselling phase, and feedback as normal.*

As a final point, do not forget the importance of experience in developing your skills. Advising and counselling can be one of the most individualised professional

---

53. See *Helping the Client*, pp. 118–20.

Figure 5.1. 'You may find that the problem lies with you, not the client.'

activities you undertake. It is often not amenable to 'off pat' solutions. It is important to reflect on your experience over time. Compare strategies that did and did not work in similar situations. Look for patterns among problem cases and 'difficult' clients. You may find that the problem lies with you, not the client.

## Parting, and beginning the continuing relationship

In the professional context, parting is not just a question of saying 'goodbye' nicely. It involves a number of discrete steps.

### Ending

First you need to consider how you start to move towards closure. Looking at your watch pointedly is one of the less subtle mechanisms that we have seen employed, but this is not usually recommended!

In all interviewing and counselling contexts, it is important to remember that a client may need some recovery time at the close of the interview. This may be particularly the case where the client has been taken through past events which are distressing, and she must now reorientate herself to the present. It is not appropriate to bring the interview too abruptly to an end in such situations. Establishing or recapping on a plan of action can help in this process; so too can some 'small talk' about everyday matters, so long as you can avoid making the transition seem false.

Second, it is also important to give the client a final opportunity to say anything else that might be of concern or importance to them. Although clients will usually be anxious to talk about the issues, cases will arise where clients are reluctant to disclose the real problem. In the medical literature there is a recognised tendency for the 'presenting symptoms' – i.e. the initially expressed reason for going to see the doctor – to turn out to be secondary to reasons that only emerge during or at the end of the consultation.[54] There is certainly anecdotal evidence of similar experiences in the law.[55] A final open question may help draw out anything that might otherwise remain unsaid.

Lastly, it should be unnecessary to say that we ought to close the interview in an appropriate fashion, but, again, research shows that we all have the capacity to forget the social graces when we get into the office, despite the fact that final impressions are important. So, do remember to see the client out before you start writing up a file note of the interview!

## Beginning

The end of the initial interview is, in most cases, only the beginning of the continuing relationship. This needs to be recognised in a number of ways.

First, intuitively or drawing on your own direct experience, what specific steps do you think you ought to take in the immediate aftermath of an interview?

### EXERCISE 5.16  Planning your next steps

*Make a short list of what action you consider necessary following a client interview.*

To some extent your tasks will be determined by the context. The steps which follow taking instructions for a conveyancing transaction will differ somewhat from litigation, for example. Even so, the following steps are normally required across most, if not all, transactions.

### Make up a file note following the interview

This should contain:

- full details of the client's personal information;
- the events leading up to the consultation etc.;[56]
- work to be done by lawyer and by client;
- advice given and advice to be confirmed.

---

54. See, e.g., P. Byrne and B. Long, *Doctors Talking to Patients*, HMSO, London, 1976.
55. In, e.g., Sherr, (1986) 49 *Modern Law Review* 323 at p. 342n.
56. Don't forget the 'seven information categories' discussed earlier in this chapter.

Most firms have a standard format. Sherr also advises including some note on the lawyer's impressions of the client, and the problem.[57]

### Review action plan and make diary entries

These should be in respect of:

- next contact; and
- deadlines agreed (if any) for later tasks/stages in the transaction.

### Send out client care letter to the client

For solicitors this is an obligation under r. 15 of the Solicitors' Practice Rules 1990.[58] This requires you to provide information to the client on fee structures and in-house complaints procedures. If you are acting on a conditional fee there is again a raft of specific information you must give to the client in writing.[59] These steps are merely preparatory to carrying out the tasks required, but should help ensure that you have a good professional basis on which to build. From here on, however, the emphasis in your relationship with the client is likely to shift (certainly in contentious work) away from focusing on the client as an information resource, and on to the discussion of strategy and objectives. This places an emphasis on the lawyer's counselling role.

## Participating

We have already seen that a commitment to counselling is a commitment to giving clients choices in the conduct of their cases. We would like to close this section by reflecting more deeply on what this means.

How far this commitment to counselling goes is an interesting and, some would say, highly politicised question. As we have seen, the classic image of the lawyer as 'professional thing-maker' (to paraphrase Maureen Cain) is one in which the lawyer is an autonomous agent whose task is to take control of the client's social problem, translate it into a legal one and resolve it. But by this act of agency, it is argued, the lawyer behaves rather like the marines who charge into occupied territory, shoot the 'baddies', liberate the 'natives' and sail away again at the first opportunity – until the next time.

Like the marines, we may have changed the material situation for the present, but we have not necessarily enabled those we have 'helped' to take command of the situation and to maintain control over their future. Moreover, it is sometimes said that counselling itself, as presently envisaged, operates as part of a 'politics of

---

57. This is rather more contentious: see Sherr's justifications in *Client Care for Lawyers*, pp. 95–6, but do consider that negative comments left on file could impose your pre-conception of the client on other lawyers and support staff in the firm.
58. See further Chapter 7, below. Additional follow-up letters should be sent after each subsequent meeting, confirming what has been agreed.
59. See Annex 14F of the *Law Society's Guide to Professional Conduct*.

control' between lawyers and clients.[60] Counselling, it is suggested, can become another, more subtle, form of control than that exercised in non-participatory forms of practice. It is very easy for the lawyer to give a semblance of choice and control to the client, while in reality she stays firmly in charge.[61]

Perhaps a more genuinely counselling–orientated role is a logical outcome of the participatory approach, and our failure to recognise this need in our clients and ourselves is explanatory of both some of the client dissatisfaction lawyers face, and of the deeper inequalities in power disclosed by current practices of lawyering. Sarat and Felstiner have started to address this issue in the context of divorce practice:

> The vocabularies of motive used by clients in divorce cases excuse and justify their conduct and place blame for the failure of their marriage, as well as for problems in the legal process, squarely on their spouses ... Their vocabulary serves to add sympathy to fees as a basis on which their lawyers' energies can be commanded ...
>
> This emphasis poses an awkward choice for lawyers. If they were to join with clients in the project of reconstructing the marriage failure ... they would be dragged into a domain that is, in principle, irrelevant to no fault divorce ... and is in fact beyond their expertise. On the other hand, if they directly challenge client characterisations ... they risk alienating their clients or deepening client mistrust. Thus most of the time lawyers remain silent in the face of client attacks on their spouses. They refuse to explore the past and to participate in the construction of a shared version of the social history of the marriage ...
>
> ... lawyers' refusal to engage with client efforts to give meaning to the past is not without consequences. It often means that clients end up dissatisfied with lawyers who do not understand or empathise with them. Furthermore, the legal construction of social relations may go far in explaining how contentious and difficult the settlement process becomes ...
>
> The vocabularies of motive used in lawyer–client interaction in divorce respond to the distinctive characteristics of that social relationship. Lawyers deploy the resources of professional position; they emphasise their experience and the expertise that experience provides as they try to limit involvement in the client's social world. While this limitation gives power to lawyers' interpretations of the social world, it cannot guarantee acquiescent clients. By repeatedly expanding the conversational agenda, clients resist their lawyers' efforts to limit the scope of social life relevant to their interaction. They manipulate attributions of blame and victimisation to counter professional authority and claims to expertise on which lawyers rely. Thus in divorce

---

60. Sherr, *Client Care for Lawyers*, pp. 112–14; for a wider analysis of the politics of control in action, see P. Harris, 'The Politics of Law Practice' in I. Grigg-Spall and P. Ireland, *The Critical Lawyers' Handbook*, Pluto Press, London 1992.
61. These concerns, and others, are echoed in current debates about empowering practice in the caring professions: see, e.g., K. Baistow, 'Liberation and Regulation? Some Paradoxes of Empowerment' (1994/95) *Critical Social Policy*, Issue 42, Winter, p. 34.

as elsewhere, law, and the images of social life with which it is associated, is deeply embedded in a conflicted and unequal social relationship.[62]

Certainly, in our view, the counselling dimension of the lawyer's role remains under-developed in current practice, perhaps because there is so little training that is genuinely counselling-orientated, and because there are perceived (and perhaps real) tensions between the role of lawyer-as-counsellor and lawyer-as-independent adviser.

## Interviewing and empathic lawyering: a (re)vision of practice?

In bringing this chapter to a close we want to move even further beyond the narrow question of interviewing skills, in order to think about the wider implications of the participatory approach to legal practice. In so doing, we will use the notion of empathy as a unifying discourse to review our approach to interviewing and to consider some radical alternatives for legal practice.

### Empathy and participation

> I only wish I could have found somebody else, a better solicitor, because I honestly thought they just didn't give a damn, couldn't care less, as though it's an everyday occurrence. Probably it is in their case but I didn't want to feel that. I mean, I didn't think that I was special, but I just wanted a little bit of – not sympathy – just concern, I think, to know what was best. I was going to them for help. I didn't know the legal position.[63]

Reading this statement, what do you think was the client's primary complaint about her solicitor?

What we think is interesting about that quote is the way in which the client's feelings about the lack of 'personal service' and 'concern' came to be translated into broader fears about the whole service she was getting. You need to think how you would prevent such a situation arising. Your ability to relate to your client at a personal level is important, as we saw in the previous chapter, in maintaining the channels of communication, and in maintaining the professional relationship once it is established.

A very important characteristic in this context is the notion of *empathy*. We have touched on this at various points in the discussion, without really explaining it. In this final section we shall suggest that empathy is the one thing that really holds the participatory approach together. Empathy operates reflexively, i.e. it informs both our perception of clients, and their perception and reception of us.

Lynne Henderson[64] has identified three distinctive features of an empathic capacity:

62. A. Sarat and W. Felstiner, 'Law and Social Relations: Vocabularies of Motive in Lawyer–Client Interaction' (1988) 22 *Law and Society Review* 737 at pp. 764–7.
63. Divorce client quoted in G. Davis, *Partisans and Mediators*, Clarendon Press, Oxford, 1988, p. 104.
64. 'Legality and Empathy' (1987) 85 *Michigan Law Review* 1574 at pp. 1579–82.

- the ability to perceive others as having their own interests or goals;
- the capacity imaginatively to experience the situation of another;
- the distress response which accompanies the imaginative experiencing of another's pain.

The conventional expectation of the professional role we adopt as lawyers is often one in which we maintain a safe 'professional' distance from our clients and their problems. This is often justified as a personal defence mechanism – we simply cannot afford to get 'involved'. We are lawyers, not social workers, it is said. Very true, but empathy does not mean actively *sharing* your client's problem/pain at a deep, personal, level: it means *understanding* and *responding* to it. At the same time it is not the same as *sympathy*. You do not have to 'take sides' to be empathic – to recognise the 'otherness' of that person's experience. Indeed, empathy can help you develop a capacity for seeing when the client might mislead you (innocently or otherwise) and help you to understand why that happens.[65] Distancing the client and objectifying her problems does not achieve that, and does not make you a 'good' lawyer. The capacity to relate to the client can be as vital as your legal knowledge, not just in terms of your own relations with such clients, but also in establishing your professional reputation:

> One of the solicitors we spoke to told us of how she had dropped one barrister from her firm's stable in favour of another who was less technically able but prepared to talk to clients in a way they were able to relate to.[66]

Empathy is something you can display throughout the relationship, not just as part of some more or less discrete 'counselling phase'. An empathic approach to interviewing also creates practical benefits in terms of the quality of information that is obtained.[67] Again, this is a good point to stop and think.

EXERCISE 5.17 **Empathic interviewing**

*Reflect on (a) the listening, and (b) the questioning techniques we have considered so far.*

*Which, if any, are particularly useful in giving an empathic response to a client?*

As you have probably gathered by now, empathic responses to the client may be many and varied. They are reflected in all the active listening techniques we have discussed in this chapter. Similarly, questioning techniques like mirroring and reflective questioning serve empathic as well as informational ends. Statements which show that you understand what the client is telling you and 'motivational

---

65. Psychologists see a close link between empathy and the accuracy of person perception: the greater the empathy the greater the accuracy. See, e.g., P. Hinton, *The Psychology of Interpersonal Perception*, Routledge, London and New York, 1993, p. 127.
66. J. Morison and P. Leith, *The Barrister's World*, Open University Press, Milton Keynes, 1992, p. 71.
67. See L. Graves, 'Sources of individual differences in interviewer effectiveness: a model and implications for future research' (1993) 14 *Journal of Organizational Behaviour* 349.

statements'[68] (e.g. explanations of why particular steps are necessary, or why you need to know certain things) also emphasise that the relationship is an empathic one.

Of course, empathy plays a central part in the lawyer's advising and counselling functions too. An empathic approach is one which recognises that legal advice has to take account of the needs of the 'whole client'. Legal problems inevitably have an emotional impact on the client, and that does not just apply to the more obvious situations in family, personal injury or criminal practice. Commercial cases too involve interaction with people who may have a strong personal commitment or involvement in a matter, and this needs to be acknowledged.[69]

## Towards a (re)vision of the relationship

At a deeper level, we would argue that empathy is central to any process of redefinition. Empathy, at least as it is starting to emerge in the academic literature, involves a call for greater contextualisation of legal disputes and legal discourse – a greater willingness to hear and engage with client stories on the client's terms, rather than just the lawyer's. In critical legal discourse this is being seen as a necessary first step in the empowerment of the client.

This may sound fine within the rarefied atmosphere of academic law, but what about the realities? Sharing power between lawyers and clients is not simply a question of saying, 'Here you are, I value your involvement, you make the decision'. Clients can, and will, turn round and say, 'Hang on, that's what I'm paying you to do'. Lawyers need to consider how they might develop practices which recognise and value the experience both sides bring to a problem, and then enable clients to participate in ways that do not smack of tokenism. Ironically, perhaps, this is already commonplace (in a sense) within large-scale commercial and corporate practice, as one practitioner has commented:

> In company/commercial work the client is aware through their own experience and so the solicitor is helped by the client. Also the possible permutations of problems have been explored before.[70]

In this context there is commonly some empathy deriving from shared values and experience – lawyers and clients are quite likely to share the same sort of background, and speak the same sort of language. It is easiest to build an empathic understanding with those who are most like ourselves. Rather more cynically, one can point out that, here, the power relationship also tends to be reversed, with the client possessing the greater bargaining power and often at least equivalent social status to the lawyer.

---

68. Binder, Bergman and Price, *Legal Interviewing and Counseling*, pp. 107–10.
69. See by way of illustration the comments in Boon 'Assessing Competence to Conduct Civil Litigation' in Boon, Halpern and Mackie, *Skills for Legal Functions II: Representation and Advice*, p. 39.
70. Cited in Boon, *ibid.*, p. 28.

In 'high street' and legal aid practices the situation may be very different (though it is not inevitable). The lawyer–client relationship may be more hierarchical in social and educational terms. Opportunities for empowering and co-operative forms of practice may be more difficult to discover, perhaps not least because our empathic capacity is limited by our experience. As Massaro suggests:

> ... we can share in only some lives, and relate to only some voices. We are part of some communities, but not others. I may be bigger than my single physical self, but I am not the world ... This vanishing point – the limit of self and the exhaustion of connection – is often the beginning point for law.[71]

If we are to move towards a more participatory style of lawyering, it will require commitment to change. We need to develop our capacity for reflection about our role as lawyers and the way we intervene in client lives.

If we are to change or develop our practices, it is important that reflection is focused and critical. It is not sufficient to stop at the level of 'Why did I do that?' Irving and Williams talk of using a 'ladder of inference'[72] as a reflective tool which is capable of drawing out the differences between your espoused theory and your theory-in-use.[73] Ask yourself these questions: [74]

- What was I trying to achieve here?
- What was it about the expected outcome that I valued?
- What assumptions am I making here?
- What beliefs do these assumptions depend on?
- Did I put those beliefs into action?

The key issue is the way in which we prioritise and implement agendas – our own and our clients. Various academics and practitioners (chiefly in the US) have proposed a variety of more or less radical practices to empower clients in these situations. At the heart of many of these developments[75] is a commitment to honouring client narrative and experience and using it as part of a collective endeavour between lawyer and client. Such practices aim to 'help the client help himself'.[76] These ideas have been operationalised in forms of community action, in

---

71. 'Empathy, Legal Storytelling, and the Rule of Law: New Words, Old Wounds?' (1989) 87 *Michigan Law Review* 2099 at p. 2122.
72. 'Critical Thinking and Reflective Practice in Counselling' (1995) 23 *British Journal of Guidance and Counselling* 107 at p. 113.
73. If you cannot remember the difference, see Chapter 2 above.
74. Irving and Williams, (1995) 23 *British Journal of Guidance and Counselling* 107 at p. 113.
75. See, e.g., Alfieri, 'The Antinomies of Poverty Law and a Theory of Dialogic Empowerment' (1987–88) 16 *New York University Review of Law and Social Change* 659; C. D. Cunningham, 'A Tale of Two Clients: Thinking About Law as Language' (1989) 87 *Michigan Law Review* 2459; P. Gabel and P. Harris, 'Building Power and Breaking Images' (1982–83) 11 *New York University Review of Law and Social Change* 369. There is an extraordinary dissonance in some of this work between high theory and low practice, so that when it comes to thinking about using client narrative, the analyses lapse into pessimism or banality: see, e.g., the papers by Alfieri and Cunningham.
76. López, *Rebellious Lawyering*, p. 52.

local law centres and other activist work. This is not that novel, though it is now dressed up in the discourses of postmodernity. There has long been a tradition of pro-active and communal legal work outside of traditional private practice. As Stephens, for example, has pointed out in the English context, pro-active law centres place emphasis –

> ...on communal control and on the use of people-working strategies in order to encourage clients to play an active role in the processing of their claims and in the running of their organised groups...[77]

There are interesting and important ways in which we can link these notions to the debate over access to justice, and the lawyer's role in facilitating access. Marc Galanter has used the participatory approach as a starting point in developing access to justice strategies. He argues that access to justice may be improved by making changes at one of four levels in the legal system: he calls these levels *rules, courts, lawyers* and *parties*.[78] Galanter also suggests that the greatest scope for increasing access lies at the level of parties.

The lack of party capability is a key barrier to greater access. Most individual litigants are 'one-shotters',[79] isolated players engaged in one-off actions who lack the institutional and structural power/access of repeat players (such as the large corporations). Lawyers could increase access by 'upgrading'[80] the party capability of litigants who would otherwise be reduced to 'one-shot' status. These techniques particularly require the organisation of parties into common interest groups, which would then enhance their capacity to seek both legal and political redress of grievances. In this sense, the lawyer's role becomes far more catalytic, and involved with 'people-working' rather than just rule-using. Bringing litigants together, helping set up community-based groups and initiatives, educating as well as giving legal advice – this involves some significant re-defining of the lawyer–client relationship.

Putting it bluntly, however, these are developments that are currently quite marginal, and divorced from the traditional centres of legal practice and experience. The challenge over the next few years will be to see whether these new discursive practices can have something to say at the centre as well as at the margin of both academic work and practice.

EXERCISE 5.18 **Concepts**

1.   *Divide into pairs.*
2.   *Each pair is to:*

---

77. M. Stephens, *Community Law Centres: A Critical Appraisal*, Avebury Press, Aldershot, 1990, p. 26.
78. 'Why the Haves Come Out Ahead' (1974) 9 *Law and Society Review* 95.    79. *Ibid.*, p. 97.
80. M. Galanter, 'Delivering Legality, Some Proposals for the Direction of Research' (1976) 11 *Law and Society Review* 225 at pp. 230–1.

(a) *define each concept, noting the page(s) on which it is discussed, and undertaking any additional research that is necessary; then*

(b) *make sure that you both understand the meaning of each concept.*

3.  *Combine into groups of four. Compare the answers of the two pairs. If there is disagreement, look up the concept and clarify it. Make sure you are all agreed on the definition and understand it.*

| | |
|---|---|
| *active/passive listening* | *counselling* |
| *empathy* | *empowerment* |
| *hypothetical questions* | *keyword questions* |
| *mirroring* | *motivational statements* |
| *open/closed questions* | *participatory approach* |
| *probing questions* | *reflective questions* |
| *six category intervention analysis* | |

### EXERCISE 5.19  Blowing the whistle?[81]

You are a trainee solicitor. Your supervising principal, Monisha, interviewed a client a week ago who has contacted the firm by email and made another appointment. Monisha is going on holiday and has asked you to speak to the client and advise her.

*Initial interview – Monisha's notes*:

**Client name:**  Maria Bertorelli.

**Address:**      14 Cumberland Ave, Bristol BS6 9UJ

Client works for Magic Mouse Company in Bristol as a financial officer.
Co. produces computer hardware and software.
3 months ago Client discovered the co. was in breach of some health & safety rules.
Client told the co. health & safety officer, but nothing done.
Client then complained to management, got nowhere, so reported the co. to the Health and Safety Executive.
HSE visited the factory, imposed expensive measures to rectify the problems.
Lilian White, managing director, summoned Client, threatened dismissal for breach of duty of confidentiality under employment contract – to keep co. secrets/ not divulge any info. about co. activities.
LW didn't carry out her threat at that time, as co. was in the middle of obtaining a vital order, but relations not good since.
Client advised we need to see contract before we can advise properly – suggested she come back when she's thought about what she wants to do.
Now Ms Bertorelli has emailed to say she has found out that the company has been selling computers which have 'illegal screen flicker' rates to developing countries. There is medical evidence to suggest that these screens cause eye

---

81. Our thanks to our colleague James Holland for this exercise.

damage. Also, the company is secretly planning a takeover in which a number of employees will be made redundant, yet the managing director has gone on record as saying this is untrue and there aren't going to be any redundancies, now or in the near future. Apparently, the factory is going to be closed. She continues:

> I feel very strongly about these practices. I want some advice on what I can do and what might happen if I disclose them. I've thought about contacting the HSE again, or the DTI, or even Customs and Excise. Over the last few months I've been writing a series of articles for a widely-read magazine, the *Global Economist*, on industrial practices in the UK and their impact on developing country economies. My next article is due to be published in three months' time. I think the best publicity for all this would be to write about it in the magazine.
>
> I realise that I'll get the sack if I disclose these matters, but I don't mind too much; it's the principle that matters, and I can get another job quite easily. But just so I know: am I right in thinking I could get compensation for unfair dismissal?

She has attached a copy of her employment contract. Clause 10 states:

## Confidentiality

10.1    *The Employee shall not (other than in the proper performance of his duties or with the prior written consent of the Board or unless ordered by a court of competent jurisdiction) at any time either during the continuance of his employment or after its termination disclose or communicate to any person or use for his own benefit or the benefit of any person other than the Company any confidential information which may come to his knowledge in the course of his employment and the Employee shall use his best endeavours to prevent the unauthorised publication or misuse of any confidential information.*

10.2    *All notes and memoranda of any trade secret or confidential information concerning the business of the Company or any of its suppliers, agents, distributors, customers or others which shall have been acquired received or made by the Employee during the course of his employment shall be the property of the Company and shall be surrendered by the Employee to someone duly authorised in that behalf at the termination of his employment or at the request of the Board at any time during the course of his employment.*

10.3    *For the avoidance of doubt and without prejudice to the generality of Clause 10.1 the following is a non-exhaustive list of matters which in relation to the Company are considered confidential and must be treated as such by the Employee:-*

      10.3.1    *any secrets of the Company;*

      10.3.2    *any information in respect of which the Company is bound by an obligation of confidence to any third party;*

      10.3.3    *marketing strategies and plans;*

      10.3.4    *customer lists and details of contracts with or requirements of customers;*

      10.3.5    *pricing strategies;*

      10.3.6    *discount rates and sales figures;*

      10.3.7    *lists of suppliers and rates of charge;*

10.3.8  *information which has been supplied in confidence by clients, customers or suppliers;*

10.3.9  *information concerning any litigation proposed in progress or settled;*

10.3.10  *any invention technical data know-how or other manufacturing or trade secrets of the Company and its clients/customers;*

10.3.11  *any other information made available to the Employee which is identified to the Employee as being of a confidential nature.*

10.4  *The Employee shall not without the prior written consent of the Board either directly or indirectly publish any opinion fact or material or deliver any lecture or address or participate in the making of any film radio broadcast or television transmission or communicate with any representative of the media or any third party relating to the business or affairs of the Company or the Group or to any of its or their officers employees customers/clients suppliers distributors agents or shareholders or to the development of exploitation of Intellectual Property. For the purpose of this Clause "media" shall include television (terrestrial satellite and cable) radio newspapers and other journalistic publications.*

1.  In your firms:
    (a)  brainstorm the law (e.g. is this defamation, privacy, contract, employment law, none of these?)
    (b)  Carry out the legal research necessary to give advice to Ms Bertorelli.
2.  Taking it in turns, advise the client (your tutor or a fellow student will play the client). The other members of your firm will observe.
3.  Feed back to each other on the following:
    (a)  Did the interaction go according to plan? Yes/no; why/why not; how, etc.
    (b)  Was a positive relationship established and maintained?
    (c)  Who was in charge?
    (d)  Was the legal advice accurate? And clearly explained?
    (e)  Did you take a good set of notes? (You will need to keep these for a follow-up exercise later.)
    (f)  Is there anything you would do differently? If so, what, and how?

EXERCISE **5.20  Review questions**

1.  *In interviewing, experience means making the same mistakes with greater confidence. Do you agree?*
2.  *During an interview a client makes a racially derogatory comment about a third party involved in his case. How do you respond?*
3.  *How far can we, or should we, go in empowering our clients to make their own decisions?*

## Learning points

*Following the model used at the end of the second section of this chapter, produce a brief summary of the principles you have derived from:*

1. *the section headed Advising and counselling; and*
2. *the section headed Interviewing and empathic lawyering.*

## Further reading

D. Binder, P. Bergman and S. Price, *Legal Interviewing & Counselling: A Client-Centred Approach*, West Publ., St Paul, Minn., 1991.

J. Heron, 'A Six Category Intervention Analysis' (1976) 4 *British Journal of Guidance and Counselling* 143.

A. Sarat and W. Felstiner, 'Law and Social Relations: Vocabularies of Motive in Lawyer–Client Interaction' (1988) 22 *Law and Society Review* 737.

A. Sherr, *Client Care for Lawyers*, Sweet and Maxwell, London, 2nd edn, 1999.

H. Twist, *Effective Interviewing*, Blackstone Press, London, 1992.

# 6

# The 'good lawyer': ethics and values in legal work

In this chapter we move on to consider what we see as a critical context in which any consideration of lawyering skills should be set: professional ethics and personal values. We saw in Chapter 1 that the very idea of a profession conventionally carries with it a collective commitment to ethical standards. Being a 'good lawyer' is about more than just technical competence, it begs the question to what ends should our skills be used? And that is an ethical question. Here we explore how this issue is addressed (or not) in the professional codes of conduct, and look at the general standards they set. We also ask you to think about whether this kind of codified ethics is enough, or whether a 'genuinely' ethical standard of professionalism needs to be based on other internal or external criteria.

## Objectives

To:

- Enable you to recognise the value conflicts inherent in legal practice.
- Introduce you to the main ethical and conduct responsibilities identified by the professional codes of conduct.
- Enable you critically to evaluate the form, focus and content of professional conduct regulations.
- Provide you with a basis for evaluating your own sense of ethics.
- Encourage you to consider the relationship between ethics and the skills of legal problem-framing and problem-solving.

## Supports benchmark statements

Students should be able to demonstrate

1. Knowledge:
   - Knowledge of major concepts, values, principles and rules of [the English legal] system
   - Ability to explain the main legal institutions and procedures of that system

2. Application and problem-solving
   - a basic ability to apply knowledge to a situation of limited complexity in order to provide arguable conclusions for concrete problems
3. Analysis, etc:
   - a basic ability to make a critical judgment of the merits of particular arguments
   - a basic ability to present and make a reasoned choice between alternative solutions
4. Autonomy and ability to learn
   - a basic ability to be able to undertake independent research in areas of law which have not previously been studied starting from standard legal information sources
5. Communication and Literacy:
   - a basic ability to read and discuss legal materials which are written in technical and complex language

## Introduction

'Sure, the law is the third oldest profession all right, in close order after whoring and pimping.'[1]

It seems to be one of life's paradoxes that law defends its status as a profession on the back of its ethical commitments, and yet lawyers are routinely condemned as a bunch of shysters who would sell their grandmothers to the highest bidder. Of course, we – as lawyers – could just shrug this off as uninformed prejudice, and carry on with the auction but while there are some very positive things to be said about the profession's ethical commitments, as we saw in chapter 1, there are clearly enough genuine issues about the professional behaviour and standards of lawyers to give the profession and others cause for concern.[2] These concerns have led in numerous jurisdictions to both greater regulation of professional behaviour, and a stronger emphasis on training in ethics and conduct.

That said, legal education in the UK has been relatively slow to develop the ethical dimension of law and lawyering, but there are signs that this is changing.[3] The Law Society's recent Training Framework Review, in its second consultation paper identifies the 'values, behaviours, attitudes and ethical requirements of a

1. D. Melinkoff, *The Conscience of a Lawyer*, West Publ., St Paul, Minn., 1973, p. 1.
2. For some recent practitioner perspectives see N. Hanson, 'A Matter of Principle' *Law Society's Gazette*, 19 August 2004; available online at www.lawgazette.co.uk.
3. See A. Boon and J. Levin, *The Ethics and Conduct of Lawyers in England and Wales*, Hart Publishing, Oxford, 1999, pp. 142–72. 'Professional Responsibility' courses became compulsory on American Bar Association-approved law degrees in the US following the Watergate scandal in the 1970s. In Australia, professional conduct was introduced in the 1990s as part of the 'Priestly 11' – the subjects identified by the Law Admissions Consultative Committee (Priestly Committee) that students are required to complete before admission to the profession. In New Zealand, law graduates seeking entry to professional training since 2001 must have first completed an undergraduate course in lawyers' ethics. In the UK, professional conduct and ethics remains a required part of vocational (post-LLB) training only.

solicitor' as one of the core components of legal education and training.[4] This may seem less than revolutionary, but ethics has not always been a formal, explicit, part of the training. Traditionally, the ethics were something that you pretty much learned – or somehow acquired – 'on the job'. It was more a matter of socialisation than education. It is perhaps this attitude more than any other that is changing.

In 1996, the Lord Chancellor's Advisory Committee on Legal Education and Conduct (ACLEC) published its *First Report on Legal Education and Training*. After emphasising the current challenges faced by the legal professions (the sorts of issues we talked about in discussing the crisis of professionalism in Chapter 1), it had this to say:

> All of the developments we have discussed above place at risk the high ethical standards of the profession, which have very much been grounded in the close-knit professional communities represented by such institutions as the Inns of Court and local law societies. As the organisations in which law is practised become larger and more complex, as competition and instability in the market for legal services increases, and as many legal practitioners experience a growing sense of insecurity, there are real dangers that professional standards will be threatened unless counter-balancing steps are taken to reinforce ethical values ... [N]o amount of external regulation of professional practice will serve as an adequate substitute for the personal and professional values and standards that lawyers should internalise from the earliest stages of their education and training. Teaching in ethical values should include more than a familiarisation with professional codes of conduct and the machinery for enforcing them ... Students must be made aware of the values that legal solutions carry, and of the ethical and humanitarian dimensions of law as an instrument which affects the quality of life.[5]

This is heady, and some would say, controversial stuff.[6] Consider:

● Are the ethical standards of lawyers something we are right to be concerned about?
● Should all law students learn something about the ethics of the profession as part of a law degree or equivalent course?
● Can teaching professional ethics, either on the LLB or in vocational training, make a difference to the ethical standards of lawyers once they get into practice?

We don't really want to discuss the possible answers to those questions right now, but make a note of what you think, and keep your answers in mind as you work through this chapter. We will come back to these questions at the end.

---

4. The Law Society, Second consultation on a new training framework for solicitors, para. 47, available at www.lawsociety.org.uk/dcs/pdf/2ndConsultationNewTraining2.pdf (last accessed 20.12.03).
5. ACLEC *First Report on Legal Education and Training*, ACLEC, London 1996, para. 1.19. (Note that ACLEC was abolished by the Access to Justice Act 1999 and replaced by the Legal Services Consultative Committee, an advisory body with less extensive powers.)
6. For academic discussion of the ethical components of the ACLEC Report, see R. O'Dair, 'Recent Developments in the Teaching of Legal Ethics – A UK Perspective' in K. Economides (ed.), *Ethical Challenges to Legal Education and Conduct*, Hart Publishing, Oxford, 1998; J. Webb, 'Ethics for Lawyers or Ethics for Citizens? New Directions for Legal Education' (1998) 25 *Journal of Law and Society* 134; and A. Boon, 'Ethics in Legal Education and Training: Four Reports, Three Jurisdictions and a Prospectus' [2002] *Legal Ethics* 34.

Given the conceptual framework we have adopted for this book we would argue that the ethical dimension of lawyers' skills should not be ignored. Schön's work itself emphasises the inevitability of what he called 'value conflicts' in professional work. Schön's choice of language here, we think, is interesting. He did not talk about ethics (or even, in ACLEC's phrase 'ethical values') but *values*. This is significant because ethics and values are not the same thing, though they do overlap. Without getting too technical about this, while we use the term 'ethics' to describe the moral standards by which we live our lives, values are much broader. They incorporate aspirations and standards that are both moral and non-moral.[7] Thus, some of our values are clearly ethical (or at least motivate action that we define as ethical), others reflect basic survival needs, others still reflect our aesthetic ideals, and so on. So, why is this important in the context of lawyering? Consider the following exercise:

### EXERCISE 6.1 Tinker, tailor ...[8]

The aim of this exercise is to help you identify the values (and remember – we are using values widely to include non-moral values) that are important to you, now, in deciding the career you would like to pursue.

1.  What is important to you in selecting a career? Write down as many things as you can think of. Focus particularly on the things that you think motivate you about a job.
2.  Look at your list. If all of these features were present in your (ideal) job, is there anything that could happen which would be guaranteed to make you leave? If so, add this thing to your list.
3.  Now, looking at your list, identify the *eight* most important factors, i.e. those that are of the greatest value to you. Number them from 1 (highest) through to 8 (lowest).
4.  Imagine you had the choice of two jobs: (a) has values 5–8; (b) has values 1–4. Which would you choose? If the answer is (a), you will need to revise your hierarchy of values until you are satisfied that you would choose job (b).
5.  What, if anything, have you discovered about your values from doing this exercise?

There are three crucial points that should come out of doing this exercise. The first is the most obvious one – that values are a big part of what motivates us.[9] They influence our attitudes and behaviours in all parts of our lives, including the job we do. This leads to a second, also somewhat obvious point, that choosing a career is itself a value-laden decision. Indeed, we would go further and say that choosing a career is one of the most important values-based (perhaps even ethical) decisions

---

7. We use the phrase 'non moral' deliberately. Non-moral is not the same as immoral or even amoral. While the term immoral obviously suggests something that is morally wrong, and amoral indicates a decision or course of action that is unconcerned with right or wrong, or action that is taken without any moral feeling, non-moral indicates values, decisions or actions which genuinely have no moral content or consequences.
8. Tutors should note that there is additional guidance on running this exercise on our website.
9. See generally M. Rokeach, *Understanding Human Values*, Free Press, New York, 1979.

we make in our lives – particularly where, as with law, choosing that career involves some commitment to a set of professional ethics. Thirdly, this exercise also draws our attention to the fact that many of the decisions we make involve choosing between our own competing values. Often we don't think of our decisions in those terms, which is why we sometimes end up with all sorts of niggling doubts or complaints after the event: it turns out that the decision we made was not a good one because it was actually inconsistent with the things we really value in a job, or relationship, etc. Identifying the values that we hold about a particular area of our lives, and assessing which of our values are most important to us (our *value priorities*) is a powerful way of ensuring that our behaviour is *congruent* (a psychological term, meaning in line with) our attitudes and values.

We now want to take this a stage further, and suggest that the idea of value priorities is useful for two particular reasons relevant to this chapter. First, it warns us that looking at a value or even a set of values in isolation is not very useful. Most real dilemmas about ethics and values are contextual and concerned with resolving specific value conflicts. Thus, Jack and Jill may both rate honesty and collegiality as important personal values, but if, in a given situation, Jill places greater store on honesty than collegiality, and Jack favours collegiality over honesty, then it is quite possible that they will come to opposing decisions on whether to blow the whistle on a work colleague who has behaved dishonestly towards their employer. Secondly, what we often have to address is not just a purely 'internal' conflict (assessing what our operative values are in this situation; deciding if they conflict, and, if so, which should have priority) but, a potential conflict between our personal values and some external standard, e.g., set down by the law, workplace rules, or a code of professional conduct. For example, Jack and Jill not only have to assess how to behave in the light of their own personal value priorities. They may also have to consider how their sense of honesty and collegiality, and other values (e.g. self-preservation) are impacted by a rule requiring employees to report misuse of company property to senior management. The problem, of course, is that in many instances, the mere existence of a prohibition is far from determinative, and such an external rule cannot, without more, guarantee an 'ethical' override of competing, personal, values.

Values have an obvious relevance to what lawyers do. Our clients' objectives will often reflect their values. Our own values will shape not only the work we choose to do, but, to some extent, how we do it. The organisation we work for will have its own (usually implicit) values.[10] Sometimes this too can lead to another kind of values-conflict, between organisational values and personal values. This may be obvious where there is a strong organisational culture, for example in bodies such as the police force, but other organisations – including law firms – will have their own,

---

10. However, note that one large law firm has recently taken the step of creating an express statement of six 'behavioural' values that are intended to shape its internal and external relationships: *The Lawyer*, 27 October 2003, p. 1; see also J. Webb, 'Managing by Values', *New Law Journal*, 13 February 2004, pp. 214–15.

Figure 6.1. 'Problem-solving is a multi-dimensional task.'

perhaps more subtle, culture, which will be a source of both acculturation (a process whereby you come to adopt the dominant values of the organisation) and conflict.[11]

Legal problem-solving is thus a multi-dimensional task. It requires us to use our skills and knowledge to resolve a range of technical and value uncertainties, in a way that is responsive to the factual, legal, ethical and other dimensions of that specific problem. You can expect to be confronted by clients – and colleagues – with objectives that may challenge your professional duties, or your personal values, or both. As we have already seen in exploring the scenarios that made up Exercise 1.6, you will certainly have cases where you will have to assess whether the problem creates an ethical dilemma for you or your firm. You may even face situations where you will have to deal with a direct conflict between your personal values and/or your professional duties and your loyalty to your firm or chambers.

Given this context, if we simply treat what lawyers do as a matter of technical competence, or 'skill', we risk losing sight of the bigger questions: for what purposes *should* lawyers use their skills, and are there things that even a lawyer *should not* do?[12]

11. Consider also your reflections on Exercise 4.12, above.
12. Richard O'Dair makes the point thus: 'The problem [with skills-based learning] as Aristotle recognised is that one may be so well-trained in bad habits as to become incapable of knowing better. If, as many think, the current mores of the legal profession leave much to be desired, this is profoundly worrying ... ' *Legal Ethics: Text & Materials*, Butterworths, London, 2001, p. 118.

In short, we start from the premise that, like it or not, as lawyers, whatever we might pretend about the non-moral nature of legal work, we are fundamentally concerned with broad moral issues of right and wrong: we are making moral choices all the time. This is not necessarily something to be afraid of. As Nathanson observes:

> To thoughtful lawyers, this can add layers of meaning and greater depth to profes-
> sional life, providing them with unexpected avenues of insight into themselves as well
> as into life's larger questions.[13]

In this chapter, we begin to address these issues. We will look, first, at the way lawyers' ethics attempts to deal with potential value conflicts, by constructing conduct rules, which prescribe the professional duties that govern lawyers' relations with their clients, other lawyers and third parties. Our intention, of course, is to get you thinking about these responsibilities experientially, so it is important to work through the exercises, which illustrate the kinds of value conflicts that can arise in legal work. We will encourage you to use this experience to think critically about the way the legal profession has dealt with ethics and values, and to consider some alternative approaches.

Let's conclude this bit of the process with a final exercise that puts a more practical slant on the values discussion we have just had – this time focusing primarily on our moral values.

EXERCISE **6.2 Does it matter?**

You should do the following exercise individually, in the first instance. There is undoubted value in then discussing the results with others *but*, because of the sensitive nature of some of the issues this exercise raises, you must be clear that you have a 'safe space' for discussion. The minimum ground rules for creating such a safe space are:

(a)    Each participant agrees to behave towards the others from a position of respect and high personal integrity and honesty.

(b)    The discussion is absolutely confidential and will not be repeated to anyone outside of the group.

(c)    The discussion is intended to encourage learning and reflection. You undertake that you will not voice opinions that are judgmental of others in the group.

(d)    Any member of the group may call a 'time out' or interrupt another member of the group if and only if they feel these ground rules are being, or are about to be, broken.

---

13. S. Nathanson, *What Lawyers Do*, Sweet & Maxwell, London, 1997, p. 137. For other discussions of the importance of lawyering as 'meaningful work' see, e.g., W. Simon, *The Practice of Justice: A Theory of Lawyers' Ethics*, Harvard University Press, Cambridge, Mass., 1998, p. 112; J. Webb, 'Being a Lawyer/Being a Human Being' [2002] *Legal Ethics* 130 at pp. 145–6.

If you cannot agree to any of these ground rules for yourself, or genuinely doubt the intention of any other member of the group to adhere to them, you probably should not discuss the outcomes of parts 1 and 2 of this exercise.

1.  Look at the following list of value statements. Don't spend too long on each item: trust your instinctive response and be honest with yourself!

    (a) Using the 1–5 scale, rate the importance of each statement to you *as a personal value*.

    (b) Now repeat this exercise, rating the importance of each statement to *the role of a lawyer*.

    (c) Compare your answers to (a) and (b). What do you find?

2.  Now, having got you thinking about your values in the abstract, let's look at some study-related activities.

| | Not at all important | | | | Very important |
|---|---|---|---|---|---|
| You should tell the truth | 1 | 2 | 3 | 4 | 5 |
| You should respect the rights of others | 1 | 2 | 3 | 4 | 5 |
| You should put the interests of family and friends before others | 1 | 2 | 3 | 4 | 5 |
| You should obey the law | 1 | 2 | 3 | 4 | 5 |
| You should be open to other views | 1 | 2 | 3 | 4 | 5 |
| You should do what you think is right | 1 | 2 | 3 | 4 | 5 |
| You should behave fairly towards everyone | 1 | 2 | 3 | 4 | 5 |
| You should put your own interests first | 1 | 2 | 3 | 4 | 5 |
| You should do what your friends or colleagues think is right | 1 | 2 | 3 | 4 | 5 |

    (a) Read the following list of activities and rate their acceptability *on the basis of your personal values only*. Note: where a statement refers to an 'assignment' assume that this means a piece of assessed coursework that counts towards your degree.

    (b) Look at those items that you have rated '1' to '3' on the scale. For each of those items, make a note of your reason(s) for giving it that rating. Are you 'comfortable' with those reasons? If not, why not? Are those reasons consistent with the value ratings you gave yourself in part 1(a)?

3.  Now, this final part of the exercise should in any event be conducted as a group discussion:

    In England and Wales, to become a member of the Law Society or one of the Inns of Court, you need to be certified a 'fit and proper person' to practise. In your view, should a person who has been found guilty of a serious assessment offence at university (cheating or deliberate plagiarism) be certified as a fit and proper person? Justify your conclusion.

|  | Totally acceptable | | | | Not at all acceptable |
| --- | --- | --- | --- | --- | --- |
| Letting a friend copy your assignment | 1 | 2 | 3 | 4 | 5 |
| Helping your girlfriend/boyfriend/ partner write their assignment | 1 | 2 | 3 | 4 | 5 |
| Copying a friend's assignment with their knowledge | 1 | 2 | 3 | 4 | 5 |
| Copying a friend's assignment without their knowledge | 1 | 2 | 3 | 4 | 5 |
| Lending your notes to a friend who missed the lecture | 1 | 2 | 3 | 4 | 5 |
| Moving a reference book you need to the wrong location in the university library | 1 | 2 | 3 | 4 | 5 |
| Tearing the pages you need out of a library textbook | 1 | 2 | 3 | 4 | 5 |
| Keeping a scarce library book your class needs for an assignment beyond its return date | 1 | 2 | 3 | 4 | 5 |
| Buying an answer to your assignment off of the internet | 1 | 2 | 3 | 4 | 5 |
| Plagiarising your assignment from a range of sources | 1 | 2 | 3 | 4 | 5 |

Tempting though it is, we don't want to propose a single set of 'right answers' to this exercise, but we will offer some pointers and further questions.

The point to part 1, of course, is to identify any differences that emerge between the personal and professional. To what extent do we think there are role-specific or role differentiated values? How do we feel about that? Part 2 forces us to focus our thinking about values onto an area that affects us (directly or indirectly) here and now. Most, but not all, of these activities break university rules. Some break the law: tearing pages out of books is clearly criminal damage; and while plagiarism is not a crime (though many would say it is 'theft' of someone else's ideas), it is inconsistent with both the moral and the property rights of the original author. How much does congruence between our values and behaviour matter to us? If we are OK about breaking some rules (perhaps because they are not 'laws' as such), how do we define the boundaries for ourselves, and others? How do we feel about the decisions we make, particularly if those situations involve some conflict with our espoused values? For example, if we say fairness is an important value, how do we justify hiding or holding onto books that our peers need as much as us?

We might argue that the issues in 2 and 3 don't really matter because we wouldn't behave like that outside of university, as if university was somehow not part of the 'real world'. Is that true, or is this just an example of what Argyris and Schön call 'distancing'? Are our values really so malleable that the situation can make a big difference to how we behave? Or are we fooling ourselves? When we get into the work environment is it a sufficient defence to say, 'I wouldn't have done X in my private life, but here it seemed OK'? You will almost certainly confront that sooner or later in your careers.

To return to our starting point, does education matter? Interestingly, a number of studies of health care professions indicate that students who are academically dishonest or act unethically in the classroom are more likely to behave unprofessionally in clinical settings.[14] This has been used to argue that curriculum changes should be introduced into health care education to promote professional behaviour and self-directed learning. It sounds familiar, doesn't it? And what about regulation? Can and should we use professional and other rules to promote 'good' values? Can we go further and rely on rules to make people 'good'? That is an underlying question we will address in the remainder of this chapter. But first we need to say a bit about the professional rules themselves.

## The regulation of professional conduct and ethics

In England and Wales both the Law Society and Bar Council, as the governing bodies of the legal professions, have promulgated rules of ethics and conduct. The Law Society's rules are compiled in the *Law Society's Guide to the Professional Conduct of Solicitors*. The last paper edition of the *Guide* (which we will refer to here as the LSG) was published by the Law Society in 1999, and is now updated online.[15] The paper version extended to some 800 pages of rules and guidance. In 2001 the Law Society set up a Regulation Review Working Party, with a remit to de-regulate and simplify the rules, so far as possible. At the time of writing, the proposed new code is undergoing a final consultation with the profession.[16]

The Bar has its own published *Code of Conduct* (the CCB). The current version of this is the seventh edition, which came into force in July 2000. It is also regularly revised and updated online.[17] It is a much slimmer document than the LSG, partly because there is not the same range of activities to be regulated by the CCB, given the more restricted kinds of work undertaken by the Bar, and partly because the approach of the CCB to regulation is more open-ended. Duties in the CCB are, for

14. L. Daniel, B. Adams and N. Smith, 'Academic Misconduct Among Nursing Students: A Multivariate Investigation' (1994) 10 *Journal of Professional Nursing* 278; G. Hilbert, 'Involvement of Nursing Students in Unethical Classroom and Clinical Behaviors' (1985) 1 *Journal of Professional Nursing* 230; M. Rhoton, 'Professionalism and Clinical Excellence among Anesthesiology Residents' (1994) 69 *Academic Medicine* 313.
15. At www.guide-on-line.lawsociety.org.uk.
16. For brief discussions of the Review, see J. Levin, 'Work in Progress – The Law Society Regulation Review Working Party' [2000] *Legal Ethics* 122–28; E. Nally, 'Simplifying the Rules' [2001] *Legal Ethics* 8–10.
17. www.barcouncil.org.uk.

the most part, defined more generally and there is not as extensive a body of notes and guidance appended to the rules, though the Bar does publish its own supplementary Written Standards for the Conduct of Professional Work and other occasional guidance.[18]

Clearly, in the context of any clinical work you might undertake (whether for live clients or simulation), these codes provide the minimum standards of conduct you should adhere to. Before looking at the codes in any greater detail, however, there are a few more general points we need to make about the regulatory and disciplinary frameworks affecting lawyers.

## The nature of professional regulation

Professional regulation is no longer a matter solely for the legal profession. While, traditionally, the legal professions have been regarded as *self-regulating*, this has increasingly become an over-simplification of the true position. Many other bodies have some degree of regulatory authority over lawyers, or at least over the legal professional bodies.[19] Consequently, much of the apparent self-regulation we see is not ('pure') *voluntary* self-regulation, rather, it is self-regulation in a *mandated* form,[20] that is, it is self-regulation that operates within a broad framework that is sanctioned or defined by government, or in which rules require some element of government approval before they come into force.

Thus, although the Law Society and Bar still have considerable autonomy in respect of lawyer discipline, they no longer have a free hand in determining the regulatory framework. The Office of Fair Trading in particular has considerable power to put pressure on the professional bodies to change or remove regulations that are deemed anti-competitive. And, more specifically, the Legal Services Commission does much to set day-to-day standards for publicly funded legal work. Further external regulation seems likely following the Clementi review of the regulation of legal services, which is due to issue its final report in December 2004.[21] Following its initial consultation, the legal professional bodies themselves, and most other published responses favour some degree of greater independent regulation – most likely in the form of a super-regulator overseeing the regulatory functions of not just solicitors and barristers, but other major providers of legal services.

18. These guidance notes are also published on the Bar's website.
19. R. Baldwin, *Regulating Legal Services*, LCD Research Series no. 5/97, Lord Chancellor's Department, London, 1997.
20. J. Black, 'Constitutionalising Self-Regulation' (1996) 59 *Modern Law Review* 24 at pp. 27–8; also J. Webb & D. Nicolson, 'Institutionalising Trust: Ethics and the Responsive Regulation of the Legal Profession' [1999] *Legal Ethics* 148 at p. 154.
21. See www.dca.gov.uk/majrep/lsr (last accessed 25.11.03). The review has generated a massive literature in the 'trade' press: see e.g. 'Clementi outlines sweeping review', *Solicitors' Journal*, 24 October 2003; 'Clementi kicks off regulatory overhaul', *Law Society Gazette*, 12 March 2004; 'LDPs get thumbs up as Clementi responses flood in', *Solicitors' Journal*, 11 June 2004; N. Rose, 'Split Personality', *Law Society's Gazette*, 15 July 2004.

## The codes of conduct

If we move on to consider the codes of conduct themselves, there are three general observations to be made about these documents.

**Ethical rules versus 'mere regulation'**

First, they involve really what are two sets of rules[22] (though the difference is not always clear from the way they are organised in the codes). The first comprises of those rules that are matters of 'mere regulation' and etiquette – for example rules which specify what can or cannot be displayed on a firm's letterhead, or rules regulating the pupillage system, or barristers' dress in court. These are not the concern of this chapter. The second kind of rules *are* concerned with what we might properly call professional ethics. They can be said to comprise three sets of duties:

- duties that a lawyer owes to the client;
- duties to the court; and
- duties to specific others or to the general public.

We will look at these duties, and the relationship between them in general terms in this chapter, though, as you have already seen from Chapter 5, we also identify ethical issues in context when we are discussing specific skills and areas of work.

**The flexibility of (some) ethical rules**

Secondly, the codes by and large do not set clear or absolute standards of behaviour. In part this reflects the nature of the issues themselves. This is not just because, as we are all well aware, any rules are open to a certain amount of interpretation. Rather, as most ethicists would accept, ethical standards, by definition, often have to be more flexible and open-textured than many other kinds of rules. It is often difficult to be categorical where ethics are concerned, because a lot of ethical dilemmas are inherently amenable to a range of reasonable alternatives rather than clear right/wrong solutions. This tendency is possibly exacerbated in the case of the lawyers' codes because they have evolved in a fairly piecemeal fashion. Many of the current rules are the result of a complex set of influences. They do not necessarily reflect clear, coherent, ethical imperatives, but are a response to political or economic pressures for change, often imposed from outside the profession, or reflect a political compromise between conflicting interests within the profession.[23] As one commentator noted, the codes represent 'a ragbag of things that have been

---

22. This distinction is developed more fully in D. Nicolson and J. Webb, *Professional Legal Ethics: Critical Interrogations*, Oxford University Press, Oxford, 1999, pp 100–1

23. See L. Sheinman, 'Looking for Legal Ethics' (1997) 4 *International Journal of the Legal Profession* 139, and 'Ethical Practice or Practical Ethics? The Case of the Vendor-Purchaser Rule' [2000] *Legal Ethics* 27.

important at some time or another'.[24] And this is where a 'regulatory' ethics or code of conduct can run into difficulties. Once we make certain 'unethical' actions subject to sanction, we have to be – or at least ought to be – specific about what improper or unlawful conduct will trigger that sanction. It cannot really be fair to sanction someone's conduct for falling below a standard that is not definable with at least some degree of certainty (note the number of qualifiers we have felt obliged to put into even this sentence!).

### The relationship with the common law

Thirdly, be aware that the codes are not entire and complete statements of what the Americans call the 'law of lawyering'. Many conduct principles are founded on Common Law principles of substantive or procedural law. Thus the law on professional negligence influences standards of professional diligence; fiduciary laws influence the rules on conflict of interests, and the laws on breach of confidence and legal professional privilege inform the standards of lawyer-client confidentiality. However, the Common Law standards and the professional standards are not always the same. The codes of conduct may set a standard that is higher or wider than the legal standard, or they will regulate only some of the issues that are potentially caught by the Common Law, leaving the legal standard as the norm for those matters not regulated by the codes. The bottom line, therefore, is that working out what one's duties are in any given situation can itself be a difficult task.

## Disciplining lawyers

Lastly, be aware, of course, that breach of the codes of conduct has disciplinary implications. Again, the rules are, and the range of institutions involved is, complex and liable to change in the light of the Clementi Review, and so we will not discuss them at any length here.[25] You should, however, be aware that both the professional bodies, and to a much lesser extent the courts have disciplinary or quasi-disciplinary functions.

### The disciplinary role of the legal professions

At present the disciplinary powers of the profession are shaped around two concepts:

- 'inadequate professional services' (IPS); and
- 'professional misconduct'.

The notion of inadequate professional services is not that clearly defined with regard to either profession. Section 37A of the Solicitors Act 1974 thus defines IPS simply as 'services which are not of the quality which it is reasonable to expect of '

---

24. Law Society interviewee, cited by J. Allaker and J. Shapland, *Organising UK Professions: Continuity and Change*, Research Study 16, The Law Society, London, 1994, p. 32.
25. For an overview (albeit now somewhat dated), see Seneviratne, ch. 4.

a solicitor; the CCB similarly describes it as 'such conduct towards a lay client or performance of professional services for that client which falls significantly short of that which is to be reasonably expected of a barrister in all the circumstances' (para. 1001). The breadth of these definitions is such that any breach of the codes of conduct is *prima facie* capable of being treated as IPS.

Nevertheless, complaints of IPS are treated as more minor than professional misconduct and will, if proven, lead to a range of lesser penalties, such as written admonishments and compensation orders. Moreover, in *R v Law Society, ex parte Singh and Choudry (a firm)*,[26] it was established that the client need not have suffered ascertainable loss or damage for the OSS or disciplinary tribunal to make a finding of IPS. IPS is dealt with in-house by the Law Society's Consumer Complaints Service, or in the case of the Bar by a variety of Bar Council panels and procedures. Professional misconduct will involve the more serious disciplinary offences, such as major failings of diligence, or breaches of the accounts rules, for which a lawyer may be suspended or barred from practice. Misconduct allegations are dealt with by the professional disciplinary tribunals.

### Conducting litigation – the role of the court

All lawyers are at least *de facto* officers of the court, and are under a variety of duties – which may apply in different degrees to the preparation of litigation as well as conduct at trial – because of that status. Many of these duties are legal rather than ethical: they are created by the courts under their inherent jurisdiction. We must stress that this is much more a reflection of the court's wide jurisdiction to supervise the conduct of litigation, than a matter of disciplining lawyers, *per se*.[27] Nevertheless, some of these duties exist also under the professional codes of conduct. Breaches of legal and ethical duties will have different consequences. Where a lawyer fails to exercise his *legal* duty to the court, the court can, and normally will, deal with that breach when it arises by virtue of its own summary procedure.[28] Breaches of the *codes* will, of course, be dealt with by the appropriate professional bodies.

At least as regards advocacy work and the conduct of litigation, the distinction between legal and ethical duties has been narrowed, both by what appears to be a growing judicial willingness to align the legal duty to the professional conduct

---

26. *The Times*, 1 April 1994.
27. *Skjevesland v Geveran Trading Co Ltd* [2002] EWCA Civ 1567, [2003] 1 WLR 912 illustrates the general judicial approach whereby complaints about a lawyer's conduct must be based on more than an alleged breach of the relevant code; there must be something about the conduct that brings it within the scope of one or other of the court's inherent jurisdictions. As Arden LJ observed, 'the content and enforcement of [the] Code [of Conduct] are not a matter for the court' [42, 49]. See similarly the observations of Staughton LJ in *Re a firm of solicitors* [1992] 1 All ER 364. Though note that there are, since 1999, statutory duties upon advocates and those authorised to conduct litigation to observe their professional rules of conduct (see ss. 27(2A)(b) and 28(2A)(b) of the Courts and Legal Services Act 1990), which could be enforceable by the courts. We return to this point briefly when we consider the advocate's duty to the court.
28. See *Myers v Elman* [1940] AC 282.

standard,[29] and by virtue of the fact that all professionals authorised to conduct litigation are now under overriding *statutory* duties to comply with their professional codes and standards for such work.[30]

The most common disciplinary power exercised by the court is probably under its 'wasted costs' jurisdiction. A wasted costs order is an award of costs against a lawyer in person, where that lawyer has displayed serious impropriety, default or negligence in bringing or arguing a case. It is used by the courts to provide judicial control over 'frivolous' or badly managed litigation.[31] That said, the courts have acknowledged that the introduction of the wasted costs jurisdiction is a significant inroad into the constitutional structure of the judicial system, and a threat to the independence of counsel. Their tendency is to construe the jurisdiction so far as possible so as not to impinge upon the advocate's constitutional position and her duty to the client.[32] You should also be aware that a court can fine or even imprison a lawyer for contempt of court in appropriate circumstances, though this is a fairly extreme and unusual sanction.

## Exploring professional conduct and ethics

As noted already, we will explore the core ethical issues in relation to three sets of duties: to the client, to the court and to others. However, we will not address them separately in quite this way, because many of the problems of ethics arise out of the interplay between these duties. So, we will be asking you to develop your understanding of professional ethics and conduct in a problem-based fashion, by working through a case study and one or two supplementary exercises. In working through these materials please be aware that, given the limited space we have for this topic, we will identify only certain key ethical obligations, not the whole range of conduct duties specified by the codes, but it will be enough to give you a sense of how the codes work, the problems that exist with a codified ethics, and a look at some of the 'big' ethical issues that arise in legal practice.

### Using the ethics case study

The following case study is in four parts and will form the main vehicle for our discussion of lawyers' ethics and conduct. It raises a number of common conduct

---

29. Thus, in *Medcalf v Weatherill* [2002] UKHL 27, Lord Rodger observed how the rules of conduct governing allegations of fraud had changed and how, accordingly, the (Common Law) duty of counsel had altered along with it [78]; see also per Lord Bingham at [21]–[22].

30. Sections 27(2A)(b) and 28(2A)(b) Courts and Legal Services Act 1990. Curiously, their Lordships made no reference to the statutory duty in deciding *Medcalf*.

31. The jurisdiction is of long standing but was extended by ss. 4, 111 and 112 of the Courts and Legal Services Act 1990. On the scope of the courts' powers, see particularly *Ridehalgh v Horsefield* [1994] Ch 205; *Medcalf v Weatherill* [2002] UKHL 27, [2002] 3 WLR 172.

32. See *Medcalf v Weatherill* [2002] UKHL 27; see also CCB 303(a); Law Society Advocacy Code, para. 6.1.

issues *and* some potential role- and value-conflicts.[33] You should aim to use the case study first as a research exercise, identifying the conduct problems that arise, and the rules that apply; use the *Law Society's Guide* for this: it is important that you get a feel for how it works and the level of advice it gives. If you want to follow this up with a textbook resource, your best bet is Boon and Levin, cited in the footnotes and 'Further Reading' at the end of this chapter, as this provides both a good level of detail and critical analysis. However, be aware that there have been a number of amendments to the codes since Boon and Levin was published in 1999. Once you have identified the basic duties, consider whether the scenario also takes you beyond the code, by raising some more fundamental ethical or value dilemmas that the codes do not really help us to resolve.

You will see also that quite often we don't actually spell out the answer in our discussion of the issues. This is deliberate, and for two good reasons. First, we don't want to tempt you into just reading through the following pages and finding our answers to the problems without doing any of the work. Secondly, often the 'answers' are not 'cut and dried' anyway, and there is some legitimate scope for disagreement – and it is often at this point that our different personal ethics and values can come into play. Again, it is valuable for you to engage with these issues for yourselves, rather than just observe us doing the work for you.

So, we begin with your introduction to Jason and his problems.

## Trouble on the High Street – Part 1

### EXERCISE 6.3 **Jason arrives**

You completed your training contract three months ago with Smith & Partners, a reputable large 'high street' firm of solicitors and are delighted to have been kept on as a newly admitted fee-earner specialising in commercial property work, including litigation. Your firm have acted for some years for a wealthy family comprising a mother, two sons and a daughter. One of the sons, Jason, has a reputation around the firm for being a difficult and demanding client.

Jason owns a small block of property on the south side of town, which he lets out on short leases. He has recently brought an action to recover rent owing under one such lease. As the most junior solicitor in the firm, the case has been passed on to you. Jason is busy proving his reputation by phoning you most days to check on the progress of his case. At present you are waiting for the other side to file certain documents in support of their defence. The procedural rules in force require submission within fourteen days; that period is about to expire but the court will generally allow a defendant extra time in such cases, provided the claimant does not object. You have always done the courteous thing in the past and allowed the

---

33. The scenario draws in large part on research by Debra Lamb and the set of ethical dilemmas she constructed out of interviews with practitioners: see D. Lamb, 'Ethical Dilemmas: What Australian Lawyers Say About Them' in S. Parker and C. Sampford (eds.), *Legal Ethics and Legal Practice: Contemporary Issues*, Clarendon Press, Oxford, 1995.

defendant's solicitors the extra time, on the basis that you may need the favour returned one day. This morning Jason phoned you to enquire how long the defendant has to put in his defence. You tell him 28 days, as you hope that will give you some peace and quiet, as you have also (rightly) told Jason that nothing else can happen in the case until the period for filing a defence has lapsed. Your strategy works, the defence is filed a week late, the case proceeds, and Jason, none the wiser, wins.

(a)    Working individually, consider:
  (i)   According to the LSG, what is your primary duty to your client?
  (ii)  What duty, if any, do you owe to the other lawyer and his/her client?
  (iii) What professional duties, if any, have you breached here?
  (iv)  Are there any broader ethical issues arising out of these events?

(b)    Discuss your conclusions in your groups, paying particular attention to any differences of opinion that arise. Consider whether each of those differences reflects different readings of the code, or different ethical or value priorities.

### Duties to the client and to other solicitors

It is a clearly established principle of professional ethics that the lawyer's primary duty, within the bounds set by the law and rules of professional conduct, is to her client. That duty is subject only to certain overriding duties to the court.

The lawyer's duties to the client are often summarised by three words: loyalty, confidentiality, and diligence. It is often said that a lawyer's primary duty is one of loyalty to the client. In the English ethics' codes, loyalty is expressed by the duty to act in your client's 'best interests' (see LSG 1.01(c)).[34] In practice 'breaches' of loyalty are likely to be dealt with as something more specific – a failure of diligence or competence, for example. Loyalty and diligence obviously go together. The lawyer–client relationship is often termed a 'fiduciary' one (i.e. based on an obligation of fidelity to the client) in which the client is obviously entitled to diligent and competent representation. The lawyer is, by definition, 'a professional who places skills and knowledge at the disposal of the client'.[35] Failures of care and skill under the codes encompass not just negligence, but any conduct which falls below the standards of competence set by the codes and professional written standards.[36]

One other point: 'best interests' is of course a flexible term, and it is your responsibility ultimately to assess what you think is in your client's best interests. The test can thus be somewhat paternalistic: you determine what is in your client's

---

34. The CCB (para 303(a)) puts it in even stronger terms: 'A practising barrister ... must promote and protect fearlessly and by all proper and lawful means his lay client's best interests.' Why do you think the CCB does that?

35. R. Cranston, 'Legal Ethics and Professional Responsibility' in R. Cranston (ed.) *Legal Ethics and Professional Responsibility*, Clarendon Press, Oxford, 1995, p. 12.

36. Insufficiently diligent and timely representation will often constitute IPS, but if it amounts to gross incompetence, it may constitute professional misconduct (see *Myers v Elman* [1940] AC 282), and possibly actionable professional negligence.

interests – though there are increasing expectations built into the conduct rules (and the Common Law) that significant decisions are made at least in consultation with the client,[37] and preferably on the client's express instructions.

In Jason's case, is there a failure of loyalty or diligence as such? Diligence really boils down to three main duties under the codes:

- The general duty to act with care and skill, proper diligence and promptness (LSG 12.03, 12.08; CCB 701(a)).[38]
- The obligation to refuse instructions where the lawyer lacks sufficient time, experience or competence to handle the matter (LSG 12.03 note 1; CCB 603(a) and (b), 701(b) and (c)).
- The duty to withdraw from the case if it later transpires that she lacks the experience or competence to deal with the matter (LSG 12.03, CCB 608(a))

There is no evidence that the second and third of these apply here. What about the first? There is an argument that you may not have been sufficiently diligent in pursuing your client's claim, but it is not, on these facts, a particularly clear cut matter. On the one hand, it might depend on how strong a rule of 'professional etiquette' it is for solicitors *not* to enforce this filing period strictly (the rule we have used is a fictitious one, so there is no way of actually finding out in this case). The more 'normal' that practice, the more difficult it may be for your client to allege a failure of diligence. On the other hand, you should always be cautious about not fully enforcing your client's rights – or at least not without their consent.

A good test is to ask yourself, what if you were to lose the case, would you, in retrospect, do anything differently? Here, you could say that has weakened your position, because you could alternatively have won on a 'technical knockout'. You might feel that is not particularly fair, but, rightly or wrongly, and subject to what we will say about duties to the court, litigation is not often concerned about being 'fair' or 'nice' to the other side. In *Griffiths v Dawson*,[39] for example, a solicitor was held to be negligent for not opposing, on hardship grounds, a divorce petition based on five years' separation, because he felt it was 'unsporting' to oppose it. As a consequence his client lost significant pension rights. The court took the view that he should have filed the defence unless specifically instructed not to do so. Obviously, the failure in diligence in *Griffiths* is greater than here, but is the underlying principle so very different? What do you think?

Did you identify any countervailing duties to lawyers or the other side that would dilute your duty to the client? You may have found out that you are under a duty to act in good faith towards other solicitors (LSG 19.01). You may well have

---

37. See, e.g., LSG para. 16.06, which creates a general duty to disclose all relevant information to the client; would you consider the passing of a deadline for your opponent's filing a defence information you should disclose to your client?

38. As noted in Chapter 5, solicitors are also under a specific duty to deal promptly with correspondence.

39. [1993] FL 315.

thought that was an extremely vague obligation and overall you would be right, though the *Guide* does add some specific illustrations of what *not* acting in good faith looks like: including failing to observe 'good manners' and 'courtesy' towards other solicitors and their staff. How far do you think courtesy ought to extend, bearing in mind that your primary duty is to your client?

Let's now take another look at how your relationship with Jason is progressing.

EXERCISE **6.4 Bayview Developments**

Jason has clearly decided that he likes you, and he has gone from being merely an occasional to quite a significant client in his own right. He now instructs you specifically and regularly to act on his behalf in a range of matters. Indeed, over time you have developed a certain respect for Jason too. To be sure he can be difficult and demanding, and he clearly has little respect for 'red tape' but he does get things done, and the amount of work he is giving you is proving to be valuable for your career. Jason is now looking to expand his business by entering into a joint venture agreement with another company: Bayview Developments Ltd. The company is interested in working with Jason on a large residential development, which they will build, while Jason's company take responsibility for the letting and management of the properties. Both companies are to underwrite the capital costs of the project, in a ratio of 60 per cent to Bayview, 40 per cent to Jason's company.

Bayview indicate that they will not enter into a formal agreement until planning permission is obtained. Consequently, plans are prepared and a detailed planning application submitted. In due course, Jason tells you that the planning application has been granted, and advises you that he has passed on this information to Bayview directly. Bayview's solicitors contact you a couple of days later, indicating that they are now ready to go ahead and prepare a joint venture agreement.

During negotiations two problems become apparent. First, it is clear that there is no minute of the Board of Directors of Jason's company authorising the company to enter into such a joint venture. You discuss this with Jason, and he acknowledges that there has been a mistake, but suggests that this was a technical oversight, that the Board will agree to producing a fictitious backdated minute, which can be produced as evidence of authority to allow the venture to proceed. You voice some doubts about both the legality and ethicality of being party to this. Half an hour later you receive a telephone call from your head of department, advising you in strong terms to be sure that you are not 'being unduly difficult about a technical breach of rules committed by an important client'. You take the hint and allow the fictitious minute to be produced and added to the case file. Two days later it becomes apparent that your client had also failed to advise Bayview that planning consent was subject to a number of conditions that would delay the project, and possibly increase costs above those projected. When you point this out to Jason in one of your (still) regular telephone conversations, he expressly forbids you to disclose the conditions to Bayview. You now have to decide what to do about this latest problem.

(a) *Consider individually:*
   (i) *What conduct rules, if any, are breached in this part of the problem?*
   (ii) *Are there other ethical issues raised by the scenario here?*
   (iii) *How will you deal with each problem/dilemma you have identified?*
(b) *Discuss your conclusions in your groups, paying particular attention to any differences of opinion that arise. Consider whether each of those differences reflects different readings of the code, or different ethical or value priorities.*

This part of the problem obviously continues to assess our duties to the client and how far our loyalty to clients should extend, particularly in situations where we are being put under pressure by the client himself, or by our superiors in the firm, to act in a particular way. Let's look at each critical issue in turn.

(i) *Who is your client?*[40] If you think the answer is obviously 'Jason', you need to think again! Whenever your client is the representative of an organisation or company, you should check that she or he has the authority to instruct you. You need to remember in these situations your client is the organisation, not the individual instructing you, and you should be careful in assuming that the interests of the two are the same. In some circumstances, if you do not check, your diligence and even your own authority to act may be called into question. Here you are told it is Jason's company and the evidence seems to point towards its being a corporate entity, but you do not know the legal form for sure. What actually is Jason's status? The answers to both these questions could make a difference to whether he has the authority in general to instruct solicitors, or even the authority on this occasion. For example, in many large companies it would be unusual for anyone other than the legal department, or perhaps the company secretary, to instruct outside counsel. Similarly, if it is a limited company or partnership certain contracts or transactions may fall outside of the scope of the business – for example, in company law terms they could be *ultra vires*, and if you do not check this, then you could put yourself and your client (the company) in a very difficult position by proceeding. This could be one reason why the minute discussed in the question is critical.

Problems of identifying the client can arise in other situations too. A common example would be where you are acting for an insured client. Depending on the circumstances, type and terms of the insurance contract your client might be the insured person, the insurer only, or both the insurer and the insured.[41]

(ii) *The backdated minute.* If backdating is, as you suspect, an illegal act, then however technical a breach it is, you are in difficult territory. The *Guide* expressly precludes you from engaging in any illegal activity (LSG 11.01). But, as a smart lawyer, you might say: it's not really my problem. My client may be in the wrong (legally or morally), but that is his problem. I have actually done nothing wrong. I have not produced a false document. I might well advise my client against such an act, but I cannot prevent it. You may even suggest that your duty of confidentiality

---

40. We could have raised this question in the last exercise too, but, as will become apparent, the answer is even more critical here.
41. See, e.g., LSG 12.06, n.1.

subsequently prevents you from disclosing your client's wrongdoing (we'll come back to this). *Do you think this is a good argument? Would you use it? Why/why not? Could it be said that, by allowing the faked minute to go into the file, you are warranting it to be genuine?*

Pretty much the same debate could arise if you thought your position was 'only' contrary to the rules and principles of professional conduct – which it could be here (see LSG 19.01 again). So, disregarding the pressure from your boss at this stage, would you have done as Jason requested, or would you have advised Bayview's solicitors of the problem? Or can you think of another option?

Well, there is a third option that is commonly used by lawyers in ethically difficult cases, and that is to advise the client that if they insist on doing *x*, then you will withdraw from acting. This is an option under both the LSG and CCB in situations where you are 'professionally embarrassed' – i.e., placed in an ethically untenable position by some person or event after you had accepted the retainer. This saves you from actually blowing the whistle on your client, but will often be enough to absolve you of formal responsibility for the wrongful act. *Would you threaten to withdraw over this matter? If so, why? If not, why not? What do you think the consequences of withdrawing would be for you, and for Jason?*

(iii)    *The undisclosed planning conditions.* Unless on the facts the conduct is fraudulent, there is little evidence of illegality here; so that issue is unlikely to arise. Is it unethical? Well, it could arguably be another breach of good faith under LSG 19.01, but that provision is almost always difficult to apply in these situations, because there is also a general expectation that the other side's lawyer should make their own necessary enquiries. In short, while you should not actively mislead another solicitor, you are not expected to do their job for them. This is sometimes a very difficult boundary question, particularly in negotiations, where the dividing line between strategically not disclosing something and actively misleading the other side can be very fine indeed.[42] Again, at this stage, you personally have not made any misleading statement to the other side, so you need to decide whether or not you have any other conduct or other ethical obligation to disclose the omission. (And, of course, you need to be aware, and advise your client of the consequences of making any statement that might induce a contract by misrepresentation.) *But what would you do if Bayview's solicitor asked you expressly about planning conditions?*

If directly asked a question, you must be very careful about saying 'no', as that would clearly be misleading. Consequently, in those circumstances, if your client still refuses to authorise disclosure of the true facts, you may have to withdraw. In some cases you may be able to deal with information problems by saying something like, 'You are advised to make your own enquiries of . . .', which serves to put the onus on the other side to find out. But you cannot sensibly do that when your own client readily has – or should – have the answer.

42. See further Chapter 9.

(iv)    *Dealing with pressure from clients and superiors.* The problem of pressure from clients is one that is commonly raised in the literature and in practice, particularly in terms of pressure from powerful, often corporate, clients whose patronage is of considerable value to the firm and maybe to your own career too. Patronage gives clients power over lawyers, with the consequent risk that the lawyer over-identifies with the client's interests in a way that undermines her ethical independence, and leads her to behave unethically or illegally for the client.[43]

The bottom line, of course, is that as a lawyer you should not allow your independence to be interfered with in this way. The principle of independence (see CCB para. 104; LSG 1.01 (a) – Solicitors Practice Rules 1990, r. 1) is a cornerstone of your ethical responsibility.[44] If you believe that what the client is asking is illegal or unethical, you are entitled – indeed required – by the codes of conduct to say no.[45] *But how do you resist the pressure?* As part of task (a)(iii) you should have tried to identify some practical solutions. If you have not done so, pause now and see what you can come up with, before reading on.

Here are some of our suggestions:

- Don't forget that the codes of conduct are also there to support you in drawing the line between what you can and cannot do for a client. You can therefore start quite legitimately by just saying 'no'. It is surprising how difficult we find this! And the reality is usually not as bad as we fear; often clients will recognise, albeit grudgingly, that you are bound by certain rules, and accept your advice.

- You can enlist the support of someone else: your client's in-house lawyer, perhaps (who will understand the professional duties you are under, and may be facing similar pressure); a more senior lawyer in your firm, or possibly by obtaining counsel's opinion – for example where you are advising that a client's proposal is actually illegal. One of the practical advantages of a divided legal profession is that barristers are more obviously independent of their lay clients, and solicitors can make use of that: clients may accept 'bad news' from a barrister in the way they might not from their own solicitor.[46]

- Ultimately, the threat of withdrawal will sometimes help focus both your client's mind on how much she wants a particular course of action, and your own. There will be times when you have to ask yourself whether you really want

43. See Nicolson and Webb, *Professional Legal Ethics*, pp. 79–80. The flip-side of over-identification is, of course, under-identification, and this may describe the experience of relatively powerless and often low status clients, who may face the consequent risk of under-representation of their interests: see *ibid.*

44. For those authorised to conduct litigation, or as advocates, there is now also a statutory duty to 'act with independence in the interests of justice' under ss. 27(2A)(a) and 28(2A)(a) of the Courts and Legal Services Act 1990, as amended by the Access to Justice Act 1999.

45. LSG 12.02 specifically states that you must not accept instructions which would require you to break the law or your professional conduct obligations.

46. The division ensures 'the client thinks you are his friend and the barrister is just doing his job': solicitor quoted by A. Boon and J. Flood, 'Trials of Strength: The Reconfiguration of Litigation as a Contested Terrain' (1999) 33 *Law and Society Review* 595 at p. 614. A number of respondents in Boon and Flood's study of litigation emphasised this function of counsel as a means of maintaining the integrity of the system and balancing the risks associated with over-identification by solicitors.

or need particular clients and the work they bring, and whether withdrawal is not just ethically appropriate, but the best thing for you too.

What if the pressure – as in our scenario – is also coming from higher up in the firm? This is by no means an unknown situation, and may be more difficult the greater the power/status gap between you and the person applying the pressure. *Is your ethical responsibility any different in this case? How would you try to deal with the problem, or would you accept 'superior orders'?*

In this situation your duties under the code of conduct are no different. Your duty to be independent is personal to you and unqualified: following 'superior orders' was no defence at Nuremberg, and it should not be here, either. As to how you might deal with the situation, to be sure the line of least resistance and the surer route to partnership may be to say nothing and get on with the job, but we're not going to advise you to do that, are we! You might have thought of some of the options we have already discussed – talking to the person in authority, in the hope that you might convince them otherwise; taking the matter to a sympathetic and still more senior member of the firm; maybe just standing by your convictions and continuing to advise your client against the course of action they propose. Maybe some of you even suggest more extreme measures, such as reporting your colleague to the Law Society, or maybe 'blowing the whistle' in some other way (which may in some cases be difficult if you are not to breach confidentiality or your contractual obligations to the firm).

What all of these actions require is a degree of responsibility and courage. It seems to us that the bottom line of being a lawyer is that YOU CHOSE THE JOB. If you are prepared to take the salary, you should be prepared to take the personal responsibility that goes with it. This is not always easy, but whoever said it would be? We overlook the extent to which lawyering, like much else in life, can demand courage, even if it is just the routine everyday kind of courage that keeps us confronting the many things that can scare us (like speaking in class, taking exams, doing job interviews, meeting intimidating clients, and dealing with bullying bosses).

Many ethicists point out that courage by itself is not a particular virtue – it can take courage to do wicked things as well as good ones. Courage only becomes virtuous when it involves taking a risk in order to do the right thing, not regardless, but well aware of the possible cost to ourselves. Derrick Bell talks eloquently about this kind of courage. A civil rights lawyer in the southern states of the US in the early 1960s, Bell was the first African American to be appointed a tenured professor at Harvard Law School. In the 1980s he undertook a very public protest over what he saw as the school's continuing failure to appoint a woman of colour to faculty. After taking two years unpaid leave of absence, he was dismissed by the university. This is some of what he says about courage:

> I am not confrontational by nature. To the contrary, I generally try hard to get along with people. After all, good relationships are comforting; hostility saps energy. Tensions in the workplace are unpleasant and render the job more difficult. And yet,

on almost every job I have held – and there have been many – issues have arisen that led me to differ with my superiors. When I differed with them, it was less out of anger than because it hurt when, in my view, their actions were misguided or unfair to me or others. I don't rise to confront every discriminatory policy or practice – but sometimes, and an individual knows when they occur, the hurt is going to simmer, slowly doing harm deep down. What is the corrective to this, if not a cure? Protest the action, speak out against the policy, openly criticize the practice.

In short, I speak out to honor myself and those whose words or actions I am protesting. By remaining silent in the face of wrong or misguided behaviour, I compound the wrong to myself by allowing the person I think is wrong to assume that his authority has vested him with an accurate sense of the situation. Challenging that embodies my duty to myself, to the person in authority, and to those in my group who have decided not to join me ...

... Sometimes I was angry at those in power, but it was not anger or vengeance that motivated my speaking out or taking action. In a sense, it was fear: I was genuinely afraid that my tacit acquiescence to decisions I thought wrong would undermine my willingness to risk criticism, alienation, and serious loss to do what I thought right.[47]

So where does this leave us? All of us have the capacity to be courageous, or not. It is our choice, *and our responsibility flows from that choice* – except perhaps in the most extreme cases where we can argue we really have been forced to act against our will. To say it is simply the fault of whoever put us under pressure, ethically speaking, misses the point: *we* have to decide whether to give in to the pressure or not, and if the ethical choice is to refuse, protest or even blow the whistle, then, as David Luban, puts it, 'you know how to whistle, don't you? Just put your lips together and blow'.[48] Perhaps the key question to ask yourself on these occasions is simply this: am I prepared to live with the choice I make, and all its consequences? (Because our choices almost invariably do have consequences, sooner or later.) This is not a counsel of perfection; you don't *have* to do the right thing, but it is a counsel against delusion. If we choose to behave unethically, at least we can grant ourselves the integrity to acknowledge it!

### Duties to others

In all of Jason's dealings so far, the person on the other side has been represented by a solicitor; what if they had been acting for themselves?

### EXERCISE 6.5 The litigant in person

Go back to the facts in Exercise 6.3. Assume that Jason's tenant was a non-lawyer acting without legal representation.

---

47  D. Bell, *Ethical Ambition*, Bloomsbury, New York and London, 2002, pp. 53–4, 56.
48.  D. Luban, *Lawyers and Justice: An Ethical Study*, Princeton University Press, Princeton, NJ, 1988, pp. 233–4.

*How, if at all, would your ethical duties and responsibilities differ if this was the case? Again, treat this first as a research exercise, then compare and discuss your conclusions within your groups.*

Solicitors owe very few express duties to non-clients. One of the exceptions is that they are under a general duty *not* to act towards anyone 'in a way which is fraudulent, deceitful or otherwise contrary to their position as solicitors' (LSG 17.01).[49] This seems to impose a standard on solicitors that extends beyond the general law against fraud and deceit.[50] Guidance to para. 17.01 suggests that its application is nevertheless pretty limited. One area it does emphasise is that solicitors must not take unfair advantage of unrepresented litigants. So, should this make a big difference to how you handle the matter in Exercise 6.3? Probably not in overall terms, though you do need to be more cautious in your dealings with an unrepresented person than with another solicitor. It would often not be unreasonable to give an unrepresented litigant some basic assistance (or at least some warning of certain risks) that you would not give another lawyer. But, in the end, you can still only assist an unrepresented litigant to the extent consistent with your duties to your own client. So, what would you actually do in this case?

**Summary so far**

- Your primary duty is to act in the best interests of your client.
- Your client is entitled to diligent and competent representation.
- You are obliged to act in good faith towards other lawyers.
- You should not deceive or take unfair advantage of other persons.
- You should not allow your client, or colleagues or any other person to interfere with the exercise of your professional independence.
- Sometimes it will take courage to maintain your independence.
- Identify others you can use as an ethical support and resource.
- Remember: if you choose to practice law, you are choosing to abide by these ethical commitments. That is your decision and it creates an ongoing personal and professional responsibility for as long as you perform the role.

49. The CCB frames barristers' responsibilities slightly differently, largely because the CCB primarily governs behaviour in court. A barrister must not engage in any conduct which is dishonest or discreditable (CCB 301) or likely to bring the profession into disrepute. She must be courteous in all her professional dealings (CCB 701), and must observe particular standards of conduct towards victims, witnesses or other third parties in court (CCB 708 (g)–(j)). Equivalent obligations apply under the Advocacy Code for solicitor-advocates.
50. This includes not just the civil and criminal law expressly on fraud and deceit, but other substantive and procedural principles which the law might use (and has used) to prevent a lawyer from taking unfair advantage of the other side in a transaction. Such principles will include the laws on implied misrepresentation and estoppel and legal duties not to mislead the court: see, e.g., J. Goodliffe, 'Fair play between lawyers' *New Law Journal*, 5 September 1997, p. 1268. Note also the general duty on parties to assist the court in achieving the Overriding Objective under the CPR; see CPR, Part 1.1 discussed in the next part of this chapter.

## Trouble on the High Street – Part 2

Now we have looked at some of the main obligations a lawyer owes his client, we can turn our attention more towards the other major professional responsibility that exists – our duty to the court. To begin that process, look at Exercise 6.6, and work through the tasks which follow.

### EXERCISE 6.6  Jason and KB Construction

A couple of days later you are still wondering how to deal with Jason's latest instructions in respect of the Bayview negotiations, when your secretary calls you to say that an angry Jason is in reception, and wants to see you urgently. You assume that he has come round to make sure you are following his instructions on the Bayview case. As Jason has no appointment, you ask your secretary to see if she can get some idea of what the problem is, and then stall him for a bit by telling Jason that you are about to take a call from another client and will not be available for the next quarter of an hour or so. You think that this might give you an opportunity to get one of your senior colleagues into the meeting to provide you with some back-up, if necessary. Your secretary calls back to say that Jason intends to wait for you and that the problem concerns an earlier property deal, not Bayview. You breath a sigh of relief, and prepare to meet Jason in one of your conference rooms.

When you walk in, Jason is pacing up and down the room. He tells you he is being sued for breach of contract by KB Construction Ltd, one of the building firms he has used. You can see that, while Jason does not mind using proceedings for his own ends, he is less comfortable being on the receiving end. The firm has issued a claim alleging that Jason is withholding a £30,000 final payment outstanding on a property redevelopment project worth £100,000. Jason's company has invoked two penalty clauses against the builder – one to the value of £15,000, on the basis that the work is not of satisfactory quality; the other, also of £15,000, for late completion of the project (by ten days). The building firm acknowledge that while there are minor faults in their work, which they value at about £2,500, these are not sufficiently serious to constitute a breach of condition such as to justify the contractual penalty clause which Jason's company invoked. Moreover, they allege that they received an oral undertaking from George Simms, the project manager, that the time penalty would not be invoked provided the work did not go more than two weeks over deadline. Jason says he has no knowledge of any such concession, and that such concessions are not standard practice for his company. However, when you press him, Jason acknowledges that George, who has now left Jason's employment, had a reputation for being 'a bit soft on the builders'.

Jason tells you that he is reluctant to settle the claim at this stage. He has had trouble with this firm in the past and he wants to 'teach them not to mess me about'. Also the Bayview and other ongoing projects Jason has have tied up most of his available capital, and he does not want to increase his borrowing to pay off the builder, if he can avoid doing so. (You begin to wonder at this point whether Jason had intended to exercise some kind of hold-back or delay on this contract almost from the outset, but you don't ask this, sensing that this might be yet another answer you might be better off not knowing.) Jason also tells you that he has heard on the grapevine that the builders themselves are in financial difficulties and so will not want a protracted fight. Jason's instructions are, as he succinctly puts it: 'Even if we can't win, string it out and screw 'em as much as you can before giving in.' 'And', he adds with a grin, 'if it helps, I've got some friends who are very persuasive. After a little chat with them, I'm sure George's recollection of events will be much clearer.'

*Working with a partner, review the text of Exercise 6.6 and consider:*

(a)   *Are you happy with the way you dealt with Jason's unexpected arrival? What did you do well; what might you have done better?*
(b)   *What issues of ethics and professional conduct does this scenario raise?*
(c)   *Taking into account the facts as your client has presented them, the relevant procedural rules and your ethical obligations, what advice will you give Jason regarding his preferred strategy?*

### Managing clients – an ethical dimension?

As new lawyers, the amount of client contact you get will often depend very much on the type of firm you work for. A lot of the big City law firms will give you very little client contact even as a newly qualified solicitor – your work will be much more about supporting and working for more senior lawyers who will actually be managing the cases and transactions. In many smaller firms you will have more client contact, and may develop your 'own' client base quite early on – perhaps even as a trainee. In Chapter 5 and Exercises 6.3 and 6.4 above we have already looked at some of the bigger ethical and conduct issues that can arise in your interaction with clients: your responsibilities for client care under PR15; your responsibilities to inform and involve your clients in decision-making, and the importance of not over-identifying with your clients. Here there is nothing as major as that, but the facts do introduce some integrity issues which relate to how we manage our clients and their expectations.

Turning specifically to task (a) in our Exercise, do you have any obligation to see Jason when he shows up? Well, no, you don't. Jason is likely to be one of many clients and many projects; if you are to manage your workload effectively, you need to be disciplined not just in scheduling your own time, but in managing clients' expectations in terms of:

● setting appointments;
● your general availability and points of contact;
● timescales for responses to letters, phonecalls, progress reports, etc.

We suggest this is not just good management practice, it is part of maintaining the integrity of your work for all your clients. Moreover, if this is a new and separate as opposed to a continuing matter, you may not even be obliged to take it on. As a solicitor you are under no obligation to accept a retainer from a client, and indeed, as we have seen, if you do not have the time or expertise, it would actually be wrong for you to do so. That said, most firms obviously try to encourage and accommodate repeat work from existing clients, and this practice will often create an expectation that you will take the work on, unless there are very good reasons for not doing so.

If you are genuinely available to a client, should you see them? This is pretty obvious, particularly if the client has an urgent concern, and has nothing much to do with ethics; it is simple courtesy and good business to do so but, again, be sure that you are clear about how much of your time your client is getting, especially as you will have other appointments and deadlines.

What about keeping Jason waiting? Again, nobody says you have to jump the moment a client says 'jump', and the idea of taking in 'back-up' to support you (provided it does that!) is probably not a bad one – though it might require some explanation to the client. But, do you think it is appropriate to get your secretary to lie to your client about why you are keeping him waiting?

You might well be surprised at the question. You may observe that it is only a 'little lie' – barely a lie at all in fact. Does it matter? Well, that's exactly the issue: does it matter? While we don't want to sound like moral prigs on this point, it is something to consider. Perhaps it will help if we start by generalising the discussion: *why do we tell lies in these sorts of situations?*

EXERCISE 6.7 **To lie or not to lie**

Think back to a social or work situation where you decided to tell a 'harmless' lie.

(a)   *What was the lie or story you invented?*
(b)   *What was your motivation for doing so?*
(c)   *What consequences, if any, did it have?*
(d)   *How did you feel about telling the lie?*
(e)   *On reflection, could you have dealt with the situation to your satisfaction without lying?*

There are times when we all tell 'little lies' because we decide that is for the best, and certainly there are times when telling the truth can cause more moral or actual harm to another than telling a lie. But most of the time we tell lies for no one but ourselves, because it is somehow 'easier' than telling the truth, or it makes us look better than the truth would, or because we don't have the self-confidence to tell it as it is, and need to dress our actions up with a 'good reason'. The lie to Jason in Exercise 6.7 is one of those – it isn't really going to do any harm, but it is also entirely unnecessary: you don't need to give Jason any reason why he has to wait, he just needs to know you will be fifteen minutes.

Of course, the real problem is not just 'little lies' but lying to clients (and others) in general – and after all, what is one person's little lie can be someone else's 'whopper' and, as someone once said, even a half-truth requires a whole lie. Ultimately, of course, this is an area where you need to assess what kind of professional behaviour is consistent with your own values. Even if you feel that you are already clear about where you would draw the line, we suggest you read the following comments in case they generate any additional issues and ideas that you have not thought about.

We sometimes wonder whether lying is a bigger occupational hazard for lawyers than for some other occupational groups. As lawyers we have a rather difficult and ambiguous professional relationship with the truth. It is part of the territory that goes with being a lawyer. That in itself would seem to be a good reason to have ethics, but a lot of the ethical rules are actually a cause of that ambiguity, not the cure.

According to the standard versions of legal ethics, we are not morally responsible for the lies – or truths – our clients tell. That responsibility remains with them – we are simply the means by which they tell their story. We don't need to know or even believe that our clients are telling the truth before we can represent them. Indeed, there are times when knowing too much of the truth can make it harder for us to do what our clients want us to do (this is one of those points that we will come back to). There is often a real tension in the legal system between truth telling and avoiding harm – particularly to your client. Perhaps as a result there is a temptation to get professionally cynical about the truth, and a tendency to see everything in shades of grey.

On the other hand, we also need to acknowledge that, ethically, our relationship with our clients is built on trust, and trust requires a (mutual) commitment to what might properly be called 'sincerity',[51] or at least some basic commitment to truthfulness. Lying to clients can be a really bad idea for good practical as well as ethical reasons:

● Lying almost always creates some kind of uncertainty – 'what did I say?'; 'could I be found out?' As Mark Twain observed, the advantage of telling the truth is that you never have to remember what you said.

● Lies on either side can undermine the relationship. You cannot do your job properly if your client tells you only half the story, or leads you off on some implausible explanation. And even your 'little lies' can, if they are discovered, create doubts and questions in the client's mind: are there bigger things that you are not being truthful about?

● Thirdly, we should not overlook that there are many situations where lying to clients and others is clearly unethical. It can be a breach of your duty under LSG 17.01, and

51. The French philosopher François La Rochefoucauld defines sincerity as 'an openheartedness that shows us as we are; it is a love of truth, a loathing for disguise': *Maximes et Réflexions*, quoted in A. Compte-Sponville, *A Short Treatise on the Great Virtues* (trans. C. Temerson), Vintage, London, 2003, p. 197.

more than that. Lying to a client is quite simply a way of manipulating that person, of getting them to do what you want. And whether you are doing it in their interest (as you see it) or in your own, your actions undermine their autonomy and independence.[52]

- And, finally, there is perhaps another ethical problem with the 'little lies', which is that we simply get used to them, and we may not see them as lies at all. We do not recognise that they each weaken our relationship with the truth, often in more subtle and insidious ways than the big lies do.

With that in mind, let's move on, because this scenario raises some really critical questions about what we can and cannot do in terms of a litigation strategy, and our relationship to the truth plays a part in this too. Jason's instructions obviously place you in yet another difficult situation. How far can – and should – you use pressure and tactical delay to force an opponent to drop a claim, or settle for less than the claim is worth? Even more critically, how should you deal with a client who seems to be proposing interfering with a witness, and, perhaps, relying on false testimony. Let us look at each of these issues in turn.

### Ethics and strategy in litigation

Conventionally, litigation strategy has been shaped by the adversary tradition, in which choice of tactics is seen primarily in technical and strategic terms. This may seem strange, because the lawyer does have an overriding professional duty to the proper administration of justice, but this duty has left unregulated many of the more dubious means by which a lawyer can pursue a client's ends in litigation. For example, bombarding an opponent with excessive amounts of paper at disclosure; trying to suppress evidence that goes against their client's interests; making incomplete or misleading responses to requests for disclosure; exploiting an opponent's misunderstandings, and being exceedingly combative in settlement negotiations, are all tactics that lawyers have employed with varying degrees of success.[53]   Jason's instructions leave you in little doubt as to what he expects: he believes KB Construction are in financial trouble already; he wants you to take advantage of that and defend the claim in such a way as to put additional time and financial pressure on the claimants, thereby forcing them either into an early – and relatively disadvantageous – settlement, or to withdraw their claim. How would you feel about doing that for a client? Is it fair? How do you square such tactics with your role as an officer of the court?[54]

The institutional response to that last question is increasingly clear: you try at your peril! In his review of the civil justice system in the mid-1990s, Lord Woolf was highly critical of the scope for tactical abuse by the parties. As he observed:

---

52. See, e.g., L. Lerman, 'Lying to Clients' (1990) 138 *University of Pennsylvania Law Review* 659.
53. See Nicolson and Webb, *Professional Legal Ethics*, pp. 172–3.
54. Traditionally, barristers are not defined as 'officers of the court', but barristers and solicitors clearly owe similar (if not identical) legal duties to the court and are both subject to its overriding jurisdiction – so the classical distinction is fairly meaningless in terms of these ethical duties – see D. Ipp, 'Lawyers' Duties to the Court' (1998) 114 *Law Quarterly Review* 63 at pp. 66–7.

Without effective judicial control ... the adversarial process is likely to encourage an adversarial culture and to degenerate into an environment in which the litigation process is too often seen as a battlefield where no rules apply. In this environment, questions of expense, delay, compromise and fairness have only a low priority.[55]

Lord Woolf's reform proposals were targeted precisely at raising the priority of these factors. His *Access to Justice* recommendations were implemented by the Civil Procedure Rules 1998 (CPR), which have made it much more difficult for lawyers to engage in time-wasting tactics and discovery abuse.[56] The key to clamping down on this has been to increase judicial supervision of pre-trial procedure, and to give judges greater powers to punish tactical abuses, for example, by more rigourous policing of disclosure, by refusing to grant extensions of time and by exercising powers to award costs against parties who try to bend or violate the rules.

The CPR also introduced the idea of an 'overriding objective' to civil litigation. The overriding objective is simply stated: it is to enable the court 'to deal with cases justly' (CPR r. 1.1(1)). Under r. 1.1(2) this is stated to include:

(a)    ensuring the parties are on an equal footing;
(b)    saving expense;
(c)    dealing with the case in ways that are proportionate;
(d)    ensuring that it is dealt with expeditiously and fairly;
(e)    allotting to it an appropriate share of the court's resources, while taking into account the need to allot resources to other cases. This is particularly reflected in judicial powers to agree or to impose a timetable for progressing a case (see CPR r. 1.4(2)).

The real ethical catch comes in CPR r. 1.3 which adds: 'The parties are required to help the court to further the overriding objective.' At the risk of stating the obvious, this means of course that it is not just the duty of the parties themselves, but of their legal advisers and advocates.[57] There is little doubt that the CPR have significantly extended the duty to the court in civil litigation. At the very least, the following assertions are consistent with rr. 1.1(2) and 1.3, and have at least some basis in authority:

● The courts will not interfere in the parties' freedom to instruct their lawyers of choice, but parties must be aware that they bear the financial risk in costs[58] of unreasonably expensive or disproportionate representation.[59] Hiring a top QC

---

55. Lord Woolf, *Access to Justice: Interim Report*, HMSO, London, 1995, p. 7.
56. For a good general overview of the operation of the CPR, see G. Slapper and D. Kelly, *The English Legal System*, Cavendish, London, 7th edn, 2004, ch. 7.
57. The same point is made explicitly by Arden LJ in *Skjevesland v Geveran Trading Co Ltd* [2002] EWCA Civ 1567, [2003] 1 WLR 912. Note also that the new professional obligations created by the CPR have been summarised and included as Annex 21I of the Law Society's Guide.
58. The indemnity principle in costs means the loser normally pays some or all of the winner's legal costs, unless the court disallows certain items, or a proportion of those items.
59. *Maltez v Lewis*, The Times, 28 April 1999.

to fight a routine county court action worth £7,000–£8,000 would probably be considered disproportionate!

- Solicitors must adhere to the rules and procedures designed to speed up the preparation and conduct of litigation. Failure to do so (whether caused by poor case management or tactical delay) may constitute a breach of the duty to the court.[60] As a consequence, your client might face a costs' penalty, or, in extreme cases you might be made the subject of a wasted costs order.

- It follows that assisting the court will include taking steps to minimise the number of applications or hearings necessary (see also CPR r. 1.4(2)(i) and Practice Direction Part 29, para. 3.5) and complying with any directions of the judge in a full and timely manner.

- Counsel should disclose to the other side, at the earliest practicable opportunity, any conflict or other cause that would enable them reasonably to object to his continuing to act.[61]

- Following the appeals in *Halsey v Milton Keynes NHS Trust and Steel v Joy & Halliday*,[62] it seems clear that litigators are under a professional duty to consider with their client whether a case is suitable for mediation or other form of alternative dispute resolution (ADR).[63]

- Once a case has come to trial, the advocate must conduct the proceedings economically; she 'must take reasonable and practicable steps to avoid unnecessary expense or waste of the court's time'.[64]

Thus, as a litigator, you face the combination of strict timetabling, together with the judicial power to give directions and control procedure *inter partes*, and a set of quite stringent duties that you owe the court. These all make it much harder than it used to be for you to operate the kind of strategy Jason has in mind. It is your duty to explain this clearly to Jason and to warn him of the risks, particularly in respect of costs, that such a strategy would incur. You should also warn Jason that he will not necessarily be able to hide behind you as much as he would like. As the *Guide* points out:

> The new rules highlight the importance for solicitors of continuing to involve their client in the proceedings ... clients are to be encouraged to attend at case management conferences whenever practicable ...[65]

You can, of course, turn this to your advantage. In presenting your preferred litigation strategy, you are assisted to a degree by the codes of conduct as well as the CPR.

---

60. See also per Lord Donaldson MR in *Langley v North West Water Authority* [1991] 1 WLR 697.
61. Per Arden LJ in *Skjevesland v Geveran Trading Co Ltd* [2002] EWCA Civ 1567 at [47].
62. [2004] EWCA Civ 576.
63. Moreover, failing to mediate, or withdrawing from mediation in circumstances which make that action unreasonable may be taken into account by the court when assessing costs – see, e.g., *Dunnett v Railtrack plc*, discussed further in Chapter 9; *SITA v Watson Wyatt; Maxwell Bentley* [2002] All ER (D) 189 as well as *Halsey v Milton Keynes NHS Trust and Steel v Joy & Halliday* [2004] EWCA Civ 576.
64. Per Lord Hobhouse in *Medcalf v Weatherill* [2002] UKHL 27 at [54].
65. Annex 21I LSG, section 2.

## Your duties to the court

Lawyers owe a wide range of duties to the court, including duties not to mislead the court, duties to assist the court with points of law or authority, and duties to obey court orders and honour undertakings given to the court.[66] These duties are generally described as 'overriding', that is they trump any apparently conflicting duties to the client or to other parties.

Although overriding, the duties to the court are also subject to the principle of lawyer independence. As a lawyer you owe duties to both your client and the court, and yet you are also independent of both. Thus, there is no obligation on an advocate to argue every conceivable point, just because that is what the client wants, and para. 603 CCB (4.1(c) of the Advocacy Code) specifically entitles advocates to withdraw if instructions seek to limit their authority to manage proceedings in court. But the duty to manage litigation, as we have seen, goes beyond this. Today, with the shift to far greater judicial control of proceedings, the litigator has a wide responsibility to the effective administration of justice. As Mason CJ observed in the Australian case of *Giannerelli v Wraith*:

> In such an adversarial system the mode of presentation of each party's case rests with counsel who, not being a mere agent for the litigant, exercises an independent judgment *in the interests of the court*.[67]

To this extent you are, in theory at least, entitled to dictate strategy to Jason. And this is both a strength and a weakness of the system. Your duty to the court helps underpin your independence from your client. But is your duty to the court also in danger of *undermining* your duty to your client? Are such broad rules, by giving a lot of power to the lawyer, as an officer of the court, hard to equate with an ethic that respects client autonomy and participation in decision-making?[68]

Putting a slightly different angle on the question, we can also ask, if you owe an overriding duty to the court, just how independent *of the court* can you be? The codes are fairly exhortatory on this one, but offer limited concrete guidance. In addition to the general principle that all lawyers should preserve their independence and integrity, they specifically stress that barristers and solicitor advocates must not allow their 'absolute independence' and 'freedom from external pressure to be compromised' and particularly must not compromise their professional standards in order to please clients, the court or a third party (CCB 307 (a) and (c); Law Society Advocacy Code, para. 2.6). This, of course, may not be easy, and even the courts acknowledge that there can be a tension, as Lord Hobhouse observed in *Medcalf v Weatherill*:

> At times the proper discharge by the advocate of his duties to his client will be liable to bring him into conflict with the court. This does not alter the duty of the advocate. It

---

66. See Ipp, (1998) 114 *Law Quarterly Review* 63.    67. (1988) 165 CLR 543, our emphasis.
68. See further Chapter 5, pp. 111–14, and Chapter 11, pp. 430–1.

may require more courage to represent a client in the face of a hostile court, but the advocate must still be prepared to act fearlessly. It is part of the duty of an advocate, where necessary, appropriately to protect his client from the court as well as from the opposing party.[69]

The principle of independence thus entitles you to make judgment calls that may not entirely accord with either the court's reading of the case, or your client's. This means that every time you take a case, you must be prepared to make that judgment. As a lawyer you can – and will – find yourself between a rock and a hard place: with a client applying pressure on one side, and your duty to the court on the other. But of course, these are not equal pressures. The critical phrase, 'where necessary, appropriately . . . ' in Lord Hobhouse's statement reminds us of where the power lies. What is 'necessary' and 'appropriate' is, ultimately, to be determined by the courts themselves.

Turning now to Jason's threat to 'influence' George's evidence, assuming it is a serious threat, what legal and ethical problems might that raise? There are several possible issues.

The first, and perhaps most obvious, concerns your overriding duty to the court. Both as an advocate and as a litigator preparing proceedings, you owe a strong 'duty of candour' to the court: in other words, you must never knowingly deceive or mislead the court (LSG 21.01; CCB 302). Knowingly allowing your client or a witness for your client to commit perjury, or knowingly destroying or failing to disclose relevant documents (or allowing your client so to act) would, for example, all constitute breaches of your duty of candour.

This kind of situation involves a common 'drawing the line' problem, triggered by the fact that your duty of candour only obliges you to disclose wrongdoing that you 'know' has occurred. 'Leon' – one of the American attorney's interviewed by Jack and Jack explains:

> The one area that comes up is whether the person you are representing is not telling the truth – even if you don't know it factually, you know it emotionally. And basically they're willing to go up and perjure themselves and you're aware of that. The general rule is, as long as you don't know as a fact that they're doing it, you can do it. But if you know as a fact that they're doing it, the rule is that you can't present that. Often in criminal situations you know your client is not telling the truth. You know it on an emotional level and a centred level, but you don't know it on a factual level . . . It's a dilemma because every lawyer has to decide where they're going to draw the line. (*What is the conflict in that situation?*) Well, the conflict is, again building a case around something that you know is not true, that you deeply believe is not true. The dilemma is drawing those lines between advocating your client's position and getting into a position where you're building up a case that you know is not true but that you

---

69. [2002] UKHL 27, [2002] 3 WLR 172 at [53].

might be able to sell. And actually in the criminal area, I'm not sure that society doesn't expect you to do that. And certainly your client expects you to do that.[70]

As Leon observes, this tends to be a critical and recurrent problem in criminal work,[71] but the duty applies to civil litigation as well. In Jason's case, you have to assess whether you 'know as a fact' that he intends to interfere with the evidence or advance a defence that is false in some material particular. If your answer is 'yes' then you cannot represent him on that basis without breaching your duty of candour. You must advise him accordingly, and if he will not adopt a more appropriate course of action, then you have no option but to withdraw.

There is a second, legal issue that you should advise both Jason and, if necessary, George about. Under Part 22 CPR, every statement of case and witness statement has to be endorsed by a statement of truth signed by the client or by their lawyer, or by the witness where it is a witness statement. The Law Society, not surprisingly, advises that you obtain the client's signature where possible, as responsibility for the statement then attaches clearly to the client. A person who knowingly makes a false claim or assertion in his statements of case or witness statement is committing a contempt of court. A solicitor who knowingly allows a false statement of truth to be made would be in breach of her duty to the court, and might conceivably also be in contempt (though this assertion has yet to be tested).

Lastly, there is a third issue that might arise from Jason's hint about his 'friends', and this takes us into yet another area of ethics: your duty of confidentiality.

### Confidentiality

As we observed earlier in this chapter, the principle of loyalty to clients is also reflected in a strong duty of confidentiality. It is said that:

> The public interest in the efficient working of the legal system requires that people should be able to obtain professional legal advice on their rights, liabilities and obligations ... To this end communications between clients and lawyers must be uninhibited ... [C]andour cannot be expected if disclosure of the contents of communications between clients and lawyers may be compelled ...[72]

Confidentiality is an obvious cornerstone of any professional relationship, and this is reflected in a wide general obligation to keep confidential *to the firm or chambers* the affairs of a client (LSG 16.01; CCB 702). Note that the obligation is not purely personal: the rules permit necessary disclosure to colleagues and staff, though, of

---

70. R. Jack and D. C. Jack, *Moral Vision and Professional Decisions: The Changing Values of Women and Men Lawyers*, Cambridge University Press, Cambridge, 1989, pp. 65–6. (The American rules in this respect are very similar to our own.)
71. See in the English context the notoriously difficult *Bridgwood* case, in which a solicitor was struck off the Roll for failing to disclose that a client was attempting to mislead the court as to their identity: see *Law Society's Gazette*, 9 November 1988, p. 53.
72. Per Lord Nicholls of Birkenhead in *R v Derby Magistrates Court, ex parte B* [1995] 4 All ER 526 at 543.

course, they are then equally bound to keep the confidence. This duty continues unless and until the client expressly permits disclosure or otherwise waives confidentiality (LSG 16.03; CCB 702). If there is no waiver, the duty of confidentiality even extends beyond the client's death.

The value of a confidentiality rule is self-evident. But the obvious question that Exercise 6.6 begs, is just how far should the duty to protect client confidentiality extend? Jason in our scenario implies that George is going to be put under some pressure, perhaps threatened with violence, perhaps even assaulted. *Is that something we should allow to happen?* See if you can work out an answer, and make a note of it before reading on.

Under LSG Chapter 16 there are a number of exceptional circumstances where confidentiality obligations give way to disclosure which is deemed to be 'in the public interest'. In practice you should be familiar with these.[73] One of these states that, if you have reasonable grounds for believing the client or a third party is planning to commit a crime involving serious bodily harm to some person, then you *may* (note: not must) break confidentiality (LSG 16.02) – it would thus not be inappropriate to tell the police, or George, the intended victim – but *only* if you anticipated that the threat involved serious bodily harm.[74] While a disciplinary tribunal might give you some latitude not to take risks with someone else's safety, it does mean that if you had evidence that Jason's friends were simply going to damage George's car, for example, then you would not be entitled to breach confidentiality. *How do you feel about that? Would your answer differ if George was a tall 15 stone ex-boxer, or a small, 60 year old man with a heart condition?*

More generally, a number of commentators point out the extent to which a strict duty of confidentiality seems to require us to do things that may seem widely inconsistent with the dictates of 'ordinary' morality. The primary example is that you are always bound by your client's disclosure of past criminality – however heinous that may be. Lawyers have used this duty to justify refusing to disclose to the grieving parents the whereabouts of their murdered child's remains;[75] or that their client has confessed to the murder of an elderly lady, for which another (and therefore innocent) man has been tried and convicted.[76]

73. Note that on 30 July 2004 the Law Society Council agreed a new draft Practice Rule, to be Rule 16E of the Solicitors Practice Rules 1990, and associated guidance: see [Draft] Solicitors' Practice (Confidentiality and Disclosure) Amendment Rule [2004] (15 July 2004). As the regulation must now be submitted for approval under the Courts and Legal Services Act, it is not yet clear when these changes will come into force. The following comments remain generally accurate for the new rules.

74. Note that draft Rule 16E (3)(ii)(A) proposes extending this exception to encompass serious mental harm as well. Obviously, this is unlikely to affect your position here.

75. This is the notorious and widely discussed 'Lake Pleasant' murder case; see, e.g., J. Chamberlain, 'Confidentiality and the Case of Robert Garrow's Lawyers' (1976) 25 *Buffalo Law Review* 221.

76. In the Scottish case of Patrick Meehan: see J. Beltrami, *A Deadly Innocence: the Meehan File*, Mainstream Publishing, Edinburgh, 1989.

EXERCISE **6.8** **In whose best interests?**

Assume you are the lawyer whose client has confessed to the murder for which Patrick Meehan has been wrongly convicted.

(a)   *List all the arguments (legal and moral) that you can think of for **not** breaching confidentiality.*

(b)   *List all the legal and moral arguments you can think of **in favour** of breaching confidentiality.*

(c)   *On the basis of those arguments, would you breach confidentiality or not? Why?*

(d)   *Read the following extract from a short article by Lloyd Snyder looking at the scope of the confidentiality rules. Compare his arguments with your own and note the differences. What do you find?*

> There are two primary arguments in favour of a broad confidentiality rule with very narrow exceptions. They may be described in short as the loyalty argument and the client disclosure argument ...
>
> The loyalty argument is based on the fiduciary relationship between the attorney and client. The attorney owes the client complete and undivided loyalty and should do nothing to undermine the interests of the client. If the client is doing something improper, or seeks to do something improper, the attorney cannot assist the client, and may have to resign from representation. The attorney also has the duty to explain the impropriety of the client's conduct and advise the client to desist. Other than advising against improper conduct and avoiding assisting the client in pursuing illegal or improper activities, the attorney should have no right to disclose or otherwise use information obtained during the representation against the interests of the client.
>
> The loyalty argument is closely related to the client disclosure argument. According to this argument, an attorney must have all the facts in regard to any legal matter in order to advise the client about his legal rights and to represent the client competently. The assurance of confidentiality acts as an inducement to the client to disclose all relevant information, even information that is embarrassing or potentially damaging. Some advocates of a broad confidentiality rule go so far as to argue that the rule actually reduces the likelihood of improper conduct, by providing counsel with sufficient information to assess the propriety of the client's conduct and convince the client not to engage in improper conduct.
>
> The argument against a broad confidentiality rule disputes both the loyalty argument and the client disclosure argument. While loyalty to a client by a fiduciary is important, it is not the only value to be considered. When a client has misused the services of an attorney in order to engage in some illegal or fraudulent conduct, the attorney should not be required to stand by and permit the client to succeed when a warning could prevent serious harm to an innocent third party. Moreover, advice to a client to avoid some improper course of action is likely to be more effective if the attorney can advise the client of her right to warn a possible victim.

Critics of broad confidentiality rules also claim that the contention that confidentiality induces clients to be forthcoming and truthful with their lawyers is unproven. There are many reasons, apart from fear of subsequent disclosure, why clients do not tell all to their lawyers. These include such factors as embarrassment and fear that their attorney will not pursue their case vigorously. There is little empirical evidence to support the claim that confidentiality induces broad disclosure. The few studies undertaken on the issue suggest that it does not.[77]

Critics further contend that whatever value may be served by confidentiality cannot justify permitting serious harm to innocent third parties. A client should not be able to prevent a lawyer from saving a third party from serious financial harm, wrongful criminal conviction, or loss of property by invoking confidentiality.

One of the factors that complicates this debate is that confidentiality, whatever its value to clients, is of great value to attorneys. It is a useful device for protecting attorneys from being compelled to disclose unpleasant or embarrassing information to others. It gives attorneys a marketing advantage over other professionals such as accountants who cannot assure their clients an evidentiary privilege or a strong professional obligation of confidentiality. Confidentiality is of undoubted value to the crooked lawyer who is willing to conspire with clients in order to further improper conduct. It is also of value to the attorney who becomes aware of a client's improper conduct and does not want to face the moral dilemma of whether to protect an innocent party rather than walk away and pocket the fees he has earned from his crooked client.[78]

(e)    *Finally, review your conclusion in (c). Have you changed your mind at all? If so, why? If not, why not?*

A final practical point: if you do intend to disclose, are you under any obligation to warn your client first? The answer to this one seems to be 'no', and obviously in some circumstances it would be very unwise to do so, as you could be putting yourself or your colleagues at risk of physical harm.[79]

---

77. See, e.g., F. C. Zacharias, 'Rethinking Confidentiality' (1989) 74 *Iowa Law Review* 351; W. H. Simon, *The Practice of Justice*, pp. 54–68 (footnoted in the original).
78. L. Snyder, 'The Battle Over the Legal Ethics Confidentiality Rule in the United States' [2001] *Legal Ethics* 98 at pp. 103–4.
79. Note that where you suspect a client may be using you to dispose of the proceeds of crime ('money laundering') or to assist in financing terrorism – both of which you are obliged to report to the authorities – you are under a positive duty not to disclose your suspicions to your client. Be aware that the law and practice on money laundering is complex, but very important. The basic legal provisions are now contained in ss. 327–33 of the Proceeds of Crime Act 2002 and ss. 18–21 of the Terrorism Act 2000, but these are supported by an extensive body of regulations (not all of which are in force at the time of writing). Unlike the earlier money laundering controls (see, e.g., Boon and Levin, *The Ethics and conduct of Lawyers in England and Wales*, pp. 259–61), the new rules are extremely wide and capable of involving most kinds of transactional work undertaken by solicitors, such as conveyancing, tax advice, corporate work, trusts and even divorce settlements – see *P v P* [2003] EWHC (Fam) 2260 – where the proceeds of crime could be involved. Proceeds of crime are also interpreted widely to include, e.g. money from robbery, tax fraud, benefit fraud, drug trafficking, the proceeds of immoral earnings and 'terrorist' funding. Current Law Society guidance is contained in the LSG, Annex 3B(1) and (2).

**Legal professional privilege**

You should be aware that confidentiality also links closely in practice to the doctrine of legal professional privilege; you cannot entirely understand one without knowing something about the other. Legal professional privilege also protects communications between lawyers and clients, but only from disclosure as evidence in legal proceedings. It therefore serves a different function from the lawyer's duty of confidentiality. Once again, the detailed rules are complicated and there is extensive case law on the scope of the privilege.[80] Privilege does not raise its head in our case study, so we will explore it through a different exercise.

EXERCISE **6.9** **Whose secret is it anyway?**

Your law firm is retained by Pharmco plc, a large pharmaceuticals manufacturer. Three years ago Pharmco engaged you to undertake a regulatory audit of its activities. In the process of so doing, you come across confidential company documents which show that the company's own research suggests results on recent drug trials, which led to the licensing of one of Pharmco's newest and most profitable products, are not reliable, and that the drug has some damaging neurological side effects that were not identified in the independent trials. You noted this in your report and advised Pharmco that a failure to disclose this information could leave the Company at risk of substantial claims from any future victims of these side-effects. You further advised that the company should adopt a document screening policy whereby all documents of a 'politically and legally sensitive nature' are reviewed by the company's in-house counsel and decisions made about whether such documents are retained or shredded on the basis of that legal advice. The company agrees to implement your policy, and shreds a number of important documents related to this product. It also shreds all its copies of your report, though you retain one copy intact, in the belief that it is subject to legal professional privilege.

Eight months ago a group action was commenced against Pharmco alleging that this same product has caused long-term neurological damage to a number of users prescribed the drug. A reference to your report was found amongst documents disclosed by Pharmco to the claimant's solicitors. They are now seeking an order compelling you to disclose your report.

*Should you disclose? Consider your answer (a) from the perspective of your personal morality and (b) from the perspective of your legal and ethical duties as a solicitor. Make a note of your answers, then read on.*

80. Most of the standard texts on evidence provide a broad treatment of the topic, and Boon and Levin, *The Ethics and Conduct of Lawyers in England and Wales*, pp. 249–53 also provides a useful summary; for a full analysis, see J. Auburn, *Legal Professional Privilege, Law and Theory*, Hart Publishing, Oxford, 2000.

In civil litigation a party is under a continuing duty to disclose all documents relevant to the case, unless those documents are subject to an immunity or privilege.[81] The main ground for claiming privilege is that the document is a confidential communication between a client and her legal adviser. As a matter of law there are actually two types of privilege: litigation privilege and legal advice privilege. In simple terms the distinction, and its significance, is as follows.

Litigation privilege, as the name implies attaches only to documents that are prepared for the '*dominant purpose*' of contemplated or actual litigation, or for other adversarial proceedings, such as arbitration. Litigation privilege:

- Cannot apply retrospectively; it does not attach to documents originally created for a non-contentious purpose but which acquire a later litigious significance.
- Can cover a wider scope of communications than the advice privilege (provided they each satisfy the dominant purpose test), including communications between a lawyer and her client, or agent or a third party, and even communications between a client and a third party.

Legal advice privilege tends to be interpreted more narrowly. It only protects communications between a lawyer and client, provided that the communications are confidential and made for the purpose of giving or seeking legal advice. The scope of what advice counts as '*legal advice*' was very restrictively interpreted by the Court of Appeal in the recent *Three Rivers* case,[82] to exclude 'commercial' or 'presentational' advice given by lawyers.[83] This decision has been overturned on appeal to the House of Lords; however, their Lordships' reasons are not expected to be given until sometime in September 2004, so you will need to follow-up this development for yourselves. The advice privilege does not protect documents passing between a lawyer and an independent third party, even if they are created for the purpose of obtaining legal advice.

There are two established situations in which legal professional privilege cannot arise:

- Where legal advice has been used to support the commission of a crime or fraud – even if the lawyer does not know that this is the client's purpose in seeking advice, the communication will be deemed not privileged on grounds of legal policy.
- in respect of expert reports prepared for proceedings under the Children Act 1989 where disclosure will be ordered if it is in the interests of the child concerned for that disclosure to take place.

One of the few ways by which privilege can be lost is by waiver. The client may waive her privilege either expressly or by implication. The English courts tend to be

81. *Vernon v Bosley (No. 2)* [1997] 3 WLR 683, and see generally CPR r. 31.16 on pre-action disclosure. Different, but extensive, rules of disclosure apply in criminal proceedings.
82. *Three Rivers District Council v Governor and Company of the Bank of England (No. 10)* [2004] EWCA Civ 218.
83. This can be a very fine distinction, particularly in the work of in-house lawyers.

quite wary of implying waiver. For example, in the case of *British American Tobacco Ltd v USA*,[84] the Court of Appeal refused a declaration that the claimants had impliedly waived their privilege over an undisclosed document by virtue of being party to an earlier consent order, which had led to public disclosure of a large number of related documents. Moreover, it has also been held that a party can waive privilege for a limited purpose only, and in such cases this should not be interpreted as a general waiver.[85]

One of the few situations where the client is deemed impliedly to waive privilege is where civil proceedings are brought against a solicitor by his client. Here privilege will be waived over all relevant documents to the extent necessary to enable the court to adjudicate the matter fully and fairly. Whether privilege can be deemed waived in respect of complaints and disciplinary proceedings is more a moot point. A solicitor is entitled under the LSG (16.02 note 12) to disclose confidential communications in response to such investigations, but can he be obliged to disclose privileged documents? This is obviously more contentious. If there was a general implied waiver, then what about the privilege that would attach to advice that the lawyer himself might receive *as a client* in respect of those proceedings? Surely it would not be fair to refuse to a lawyer the right that any other citizen can assert before any other court or tribunal? But doesn't the preservation of a general privilege at the same time risk destroying the prospects of success of at least some such disciplinary investigations? Well, yes it does. Nevertheless, the Privy Council has asserted that the public interest in the privilege overrides the countervailing public interest in maintaining the integrity of the profession, and while the privilege may be waived, it should not be overridden without clear statutory authority.[86] In all other respects, privilege cannot be waived by the lawyer, even if he or she is the creator of the relevant document.

So, let us apply these principles to the facts in Exercise 6.9. The exercise raises a difficult technical problem that is of considerable significance in commercial practice where, post-Enron, the role of lawyers in hiding corporate misconduct is becoming an increasingly sensitive political and regulatory issue.

There are two main questions you should have considered here: Is the document capable of attracting privilege? If so, is there any basis on which privilege could or should be denied?

(i)    *Is the document privileged?* In our view the document cannot attract litigation privilege. The crucial question in this regard is whether litigation existed or was

---

84. [2004] EWCA Civ 1064. It should be noted that the Court of Appeal's judgment runs counter to rulings given in related litigation in Australia and the US.
85. 'It must often be in the interests of the administration of justice that a partial or limited waiver of privilege should be made by a party who would not contemplate anything which might cause privilege to be lost, and it would be most undesirable if the law could not accommodate it', per Lord Millett in *B and Russell McVeagh McKenzie Bartleet & Co v Auckland District Law Society and Judd* [2003] UKPC 38.
86. *Ibid.*

reasonably in contemplation at the time the document was created. The facts here are not dissimilar to those in *USA v Philip Morris Inc and British American Tobacco (Investments) Inc.*[87] BAT was (and at the time of writing still is) a party to major litigation in the US in which the US government is seeking $280 billion from the tobacco companies alleging that they have operated in an unlawful enterprise to deceive and defraud the American public about the risks of smoking. Letters of request were issued in the Royal Courts of Justice in respect of a document produced by Andrew Foyle, an English solicitor who had acted for BAT between 1985 and 1994, and had allegedly played a key role in developing BAT's document retention policy. The Court of Appeal upheld the decision at first instance that there had to be more than just a distinct possibility of litigation for the litigation privilege to apply (the judge had also held that, without further information about the document itself it was not possible to determine whether it was governed by the advice privilege). The same applies to Exercise 6.9. On the facts as you have them, it is difficult to assert for sure that the document would attract advice privilege – you need to look at the document.

(ii)   *If it does attract the advice privilege, is there any basis on which privilege should be waived or refused?* Let's deal with waiver first, though on the facts it is unlikely to be in your or your client's best interests. Remember what we have already said: as a lawyer you cannot waive your client's legal professional privilege. Obviously, a client needs to be advised of any litigation risks (including self-incrimination) that might arise from waiving privilege, but the decision is entirely your client's, and there is no basis upon which you can prevent waiver. In this sort of situation you may want to consider whether you are sufficiently independent or whether there is a risk of a conflict between your interests in the matter and your client's. It may therefore be sensible and proper to recommend that your client seeks independent legal advice on the question whether the document is privileged, and whether any such privilege should be waived.

The second question is whether your advice falls within the crime/fraud exception. This has been construed widely enough to include civil as well as criminal fraud and other purposes 'of effecting iniquity'.[88] Quite how far the courts would be prepared to take this idea of iniquity is open to question, and there is apparently no English authority directly on the situation raised by this exercise. Nevertheless, it seems to us that there is an arguable point here. Document destruction could amount to an attempt to pervert the course of justice or (if the documents are destroyed after proceedings have commenced) contempt of court.[89] If, on the facts, a policy of destroying documents constitutes an attempt to pervert the course of justice or a (criminal) contempt, it seems reasonable to suggest that the document initiating that policy could itself fall within the crime/fraud exception, provided it clearly advocates a criminal policy – if it does not go that far and simply delegates those policy decisions in-house, then we think it

87. [2004] EWCA Civ 330.    88. *Barclays Bank plc v Eustice* [1995] 4 All ER 511.
89. Cp. the discussion in the Court of Appeal of Victoria, Australia, in *British American Tobacco Australia Ltd v Cowell* [2002] VSCA 197.

doubtful that privilege would be lost from *this* document. Responsibility for any criminal acts would most likely remain in-house. So, again, the decision very much turns on what the document actually says.

Obviously, this is a very technical legal problem, but underlying it there are significant issues of ethics. Remember that, as a lawyer (whether in-house or external counsel) advising on a document retention policy, you cannot advise your client to do what is not lawful. To do so is clearly contrary to basic principles of professional conduct.

Even if your and your client's actions are not clearly unlawful, there is still a larger ethical question. Should lawyers use confidentiality and privilege to mask what many ordinary people would see as evasions of corporate social responsibility?

This seems to be one of those areas that begs questions about where we draw the line between an amoral and an immoral professionalism. There is a real danger that these sorts of practices reinforce the view that, as Melinkoff hints, lawyers will simply prostitute themselves to anyone prepared to pay a fat enough fee. The reality to be fair is probably more complex than that. Sometimes we can get so caught up with the relationships and the process of just doing the work, that we lose objectivity. As Eames J observed in the Victorian Supreme Court's decision in the *McCabe* case, 'the long-standing and very close association between in-house lawyers [at BAT] and private practitioners had the potential for blurring the roles and responsibilities of lawyers'.[90] Sometimes we may simply cave in to pressure from powerful patronage clients; sometimes, perhaps most worrying of all, we may experience a complete moral 'blind spot' and not see that there could be anything dubious in our actions. Should the profession issue guidance on this matter? Is even more regulation the answer? Discuss this in your groups.

### Summary so far

- Remember that your duty to the court can override your duty to your client.
- You owe the court a duty of candour.
- You must, under the CPR, assist the court to deal with cases justly.
- You owe your client a strong and continuing duty of confidentiality, which is supported in litigation by the doctrine of legal professional privilege.
- But be aware of the limits of both confidentiality and privilege.
- Think carefully about the ethics of the everyday things you do: the 'little lies' and obfuscations; our capacity to use our skills to manipulate our clients and others, often in

---

90. *McCabe v British American Tobacco* [2002] VSC 73; reversed in *British American Tobacco Australia Ltd v Cowell* [2002]VSCA 197. As a result of *McCabe*, however, the Victoria state legislature introduced s. 142A of the Legal Profession Regulation 2002, prohibiting lawyers from destroying or moving or advising a client to destroy or move relevant documents where proceedings are 'likely' to be commenced.

quite 'minor' matters; the way we prioritise some relationships over others; the capacity we have to lose our objectivity. All of these can undermine our professional integrity.

## Trouble on the High Street – Part 3

In this last part of the case study we turn to the remaining 'big issue' of professional conduct – conflicts of interest. Quantitatively, at least, conflicts are one of the most important aspects of professional conduct. Empirical research both here and in the US emphasises that conflicts of interest are a pervasive problem.[91] As legal practice becomes more specialised, potential conflicts arise in those niche areas where clients are all chasing the services of the relatively few individuals and firms with the expertise to do the work. Solicitors themselves can also become a source of role conflict, for example, by moving firm, or getting financially or managerially involved in their client's business. With Exercise 6.10 we begin the discussion by exploring a fairly common example of a conflicts problem.

EXERCISE **6.10  Bayview strikes again**

A colleague from your firm's tax department phones you to say that she had heard you were acting against Bayview. She asks whether you realised that, up until three years ago, Bayview was called RLW Property Inc. Ltd and had used this firm for some tax advice, and one or two small litigious matters. Your firm have not acted for Bayview since the change of name. Your colleague questions whether, as a result, you are 'conflicted' in your representation. You immediately see this as a way out of your quandary and call Jason to tell him that you will have to cease acting for him in this transaction, as you have just discovered that it creates a conflict of interest for your firm. Jason is not happy, and cannot understand why there is a problem: after all, your firm no longer acts for Bayview, and you were never involved in that work anyway. In fact, Jason adds, how can there be a conflict when Bayview and his company not only want the same thing, but Jason's sister, Eloise, is about to join the board of Bayview as a non-executive director, and wants to suggest that you act for *both* Bayview and Jason's company in seeing this deal through. At this point you ask Jason to excuse you for a moment, and you put your telephone down while you decide who to call first: the Law Society's ethics helpline, or the Samaritans . . .

(a)   *Define in general terms what 'conflicts of interest' means in the context of professional legal ethics.*

(b)   *What are the conflicts problems created by this question?*

---

91. Unusually for the ethics literature, there are two book-length empirical studies: J. Griffiths-Baker, *Serving Two Masters: Conflicts of Interest in the Modern Law Firm*, Hart Publishing, Oxford, 2002; and S. Shapiro, *Tangled Loyalties: Conflict of Interest in Legal Practice*, University of Michigan Press, Ann Arbor, Mich., 2002; see reviews respectively by J. Flood (2003) 66 *Modern Law Review* 944 and J. Webb (2003) 30 *Journal of Law & Society* 472.

(c)    *How would you propose resolving those problems in this case? Discuss this in your groups and make a note of your preferred solutions before you read on.*

## Conflicts of interest

The basic notion of a conflict of interest is quite simple:[92] a lawyer should not represent a client where the material interests of that client are opposed either to her own interests, or to the interests of another client. The conflict of interest rules exist (in theory at least) to reinforce lawyer fidelity to clients and to protect client autonomy.[93]

Turning to the facts of Exercise 6.10: you are told that your firm has ceased acting for Bayview, so it seems that the matter starts out as a problem of what we would call 'successive representation'. Principle 15.02 LSG precludes a solicitor or a firm of solicitors from acting against an existing or former client once that client has imparted confidential information to her/them. There is no time limit to this duty, so it prevents firms from taking on new business from prospective clients where that would create an actual or potential conflict with the interests of an existing or former client. The critical issue, however, is not just whether your firm has acted for Bayview, but whether it has, in the process, acquired relevant confidential information about that client. By relevant, of course, we mean relevant to this later, potentially conflicting, transaction. All we know here is that Bayview, in its former guise, had used your firm for both tax and litigation advice. So, on the face of it, these are different kinds of matter, but that still does not preclude the possibility that your firm might hold confidential financial information on Bayview that could, for example, give you an unfair advantage over them in negotiations. Strictly, if there is such a conflict you should withdraw. In this way the conflict rules protect you from having to balance or choose between two general and potentially conflicting duties: to preserve the confidentiality of your former client (Bayview) *and* to disclose all relevant information to your existing client, Jason. However, in practice, some law firms would seek the consent of both parties and continue to act by creating an internal 'information barrier' or 'Chinese Wall' within the firm, to stop confidential information being shared inappropriately.[94] Under the letter of the existing LSG, this strategy is allowed in only very limited circumstances, and not in the case we have described here.

Does it make any difference that you have never acted for Bayview personally? Again, strictly, no, it does not under the present rules. Subject to some very limited exceptions, the conflict generally binds the firm not just the individual solicitor. Nowadays, most firms use computerised or manual conflict tracking systems to try and identify cases where there is a risk of successive representation problems. In

92. For similar definitions, see Boon and Levin, *The Ethics and Conduct of Lawyers in England and Wales*, p. 267; Griffiths-Baker, *Serving Two Masters*, p. 1.
93. Boon and Levin, *ibid.*, p. 267.    94. See Griffiths-Baker, *Serving Two Masters*.

this instance yours does not seemed to have worked, perhaps because no one has picked up Bayview's change of name.

Let's turn now to Eloise and Jason's suggestion that you act for both entities. This would potentially turn our conflict into a 'simultaneous representation' problem. However, that does not make the situation any better! Technically, it would create what we call a 'same matter' conflict, that is, one where you are seeking to represent separate clients who have or are likely to have 'adverse' or opposing interests in the same matter. In this case, given the information you have already have about Jason's behaviour in this transaction (see Exercise 6.6), there is strong evidence that the interests of the two parties *are* adverse, and you should refuse to act for both, with a quiet word to Jason, explaining why! In this context, the conflicts principle thus seems entirely appropriate and commonsensical: you cannot act in the best interests of two people whose interests conflict with each other.

That said, the existing conflicts rules have been widely criticised as too restrictive and overly complicated. Applying the conflicts rules has been complicated by the fact that there is a lot of case law which address the fiduciary principles and legal implications of conflicts of interest independently from the generally higher standards imposed by the professional code of conduct.[95] The rules in the LSG also tend, it is sometimes said, too readily to *assume* that the interests of each side to a transaction are necessarily opposed. They therefore, perhaps unfairly, preclude the possibility of the parties consenting to joint representation with adequate information safeguards in appropriate cases.

The Law Society has finally bowed to pressure, particularly from commercial firms, for a change in the rules. A new draft Practice Rule 16D[96] proposes aligning the professional rules more closely to the Common Law standard,[97] which already operates a principle of allowing joint representation, provided there is a common interest between the parties and 'informed consent' to such transactional representation. The new rules and guidance also extend the legitimate use of information barriers, and spell out for the first time the steps firms should take to make them effective. Information on the new rules will appear on our website as they come into force.

In addition to the generic rules we have looked at here, there are other rules governing conflicts in specific contexts – notably in respect of some solicitor-client conflicts and in regard to conveyancing transactions – which restrict the possibility of joint representation in such areas of practice. Even if the proposed reforms take

---

95. This overlap has evolved because the fiduciary principles are used specifically by the courts to prevent disclosure of confidential information, or to avoid transactions tainted by a conflict of interests. By contrast, as we have seen, the conduct rules are a disciplinary matter only. The fiduciary rules also apply to a range of professional service providers, not just lawyers. Note that the duties under the CCB are much closer to the Common Law position than many of the existing LSG principles.

96. See [Draft] Solicitors Practice (Conflict) Amendment Rule [2004] (15 July 2004).

97. See notably the leading case of *Prince Jefri Bolkiah v KPMG* [1999] 2 AC 222. See also *Loch Shipping v Richards Butler* [2002] EWCA Civ 1280 for a useful summary of the principles to be applied following *Bolkiah*.

effect, a number of these specific rules are retained, so the regulations are likely to remain quite complex.

*Summary*

- Your are under a duty not to act, or if necessary to withdraw from acting, where your representation creates a conflict of interest.
- Conflicts may arise either between your own interests and those of your client, or between the interests of two different clients.
- Conflicts between clients may arise out of either successive or simultaneous representation.
- In some exceptional circumstances joint representation does not create a conflict of interest, or the conflict may be avoided by the creation of 'information barriers' within the firm.

Conflicts of interest are probably the most obviously 'regulatory' of the rules we have considered. Many ethicists would not treat conflicts as generating significant ethical as opposed to regulatory problems. As we have sought to show, this is less true of the other problems we have explored in this chapter, which may be particularly troubling because they generate not just rule- but value-conflicts for us.

Sometimes it may even seem that the conduct rules provide the least ethical help when it is most needed – in the 'grey' areas within and between the rules, and in those areas where the biggest gaps between professional and 'ordinary' morality occur. This lead us to the next theme of this chapter.

## Should we rethink legal ethics?

We have so far looked at ethical dilemmas largely from within the framework established by the codes of conduct. We have suggested a number of specific ways in which that framework might be deemed problematic; we have even touched on, but not yet discussed, some of the problems underlying that conceptual framework. What we have probably left you with, so far, is a certain amount of bewilderment. Here are a lot of rules that seem to be of difficult if not downright doubtful application; the underlying rationale may not always seem clear; you may even be thinking, what have these rules actually got to do with ethics anyway! As a way into getting rather more clarity about the issues and problems with legal ethics, we can begin by thinking a little more carefully about the nature of ethical problems and decision-making.

### Ethics and problem-solving

Let's begin the inquiry by thinking about the kinds of problems which you have just observed and experienced, and the extent to which they create genuine ethical dilemmas rather than mere technical problems for us. We use the term 'dilemma' quite deliberately here. The crux of a *real* ethical dilemma is that, for some reason (e.g. the absence of moral principles, or a conflict of duties, or some value uncertainty/conflict) we do not know what morality requires of us.[98] Many apparent ethical dilemmas in practice are not dilemmas, nor are they particularly about ethics. As we have already seen, if I know what is the right or good thing to do, and I am under pressure (from my client or whoever) to do something else, that is not an ethical dilemma. I know what is the ethical thing to do; the problem is simply whether I choose to do it. Knowing the ethical solution is relatively easy; choosing it may be less so!

Real conflicts of duties should be fairly rare *within the framework of a codified ethics,*[99] not least because well-designed codes usually attempt to construct rules of priority (e.g. 'the duty to the court trumps the duty to the client') to prevent a true dilemma from arising, or offer overriding ethical principles which provide guidance in resolving conflicts or ambiguities in the rules. But what about where the conflict or uncertainty exists between the duties laid down in the code and your personal morality, what do you do?

EXERCISE 6.11 **My station and its duties**

Assume that you are a barrister. You have been asked to defend the leader of a small and highly radical black separatist organisation. At the end of a public meeting in Birmingham last week he was reported as warning ' . . . the white man and his Indian lackey, if you try to keep us in your ghettoes, we will put you in your graves'. He has been charged with the offence of inciting racial hatred. From the case papers it seems unlikely your client has a substantive defence. However, it is equally clear that there are procedural flaws which could offer you a technical defence that would lead to the charges being dropped.

(a) *Would you take the brief? If so why, if not why not?*
(b) *If you take the brief, will you try to get the charges thrown out on a technicality or not? Consider your answer from the perspective of (i) the code of conduct and (ii) 'ordinary' or 'common' morality.*
(c) *What values do you think you are prioritising in making your decision?*
(d) *Why are you prioritising them? Give reasons.*
(e) *If possible, contrast your answers with those of other members of your group. What conclusions can you draw from this about the scope of 'role' and 'common' morality?*

As a 'pure' professional conduct problem, this is not particularly difficult. What may make it more difficult for some people, though not necessarily everyone, is the potential conflict between what seems to be required by the role morality, and what may be acceptable to general moral beliefs and principles – what we have called common morality. In resolving the ethical dimension of this problem, we need to think about what it means when we say there is a separate sphere of 'professional

98. E. Lemmon, 'Moral Dilemmas' (1962) 71 *Philosophical Review* 139–58.
99. This qualifier (in italics) is important for reasons that will soon become apparent.

morality'. In essence this seems to involve two claims: (i) that there is a morality that attaches to that role; and (ii) that morality is distinguishable from any ordinary or personal moral principles we may hold. This idea is characterised in ethical theory by the 'separatist thesis'.[100] Separatism is not necessarily an argument for amoral professionalism. But it does argue that ends, which may not be morally justified on their own or as a part of 'ordinary ethics', may be justified by the profession's own moral values. On this basis one could argue that there should be no real clash between personal and professional ethics, since the latter can operate within a sphere that is autonomous. There is thus nothing wrong with us saying that our morality responsibility is, in practice, defined by the ethical code and the underlying legal rules, and nothing more. It is therefore fine to represent a client belonging to an extremist political group advocating, say, class war or racist violence, so long as that client does not require you to do anything illegal or contrary to the code. This is an attractive argument at one level, since it does prevent each of us behaving like a kind of moral police, and creating a situation where unpopular causes potentially go unrepresented, and, as we hinted once before, there is a bottom line: to put it bluntly, if you don't like the morality, don't take-on the role: indeed, as Beyleveld and Brownsword put it, 'the failure to observe the role-morality is a failure to play the role'.[101] No-one made you become a lawyer.

On the other hand, legal ethicists question this emphasis on role morality, at least as it plays out in the standard conception of neutral partisanship. There is a concern that separatism actually discourages actors from questioning their (and their profession's) underlying framing of the role. It is also inclined to emphasise social conformity over (individual) moral integrity and may too readily allow people to escape moral responsibility for their actions not just through a simple and unthinking allegiance to the role but, in an increasingly bureaucratic culture, by allowing responsibility to fall 'between the players'.[102] Particularly through its emphasis on the role morality of neutral partisanship, it can require lawyers to be no more than amoral technicians: it breeds a compliance culture; narrowly concerned with interpreting and applying technical obligations, rather than asking whether the activities expected of a lawyer are good or bad. There is a growing sense in the ethics literature that this is problematic. As we have seen, lawyers are not generally required or expected to put wider third party or public interests before the interests of their clients, even where their clients may possess, perhaps even have disclosed to their lawyer, information about the whereabouts of a missing body, a pending financial crisis or the causes behind environmental or public health disasters.[103]

100. See A. Gewirth, 'Professional Ethics: The Separatist Thesis' (1986) 96 *Ethics* 282.
101. *Law as a Moral Judgment*, Sweet & Maxwell, London, 1986, p. 408.
102. See Luban, *Lawyers and Justice*, pp. 121–4.
103. See, e.g., Simon, *The Practice of Justice*, pp. 4–7; Boon and Levin, *The Ethics and Conduct of Lawyers in England and Wales*, pp. 211–13; Nicolson and Webb, *Professional Legal Ethics*, pp. 107–9, 111 and 272–5 (indicating how harm to others could play a bigger role within a contextual approach to ethics).

This brings us back to the questions of our own moral autonomy. Like it or not, whatever the theory says, we are exposed to being associated *morally* with both the causes we represent and the way we represent them. Many ordinary people simply do not seem to find the theory that lawyers are morally non-accountable plausible. Moreover, there is a concern that this amoralism can spill over into our personal lives 'becoming its own impoverished morality by default'.[104]

To be fair, the target here is not all role morality *per se*. Even the sternest critics seem to accept the *prima facie* validity of some notion of role-differentiation, while expressing concern at some of its grosser manifestations. One particular target is its translation into a detailed, disciplinary code of conduct. Codification encourages what William Simon calls a 'categorical' approach to ethical decision-making:

> Such decision-making severely restricts the range of considerations the decisionmaker may take into account when she confronts a particular problem; a rigid rule dictates a particular response in the presence of a small number of factors. The decisionmaker has no discretion to consider factors that are not specified or to evaluate specified factors in ways other than those prescribed by the rule.[105]

By removing this essential feature of discretion it is said, a codified ethics anesthetises moral conscience.[106] It also puts lawyer and client into separate moral universes, neither needing to engage with the values of the other.

A number of the writers we have already discussed argue against this categorical model.[107] Drawing on a number of different ethical theories[108] that are critical of the conventional duty-based approach, they take the view that, if we are to improve the ethical performance of the legal profession, we do not need more rules, more strictly enforced. This does not mean that they want lawyers to be publically *un*accountable for what they do. It does mean that they are trying to construct a different approach, which requires lawyers to engage more deeply with the ethical nature of the role. Their plea is thus for a much more 'situational' or 'contextual' approach. This kind of approach seems more in line with the emphasis on contextual reasoning and reflection that is found in modern applied ethics, where it is said that:

---

104. A. Hutchinson, 'Legal Ethics for a Fragmented Society: Between Personal and Professional' (1998) 5 *International Journal of the Legal Profession* 175 at p. 186.
105. Simon, *The Practice of Justice*, p. 9.
106. D. Nicolson, 'Mapping Professional Legal Ethics: The Form and Focus of the Codes' (1998) *Legal Ethics* 51 at p. 67.
107. Chiefly, Simon's work in the US, Hutchinson's work in Canada, and Nicolson and Webb's writing in the UK. Compare also C. Sampford and S. Blencowe, 'Educating Lawyers to be Ethical Advisers' in Economides (ed.), *Ethical Challenges to Legal Education and Conduct*, p. 315 at pp. 330–4. Stan Ross's work in Australia shares some characteristics with these critiques, though it also starts from a significantly different premise – essentially reflecting a 'gnostic' (religious or spiritual) perspective on lawyering. See S. Ross, *Ethics in Law: Lawyers' Responsibility and Accountability in Australia*, Butterworths, Sydney, 1998.
108. Such as virtue ethics, feminist ethics – particularly the ethic of care, and postmodern perspectives on ethics; see Nicolson and Webb, *Professional Legal Ethics*, ch. 2 for an overview of these traditions.

>The methods which applied ethics can make its own may be compared to those of a designer who starts with a blueprint, but has to adapt it to the materials to hand and to the situations in which it is required.[109]

These critical perspectives share a number of features:

- They emphasise the importance of morally activist lawyering – i.e. that lawyers are implicated in both the means and ends of representation, and should, if necessary, engage clients in moral dialogue about those means and ends.
- They tend to emphasise the development of moral character, and the significance of education in developing moral character more than traditional approaches.
- They tend to reject neutral partisanship as a universal characterisation of the lawyer's role. In this sense they adopt a much more pluralistic approach to the underlying values of lawyering.
- They do not necessarily reject the idea of a codified ethics, but they tend to have a different approach to the regulation of ethical responsibilities from the existing codes (though perhaps closer in spirit to what the Law Society's Regulation Review Working Party originally set out to achieve). This is often framed in terms of a greater emphasis on general principles, allowing for more contextual reasoning in specific situations.[110] It may also focus less on minimum (disciplinary) standards of conduct and more on 'aspirational' or 'best practice' standards. The aim of such endeavours is explicitly to create what May calls 'an ethic of responsibility' that demands 'a wide discretion concerning what is required to be a responsible person, rather than an emphasis on keeping an abstract commandment or rule'.[111]

While these critical approaches are becoming more the orthodoxy in legal ethics scholarship, they have had limited impact on the real world of practice to date. In aiming for high aspirational standards, in regulation, education and professional decision-making, they are open to the criticism of setting targets that are too hard for the professions to meet,[112] or are just unrealistic in the harsh commercial environment that exists today. At the same time, we know that there are already lawyers who aspire to styles of lawyering that draw on different values from the modern orthodoxy of professionalism.[113]

---

109. B. Almond, *Introducing Applied Ethics*, Blackwell, Oxford, 1994, p. 8.
110. This could take a number of different forms, from a more traditional 'Platonic' approach, which might attempt to create a hierarchical structure of principles, duties and obligations – an approach which seems to have been influential in shaping 'principled' approaches to bio-ethics (see T. Beauchamp and J. Childress, *Principles of Biomedical Ethics*, Oxford University Press, New York, 5th edn, 2001) to more 'postmodern' approaches which propose a multi-layered approach identifying underlying values, general principles and 'contextual factors' which should be taken into account when making decisions (see, e.g., Nicolson and Webb, *Professional Legal Ethics*. pp. 280–3).
111. L. May, *The Socially Responsive Self: Social Theory and Professional Ethics*, University of Chicago Press, Chicago, 1996, p. 88.
112. See, e.g., Griffiths-Baker, *Serving Two Masters*, p. 185.
113. See, e.g., N. Cahn, 'Styles of Lawyering' (1992) 43 *Hastings Law Journal* 1039; S. Scheingold and A. Bloom, 'Transgressive Cause Lawyering: Practice Sites and the Politicization of the Professional' (1998) 5 *International Journal of the Legal Profession* 209.

Should we be aspiring to a more ethical professionalism? That is for each of you to decide in your own lives, whether you practice law or enter a different field. We all have to address our ethics and values at some point in our lives, and whether you practice law or not, your own values will have been influenced by your experience at law school. We simply leave you with an observation from an essay written by an American law student, a paper incidentally much influenced by an 'ethic of care' perspective:

> I cannot be sure that thinking about the world differently will change it, but I can be sure that apathy will doom me to an existence of perpetual submission . . . Who knows what we may discover in ourselves and others if we learn to break free of the myriad, repressive, ideological, constructs we have internalised and justified for so many years. Of course there are risks. Who knows whether we will inadvertently box ourselves into new and equally stifling ideologies in our attempts to break free from old ones? I don't. But I do find using fear of the unknown to justify inaction . . . pathetic and offensive.[114]

EXERCISE **6.12  Concepts**

In this chapter we have discussed a number of concepts. We list the main ones below. The procedure for learning these concepts is as follows:

1. *Divide into pairs.*
2. *Each pair is to:*
   (a) *define each concept, noting the page on which it is discussed, and*
   (b) *make sure that both members of the pair understand the meaning of each concept.*
3. *Combine into groups of four. Compare the answers of the two pairs. If there is disagreement, look up the concept and clarify it until all agree on the definition and understand it.*

| | |
|---|---|
| *Ethics* | *Separatist thesis* |
| *Values* | *Moral activism* |
| *Neutral partisan* | *Conflicts of interest* |
| *Cab rank principle* | *Duty of candour* |

EXERCISE **6.13  Review questions**

1. *Legal education, according to Roger Cramton, suffers from:*

   > *. . . a pragmatism tending toward an amoral instrumentalism . . . an individualism tending toward atomism, and a faith in reason and democratic processes tending toward mere credulity . . .*[115]

---

114. K. Worden, 'Overshooting the Target: A Feminist Deconstruction of Legal Education' (1985) 34 *American University Law Review* 1141 at p. 1165.
115. 'The Ordinary Religion of the Law School Classroom' (1978) 29 *Journal of Legal Education* 247 at p. 262.

    (a) *What does Cramton mean by this? Refer to his article, and your notes on this chapter.*

    (b) *Do you agree?*

2.   *Elvis Presley reputedly said 'values are like fingerprints. Nobody's are the same, but you leave 'em over everything you do.'*

    *Discuss this statement in the light of the issues raised by this chapter.*

3.   *In looking at your duties to the court and the client in litigation, we focused on civil proceedings. Assume for now that you exclusively undertake criminal defence work:*

    (a) *Do you think as a criminal defence advocate you are more or less entitled to act as a 'zealous advocate' for your client. Why?*

    (b) *You are the duty solicitor representing a client in a shoplifting case before the magistrates. Your client has admitted to you that he has a number of previous convictions for theft of which the prosecution are unaware. Your client has not disclosed that he has changed his name since his last prosecution two years ago, and his 'alias' has not been picked up by criminal records. Your client intends to plead guilty to the charge. The case is about to be called.*

    *Do you (please give your reasons):*

    i. *Say nothing and offer mitigation on the basis that your client is a first offender?*

    ii. *Say nothing but make no reference to his apparent lack of offending in mitigation?*

    iii. *Disclose the error to the prosecution before the case is called?*

    iv. *Withdraw and advise the client to find another solicitor?*

4.   *At the start of the chapter we asked:*

    ● *Are the ethical standards of lawyers something we are right to be concerned about?*

    ● *Should all law students learn something about the ethics of the profession as part of a law degree or equivalent course?*

    ● *Can teaching professional ethics, either on the LLB or in vocational training, make a difference to the ethical standards of lawyers once they get into practice?*

    *Without looking at your previous answers, write out answers afresh to these questions. Now compare these with your original answers. What have you learnt?*

## Further reading

A. Boon and J. Levin, *The Ethics and Conduct of Lawyers in England and Wales*, Hart Publishing, Oxford, 1999.

D. Nicolson and J. Webb, *Professional Legal Ethics: Critical Interrogations*, Oxford University Press, Oxford, 1999.

R. O'Dair, *Legal Ethics: Text & Materials*, Butterworths, London, 2001.

W. Simon, *The Practice of Justice: A Theory of Lawyers' Ethics*, Harvard University Press, Cambridge, Mass., 1998.

# 7

## Clarifying language: making sense of writing

All of you who read this book are experienced writers. But how well do you write? This can only be judged by looking at a text through the eyes of the reader. You will analyse a number of texts to identify their audiences and purposes. We encourage you to pick out organisational and linguistic features which clarify or obscure meaning. We explore the concepts of correctness, appropriateness and standard English. We provide exercises and examples which allow you to reflect on, articulate and develop your tacit knowledge of how to write clearly, concisely and correctly.

## Objectives

To:

- Identify and describe differences between the spoken and written language.
- Recognise different styles of writing and judge when each is appropriate.
- Identify strengths and weaknesses in your writing and develop strategies for improvement where necessary.
- Plan your writing to take account of the needs of your reader.
- Emphasise the need for clarity and the value of plain English at all times.
- Use style, grammar and vocabulary which is appropriate to your task.

## Supports benchmark statements

Students should demonstrate a basic ability:

### 6. Communication and literacy

- To understand and use the English language proficiently in relation to legal matters.
- To present knowledge or an argument in a way which is comprehensible to others and which is directed at their concerns.
- To read and discuss legal materials which are written in technical and complex language.

## Why it is important to write well

Practising lawyers and law students spend a lot of their time writing. By now, you are well-versed in the skills of legal discourse (the language and method of reasoning used by lawyers), practising it constantly in essays, problem analyses, exam answers and lecture notes. It has become part of your tacit knowledge.

These forms of writing are read and evaluated by your tutors, who are themselves lawyers. As practising lawyers, however, you will also be writing for others who are not familiar with the language and reasoning of the law.

EXERCISE 7.1  **What, when and why?**

*List the forms of written communication you think you will need in your work as a lawyer. Then compare your list with ours which follows.*
    You will need to be able to:

- Take a clear, comprehensible set of *notes* (in what circumstances, and why?).
- Write *letters* which the recipients (who are they?) will understand.
- *Draft* (compose) *legal documents* (such as, and who for?).
- Write *opinions* (barristers) (who for?).

As we saw in Chapter 3, communication is about getting the message you want across to your recipient. Developing a fluent written style will save you and your reader a lot of time, irritation and misunderstanding . . .

Figure 7.1a

. . . with writing, you don't get a second chance to get your message across . . .

Figure 7.1b

EXERCISE 7.2 **Which is dense? The reader or the text?**

Below are three written texts. For each one:

(a)  *Read quickly to discover the meaning, then more carefully to get the detail.*
(b)  *Did you sort out the meaning after:*
   *(i)  the first reading?*
   *(ii)  the second reading?*
(c)  *Who do you think are the intended readers?*
(d)  *Note down which features you think make the text difficult to understand, giving reasons.*

1. Where particulars of a partnership are disclosed to the Executive Council the remuneration of the individual partner for superannuation purposes will be deemed to be such proportion of the total remuneration of such practitioners as the proportion of his share in partnership profits bears to the total proportion of the shares of such practitioner in those profits.[1]

2. SECTION 21, CONSUMER PROTECTION ACT 1987
   Meaning of 'misleading'
   21(1) For the purposes of section 20 above an indication given to any consumers is misleading as to a price if what is conveyed by the indication, or what those consumers might reasonably be expected to infer from the indication or any omission from it, includes any of the following, that is to say –

1. Taken from Sir Ernest Gowers, *The Complete Plain Words*, Penguin, London, 1986, p. 2.

(a) that the price is less than in fact it is;

(b) that the applicability of the price does not depend on facts or circumstances on which its applicability does in fact depend;

(c) that the price covers matters in respect of which an additional charge is in fact made;

(d) that a person who in fact has no such expectation –

    (i) expects the price to be increased or reduced (whether or not at a particular time or by a particular amount); or

    (ii) expects the price, or the price as increased or reduced, to be maintained (whether or not for a particular period); or

(e) that the facts or circumstances by reference to which the consumers might reasonably be expected to judge the validity of any relevant comparison made or implied by the indication are not what in fact they are.

3.  . . . ideas which stress the growing importance of international co-operation and new theories of economic sovereignty across a wide range of areas – macro-economics, trade, the environment, the growth of post neo-classical endogenous growth theory and the symbiotic relationships between growth and investment in people and infra-structure, a new understanding of how labour markets really work and the rich and controversial debate over the meaning and importance of competitiveness at the level of individuals, the firm or the nation and the role of government in fashioning modern industrial policies which focus on maintaining competitiveness.[2]

**Analysis of text 1**

This text was written for ordinary people, not experts. Writing like this is inefficient, because the writer, or someone else, will have to take time to explain the meaning. Why is it so difficult to grasp the meaning on a first reading?

First of all, it is all one sentence (57 words), so that by the time you get to the end, you have forgotten the beginning.

Secondly, any sentence should contain one or more verbs. These tell you what is happening, to whom, where, when, etc. Verbs give life and movement to the ideas being expressed. In this text there are only three verb phrases:

*. . . are disclosed . . .*
*. . . will be deemed to be . . .*
*. . . bears . . .*

2.  Taken from a speech made by Shadow Chancellor Gordon Brown and quoted in the *Daily Mail*, 28 September 1994, and the *Guardian*, 7 December 1994. The *Guardian* further reported that Gordon Brown won the Plain English Campaign No Nonsense Award 1994 for this 'long-winded drivel'. It appears the speech might have been composed by a researcher, Ed Balls. This prompted then President of the Board of Trade Michael Heseltine to announce to the 1994 Tory Conference: 'It wasn't Brown's – it was Balls'.' (See *Daily Mail*, 7 December 1994).

Furthermore, the first two are passive verbs. Active verbs are made passive by inverting subject and object and changing the form of the verb, as in the following example:

ACTIVE: *The dog* (subject) *bit* (verb) *the man* (object);
PASSIVE: *The man* (now the subject) *was bitten* (verb) *by the dog* (now called the agent!).

Although these two sentences appear to have the same meaning, the passive draws your attention to what happened at the expense of the person or thing carrying out the action. It therefore has the effect of making the message impersonal. Moreover, the passive form increases the length and complexity of the sentence. This may make it more difficult to understand.

In 'officialese' often no subject is expressed, so that the active form can't be used. Try putting this phrase from Text 1 into the active form:

Where particulars of a partnership are disclosed to the Executive Council...

Congratulations if you managed it and it still sounds acceptable. We couldn't. This device of omitting the subject is common in such writing. It gives the impression that a sequence of actions takes place without any human intervention causing them, or seeing them to a conclusion. This is why such writing seems to represent the cold, remote, inhuman face of bureaucracy. Moreover, there is no obvious person to blame when things go wrong!

Thirdly, Text 1 makes up for the lack of verbs with cumbersome and complicated noun phrases:

... *particulars of a partnership*...
... *the remuneration of the individual partner for superannuation purposes*...
... *such proportion of the total remuneration of such practitioners*...
... *the proportion of his share in partnership profits*...
... *the total proportion of the shares of such practitioner*...

The effect is to make the meaning obscure, and the content dry and uninteresting. It reads like a list rather than a series of dynamically connected ideas.

We suggest the following plainer English translation, but only tentatively: we aren't sure the meaning is right. We use 'your' because this text is taken from a reply to a letter of inquiry.

*Your superannuable income will be proportionate to your share in the partnership profits.*

Sir Ernest Gowers suggests the following as a possible meaning:

*Your income will be taken to be the same proportion of the firm's remuneration as you used to get of its profits.*

You will see that we don't agree on the meaning of the text. Is it because we are stupid, or because the text is incomprehensible?

**Analysis of text 2**

The paragraphing and numbering in this text aids clarity to the extent that a large block of print is broken into smaller blocks which are easier on the eye. However, smaller chunks do not make the text any more digestible. Why not?

The main point of the text is made in the first few lines. The rest is a list of situations which qualify the main point. We assume that the intention of the writer in sub-dividing the points was to make the message clearer, but the use of subordinate clauses (sentences within sentences) and repetitions spoils the intention. The effect is to pack in far too much information to grasp at a first reading.

Unlike Text 1, this text is written for experts who will take time to scrutinise it in great detail to discover its meaning and check for ambiguity. The drafter therefore has to ensure that the text is precise, unambiguous and comprehensive. She will use words and phrases that have acquired special meanings through legal convention and precedent. For example:

> *For the purposes of section 20 above . . .*

In the view of Sir Ernest Gowers:

> If it is readily intelligible, so much the better; but it is far more important that it should yield its meaning accurately than that it should yield it on first reading, and legal draftsmen cannot afford to give much attention, if any, to euphony or literary elegance. What matters most to them is that no one will succeed in persuading a court of law that their words bear a meaning they did not intend, and, if possible, that no one will think it worth while to try.
>
> All this means that their drafting is not to be judged by normal standards of good writing . . . [3]

Do you agree with this view? We will be looking in detail at the language of legal documents in Chapter 8.

**Analysis of text 3**

We would like to put Text 3 into plain English for you, but we don't know what it means. This is the kind of obfusc babblegab you will probably have come across in articles and textbooks, and which we hope you do not imitate!

Much of the discussion we had about Text 1 is relevant here. In a sentence (or part of a sentence) of 93 words, there are only three verbs: *stress, work, focus.* Ponderous and inelegant noun phrases proliferate, for example:

> . . . *the growth of post-neoclassical endogenous growth theory* . . .

There is a danger that once you allow these streams of noun phrases to pour forth, they form themselves into lists and give you little flexibility to vary the structure

---

3. Sir Ernest Gowers, *The Complete Plain Words*, p. 6.

and rhythm of your writing. This is, inevitably, a turn-off for the readers. Any stimulating ideas the writer intended to communicate have been lost in their expression.

The writer could liven the text up and make it more intelligible by breaking it into smaller units and using fewer abstract words and more verb phrases. How many people understand the terms 'post-neoclassical' and 'endogenous growth theory'? It's one thing to use these terms amongst the small group of people who understand them, it's quite another to use them in a speech intended for wider circulation. This speech was delivered to economists, but the writer must surely have anticipated that information on Labour Party economic policy would be widely reported.

Let's now look at a text that gets its message across in quite a different way

EXERCISE 7.3  **Lord Lucid**

Read Lord Denning's judgment in *Mitchell (George) (Chesterhall) Ltd v Finney Lock Seeds Ltd* (1982) 3 WLR 1036 (CA). In particular, read 1043A to 1045F and, in pairs, discuss the following:

(a)   *Who are the likely readers?*
(b)   *When this case reached the House of Lords, Lord Bridge referred to Lord Denning's 'uniquely colourful and graphic style'.[4] Using examples from the text, identify the features of this style and compare the text with those you studied in 7.2.*

This text is a brief summary of the law on exemption clauses, intended for other lawyers to read, so you might expect it to be as inelegant and unexciting as the texts in 7.2. On the contrary, one can't help wishing Lord Denning had written a textbook on contract law. What makes it such an enjoyable read?

It's enjoyable because it's not a struggle. Sentences are a reasonable length, and simple in structure. There are no surplus words or phrases. Lawyers deal in abstractions, and Lord Denning is no exception. However, he uses an old device to catch our imagination and keep our attention. He tells us a story of heroes and villains. The story is full of illustrations and imagery. He turns abstract concepts into images which become tangible and real to the reader. The notion of freedom of contract, which law students spend some hours conceptualising and attempting to understand, becomes an 'idol', worshipped by the legal establishment. The 'true construction of contracts' is a 'secret weapon' with which to stab the idol in the back:

> Faced with this abuse of power – by the strong against the weak – the judges did what they could to put a curb upon it. They still had before them the idol, 'freedom of contract'. They still knelt down and worshipped it, but they concealed under their cloaks a secret weapon. They used it to stab the idol in the back. This weapon was called 'the true construction of the contract'.[5]

---

4. (1983) 2 All ER 737 at 741.    5. At 1043.

Masses of verbs move the text along, and there is hardly an abstract noun phrase in sight.

What distinguishes this writer from those in 7.2 is the impression that this writer has a clear point of view about the subject. Is Lord Denning less objective than his colleagues in the House of Lords, with their 'indigestible' speeches? Or is he just more open about the values he brings to bear on his decisions?[6]

To reinforce the points made so far, we end this section with part of a bible story and Richard Wydick's translation of it into gobbledygook:

> [A]s the Lord commanded . . . he lifted up the rod and smote the waters of the river . . . and all the waters that were in the river were turned to blood. And the fish that were in the river died; and the river stank, and the Egyptians could not drink the waters of the river; and there was blood throughout all the land of Egypt. (Exodus 8:7)

Here is the information described in the language of a modern environmental impact report:

> In accordance with the directive theretofore received from higher authority, he caused the implement to come into contact with the water, whereupon a polluting effect was perceived. The consequent toxification reduced the conditions necessary for the sustenance of the indigenous population of aquatic vertebrates below the level of continued viability. Olfactory discomfort standards were substantially exceeded, and potability declined. Social, economic and political disorientation were experienced to an unprecedented degree.[7]

## Learning from your writing experience

The purpose of Exercise 7.2 was to encourage you to pick out characteristics of effective and ineffective writing. Those we identified which help to obscure meaning were:

| | |
|---|---|
| *Long sentences* | |
| *Complex sentences* | – passives |
| | – verbs turned into nouns/noun phrases (nominalisations) |
| | – subordinate clauses |
| *Repetition* | |
| *Difficult vocabulary* | – abstract concepts |
| | – technical terms |

It should now be clear that to get your message across you must have your readers and their feelings in mind. If the readers are bored, irritated, frustrated or switched off, they are less likely to be persuaded by the message – if indeed they can grasp it.

---

6. For further discussion on this point, see J. Holland and J. Webb, *Learning Legal Rules*, Oxford University Press, Oxford, 2003, pp. 118–21.
7. R. Wydick, 'Plain English for Lawyers' (1978) 66 *California Law Review* 727 at p. 737.

If you are faced with a text that you find almost impossible to grasp, don't lose confidence in your intellectual abilities. It may be that ideas expressed in some texts are intellectually very demanding, but in many cases the fault will lie with the writer. It is not that you are too stupid to grasp the thoughts of a great expert. Rather, obscure writing is at worst a sign of the writer's muddled thinking or pretentiousness, or at best the result of bad planning.

Think now about your own writing skills. You are all writers of 15 or more years of experience. Or have you had one year's experience 15 times over? Are you complacent about your writing ability? How consciously do you reflect on and refine your writing? Do you make the kinds of mistakes poor writers make? Do you write with your reader in mind? Writing is so much a part of our tacit knowledge that it is easy to take the skills involved for granted. Think about your essay-writing. Are your arguments fluent and clearly linked? If not, why not? Is it because you don't express yourself well, or because you haven't clearly thought them out, or a bit of both?

### EXERCISE 7.4 Do you suffer from verbal diarrhoea?

(a) *Choose a partner, and an extract from an essay you have written recently.*
  (i) *Read your text carefully.*
  (ii) *Note down which features aid or impede clarity, giving reasons.*
  (iii) *Give your text to your partner and ask her to do the same.*
  (iv) *Compare notes with your partner and discuss ways of improving your text.*
(b) *If you are still on speaking terms with your partner, carry out stages (a)(i)–(iv) with your partner's text.*
(c) *Make an entry in your learning diary. Make sure you include an action plan on what changes to make to the next piece of writing you draft.*
(d) *Remember to carry out your action plan.*

As we have seen, poor writing is a reflection of the writer's failure to take her readers into account. If you can, put yourself in your reader's shoes and imagine them being sympathetic to and interested in your message. In other words, write as if you are talking to your reader. One way of doing this is suggested by Jane Mace:

> To do this, I have to create the idea of a reader as if he or she were here in the room, nodding as I speak, disagreeing with what I say, asking me questions and prompting me to say more.[8]

The proficient writer's aim is therefore to make sure the reader understands the message easily and precisely. This involves:

---

8. J. Mace 'Writing and Power: Influence and Engagement on Adult Literacies' in D. Boud and N. Miller, *Working with Experience: Animating Learning*, Routledge, London, 1996, p. 173. See also Plain English Campaign, 'Suggestions for clear writing', *Plain English Course Workbook* 2002, p. 11.

---

- KNOWING EXACTLY WHAT YOU WANT TO SAY.
- SELECTING THE FORM OF ENGLISH THAT IS APPROPRIATE FOR THE READER AND THE PURPOSE.
- SAYING EXACTLY WHAT YOU MEAN TO SAY.

---

## Know exactly what you want to say

### EXERCISE 7.5  **The brick exercise**

*(a)   Briefly note down what you think are the main differences between the spoken and written language.*

*(b)   For this part of the exercise, follow your tutor's instructions.*

## Differences between the spoken and the written language

Many writers (does this include you?) think that in writing you use less common words and phrases. Why? They add formality, courtesy, dignity, and demonstrate the writer's high level of education, adherents to this mistaken belief might reply. Unfortunately, adherence to this view is the main source of gobbledygook and babblegab. We analysed some examples in Exercise 7.2. Here are some further examples of officialese:

> *Prior to collecting your vehicle, please ensure you pay for your parking at the machines located in each bus stop in the car park. Credit card payments in excess of £130 and payment by cheque can only be dealt with at the administration building situated at the exit.*
>
> *We are embarking on measures to resolve the issue at the earliest opportunity.*
>
> *Please ensure noise is restricted to an absolute minimum in the vicinity of the quiet study locations.*

The Brick Exercise should have demonstrated the necessity for clarity and precision in writing. Certain features which aid understanding in a conversation are absent from written communication. What are these missing features? You should remember them from Chapter 3.

- *Body language* This tells the participants the state of mind and level of understanding and interest of the other participants.
- *Prosodic features* These include stress, intonation, pauses and wordless sounds – *ugh, ooh, ouch, um*, which convey meanings such as disgust, surprise, excitement, embarrassment, the need for time to think, and so on.
- *Immediate response* In conversation, the participants can respond immediately to what is said, and a speaker can modify what she says in the light of that response.

It is this combination of body language, prosodic features and immediate response which makes speech so much easier to understand than writing. Whereas in speech you can think as you go along, in response to the reactions of your listener, when writing you need to get it right first time. To do that, you must think and plan in advance.

Since your aim will always be clarity and precision, as a general rule you should avoid less common words and phrases. Otherwise, your reader may think you pompous, ponderous, prolix and over-formal. This is not a good way to start or maintain a relationship.

## Planning

Research into successful writing strategies tells us that writing is not a linear process. Instead, writers use a circular, reflective approach:

> Perhaps the most powerful writing strategy is to take a problem-solving approach to writing which focuses on the three goals common to every writer: understanding of the issues to be discussed, effective communication of that understanding to the reader and persuading the reader to respond. Implicit in this approach is thinking the problem through, generating ideas and revising them, organising ideas in a logical framework, analysing the reader, monitoring whether the paper achieves the writer's goals and making the necessary changes.[9]

So why not begin by having a good think about the purpose of the communication?

**Why are you writing?**

What do you want to happen as a result of it? For example, are you writing to persuade a client to take a particular course of action? If so, your message must be sufficiently comprehensive and clear that the client can make a decision quickly, preferably with no need for further discussion.

**Who are you writing to?**

You will be more likely to get the response you want if you aim to establish and maintain a fruitful relationship with your reader. Be aware of her needs as well as her status, and vary your language and style accordingly. Put yourself in her shoes and ask yourself what's in it for her.

The following factors will determine the way you write:

(a)  *How well do you know your reader?* Are you on first name terms? Would he like to be addressed as J Webb Esq, or would he find such formality unfriendly?

(b)  *What is his attitude towards you?* Is he on your side or the other side? Is he a fellow professional?

(c)  *What will his attitude be to the message?* Is the news good or bad? Is he likely to be hostile?

(d)  *How easily will he understand the information?* Is it very technical or detailed?

---

9. A. Hasche, 'Teaching Writing in Law: A Model to Improve Student Learning' (1992) 3 *Legal Education Review* 267 at p. 270.

*(e)    How well can he read?*

*(f)    How well does he understand English? Is it his mother tongue?*

EXERCISE **7.6**  **Plain thinking**

1.    *(a)  A client has instructed you to petition for divorce. In a letter to her describing the legal procedure, explain the term* DECREE NISI.

*(b)  A friend of yours runs a business designing computer software. He wants to know what emergency measures could be taken to stop a rival organisation selling his designs. He would like you to email him your reply. You want to suggest the use of a* SEARCH ORDER. *How would you express this?*

*(c)  Your client is about to embark on a long and complex personal injury claim. Write and explain to her what is involved in a* CONDITIONAL FEE AGREEMENT.

*(d)  You occasionally write for a local newspaper as their legal correspondent. They have asked you to write a piece for their readers about a recent case where a man was pushed down the stairs by his sleepwalking wife. How would you explain the defence of* AUTOMATISM?

*(e)  A fellow student has been seriously injured during a rugby match and wants compensation. Write and tell him about* VOLENTI NON FIT INJURIA.

2.    *In small groups:*

*(a)  Compare your written versions.*

*(b)  Discuss the methods and techniques you used to explain the legal terms.*

*(c)  Discuss and note down what you have learnt from this exercise.*

*(d)  If you were asked to repeat Exercise 1, what changes would you make to your approach?*

One fundamental point you may have discovered from this exercise is that you have to be absolutely clear about the meaning of technical terms yourself, before you can convey their meaning to others! Legal language is part of your social knowledge, yet it is only when you have to explain its meaning to lay people that you realise how much of it is not yet tacit knowledge. You may have mugged up *automatism* for a criminal law exam in the first year, and promptly forgotten it when you moved on to 'learn' contract. It is only when you have had to deal with it in the swamp that it gradually becomes part of your tacit knowledge.

EXERCISE **7.7**  **Who is my reader?**

Below are three letters written by solicitors, and a notice. Read these texts and in small groups discuss the questions that follow.

1.    Dear Sirs,
       *Burke v Melford Limited*
       WITHOUT PREJUDICE
       Thank you for your letters of 20 March and 2 April.

We note that Ms Burke has rejected the Part 36 offer and that the matter may well have to proceed to trial.

Incidentally, we think the cases you have pointed out in Westlaw have quite the opposite effect from the one you intended. We think those reports show that rather more serious injuries than those suffered by your client might achieve awards in the region of £10,000 to £15,000. Ms Burke's injury was not in the same category as the other claimants you referred us to.

For example, your client suffered a fracture which was only slightly displaced and this is why it was left to unite naturally. Your client was in hospital for only two days.

Mr Maple sustained a triple fracture of the ankle which needed fixing internally with plate and screws. His walking was limited to about half a mile, and there was a 5 percent risk of osteo-arthritis developing.

Mrs North underwent no less than five operations under general anaesthetic over a period of four years. The serious and permanent disabilities and disfigurement she suffered put her in a wholly different category to Ms Burke.

The same comment applies to the award to Ms Hazelwood by the CICB last July.

We will put your proposal to our clients and will let you know their response shortly.

Yours faithfully

2.   Dear Mrs Thornhill,

*Road Traffic Accident – 25 June 200.*

We understand from the Police Report that you were present at the scene of this accident and made a statement to the police.

We are acting for Molars Ltd, the company whose van was involved in the accident. The driver of the other vehicle has begun legal action against Molars Ltd, alleging that their employee, the van driver, was negligent.

As you were a witness to the accident, it is possible that we will want to call you to give evidence at the trial. We would like to fix the date of the trial at a time which is convenient to the people involved.

Could you therefore please let us know if you move house, and any dates that you will be unavailable for the rest of this year.

We will do our best to inconvenience you as little as possible. A pre-paid envelope is enclosed for your reply.

If you would like to discuss this further, please feel free to contact Ms Zoë Smith at this office.

Yours sincerely

. . . . . . . . . .

3.   Dear Sir,

*Copyright Claim*

*WITHOUT PREJUDICE*

Thank you for your letter dated 22 February 200 . . .

In response to your claim for £200, we are prepared to offer £50 in full and final settlement of all your claims in relation to the multiple reproduction of the print of the cassette sleeve. This represents the notional royalty which you would have received for all prints made and represents your likely loss in law if a copyright claim was successfully made out by you. We do not accept that the items listed by you next to your claim for £150 represent any part of your likely loss in law if a copyright claim was successfully made out by you.

This offer remains open for acceptance for 14 days from the date of this letter. Acceptance is only valid when received in writing by us.

We hereby put you on notice that we are aware that you have been making recordings of some of our concerts without our permission. We consider this activity to be in breach of our rights in our live performances as contained in the Copyright Designs and Patents Act and give you formal notice to refrain from this activity forthwith. In addition, we hereby reserve all of our rights in relation to your unlawful recordings of the concerts concerned.

Yours faithfully,

. . . . . . . . . .

4.    This notice was sent to a resident who was late with her council tax:

---

### Please Note

YOU HAVE LOST YOUR RIGHT TO PAY BY INSTALMENTS.

IF PAYMENT OF THE FULL AMOUNT SHOWN IS NOT MADE WITHIN SEVEN DAYS A SUMMONS WILL BE ISSUED. THIS WILL INCUR ADDITIONAL COSTS OF £24.50.

---

### Questions

(a)    What is the purpose of the communication?
(b)    Who is the reader?
(c)    What do the language and style tell you about the relationship between writer and reader?
(d)    What do you think will be the attitude of the reader to the writer and the message?
(e)    To what extent does the writer take the reader's needs into account?
(f)    If you were the recipient, how would you respond to the communication?
(g)    Has the writer achieved her purpose?

Now that you know your reader, move on to consider:

DO YOU HAVE ALL THE *INFORMATION YOU NEED*?

Is it accurate, or is there anything that needs checking? Is it complete?

WHAT IS THE BEST WAY TO *ORGANISE* THE INFORMATION FOR THIS READER?

You won't achieve your purpose if the recipient throws your letter in the bin or puts it on one side, probably to be forgotten. To get a quick response, you need to capture her interest and keep it. You can do this by making it clear why the message is important to her and how a reply will benefit her. Look again at the letters in Exercise 7.7. The writers are concise and get straight to the point. The recipients should be able to read, understand and act on the information at one reading.

If your purpose is to provide information, consider the effect the information will have on your reader. Is the news good or bad? If good, don't waste the reader's time with preliminaries. Get straight to the central point. If the news is bad, prepare the recipient for disappointment by giving some neutral or positive information first. Try to end on a positive note, for example, by offering a possible alternative solution.

If your purpose is to persuade the reader to a course of action, you need to make the benefits to the reader clear straight away. Point out the drawbacks of failing to follow the course of action.

Whatever your purpose, you must structure the content of the message so that it can be understood easily and unambiguously. Each paragraph should deal with one main topic, and should be clearly linked to the preceding and following paragraphs. We look at paragraphing in detail later in this chapter.

EXERCISE 7.8 **Golden bull**

Have a look at this letter from X . . . . . . District Council

> Dear Sir
>> Re:
> I thank you for your letter dated 29 April 2002.
> Under Rule 312 of the Land Registration Rules every notice issued or sent by the Land Registry must fix a time within which any act or step required by such notice to be done or taken thereunder is to be done or taken, and shall state what will be the consequence of any omission to comply therewith. The notice period is therefore discretionary and fixed by the Land Registry. In this particular case the Registry have allowed for a notice period of twenty one days plus a further period of seven clear days for the delivery of the notice to ourselves which is allowed by Rule 313 of the Land Registration Rules 1925.
>> If no objection is received from ourselves the Land Registry will presumably proceed to register the title in the name of Mr . . . . . . . .
>> If however we were to object then the Land Registry would take into consideration our objection and the reasons for that objection before deciding whether or not the registration should proceed.
>> The Council's position is that they have no objection to the application and presumably unless any other objections are received, the registration can proceed.
>> Yours faithfully.

1.   What do you think is the purpose of this letter? Has the writer achieved it?
2.   What question is this letter attempting to answer?
3.   Is the information organised in a way which facilitates understanding?
4.   Comment on the language of the letter.

This letter received a Golden Bull award from the Plain English Campaign in 2003 as an outstanding example of gobbledygook. The reader is drowning in legalese by the end of the second paragraph, and to what purpose? The writer's intention, surely, was to answer a question raised by the recipient in a previous communication. However, it is not until the final paragraph that we have any idea what that question is. The reader looking for an answer has to wait until the end of the letter, having waded through a mass of unintelligible irrelevance. A frustrating experience indeed.

The letter is an excellent example of a text written without the reader in mind. Instead it reflects the thought processes of the writer – the steps *s/he* went through to get the answer. S/he takes the reader through these steps, whether the reader likes it or not. A structure which provides the answer at the beginning is preferable from the reader's point of view. It gives him a context in which to understand the information that follows because he can see where it flows from and where it leads back to. Furthermore, it demonstrates sensitivity to the reader's needs, so that a constructive relationship is more likely to develop. In short, a communication is unlikely to achieve its purpose if it is organised in a form which is convenient for *you*, not the recipient. By all means take the reader through the law – but only *after* you have answered their question.

### How should the information be presented on the page?

Closely spaced, unbroken blocks of print are hard on the eye and will turn the reader off. Use headings, subheadings and a numbering system if you are presenting a large amount of information.

## Summary

**Knowing what you mean to say involves:**

KNOWING YOUR PURPOSE
KNOWING YOUR READER
KNOWING YOUR INFORMATION
KNOWING YOUR ORGANISATION
KNOWING YOUR LAYOUT

## Selecting appropriate language

EXERCISE 7.9  **Who speaks good English? It is I!**

*In groups of three or four, discuss the following:*
(a)   *What is good English?*
(b)   *Who speaks it?*
(c)   *What is bad English?*
(d)   *Who speaks it?*
(e)   *What are your pet hates in language use?*
(f)   *Why do you hate them?*

### Select an appropriate variety of English

Language experts agree there is no satisfactory definition of a 'language'. This applies as much to English as it does to any other language. English is the first language of about 400 million people worldwide, the second language for a further 350 million, and another 100 million use it fluently as a foreign language. More radical estimates suggest an overall figure of over 1 billion English users throughout the world.[10] As you know, there are significant differences in the English language, depending on where it is spoken. The English of an American is not quite the same as the English of a person from the Indian sub-continent, and that of an Australian differs from the language of an English person. American English, Indian English and Australian English are different *varieties* of English.

Differences in spoken English can be heard at a much more local level. Many people in the UK learn a language as children which is very different from the kind of English heard on the BBC. These local varieties, or dialects, of English are highly complex, rule-governed ways of communicating. In other words, they have grammars.

When asked who speaks good English, many will say 'the Royal Family', or 'BBC newsreaders and commentators', because they speak standard English, which is 'accent-free', and therefore 'better' than other varieties.

How do language experts respond to this?

It is well-known to nearly everybody in the English-speaking world that most of us pronounce the language very badly. But, here again, the strongest complaints are usually reserved for the way in which other people pronounce, since it is obviously people from other cities, countries, age groups and social classes who really make a mess of things and have the most appalling accents, voices, drawls, twangs, whines and burrs. As linguists, we think that this widespread belief, like so many others that have to do with language, is mistaken. In fact, almost all of us pronounce our native language, whatever it is, very well indeed . . .

Some words in English have more than one pronunciation. Some of us, for instance, say 'ecconomics' while others say 'eeconomics'. This doesn't seem to bother anybody. With other words, however, passions are roused, and one pronunciation is condemned as wrong, illogical, ignorant, ugly and careless, while the other is praised as correct. Should we say '*con*troversy' or 'con*tro*versy'? Should it be 'Covventry' or 'Cuvventry'? Is it 'offen' or 'offten'? Does it matter? Will it make any difference to anything important if everyone starts saying 'irre*voc*cable' rather than 'irre*vvo*cable'?

[Accent] refers . . . to the way particular vowels and consonants of a language are pronounced, and to the intonation or sentence melodies employed. Because accent refers in this way to pronunciation, everybody, without exception, has an accent. Complainers, of course, often talk as if only other people have accents – and usually

10. See D. Crystal, *The Cambridge Encyclopedia of Language*, Cambridge University Press, Cambridge, 2nd edn, 1997, p. 360.

rather funny ones at that – but if they pronounce vowels and consonants when they speak, and we have to assume that they do, they must have accents also. An accent, then, is not something to be ashamed of, because everyone speaks with an accent.

. . . we use people's accents to find out things about them. If you can tell whether somebody is a Geordie, Australian, Cockney, upper-class, etc, when they speak, then you are able to do this mostly – and most quickly – from the accent . . .

But we do more than use accents as clues. We also pass judgments on them. We say that some people are 'nicely spoken', that others are 'affected' in their speech, and that yet others have 'ugly' accents. As linguists, we believe that judgments of this type are almost entirely social judgments, based on what we know, or think we know, about the accent in question and where it comes from. We do not believe that these judgments are in any way truly aesthetic.[11]

One example of a pet hate, particularly amongst older people, is the use of the glottal stop: -? instead of -t. They regard this as 'lazy' or 'sloppy' pronunciation. In fact, speakers using glottal stops follow quite clear linguistic rules. Their use depends on the position of -t in the word. So, for example,

bu?er (butter), bo?om (bottom), bi?e (bite), biscui? (biscuit),

but not

?ank (tank), ?eacher (teacher).

In the UK the standard English accent, or 'Received Pronunciation' (RP) is perceived as the most prestigious, because it is used by the influential, the wealthy and the educated. An experiment was carried out with a lecturer who could speak both RP and a strong regional accent. He gave the same lecture several times to a series of different audiences who did not know the real purpose of the experiment. The lectures given in RP were judged by most listeners to be superior in content to those delivered in the regional accent![12] Do we therefore judge the authenticity of news reporting by the accent of the newsreader? Are witnesses in court who speak RP more believable than those who don't?[13]

Of course, standard English doesn't only differ in pronunciation from other accents. You will hear lots of people speak the standard language, not in RP but in regional accents. Standard English is also a dialect, which differs grammatically from other dialects of English. Although it is only one dialect among many, like RP standard English is perceived as superior to non-standard forms, because it is the dialect used in all our national institutions, taught in school, learned by non-English speakers and used in international communication.

11. L. Andersson and P. Trudgill, *Bad Language*, Blackwell, Oxford, 1990, pp. 19–20, 21–2. See also D. Freeborn, P. French and D. Langford, *Varieties of Language; An Introduction to the Study of Language*, Macmillan, Basingstoke, 1986, pp. 81–4.
12. This experiment is described in Freeborn, French and Langford, *Varieties of Language*, p. 17.
13. See Chapter 3. We discuss this particular question in more detail in Chapter 10.

No matter which spoken variety you learned as a child, you are expected to be able to use the standard written variety. However, in your work as a lawyer you will probably communicate with people who do not speak or write standard English. Will you perceive them as inferior for that reason? Or their language as incorrect?[14]

## Select an appropriate register

*Register* is a technical term used in linguistics to refer to the language we use in situations. Suppose, for example, that your dialect is standard English. In one day you will use and move between a number of registers of standard English, depending on where you are and who you are talking or writing to. You will use different language to your child, your partner, your law lecturer, your employer, your best friend, your clients, the judge, and your colleagues. As a barrister you will use different language with your colleagues in court from that you would use with them in chambers or over lunch. You adapt your standard language to suit each occasion and to reflect the kind of relationship you have with your audience.

Occupations and activities have their own specialised language registers. Thus, rugby players participate in *loose mauls, rucks* and *turnovers.* Linguists discuss *syntax, whiz deletion* and *register.* And lawyers? *For the purposes of the aforesaid it is submitted that the said professionals may be in flagrante delicto hereunder. Res ipsa loquitur.* As this example demonstrates, we are not talking only about vocabulary. Grammatical structure also changes between registers. This is clearly illustrated in the following extract from a radio sports commentary:

> . . . and here's Ljungberg – sprinting forward – and took the ball past one defender – ran into another – with a clear pass straight to Dennis Bergkamp – right side into the penalty area – Henry waits – Bergkamp tackle – ball breaks to Lauren – in it goes to Parlour – and once more a Southampton player's down injured inside his penalty area – but play progresses . . . [15]

To capture what is happening as it's happening, commentators omit words which would normally be necessary to make sentences 'grammatical.'

A register may also contain slang. Police officers may talk of sending out the *yobbo van,* and teachers in higher education may refer to 'resource-based learning' as *fo-fo* (unabbreviated form unprintable – please consult your tutor).

Command of a register can signify your membership of a closely-knit group and increases group cohesion by keeping out those who don't belong. For example, users of technical language justify the need for it in the interests of precise and accurate definition, and shorthand. However, we need to think long and hard

---

14. For opposing views on the status of standard and non-standard forms, see extracts from P Trudgill *Accent, Dialect and the School,* Edward Arnold, London, 1975, and J. Honey, *The Language Trap: Race, Class and the 'Standard English' Issue in British Schools,* 1983, both cited in Freeborn, French and Langford, *Varieties of Language,* pp. 20–1. See also S. Pinker, *The Language Instinct,* Penguin, Harmondsworth, 1994, ch. 12.
15. Alan Green, Radio Five Live, 17 May 2003.

about how much of it is actually necessary, and to what extent we use it to mystify outsiders.[16]

Outsiders, and some insiders, refer to specialised vocabularies as *jargon*. This word was:

> ... first used, in the late fourteenth century, in the sense of the twittering of birds. From this it passed on naturally to mean talk one does not understand, or gibberish, and so to any form of speech or writing filled with unfamiliar terms or peculiar to a particular group of persons.[17]

EXERCISE 7.10  **Le mot juste**

Here are some words and phrases which lawyers are fond of using. Which are essential to the legal register, and why?

| | | |
|---|---|---|
| *ultra vires* | *inter alia* | *prima facie* |
| *Calderbank letter* | *aforementioned* | *certiorari* |
| *affidavit* | *pursuant to* | *fee simple* |
| *conveyance* | *disbursements* | *lessor* |
| *the said agreement* | *hearsay* | *voire dire* |

## Select an appropriate level of formality

Degrees of formality, informality and tone are aspects of register since they are determined by context. For example, consider the move from formal language to slang in Figure 7.2:

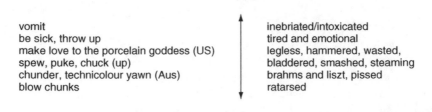

FORMAL

vomit
be sick, throw up
make love to the porcelain goddess (US)
spew, puke, chuck (up)
chunder, technicolour yawn (Aus)
blow chunks

inebriated/intoxicated
tired and emotional
legless, hammered, wasted,
bladdered, smashed, steaming
brahms and liszt, pissed
ratarsed

INFORMAL (SLANG)

Figure 7.2

16. 'Since lawyers are a prestigious elite group, using the language of the law can be a claim to this prestige .... Furthermore, if the language needed to operate within a specialist field is unintelligible to non-specialists, this creates the need for the services of a specialist to mediate between ordinary people and the specialist field. Put crudely, it makes work and money for lawyers': J. Gibbons, *Forensic Linguistics: an Introduction to Language in the Justice System*, Blackwell, Oxford, 2003, p. 37.
17. K. Hudson, *The Jargon of the Professions*, Macmillan, London, 1978, p. 10.

As we have said, the level of formality and the kind of tone you adopt will depend on the relationship you want to establish or maintain with your reader and what your perception is of the reader's expectations. You may choose to use a formal style with plenty of legal language to resolve a dispute quickly. For example, the tone of Letter 3 in Exercise 7.7 is hostile. A lawyer drafted it, but it was signed by the clients. They wanted to make it clear to the recipient that they had taken legal advice. The tone puts the recipient in a very poor bargaining position. Since it will cost him more than £50 to consult a solicitor, he has little choice but to accept the offer.

Used in this way, legal language and tone can be extremely powerful. If the writer had conveyed the message in a friendly, courteous tone the recipient might still be prevaricating. We discuss the power of legal language in drafting in more detail in Chapter 8.

## Select gender-neutral language

The well-known rule that the masculine includes the feminine is based on the belief that language is neutral. It is not. Look at the following three examples:

*Every solicitor in private practice should ensure his complaints procedures are clearly set out in writing.*

*There are so many conflicting cases in this area of contract law that the businessman cannot be certain what the law is.*

*Anyone who has reasonable grounds for complaint should send his objections to Head Office.*

The constant use of *he, his, him* perpetuates an ancient linguistic convention[18] which many people now find offensive. When we want to refer to a person whose gender is unspecified, what good reason is there to choose the masculine pronoun instead of the feminine? For those of us who hold stereotypical views about gender roles in society, perpetual use of the masculine pronouns serves only to reinforce them. In the sentences above, try changing the masculine forms into feminine. Does it sound strange? If so, why?[19]

There are a number of ways to avoid masculine forms. Many writers prefer to use *they* and *their*, etc:

---

18. Some Romance and Germanic languages have gender neutral pronouns: for example, French *on*, English *one* and German *man*. Both the French and English versions are derived from the Latin *homo*, meaning *man*. Throughout the ages people have extended the meaning to include both genders, so *homo* comes to have the general meaning of *human*, irrespective of gender (cf *homo sapiens*, *homo erectus*, etc). The fact remains, however, that these words are derived from a word which means *man* and is grammatically masculine.

19. Interestingly, the number of women qualifying as solicitors increased by 85 per cent from 1990 to 2000. In 1999/2000 53.1 per cent of newly qualifying solicitors were women, compared to 46.6 per cent in 1990. Between 1991 and 2001 the number of women holding practising certificates has more than doubled, having increased by 128.5 per cent: *Trends in the Solicitors' Profession: Annual Statistical Report*, Law Society, London, 2000, p. 72, and 2001, p. 5.

*Anyone who has reasonable grounds for complaint should send their objections to Head Office.*[20]

Others may choose to rewrite the sentence using you, your, etc:

*If you think you have reasonable grounds for complaint you can send your objections to Head Office.*

The plural may be possible:

*All solicitors in private practice should ensure their complaints procedures are clearly set out in writing.*

Some writers use roughly equal numbers of *he, she, his, her,* etc. Others deliberately use the feminine forms to challenge the stereotypical view. In this book we use the feminine forms most of the time.

The following is gender neutral, but inelegant, so we don't recommend it:

*Anyone who has reasonable grounds for complaint should send his or her objections to Head Office.*

Other gender neutral usages are criticised for their ugliness and inelegance: for example, *humankind, significant other.* In this book we reluctantly use *drafter* for *draftsman.* There seems to be no elegant alternative.

Businessman, salesman, fireman, policeman, when used generically, can be replaced by *businesspeople, salespeople, fire fighters, police officers.*

## Summary

**Selecting appropriate language for your communication means thinking about:**

VARIETY

REGISTER

TONE

GENDER NEUTRALITY

## Say exactly what you mean to say

### EXERCISE 7.11 Grasping grammar

Note down in a few sentences what you understand by the word 'grammar'. Discuss your answers with your group. Can you reach a consensus about the meaning? If so, what is it?

---

20. This usage has apparently been normal in English for centuries. It is found most frequently in informal language, but also in formal written English; see M. Swan, *Practical English Usage,* Oxford University Press, Oxford, 2nd edn, 1995, p. 529.

## Getting the fundamentals right

Do you remember our earlier discussion about the status of standard English and other dialects? Grammar is at the heart of this debate. For linguists, the main meaning of 'grammar' is a *description* of the rules which underlie a speaker's ability to understand, speak and (possibly) write a given language. Linguists therefore treat all grammars as equally valid, and prefer to talk of 'appropriate' and 'inappropriate' grammar.

In its popular sense, 'grammar' is a set of rules which *prescribe* how users should speak and write. Those who believe in the superiority of standard English tend to talk of its grammar as 'correct' whilst the grammars of other dialects are 'incorrect'.

EXERCISE 7.12 **Bad grammar**

In small groups, discuss the examples of written English below. Identify the features which make each text 'inappropriate', or 'incorrect'.

1.   Graffiti from the London Underground:

*I woz ere*
*Ere I woz*
*Woz I ere?*
*Yes, I were*

2.   *want pizza don't any on I anchovies my*
3.   *He failed to entirely avoid the oncoming car.*

In 1 the meaning is clear, and the text is perfectly punctuated. However, we can all recognise this as non-standard English, because the spelling is incorrect. There is also a grammatical mistake of subject/verb agreement in the last line.

Example 2 is nothing more than a meaningless list of words. If someone said it to you, you would need time to sort it out into some logical meaning. And this is a very simple sentence. Imagine the difficulties of sorting out much more complex and abstract sentences. This example illustrates the most fundamental rule of English grammar: that relationships within sentences are governed by rules of word order. Break this rule substantially and you get nonsense. Native English speakers whose language has developed normally do not make mistakes like this. The rules of word order are part of our tacit knowledge, and we apply them correctly, even though we might not be able to say what they are.

There appears to be a problem with word order, too, in 3. It may look perfectly all right to you. It seems to get its message across clearly (and more concisely than the first example!). However, it breaks a well-known 'rule':

Never split an infinitive.

Those who cleave to this rule would say the 'correct' form is:

*He failed entirely* to avoid *the oncoming car.*

However, a change in the word order here changes the meaning. The first version suggests a slight impact, whilst the second suggests a full impact. Thus, splitting or not splitting in such a case may communicate the wrong information.

The rule about not splitting the infinitive is not a grammatical rule at all. It is a stylistic preference, and is therefore a matter of taste rather than correctness or incorrectness. As Bryan Garner notes, confusing grammar with style has led to a 'legacy of bad writing advice':

> The pedantic 'rule' to never split an infinitive, for example is a superstition that just won't die. So too that a preposition is a taboo part of speech to end a sentence with. And forget the idea that a conjunction should never start a sentence. Any writer can benefit from unlearning such baseless nonsense.[21]

Nobody is born with the written variety of English as their mother tongue, so for all of us there is an element of 'foreignness' about it. Admittedly, if we are used to using standard English in our everyday lives, the similarities between that and written English help us enormously. The point, however, is that when we learn a new language we need rules and conventions which we can follow and trust. Some of these are plainly necessary, others are not. Those that are plainly necessary are to do with 'grammar'.

The following are the most important rules you must abide by: otherwise you will be using this variety of English incorrectly.

## Use complete sentences

Unlike the spoken language, written English demands that we use full sentences to convey our meaning. If you are not using these you are not respecting the way that the language encompasses elements of sense and meaning. Here is the final paragraph of a letter sent to Caroline by a former bank manager:

> I trust that this letter will put things in perspective and *where in finality you find it needful for our offered support to come from elsewhere.*

When you have read to the end, you expect more words, not a full stop. The italicised part is not a full sentence. By full sentences we mean ones that contain a *subject* and a *verb* and any necessary *objects*.

The SUBJECT usually appears before the main verb in statements and after the main verb in questions:

*Jim* was stopped by the police on the way home last night.
Where was *Jim* stopped by the police?

---

21. B. Garner, *The Redbook: A Manual on Legal Style*, West Group, St Paul, Minn., 2002 p. 123.

All the following can be subjects:

| A noun: | *Hang-gliding* is dangerous. |
|---|---|
| A noun phrase: | *Endogenous growth theory* is dangerous. |
| | *The cost of mortgages* is going down. |
| A pronoun: | *It* isn't possible. |
| | *Who* wrote that rubbish? |
| A subordinate clause: | *What you wrote* was perfectly acceptable. |

The VERB must agree with its subject. In standard English there is little variation in the form of verbs. An exception is the third person singular of the present tense. For example: *I sing, she sings.*

Other exceptions are the verb *to be*, for example:

*I am, she is, you are,* etc.
*I was, you were,* etc.

Modal verbs don't change at all:

*must, can, may, might, shall, will, ought, should, would, could.*

Some verbs have to be followed by an OBJECT, others don't. For example,

*He sang* is correct, but
*I don't want* is not.

The following are all acceptable sentences:

*He sang.*
*He sang the national anthem* (object: WHAT did he sing?).
*He sang in the bath* (adverbial phrase: WHERE did he sing?).
*He sang out of tune for several hours* (adverbial phrases: HOW did he sing, and for HOW LONG?).
*He sang everything that we wanted him to sing* (object: WHAT did he sing?).

Note that some sentences may be complete though they omit the subject. The subject is implied, for example, in the politeness formula sentence *Thank you,* and in commands:

(I) *Thank you for your letter.*
(You) *Go to your room.*
*Don't* (you) *park on double yellow lines.*
*Never* (don't you ever) *split an infinitive.*

The following sentences are unacceptable. What is missing?
*With reference to your letter of 21 March.*
*Thanking you for your kind attention.*
*Unfortunately being unavailable at the time I wanted to see her.*

The first has no verb at all. In the second, *thanking* does not imply the subject *I* and so is not a verb. It would be acceptable to say:

*Thank you for your kind attention.*

The first part of the third sentence is wrong. *Being* does not imply the subject *she*, and so the subject must be expressed, and then the verb must agree with it:

Unfortunately *she was* unavailable at the time I wanted to see her.

In some contexts, such as story-telling and conversational style, incomplete sentences may be acceptable in written English. For example:

*Out of winter into spring.*
I sat in the public gallery, studying the defendant's face, as the jury gave their verdict. *Guilty.*
What do you think of this chapter so far? *Rubbish.*

**Observe the rules of syntax (word order)**
*Syntax* is the way in which words are arranged to show relationships of meaning within (and sometimes between) sentences.[22] In highly inflected languages, like Latin, the meaning is derived from the different word endings, which indicate the relationship between one word and another. English has very few inflections. We noted above that English verbs vary their form very little. They add *-s* or *-es* for the third person and most add *-ed* for the past. Most nouns add *-s* or *-es* to make the plural. That's about all. We therefore derive the meaning of an English sentence not from word endings but from the order of the words in the sentence.

Using word order intelligently therefore enables you to write your meaning more correctly. To tie yourself down with unnecessary 'rules' like not splitting the infinitive restricts your capacity to be precise, as the example on p. 227 demonstrated.

Some words may look benign but can cause trouble. For example:

The prosecutor *only* stood up when the magistrates entered the court room.

This sentence can have several meanings:

*The prosecutor had been sitting down up until that point.*
*Nobody stood up except the prosecutor.*
*The prosecutor did nothing except stand up: she did not speak, smile, etc.*

Careful planning of the word order will enable you to express the meaning you want. Where would you put *only* to get each of the three meanings above? Or do you have to make more radical changes to the sentence?

22. Crystal, *Cambridge Encylopedia of Language*, p. 94.

In the next chapter we shall see the liberties legal drafters take with word order to try to ensure precision.

## Use appropriate punctuation

Punctuation helps us make sense of written language by breaking it up into smaller units. Furthermore, as we noted during the Brick Exercise (7.5), the prosodic features which aid our understanding of the spoken language are absent from the written. If spoken, the meaning of

*The prosecutor only stood up when the magistrates entered the court room.*

would be understood quite clearly from intonation and emphasis on particular words and syllables. Precise word order is one way of compensating for loss of prosody; punctuation is another. See how punctuation alters the meaning in this sentence:

*The judge said the accused was the most heinous villain he had ever met*
*The judge, said the accused, was the most heinous villain he had ever met.*

Intonation and emphasis would make the meaning clear if either of these sentences were spoken.

EXERCISE 7.13 **Some people just don't know when to stop**

*Briefly write down when you would use the following punctuation marks:*

*(a)    a full stop;*
*(b)    a comma;*
*(c)    a semi-colon;*
*(d)    a colon;*
*(e)    an apostrophe.*

Full stops don't usually cause trouble. The rule is straightforward as long as you understand the rules for sentences. We use full stops to separate sentences. Each new sentence starts with a capital letter and ends with a full stop.

*I met Mrs James in the supermarket. We decided to go for a cup of coffee together. Over coffee she began to tell me about her divorce.*

Commas separate words, phrases and clauses. They signify short pauses and changes in intonation in the spoken language.

The example above of the judge and the accused shows how using and not using commas can affect meaning. Moreover, your meaning may be obscured if your sentence is top-heavy with commas. For example:

*There may be some difficulty, as I have already indicated, if, as you wish, you insist on inserting Clause 5b, in its present form, into the contract, without some modification, which takes account of the present law.*

We wouldn't want this writer to draft our contracts. She is extending the sentence length to accommodate new thoughts as they come to mind. The comma is not a substitute for thinking and planning. What would you do to make this message readable?

Cutting out a few commas won't do. The sentence needs re-thinking. Here is one possible alternative:

> *If you wish to include clause 5b in the contract, we will have to alter it to make it comply with the law.*

Commas don't function as full stops and so shouldn't be used to link sentences. You can link two sentences with a co-ordinating conjunction (e.g. *and, but, for*), or make a sentence break with a full stop. For example,

> *I shall discuss two recent cases, the first was decided a month ago, the second only yesterday.*

can be rewritten as:

> *I shall discuss two recent cases. The first was decided a month ago and the second only yesterday.*

Similarly,

> *You must put your application in within 28 days, otherwise you will lose the right to make a claim.*

should be rewritten thus:

> *You must put your application in within 28 days. Otherwise you will lose the right to make a claim.*

Alternatively, it is possible to use a co-ordinating conjunction which means the same as *otherwise*:

> *You must put your application in within 28 days, or you will lose the right to make a claim.*

If you don't want to make a complete break between the sentences above, can you use a stop that is less full – a colon or semicolon? You can use a semicolon where you think a sentence is too closely related to what has gone before to be cut off by a full stop. However, these situations are rare.

> *I could hear footsteps behind me; then they stopped.*

Use of the semicolon here heightens the tension. Generally, however, they aren't necessary because we have the full stop.

The colon is used to precede an explanation, and so can be used in the sentence above. A colon can also introduce a list. For example:

> *There are three main ingredients for batter: flour, milk and egg.*

Apostrophes cause a lot of trouble. You find them in all sorts of places where the rules say they should not appear at all. This is probably because apostrophes represent nothing that is heard in the spoken language. Other punctuation highlights intonation, emphasis or pauses. Apostrophes are purely a written convention.

In fact, the rules are quite straightforward. In spoken English we generally indicate possession by adding -*s* to the 'possessor'. In writing the -*s* is retained, but we add an extra feature – an apostrophe. For example:

> *The dog's biscuits*
> *The dogs' biscuits*
> *Mary's paintings.*

In speech the first two examples sound exactly the same and we would have to judge the precise meaning from the context. The written form tells at a glance whether we are talking about one dog or more.

Because apostrophes are usually unnecessary to understanding, many people think them old-fashioned. It may be because attitudes are changing that there is so much uncertainty about how to use them. Some people mistakenly add apostrophes to verb endings and noun plurals:

> *This shop offer's fresh vegetables' at very low prices.*

Apostrophes should never be used in this way. If you want to be thought of as an educated writer, you need to learn to use them correctly. The rules are as follows:

1. Singular nouns and plural nouns which don't end in 's': put the apostrophe before the 's':

   > The *dog's* biscuits
   > A *woman's* right to choose
   > *John's* neighbours
   > The *men's* changing room.

2. Plural nouns ending in 's': put the apostrophe after the 's':

   > The *judges'* wigs
   > The *dogs'* biscuits.

3. Singular nouns ending in 's': put the apostrophe after the 's'. You can add another 's':

   > *James'* knuckles, or
   > *James's* knuckles.

   We also use the apostrophe to measure a period of time:

   > five *weeks'* work,
   > seven *days'* holiday;

to refer to places and premises:

> Make an appointment at the *dentist's*.
> Shall we go and eat at *Brown's*?

It is also, rather unexpectedly, used in the following way:

> He is a friend of *George's*.

This seems mainly to be used for relationships and in sentences where an alternative would be to use *one of*, as in

> He is one of *George's friends*.

Where we combine subject and verb to make one word, we use an apostrophe. This is called elision. For example:

> *She's* never going to marry him!
> *John's* going to Australia.
> *Who's* going with him?
> *Who'd* want to go there?

A second kind of elision is when some verbs are made negative:

> *haven't, couldn't, don't, mustn't, wasn't*, etc.

Note that the apostrophe goes where the *-o* should be, not between the words. It marks the dropping of the letter *-o*, not the boundaries between the words.

A frequent mistake is to confuse the following:

> *whose* (the possessive pronoun) and
> *who's* (short form of *who is* or *who has*)

as in

> *Whose bike is this*? (answer: Kate's)
> *Who's coming to lunch*? (Who is coming to lunch?)
> *Who's got the Watson file*? (Who has got, etc)

If the version you are using cannot be expanded to *who is* or *who has*, then you must use *whose*. The same rules apply to *its* and *it's*.

EXERCISE **7.14  Whose who?**

*Put the appropriate form into the following:*

- Have you heard who__ been made redundant?
- Do you know who__ writing that is?
- You know Jenny's car? Well, it__ for sale.
- It__ mileage is very low.
- Can you tell me who__ taken my wig?
- Put that down. You don't know where it__ been.

Many of you probably apply the rules of punctuation correctly, even if you are not in the habit of articulating them. If we insult your intelligence, we apologise. However, it is important to remember that selecting appropriate punctuation marks is not a matter of taste or cosmetics. These marks carry meaning and so have an important grammatical function. Punctuation is part of your 'grammar'.

We shall see in Chapter 8 how the traditional reluctance of lawyers to use punctuation in legal documents has contributed to the unintelligibility of these texts.

## Use correct spelling

Sorry, folks! Spelling is one of those conventions we just have to observe. It is not acceptable to experiment: it is either right or wrong.

What makes English spelling so difficult is that words are not spelt as they are pronounced. There are two main reasons for this: firstly, the spelling system introduced by the Normans was mixed with the system we used before the Conquest. This accounts for two different spellings for the same sound, for example -*se* and -*ce*:

*mouse, mice.*

Furthermore, we also have two sounds for the same spelling, for example -*g*:

*get, gender*
*gift, gin.*

The second reason is that pronunciation has changed, but spelling hasn't. In the Middle Ages those few people who could write spelt words in different ways. However, a fixed and uniform system of spelling began to be established with the introduction of printing in the fifteenth century. In the eighteenth century English dictionaries adopted this standard system. This is largely the system we use today: a fossil, unaffected by major changes in pronunciation which have taken place since the fifteenth century.

We see examples of this fossilisation in:

*liGHt, Knee, douBt, saLmon.*

We spell *meat* and *meet* differently because in the past *ea* and *ee* were two different sounds. Can we therefore say that all words where *ea* and *ee* occur sound the same? Think of other examples:

*read, reed*
*dear, deer.*

But compare:

*great, greet*
*head, heed.*

We therefore can't rely on a clear rule. English spelling has few 'rules', and those there are may be outnumbered by the exceptions to them. No wonder writers have problems. Since there are so few rules, learning to spell in English is largely a matter of memorising. We do not use the intellectual processes which are necessary to acquire the complex linguistic skills of grammar and punctuation.

It is therefore quite untrue to say, as many do, that poor spelling is a sign of intellectual incompetence. Nevertheless, incorrect spelling is unacceptable in written standard English. If you send a letter to a client asking:

*Where woz your daughter the night your house woz burgled?*

your client is likely to withdraw her instructions, thinking you uneducated, incompetent or unprofessional. If you have difficulties with spelling, always use a dictionary or a spell-checker.

## Summary

**Saying what you mean to say means getting the fundamentals right:**

USE APPROPRIATE GRAMMAR (STANDARD WRITTEN ENGLISH)
WRITE COMPLETE SENTENCES
WITH CORRECT WORD ORDER
AND APPROPRIATE PUNCTUATION
USE CORRECT SPELLING (STANDARD WRITTEN ENGLISH)

## Moving towards artistry

Following the fundamentals will not of itself lead you to write acceptable and comprehensible English. Good writing is the result of good judgment about:

- CLARITY;
- PRECISION;
- ELEGANCE.

There are no hard and fast fundamentals for this. You have to develop your own views and test them in practice. However, there are certain things you should concentrate on which will help you develop your judgment.

### Vocabulary

You may find it useful at this point to go back and re-read the texts and discussion on Exercise 7.2. Remember, what you should be aiming for is to make your meaning clear as rapidly and straightforwardly as possible. What you should avoid is the appearance of pomposity and formality which certain words and phrases tend to give to writing. This can create a barrier between you and your reader. For the same reason you should avoid long-windedness, unnecessary technical terms and antiquated language, particularly Latin! This 'legalese' has given lawyers a bad name.

When we discussed the Brick Exercise (7.5) we suggested that writers should avoid infrequently used words and phrases. The words and phrases below, once rarely used, have become common both in speech and writing, particularly officialese. For example:

*commence* (begin)
*utilise* (use)
*facilitate* (help, assist)
*at a later date* (later)
*prior to* (before)
*on a regular basis* (regularly)
*in the final analysis* (finally)
*subsequent to* (after)
*until such time as* (until)
*at this moment in time* (now, at present, currently)
*as a matter of urgency* (urgently)
*and while we are on the subject* (furthermore)
*in the vicinity of* (near)
*for the purpose of* (to)

Richard Wydick has some sensible advice:

*Every time you see one of these pests, swat it.*[23]

Can you think of other pests which you are in the habit of using?

In speech some of these phrases are used as gap fillers while the speaker prepares to introduce a new topic or thinks out what she is going to say next. In writing this padding device is often used to introduce a new topic, or to link paragraphs. For example:

*As far as your purchase is concerned*, we will deal with it as a matter of urgency.
*With regard to your request for* further and better particulars, we enclose herewith a statement ...
*As I have already said,* ... (so why repeat it?)
*As I mentioned earlier,* ...

Try to avoid these clumsy devices. Concise language will bring elegance to your writing. Imprecise language will dilute the force of your message.

The same goes for redundant words and phrases. What we are talking about here is the insertion of unnecessary words and phrases as padding. For example:

*close proximity*
*duly incorporated*
*I enclose herewith*
*forward planning*

23. R. Wydick, 'Plain English for Lawyers' (1978) 66 *California Law Review* 727 at p. 731.

*unfilled vacancy*
*null and void*
*last will and testament.*

If it is possible to cut out a word without altering the meaning of the sentence, cut it out. Which words are redundant in this sentence?

*Relatively few people can afford the cost of taking a case through the civil courts.*

## New use or misuse?

Another problem with using big words to impress the reader is that you have to be absolutely sure you know what they mean. Can you spot the fault in the following sentence?

*I have been invited to partake in a group session on experiential learning.*

The writer uses *partake* when she means *participate*. This is what is known as a *malapropism*, named after the character Mrs Malaprop in Sheridan's play *The Rivals*. Sheridan took her name from the French *mal à propos* which means 'inappropriate'. She kept using and misusing long, learned words.

The *partake/participate* confusion is now quite common in speech. So is it still a malapropism, or does it denote a change in the meaning of *partake*? Linguists Lars Andersson and Peter Trudgill address this problem:

> As we have seen, languages are socially based systems and individuals. If a single person such as Mrs Malaprop misuses a word, this is a problem for she cannot unilaterally decide to change the meaning of words. In the case of Mrs Malaprop herself, the usual effect is comic, but of course confusion could also result. The moral is that trying to use fancy language can easily lead someone into looking very foolish. Mrs Malaprop would have been much better advised to stick to her own everyday language.
>
> Notice, however, that if everybody used the same malapropism, then it would by definition no longer be a malapropism … The fact is that words mean what speakers use them to mean. Formerly, for example, all speakers of English … used the word nice to mean 'ignorant', 'foolish'. Gradually the usage went through a series of changes so that the meaning became by turns 'shy', 'delicate', 'fine', and finally 'pleasant'. Anyone wanting these days to use nice with its original meaning would be making just as bad a mistake as Mrs Malaprop.[24]

24. L. Andersson and P. Trudgill, *Bad Language*, Blackwell, Oxford, 1990, p. 150. Another current misuse commonly found in speech is 'off my own back', as in 'I did all that entirely off my own back.' The 'correct' version is 'off my own bat', meaning *on my own*, *without help*. Are the Malaprops confusing it with the phrase 'making a rod for your own back', which of course means something entirely different? What do you think is the derivation of 'off my own bat?' It's pretty obvious but if you can't guess, look it up in the *Cassell Dictionary of Slang* or ask persons of a certain age steeped in traditional English summer sports.

Andersson and Trudgill comment that although confusion may arise whilst words are changing their meanings, complete misunderstanding is unlikely.[25]

Grammatical forms also undergo change. For example, the prescriptive rules on *less* and *fewer* tell us to use *less* with uncountable nouns (which because they are uncountable, have no plural forms), as in:

> If you drive at a steady 55mph, you use *less petrol.*
> Everyone should pay *less income tax.*

Countable nouns, which have plurals, should be preceded by *fewer*:

> There are *fewer people* here than there were yesterday.
> Higher pay settlements mean *fewer jobs*, says the government.

However, it is now very common in speech to say *less* instead of *fewer*:

> *Less people.*
> *Less jobs.*

This usage has found its way into writing, too. It looks like a sensible language rationalisation – why have two forms when we could use one, without any misunderstanding? The problem is, when a language change like this is happening, it is difficult to know at what point the new usage becomes acceptable. Some people see the 'misuse' as a sign of poor education.

Another grammatical change is now found very frequently in writing, as well as speech. Here is an example:

> If you require any assistance, please contact *myself* or my assistant.

Your tacit knowledge, once surfaced by yourselves,[26] will tell you that these reflexive pronouns *-self, -selves*, as in:

> *She washed herself in ass's milk.*
> *Go and clean yourselves up.*
> *We can't go there by ourselves.*
> *He has a very fine opinion of himself.*

are grammatical because in each case the pronoun refers to the subject of the sentence. We'll call this Rule 1. Note that the rule is not always consistently followed. For example,

> *Have you got any money on yourself?*

sounds distinctly odd!

---

25. For an illuminating example of this, see their discussion of the development in meaning of the word *interested* and its negative forms *disinterested* and *uninterested*: Andersson and Trudgill, *Bad Language*, pp. 151–4.
26. You may need a grammar book to help you. We did.

Rule 2: The reflexives can also be used in another way to give emphasis, as in:
Are you sure he got my message? Yes, I took it round there *myself*.
However, the traditional rules do not allow their use as object pronouns *you, me, him, her, us, them*. Yet this is what is happening. If words mean what people use them to mean, then the frequency of this usage signifies a language change. But is this usage acceptable in standard written English? It certainly makes some people grind their teeth. Why?

We looked for this usage in a fairly recent grammar book[27] and found a reference to it after certain words and phrases, such as *as for, like, but for, except for*:

> *As for me/myself, I'm going home now.*
> *Heavy drinking is not a good idea for someone like me/myself.*

and in co-ordinated noun phrases, such as:

He showed us a picture of *him and Kate*.
He showed us a picture of *himself and Kate*.

Is *please contact myself or my assistant* covered by this second situation? *Myself or my assistant* is a co-ordinated noun phrase, like *himself and Kate*. But can you spot the difference? In the latter *himself* points back to the subject *he*. This sentence can therefore fall into our Rule 1, as would

> *He showed us a picture of himself.*

However, in

> *If you require any further assistance, please contact myself or my assistant.*

the subject of the sentence is *you*. Similarly, in the extremely inelegant

> *Your tacit knowledge, surfaced by yourselves, will tell you, etc . . .*

the subject is *your tacit knowledge*. The 'misuse' therefore does not seem to be a gradual extension of pre-existing rules, but a complete defiance of them. This is what may boggle the mind and grind the teeth of prescriptive grammarians. Nevertheless, the latest edition of Swan's *Practical English Usage* acknowledges this use in co-ordinated noun phrases such as

> *There will be four of us at dinner: Robert, Alison, Jenny and myself.*

although Swan is silent on whether it is acceptable in standard written English.[28] If, like us, you prefer to avoid it, you can write *Please contact me or my assistant*.

A more recent grammatical 'misuse' quite common in speech and unfortunately creeping into the written language is to replace the past forms of modal

27. G. Leech and J. Svartik, *A Communicative Grammar of English*, Longman, London, 1994, pp. 335–6.
28. Swan, *Practical English Usage*, p. 486.

verbs *could have*, *would have*, *should have*, *must have*, *may have*, *might have*, *ought to have* with *of*. For example:

A: *You could of told me you were arriving on the early train.*

B. *Didn't you get my email? I sent it two days ago, so you should of.*

A. *I never. But I might of deleted it by mistake.*

B. *You must of.*

Using *of* instead of *have* is grammatically incorrect. Why is this usage taking hold? In speech the *have* of *must have*, *should have*, etc is normally unstressed: we can express this in informal writing as *must've*, *should've*, etc. Similarly, *of* is almost always unstressed, for example:

the law *of* torts

a game *of* chance

where *of* is pronounced like *'ve* in the examples above. We think that because the two sounds are identical in speech, some people confuse them in writing.[29] Don't!

## Sentence length and complexity

As you have learnt from your own reading experience, long sentences tire and confuse the reader. Yet too many short sentences one after another make the content disjointed and your writing look simplistic. The secret of good writing is to vary the length of your sentences. However, it is difficult to say what makes a 'long sentence' because readers have different levels of reading ability. One reader might find a sentence of 12 words difficult to understand, while another might find it childish and patronising. The average reader seems happy with sentences of 15 to 20 words, but this is only a rough guide.

Moreover, the number of words alone doesn't determine the level of understanding. This will depend also on how complex the sentence is. In Exercise 7.2 we noted that lengthy abstract noun phrases (nominalisations) are difficult to process because they compress a number of ideas into few words. If we replace them with verbs, the sentence will probably be longer, but more comprehensible.

The passive is another grammatical feature we looked at in Exercise 7.2 which can obscure meaning. Should you use it, and if so, when? You can use the passive to emphasise an action, irrespective of who carried it out if the action is clearly more important than who did it. For example, a newspaper reporter at the scene of an accident might well write:

*The injured woman was taken away in an ambulance.*

because she is more interested in reporting the events at the scene. A close friend or relative of the injured woman, however, would probably look at it differently. They might say:

*They took her to hospital in the ambulance.*

---

29. In other words, where they *should of* written *should have*, they write *should of*, which they *shouldn't have*.

In scientific and academic writing we use the passive because we are not usually interested in who carried out the activity:

*Water was mixed with mud and heated.*

This style of writing is supposed to denote academic rigour, because it appears to be impersonal and objective. For example:

*It is submitted that . . .*
*It is argued that . . .*

is preferred to:

*I think that . . .*
*I feel that . . .*

Bear in mind that the passive puts distance between you and the recipient of your message. Use it sparingly.

Another very confusing feature is the overuse of negative forms. For example:

*Members of the jury, is it not improbable that in the circumstances he would not have been unable to avoid the attack?*

As members of the jury are we supposed to think that he could or could not have avoided the attack? It will take us some time to decide, by which time the advocate will have gone on to the next point, or beyond.

The sentence is not particularly long, but there are five items in it which convey negative meaning: *not, im-, not, un-, avoid.* The reader has to decipher which negatives cancel each other out. Furthermore, when you compose something as complicated as this, how can you know you are expressing the meaning you want to express? Make sure your sentences make sense.

Other sentences difficult to grasp on a first reading are those with a number of subordinate clauses. Subordinate clauses are 'sentences within sentences' and consequently make heavy demands on the reader's memory. For example:

*Mr Hughes, who is a well-known local solicitor, having been stopped by the police on his way back from lunch at a nearby pub where he had had some drinks with a few colleagues, will have to go to court because of the positive breath test and could lose his licence.*

Far too much information is packed into this one sentence, and it is hard to keep track of the sequence of events. It doesn't help that the subject, *Mr Hughes,* is separated from its main verb *will have to* by several other ideas.

There are seven separate ideas in this sentence. You could write each of them as a separate sentence, but your writing would look childish. You don't need to avoid subordinate clauses altogether, but the more you put into your sentence, the harder it will become to understand it. Why not start from scratch with this one and sort out the order of events?

If you do this, you will probably find you don't need to put each idea into a separate sentence. Most readers are capable of taking in more than one idea for each sentence. You have to use your judgment about whether you are overloading them or not.

Just as we have to take care about expressing different ideas within sentences, so we have to make sure our sentences are linked in some way. Each sentence, either in its sense, or by the use of linking words, should follow logically from the sentence which preceded it. What is the problem with these two sentences?

*Vicky failed her degree. She did very well in Trusts.*

They seem to be contradictory because they are not linked in a way which shows the desired relationship between the two ideas. We can rewrite them to show that there is a logical relationship between the two ideas:

*Vicky failed her degree, although she did very well in Trusts.*

EXERCISE **7.15 Sense and nonsense**

1.  *Rewrite the text below, making sure the sentences follow logically from each other. You don't have to use the same number of sentences.*

    Usually a litigant will only go to court if advised that she has an arguable case. Do their lawyers read the same law? Why are people prepared to go to court when statistically they only have a 50 per cent chance of success? What is it about legal disputes which means that both parties can be certain enough of the truth of their claim and the legal merits of their case to go to court? In any legal argument that gets to court someone wins and someone loses.[30]

2.  *Choose a partner and compare versions:*
    *(a) Does your new version make sense? If so, why? If not, why not?*
    *(b) What have you learnt from this exercise which you will use in your own writing?*
    *(c) Record an action plan in your learning diary.*
    *(d) Remember to put your plan into action the next time you write anything that will be read by others.*

## Paragraphing

Paragraphing is the skill of constructing documents whose contents flow in a logical order. Each paragraph should deal with one main topic, which is then developed in the rest of the paragraph. You probably all know this, but do you do it?

The rules for linking paragraphs are the same as for sentences. To give your text a coherent structure, each paragraph should be linked to the previous and the following paragraphs.

Some people write a series of paragraphs of just one sentence.

---

30. Adapted from J. Holland and J. Webb, *Learning Legal Rules*, Oxford University Press, Oxford, 2003, p. 99.

This is a sign of poor writing.

This is because the writing seems disjointed.

The reader has to struggle to make connections.

It looks simplistic.

Get the picture?

However, long, unbroken blocks of print which contain a large amount of information also put a strain on our information processing abilities. We must struggle to extract and make connections between pieces of information.

Above we advised you to vary the length of your sentences. Do the same with your paragraphs. A paragraph consisting of one sentence is therefore perfectly acceptable once in a while, but not as a general habit.

Every paragraph has a topic sentence, usually at or near the beginning. This sentence encapsulates the main point of the paragraph. As long as you have planned your content carefully you should not find it difficult to decide what goes into the topic sentence of each paragraph. What is more difficult is to relate the other sentences in the paragraph to the topic sentence and to each other.[31]

EXERCISE 7.16  **Link-hunting**

*Read this text carefully and answer the questions that follow. Then compare your answers with others from your group.*

**The thrill of the manhunt**

The abolition of hunting is, quite literally, a Utopian ideal. The inhabitants of Sir Thomas More's island rejected the thrill of the chase 'as a thing unworthy to be used of free men'.

Nearly 500 years on, John McFall MP hopes that Parliament will follow their example by giving a second reading to his Wild Mammals (Protection) Bill. His opponents, predictably enough, have accused him of hypocrisy. Why ban fox-hunting but allow shooting and fishing? Why legislate to 'protect wild mammals from certain cruel acts including being taken, killed or injured by the use of dogs' while doing nothing about the cruelty of other predators? It is 'disgraceful', one pro-hunting man thundered this week, that the RSPCA hasn't lifted a finger to campaign on behalf of wild birds, which are 'lured to bird tables with peanuts, then caught by domestic cats and taken half-alive to be tortured'.

Fair enough. Our attitudes to animals are indeed inconsistent. People who seethe with indignation at the sight of a fur coat made from farmed mink will happily swagger about town in leather jackets. Many self-styled 'vegetarians' are quite willing to gorge themselves on smoked salmon. Even vegans may be on shaky ground: after watching

---

31. If you find paragraphing difficult, try the exercise on paragraph analysis in C. Maughan and M. Maughan, 'Legal Writing' in J. Webb et al., *Lawyers' Skills*, Oxford University Press, Oxford, 2004, pp. 35–9.

David Attenborough's Secret Life of Plants, can anyone be sure that cabbages and carrots have no feelings? In a real Utopia, we should all eat nothing but salt – except that, as G K Chesterton once predicted, some smart aleck would then ask 'why should salt suffer?'

Hunters should, however, think twice before making too much of these inconsistencies, lest they be expected to follow through the logic of their own position. If, as they say, it is wrong for Parliament to outlaw blood sports, why don't they demand the repeal of laws against bear-baiting and otter-hunting? And why hasn't the British Field Sports Society re-introduced the noble art of pig-sticking – which is a far more equal battle of wits, setting a lone hunter against a large and dangerous hog?

Why, come to that, should the nanny state prevent us indulging in the ancient and once popular pastime of cock-fighting? When I proposed this the other day to a hunting zealot of my acquaintance, she squealed with outrage: 'Oh no, it's cruel!'

Quite so. The solution, I suggest, is to find humane – or rather human – alternatives. Near where I live in East Anglia there is a pack of bloodhounds which pursues runners across the fields every weekend, to the great enjoyment of all concerned. Sub-aqua enthusiasts could be recruited to swim around Scottish lochs, occasionally rising to the bait of a dry-fly. Viscount Whitelaw showed what could be done on the grouse-moors when, a few years ago, he fired a volley of shotgun pellets into the backside of Sir Joseph Nickerson; Sir Joseph seemed none the worse for the ordeal.

And here's an even better idea: why doesn't some animal-lover invent a 'sport' in which two men climb into a ring and punch each other to a pulp? It might lack the gory excitement of the old cock-fights and dog-fights, but at least no one would try to ban it.[32]

1.  (a) *Identify the topic sentence in each paragraph.*
    (b) *Taking each paragraph in turn, identify the words and phrases which:*
        (i) *link sentences within paragraphs, and*
        (ii) *link paragraphs.*
    *For example:* and, or, but, however, moreover, on the other hand, therefore, although.
    (c) *Are there any sentences which are not linked by such words or phrases? If so, how are they linked?*
2.  *Now try this exercise, with a partner, on some of your own writing.*
    (a) *Separately, look at two or three paragraphs you have written.*
    (b) *Then compare your results.*
    (c) *Do you agree on the topic sentence? What linking devices are used? Do they help clarify or obscure the meaning?*
    (d) *Now do the same with two or three paragraphs written by your partner.*

32. Taken from the *Guardian*, 1 March 1995. The author is Francis Wheen.

It is, of course, possible that you will disagree with your partner about which sentence is the topic sentence. Your interpretation of a paragraph may differ from the one the writer intended. The lesson to be learned here is that there is more likely to be agreement on the meaning when the text is written clearly and coherently. It is much more difficult to agree where the writer's meaning is obscure.

So far in this chapter we have considered a number of characteristics of writing. It may be useful now to formulate a 'rule' for *saying what you mean to say*. We call ours the *three cs*:

---

**BE     CLEAR**
**CONCISE**
**CORRECT**

---

This involves:

- Writing complete sentences, but:
- Avoiding over-long and complex sentences;
- Using frequently used words and phrases instead of infrequently used ones;
- Cutting out redundant words and phrases;
- Avoiding clumsy and inelegant words and phrases;
- Not using the legal register unless:
  (a) there is no alternative, and
  (b) the reader will understand it;
- Making sure you know what your words mean;
- Using accepted grammatical forms;
- Using correct syntax;
- Using appropriate punctuation;
- Spelling correctly;
- Structuring paragraphs with topic sentences;
- Structuring paragraphs with linking devices.

Now, in the next exercise, try applying these guidelines to some poor writing.

EXERCISE 7.17 **Take out the rubbish**

*In small groups:*

1.  *Note down what is wrong with the following texts. Give reasons for your answers.*
2.  *Then rewrite each text so that it is clear, concise and correct.*
    (a)  The defendant denied that she was in breach of contract as alleged by the claimant.

(b)    It is of supreme and paramount importance to our education programme, inter alia, that classes be kept at minimum levels.

(c)    Prior to collecting your vehicle please ensure you pay for your parking at the automatic machines located at the administration building which is situated at the exit.

(d)    Looking forward to meeting with you next week. In the meantime do not hesitate to contact Ms Bloggs or myself at any time should you have any specific queries.

(e)    Whenever there is a body laying in front of his jurisdiction, the coroner must be informed.

(f)    I have given implicit instructions to my staff to keep noise to an absolute minimum due to the close proximity of residential properties.

(g)    A recent report complained that the Crown Prosecution Service was the victim of a great deal of unwarranted criticism. Whenever there is a cock-up they always get the blame.

(h)    The jury also provide a freshness to our system of justice because they are unbiased and therefore their mind is open and enables them to be objectionable.

(i)    The conclusion which has been reached by my client is that if there is a continuation of your insistence on this position, the termination of the contract will be taken into serious consideration by her.[33]

(j)    Subject to banning right turning movements out of East Lane into King's Road ground level crossing facilities across King's Road, south of East Lane, could be provided by means of a staggered green man facility.[34]

(k)    We are embarking on measures to resolve the issue at the earliest opportunity.

(l)    He is a distinguished academic and an imminent politician.

(m)    There was a discussion yesterday on the worrying of sheep by dogs' in the minister's room.

(n)    Mr Maplethorpe, a magistrate, who was well-known for the severity of his views on drunk driving and who made it a point of principle to give the maximum sentence for such offences, particularly when faced with re-offenders, being absent from the meeting that day, a very unusual occurrence for him, was elected chairman of the bench.

(o)    A copy of this letter is attached for you to send to your insurers. Finally we expect an acknowledgement of this letter within 21 days by yourselves or your insurers.

(p)    The Defendants case would of been assisted in the event that this evidence had been disclosed prior to the commencement of the trial.

(q)    The remedies for innocent misrepresentation are rescission and damages, awarded at the courts discretion.

33.    Our thanks to Richard Wydick for this one, which 'clanks along like a rusty tank': (1978) 66 *California Law Review* 727 at p. 745.
34.    And to the Plain English Campaign for this one; *Utter Drivel*, Robson Books Ltd, London, 1994, p. 86.

(r)    I have a list of the shareholders of the company, who's participation in the share capital exceeds 10 per cent.

## Self-edit your writing

Self-editing helps you to develop the skill of looking at what you have written through the eyes of your reader. Getting into the habit of self-editing is a matter of attitude. It can be frustrating and time-consuming to have to rewrite sections of your draft, but the more strict you are with yourself about this, the faster you will achieve artistry.

You may have learned from doing these exercises that it helps to read a draft aloud to yourself, or preferably, to someone else. Better still, ask them to read it aloud to you. This is probably the most revealing strategy to use, because you will hear all your mistakes read out and you will know immediately whether the content is clear and logical. This can be very embarrassing, but at the same time illuminating and instructive.

By now you should be able to draft your own self-editing checklist. This should contain questions you must ask yourself about your text after you have composed one. Try to answer the questions honestly.

EXERCISE 7.18  **Self-editing**

1.    *In pairs, draft a self-editing checklist. Be clear, concise, correct.*
2.    *Compare your list with ours at the end of this chapter. If you think it necessary, revise your list.*
3.    *Try your list out on your next piece of writing. Is it adequate? If not, make any necessary changes.*

## Writing letters

There is certain technical information you need to know before you begin to practise drafting legal letters.

### Writing to clients: client care[35]

Practice Rule 15 of the Law Society's Guide aims to improve communications between solicitors and their clients. It imposes obligations on solicitors to give their clients certain basic information early on in the relationship and throughout the case:

Solicitors shall:

a.    give information about costs and other matters, and
b.    operate a complaints handling procedure,

35.  See Law Society, *The Guide to Professional Conduct of Solicitors*, Law Society, London, 1999, ch. 13.

in accordance with a Solicitors' Costs Information and Client Care Code made from time to time by the Council of the Law Society...

A client must be told who is dealing with his case, and must be kept up to date on how the case is progressing. He must be given a name in the firm to contact if he has a complaint, and details of the firm's complaints procedure. In addition, a client must know at the time of instructing a solicitor what the solicitor is going to charge for her services. As the case progresses, the client must be kept informed about costs.

## Writing to other people

### The letter of claim (formerly known as 'letter before action')

Under the Civil Procedure Rules, pre-action protocols have been created which set out the steps the parties should take to communicate with each other about a prospective claim.[36] The aim of a protocol is to encourage the parties to exchange information early and avoid litigation by settling the claim without any further action. Litigation is seen as the last resort. The first step is for the claimant to send a letter of claim to the defendant, informing him about the dispute. The letter should state the facts of the claimant's case, the loss or injuries suffered, and the remedy she is seeking. The Personal Injury Protocol contains a standard format for the letter of claim, intended to be clear enough for the recipient to understand and take the necessary steps.[37] It is unfortunate that rules of court are needed to make lawyers draft clearly, especially as the concept of the letter of claim is familiar and the content is not particularly complex.[38] We can commend the specimen letter for avoiding legalese, but officialese is not entirely absent; see the final paragraph quoted as sentence (o) in Exercise 7.17 above.

As a lawyer you will, of course, write lots of different kinds of letters. Some will seek information, others will provide information, negotiate or set out the terms of a settlement. Negotiations towards the sale or purchase of land, for example, should be headed SUBJECT TO CONTRACT.

WITHOUT PREJUDICE at the top of the letter allows parties to negotiate freely without the risk of damaging their case. If negotiations subsequently fail and the case goes to court, no 'without prejudice' correspondence will be included in the bundle of documents for court.

EXERCISE 7.19  **Joyless in the Maldini**

You have been instructed by Margaret Foster, who came to ask your advice about a possible claim against a tour operator. Ms Foster told you she booked a package

36. CPR (1998) Vol. 1 C1–001. Protocols in force at the time of writing are Personal Injury, Clinical Negligence, Professional Negligence, Construction and Engineering Disputes, and Defamation.
37. At C2–016. For an example, see Inns of Court School of Law, *Civil Litigation*, Oxford University Press, Oxford, 2003, ch. 2.
38. Compare the comment by Boyle et al., *A Practical Guide to Lawyering Skills*, Cavendish, London, 2003, p. 46.

holiday for her family with Joyful Tours Ltd in April this year. The holiday was for two weeks in the Maldini islands, from 14 July to 28 July. The hotel was described as follows:

> *All 60 rooms are air-conditioned and comfortably furnished. Each has a mini fridge-bar, shower and wc. All rooms have a verandah opening on to the beach. There is an air-conditioned restaurant, a bar and a club house. There is a wide range of water sports, including scuba diving. Regular evening entertainment includes live bands. For a change of scene a ferry service operates to the neighbouring island of Voss.*

The air-conditioning in the Fosters' hotel rooms did not work. The children's verandah opened on to a noisy building site, with no sea view. The bar was closed for nine nights of their stay. Bob, Margaret's son, particularly wanted to learn to scuba dive, but was told this facility was not available. No other water sports were offered either. There was only one disco held in the club house, and not one live band appeared during their stay. Desperately searching for a change of scene by visiting Voss, they found there were no ferries operating.

Margaret complained several times to the Joyful Tours representative in the hotel, but nothing was done. The family came home miserable and depressed. One of Joyful Tour's booking conditions states:

> *. . . In the unlikely event that matters cannot be resolved to your satisfaction in the resort, details of your complaint should be notified in writing to our Customer Relations Department at our Manchester Head Office within 28 days of returning from the resort. We will not accept liability in respect of claims which we receive after that date.*

Margaret wrote to Joyful Tours to complain, but not until 19 September.

*In pairs:*

(a)    *Carry out the necessary research. Mind map or flow chart the information you think you need to give Ms Foster.*
(b)    *Draft a letter to Ms Foster, confirming her instructions and explaining the legal position.*
(c)    *Draft a letter to Joyful Tours.*
(d)    *Give your letters to your tutor.*

## Good writing makes sense

We hope we have made it clear in this chapter that you should never under-estimate the importance of good writing. Because you have been writing for so long as part of your education, it is easy to assume you are good at it, or at least that your skills are adequate. We have seen many examples in this chapter of poor writing composed by ostensibly well-educated people who must have been writing for years.

We hope your study of this chapter has provided you with some insight into how language works. In our experience, students frequently recognise that they are poor writers, but cannot pinpoint their weaknesses. We think that it helps to identify weaknesses and put them right when you have some idea of the functions of grammar and punctuation.

We have tried to dispel some of the popular misconceptions about language. That punctuation is part of your grammar, for example, may have come as a surprise to some of you. It is easy to think that punctuation errors are unimportant, whereas they are necessary and useful markers of meaning.

Similarly, it may have surprised some of you that you learn the fundamentals of grammar without being formally taught. Or that writing which makes the reader struggle to get the meaning denotes ineptitude or muddled thinking rather than elegance and sophistication. Remember too that if you have a problem with writing, it may not be because of linguistic expression alone. It may be that you have not thought through clearly in advance what it is you want to say.

EXERCISE 7.20 **Concepts**

In this chapter we have discussed a number of concepts. We list the main ones below. The procedure for learning these concepts is as follows.

1.   *Divide into pairs.*
2.   *Each pair is to:*
     *(a) define each concept, noting the page on which it is defined and discussed, and*
     *(b) make sure that both members of the pair understand the meaning of each concept.*
3.   *Combine into groups of four. Compare the answers of the two pairs. If there is disagreement, look up the concept and clarify it until all agree on the definition and understand it.*

| | |
|---|---|
| *register* | *dialect* |
| *syntax* | *grammar* |
| *accent* | *malapropism* |
| *sentence* | *topic sentence* |
| *officialese* | *jargon* |
| *standard English* | *correctness* |

EXERCISE 7.21 **More rubbish**

*In small groups:*

1.   *Note down what is wrong with the letter below. Give reasons for your answers.*
2.   *Rewrite the letter. (You should be able to infer the context.)*
3.   *Exchange redrafts with another group.*

4.  *Mark their redraft. Underline or highlight good and bad points, and give a mark out of 10.*
5.  *Return the redraft to the group and give constructive oral feedback.*
6.  *Note down anything you will do differently next time.*


Fleeceham & Bankitt
Solicitors
Blur Buildings
Narrow Street
Bristol BS45 5OJ
6 March 200 . . .


Dear Sirs,

*Re: Gary Francis Dobbs*

We are in receipt of your communication dated 28 February 2000 . . . , for which we are grateful. As is doubtless known to yourselves, the discussions between myself and the aforementioned client attract Legal Professional Privilege which it is incumbent on the client to waive, rather than ourselves.

In order to facilitate your enquiries, we have taken it upon ourselves to take matters further by re-establishing contact with Mr Dobbs, at present resident in Grabham remand centre. Mr Dobbs expressed to us his lack of opposition to such waiver of Privilege, the effect of which being that we are enabled to bring the content of such Privileged information to your attention.

My initial personal contact with this client took effect at 7.57 pm precisely, in a cell at Grasston Police Station. During this brief interlude between interviews Mr Dobbs gave me the impression, in somewhat garbled dialect, that he was not a well man. I apprised him of the forthcoming situation of the interview and reassured him that my presence there was assured. Mr Dobbs did not make any admissions at this premature stage. Nor did he appear, to my surprise, unduly becalmed by my assurance of accompaniment at the interview.

Mr Dobbs continued to seem somewhat disfunctional throughout DC Binks's postulations, and rather lacked self-composure in my view, in consideration of the fact that the posture on the part of the Police Officers did not convey an impression of undue pressure or threatening aspect.

During the interval, we had time for a little chat. Mr Dobbs told me that he had indeed taken the Car and driven it for some distance, as alleged by the Police Officers. I must say at this point, however, that comprehension of Mr Dobbs's strange speech patterns was not automatic. Probing for understanding did not appear to be received with equanimity on his part, for some reason I know not what of.

I advised him in plain and simple English to come clean with me on the Aggravated Vehicle Taking business. The great proportion of my time was taken up in attempting at considerable length and clarity to put across the merits as regards sentencing of admitting the aggravated facts in issue if indeed facts they be. If not, however, I explained at great length, he should be forearmed to treat the stipulations and ramifications of the Officers with considerable disdain in pursuit of denial.

What I said to him I fear made little sense. He was in a condition of extreme agitation and dejected. His replies to my exhortations were convoluted and to some extent non-existent. Thus I cannot report them to you with any precision or intelligibility.

I wish to inform you that should you require any further assistance from myself, from the 15th until the 22nd of March I shall be attendent and presenting a Paper at a symposium in Seattle, USA, the subject of which is delineated as 'Solicitor–Client Discourse: Semantic and Lexical Variables in Police Station Narratives'. I shall therefore unfortunately be unable to attend upon any needful requirements of yourselves.

Yours faithfully,

... ... ....

## EXERCISE 7.22  Blowing the whistle? Part II[39]

Maria Bertorelli has phoned your firm to say she has heard nothing from you. Although her English is good, it is not her first language and she is not sure she understood everything you told her at the meeting two weeks ago.

1.  *In your groups, write a letter to Ms Bertorelli confirming the advice you gave her at the meeting.*
2.  *Exchange letters with another group.*
3.  *Underline or highlight good and bad points and give a mark out of 10.*
4.  *Return the letter to the group and give constructive feedback on the following:*
    *(a) Does the letter achieve its purpose?*
    *(b) Is all the information accurate and relevant?*
    *(c) Are style and tone appropriate?*
    *(d) Is the information organised appropriately?*
    *(e) Is the language clear, concise and correct?*
5.  *Note down anything you will do differently next time.*

## Review question

*Discuss the following quotation:*

[T]here are no important propositions that cannot be stated in plain language ... The writer who seeks to be intelligible needs to be right; he must be challenged if his argument leads to an erroneous conclusion and especially if it leads to a wrong action. But he can safely dismiss the charge that he has made the subject too easy. The truth is not difficult. Complexity and obscurity have professional value – they are the academic equivalents of apprenticeship rules in the building trades. They exclude the outsiders, keep down the competition, preserve the image of a privileged or priestly

39.  See exercise 5.19.

class. The man who makes things clear is a scab. He is criticised less for his clarity than for his treachery.[40]

## Learning points

(a)    *Select an assignment that you are planning to write in the next few weeks.*
(b)    *What changes will you make to your approach, and why?*

## Further reading

Sir Ernest Gowers, *The Complete Plain Words*, Penguin, London, 1986.

M. Swan, *Practical English Usage*, Oxford University Press, Oxford, 1995.

J. Ayto, *The Oxford Essential Guide to the English Language*, Oxford University Press, Oxford, 1998.

Plain English Campaign, *Plain English Course Workbook*, Plain English Campaign, 2002.

M. Cutts, *Plain English Guide*, Oxford University Press, Oxford, 1999.

R. Wydick, *Plain English for Lawyers*, Carolina Academic Press, US, 1985.

C. Maughan and M. Maughan, 'Legal Writing' in J. Webb, C. Maughan, M. Maughan, M. Keppel-Palmer and A. Boon, *Lawyers' Skills*, Oxford University Press, Oxford, 2004.

B. A. Garner, *The Redbook: A Manual on Legal Style*, West Group, St Paul, Minn., 2002.

F. Boyle, D. Capps, P. Plowden and C. Sandford, *A Practical Guide to Lawyering Skills*, Cavendish, London, 2003, pp. 1–53.

M. Costanzo, *Legal Writing*, Cavendish, London, 1993.

P. Rylance, *Legal Writing and Drafting*, Blackstone, London, 1994.

H. Brayne and R. Grimes, *Professional Skills for Lawyers: A Student's Guide*, Butterworths, London, 1998, pp. 23–90.

## Self-editing checklist for writing

Purpose:

What is the purpose of this communication?
Have I adapted style and content to suit the reader's needs?
Have I dealt with all the issues?
Have I answered all the questions raised?
Have I gone into enough/too much depth?
Have I repeated myself unnecessarily?

Content:

● Is all the information accurate?
● Is all of it relevant?

---

40. J. K. Galbraith, *Writing, Typing and Economics*, Atlantic, 1978, p. 105.

## Style:

- Is the style too formal/informal?
- Will my tone produce the desired response?
- Is it friendly, courteous, helpful, frank?
- Is it peremptory, hostile, rude?

## Layout:

- Is the layout appropriate for the purpose and content?
- Is it set out in manageable blocks?

## Structure:

- Is the information organised appropriately?
- Are the sentences short enough?
- Does the order of sentences and paragraphs make sense?
- Does each paragraph contain just one main idea?
- Is there a link between each paragraph and the next?
- Are there links between sentences in each paragraph?

## Language:

- Have I used plain language – clear, concise, and correct language that the reader can easily understand?
- Have I omitted words and phrases which are
    - infrequently used;
    - inelegant;
    - redundant;
    - unnecessarily technical;
    - unnecessarily abstract;
    - verbose?
- Is the grammar appropriate for the purpose?
- Are punctuation and spelling correct?

# 8

## Manipulating language: drafting legal documents

The language of legal documents has unique features which are closely linked with its purposes. A legal draft is a correct and complete statement of a legal relationship, so legal drafters are much more concerned with making that statement comprehensive than comprehensible. A drafter wants to guard against the possibility of litigation arising from her draft more than she wants it to be elegantly written and easily understood. The extent to which the often complex requirements of the draft can be rendered in elegant, easily understood English is the measure of the drafter's artistry.

## Objectives

To:

- Examine the purposes of legal document drafting.
- Analyse the linguistic, organisational and contextual features of legal language.
- Determine what is essential for precision and clarity, and discard what is not.
- Establish a general set of principles for drafting in plain English.
- Apply these principles when redrafting and drafting documents.

## Supports benchmark statements

Students should demonstrate a basic ability:

6. Communication and literacy
- To understand and use the English language proficiently in relation to legal matters.
- To present knowledge or an argument in a way which is comprehensible to others and which is directed at their concerns.
- To read and discuss legal materials which are written in technical and complex language.

7. Other key skills
● To produce word processed text and to present such work in an appropriate form.

## Legal documents are precision instruments

Why are legal sentences so grammatically complex? Why do lawyers

● Use unusual word order?
● Use mammoth sentences (sentences within sentences)?
● Repeat themselves?
● Use the passive?
● Use complex nominalisations instead of verbs?

In Chapter 7 we argued that clarity and precision are at the heart of artistry in writing. In legal document drafting, however, these two elements are apparently in conflict. Why is this so? To answer this question we must look at the functions of drafting.

> Legal language does not only have a communicative function. In both its written and oral forms, it is the primary *tool* of the legal professional. Unlike physicians who have instruments and procedures, engineers who have blueprints, computers and processes, and scientists who have laboratories, lawyers have only legal language. In fact, lawyers call their legal documents 'instruments'. True, all professions have a body of thought and theory that is embodied in language, but for lawyers there is only *one* way of accessing this knowledge – through legal language.[1]

Let's have a look at one of these 'instruments'.

EXERCISE **8.1 Runaway trolleys**

*Read the following text and answer the questions.*

The Litter (Northern Ireland) Order 1994 Schedule 1: Abandoned Shopping and Luggage Trolleys

1.
　　(1) Subject to sub-paragraph (2), this Schedule applies where any shopping or
　　　　luggage trolley is found by an authorised officer on any land in the open air
　　　　and appears to him to be abandoned.

---

1. V. Charrow, J. A. Crandall and R. Charrow, 'Characteristics and Functions of Legal Language' in R. Kittredge and J. Lehrberger (eds.), *Sublanguage: Studies of Language in Restricted Semantic Domains*, De Gruyter, Berlin, 1982, p. 181.

    (2)  This Schedule does not apply in relation to a shopping or luggage trolley found on the following descriptions of land, that is to say –

      (a)  land in which the owner of the trolley has an estate;

      (b)  where an off-street parking place affords facilities to the customers of shops for leaving there shopping trolleys used by them, land on which those facilities are afforded;

      (c)  where any other place designated by the district council for the purposes of this Schedule affords like facilities, land on which those facilities are afforded; and

      (d)  as respects luggage trolleys, land which is used for the purposes of its undertaking by a statutory undertaker.

2.  *Power to seize and remove trolleys*

    (1)  Where this Schedule applies in relation to a shopping or luggage trolley, the district council may, subject to sub-paragraph (2), –

      (a)  seize the trolley; and

      (b)  remove it to such place under its control as the council thinks fit.

    (2)  When a shopping or luggage trolley is found on any land appearing to the authorised officer to be occupied by any person, the trolley shall not be removed without the consent of that person, unless –

      (a)  the council has served on that person a notice stating that the council proposes to remove the trolley; and

      (b)  no notice objecting to its removal is served by that person on the council within the period of 14 days from the day on which the council served the notice of the proposed removal on him.

(a)  *Can you grasp the meaning on a first reading?*

(b)  *Why/why not?*

(c)  *Who is the text written for?*

(d)  *Who are the likely readers?*

(e)  *What is the purpose of the document?*

(f)  *Agree definitions of 'luggage trolley' and 'shopping trolley'. Draft your definitions in the style of the Schedule.*

(g)  *Compare your draft with the original; s. 5 of the Schedule.*

Nobody reads documents like this out of choice. We only read them if we have to. Their purpose is to provide a comprehensive and correct statement of the law. Legal drafters know that their creations will be scrutinised at length and in silence by legal experts who will often be intent on finding some loophole or ambiguity which will advance their argument or their client's case. It is therefore vitally important to get the law right.

There are those who take the view that any thought or idea can be expressed in an immediately comprehensible way. We don't agree. Haven't you ever had a thought which you couldn't put easily into words? Sometimes our thoughts are too sophisticated to be rendered by the language we have at our disposal. Legal drafters often find themselves in this position and consequently have to stretch, twist and curl the language to embrace all possible meanings and interpretations which can be ascribed to their documents. Headline writers do this to create ambiguity:

STIFF OPPOSITION EXPECTED TO CASKETLESS FUNERAL PLAN

DRUNK GETS NINE MONTHS IN VIOLIN CASE

QUEEN MARY HAVING BOTTOM SCRAPED

COLUMNIST GETS UROLOGIST IN TROUBLE WITH HIS PEERS

IRAQI HEAD SEEKS ARMS[2]

Presumably, the headline writers knew which meaning of *stiff, violin case, bottom, peers* and *head* they had in mind. This is precisely the kind of ambiguity that legal drafters need to avoid. How are they to do this?

To be so precise as to avoid ambiguity, whilst at the same time covering every foreseeable eventuality is extremely difficult. This is why many drafters stick to boilerplate.[3] It is certain and therefore safe. They don't want to take the risk of litigation which could arise if in the name of clarity, brevity and elegance they experiment with untested language.

This is the key issue in this chapter. Up to this point we have argued that getting your message across to your recipient quickly and easily is the primary purpose of speech and writing. We have recommended respect for the needs and abilities of your audience and the use of plain English in writing. In drafting, we have to make sure that what we say is comprehensive and correct in law and fact, before considering the likely needs of the reader. In fact, we have to assume that our readers are capable of understanding what we write, because we are not going to alter it to make it more accessible.

Naturally, we believe you should aim for clarity as well. Mastering the techniques of precision will make you technically competent, but add clarity and you will be developing your artistry. You can be innovative with language without having to experiment with untried forms.

So you should still have your reader in mind. An 'authorised officer' or 'statutory undertaker' may need to read the trolley regulations. She may not have time to consult a lawyer or indeed may not have access to one.

## Legal documents and the three Cs

Imagine a council employee wants to deal with a complaint from a resident who keeps finding empty shopping trolleys in his garden. How easily will she find her way round this document? In comparison with many older statutory instruments, this one is a model of clarity. There is plenty of punctuation which breaks up sentences into manageable blocks and helps with meaning. No block of print is

2. Taken from S. Pinker, *The Language Instinct*, Allen Lane, London, 1994, p. 79.
3. '... a standard provision that is routinely added to a particular type of document': P. Tiersma, *Legal Language*, 1999, p. 59. See also Charrow, Crandall and Charrow, *Sublanguage*, p. 178.

longer than three lines, and generally, each section and sub-section deals with only one idea. The word order follows the patterns of standard English with one or two exceptions: s. 1(2)(d), for example. It would be more usual to say:

> ... land which is used by a statutory undertaker for the purposes of its undertaking.

Nevertheless, some parts of the document are long-winded. For example:

| | | |
|---|---|---|
| 1(2)(d): | ... which is used *for the purposes of* its undertaking ... | Won't *for* do? |
| 1(2): | ... in relation to.. . | Won't *to* do? |
| and | ... that is to say – | Is this necessary? |

A bit of tinkering in these examples will reduce redundant words and phrases. However, we have to think a little harder before we abandon the cumbersome phrase at the end of the following section:

> 1(2)(c) where any other place designated by the district council for the purposes of this Schedule affords like facilities, *land on which those facilities are afforded;*

A more elegant rendering produces:

> any other land designated by the district council which affords like facilities;

The ambiguity here makes it clear that the cumbersome phrase is not superfluous. Using *which* or *who* will bring elegance to writing, but these words can be dangerous for legal drafters. It must be quite clear which preceding item these words refer back to. This is why legal drafters have avoided the usual ways of linking an item either to what follows or what has gone before. Legal documents therefore seem to be unnecessarily repetitious, and hard to read as a result.

An unfortunate by-product of this concern for precise reference is a host of ugly words and phrases which have come to characterise boilerplate: *aforesaid, hereinbefore, the said facilities*, for example. These allow the drafter to avoid ambiguities which could arise from using ordinary English linking words like *he, she, it, them, their, this, that, which, who*, etc. However, these archaic usages have become so entrenched in the legal register that lawyers use them in situations where no ambiguity would arise. For example:

> *By an oral agreement made ........ the Defendant, in the course of his said business, agreed with the Claimant that he would carry out various building and redecoration works to the Claimant's said flat for a total price of ....... . The said agreement was evidenced ... by a letter from the Defendant ...*
>
> *At all relevant times the Defendant knew that the said works were required by the Claimant in order that he could let the said premises immediately after the conclusion thereof.*

> *There were* ..... *the following express terms of the said agreement:*
> .......*That the Claimant would pay the said price by means of one payment of* ....*imme-
> diately prior to the commencement of the said works, and the balance of* .... *upon the
> completion thereof.*[4]

Are all these *saids* really necessary? And couldn't we use '*this* agreement', '*these*
works, '*agreed* price'? Or would the gravitas of the law be irredeemably shaken by
the use of these ordinary words? We shall return to this point shortly.

Now have a look at s. 1(2)(b):

> where an off-street parking place affords facilities to the customers of shops for leaving
> there shopping trolleys *used by them*, ...

*Used by them* is inelegant, but we should be grateful that modern drafting is
beginning to abandon forms like *by the said customers* and use *by them* instead
where it is quite clear who is referred to. The plain English campaign is clearly
making its mark!

There are other examples in this text. In s. 2(2)(b) we have *that person* and *by
him* rather than *the said person* and *by the said person*, or *by that person*. In s. 1(2)(c)
the drafter uses *like facilities* instead of repeating the whole phrase:

> to the customers of shops for leaving there shopping trolleys used by them.

Is *like* sufficiently safe? Why didn't she use *such*, a very common word in such
writing? Do they mean the same?

*As respects* in s. 1(2)(d) is a usage we haven't come across before. It seems to
replace the officialese *in respect of* but does not improve on it.

Let's turn now to a sub-section that is hard to grasp. In s. 2(2)(b) the drafter
crams a number of ideas into one sentence. No wonder the sentence lacks clarity.
How many ideas can you list in this sentence? We counted at least four: the trolley
'shall not be removed unless':

1.   that person has not served a notice on the council;
2.   this notice objects to removal;
3.   this notice must be served within 14 days;
4.   from the date the council served its removal notice on that person.

Not surprisingly, the normal rules of English syntax cannot cope. The rules have to
be bent and twisted, and the reader has to study the text carefully to sort out the
grammatical relationships which give the clues to meaning.

Interestingly, Latin would have coped much better with s. 2(2)(b). Meaning in
Latin is determined not by the word order, as in English, but by word endings.

---

4.  This is an extract from an example draft in W. M. Rose, *Pleadings Without Tears*, Oxford
    University Press, Oxford, 2002, pp. 49, 54. Now that the CPR encourage lawyers to write in
    plain English, we were surprised to find that these archaic forms are still used. However, the Inns
    of Court School of Law Drafting Manual recommends deleting 'said' if there is no possible
    ambiguity: (2002) p. 5.

Deciphering long sentences was therefore not difficult. The noun and case forms of Latin showed quickly and concisely the internal relationships of ideas in a sentence. An idea which might need eleven words in English could be expressed in five. For example:

> de minimis non curat lex:    the law does not concern itself with things of little importance

Many legal documents used to be written in Latin, where it is possible to incorporate a large number of ideas into one sentence. To do the same in English needs far more words. Perhaps it is the old lawyers' love of Latin which has left us the legacy of interminable legal sentences which only an expert can understand, and then with difficulty.

A further motivation for long sentences is the lawyer's preference for placing all information on a particular topic in one self-contained unit:

> Presumably, this tendency reduces the ambiguity that might result if conditions on a rule or provision are placed in separate sentences. Legal drafters seem to fear that if they place a condition or a rule in a separate sentence directly following the statement of the rule, some lawyer will later be free to argue that the condition does not apply.[5]

Turning now to the vocabulary of these regulations, you won't have found any archaisms. Nevertheless, there are words and phrases with technical meanings which a lay person may not have come across. For example:

> *estate*
> *land*
> *authorised officer*
> *statutory undertaker*
> *under its control*
> *thinks fit*

*Seize* is an interesting, metaphorical usage. It doesn't sound like legalese. Rather, it conjures up an image of an authorised officer grabbing hold of a trolley, shouting 'come here, you . . . !' Do you think the drafter should have used the more neutral *take possession of*?

Reading s. 1(2)(d), a lay reader may be forgiven for missing the connection between luggage trolleys and funeral parlours. As far as we know, corpses are not transported in luggage trolleys!

Help is at hand in the interpretation section, which defines *statutory undertaker*. Moreover, our council employee will find herself described in the definition of *authorised officer*. The other terms in the list are not defined. Can she get the meaning from the everyday English definitions? If not, will a dictionary help?

---

5. P. M. Tiersma, *Legal Language*, p. 56.

Let's try this out with the word *estate*. The *Oxford English Dictionary* gives us thirteen meanings. Number 11 is the legal meaning:

> The interest which anyone has in lands, tenements, or any other effects; often with qualifying words or phrases as *an estate upon conditions, in fee, for life, of inheritance, tail from year to year, at will,* etc. *Real estate,* an interest in landed property; *Personal estate,* an interest in moveables . . .

Will a law dictionary explain this definition in terms comprehensible to the lay person?

> 'Estate' has two meanings. In its narrower meaning it denotes the fee simple of land and any of the various interests into which it could formerly be divided at law, whether for life, or for a term of years or otherwise: and, where there was an estate at law, there could be a corresponding estate in equity. In its wider meaning it denotes any property whatever and is divided into real and personal estate.[6]

To interpret these entries correctly you surely have to be familiar with the legal register.

*Under its control*: will the officer tie the trolley up to prevent it escaping? This phrase has a specific legal meaning which will probably elude anyone not well-versed in the discourse of law. The same is true of *think fit*.

We can't comment on how the information is organised in this document, because we have only quoted two sections of it. However, we can see that the information itself is not particularly complex. You probably paraphrased the content very quickly. It is therefore relatively easy to draft it in a manner that the reader finds comprehensible. Although you may have concluded that a lawyer will need to explain certain terms to a lay person, this shouldn't be too difficult a task.

Nevertheless, when the drafter tries to cover a number of ideas in one sentence, as in s. 2(2)(b), it obscures the meaning. Do you remember Text 1 in Exercise 7.2? How could you forget it?

> Where particulars of a partnership are disclosed to the Executive Council the remuneration of the individual partner for superannuation purposes will be deemed to be such proportion of the total remuneration of such practitioners as the proportion of his share in partnership profits bears to the total proportion of the shares of such practitioner in those profits.

This text is so impenetrable that we weren't able to agree on the meaning. Normal English structure can't do justice to such complex subject matter. Let's look now at part of a regulation which is not as immediately accessible as the trolley regulations.

---

6. J. Saunders (ed.), *Words and Phrases Legally Defined*, vol. 2, Butterworths, London, 1989, pp. 175–6.

EXERCISE **8.2** **Unravelling the regs**

Gerry is a family friend who comes to ask your advice. His father, George, is 87 years old and lives in a residential home for the elderly. Gerry is legally entitled to act for George in matters of social security.

Income support was paid to George from the date he entered the home (December 2000). At that time George's house was put on the market, but was not sold until July 2002. All but £4,000 of the proceeds of sale were paid to Gerry and his sister, Jane. This was to repay them:

(a)    for money they spent on looking after George and his house for several years until he entered the residential home,
(b)    for money they had spent renovating and decorating the house to get it ready for sale,
(c)    for legal fees and selling costs.

Therefore, only £4,000 was paid directly to George.

Gerry has received the following notification from the Social Security Adjudication Officer:

> The claimant is not entitled to Income Support from 14 July 2002. This is because he is treated as possessing capital which exceeds the prescribed amount of £8,000.

When Gerry phoned the social security office for an explanation, he was told that the Adjudication Officer considered that items under (a) and (b) were not proper deductions, but had been made solely to secure George's entitlement to income support. Gerry was referred to the following provisions:

●    Section 134 of the Social Security Contributions and Benefits Act 1992.
●    Regulations 45 and 51 of the Income Support (General) Regulations 1987.

Gerry started to read Regulation 51, but gave up after sub-section 2 and consulted you.

> Notional capital
> 51(1) A claimant shall be treated as possessing capital of which he has deprived himself for the purpose of securing entitlement to income support or increasing the amount of that benefit except—
>
> (a)    where the capital is derived from a payment made in consequence of any personal injury and is placed on trust for the benefit of the claimant; or
> (b)    to the extent that the capital which he is treated as possessing is reduced in accordance with regulation 51A (diminishing notional capital rule).
>
> (2) Except in the case of –
>
> (a)    a discretionary trust;
> (b)    a trust derived from a payment made in consequence of a personal injury; or
> (c)    any loan which would be obtainable if secured against capital disregarded under Schedule 10,

any capital which would become available to the claimant upon application being made but which has not been acquired by him shall be treated as possessed by him but only from the date on which it could be expected to be acquired were an application made.[7]

Gerry wants you to tell him how the Adjudication Officer could have reached this decision.

*In small groups:*

(a)    *Paraphrase s. 51(1) and (2), noting how long this process took you.*
(b)    *What features make this text more difficult to understand than the trolley regulations? Give reasons.*
(c)    *When you have done the research, draft a letter to Gerry, explaining the legal position.*
(d)    *Compare your draft with another group's draft and feed back.*
(e)    *Discuss the purposes of Exercises 7.1, 7.2 and 7.3, and what you have learnt from the exercises about drafting.*

What has to be put down in words in reg. 51 is extremely complex. To start with, you have to grasp the central notion: that the law treats you as having capital even though in reality you haven't! It is not easy to get your head round this apparently illogical proposition.

Your work on Chapter 7 and your analysis of the trolley regulations here will have enabled you to identify the linguistic features which impede understanding, so we don't propose to discuss them again here. The tortured sentence structure speaks for itself.

To add to the complexity, the reader may have to refer to other sources (reg. 51A, Schedule 10). After the further six sub-sections in s. 51 which we haven't quoted, there is a list of words and phrases in which the reader is referred to various other pieces of legislation to find their definitions. To interpret the meaning, it is therefore necessary to refer to sources other than the provision itself.

Why have we asked you to analyse legislation in these exercises, when you are much more likely to be drafting contracts, wills and statements of case? Since we can't expect lay people to find their way round this legislation without expert help, it is vital that the experts understand it. Then they have to be able to explain its meaning to non-experts. How sure are you that your explanation to Gerry was completely accurate and comprehensive? If as a result of your investigations you concluded that Gerry could successfully appeal the Adjudication Officer's finding, would you suggest to him that he argues the appeal before the tribunal himself? Or will he need representation?

Working through these exercises should have made it clear that with subject matter as complicated as this and where it is necessary to cross-reference from a number of sources, drafting a version which makes sense (even to lawyers) will be impossible. Yet your client is going to expect that you can do this even if in many

---

7. Income Support (General) Regulations 1987.

cases you would have to consolidate all the sources before you could attempt something intelligible.

Consolidation, of course, is a task for a higher authority. This brings us to our next point of discussion on the purpose of drafting.

## Legal language is powerful stuff

It is axiomatic that ignorance of the law is no excuse. Yet the provisions we have quoted demonstrate that ignorance of the law ought to be a very good excuse. We are governed by regulations that may be inaccessible to those appointed to enforce them, as well as to all of us who are expected to obey them. For reasons we have discussed, the designers of these instruments are not concerned about the reader's level of understanding. Their creations put the law into action. If what you do is contrary to regulation A which must be read in conjunction with regulation B as amended by regulation C, you are guilty. Likewise, if you put your signature to a contractual document you may experience the full force of the Law (note capital L) if you don't keep to its terms.

> ... because bureaucrats communicate with the rest of the world on unequal terms – because they possess the power – they do not have to listen to non-bureaucrats. Outsiders must deal with the bureaucracy on its own terms. Consequently, bureaucrats may forget how to organise their ideas, write, and speak like ordinary people. Sometimes, they may consciously use bureaucratese to exclude outsiders, or to enhance their own power by mystifying outsiders.
>
> Because of the power of the government over ordinary people, bureaucratic language (including the written variety) is effectively a prestige dialect. Even though many people dislike it, even ridicule it, many others consider it valuable, and worth emulating. The news media are quick to take up bureaucratic jargon and use it as their own, contributing to its spread and further enhancing its prestige.[8]

As Veda Charrow says, many bureaucrats are lawyers, who both interpret and perpetuate the legalese that gives life to the bureaucracy. But can we expect them to stop using this high status dialect? Learning to think like a lawyer takes years of training, and some years of experience to refine. However, if some of the examples we have looked at represent how lawyers think, law schools should be very worried indeed. As American attorney Ronald Goldfarb puts it:

> Something very strange happens when human beings enter law school. At some point during their three years, students pick up the notion that in order to be a lawyer, one must learn to speak and write like a lawyer. No one actually tells law students this is a requirement to pass the Bar, but inevitably the message reaches them.

---

8. V. Charrow, 'Language in the Bureaucracy' in R. Di Pietro (ed.), *Linguistics and the Professions: Advances in Discourse Processes*, vol. 8, Ablex, Norwood, NJ, 1982.

Nothing is done in law school to cure the problem, in fact it is compounded. What students read in law school are law review articles, legal treatises and judicial opinions. In the most part this is a collection of turgid, overblown, pompous, technically incompetent prose.

By the end of three years, students can barely get through a letter or a conversation without dropping a few 'notwithstandings', 'heretofores' and 'arguendos'. Everything they have seen and heard for three years leads them to assume this lingo is expected of them.[9]

Arthur Symonds lampooned a lawyer's 'supernatural incantation' for the simple statement *I give you this orange*:

> Know all men by these presents that I hereby give, grant, bargain, sell, release, convey, transfer, and quitclaim all my right, title, interest, benefit, and use whatever in, of, and concerning this chattel, otherwise known as an orange, or citrus orantium, together with all the appurtenances thereto of skin, pulp, pip, rind, seeds, and juice, to have and to hold the said orange together with its skin, pulp, pip, rind, seeds, and juice for his own use and behoof, to himself and his heirs in fee simple forever, free from all liens, encumbrances, easements, limitations, restraints, or conditions whatsoever, any and all prior deeds, transfers or other documents whatsoever, now or anywhere made to the contrary notwithstanding, with full power to bite, cut, suck, or otherwise eat the said orange or to give away the same, with or without its skin, pulp, pip, rind, seeds, or juice.[10]

This may be humorous exaggeration, but the point is made. Using this dialect shows you are an expert. Expertise denotes power and prestige. By relinquishing their boilerplate lawyers reduce the gap between them and ordinary mortals.

We referred earlier to the gravitas of certain legal English. There are features of legal discourse and culture which are reminiscent of religious ritual. Until recently, for example, the remedies an injured party seeks used to be listed in what was known as the 'prayer'.[11] When judges or magistrates enter the court room, we are ordered to 'all rise'. We half expect them to ask us to remove our hats. The majesty of the court is reinforced through the unusual form of headdress worn by judges and barristers. Anyone who wore this somewhere other than a court room would probably be the object of ridicule. Recently, however, newly appointed solicitor-advocates wanted to adopt this ritual. The Bar objected.

> And as in some religions, where it is not necessary (or perhaps even desirable) to understand the meaning of the rituals in order to be impressed by the power of the deity, it is not necessary for the lay person to understand the law in order to

9. R. Goldfarb, 'My Secretary, Hereinafter Referred to as Cuddles  ' (1978) 5 Barrister 10.
10. *Mechanics of Law-Making*, 1835, quoted in J. D. Gordon III, 'How Not To Succeed in Law School' (1991) 100 *Yale Law Journal* 1678 at p. 1689.
11. The 'prayer' is no longer required under the new Civil Procedure Rules, since the remedies now appear on the claim form (formerly known as the 'writ'). Nevertheless, the ICSL Drafting Manual suggests that both the term and the format are still widely used: (2002) p. 50.

be impressed by the power of the law. As with religion, the law has trained inter-mediaries – lawyers – who will interpret, even intercede for us.[12]

It is not only the bureaucracy that deals with us on unequal terms. Since the use of standard form contracts became widespread, there has been concern that the recipients of these have no choice but to accept the terms, however unreason-able.[13] Judicial decisions, statutes and, more recently, EC Directives have sought to redress the balance. Regulation 6(2) of the Unfair Terms in Consumer Contracts Regulations 1999 requires businesses to draft terms in 'plain and intelli-gible language'. To improve clarity, the Office of Fair Trading (OFT) negotiates revised terms with business contractors. The OFT has kindly allowed us to reprint recent examples of revised terms which the businesses concerned are now using:

> ORIGINAL TERM: This Agreement and the benefit and advantages herein contained are personal to the Member and shall not be sold, assigned or transferred by the Member.
>
> REVISED VERSION: Membership is not transferable.
>
> ORIGINAL TERM: Title to property in the goods shall remain vested in the company (notwithstanding the delivery of the same to the Customer) until the price of the Goods comprised in the contract and all other money due from the Customer to the Company on any other account has been paid in full.
>
> REVISED VERSION: We shall retain ownership of the goods until you have finished paying for them.
>
> ORIGINAL TERM: Lessor shall not be liable for loss or damage to any property left, stored or transported by Hirer or any other person in or upon Vehicle either before or after the return thereof to Lessor. Hirer hereby agrees to hold Lessor harmless from, and indemnify Lessor against all claims based on or arising out of such loss or damage unless caused by the negligence of Lessor.
>
> REVISED VERSION: We are only responsible for loss or damage to property left in the vehicle if the loss or damage results from our negligence.[14]

Boilerplate has played its part in inventing long, complex and incomprehensible documents. Figure 8.1 sets out BT's conditions for telephone service. In 1990 you would have been required to sign this document if you wanted to use a telephone in your home.

---

12. V. Charrow, J. A. Crandall and R. Charrow, *Sublanguage*, p 181. On the non-verbal commu-nication of power in the courtroom, see the description by P. Goodrich, 'Modalities of annun-ciation: an introduction to courtroom speech', in R. Levelson (ed.), *Law and Semiotics*, vol. 2, Plenum Press, New York, 1988, pp. 143–65.
13. See, e.g., F. Kessler, 'Contracts of Adhesion – Some Thoughts About Freedom of Contract' (1943) *Columbia Law Review* 629; Lord Reid in the *Suisse Atlantique* case [1966] 2 All ER 61 at 76; Lord Diplock in *Schroeder Music Publishing Co Ltd v Macaulay* [1974] 3 All ER 616 at 624; Law Commission *Second Report on Exemption Clauses in Contracts* (1975) No 69; G. Gluck, 'Standard Form Contracts: The Contract Theory Reconsidered' (1979) 28 *International and Comparative Law Quarterly* 72.
14. For further examples, see http://www.oft.gov.uk.

# Conditions
# for Telephone service

**(applicable only to telephone exchange line customers)**

**1  For definitions see paragraph 27**

**2  Provision of service**

2.1  We agree to provide you with service on the terms and conditions of this contract.

2.2  For operational reasons we may vary the technical specification of service.

2.3  It is technically impracticable to provide service free of faults and we do not undertake to do so. We do undertake however certain obligations with regard to a failure of your line: see paragraph 8 below.

2.4  Requests made to us relating to the provision of service are to be made or confirmed in writing if we ask.

2.5  We accept liability for failure to provide your line by any date agreed for its completed provision or to restore service after a failure of your line subject to sub-paragraph 21.2 and the other terms and conditions of this contract but any other date proposed by us or you is to be treated as an estimate only and we accept no liability for our failure to meet it.

2.6  If we agree any change in service, this contract is to be treated as varied accordingly.

**3  Classification of lines**

We will classify or reclassify your line as a business or residential line according to the main purpose for which the line or your premises are used.

**4  Shared lines**

On occasion we may, for operational reasons, change a shared line to an exclusive line.

**5  Minimum period of service**

The minimum period of service (beginning on the day when service is first made available) is 12 months or the applicable period set out in our Price List but it does not prevent us from exercising our rights to suspend service, or you or us from terminating this contract or the provision of a service or facility under it.

**6  Our general powers**

We may:

6.1  whenever necessary for operational reasons, change the name or number of the exchange serving your line, or its number, or any other name, code or number allocated in connection with service;

6.2  in an emergency, suspend service temporarily in order to provide or safeguard service to a hospital or to the emergency, or other essential, services;

6.3  temporarily, suspend service for the alteration of our apparatus to permit the passage of vehicles with abnormal loads;

6.4  temporarily suspend service for repair maintenance or improvement of any of our telecommunication systems and any poles, brackets, cabinets or ducts supporting or enclosing them; and

6.5  give instructions about the use of service which we think reasonably to be necessary in the interests of safety, or of the quality of service to our other customers;

but before doing any of these things we will give as much written or oral notice as is reasonably practicable in the circumstances, and we will restore service as soon as is reasonably practicable after temporary suspension.

**7  Your responsibility for your line**

You are responsible for your line (including any associated poles, brackets, cabinets or ducts) within the boundary of your premises and for its proper use: if it is lost, destroyed or damaged (except for fair wear and tear) you must pay our charge for its replacement and/or repair. You must not interfere with it nor permit anybody else (except someone authorised by us) to do so.

**8  Failure of your line**

8.1  If you report a failure of your line, we undertake, subject to paragraph 21 and other terms and conditions of this contract, to correct it not later than two whole working days after it is reported.

8.2  if we do work to correct a reported failure of your line and find there is none, we may charge you for the work.

8.3  if we agree to attend to a fault outside the normal working hours of the fault repair service we are otherwise contracted to provide for you, you must pay a charge based on our applicable Time Related Charge set out in our Price List.

Figure 8.1.

### 9 Connection and use of your equipment with our telephone system

You may connect your equipment to your line only by means of a socket installed and maintained by us unless we agree otherwise and we may withdraw our agreement by reasonable notice. Your equipment must not be used with your line (whether connected or not) except in accordance with our appropriate terms and conditions for the attachment of customers' equipment to our telecommunication systems in force from time to time, which form part of this contract. You can see or obtain copies at any of our District Offices. In addition, you must not allow any other person to do any of the things forbidden by this paragraph.

### 10 Electricity

If we ask you, you must provide at your expense a suitable mains electricity supply, with connections where we need them, to enable us to provide you with service.

### 11 Phone Books

We will allocate a number to your line and, unless you ask otherwise, we will make a free standard form entry for each line or line group identified by the same telephone number as soon as is reasonably practicable in your appropriate area Phone Book. Any special entry is agreed subject to the additional terms and conditions and relevant charges in our Price List.

### 12 Mis-use

12.1 You must not use or permit anyone else to use service:

    12.1.1 to send a message or communication which is offensive, abusive, indecent, obscene or menacing, or

    12.1.2 to cause annoyance, inconvenience or needless anxiety; or

    12.1.3 in breach of instructions we have given under sub-paragraph 6.5.

12.2 If we suspend service for contravention of sub-paragraph 12.1, we can refuse to restore it until we receive an acceptable assurance from you that there will be no further contravention.

### 13 Charges for service, your responsibility for them and value added tax - general

13.1 You must pay on demand the charges for service which appear, or are calculated according to the rates which appear, or are otherwise mentioned, from time to time in our Price List. When we make a change to those charges or rates we will publish details (including the operative date) in our Price List as soon as possible and in any event not less than 2 weeks before the change is to take effect unless the charge is payable only by you in which case we will give you not less than 2 weeks' notice of the change.

13.2 Unless this contract provides otherwise you are responsible for all charges set out in our Price List for service provided for you; in particular, for charges for calls and other telephone services and facilities made or requested from your line, or obtained by the use of any name, code or number allocated to you under this contract or of one of our British Telecom Charge Cards associated with your line, whether they are made, requested or obtained by you or any other person.

13.3 Unless our Price List provides otherwise, all charges for service are exclusive of value added tax for which, if it is applicable, an amount will be added to your bill.

13.4 The charges for any call are those calculated by us using details recorded at our exchange only.

13.5 We may allow you to pay charges by instalments, but you must pay all unpaid instalments when this contract is terminated.

13.6 If at your request we apply a special low user tariff to your line, we will cease to apply it immediately without notice if we become aware that your line does not qualify and may charge you retrospectively at the normal rate.

### 14 Rental

14.1 You become liable to pay rental on the day on which we first make service available for you.

14.2 Except for temporary service you must pay rental in accordance with our billing cycle. If we begin, or cease, service on a day which is not the first or last day of the period by reference to which we charge rental we apportion rental on a daily basis for the incomplete period. Rental is normally payable in advance but we may on occasion bill you in arrears.

Figure 8.1. (cont.)

## 15 Deposits and payments in advance

**15.1** We may ask you for a payment in advance not exceeding the connection charge and rental for the minimum period of service for the service requested, before service is provided.

**15.2** We may ask you for a deposit at any time, as security for payment of future bills, in accordance with guidelines which we publish from time to time. We can hold it until payment of all you owe us, though we may use all or part of it for payment of any charges due. When we repay a deposit or part of a deposit we will add interest at the rate, whether expressed as a percentage or a formula published in our District Offices for the period in question.

## 16 Cancellation

You may give us notice to cancel this contract, or a service or facility asked for under it, before service or the particular service or facility is provided as the case may be but we may make a charge for abortive work done and/or money spent to meet your requirements.

## 17 Default

**17.1** If you:

**17.1.1** do not pay any charge within 28 days of it falling due or break this contract in any other way; or

**17.1.2** do not pay any charge for any Telephone, Telex or Private Service within 28 days of it falling due to us under another contract with us; or

**17.1.3** are subject to bankruptcy or insolvency proceedings;

we can (without losing or reducing any other right or remedy) suspend service (including partially) temporarily without notice, though you remain liable to pay rental during the suspension, or terminate this contract by immediate notice. If we suspend service because you do not pay any charge, then any further suspension within a period of 12 months following restoration of service may take place 14 days after your failure to pay instead of after 28 days.

**17.2** "Bankruptcy or insolvency proceedings" means bankruptcy proceedings or in Scotland sequestration proceedings, becoming insolvent, making any composition or arrangement with creditors or an assignment for their benefit, any execution, distress, diligence or seizure; or if you are a company, being the subject of proceedings for the appointment of an administrator, going into liquidation whether voluntary or compulsory (except for the purpose of amalgamation or reconstruction) or having a receiver or administrative receiver of any assets appointed.

**17.3** On termination under this paragraph, as well as other sums payable up to the end of the contract, you must pay us the rental which would have been payable for the remainder of the minimum period of service at the rate in force at termination but we will make due allowance for any rental you have paid in advance for a period ending after the termination date or the end of the minimum period of service whichever is later, and make a repayment where appropriate.

**17.4** You continue to be liable to pay all charges which are due for service during any period in which you do not comply with this contract.

**17.5** If we waive a breach of contract by you, that waiver is limited to the particular breach. Our delay in acting upon a breach is not to be regarded in itself as a waiver.

## 18 Termination of service by notice

At any time after service has been provided this contract or the provision of any service or facility under it can be ended:

**18.1** by one month's notice by us;

**18.2** by 7 days' notice by you, unless this contract provides otherwise.

If we give notice, you must pay rental up to the expiry date of the notice. If you give notice, you must pay rental until 7 days after the date we receive the notice or until expiry of the notice, whichever is later, except that you must pay rental for the remainder of any minimum period of service at the rate in force at termination unless you have given notice because of an increase in the rate of rental. Your notice does not avoid any other liability for service already provided. Whoever gives the notice, we will repay or credit to you the appropriate proportion of any rental paid in advance (unless it is for

Figure 8.1. (cont.)

part of the minimum period of service) for a period ending after your liability for rental ceases.

### 19 Permission to enter property

You must allow anyone accredited by us, on production of official evidence of identity and authority, reasonable access to your premises at all reasonable times for the purposes of this contract, and you must obtain the permission of any other person which is needed. We will try to comply with your reasonable require- ments as to safety of people on your premises.

### 20 Arbitration

If a dispute between you and us about this contract does not involve a compli- cated issue of law, an issue of quantifica- tion or of mitigation of loss, or a sum exceeding £5,000, you may refer it to arbitration by the Chartered Institute of Arbitrators under procedures agreed between us and the Institute, details of which appear in our Code of Practice for Consumers.

### 21 Our liability

21.1 We do not exclude or restrict liabili- ty for death or personal injury resulting from our negligence.

21.2 Our liability for default in the provi- sion of service whether in contract, tort, delict or otherwise (including liability for negligence) is limited to loss or damage caused by our fail- ure:

21.2.1 to provide your line by any agreed date for its completed provision; or

21.2.2 to restore service after a fail- ure of your line;

and arises on the third working day after the agreed date or after the day on which you report the failure of your line to us. It is limited to:

21.2.3 £5 without proof of loss for each complete working day (or part of a day) once liability has arisen until your line is provided or service is restored excluding any working day (or part of a day) in a period of failure by us caused and/or continued because you do not provide us with any access to your premises or other rea- sonable assistance necessary for the purpose and under your control or because you

agree to the delay; or (at your choice)

21.2.4 damages for breach of con- tract consisting of the actual financial loss sustained by you on or after that third working day, and caused by our failure continuing on or after that day, up to £5,000 if your line is a business line or up to £1,000 if your line is a residential line;

for each line concerned (whether provided under this or another con- tract), subject to a maximum of £20,000 for all such lines for each incident or related series of incidents at any one set of your premises;

but we are only liable if you make your claim in writing, unless we agree otherwise, within 2 months of the completed provision of your line or the restoration of service.

21.3 We will not be liable under or in con- nection with this contract whether in contract, tort, delict or otherwise (including liability in negligence):

21.3.1 for any default in the provi- sion of service; or

21.3.2 for any indirect or conse- quential loss, corruption or destruction of data, any loss of business, revenue or prof- its, anticipated savings or wasted expenditure or for any financial loss whatever;

except as provided by sub-para- graphs 21.1 and 21.2;

and any liability or ours whatever its nature except liability under sub- paragraph 21.1 whether in contract, tort, delict or otherwise (including liability for negligence) is limited to £1,000,000 for any event or related series of events and £2,000,000 for all events in any period of 12 months.

21.4 In performing any obligation under this contract our duty is only to exer- cise all the reasonable care and skill of a competent telecommunication service provider and in a case falling within sub-paragraph 21.2 (but not in any other case) the burden of proof that we have done so is upon us.

21.5 Each provision of this paragraph limiting or excluding liability oper- ates separately in itself and survives independently of the others.

Figure 8.1. (cont.)

**21.6** Sub-paragraph **21.2** does not apply to a line providing automatically for the recording of calls to you for which you are to pay all or part of the charges or used primarily in connection with a service which you provide to callers and where we pay you for each call made to that service.

**21.7** We may pay a sum payable under sub-paragraph 21.2 not exceeding £25 by a credit to your account.

**21.8** In our Districts where 24 hour fault reporting is available for all customers, a fault reported outside the working hours of a working day for our fault repair service applicable to you will be regarded as reported during the working hours of the next working day.

## 22 Indemnity

You must indemnify us against any claims or legal proceedings arising from your use of service which are brought or threatened against us by another person.

## 23 Variation of terms and conditions

We can from time to time change the terms and conditions of this contract other than the charges payable under it by a document referring expressly to this paragraph and signed by a duly authorised employee of ours. We will publish details of any change (including the operative date) in each of our District Offices as soon as possible and in any event not less than 2 weeks before any change is to take effect, except that if the change is made to a provision of this contract limiting or excluding our liability for breaches of our duty to you (in contract, tort or delict) we will give you not less than 2 weeks' notice of the change.

## 24 Limitation on assignment

You must not assign the benefit of this contract in whole or in part.

## 25 Giving notice

A notice given under this contract, except under paragraph 6, (including a bill sent by us to you) must be in writing and may be delivered by hand or sent by telex or prepaid post to the addressee at the following addresses.

**25.1** To us: the address of our District Office shown on our order form which leads to the making of this contract or on your last bill or any alternative address which we notify to you at any time.

**25.2** To you: the address to which from time to time you ask us to send bills, the address of your premises, or if you are a limited company, your registered office.

## 26 Matters beyond our reasonable control

We are not liable for any breach of this contract where the breach was caused by Act of God, insurrection or civil disorder, war or military operations, national or local emergency, acts or omissions of government, highway authority or other competent authority, our compliance with any statutory obligation or an obligation under a statute, industrial disputes of any kind (whether or not involving our employees), fire, lightning, explosion, flood, subsidence, weather of exceptional severity, acts or omissions of persons for whom we are not responsible (including in particular other telecommunication service providers) or any other cause whether similar or dissimilar outside our reasonable control.

## 27 Definitions and application

**27.1** In this contract unless the context otherwise requires:

"we" and "us" means British Telecommunications plc;

"you" means the customer with whom we make this contract including a person reasonably appearing to us to act with that customer's authority;

"failure of your line" means any failure of your line causing you continuous total loss of the ability:

– to make a call; or

– to receive a call;

"line" means a telephone exchange line and ancillary apparatus and in particular, does not include your equipment;

"provision of your line" includes reconnection of your line after temporary disconnection at your request;

"service" means telecommunication service provided by means of the line connecting your premises to our telephone exchange and the rest of our public switched telephone network and telephone service provided to you when you use a British Telecom Chargecard associated with your line and any ancillary or related services but not AccessLines together with, where applicable, services or facilities listed in the Telephone Service sections of our

Figure 8.1. (cont.)

Price List provided by or in connection with your line;

"working day" means a complete calendar day on which we would normally do work to provide an exchange line for you or to repair faults in accordance:

– with our standard fault repair service (work carried out 0800-1700 hours Monday to Friday excluding Bank and Public holidays which we observe); or

– with any alternative fault repair service we have contracted to provide for you;

except that if the working hours of the fault repair service applicable to your line are 24 hours per day seven days per week, for the purpose of sub-paragraph 21.2 a working day is each period of 24 hours calculated from the time a fault is reported;

"your equipment" means equipment, including in particular additional sockets and related wiring, which is not part of our public switched telephone network and which you use or intend to use for service;

"your premises" means the premises at which service is or is to be provided under this contract; and

words in the singular include the plural and vice versa.

27.2 Our Price List contains definitions,

notes, terms and conditions which form part of this contract where relevant. You can see copies or obtain extracts at any of our District Offices.

27.3 We will provide you with telephone service only on these "Conditions for Telephone Service" which set out our entire contract with you.

NOTE

(This note is for information only and does not form part of our contract with you).

We run our public switched telephone network under a licence, issued under the Telecommunications Act 1984, which contains conditions which we must observe in providing service and which are enforceable by the Director General of Telecommunications. Copies are obtainable from HMSO.

**AccessLines**

AccessLines are provided on British Telecommunications plc's Conditions for Private Service. They contain limitations and exclusions of liability, in particular (but not only) for loss of profits, business or anticipated savings, or for any indirect or consequential loss whatsoever and those limitations and exclusions differ from those for Telephone Service. The Conditions may be seen or obtained from any District Office. Charges for AccessLines will appear on the bill for you Telephone Service.

Figure 8.1. (cont.)

Does it really need to be so long and dense? Don't worry, we won't ask you to analyse it ... yet!

Pressure from politicians, judges, and consumer groups over issues of bargaining power have been effective in encouraging the move towards plain English in legal documents. The trolley regulations we analysed earlier are evidence of this. In the mid-1990s BT redrafted its Conditions for Telephone Service and produced a clear and concise plain English version. But what is plain English? What is legal English? And how can we reconcile the apparently conflicting demands of clarity and precision? Answers to these questions will provide us with a strategy for drafting.

## Legal language is not plain language

EXERCISE **8.3  Plain reflection**

(a)   *Write a definition of plain English, then compare your definition with another student's. If it helps, refer to Chapter 7 again.*

(b)    *Think about what you have so far read of this chapter. Make a list of the factors you think contribute to the impenetrability of legal writing.*

Lawyers themselves are not as expert in language as they would have us believe. They seem to misunderstand the nature of linguistic complexity. Studies have shown that when lawyers are asked what makes legal documents incomprehensible, they tend to put it down to technical vocabulary and the complexity of legal concepts.[15] Moreover, until recently, lawyers who have researched legal language largely concentrated on vocabulary – terms of art, latinisms, and archaic, formal and infrequent words and phrases.[16] See figure 8.2.

Cutting out archaisms and superfluous expressions will help, but is only tinkering with the problem. You should remember from your analyses of officialese and academic writing in Exercise 7.2 that there are also grammatical and organisational features of the language which inhibit understanding. These are common in legal language too. As we pointed out at the beginning of this chapter, lawyers draft mammoth sentences, use unusual word order, repeat themselves, use complex noun phrases instead of verbs, and where they do use verbs, use passive rather than active forms. Let's look more closely at this process, beginning with an everyday English example:

*The dog bit the boy because he pulled its tail. The boy screamed very loudly and fell over.*

No difficulty in grasping the meaning here, the grammar is straightforward. There are four ideas:

1.    *The boy pulled the dog's tail.*
2.    *The dog bit the boy.*
3.    *The boy screamed very loudly.*
4.    *The boy fell over.*

The word order makes clear who did what to whom. Idea 2 is linked to 1 by the conjunction *because;* ideas 3 and 4 form a separate sentence, linked by *and*. Each event is conveyed by an active verb. But what happens if we rewrite as follows?

*The loudly screaming boy bitten by the dog for pulling its tail fell over.*

This version illustrates how the word order of a grammatically complex sentence can vary in English. As a result, the reader needs longer to fathom out the meaning. If the reader is not a native English speaker, he would find it difficult, if not impossible, to discover the four ideas. All four are crammed into one sentence. The normal syntactical rule that subject and verb are close together is broken: the subject *loudly screaming boy* is separated from its verb *fell over* by eight words. The active verb *bit* is now passive, so the usual subject/verb/object order is reversed. The phrase *for pulling*

---

15. For example, R. Charrow and V. Charrow, 'Investigating Comprehension in Real-World Tasks', paper presented at Linguistic Society of America Annual Meeting, Philadelphia, December 1976.
16. For example, D. Mellinkoff, *The Language of the Law*, Little, Brown & Co, Boston, 1963.

*its tail* is harder to grasp than the original because important clues as to meaning are left out; you are left wondering *who* did the pulling. The noun phrase *loudly screaming boy* does not make clear whether the boy was screaming before or after the biting; is it possible the dog bit him to shut him up? Moreover, the sentence is hideously ugly. Surely no literate person writes (or speaks) like this – do they?

Veda and Robert Charrow isolated a number of these features in their study of the comprehensibility of Californian standard civil jury instructions.[17] These instructions are given orally by the judge before the trial starts. The Charrows then redrafted the instructions, eliminating the features that apparently gave trouble. Comprehensibility increased on average by 35–40 per cent. These results don't seem particularly encouraging. Is it because the concepts are so complex? Here is one of the original instructions:

> You must never speculate to be true any insinuation suggested by a question asked a witness.

There are too many ideas pushed into one sentence and normal syntax can't take it. Nobody would normally speak or write like this. In the jargon of linguistics, this writer uses multiple embeddings with whiz deletion! This means there are sentences within sentences which leave out the *Wh-* words *which* or *who*. It is these words which help us process the information more easily by showing the relationship between the ideas:

> any insinuation which is suggested by a question which is asked a witness.

There are three ideas in the sentence:

1. when a lawyer questions a witness;
2. if the question contains insinuations;
3. you must never think that those insinuations are true.

It is what is left out which increases the unintelligibility, along with the passive verbs *suggested* and *asked*.These are truncated passives, i.e. passives where we aren't told who the agent is. Charrow and Charrow rewrite as follows:

> If a lawyer's question to a witness contained any insinuations, you must ignore those insinuations.

This example destroys another common preconception about language: that the longer the sentence, the more difficult it is to process. Rewriting sentences like this in comprehensible English will mean making them longer. The same is true of our *dog bit boy* example discussed earlier.

---

17. 'Making Legal Language Understandable: A Psycholinguistic Study of Jury Instructions' (1979) 79 *Columbia Law Review* 1306–74.

We have come across the language of US jury instructions before, in Chapter 3.[18] You may have identified the underlying tension between language appropriate for the lay audience (jurors) and that appropriate for the legal audience (fellow judges and lawyers).[19] In contrast to the relative freedom enjoyed by English judges to explain in plain language, their US counterparts are restricted by the need for legally watertight language. Consequently, jurors may hear the instructions once only, and if they ask for explanation, will simply hear the words repeated. As English and Sales point out,

> The legal system has … foisted upon jurors instructions that have been criticized as abstract and generic … Jurists persist in administering these instructions to jurors because they have survived on appeal to a higher court … The view that jurors remember and understand any instruction given them, and that therefore it is more important to focus on an instruction's survivability on legal appeal than on its comprehensibility, is ill-informed.[20]

Looking again at the instruction we quoted in Exercise 3.9, what are the features that obscure the meaning?

> Discrepancies in a witness's testimony or between his testimony and that of others, if there were any, do not necessarily mean that the witness should be discredited. Failure of recollection is a common experience, and innocent misrecollection is not uncommon. It is a fact, also, that two persons witnessing an incident or a transaction often will see or hear it differently. Whether a discrepancy pertains to a fact of importance or only to a trivial detail should be considered in weighing its significance.

| Grammatical Features | |
| --- | --- |
| Abstract nouns and noun phrases in place of verbs (nominalisations) | 'failure of recollection, fact of importance', |
| Multiple negatives | 'innocent misrecollection is not uncommon', |
| Unusual word order | 'Whether a discrepancy … its significance'. |

A feature that we haven't discussed before is the misplaced adverbial. This is a word or phrase which is inserted into a part of the sentence where you would not expect to find it. It may break up the normal subject–verb–object word order and the break is often marked with commas. In legalese you often find these between subject and verb. For example:

| | |
| --- | --- |
| Discrepancies … | (Subject) |
| if there were any, | (Adverbial) |
| do not necessarily mean … | (Verb) |

18. See Exercise 3.9.
19. Forensic linguist John Gibbons refers to this tension as the 'two audience dilemma' in *Forensic Linguistics*, Blackwell, Oxford, 2003, p. 174.
20. P. W. English and B. D. Sales, 'A Ceiling or Consistency Effect for the Comprehension of Jury Instructions' (1997) 3 *Psychology, Public Policy, and Law* 381–401.

There is also an organisational problem in this paragraph. It is not clear how the subject matter relates to the jurors. 'What's this got to do with me?' a juror might ask. 'What am I supposed to do?' The Charrows' modified version makes this relationship clear by addressing them directly:

> As jurors, you have to decide which testimony to believe and which testimony not to believe.
>
> You may be tempted to totally disbelieve a witness because he contradicted himself while testifying. Keep in mind, however, that people sometimes forget things, and end up contradicting themselves.
>
> You might also be tempted to totally disbelieve a witness because another witness testified differently. But keep in mind also that when two people witness an incident they often remember it differently.
>
> When you are deciding whether or not to believe a witness, you should consider whether contradictions or differences in testimony have to do with an important fact or only a small detail.

These examples show that understanding does not depend on the ease or difficulty of comprehending individual words and sentences, but on how they relate to each other in a text.

A large number of US studies confirm the Charrows' findings that standard instructions are poorly understood by jurors and mock jurors; rewriting them in plain English leads to better understanding.[21] Fundamental Common Law notions frequently misunderstood are 'reasonable doubt', 'the presumption of innocence', and 'the burden of proof'. That this happens at all is worrying, but particularly so in states like California and Tennessee, which have the death penalty.[22] The 1995 Tenessee instruction on reasonable doubt states:

> Reasonable doubt is that doubt engendered by an investigation of all the proof in the case and an inability after such investigation to let the mind rest easily as to the certainty of guilt. Reasonable does not mean a captious, possible or imaginary doubt. Absolute certainty of guilt is not demanded by the law to convict of any criminal

---

21. A lot of recent work has been done on reforming and rewriting jury instructions. The California jury instructions task force, set up after the O. J. Simpson trials, has made changes to civil instructions which came into effect in September 2003 (24 years after the Charrows first published their plain English versions!) For example, the phrase 'Failure of recollection is common. Innocent misrecollection is not uncommon' has been replaced by 'People often forget things or make mistakes in what they remember'. Changes to criminal instructions are due to be approved in 2005. Is it fear of oversimplification and loss of legal effect that has delayed this process for so long? (See http://www.plainenglish.co.uk.)
22. There is evidence that jurors with lower levels of comprehension are more likely to impose the death penalty. See Gibbons, *Forensic Linguistics*, pp. 178–9, and Triesma, *Legal Language*, pp. 231–40.

charge, but moral certainty is required, and this certainty is required as to every proposition of proof requisite to constitute the offense.[23]

This is a classic illustration of the 'two audience dilemma'. If you are unfamiliar with law and complex written language like this, you will have difficulty grasping the meaning.

Moving on now to a different context, let's analyse a small piece of contract boilerplate.

EXERCISE **8.4 Clause analysis**

The text below is taken from a precedent which the author suggests can be used for drafting a contract of employment in the publishing and multimedia business.[24] We have numbered the lines of the text to give you points of reference in your analysis.

(a) *Read the text and paraphrase the content. Note down how long this process took you.*
(b) *What is its purpose?*
(c) *Who is it written for?*
(d) *Who are the likely readers?*
(e) *Comment on:*
   (i) *layout;*
   (ii) *punctuation;*
   (iii) *sentence length;*
   (iv) *word order;*
   (v) *sentence complexity;*
   (vi) *vocabulary.*
(f) *Imagine you have to explain the meaning of the clause to a newly engaged employee of the company. What would you say?*
(g) *Redraft the clause in plain English.*

15. Intellectual property

The entire copyright and all other rights including without limitation design rights registered design rights patent rights trade mark rights rights of action and all other rights of whatsoever nature in and to any and all material invention or process of whatever description created or produced by you whether alone or in collaboration with others in the performance of your duties whether or not during the working hours specified in paragraph 1 and whether or not at the location referred to in paragraph 9.1 or at any other location shall vest in the Company absolutely from the moment of creation and the Company its successors assignees and licensees shall be the sole absolute unencumbered legal and beneficial owner throughout the world of all rights in all such material for the full period during which such rights may now or at any time in the future subsist under the laws in force in any part of the world.

---

23. Tennessee Pattern Jury Instruction – Criminal 1995: 7.14, quoted in B. K. Dumas, 'US Pattern Jury Instructions: problems and proposals' (2000) 7(1) *Forensic Linguistics* 49–71. Dumas offers a more comprehensible, albeit longer version.
24. Taken from M. Henry, *Publishing and Multimedia Law*, Butterworths, London, 1994, p. 792.

The main grammatical features we have been discussing:

- nominalisations;
- multiple embeddings;
- truncated passives;
- noun lists;
- unusual word order;

are all found in other professional varieties, such as academic and bureaucratic writing. There are features, however, which we find only in legal English. For example, a rule of English word order tells us that an adjective precedes its noun:

- *legal language;*
- *ugly expressions.*

In the term of art *fee simple*, however, we use French word order, but we pronounce it as English, not French. Is there something about the development of legal English that accounts for such unique usage?

## Legal language is unduly peculiar

Richard Wydick tells us that criticism of lawyers' writing is not new:

> In 1596 an English chancellor decided to make an example of a particularly prolix document filed in his court. The chancellor first ordered a hole cut through the centre of the document, all 120 pages of it. Then he ordered that the person who wrote it should have his head stuffed through the hole, and the unfortunate fellow was led around to be exhibited to all those attending court at Westminster Hall.[25]

Although we don't deal with poor writers in this way now, probably the characteristics of prolixity then were much the same as they are now. Legal language has not changed in the way that the standard variety has.

### Lawyers, not the people, decide what words mean

Ordinary language changes through usage. New forms take the place of old ones, and other forms change their meaning. In Chapter 7 we looked at the meaning of *nice* and how it has changed over time. The word *gay* is another example. No one would now use this word in its former meaning of *cheerful, lively* because it would confuse the recipient of the message. Old forms we no longer use include, for example, the third person singular present tense of verbs *-th*, as in *he hath* (he has). The new forms then become acceptable in the standard written variety.

Because we do not normally speak or write legal English, it has developed much more slowly. Meanings are imposed on the users by courts, legislatures and other agencies. To ensure precision, lawyers are reluctant to depart from them and create new forms. Reliance on these past, static forms gives legal language its archaic

---

25. R. Wydick, 'Plain English for Lawyers' (1978) 66 *California Law Review* 727 at p. 727.

flavour. Lawyers won't let them die! They prefer to retain archaisms like *herein-after, aforesaid* and *witnesseth*.

Lawyers have also shown a liking for tautology. For example:

- null and void;
- goods and chattels;
- terms and conditions;
- perform and discharge;
- will and testament.

These usages show the dominance of Latin and French over legal language for centuries. Where there were English and Latin or French words for the same item, there was often doubt as to whether the words meant exactly the same. To be safe, lawyers used both.

The legal register still contains both Latin and French legal terms which survive in their original forms, though not in their original pronunciation. What examples can you think of? Are you sure you use them all correctly?

Figure 8.2. If a Minister has ultra virus the Divisional Court will squash it.

Imposing specialised meanings on particular words and phrases has led to differences between ordinary and legal English concepts. The concepts of *negligence, assault,* and *consideration,* for example, all have specific legal meanings which are different from those understood by non-lawyers. What other examples can you think of?

Moreover, to promote precision a statute may declare that a specific term be interpreted in a particular way. A somewhat extreme example is quoted by Peter Tioroma.

Such concerns must have inspired the highly contorted definition of **buttocks** in a Florida ordinance aimed at reducing the amount of exposed flesh in establishments featuring nude or nearly nude dancers. To require dancers to **cover** their **buttocks**, without more, would only invite them to skirt the rule by wearing the skimpiest covering possible, leaving virtually nothing to the imagination. The county thus deemed it prudent to define **buttocks** as precisely as possible:

> The area at the rear of the human body (sometimes referred to as the gluteus maximus) which lies between two imaginary lines running parallel to the ground when a person is standing, the first or top of such lines being one half-inch below the top of the vertical cleavage of the nates (i.e. the prominence formed by the muscles running from the back of the hip to the back of the leg) and the second or bottom line being one half-inch above the lowest point of the curvature of the fleshy protuberance (sometimes referred to as the gluteal fold), and between two imaginary lines, one of each side of the body (the outside lines), which outside lines are perpendicular to the ground and to the horizontal lines described above and which perpendicular outside lines pass through the outermost point(s) at which each nate meets the outer side of each leg . . . (J. Smith, 'Using 328 words when, in the end, just one would do', LA Times, May 18 1992).[26]

Nevertheless, drafters do not set out specific meanings all the time. They may have good reasons for being imprecise. Consider the following example, taken from our old friend, the Litter (Northern Ireland) Order 1994:

1. Subject to paragraph (4), if any person, being a person in charge of a dog, permits the dog to deposit its excrement in any place prescribed by regulations, he shall, subject to paragraph (2), be guilty of an offence.
2. It shall be a defence for a person charged with an offence under paragraph (1) to prove that –
   a. he took all reasonable precautions and exercised due diligence to avoid the commission of the offence; or
   b. he made a reasonable attempt to remove the excrement.

### EXERCISE **8.5 Shovelling excrement**

*You are a local councillor. The Responsible Dog Owners Association asks you to explain this regulation to them in plain English. What will you say?*

You won't have found it easy to be precise, because the deliberate use of the elastic concepts *reasonableness* and *due diligence* allows matters to be decided on a case by case basis. The Association, which wants a straight answer about what constitutes a valid defence, will not be happy.

Do you think this regulation should provide a defence at all? We are sure many of you will have strong views on this. Inhabitants of Britain either love or hate dogs but are rarely indifferent, even if we can all agree to hate their deposits. Legislatures

26. *Legal Language*, p. 118.

and government agencies have to balance up conflicting interests, about which there may have been widespread public discussion and intensive lobbying by pressure groups. In situations like this it will be left to the courts to set the boundaries, so decisions will not be seen as 'political'.

Contract terms may be drafted in such a way as to leave their meaning unclear. This is usually done to give an advantage to the party drawing up the contract. For example:

> The Company reserves the right to make alterations to your normal working hours in order to meet its business commitments.

## Put yourself in her position: deriving meaning from context

In ordinary English writing, readers infer meanings from context. We imagine ourselves or others in the situation described either by the words themselves, or by what went before. If we replaced

> leaving there shopping trolleys used by them

in s. 1(2)(b) of the trolley regulations with

> leaving their shopping trolleys there

as we briefly threatened to do on p. 261, we would infer that *their* means *customers'* shopping trolleys, but that the customers don't own them, because shopping trolleys are always owned by stores, never by customers. The relationship between customer and shopping trolley is quite clear.

Because lawyers have to make the words themselves clear in case other lawyers challenge the meaning, their discourse demands that they try to derive meaning entirely from the words they use. They must therefore avoid the possibility of alternative interpretations from context. Only when the meaning is ambiguous or uncertain do they turn to context for an interpretation.

### EXERCISE 8.6 Natural meanings

*In small groups, discuss:*

(a)   *Which devices of statutory interpretation exclude inferences from context?*
(b)   *Which don't?*

It isn't easy to exclude context when it plays such an important part in helping us to process meanings. Because lawyers have to go to some lengths to obliterate it, they have developed the skills of understanding and classifying information without using it. Unfortunately, this can lead them to make assumptions about lay people's abilities to do the same.

The jury instructions we looked at earlier are an example. Drafters of documents assume readers (or listeners) know the purpose of the document, and so don't state it. However, people who are unfamiliar with the criminal justice system and who are not clear about their role in it will not be able to work out how the instructions relate to them unless they are clearly told what their role is.

You are all probably familiar with the police caution given to suspects before questioning. When it was being revised a few years ago, the first draft was as follows:

> You do not have to say anything. But if you do not mention now something which you later use in your defence, the Court may decide that your failure to mention it now strengthens the case against you. A record will be made of anything you say and it may be given in evidence if you are brought to trial.

Apparently, it was discovered in a survey that 60 per cent of A level students could not understand it, so an attempt was made to simplify the draft. Here is the final version (PACE Code of Practice C Para. 10.4):

> You do not have to say anything. But it may harm your defence if you do not mention when questioned something which you later rely on in court. Anything you do say may be given in evidence.

The main criticism of the first draft was that there were too many words in it. Is this the problem?

EXERCISE 8.7   **Caution! Unforeseen hazard ahead!**

*In small groups, answer the following questions:*

(a)   *Why did it become necessary to revise the caution?*
(b)   *What was the legal position of a suspect who declined to answer police questions*
    (i)  *before*
    (ii) *after the new caution?*
(c)   *Which features impede understanding in the first version above? Give reasons.*
(d)   *To what extent is the final version an improvement on the first? Give reasons.*
(e)   *If you think the final version has deficiencies, how would you remedy them?*

The way this problem has been dealt with demonstrates once again that lawyers misconceive what is complex in legal language. The problem here is not sentence length, but that both these drafts are pieces of legal discourse. As such they cannot be easily understood by outsiders. You have to be familiar with the world of the lawyer and the legal register to grasp these concepts.[27] *It may harm your defence –* what will this mean to someone who has never been inside a criminal court and knows nothing of criminal procedure? Similarly, *something which you later rely on in court –* what is meant by *rely on*?

---

27. For more discussion on this, see R. Eagleson, 'Plain English: Some Sociolinguistic Revelations', in S. Romaine (ed.), *Language in Australia*, Cambridge University Press, New York, 1991, pp. 362–72 at p. 369.

How can it happen that with something as important as this, when in many situations a lawyer will not be there to advise, the drafter is talking to a lawyer when she should be addressing the suspect?

In setting the scene in the courtroom it appears the writer ignored the listener's perspective. If she had put herself in the suspect's shoes, she would have been able to anticipate the barriers to understanding. Is this simply a failure to grasp the importance of context, or is it a reflection of the view held by many lawyers that legal concepts are too complex to be understood by ordinary people?

As part of the Document Design Project at the American Institutes for Research, a group of researchers redesigned the District of Columbia Medicaid form. People on welfare had to fill in this form to get money to pay for health care. One factor the researchers found which impeded the recipients' understanding of the original form was that they understood a term differently from the meaning the drafter intended:

> One kind of change which we made was simply at the word level, to take account of special audience characteristics. The MRF audience is comprised of people who are poor, not well-educated, often old, and frequently speakers of a non-standard dialect, or not native speakers of English. Problem analysis showed that these people tend to misinterpret the term 'family member', which recurs in important questions throughout the form. Or rather, they misinterpret the term relative to the dialect of the document designer. The designer intends the phrase to refer to people in the immediate, nuclear family of the Medicaid recipient, all covered by a common Medicaid card. This meaning is not spelled out, but is implied by listing the names of the people covered and placing them in a box labelled 'family members' near the top of the form. The designer assumes the meaning is clear not only because of this graphical definition, but also because the phrase itself is simple, familiar, and has a unique meaning to the designer. People in the Medicaid population, however, have extended families – a network of kin, often reared together, and all considered immediate family. As might be expected, many respondents answered questions about family employment and resources as if those questions referred to nephews, cousins, sisters-in-law, and others not covered by the recipient's Medicaid.[28]

This presumably happened because the drafter either knew nothing of the experience and way of life of the readership, or for some reason decided to ignore these.

People who have to explain complex ideas and procedures to others often help them understand by making abstract concepts concrete. Jesus and other religious leaders have done it for thousands of years. Lord Denning did it with freedom of contract, as we saw in Chapter 7. Even law teachers do it. Revision of the Medicaid form at the sentence level was based on a particular method called the 'scenario

---

28. V. Charrow, V. Holland, D. Peck and L. Shelton, *Revising a Medicaid Recertification Form: A Case Study in the Document Design Process*, American Institutes For Research, Washington DC, 1980, cited in L. Campbell and V. Holland, 'Understanding the Language of Public Documents Because Readability Formulas Don't', in Di Pietro, *Linguistics and the Professions*, pp. 157–72.

principle'.[29] Readers were asked to explain the meaning as they went along, in an effort to understand. They tended to convert the information into a small dramatised scenario – a scene in which somebody does something:

> Take, for example, a paragraph headed 'Applying for Bank Loans,' and starting 'The procedure to apply for bank loans consists of . . . ' A reader might turn the preceding into, 'Now say I wanted to apply for a bank loan, then I would . . . ', or 'Now this fellow wanted to apply for a bank loan, then he . . . ' In trying to understand what the regulation said, readers expressed abstract definitions (with a nominalisation like 'procedure' as subject) in the form of a story-like event (with a human agent as subject doing an action in a time and place context). The event frame makes information concrete, imageable, and familiar through relationships like agent–object and action–goal. This frame seems to be a basic structure of experience and a way we naturally think.[30]

Nobody (apart from law students?) reads legal documents to learn definitions. We read them to engage in human activities: to find answers to questions, to make decisions and carry them out. In the earlier exercises where we asked you to paraphrase and explain legal provisions, did you use the scenario principle? Or did you fiddle about with abstract legal concepts and then attempt to translate them into real life contexts? Which will be your starting point for your drafting?

## Does it matter what it looks like? Layout and punctuation

According to Crystal and Davy,[31] the content of early legal documents was usually set out on parchment in one solid block of writing, the lines extending from margin to margin. This unbroken format may have been used to economise on parchment, or to defeat fraudulent insertions or deletions by leaving no spaces. The advent of printing did nothing to make the format more accessible.

Most early documents were written in Latin, which as we noted earlier, has a periodic structure. This means that the relationship between main and subordinate clauses is clear from the word forms and endings. It was therefore quite acceptable to draft long sections of a document, or even a whole document, in one sentence.

As these documents were read, not spoken, there was no need for punctuation to show the reader where to pause. It is interesting that proclamations, written to be spoken out loud, were always properly punctuated.[32] Furthermore, punctuation could be added to change meaning, and so having none at all prevented forgeries.

The regulations we have looked at in this chapter reveal the modern tendency of legislation to use punctuation, headings and numberings to separate provisions. It

29. See L. Flower, J. Hayes and H. Swarts, 'Revising Functional Documents: The Scenario Principle', *Document Design Project Technical Report No 1*, Carnegie–Mellon University, Pittsburgh, Pa., 1980.
30. Campbell and Holland, 'Understanding the Language of Public Documents', pp. 165–6.
31. D. Crystal and D. Davy, *Investigating English Style*, Longman, London, 1969, pp. 193–217.
32. *Ibid.*, p. 200.

recognises that the reader will rarely want to read the whole instrument and thoroughly digest all of it. Breaking the provisions up into separate items makes it easier to scan the document and find the provisions you are looking for.

## Isolated sentences

Besides being long and complex, legal sentences are self-contained. This means they stand on their own, neither linked to what precedes or follows them. This is necessary because each action or requirement is dependent on a series of conditions which must be fulfilled before it can happen. That's it. Nothing else is relevant. You then go on to the next action or requirement, and then the one after that.

Earlier in the chapter we suggested that this lack of linking is responsible for cumbersome repetition in legal writing. In standard written English ideas are linked by logical progression and the use of linking words and phrases. This gives coherence to a text. We discussed this in some detail too in Chapter 7.

By treating each sentence as a separate item, legal ideas are isolated from each other. The writing is disjointed and may read like a list. Documents therefore seem to lack coherence. The reader has to struggle to make connections between items and their place in the text as a whole, as well as put up with unnecessary repetition.

In fact, legal documents are coherent, in a way which is closely linked to their purpose. They are written records which lawyers use for reference. This means that, for example, readers will not normally scan a new piece of legislation to get a rough overview – they can get this from journals and commentaries. They will scan to find out which sections of the document are likely to give them the answers they want to specific questions, then take time to study those parts in detail. This process is easier if each section is set out separately from every other.

## Coherence and word order

We mentioned earlier that in everyday writing (and speech) the subject appears at or near the beginning of the sentence, followed closely by its verb. Legal drafters, however, put words, phrases and clauses in unusual positions. The usual underlying logical structure of a legal sentence is

If (or when) X, then Y shall be Z, or Y shall do Z.

- X is a set of conditions or circumstances (if? when? where?);
- Y is the agent (who?);
- Z is the state or action (what?).

This structure is sometimes known as a *legislative sentence*, or *legislative thought*.[33] Here is a simple example:

33. See, e.g., P. James and R. Goncalves, *Modern Writing For Lawyers*, Continuing Legal Education, Society of British Columbia, Vancouver, 1993, p. 145; also N. Gold, K. Mackie, W. Twining (eds.), *Learning Lawyers' Skills*, Butterworths, London, 1989, p. 132.

> If the work is cancelled by the customer,        (X)
> the contractor                                   (Y)
> is entitled to make the following charges . . .  (Z)

Look back to reg. 51(2) on notional capital in Exercise 8.2. It begins with a list of exceptions. Besides feeling confused, a lay reader might well wonder why it takes so long to get to the point.

Normal English word order would be Y, Z, X. Why the difference? In legal sentences the X component often appears at the beginning of the sentence to enable the reader to discover early on whether she is interested in this provision or not. If not, she is spared the agony of having to read on! If she is unfortunate enough to have to struggle on, by the end she may well have been floored by a monstrous and nightmarish sentence which spawns vast strings of embedded clauses and phrases. These overwhelm the subject of the sentence and swallow up part of its verb. She may hunt in vain, but won't find the verb until it is disgorged many lines further on.

Can you make out the underlying structure in this complicated legislative thought? Section 2(1) of the Official Secrets Act 1911:

> If any person having in his possession or control any sketch, plan, model, article, note, document, or information which relates to or is used in a prohibited place or anything in such a place, or which has been made or obtained in contravention of this Act, or which has been entrusted in confidence to him by any person holding office under His Majesty, or which he has obtained owing to his position as a person who holds or has held office under His Majesty, or as a person who holds or has held such an office or contract –
>
> (a)    communicates the sketch, plan, model, article, note, document or information to any person, other than a person to whom he is authorised to communicate it, or a person to whom it is in the interest of the State his duty to communicate it, or
>
> (b)    retains the sketch, plan, model, article, note, or document in his possession or control when he has no right to retain it or when it is contrary to his duty to retain it:
>
> that person shall be guilty of a misdemeanour.

The X component in s. 2(1) is introduced by *If.* The subject of this clause is *any person*. We then have to read another 96 words before we come upon its verb *communicates*. You therefore have to keep the opening words in mind all the way to (a). The X component is made up of a number of sub-clauses, so that by the time we get to Y and Z, the drafter thought it necessary to remind us who the subject is: *that person* (Y).

Why not use normal English word order? Components Y and Z are so simple and brief that the reader can easily check the provision for relevance. Here is the underlying structure, using normal word order:

> a person(Y) is guilty of a misdemeanour(Z) if . . . (X).

This does not help with the complexity of the X component, however. Now try and work out the relationship of the sub-clauses in the X component to each other. You will see then that the relationships between the numerous *or* and *which* clauses can be clarified by using lists and numbering.[34]

But is it that simple? Where drafters use a co-ordinating conjunction, such as *or* or *and*, they appear to join two legislative sentences in one provision. This can be confusing for the reader, who has to work out whether the provision covers one right or obligation with a number of X components, or two distinct rights or obligations. You can find an example of this in the intellectual property clause you redrafted in Exercise 8.4. If you are sure that the provision deals with two rights, you should split them into two separate legislative sentences.

## Interceding with the Deity: pleadings

In the past, civil proceedings were set out in formal documents known as 'pleadings'. The Civil Procedure Rules 1998 established a new approach to civil litigation, intended to convert a culture thought to be overly adversarial to a new spirit of openness and cooperation. The overriding objective is to enable courts to deal with cases justly; to this end, the parties and their lawyers should ensure as far as possible that both sides are on an equal footing – no withholding of information, no surprises, no unnecessary expense or delay – so that cases will be won or lost on their merits.[35] 'Statements of case' have now replaced 'pleadings' in the CPR, but their function is substantially the same: to set out the material facts and allegations of your case against another party or parties. And just as in the past, there are formal rules and conventions which prescribe the form and content of each document.[36]

In civil proceedings the most important pleadings you will draft are:

1. The *particulars of claim*, which states the claimant's case and the remedy she is seeking. Boyle et al. paraphrase this thus:

   > These people were involved . . . this happened . . . as a result I have suffered . . . so this is what I want from you . . .[37]

2. The *defence*, which sets out the facts denying the claimant's claim, paraphrased thus:

   > In reply to your claim I agree . . . . I deny . . . because . . . I'm not sure what you're talking about and I want you prove it . . . So I won't give you . . .[38]

In criminal proceedings at Crown court the offences the defendant is charged with are set out on the *indictment*.

The pleadings limit the issues to be tried, so that if you forget to raise an issue on the draft, you can't raise it unless the court gives you leave. Essentially your draft should:

---

34. Section 2(1) was repealed by the Official Secrets Act 1989, which defines six categories of official information.
35. See CPR r. 1.1.    36. See CPR Practice 5, para. 2; r. 16.4; Practice Direction 16, para. 3.
37. *A Practical Guide to Lawyering Skills*, p. 193.
38. *Ibid.*, p. 194.

- Summarise your case            BE CONCISE
- Clarify your case              BE CLEAR
- Be logically organised         BE CORRECT
- Contain all the issues to be raised    BE COMPLETE

Although pleadings are the most formal documents you will draft, the drafting skills are the same as those you need for other kinds of legal documents. You have to draft pleadings carefully, because a poor draft suggests you haven't prepared your case properly. A concisely worded, comprehensive draft is more likely to focus the judge's attention on the strengths of your case. If you omit a material fact or get something wrong, the case could be lost. For example, the defendant may go free if you draft the indictment incorrectly.

Note, too, the comments of William Rose:

> You may ask, 'Well, what is the point of elegant drafting? After all, so long as I have made myself clear, why should style be of any relevance?' The answer can be summed up in one word – authority.
>
> Assuming a basic legal competence, the most important additional attribute that will distinguish good pleading (or advocacy for that matter) from the mundane, is authority. To be able to stamp your mark on the case, pick it up by the scruff of its neck, dictate the action, and essentially show yourself to the Court to be in command and the master of your subject, gives you an incalculable advantage over your opponent. For a start, and have no doubt about this whatsoever, it shows! Your opponent will know, the Judge will know, and if you are at the Bar your solicitor will know. In terms of prestige, and sheer psychological 'clout' you are ahead. Don't be mistaken, these things matter.[39]

There are a number of detailed practical guides on the technique of drafting pleadings. Here are a few of them:

> The Inns of Court School of Law: *Drafting*.
> 'Legal Drafting: Formal Documents' in Boyle et al, *A Practical Guide to Lawyering Skills*.
> W. M. Rose *Pleading Without Tears: A Guide to Legal Drafting*.

We suggest you consult at least one of these before you attempt the next exercise. You may also find it useful to look at CPR, r. 16.4.

### EXERCISE 8.8  Major surgery[40]

*Read the following extract from a draft statement of case.*

*(a)    Which material should not be pleaded? Give reasons.*

*(b)    Comment briefly on the style.*

---

39. W. M. Rose, *Pleading Without Tears: A Guide to Legal Drafting*, Oxford University Press, Oxford, 2002, p. 10.
40. Adapted from the Inns of Court School of Law, *Drafting*, Oxford University Press, Oxford, 2002, pp. 28–30.

IN THE HIGH COURT OF JUSTICE          CLAIM NO. 2002 HC 8332
QUEENS BENCH DIVISION
BETWEEN

RICHARD WILLIS                          <u>Claimant</u>

and

DENNIS UNDERWOOD                        <u>Defendant</u>

PARTICULARS OF CLAIM

1.  On 1st May 2002 at about 9.00 pm, there was a really nasty accident on the A45 in
    Warwickshire. The Claimant, Richard Willis, who lives at 27 Mead Close,
    Stratford-upon-Avon, was driving his Jaguar motor car registration L208 RGD.
    He had only bought the said car a few days earlier and was very proud of it, so he
    was driving carefully, lawfully and safely. It was quite dark.
2.  With the Claimant in his Jaguar motor car were his wife Helen and his two
    children Jennifer, aged 8 and Nigel, aged 5. They were returning from a visit to the
    Claimant's wife's mother. The Claimant had not been drinking alcohol. As the
    Claimant proceeded in a westerly direction along the A45 highway he was
    travelling at about 45 mph, when at the junction of the highway with Offchurch
    Lane, near Drexford, the accident hereinbefore referred to occurred.
3.  Drexford is in Warwickshire and it was accordingly the Warwickshire police who
    were called to the scene. PC Edwards of the Warwickshire Police will say that the
    position of the vehicles and the tyre marks showed that the said collision was
    caused by the erratic driving of the Defendant, Mr Dennis Underwood, who lives
    at 12 The Hawthorns, Solihull, West Midlands.
4.  According to PC Edwards, Mr Underwood drove his vehicle, which was a
    Rover Metro motor car registration number Y283 KEN, into the Claimant's
    motor car by emerging from Offchurch Lane while the Claimant's car was
    passing.
5.  There were several witnesses to the said accident who all gave statements to the
    Warwickshire Police. One witness, Surinder Singh, will say the said collision was
    caused by Mr Underwood.
6.  Since the Claimant and Defendant were both using the public highway at the same
    time, it was reasonably foreseeable that an accident might occur if either of them
    failed to take reasonable care. Accordingly the Defendant owed the Claimant a duty
    of care and this claim is founded on his negligence (*Donoghue v Stevenson*).

The Claimant had no way of knowing that another driver would be so stupid or that
an accident was about to occur and so was unable to take avoiding action. The said
accident was therefore caused solely and absolutely by the appalling negligence of
the Defendant.

PARTICULARS OF NEGLIGENCE

The Defendant owed a duty of care and did not take proper care for the safety of other users of the highway. This means he was negligent. There were many ways in which he could have avoided the accident, but the Claimant will say he was particularly at fault in that:

a.    He did not look where he was going. The Claimant's car had its lights on and the Defendant should have seen it, but nevertheless drove on to the A45 highway from Offchurch Lane without looking to see if the road was clear. In breach of the Highway Code he was therefore not keeping a proper or indeed any look-out.

b.    He was on a minor road and the Claimant was on a major road. The Defendant should therefore have given way to the Claimant but failed to do so. If he had been driving with due care and attention he would have been alert enough to give precedence to the Claimant's car at the junction. Although it was dusk, nevertheless it was not entirely dark, and the Claimant had his lights on: accordingly the Claimant will say *res ipsa loquitur*.

c.    He was at a stop sign, but the skid marks show he failed to stop. He also made no attempt to steer or otherwise control his car so as to avoid the said accident.

d.    The Defendant's negligence resulted in him striking the Claimant's motor car. The Defendant was injured in the accident, but the Claimant is not responsible for that.

e.    As respects all the matters aforesaid, the Claimant suffered pain and injury, but his wife and children were unhurt. The accident also meant that the Claimant sustained loss and damage. This loss and damage was all reasonably foreseeable and the Defendant is liable to compensate the Claimant for it. The Claimant suffered *inter alia* a fractured ankle.

## The illiteracy of the well-educated

Robert Eagleson quotes the following example of typical legalese:

> In default of the appearance of the objector before the Tribunal for the purpose of review, the Tribunal shall . . .

Translated into clear English, this means

> If the objector does not appear before the tribunal . . . [41]

Why is it that lawyers and other professionals turn verbs into complex and ponderous nominalisations and add lots of superfluous words? We don't speak or write like this when our purpose is to communicate. Has our training and experience made this our natural mode of communication? Do we think naturally in nominalisations? Or do we translate from the normal to the abnormal? If so, we tend to make meanings and concepts much more complex than they are in reality, because, as we have seen, the language is so ill equipped to cope.

41.  R. Eagleson, 'Plain English', pp. 366–7.

Eagleson continues:

> What is worrying is that it is the educated who appear to be afflicted with the disease of gobbledegook. They have a restricted view of language, allowing its communicative role and the rights of audience to be discounted. They are frequently trapped in their own linguistic conceits, enmeshed in words, deceiving themselves and others into believing that they are saying something. As enterprises to rewrite the Takeovers Code and insurance policies have shown, they are at times saying not what they intend, but the sheer convolution has hidden the error. The thrust for plain English reveals that ironically it is the professionals who are linguistically disadvantaged. While sadly they may be disadvantaging others in the community by not setting out their rights and responsibilities clearly, it is they who are in need of instant help . . .
>
> Plain English is not about helping the less well-educated and less fortunate in the community; it is also about releasing the more able.[42]

Now you are released, you can work towards creating a strategy for drafting.

## Defining your drafting principles

By the time you reach this point you should have a clear idea about the purposes of drafting and how to achieve them. Now you are in a position to design a general set of drafting objectives. Use these objectives:

(a)    every time you begin to plan a draft;
(b)    as you revise your draft; and
(c)    after you have completed your draft.

### EXERCISE 8.9  A general checklist for drafting

*In pairs, draw up a checklist of your drafting objectives. You may want to use the following materials to help you:*

1.    *Your self-editing checklist for writing.*
2.    *The Law Society Legal Practice Course standards for writing and drafting, reproduced below:*

Students should have developed a basic skill in the preparation and drafting of a range of documents and should be able to formulate and present a coherent piece of writing based upon facts, general principles and legal authority, in a structured, concise and where appropriate, persuasive manner.

**Students should be able to draft documents that:-**

1.    meet the client's goals, carry out the client's instructions and address the client's concerns;
2.    maintain a standard of care which protects the interests of the client;

---

42. *Ibid.*, p. 372.

3.     deal appropriately with client care and professional conduct issues;
4.     accurately address all the relevant legal and factual issues;
5.     where appropriate, identify relevant options, including the costs, benefits and risks of those options;
6.     where appropriate, demonstrate a critical use of precedents;
7.     are logically organised;
8.     form a consistent and coherent whole;
9.     follow the rules of grammar;
10.     demonstrate appropriate use of language;
11.     are succinct and precise;
12.     meet any formal legal or other requirements.

**Students should be able to explain the principles and criteria of good drafting practice and should be able to:-**

1.     identify pieces of drafting where those criteria are either met or not met;
2.     modify their own drafting errors to meet these criteria;
3.     transfer drafting principles or criteria learned in one context to other contexts;
4.     use techniques for appraising and developing their own writing and drafting style.

Students should have developed basic skill in the use of precedents, in setting out documents, in drafting clauses and should be able to write letters to lawyers, other professionals, clients and other non-lawyers.[43] The main headings we came up with are:

- PURPOSE
- READERSHIP
- CONTENT
- PROCEDURE
- LAYOUT
- STRUCTURE/ORGANISATION
- LANGUAGE
- STYLE

You may have decided you need a more detailed checklist than the Law Society's, but that some of the detailed questions in your writing checklist are inappropriate for legal documents.

The *Purpose* Heading needs to be adapted to the specific purposes of drafting we have discussed. Most drafting manuals suggest the Law Society guideline (a). However, we have seen that in some standard form contracts the client's goals may not always correspond to those of the readership or the public as a whole. There may therefore be ethical issues you need to think about.

---

43. Version 9, 2003.

Given our earlier discussion about the organisational characteristics of legal documents, you may have dispensed with the need to link ideas.

Our checklist is more detailed than the Law Society standards, because we think it is helpful to be able to answer very specific questions about your drafts. Some of the questions overlap, but we wanted to make the list comprehensive:

### Purpose

What are my client's goals?
How is the document going to be used?
What does the client expect it to accomplish?
What are the client's instructions?
Have I carried them out?
Does the client understand the document?
Who are the readers?
Will they understand the document?
Does it matter if they don't?
Is it clear to all readers what the document is for/how it affects them?

### Content

Have I covered all the relevant law?
What legislation applies?
What case law applies?
What are the possible legal pitfalls?
Have I understood the relevant law correctly?
Have I drafted it accurately?
Does the document cover all contingencies?
Is it precise?
Is there any ambiguity? In meaning? In syntax?
Is it vague in the right places?
Have I repeated myself unnecessarily?
Do any provisions contradict each other?

### Procedure

Are there any formal legal requirements?
If so, have I met them?
Have I used a precedent?
If so, have I modelled my draft on it?
Or have I checked my draft against it?

### Structure

Is the document organised into a coherent whole?
Does the material follow a logical sequence?
Is the material divided into appropriate categories?
Does each category/heading/section/paragraph/sentence contain –

(a) relevant material?

(b) just one idea?

Have I used legislative sentences where appropriate?

Are any sentences too long?

Have I used normal English word order?

If not, does the syntax make sense?

Do I need to make the purpose of the document clear?

Have I given the same word the same meaning throughout?

## Layout

Is this appropriate for the purpose and content?

Is it set out in manageable blocks?

Have I used appropriate headings, subheadings, numbering?

Do the headings accurately and concisely describe what follows?

## Language

Have I followed the 'three Cs'?

Is my grammar appropriate for the purpose?

Have I used unnecessary

- sentences within sentences?
- nominalisations?
- passives?
- multiple negatives?
- misplaced adverbials?
- word lists?

Have I omitted words and phrases which are

- redundant?
- unnecessarily technical?
- archaic?
- verbose?

Is punctuation correct?

Have I used too much/too little for the purpose?

Is spelling correct?

## Style

Is the style too formal/informal for the purpose?

Will the tone produce the desired response?

## Effect

Have I done everything possible to protect the client's interests?

Do I understand what I have drafted?

Do I find it convincing?

You may find the length of this list daunting. As you become more confident and experienced in drafting, you will find you can discard much of the detail.

## Putting principles into practice

### EXERCISE 8.10  Have a go

You are legal adviser to Long Haul Tours, a newly formed company setting up in the travel business. They have instructed you to draft a booking form for their new 200–package holiday brochure. The company is a member of the Association of British Travel Agents.

The company is particularly concerned to have maximum protection against possible claims by customers should the company cancel or make last minute alterations to bookings. On the other hand, it is keen to prevent customers cancelling or altering bookings, if possible.

1. *In small groups, brainstorm how to go about the task and discuss possible approaches and methodologies.*
2. *Individually, decide which methodology you prefer and why. Make a note in your learning diary on your preferred methodology.*
3. *In your group:*
    *(a) Decide which methodology you are going to use.*
    *(b) Draw up an action plan and show it to your tutor, remembering to define your objectives.*
    *(c) Do the necessary research.*
4. *In preparation for a meeting with the client, draft notes explaining the content and effect of the cancellation clauses you are preparing to draft.*
5. *Draft these clauses (preferably word-processed). Check you have achieved your objectives.*
6. *Exchange drafts with another group and analyse their draft.*
7. *Feed back to the group on their draft, and receive feedback on yours.*
8. *Discuss with the whole group what problems you experienced in the exercise and what you did to overcome them. Use this information for your learning diary entry.*
9. *Your tutor will give each group a booking form. Read it carefully. Would you make any changes to:*
    *(a) your draft, and*
    *(b) the booking form*
    *as a result of the practical work and analysis you have carried out for this exercise? If so, what changes?*

## Defining your approach

There are a number of ways you could go about planning this draft. Pragmatists will probably favour dashing off to the nearest travel agent to get specimen booking forms. Theorists may have suggested researching the relevant law first. Activists will have taken a leading role in the brainstorming session and might even have suggested having a go at drafting from scratch. Reflectors will have thought carefully about all the approaches you discussed before deciding eventually which one to go for.

All these methodologies are equally valid. Select whichever one you think will work best for your group.

### Aim to be a critical composer, not a complacent copier

Even for accomplished writers, drafting is difficult and time-consuming because it involves so much detail. One thing you will need to decide is how to use formbooks and precedents. These are useful for getting started on a draft, as are examples of booking forms in this particular case. They will save you a lot of time and will help to boost your confidence. Furthermore, they help you structure your draft and check you haven't left anything out. As you become more confident and experienced, however, you will not improve your drafting skills sufficiently to become proficient if you rely too heavily on 'off the shelf' precedents. Try to develop your own style as early as possible.

Slavish copying of formbook precedents can be dangerous. You may fail to recognise or analyse a potential problem if you rely too heavily on them. You must evaluate a precedent as carefully as you do your own writing.

You will find that once you can draft with precision, clarity and elegance, you can draft anything. However, keep in mind that the quality of your drafting will be determined as well by the quality of your research and preparation.

We end this chapter with views on drafting from two practitioners: a barrister in commercial practice and a trainee solicitor. Interestingly, neither view seems to reflect any concern for the readers.

> If you're a novelist or an academic, plagiarism is a dirty word, but if you're a practitioner it isn't ... whether you're copying your own precedent, a textbook precedent or somebody else's precedent or if you get six precedents that are roughly in the area but not quite and you chop and change between them ... so long as you've got a draft that is the right answer and is going to progress that case the step required and you get that back quickly ... that's what you're being paid for – getting the right information down on paper and back to the client as quickly as you can ... yes, the solicitor client ... That's a better service than locking yourself up and attempting to do it all out of your own head.[44]

> ...most drafting exercises on the LPC were unproblematic. The reality is that much drafting in real life is not so straightforward. There are often additional points that must be covered or quirks in the information that you are given so that precedents fail to be of use. Only experience enables you to deal quickly and efficiently with drafting.[45]

We hope that these last two chapters have convinced you of the importance of keeping your reader in mind when planning to draft. We recommend you use

---

44. Quoted in J. Morison and P. Leith, *The Barrister's World*, Open University Press, Milton Keynes, 1992, p. 96.
45. Trainee solicitor Nick Oliver, in *Legal Aide*, Trainee Solicitors' Group, Spring 1995, p. 4.

formbooks critically and discard bits of boilerplate which are archaic and super-fluous. Plagiarism is quick and easy, but the results are almost invariably ugly, ponderous and incomprehensible to the reader.

EXERCISE **8.11**  **Concepts**

In this chapter we have discussed a number of concepts. We list the main ones below. The procedure for learning these concepts is as follows:

1.  *Divide into pairs.*
2.  *Each pair is to*
    (a)  *define each concept, noting the page on which it is discussed, and*
    (b)  *make sure that both members of the pair understand the meaning of each concept.*
3.  *Combine into groups of four. Compare the answers of the two pairs. If there is disagreement, look up the concept and clarify it until all agree on the definition and understand it.*

| | |
|---|---|
| *boilerplate* | *context* |
| *tautology* | *truncated passive* |
| *nominalisation* | *scenario principle* |
| *archaism* | *legislative sentence* |
| *pleadings* | *whiz deletion* |
| *bureaucratese* | *misplaced adverbial* |
| *term of art* | |

EXERCISE **8.12**  **Analysis**

*In your groups: compare Clause 7 of the more recent BT Conditions for Telephone Service with Clauses 13, 14, and 15 of the earlier BT conditions on pages 270–1. (Your tutor will give you a copy.) In particular, comment on:*

–  *punctuation*
–  *sentence length*
–  *word order*
–  *sentence complexity*
–  *vocabulary*

*and give examples to show how these features influence readability.*

EXERCISE **8.13**  **Boilerplate redrafting**

1.  *In your groups, read the business tenancy clause below.*
2.  *Summarise the legislative thought in no more than 60 words.*
3.  *Redraft the clause in plain English. When you are satisfied with your draft, write it on an overhead transparency.*
4.  *All groups should then show their redrafts to the whole group and feed back.*

2. Payment of insurance

In the event of the demised premises or any part thereof or any of the adjoining or adjacent premises of the Council or any part thereof respectively being damaged or destroyed by fire at any time during the term hereby created and the insurance money under any insurance effected thereon being wholly or partly irrecoverable by reason solely or in part of any act or default of the lessee its agents servants or workmen or of persons occupying or being upon the demised premises or any part thereof with the authority or permission of the lessee then and in every such case the lessee will forthwith in addition to the rent pay to the Council the whole or (as the case may require) a fair proportion of the cost of completely rebuilding or reinstating the same and any dispute as to the proportion to be so distributed by the lessee or otherwise in respect of or arising out of this provision shall be determined by a single arbitrator in accordance with the provisions of the Arbitration Acts 1950 1975 and 1979 or any statutory modification or reinactment thereof for the time being in force.

EXERCISE **8.14**  **What is reasonable doubt?**

Go back to p. 279 and re-read the jury instruction on reasonable doubt.
  *In your groups:*

1.  *Briefly identify the features which make the instruction difficult to understand.*
2.  *Discuss Dumas' revised version, noting the features which make it more intelligible. (Your tutor will give you a copy.)*
3.  *Finally, compare both versions with the English law instruction on reasonable doubt. (Look this up.) What are the similarities and differences?*

## Review questions

1.  Below are two extracts which discuss the problem of obscurely drafted legislation. The first is taken from an article written by Francis Bennion around the time Lord Woolf was working on his reforms of the civil justice system:

    A prime cause of the horrendous cost of legal advice and litigation, now under investigation by Lord Woolf, is the obscurity of the law . . .
      . . . my advice to Lord Woolf is this. Do not look for savings by trying to make the law easier for lay persons to understand. Instead, make it easier for lawyers to use.[46]

    The second is a comment by Lord Harman on the Housing Act 1957 (now repealed):

    To reach a conclusion on this matter involved the court in wading through a monstrous legislative morass, staggering from stone to stone and ignoring the marsh gas exhaling from the forest of schedules lining the way on each side. I regarded it at one time, I must confess, as a Slough of Despond through which the court would

46. *The Times*, 24 January 1995, p. 35.

never drag its feet, but I have by leaping from tussock to tussock as best I might, eventually pale and exhausted, reached the other side.[47]

(a) *Do you agree with Francis Bennion's view? Why/why not?*

(b) *How would you make the law easier for lawyers to use?*

(c) *Summarise the differences between plain English and legal English. How do these differences reflect the differing priorities of each type of writing?*

2. '. . . it is actually harder to be absolutely unambiguous in plain English than in the kind of language used in the past.'[48] *Do you agree with this view?*

## Further reading

The Inns of Court School of Law, *Drafting*, Oxford University Press, Oxford, 2004.

'Legal Drafting: Formal Documents' in Boyle et al., *A Practical Guide to Lawyering Skills*, Cavendish, London, 2003, ch. 6.

'Drafting Legal Documents' in Webb et al., *Lawyers' Skills*, Oxford University Press, Oxford, 2004, ch. 4.

W. M. Rose, *Pleading Without Tears: A Guide to Legal Drafting*, Oxford University Press, Oxford, 2002.

E. Doonan and C. Foster, *Drafting*, Cavendish, London, 2001.

P. Butt and R. Castle, *Modern Legal Drafting: A Guide to Using Clearer Language*, Cambridge University Press, Cambridge, 2001.

M. Asprey, *Plain Language for Lawyers*, The Federation Press, Sydney, NSW, 1996.

M. Adler, *Clarity for Lawyers*, Law Society, London, 1990.

B. K. Dumas, 'US Pattern Jury Instructions: Problems and Proposals' (2000) 7(1) *Forensic Linguistics* 49–71.

47. *Davy v Leeds Corporation* [1964] 3 All ER 390 at 394.
48. Inns of Court School of Law, *Drafting*, p. 4.

# 9

## Handling conflict: negotiation

Negotiation is an interactive social process that we regularly engage in. You have therefore become well versed in the skills of negotiating long before you get to this chapter. Our task here is to enable you to identify your skills and transfer them to the context of legal practice. You will consider the broad range of situations in which lawyers negotiate, and how effective they are as negotiators. You will have a chance to identify what type of negotiator you are before we introduce you to three negotiating strategies: win/lose, win some/lose some, and win/win. You will try out these strategies in specific legal situations and assess their strengths and weaknesses. Finally, we ask you to consider your own position in the light of the often conflicting ethical and commercial pressures of a busy law practice.

### Objectives

To:

- Recognise the importance of negotiation in legal practice.
- Consider the part negotiation plays in dispute prevention and resolution.
- Identify and analyse your negotiating behaviour and personality.
- Analyse the negotiating process and its ethical implications.
- Examine zero-sum and creative strategies of negotiation.
- Assess which strategies are appropriate in which situations.
- Practise negotiation planning, strategies and skills in legal contexts.
- Develop an understanding of how to negotiate ethically.

### Supports benchmark statements

Students should demonstrate an ability:

2. Application and problem-solving
- To apply knowledge to a situation of limited complexity in order to provide arguable conclusions for concrete problems.

4. Analysis, etc
- To recognise and rank items and issues in terms of relevance and importance.
- To make a critical judgment of the merits of particular arguments.
- To present and make a reasoned choice between alternative solutions.

5. Autonomy and ability to learn
- To act independently in planning and undertaking tasks.

7. Other key skills
- To work in groups as participants who contribute effectively to the group's task.

## Making decisions and resolving conflict

In its broadest sense, negotiation is a form of decision making. It is the process of bargaining to reach an agreement in any situation where the views of more than one person have to be taken into account. We engage in this interactive process constantly when we are with other people:

– Do you fancy a coffee?
– Yes, but I'll get them.
– No, it's OK. You paid last time.
– OK, thanks.


– Your car looks like a bit of a rust box to me. I'll give you £500, take it or leave it.
– Leave it out. There's not an ounce of rust on it.
– £550, that's my final offer.
– OK. It's a deal.

Now consider the following exercise:


EXERCISE **9.1 Conflicts of interest**

The Joneses, a close-knit and harmonious family, have just won £20,000 on the national lottery. Not surprisingly, at the time they bought tickets they didn't decide what they would do with the money if they won.

Phil wants to buy a new car. He has to travel a long way to work, and his old banger is always breaking down. His boss is beginning to get angry about his lateness.

Debbie, his mother, wants to spend the money on a good holiday for the whole family. They haven't had a holiday abroad for several years.

Ray, his father, wants to use the money to pay off some of the mortgage on the family home.

Sarah is applying to university and wants the money to tide her over the three years until she gets a job. This would mean she would not have to depend on Debbie and Ray.

Rebecca thinks all the family members who are working should give up their jobs and start their own business, making and delivering pizzas.

The family has arranged to meet and discuss what they are going to do with the money.

(a)    Role play: the family meeting.
    (i)    Form groups of five if possible; four if necessary. Allocate a role to each member of the group, leaving out one of the roles if you are a group of four. Change the gender of the roles as necessary to suit your group.
    (ii)    You have 10 minutes to prepare your role. You can make up facts as appropriate to your role.
    (iii)    Role play as if you were at the family meeting.
(b)    'Families' feed back to large group.
    (i)    Did you reach a decision? If so, what was it?
    (ii)    Did everyone agree with it? Why/why not?
    (iii)    How was the decision reached? Analyse carefully what strategy/ tactics each role player used to try and get what they wanted.
    (iv)    Analyse the thoughts and feelings of each role player during the meeting.
    (v)    Did any role player plan their strategy in advance? If so, did they stick to it in the meeting? Why/why not?
    (vi)    If you didn't reach a decision, why was this?
    (vii)    Have you learnt anything new:
       – about negotiation within a family group?
       – about yourself as a negotiator?

The scene you have just acted out involved much more than simply group problem-solving. The participants have various needs and goals which are in conflict with those of the other participants. You may have noted that different people use different strategies to try and get what they want. We learn these strategies in childhood. Those of you who are parents will know the subtle means by which your children manipulate you to get what they want and no doubt you have a range of techniques for handling conflicts with them.

Even from these simple examples, we can begin to see how negotiation can operate in two rather different ways. First, it can act as an alternative to conflict – we can see a potential conflict arising and deploy negotiation to prevent it – here negotiation becomes a *conflict-blocking* device.[1] Secondly, where a conflict has already developed, we can use negotiation to manage and ultimately thereby to diffuse it – hence negotiation can also be a *conflict-managing* and *conflict-resolution* device. The distinction between conflict-blocking and conflict-managing/resolving can be strategically significant, as we shall see, but while there are differences, there is also one overriding similarity: to be effective, negotiation requires some element

---

1.  Here we are using the term conflict-blocking in a rather different sense from Stephen Nathanson's discussion of the lawyer's role as either 'playing-out' or 'blocking' conflict in *What Lawyers Do*, Sweet & Maxwell, London, 1997, discussed in Chapter 1, above.

of *collaborative problem-solving*. The quality of a negotiated outcome thus depends fundamentally on how effective we are – as negotiators – in overcoming whatever barriers to agreement exist in a given situation.

## How do you deal with conflict?

How you act in a conflict, or a situation ripe for conflict, will be determined by a range of personal influences, including how you perceive the situation, the relationship you have with the other people involved, the importance you attach to your preferred outcomes, and your own 'style' of dealing with conflict. These together will help shape your overall 'conflict strategy'.

If it is a 'one-off' interaction, like advertising your car in the paper and selling it to whoever makes the best offer, you are unlikely to meet the buyer ever again. You may therefore think you can get away with some tough bargaining to obtain the highest price. If, on the other hand, you have conflict at work, at home or with friends, a harmonious future relationship will usually be more important to you than getting everything you want. You are therefore more likely to compromise to reach agreement.

Negotiation thus commonly involves balancing two conflicting desires: to achieve all your goals, and maintain co-operation in the future. Which is more likely to satisfy your longer term needs? Your assessment of the relative importance of achieving short term goals and maintaining relationships will influence your behaviour during negotiation.

EXERCISE **9.2 The shark and the turtle**

The purpose of this exercise is to help you reflect on the ways you have learned to manage conflicts and how they compare with the methods that others use.[2]

1.  *Form groups of four – this exercise works best if your partners are people you have worked with before.*
2.  *Your tutor will give each of you a questionnaire. Working individually, complete the questionnaire without conferring with the other members of your group.*
3.  *Read the text on conflict strategies below.*
4.  *Write the names of the other members of your group on separate slips of paper, one name to a slip. On each slip of paper, write the conflict strategy that you think best fits the actions of the person named.*
5.  *Pass each slip to the person whose name is on it. Each of you should receive three slips of paper describing the conflict strategy the other group members ascribe to you.*
6.  *Add up your score on the questionnaire, using the table given you by the tutor. The highest score will indicate the strategy you use most frequently. The second highest score indicates the strategy you use as a back-up when your first one fails.*

---

2.  Taken from D. Johnson and F. Johnson, *Joining Together: Group Theory and Group Skills*, Allyn & Bacon, Boston, Mass., 8th edn, 2003, pp. 385–7.

7.  *Tell the group your questionnaire results, comparing them with their descriptions of your style on the slips of paper. Ask the other group members for examples of how they have seen you act in conflicts. Repeat this feedback procedure for all group members.*
8.  *Discuss the strengths and weaknesses of each of the conflict strategies.*

### Strategies for managing conflicts (figure 9.1)

*The turtle (withdrawing)*
The turtle withdraws into its shell to avoid conflict rather than face up to it. Turtles will keep away from anyone involved in a conflict, even if this means damaging a relationship with that person. Inter-personal goals are not important to them.

*The shark (forcing)*
The shark wants to win and the opponent to lose. Sharks will try to force opponents to accept their desired outcome to the dispute and won't mind sacrificing relationships to that goal. Sharks attack, overwhelm and intimidate opponents. They see losing as failure and inadequacy.

*The teddy bear (smoothing)*
Teddy bears smooth over conflict and will abandon their goals in order to preserve relationships. They want others to accept and like them.

*The fox (compromising)*[3]
The fox wants to meet in the middle. She wants a mutually acceptable agreement and is prepared to sacrifice part of her goals and relationships to achieve it. In short, agreement is an end in itself for the fox.

*The owl (confronting)*
Owls confront problems (not people!). Both their goals and relationships are very important. They view conflict resolution as a means of eliminating tension and negative feelings, and look for a solution which yields the best result for both sides.

Besides your personal strategy, there are external factors which influence how you act. Within the group – organisation, family, friendships, or community – there are rules and conventions which determine how negotiation should operate. These may be explicitly agreed: for example, Standing Orders which determine how local council meetings are to be conducted. Or they may be implicit. For

---

3. We acknowledge that the choice of the 'fox' label for this characteristic seems rather strange. Through much English and European folklore the fox has acquired a much less attractive reputation, as a sly and untrustworthy creature, but this is clearly not what Johnson and Johnson have in mind. Perhaps it reflects a US/European cultural difference that we are unaware of.

Figure 9.1. Conflict strategies

example, it might be acceptable to throw a tantrum at home during a family row, but it would be thought quite unacceptable to do so at a company board meeting.

Moreover, it might be clear to everybody involved that certain things are simply not negotiable. For example, a couple living together may have agreed that infidelity by one or the other is not acceptable, so that if it happens, they will decide to split up.

A further significant factor which can influence the process and outcome of negotiation is the bargaining positions of the participants. Age, gender, education and values may bring about subtle and imperceptible shifts of power from one participant to another and back again. These can affect the course of the negotiation and indeed may be the source of the conflict. By virtue of their position, parents know they can resolve a dispute so that their child gets nothing. Employers can drive hard bargains on pay and conditions when jobs are in short supply. Bosses can bully, sexually or racially harass junior employees or trainees and feel they can get away with it. Can you think of other factors external to the conflict itself which might influence the course and outcome of negotiation?

## The context of legal negotiation

In understanding how legal negotiation fits into our whole pattern of disputing and conflict behaviours, we need to think about the trajectory that disputes take. Not every dispute, of course, ends up in court, and there are methods of conflict resolution which do not involve negotiation at all. You can 'settle' a dispute by head-butting your opponent, or you can walk away from it, like the turtle. At the other extreme are the formal methods of adjudication – the courts, whose decisions are not negotiable. We can thus think of disputing in terms of a pyramid of events, in which the many minor disputes, perceived grievances and upsets of everyday life are at the bottom and litigation is at the top.[4] We routinely put up with much of what is at the bottom, or find informal ways of dealing with it. But what is it that converts some events into legal disputes?

### Naming, blaming, claiming ... and negotiating

Felstiner, Abel and Sarat characterise the shift from event to dispute as the product of a process of 'naming, blaming and claiming'.[5] An individual who suffers a 'perceived injurious event' first has to see it as a grievance rather than, say, an act of fate or their own fault. 'Naming' is thus the critical first stage of translating that event into a grievance. Many potential grievances go unperceived and hence unnamed – for example, breaches of product warranty that are never identified by purchasers. The second stage of the trajectory involves 'blaming'. We may be aware of a grievance, but unable to act on it unless there is another person or institution that we can identify as being 'at fault' or otherwise responsible. It is only when those grievances are voiced to the offending person that the third phase begins and they become 'claims'. Consequently, many claims will not crystallise, either because the potential claimant cannot identify the person at fault (the hit-and-run driver, or the con-man who has disappeared without a trace), or because she lacks the will, or the knowledge of potential remedies to pursue it.[6] One of two things will happen to claims which

---

4. M. Galanter, 'Reading the Landscape of Disputes: What We Know and Don't Know (and Think We Know) about Our Allegedly Contentious and Litigious Society' (1983) 31 *UCLA Law Review* 4.
5. W. Felstiner, R. Abel and A. Sarat, 'The Emergence, and Transformation of Disputes: Naming, Blaming, Claiming ... ' (1980–81) 15 *Law & Society Review* 631.
6. Early studies in Australia and the US showed a similar pattern of variation between the types of dispute most likely to result in litigation. Matrimonial disputes gave rise to the most litigation, followed by tortious claims for personal injury. By contrast grievances about discrimination

are pursued; either the claims will be accepted, and some restitution offered, or they will be denied. Only those claims that are denied ultimately become disputes in the sense that we are using the term. But even then not all disputes will end up in court. Recourse to litigation is only one of a number of informal or formal means of settling disputes, and many more disputes will be settled by some form of negotiation than will actually be litigated. This is where the lawyers come in.

### EXERCISE 9.3  Negotiate? What for?

*In pairs or small groups, discuss:*

1.  *In what circumstances do legal practitioners negotiate, and why?*
2.  *In each circumstance you have identified, who will the lawyer negotiate with, and on whose behalf?*
3.  *In those circumstances you have noted which could lead to trial, what advantages do you think negotiation has over court action? Are there any disadvantages?*

Since the practice of law is one of the ways we manage those social relations, it is hardly surprising that lawyers in practice spend a great deal of their time planning and carrying out negotiations. They negotiate with their clients and they negotiate on their behalf, by phone, letter, fax and face to face. They negotiate with the other side's lawyer and lay experts such as social workers and doctors. In face-to-face negotiation with an opponent they may have the client present and participating, or do it without the client. They may conduct the negotiation through a mediator. However it is done, we know that well over 90 per cent of civil cases are settled or withdrawn before trial. Why should this be so?

Research suggests that the decision to pursue litigation is shaped by a complex mix of motivational, economic and institutional factors.[7] In personal injury claims, for example, a number of factors may persuade the client not to go as far as trial. It may be difficult to predict the trial outcome, because certain facts may be difficult to prove, or there is a conflict of medical evidence; a claimant may need compensation more urgently than the trial process will allow, the client may not be able to afford to litigate, or the client may not want to ruin an existing relationship with the opponent.

Businesses may have a different propensity to sue than individuals, because of the different transactions engaged in and interests to be protected. Large companies have both the resources and the inclination to use legal *fora* (aggressively, if need be) to protect their name, reputation and intellectual property rights. For an example of this, consider the recent 'Napster Wars' launched by the music industry against the wave of music 'piracy' sparked by the increased availability of music downloads on the web using MP3 and P2P

resulted in the least litigation: see R. Miller and A. Sarat, 'Grievances, Claims and Disputes' (1981) 15 *Law & Society Review* 525; M. Fitzgerald, 'Grievances, Disputes and Outcomes' (1983) 1 *Law in Context* 15. What factors do you think might account for this difference?

7.  R. Cranston, 'What Do Courts Do?' (1986) 5 *Civil Justice Quarterly* 123 at pp. 126–8.

software.[8] But at the same time there is substantial evidence that business people tend not to use contract law remedies and court action when resolving disputes with other businesses. Often they will find excuses to suppress potential disputes and will renegotiate contracts, rather than seek enforcement of existing terms, in order to preserve long-term relationships. Often this is because they place the preservation of these relationships as central to achieving their long-term goal: to be, or continue to be, successful in business.[9]

The importance of negotiation to civil practice is such that Marc Galanter coined the term 'litigotiation' to describe the approach of civil litigators to their work.[10] What Galanter means by this is that negotiation has itself become an integral part of the litigation strategy; indeed in his view the 'hard law' is itself only one of the tools lawyers use in playing the litigotiation game. (And as we shall see later in the chapter, there are a number of issues around what happens to the negotiation process in the lawyer's embrace.) Moreover, in England, the Civil Procedure Rules 1998 have increased the emphasis on settlement as part of Lord Woolf's attack on what he saw as the excessively adversarial culture of civil litigation. Research to date suggests that although the reforms have not engendered a total culture change among litigators, they have significantly reduced the volume of civil proceedings.[11] Furthermore, in many areas of work the Woolf reforms seem to have increased the amount of co-operation and settlement between parties and led to earlier settlement than under the old regime.[12]

8.  See, e.g., J. Alderman, *Sonic Boom. Napster, MP3 and the New Pioneers of Music*, Perseus Publ., Cambridge, Mass., 2001; L. Marshall, 'Metallica and Morality: The Rhetorical Battleground of the Napster Wars' (2002) 1 *Entertainment Law* 1.

9.  See S. Macauley, 'Non-Contractual Relations in Business: A Preliminary Study' (1963) 28 *American Sociological Review* 55 at p. 61; also 'An Empirical View of Contract' [1985] *Wisconsin Law Review* 465. See also H. Beale and A. Dugdale, 'Contracts Between Businessmen: Planning and the Use of Contractual Remedies' (1975) *British Journal of Law and Society* 18; P. Vincent-Jones, 'Contract Litigation in England and Wales 1975–1991: A Transformation in Business Disputing' (1993) 12 *Civil Justice Quarterly* 337.

10. M. Galanter, 'Worlds of Deals: Using Negotiation to Teach about Legal Process' (1984) 34 *Journal of Legal Education* 268 at p. 268.

11. The number of claims issued in the County Court and High Court fell gradually but consistently in the three years since April 1999. In contract and tort cases in the County Court, the average number of claims for the two-year period May 1999 to April 2001 fell by 20 per cent. In the High Court the total number of claims in 2001 was 19.6 per cent lower than in 2000 – Lord Chancellor's Department, *Civil Justice Reform Evaluation – Further Findings* (August 2002) at www.lcd.gov.uk/civil/reform/ffreform.htm, paras 3.1–3.12 (last accessed 27 March 2003).

12. See T. Goriely, R. Moorhead and P. Abrams, *More Civil Justice? The Impact of the Woolf Reforms on Pre-Action Behaviour*, Research Study 43, The Law Society and Civil Justice Council, London, 2002. In a survey of 100 senior litigators conducted by Market and Opinion Research International (MORI) in 2000, 76 per cent of those surveyed were of the opinion that the CPR had caused positive changes in settlement culture; 47 per cent reported that cases were settling more quickly than under the old rules; 40 per cent reported little or no change, and only 5 per cent complained that cases were being resolved more slowly than before the Woolf reforms took effect – see www.mori.com/polls/2000/cedr2.htm (accessed 26 March 2003). The LCD data in *Further Findings*, para. 4.3, also indicate an increase in settlements before the day of hearing – the proportion rising from 50 per cent (July 1998–June 1999) to 69 per cent (November 1999–December 2001). Data on the cost implications of the reforms is less certain. Goriely et al.

While we associate negotiated settlements primarily with civil proceedings, negotiation may feature in criminal proceedings too. Although we have no formal procedure of charge or plea bargaining in the UK, prosecution and defence lawyers are known to agree deals as a way of ensuring conviction while limiting the costs of criminal prosecution, and (from the defence perspective) as a means of reducing sentence by entering a guilty plea, perhaps to a lesser offence than that originally charged.[13]

## The growth of Alternative Dispute Resolution[14]

Concerns about the cost, delay and general stress engendered by litigation have led policy-makers not just to seek methods for enabling more settlement in litigation, but to encourage alternative methods and *fora* for resolving disputes. Alternative Dispute Resolution (ADR) mechanisms have expanded rapidly during the last thirty years, principally in the US. In the UK their development is rather more recent, and, again the Civil Procedure Rules have done much to extend ADR mechanisms in the civil justice system. Some methods, like arbitration and the use of tribunals, have a long history and are perhaps not that alternative – many people would see them as just less formal ways of judging. Others, such as early neutral evaluation, the mini-trial and mediation are new – at least to the Western legal traditions. ADR can be seen quite pragmatically as a means of relieving overloaded courts and improving access to justice. However, its supporters suggest it has a more valuable social contribution than that. While its growth is perhaps one symptom of what Schön calls the crisis of confidence in professional knowledge and status,[15] the supporters of ADR also view ADR more

report some evidence that cases are being settled at lower cost; however the LCD's *Further Findings* report took the view that 'it is still too early to provide a definitive view on costs ... with statistics difficult to obtain and conflicting anecdotal evidence' (para. 7.1). What is clear is that the CPR have led to a greater front-loading of costs, as more work now needs to be done at an earlier stage. This may consequently *increase* costs relative to the pre-CPR regime in some cases that settle.

13. The Report of the Royal Commission on Criminal Justice (Cm. 2263, 1993, paras. 41–58) proposed a more formalised system of plea bargaining along the lines of the American system. This proposal has not been adopted, but s. 48(1) of the Criminal Justice and Public Order Act 1994 implements Recommendation 156 of the Royal Commission that earlier guilty pleas should attract higher sentence discounts. When deciding sentence, the court can take into account at what stage in the proceedings the offender indicated his intention to plead guilty, and the circumstances in which he gave the indication. For recent discussion of plea bargaining, see generally A. Sanders and R. Young, *Criminal Justice*, London, Butterworths, 2nd edn, 2000, and M. McConville, 'Plea Bargaining: Ethics and Politics' (1998) 25 *Journal of Law & Society* 562. An interesting, but rather depressing account (in our view!) of practitioners' justifications for plea bargaining is A. Mulcahy, 'The Justifications of Justice: Legal Practitioners' Accounts of Negotiated Case Settlements in Magistrates' Courts' (1994) 34 *British Journal of Criminology* 411.

14. For a discussion of the development and characteristics of Alternative Dispute Resolution mechanisms, see K. Mackie (ed.), *A Handbook of Dispute Resolution*, Routledge, London, 1991; M. Palmer and S. Roberts, *Dispute Processes: ADR and the Primary Forms of Decision-Making*, Butterworths, London, 1998; K. Stone, *Private Justice: The Law of Alternative Dispute Resolution*, Foundation Press, New York, 2000; E. Carroll and K. Mackie, *International Mediation – The Art of Business Diplomacy*, Kluwer, The Hague, 2000.

15. See Chapter 1, above.

positively, as being capable of producing *better* outcomes than litigation in many cases.

Resolving disputes in the formal tradition of black-letter law adjudication is not always an appropriate response in a society whose citizens and communities expect to regulate their own lives and collaborate in conflict resolution. As Tony Marshall says, painting a conflict in terms of legal rights and wrongs is often unrealistic and an over-simplification of conflict. Moreover:

> In practice the law can be said to set a bad example – the use of socially condoned violence. Law is perhaps the most civilised way we have of fighting; but it is still fighting. It is unfortunate that law has become the predominant representation of conflict resolution in modern society.[16]

Of course, there are situations where court action is preferable to more informal mechanisms of dispute resolution. Take, for example, abuses of fundamental human rights, serious criminal behaviour, or the need for clear statements of public values and the policies which support them.[17] All these may best be satisfied by a legal judgment. ADR does not declare or develop the law, does not happen in full view of the public, and may not even yield a resolution if the process breaks down. Many working in the dispute resolution field would acknowledge this, and prefer to think of dispute resolution more holistically, so that the search is for *appropriate* dispute resolution in every case, rather than a matter of choosing between litigation and something that is simply 'alternative' to that.

## ADR and negotiation

Most ADR mechanisms involve a neutral third party as some kind of decision-maker, information-giver or facilitator. A key variable distinguishing between ADR techniques is whether or not the third party has the power to determine the dispute.[18] The decisions of arbitrators are normally determinative and binding; an ombudsman's decision may be binding or non-binding, depending on the nature of the scheme. Some ADR techniques, by contrast, are designed purely to facilitate the parties in their own negotiation and settlement processes. Early neutral evaluation, for example, is always non-binding. It uses a third party (say a barrister, judge or some other expert) to evaluate the likelihood of a claim, or part of a claim, succeeding. The third party reports her decision, so that the parties can re-enter their own ('partisan') settlement negotiations with a greater sense of realism about the likely outcome.

The most widely used facilitative ADR mechanism is mediation. It goes beyond using a neutral third party to provide information, since the process is designed

---

16. T. Marshall, 'Neighbour Disputes: Community Mediation Schemes as an Alternative to Litigation', in K. Mackie (ed.), *Handbook of Dispute Resolution*, p. 64.
17. See O. Fiss, 'Against Settlement' (1984) 93 *Yale Jaw Journal* 1073.
18. See, e.g., the typology of dispute resolution processes in S. Goldberg, F. Sander and N. Rogers, *Dispute Resolution*, Aspen Law & Business, New York, 1992, pp. 4, 5.

pro-actively to enable settlement through a process of 'assisted negotiation'. The mediator's task is to work with the parties in negotiating a mutually acceptable agreement through the mediation process itself. Some of you may be aware of the part mediation plays in matrimonial disputes.[19] It is also of growing importance in civil and commercial disputes, where the Civil Procedure Rules contain a number of provisions encouraging the courts and the parties to use ADR (in practice this tends to mean mediation or early neutral evaluation).[20] Moreover, mediation is also evolving beyond this conventional conflict-resolution role, to take on more of a conflict-blocking function. As an example of this today 'deal mediators' utilise ADR techniques 'up-front' to broker commercial deals and international contracts *before* any potential disputes arise.[21]

Given the importance of mediation in the modern civil justice system, and the similarities between negotiation and mediation as processes, we will conclude this chapter by looking in more depth at the role of the lawyer in supporting clients in mediation.

## What clients want from negotiation

What do you think a client wants most from a negotiation? Clearly, she wants the dispute resolved. But what does that mean? Research on client satisfaction with methods of alternative dispute resolution indicates that procedures can be at least as important to clients as outcomes.[22] In other words, they are less interested than we might expect in getting everything they want from the negotiation, or litigation. They may not even be that interested in the money – sometimes an apology or acknowledgment of the harm caused will be as, if not more, important.[23] Normally, they want

19. See, e.g., G. Davis, *Partisans and Mediators: The Resolution of Divorce Disputes*, Clarendon Press, Oxford, 1988.
20. Under CPR r. 1.4 (1), the court must further the overriding objective by actively managing cases. This may include (para. 1.4(2)(c)) 'encouraging the parties to use an alternative dispute resolution procedure ... '. Furthermore, a party to proceedings may specifically request an order staying proceedings to enable the parties to settle the case by means of ADR CPR r. 24.5. Where a party has refused to mediate, and the court deems that refusal unreasonable, then the court may penalise that party in costs in respect of those proceedings under powers in CPR r. 44.3: see *Dunnett v Railtrack* [2002] EWCA Civ 302, [2002] 2 All ER 850; *Leicester Circuits Ltd v Coates Brothers plc* [2003] EWCA Civ 333; but note also *Halsey v Milton Keynes NHS Trust and Steel v Joy & Halliday* [2004] EWCA Civ 576.
21. M. Hager and R. Pritchard, 'Deal Mediation: How ADR Techniques Can Help Achieve Durable Agreements in the Global Markets', *The CEPMLP Journal*, vol. 6, at www.dundee.ac.uk/cepmlp/journal/html/article6–12.html (last accessed 6 April 2003).
22. For an overview of the research, see T. Tyler, 'Procedure or Result: What Do Disputants Want from Legal Authorities?, in K. Mackie (ed.), *Handbook of Dispute Resolution*, pp. 19–25. See also H. Genn, *Mediation in Action*, Calouste Gulbenkian Foundation, London, 1999, pp. 31–2. Note that much of the research focuses on private rather than corporate clients. We are aware in writing this that there is a danger in assuming that all clients want the same thing.
23. This is not always high on the lawyer's agenda: cf. the comments of one mediator reported by Linda Mulcahy: 'I said to him [defendant's solicitor] at one stage ... "Do you think there are ways of making your offer more appealing to the plaintiff?" and he said: "You mean add more

to be treated with courtesy and respect, and to participate actively in the process;[24] they want their emotional needs acknowledged as part of this process.[25] This means having the opportunity to put their cases and have their views listened to by the lawyers, judges, or mediators who are working after all to resolve *their* problems. Disputants value having some control over the outcome of their dispute and, moreover, if they do, they are more likely to be satisfied that the outcome is fair.[26]

Do not also assume that lawyers and clients will necessarily agree on what is fair. You (as a lawyer) may take the view that the informal procedures of ADR do not offer parties the safeguards provided by the formal procedures of litigation. For example, a common criticism of informal plea bargaining is that the offender's lack of bargaining power in this situation may force him to make a decision against his own best interests. Yet can we necessarily assume the offender sees it in the same way? Isn't it possible he may view the chance to have a say in the outcome of his case as far more 'just' than having a decision imposed on him by a court? At the very least the lawyer should check that the client's view of what is fair and just accords with her own.

If we look at dispute resolution from the client's point of view, we should not be surprised at these findings. After all, it is the clients, not their lawyers, who have to live with the outcome.

## What lawyers want from negotiation

Lawyers are in an ambiguous position. Technically, they are only the agents of their client, but they are also the managers of the litigation or other dispute. They are the ones primarily responsible for the outcome, and for advising on the means of getting there. This gives them considerable situational power, but also a lot of responsibility, responsibility that may often make them cautious and risk-averse in selecting dispute resolution strategies, and perhaps even specific outcomes. At the same time, as Goodpaster points out, 'accountability to another leads one to greater advocacy than is the case when acting for oneself'.[27] This sense of partisanship may be enhanced by the ethical duty to act in the client's 'best interests' and by a training that often encourages them to see disputes primarily in 'win–lose' terms. Conventionally, 'thinking like a lawyer' means thinking adversarially. While it would be wrong of us to over-generalise, this can have a significant impact on both the lawyers' and the parties' ability to shape how the dispute is perceived and managed once it is handed

money?" and I said "No. I mean is there anything you could give the plaintiff that you would not have to pay for?" And he said "such as?" and I said "an apology?" After a while he said: "Have they asked for that?" And I thought: "Are you on this planet? Were you in that room?"': 'Can leopards change their spots? An evaluation of the role of lawyers in medical negligence mediation' (2001) 8 *International Journal of the Legal Profession* 203 at pp. 216–7.

24. 'Those with problems value the opportunity to present their problems to authorities. By allowing disputants to bring their problems to them, authorities are reaffirming the disputants' social standing and their right to call on the authorities for help.' Tyler, 'Procedure or Result', p. 22.

25. See further the discussion below at pp. 315–16.

26. Compare Genn, *Mediation in Action*, pp. 32, 34.

27. G. Goodpaster, 'Lawsuits as Negotiations' (1992) 8 *Negotiation Journal* 221 at p. 223.

over to the lawyers. Even though many litigators would argue that they are focused on settlement, it may be 'settlement' largely as defined by the adversarial context. Unless they are pulling their punches, they will be looking for a solution that can be presented to the client as a victory, or at least not a defeat ('it's the best we could get in the circumstances').[28] There is a risk that lawyers will be inclined to think of settlement, when not thinking about 'winning' the negotiations, largely in terms of 'compromise'.[29] The problems with this will become more apparent as we progress.

## Mind the gap[30]

The fact is that lawyers and clients may approach not just negotiations, but the whole process of dispute resolution with rather different world views. Not surprisingly, perhaps, lawyers tend to focus on the legal issues. They may therefore sidestep the relational and emotional dimensions of the dispute that are often important to the client.[31] In this sense there may be a significant gap between lawyer and client perspectives on what needs to be addressed in achieving settlement or resolution of a dispute.

Research by Austin Sarat and William Felstiner, among others, provides evidence that client and lawyer perceptions of the reality and function of negotiation differ in other respects.[32] They recorded conversations between clients and their lawyers involved in divorce cases. From these they formed the conclusion that while clients concentrate on what happened in the past and the failure of their marriage, lawyers focus on the future: the legal issues of getting the divorce and making arrangements about children and property.

> Lawyers avoid responding to these (the clients') interpretations because they do not consider that who did what to whom in the marriage is relevant to the legal task of dissolving it. In this domain clients largely talk past their lawyers, and interpretive activity proceeds without the generation and ratification of a shared understanding of reality.[33]

28. Compare D. Rosenthal, *Lawyer and Client: Who's in Charge?*, Transaction Books, New Brunswick, NJ, revised edn, 1977, p. 111.
29. See, e.g., P. McGarrick, 'What's alternative about ADR?' *Law Society's Gazette*, 11 March 1992, p. 2.
30. This phrase is used by C. Cunningham, 'A Tale of Two Clients: Thinking About Law as Language' (1989) 87 *Michigan Law Review* 2459 at p. 2469.
31. But it is also apparent that lawyers display a certain ambivalence to emotion. On the one hand, the client's emotions are likely to be seen as something messy that get in the way of effective dispute resolution, but, on the other, the lawyers themselves may well generate and employ a degree of emotion – particularly anger – as part of their own adversarialism. As one American study of mediation reports, the key issue in many mediations is 'to get past the angry attorneys': D. Golann, 'Is Legal Mediation a Process of Repair – or Separation? An Empirical Study, and Its Implications' (2002) 7 *Harvard Negotiation Law Journal* 301 at p. 329.
32. A. Sarat and W. Felstiner, 'Law and Social Relations: Vocabularies of Motive in Lawyer–Client Interaction' (1988) 22 *Law and Society Review* 737; also 'Law and Strategy in the Divorce Lawyer's Office' (1986) 20 *Law and Society Review* 93; J. Griffiths, 'What Do Dutch Lawyers Actually Do In Divorce Cases' (1986) 20 *Law and Society Review* 135; S. Merry and S. Silbey, 'What Do Plaintiffs Want?' (1984) 9 *Justice System Journal* 151.
33. Sarat and Felstiner, (1988) 22 *Law and Society Review* 737 at p. 742.

Here is an extract from one conversation, followed by the authors' comments:

Client: There was harassment and verbal degradation. No interest at all in my furthering my education. None whatsoever. Sexual harassment. If there was ever any time when I did not want or need sex, I was subject to, you know, these long verbal whiplashings. Then the Bible would be put out on the counter with passages underlined as to what a poor wife I was. Just constant harassment from him.

Lawyer: Mmn uh.

Client: There was . . . what I was remembering the other day, and I had forgotten. When he undertook to lecturing me and I'd say, 'I don't want to hear this. I don't have time right now,' I could lock myself in the bathroom and he would break in. And I was just to listen, whether I wanted to or not. And he would lecture me for hours. Literally hours . . . There was no escaping him, short of getting into a car and driving away. But then he would stand outside in the driveway and yell, anyhow. *The man was not well* (emphasis added).

Lawyer: Okay. Now how about any courses you took?

> This lawyer does not respond to his client's attribution of blame or characterisation of her husband; no negotiation of reality occurs. The 'okay' seems to reflect the end of his patience with her description, and he abruptly changes the subject.[34]

These conversations took place in the context of no-fault divorce. Engaging with the client in reconstructing the past is therefore irrelevant and time-wasting for the lawyer, because there are no legal issues of marriage breakdown to resolve.

However, in a fault-based system the lawyer will want to discuss the details of the marriage failure with the client. This is necessary to identify the relevant legal issues and to check the accuracy of the client's description of her ex-partner's behaviour and character. Client–lawyer interests therefore seem to coincide. How much does it matter if the client interprets the lawyer's interest in the marriage failure as motivated by sympathy and support, when in fact it is motivated by issues of law and fact?

In the case of no-fault divorce, however, the needs and perceptions of client and lawyer do not even appear to coincide. It is as if they are –

> in effect largely occupied with two different divorces: lawyers with a legal divorce, clients with a social and emotional divorce. The lawyers orientate themselves towards legal norms and institutional practices, the clients towards the social norms of their environment.[35]

When articulating and developing your approach to negotiation, you clearly need to be aware of gaps like these. Can they be bridged, and if so, how? Is it the responsibility of the lawyer to bridge them, for example, by developing an ethic of care?[36]

---

34. *Ibid.*, pp. 44–5.    35. J. Griffiths, (1988) 20 *Law & Society Review* 135 at p. 155.
36. See S. Ellmann, 'The Ethic of Care as an Ethic for Lawyers' (1993) 81 *Georgetown Law Journal* 2665.

What are the 'business' implications? In a busy practice, will you be given the time to listen to and empathise with your client? Or will there be too much pressure on you to 'process' as many clients as possible to earn more fee income for the practice?

It is essential to keep these questions in mind as we work through the principles and practice of negotiation.

## Learning the art of lawyer negotiation

At the start of this chapter we pointed out that we have all been negotiating from a very early age. Negotiation is such a 'natural' process that we are hardly aware we are doing it a lot of the time. Until recently, lawyers received no training in legal negotiating skills, but were left to pick them up 'on the job'. This they had to do by building on the tacit knowledge they had gained throughout their lives. It was a haphazard and difficult process for many. We want you to begin the process now, so that when you come to negotiate professionally you will have a starting point for the development of your own artistry.

That said, we need to keep in mind that lawyer negotiation is not necessarily the same as day-to-day negotiating in other spheres. Lawyer negotiation involves four distinctive attributes:

- Lawyer negotiations are *representative* negotiations – you are acting on behalf of a client to whom you owe certain duties and responsibilities.
- It follows that lawyer negotiations as a process are more complex than simple bi-lateral negotiations – they involve both *inter-party* (between the representatives of each side) and *intra-party* (between lawyer and client) negotiations.
- Lawyer negotiations may be either *facilitative* (i.e. deal-making) or *settlement* negotiations. These contexts may, to some extent, demand different strategies, perhaps even some different skills.
- Lawyer negotiations always take place *'in the shadow of the law'*. Legal rules (substantive and procedural) create a context for and, to some degree a style of negotiation. This is particularly true of settlement negotiations.

Negotiating with 'the other side' can only begin once a sometimes quite complex set of decisions have been made about one's own case. This is not just a matter of assessing what the law says. As Eekelaar, Maclean and Beinart[37] observe, lawyers have first to negotiate their own position based upon three key elements: (1) their perception of the client's interests; (2) the client's instructions, and (3) the normative standards – law and ethics – which provide the framework of rules and entitlements within which the lawyer must operate. The 'decisional matrix' provided by these elements will vary from case to case. As Eekelaar et al. explain,[38] the ideal negotiating position evolves from the convergence of all three elements,

37. J. Eekelaar, M. Maclean and S. Beinart, *Family Lawyers: The Divorce Work of Solicitors*, Hart Publishing, Oxford, 2000, pp. 88–101.
38. *Ibid.*, p. 91.

but there will be cases where the normative standards are, to some degree, at variance with the client's interests, and also cases where the client's instructions converge with neither the normative standards, nor the client's best interests. In these situations the lawyer either needs to work hard with the client to achieve alignment, so far as possible, or, so far as legally permissible, she must ultimately allow client instructions to prevail.

With this background in mind we shall look at the process of negotiation as a series of steps:

1.  Identify the critical issues.
2.  Select a negotiating strategy and style.
3.  Sort out your ethics.
4.  Work out your tactics.
5.  Keep your act together during the negotiation.
6.  Keep a negotiation journal.

## Step 1: Identify the critical issues

By 'critical issues' we mean those issues (legal and non-legal) which must be resolved if the dispute as a whole is to be resolved and the parties are to reach agreement.

EXERCISE **9.4  What is there to negotiate about?**

The purpose of this part of the exercise is to identify the critical issues in the five cases which follow.

(a)  *Form groups of four or five. Each group should then split into two sub-groups, A and B. Sub-group A will represent one party to each dispute, Sub-group B will represent the opposing party:*

| SUB-GROUPS A | SUB-GROUPS B |
| --- | --- |
| *Wilf* | *Pam* |
| *Employer* | *Frances* |
| *Carol* | *Bob* |
| *Maxine* | *John* |

For Case 4, *divide your group so that Randall, the Chairman, and Cliff are all represented.*

(b)  *Each sub-group should list the critical issues in each of the five cases.*
   1.  Wilf, a third year student, has lived at 9a Woodbridge Way for three years under a tenancy agreement with Pam. Wilf owes Pam £1,200 in back rent because he has got into debt and hasn't paid any rent at all for the last few months. He is preparing for his final exams in two month's time.

Pam has given Wilf notice to quit, convinced that she will get no more rent out of him. She was reluctant to do this, because up to now Wilf has been a model tenant. Last year when Pam was going to have the flat decorated, Wilf offered to do it for a small charge if she paid for all the materials. He decorated the whole flat and Pam paid him £100.

The neighbours were unhappy at first when they knew a student was moving in, but they have never had any reason to complain about noise, or anything else. All the neighbours are very friendly with Wilf and have told Pam they will be sorry to see him go.

2. Frances is a recently qualified chartered accountant who got a job with a prestigious firm in the City. Two months after she started the job, she found she was pregnant. Her relationship with the baby's father had ended when she moved down to London to take the job.

   Frances decides she wants to have the baby and keep her job, because her career prospects with this firm are excellent. After she has told her employer she is pregnant, the partners meet and decide to terminate her contract. The reason they give her is that the time off she will need for the birth etc., will mean she can't complete her probationary period. They advertise for a new accountant immediately.

3. Bob and Carol have been married for ten years and have three children, aged 8, 6 and 3. Carol is a talented painter who had two successful exhibitions before she got married, but hasn't done any serious painting since she had the children. Over the years she has become increasingly resentful about the lack of opportunity to pursue a career.

   Bob works for an international oil company and is often abroad. He has therefore played little part in looking after the children. However, the family is well off, and Bob repeatedly suggested to Carol that they employ a nanny to live in and look after the children. Carol always refused, saying she didn't want a stranger in their house. She would rather her husband was home more.

   Six months ago, Carol started an affair with Rachel. Bob found out and made her leave the family home. Rachel agreed that Carol could live with her for the time being. The couple are the main source of gossip in the village where they live.

   Bob will not allow Carol to see the children at all, and has begun divorce proceedings.

4. On the eve of a major cup final, Randall Dolph, the captain of Melton FC, was interviewed by the press. Off the record, he called the club Chairman a 'fat old fart, who knows absolutely f*** all about football'. One tabloid newspaper printed the statement, and now the story is headline news. The Chairman is extremely concerned about his public image and credibility, and goes on record as saying he wants Randall sacked from the club. He instructs Cliff, the team manager, to drop Randall from the team. If Cliff refuses, the Chairman says, he will be sacked. The Chairman has also begun proceedings against the tabloid newspaper.

   In the meantime, the players have refused to play in the cup final unless Randall is reinstated. If the match doesn't go ahead, the club will incur a large financial penalty and lose important income. They may even be expelled from their league. The supporters club has threatened to boycott all matches unless the Chairman resigns immediately.

5. When Maxine Krantz was driving down Stapleton Road one evening last May, she knocked a cyclist off his bike. Stapleton Road is quite wide, but there were cars parked on both sides of it. In her statement to the police Maxine said the cyclist pulled out in front of her from behind a parked car as she was beginning to overtake him.

John Rose, the cyclist, said Maxine was driving too fast, otherwise she could have stopped. Also, there was not enough room for her to overtake at that point. John's kneecap was broken, his bike was damaged, and his clothes ruined. Maxine has not been prosecuted.

Maxine doesn't want any publicity, because she is well known in the area and a local magistrate.

John is due to start a new job in Australia in two months' time.

*In your sub-groups:*

(c)   *Get together with another sub-group which is advising the same parties. Compare findings and try to agree a final list of the critical issues for each case.*

(d)   *Now list what you think are the critical issues for the other side in each case. Then discuss your list with your opposing sub-group.*

(e)   *With your opposing sub-group, try to agree:*
      *(i)  a list of critical issues, and*
      *(ii)  their order of importance.*

Your identification of the critical issues should have provided you with a clearer idea of the possible outcomes of each dispute.

You may not have been able to agree on the order of outcomes. Nevertheless, you should now be in a position to advise your clients what their options are. In real situations you would do the next part of the exercise together with your clients, having discussed their objectives with them.

(f)   *In your sub-groups: rank your options in each case, from the best possible outcome down to the least desirable. Can you justify this ranking? Don't forget that any assumptions you make about your client's needs or interests would, in a real situation, have to be articulated and checked. Try to determine in each case your client's likely bottom line: the lowest acceptable option.*

(g)   *Are there any reasons why negotiations might fail? If so, what are they?*

(h)   *What are your choices, if any, if you don't reach agreement?*
      You must be prepared for negotiations to fail. This means you need to work out the best possible and practical course of action should this happen – we call this your Best Alternative to a Negotiated Agreement (BATNA).[39] Your BATNA may be court action, or it could be some alternative like arbitration or mediation.

(i)   *Compare your rankings with those of your opponent.*

(j)   *Feed back to tutor and whole group.*

---

39. See R. Fisher and W. Ury, *Getting to Yes: Negotiating An Agreement Without Giving In*, Business Books, London, 1991, p. 104.

You should now be in a position to think out your negotiating strategy – how you intend to get what your client wants.

Incidentally, don't worry that you haven't researched the law yet. We are concerned here to get you thinking generally and creatively about how to use negotiation to resolve legal conflicts.

However, before we move on to strategy, compare your list of critical issues with ours. We aren't going to work through all the cases, but we shall illustrate the purpose of the exercise so far with Case 1, and make some general points.

CRITICAL ISSUES

| PAM | WILF |
| --- | --- |
| Can she evict Wilf? | Can Pam evict him? |
| Does she want to evict him? | Does he have anywhere to go? |
| Does she want to lose a good tenant? | Where can he live while doing his exams? |
| Does it matter if they part on bad terms? | Does it matter if they part on bad terms? |
| Is there any way she can get the money? | Is there any way he can pay? |
| – all of it? | – all of it? |
| – some of it? | – some of it? |
| – when? | – when? |
| – how? | – how? |
| Can he pay rent in the future? | Can he pay rent in the future? |
| How long will he stay? | How long will he stay? |
| Does she mind the bother of getting a new tenant? | |

You may have thought of others, or considered some of these not critical.

On the information you have, there are a number of issues the parties have in common which could be a starting-point for negotiation. It may come down to Pam deciding how important this source of income is to her. We can't judge this without knowing more about her financial circumstances. If it is the priority, then negotiations may not be successful.

POSSIBLE OUTCOMES

| PAM | WILF |
| --- | --- |
| Wilf is evicted and she gets a new tenant quickly who can pay. Wilf pays the debt off immediately by getting a loan. | Pam lets him stay rent-free until his exams are over. Either she writes off the debt or he pays it off by instalments. |

| | |
|---|---|
| As above, Wilf pays the debt off by instalments. | As above, he pays a minimal amount until he leaves. |
| As above, she writes off part of the debt: failing that, all of it. | As above, he owes full rent until he leaves. |
| Wilf stays until exams are over, pays full rent from now, and arrears by one of the methods above. | He is evicted, debt is written off. |
| | As above, pays off part of the debt in instalments. |
| Wilf stays as long as he likes; come to some flexible arrangement about rent. | As above, has to get loan to repay debt. |
| BATNA – Court order for possession. | BATNA – Arranges to stay with friend until exams over. |

Wilf's real BATNA could be a moonlight flit, but as his lawyer you shouldn't have advised him to do this!

It is worthwhile identifying the contingent or contextual factors that will have influenced your options in each situation. Four of the cases depend on whether an established relationship should continue. In Bob's and Carol's case, it will have to continue in some form or other. The personal injury claim is a 'one-off' situation, so the relationship of the parties is probably not an issue. On that basis, litigation may look like an attractive option.

However, on the information you have so far on the personal injury claim, the outcome if the matter went to court is very uncertain. The issue of liability is unclear, before you even get to quantum. In Cases 1 and 2 the legal issues are clear. Case 4, however, differs from the others not only because at least three parties are involved; here the legal issue – defamation – is peripheral to the conflict. The parties will have to negotiate, and fast, if they want to avoid a debacle, as sports commentators are fond of describing such an event.

We summarise these contingent factors as follows:

1. DOES THE RELATIONSHIP HAVE TO CONTINUE?
   DO THE PARTIES WANT IT TO?
2. IS THIS MAINLY ABOUT MONEY?
   IS THE AMOUNT CERTAIN OR UNCERTAIN?
3. WHICH IS LESS TROUBLE: SETTLEMENT OR LITIGATION?
   – NOW? COST, DELAYED DECISION, CONTROL?
   – THE FUTURE?
4. IF WE GO TO COURT: IS THE OUTCOME CERTAIN?

You will probably have found that your order of preferred outcomes in every case is fairly speculative, because you haven't got enough information to go on. What is more important at this stage, however, is to recognise that your intuition and experience have guided you to prefer some options over others. Your knowing-in- action will similarly inform your choice of negotiating strategy.

EXERCISE **9.5 Pam and Wilf**

*In the large group:*

1. *Select two volunteers to do the negotiation, one to role play Pam's lawyer, the other one to represent Wilf. The volunteers have 10 minutes to prepare their roles.*

   *To prepare for the negotiation, the role players will need to look at a profile of their client on the website. Naturally, they may only look at the profile of their own client! If any more information is needed, they may make it up, provided it is consistent with the information in the profile.*

   *The rest of the group will be given both profiles.*

2. *The lawyers carry out the negotiation.*

3. *Feed back in the following order:*

   *(a) Pam's lawyer;*

   *(b) Wilf's lawyer;*

   *(c) members of the group;*

   *(d) tutor.*

   *The lawyers should try to answer these questions:*

   *(i) What was the best possible outcome for your client? Did you achieve it?*

   *(ii) Are you completely satisfied with the result? Why/why not?*

   *(iii) Does the outcome benefit both parties? Why/why not?*

   *(iv) What kind of relationship did you want to build with your opponent? Give reasons. Did you establish the relationship you wanted? Why/why not?*

   *(v) What was your opening stance? Why?*

   *(vi) Did you share information with your opponent? Why/why not?*

   *(vii) Did you obtain any information from your opponent? Why/why not?*

   *(viii) Did you make any concessions? Which? Why/why not?*

   *(ix) During the negotiation, did you feel:*

     *– upset?*

     *– angry?*

     *– confident?*

     *– strong?*

     *– weak?*

     *– pressured?*

     *– hostile?*

     *– any other emotion? Which?*

     *If so, at what point, and why?*

   *(x) Is there anything you would do differently if you carried out this negotiation again? If yes, what and why?*

## Step 2: Select a negotiating strategy and style

Should you negotiate on the merits of the case as a whole, or on the basis of getting the best for your client at the expense of the other side? When should you consider compromise? We summarise the negotiating strategies below and then go on briefly to describe their main characteristics. A great deal has been written about these strategies.[40] You will find that writers differ in their descriptions and terminology (as we show in the box below), and this can be quite confusing. For example, some understand 'co-operative' strategy to mean both strategies two and three below, as opposed to the 'competitive' strategy of number one.

**Negotiation strategies: the naming of parts**

1.  WIN/LOSE                (competitive, adversarial, positional, zero-sum).
2.  WIN SOME/LOSE SOME      (compromising, co-operative, collaborative).
3.  WIN/WIN                 (problem-solving, integrative, principled, creative).

You may be surprised to learn that there is a fourth strategy which we call LOSE/LOSE; but more of that later.

### The win/lose approach

This is the courtroom model and so is as admirably suited to lawyers, you may think, as it is to sharks. The participants are adversaries, the goal is victory. The prize is a bigger share of a fixed cake. Therefore, any gain for the winner means a corresponding loss for the loser. Game theorists consequently refer to this model as 'zero-sum' bargaining.[41]

The negotiator may not go in hard, but will certainly take control from the beginning. She will try to get the opponent to make the first of a number of concessions. She will be slow to reveal information and will exaggerate the strength of her client's position. She may appear conciliatory so as to get all the information she needs from the opponent. She takes up a strong, uncompromising position and keeps the pressure on the opponent to make concessions. However, she is not overtly aggressive. She may be argumentative, but will remain within the bounds of courteous and ethical conduct.

### The win some/lose some approach

This approach recognises that you need to give in order to get. It may start from a win/lose position and then negotiators come to realise that neither party has a chance of winning outright. They therefore have to decide what is important and what can be given away. The objective is to achieve a solution which is satisfactory to both sides. Co-operative negotiators seek to establish and maintain a friendly relationship with the opponent, so that they can look for common ground and shared interests (the fox).

---

40. See, e.g., G. Williams, *Legal Negotiation and Settlement*, West Publishing, St Paul, Minn., 1983; R. Fisher and W. Ury, *Getting to Yes*; D. Lax and J. Sebenius, *The Manager as Negotiator: Bargaining for Co-operation and Competitive Gain*, Free Press, New York, 1986; C. Menkel-Meadow, 'Legal Negotiation: A Study of Strategies in Search of a Theory' (1983) *American Bar Foundation Research Journal* 905. See also the skills guides recommended in the Further Reading section at the end of this chapter.
41. See, e.g., R. Axelrod, *The Evolution of Co-operation*, Basic Books, New York, 1984.

## The win/win approach

All the approaches so far described involve a large element of 'positional' bargaining – a process which involves each party taking a position and moving (or not) to a compromise by an exchange of gains and concessions. It fits the essentially adversarial character of lawyering.

On the face of it, the win/win approach favours the co-operative, collaborative style of bargaining, but appearances can be deceptive. Instead of being satisfied with compromise, its objective is mutual gain. In this respect win/win owes something to game theory and particularly Axelrod's 'Tit-for-tat' (TFT) or 'conditional co-operation' strategy.[42] TFT has been shown by game theorists to be an extremely robust negotiating strategy in environments where there is the potential for both co-operation *and* exploitation (Axelrod calls the latter 'defection'). This is because TFT starts from an assumption of co-operation but also punishes defection with future non-co-operation. TFT thus supports the generation of win/win outcomes in three ways:[43]

- TFT is *never* the first to defect. It always assumes a co-operative style, geared to creating a fair agreement through an open negotiating process.
- But co-operation is always *conditional* on reciprocity. If the other side defects, TFT *will* retaliate.
- Lastly, TFT is *forgiving*. If the other side shows good faith it will return to being co-operative.

Fisher and Ury describe a process of win/win negotiating that they call 'principled' negotiation, or negotiation 'on the merits'.[44] They see the process not as a contest in which the parties haggle over their positions, conceding a bit here and a bit there, but as a shared problem in which the best possible solution must be obtained for both sides. The danger of the positional approaches is that the parties can overlook other options and common interests as they get locked into argument over slight shifts of position. Principled bargaining, on the other hand, is 'designed to produce wise outcomes efficiently and amicably'.[45] So, let us now consider how principled negotiating actually works.

Fisher and Ury define four key rules:

1.  SEPARATE THE PEOPLE FROM THE PROBLEM.
2.  FOCUS ON INTERESTS, NOT POSITIONS.
3.  INVENT OPTIONS FOR MUTUAL GAIN.
4.  INSIST ON OBJECTIVE CRITERIA.

---

42. Ibid.
43. See A. Boon and J. Levin, *The Ethics and Conduct of Lawyers in England and Wales*, Hart Publishing, Oxford, 1999, p. 329.
44. Fisher and Ury, *Getting to Yes*.    45. *Ibid.*, pp. 10–11.

*Separate the people from the problem*

This rule appreciates that human beings are creatures of strong emotions who often have radically different perceptions and have difficulty communicating clearly. Emotions typically become entangled with the objective merits of the problem. Taking positions just makes this worse because people's egos become identified with their positions. Hence, before working on the substantive problem, the 'people problem' should be disentangled from it and dealt with separately. Figuratively, if not literally, the participants should come to see themselves as working side by side, attacking the problem, not each other.[46]

Separating the people from the problem is far from easy. Do you have any suggestions as to how to go about this?

*Focus on interests, not positions*

The parties' interests may not all conflict. You won't discover their compatible interests unless you look behind their apparently opposed positions. To understand their real interests, ask 'why'? not 'what'. You are then more likely to find out what it is they really want.

> Consider the story of two men quarrelling in a library. One wants the window open and the other wants it closed. They bicker back and forth about how much to leave it open: a crack, halfway, three-quarters of the way. No solution satisfies them both.
>
> Enter the librarian. She asks one why he wants the window open: 'To get some fresh air.' She asks the other why he wants it closed: 'To avoid the draught.' After thinking a minute, she opens wide a window in the next room, bringing in fresh air without a draught.[47]

*Invent options for mutual gain*

In negotiation we distinguish broadly between integrative and distributive solutions. To use a simple analogy, the difference is between looking at how you divide up a cake (a distributive question) and seeing if there are ways of making the cake bigger. Adversarialism encourages distributive solutions – it is often easier (especially in litigation where the focus is on compensation for harm done) to haggle over the size of a slice than to re-define the cake. Looking to expand the cake will involve creative processes of brainstorming and lateral thinking. Examples of integrative problem-solving might include:

● Persuading a client to offer an apology to the opponent.
● In an employment dispute, suggesting a change in the (former) employee's file to show that he resigned, rather than being dismissed, in exchange for an undertaking by the employee not to compete with his former employer.

46. *Ibid.*, p. 11.   47. *Ibid.*, p. 41.

- In a partnership dispute, brokering an agreement between the parties to divide up the intellectual property of the firm according to each partner's relative needs, rather than by the share allocated by the partnership agreement.
- In catastrophic personal injury claims, using the flexibility of a structured settlement to meet the needs of a claimant while seeking to limit the immediate (cash) cost to the insurer.

Think up in advance of the negotiation the widest range of possible solutions which promote shared interests and reconcile conflicting ones. We encouraged you to try this in Exercise 9.4.

Why do you think it is important to do this in advance?

*Insist on objective criteria*
Negotiations can become a contest of wills or a conflict of opinion in which neither side wants to lose face. You can avoid this if you establish an independent basis for settlement, such as market value, expert opinion, custom or law. A fair settlement based on objective criteria will be more acceptable to both sides.

You may have already decided which of the three strategies we have outlined fits best with your assessment of your negotiating personality. Owls will tend to go for win/win, for example. However, you need to experiment with all three to see how they work. They are not mutually exclusive, and no single strategy will succeed in every case. You must recognise which strategy is appropriate for a particular case and a particular opponent. Aim to become conversant with all of them. Furthermore, you need to be able to recognise which style your opponent is using.

EXERCISE **9.6 Have your cake and eat it** ...

*In your groups:*

(a) *Discuss the advantages and disadvantages of each strategy.*
(b) *List the advantages and disadvantages of each on separate pieces of flipchart. Then compare your list with those of other groups.*
(c) *Divide into pairs. Choose one of the negotiating scenarios:*
   - *Frances/Employer*
   - *John/Maxine*
   - *Chairman/Randall/Cliff (you will need to form a threesome for this one)*
   - *Bob/Carol*
     *and prepare the negotiation (20 minutes). For further information, consult the profiles on the website. Remember not to look at your opponent's profile!*
(d) *Role play the negotiation.*
(e) *In your pairs, answer the following questions:*
   (i) *Was the negotiation successful? Why/why not?*
   (ii) *What strategy did each of you plan to use, and why?*
   (iii) *Did you alter your strategy during the negotiation? If so, why?*
   (iv) *What, if anything, will you do differently next time?*

We summarise the strengths and weaknesses of the three negotiating styles below. The list is not comprehensive.

### THE WIN/LOSE STYLE OF COMPETITIVE BARGAINING

| STRENGTHS | WEAKNESSES |
|---|---|
| Makes clear you are out to win. | Can produce tension. |
| May get result close to opening position. | May irritate opponent. |
| Effective against weak opposition. | May divide parties further. |
| Most likely to get concessions. | Can result in deadlock. |
| Results may impress clients and colleagues. | Loses sight of mutual interests. |
| Can get the best result for client. | Exchanges may become emotional. |
| | Negotiator may build up reputation which antagonises future opponents. |

### THE WIN SOME/LOSE SOME STYLE OF CO-OPERATIVE BARGAINING

| STRENGTHS | WEAKNESSES |
|---|---|
| Likely to result in settlement. | May give away more than necessary. |
| Settlement more likely to be fair. | Strengths of case may not be pushed. |
| May improve parties' relationship. | May appear 'weak' and be exploited by win/lose opponent. |
| Friendly, trusting atmosphere may encourage opponent to make concessions. | May accept easy option, not the best one. |
| Results may benefit both sides. | May not get the best for client. |

### THE WIN/WIN STYLE OF PRINCIPLED NEGOTIATION

| STRENGTHS | WEAKNESSES |
|---|---|
| Can explore options which positional bargaining obscures. | Opponent may not use it and so not respond. |
| Avoids haggling and bickering. | No safety net of the 'bottom line'. |
| Can get best possible result for both sides. | Only works if there are compatible interests. |
| Bargains on objective criteria. | Negotiation stages not clearly defined. |

We hope that by this stage you are beginning to get an idea of these approaches and styles. You may have made up your mind that a particular one does not suit you, and so you won't use it. Consider that, in so doing, you set limits on your own development and effectiveness as a negotiator. To be sure, the ability to switch and merge different styles and strategies takes time to develop, but your target as an experienced legal negotiator, must be to use all three, and if necessary, use them at different points during the same negotiation.

The next exercise should give you some further insight into how the strategies work.

### EXERCISE 9.7  The Red–Blue exercise[48]

*In your groups:*

1. *Discuss what factors make a negotiation successful. Consider in particular the behaviour and characteristics of an effective negotiator.*
2. *Summarise your findings on flipchart.*
3. *Form yourselves into new teams. There must be an even number of teams, e.g. A plays B, C plays D, E plays F etc. Each game will need one person to act as a 'go-between'. Each game should be played as far away as possible from the others, as it can get very noisy!*

   The rules for each game are as follows:

   OBJECTIVE: To end the game with the highest possible positive score for your team.

   1. There are two teams.
   2. There are ten rounds.
   3. Your team will choose to play either red or blue at each round.
   4. When your team has decided on its colour for that round, tell the go-between. You will be told what your opponents have played only when both teams have decided. It is the combined colours that determine your respective scores.

| PLAY | | SCORE | |
| --- | --- | --- | --- |
| *GROUP A* | *GROUP B* | *SCORE A* | *SCORE B* |
| Red | Red | +3 | +3 |
| Red | Blue | −6 | +6 |
| Blue | Red | +6 | −6 |
| Blue | Blue | −3 | −3 |

48. This is one of the many variations on the Prisoner's Dilemma Game (PDG), invented in about 1950 by Merrill Flood and Melvin Dresher. M. Deutsch used the PDG to study the issue of trust in situations of conflict; see for example 'Trust and Suspicion' (1958) 2 *Journal of Conflict Resolution* 265–79. The PDG has been extensively studied by mathematical game theorists, and game theory has also become an important theoretical perspective in studying negotiation strategy: see D. Luce and H. Raiffa, *Games and Decisions*, Wiley, New York, 1957; also Axelrod, *The Evolution of Co-operation*.

You will be scored as follows:

5. You can have a conference with the opposing group after the fourth round. However, this can only take place if both groups wish it.

6. You can have another conference after the eighth round, if both groups choose to do this.

7. The ninth and tenth rounds score double, i.e.:
   - If both groups play Blue, each scores −6;
   - If one group plays Blue, the other Red: Red = −12; Blue = +12;
   - If both play Red, each scores +6.

   Use the score sheet in Figure 9.2 and fill it in after each round, entering both your score and that of the opposing team. Remember that at the conference points you may only negotiate if both sides agree. You are only playing your opponents. The other pairs of groups are not part of your game.

   Your tutor will put all the scores up on the white board.

4. *Return to your original groups. Display the flipchart your group did for part 2 of the exercise somewhere where all the other groups can read it.*

5. *Game teams feed back to the large group:*
   - *What was the objective of the game?*
   - *Does your score reflect that objective?*
   - *How does your score compare with your opponents'?*
   - *Briefly describe the course of your game and why your team acted as it did. Were there any disagreements about strategy within the team? What are your feelings, both towards your opponents and towards other members of your team?*
   - *What do you think was the purpose of the game?*

| | Colour played | | Score | |
|---|---|---|---|---|
| Round | A | B | A | B |
| 1 | | | | |
| 2 | | | | |
| 3 | | | | |
| 4 | | | | |
| **Conference Point** | | | | |
| 5 | | | | |
| 6 | | | | |
| 7 | | | | |
| 8 | | | | |
| **Conference Point** | | | | |
| 9 (score double) | | | | |
| 10 (score double) | | | | |
| **TOTALS** | | | | |

Figure 9.2.

    –  *How does your 'flipchart for effective negotiation' compare with the way you played*
       *this game? Do you detect any discrepant reasoning?*

6.   *Further Reflection-on-Action. When you have had more time to reflect, make a detailed*
    *entry in your learning diary about this exercise. What have you learned from the*
    *experience? Please show your diary to your tutor for comments.*[49]

We dropped a hint earlier about a fourth strategy, which we called lose/lose. It has
to do with saving face, i.e. we would rather win than lose, but if we are going to lose,
we shall drag the other side down with us. A negotiator will consciously and
deliberately decide to outdo her opponent, even if it means ending up with an
unsatisfactory outcome herself. These sharks[50] prefer competition so strongly that
they will not forgo it in exchange for a mutually much more beneficial outcome,
even if this means they and their clients receive substantially less as a result. Win/
lose is so ingrained that they think they have won because they haven't lost as much
as the other side. Their reward lies in beating their opponents.

This brings us neatly to our third step in learning the art of negotiation.

## Step 3: Sort out your ethics

While the official code of conduct prescribes a zealous pursuit of the client's interests,
the informal norms and the realities of professional life prompt compromise and
co-operation. Unfortunately, clear guidelines for helping attorneys decide which path
to take are nonexistent.[51]

This writer is talking about the divorce process in the US, but you might want to
consider whether the point is a general one that applies equally to the UK. If Kressel
is right, how can you reconcile this conflict? You have probably been discussing
these questions already, before you reached this point.

Does it mean you must use the win/lose strategy? You may think that getting a
settlement which is fair to both sides is not the same as maximising your client's
interests. Is principled negotiation a realistic and ethical strategy in legal disputes?
The cake, whatever its size, will have to be shared out in the end. Can you get the
best for your client and yet avoid positional bargaining?[52] And should you use it
where there are serious imbalances of power between the parties?

In 1987 Hazel Genn published a study of negotiated settlements in personal
injury claims between claimants' solicitors and defendant insurance companies.
She found that claimants are disadvantaged from the start because of the impreci-
sion and uncertainty of the law of negligence and the problems of proof. These

---

49. In all the years that we have played Red–Blue with our students, the results are nearly always the
    same. There are a number of things that you can learn from them about negotiation, but it would
    give the game away to mention them here. Tutors: please consult the website.
50. Are lawyers and law students included among their number?
51. K. Kressel, *The Process of Divorce: How Professionals and Couples Negotiate Settlement*, Basic
    Books, New York, 1985, p. 59.
52. Lax and Sebenius call this 'the negotiator's dilemma': *The Manager as Negotiator*.

factors put pressure on claimants to avoid the risks of trial and compromise their claims. The inequality increases because not only are insurance companies specialist and experienced 'repeat players' in negotiation and litigation; they have greater financial resources to collect the information needed to resist the claim.[53] Therefore, although the parties may have a common interest in saving time and money by not going to court, their fundamental interests are diametrically opposed.

> ... the nature of personal injury claims settlement is inherently adversarial. The plaintiff wants to maximise his damages, while the defendant wants to avoid or minimise payment ... In this contest the very idea of co-operation between the parties appears misconceived and many specialist personal injury solicitors recognise this fact ... although insurance companies encourage co-operation rather than confrontation and prefer matters to be settled without the commencement of court proceedings, they will take advantage of their opponent if the opportunity is presented. The desire for co-operation among insurance companies therefore appears largely opportunistic; and for plaintiffs' solicitors to postpone the commencement of proceedings in the interests of co-operation, or to be drawn into longer-term co-operative relationships, may not be in plaintiffs' best interests, unless claims are weak or of low value.[54]

This seems to suggest that the 'ethical' choice is the win/lose approach in claims against a 'powerful' defendant. If you accept this view, then you will have to learn to use the strategy effectively if you are acting for the claimant, and to resist it effectively if you are acting for defendants![55]

In theory, win/win lends itself to situations where the relationship between the parties has to continue after the conflict has been resolved. It is therefore seen as a more 'natural' strategy for negotiation and mediation in matrimonial and commercial disputes, for example, where the conflict is about much more than money. However, if such disputes are negotiated by lawyers rather than mediated by a neutral third party, win/win may be thwarted if the lawyers insist on keeping information from the other side as their 'secret weapon', rather than revealing it.

Talking about the divorce process, McEwen, Mather and Maiman give us some insight into the lawyer's role conflict:

> The demands of trial preparation and of negotiation are not entirely consistent ... Lawyers must decide, for example, between aggressively using formal legal procedures such as discovery and embarking on co-operative, informal efforts at information sharing; between taking extreme positions and making 'reasonable' offers; between being open and honest about underlying interests and goals or keeping

---

53. See H. Genn, *Hard Bargaining: Out of Court Settlement in Personal Injury Actions*, Clarendon Press, Oxford, 1987, pp. 161–69.
54. *Ibid.*, p. 166.
55. But see A. Paton, 'How to Create a Win/Win Situation', *Post Magazine*, 28 April 1994, pp. 28–9, where the author describes the successful mediation of a personal injury claim.

them hidden; and between engaging in strategic behaviour that imposes costs and pressures on the other party and minimising posturing and costs for both parties.[56]

The apparent demands of negotiation strategy can create some major ethical dilemmas that are barely addressed by the professional codes of conduct. A key question, for example, is, how legitimate is it to engage in what we might call 'strategic deception' in negotiation. Consider the following short exercise.

EXERCISE 9.8  **How low can you go?**

Assume you are representing a client in 'without prejudice' (oral) negotiations. Your opponent asks you a question, the honest answer to which you fear could damage your client's interests and weaken your position in the negotiation. Do you:

1.   answer fully and honestly, reminding your opponent that your answer is without prejudice at this point?
2.   Refuse to answer, because you consider that it is not in the interests of your client to do so?
3.   Provide a partial answer that is not untrue but does not disclose the full position, and so could be construed as misleading by omission?
4.   Provide an answer that is partially true but which also contains some positively misleading 'information', designed to try to reduce the damage to your bargaining position?
5.   Lie outrageously and hope you don't get caught out?

(a)   *Make a note of:*
   (i)   *which option you think intuitively is likely to be in the best interests of your client;*
   (ii)   *which option you think is the course of action most likely to be consistent with your professional duties (without looking it up!);*
   (iii)   *what option best meets your own personal standards of conduct.*
(b)   *Compare your answers with those of others in your group, then*
(c)   *See if you can find out which course of action is most consistent with the professional codes of conduct.*

This is not just an academic conundrum, but a real day-to-day problem which, it is at least arguable[57] (though the codes of conduct are vague in the extreme), exposes lawyers to a potential conflict of interest between their duties to the profession and to the client.

Does the sharing of information produce yet another conflict of interests? Suppose you are representing Bob, and at some stage during the negotiation, he

---

56.  C. McEwen, L. Mather and R. Maiman, 'Lawyers, Mediation and the Management of Divorce Practice' (1994) 28 *Law and Society Review* 149 at p. 157.
57.  See the discussion in R. O'Dair, *Legal Ethics: Text and Materials*, Butterworths, London, 2001, ch. 8; Boon and Levin, *The Ethics and Conduct of Lawyers in England and Wales*, pp. 331–5.

tells you he has just inherited £50,000 worth of shares from his deceased grandmother, but Carol mustn't know about it? How will you respond? If you fail to persuade him to reveal this information, you will have to confront the fact that it will no longer be possible to reach an agreement that is fair to both parties. Ironically, the conflict might be resolved for you by Carol's lawyer setting in motion the formal procedures of disclosure.

Moreover, what do you do if your client is being totally unreasonable? If you challenge her expectations, you can leave yourself open to the charge of not acting in her best interests. Of course, you can use the law as an excuse to give unwelcome advice in cases where the law is clear. However, in many situations it isn't. In divorce negotiation you may have to bear in mind the interests of the children and the extent to which they compete with those of their parents. This is an area where strong emotions can influence clients to make unrealistic and unreasonable demands. You have to be clear on where to draw the line between your natural inclination to support your client through a testing and emotional time, and the need to convey possibly unpalatable alternatives.

The final point on the subject of you and your ethics is one we have talked about earlier in the chapter: the extent to which you allow your client to participate in the negotiation process.[58] This will be determined firstly by your duties to advise and inform her, to obtain her instructions and to carry them out. You therefore have to be absolutely clear about what your client wants from negotiation. Remember to 'mind the gap': know, respect and support your client's view of the situation.[59]

Secondly, you will have to make decisions about negotiation strategy and tactics, and whether or not you will let the client have a say in these matters. This is difficult, because you need to be as flexible as possible. For example, you might need to vary your strategy and tactics during the negotiation.

Next, do you want the client to be present during the negotiation? Will she cramp your style? Certainly, until you are experienced, you might prefer to do it without her. If the other side's lawyer is someone you know well and trust, could the client feel left out, or think you too friendly with 'the opposition'?

You at least need to think about these issues, even if you can't easily resolve them.

EXERCISE **9.9 Hidden messages**

The following text contains extracts from a negotiation carried out by two students on Case No. 5, John Rose and Maxine Krantz. The defendant insisted that she did

---

58. For a relatively rare example of a paper arguing for a participatory approach to negotiation, see R. Cochran Jnr, 'Legal Representation and the Next Steps Toward Client Control: Attorney Malpractice or the Failure to Allow the Client to Control Negotiation and Pursue Alternatives to Litigation' (1990) 47 *Washington & Lee Law Review* 819.

59. In practice, your client cannot participate fully all of the time. She will not be present when you are on the phone to the other side's lawyer and may not entirely understand details of expert evidence and complex legal procedures. Your heavy caseload will mean you may not always be able to explain and inform as often as you would like to.

not want her insurance company involved. Assume that the lawyers have not met each other before.

*In your groups, read the text and discuss the questions which follow.*

C: Hello there.

D: Hello.

C: Thank you for instigating this negotiation, I'm sure we can sort things out. I thought I might kick things off by just running through my client's case – basically put on the table for you the kind of settlement we're looking for, which will make my client happy.

D: That's fine.

C: If we perhaps do a quick résumé of the facts. The accident happened on ... *(C briefly summarises the facts of the accident and description of the injury. Both agree on these.)* We are alleging your client was negligent under several headings, actually. Basically we're contending that your client was guilty of careless driving under s. 3 of the Road Traffic Act, and failed to observe the highway code by not leaving adequate clearance for a cyclist, which should be somewhere in the region of at least three feet.

D: Right ...

C: So that's the case we're making out. One other thing: as yet we haven't got ...

D: *(interrupts)* Would you mind me coming in now, and leaving the detail. There are one or two things I want to come back to. First of all, obviously, the facts as you describe them, I'm quite happy with. But the manoeuvring between vehicles – you said what was happening when your client was hit from behind – the evidence I'm looking at ...

C: *(interrupts)* The accident report, I was going to refer to that ...

D: ... the accident report. As you know, Mrs Krantz has disclaimed all responsibility and alleges it was entirely the fault of your client. *(Meanwhile C is murmuring and interrupting.)*

C: Can I just ask in that case: on what grounds is she saying she is not liable?

D: This is what I was coming to – that your client was at fault, that he was negligent himself. Can I ... *(Lawyers go into the facts of the accident in minute detail, looking at the statements, then do the same with the details of the injury. Then they agree to accept the evidence of the medical reports.)* ... You quoted to me various provisions of the Road Traffic Act, presumably in support of your claim of negligence.

C: That's right.

D: I too have researched the Road Traffic Act, and though it's a fruitless exercise to read it all, there are offences which Mr Rose might have committed. What I'd like to say is there were no charges brought against my client, so I don't ...

C: No, and likewise none against my client, but I think we must look at the overall evidence. I don't think that anyone at any stage has been guilty of any offence, and one must realise that as my client was the most likely of the two to be injured, the onus was on your client to drive carefully and considerately. What I would like to do, unless you've got any more points there . . .

D:  No, I was responding . . . , right . . .

C:  Obviously I refute any allegation that my client was negligent. It's difficult to imagine how he could have been, considering he was actually in front of the vehicle that your client was driving. However, a few points that I can come up with in the road accident report, perhaps you could help me with these . . . *(There follows another detailed examination of the facts of the accident.)*

D:  I think I have to concede that given that your client is the more vulnerable road user, that . . . we would like to discuss that there was fault on both sides. I would like you to move towards me and accept that there was fault on both sides. If I continue here . . .

C:  Well, um, there are several points that we do have to discuss, can I run through them?

D:  Well, yes, can I say then I'm conceding that there was certainly fault on our side. What I want to establish from you is that there was also fault on your side.

C:  Um . . . in what way? Can you actually elaborate?

D:  Yes, certainly. I won't refer to the Road Traffic Act unless you want me to.

C:  No, I just wonder what your general contention of contributory negligence is *(There follows another detailed discussion of facts and statements.)* I think I tend to agree with you that there may be just perhaps a small amount of blame on the part of my client, because he does actually say that he was manoeuvring in between two parked vehicles.

D:  I wonder if we're getting a little bit stuck in that these two statements come down to my client's word against yours and who is the court going to believe. *(Lawyers go on to discuss the independent witness statement and how unhelpful it is.)* Can we see where we are now? We have agreed there is fault on both sides.

C:  I'm relatively happy that I've established that my client is not totally to blame if . . .

D:  So shall we move on?

C:  I believe you've already received a statement . . . *(Lawyers confirm C's figures for the special damages claim.)* We are looking for damages in the region of £3,000 to cover pain and suffering and future loss of amenity.

D:  Right.

C:  That is obviously on top of the special damages figure, so the total is £4,765 now, and I think we can negotiate on that to a certain extent, but that's my opening gambit.

D: Right. We'll accept the special damages. We are looking for contributory negligence from your client to reduce the overall figure – say 50:50.

C: Right, well there's absolutely no way we can accept 50 per cent liability. If that's your contention, we're quite happy to take it all the way into court and let the court assess the damages, based on the evidence. I think possibly I'd go so far as to say maybe 20 per cent contributory negligence.

D: (pause) You've got to move more towards me, Mr Brown.

C: Well, I . . . Good heavens, is that the time? I'm afraid I'll have to leave in a minute. I've got another appointment.

D: If you want me to, I'll make you an offer, then. I'll concede your starting at 20 per cent. I need more from you and we can't agree a settlement like that. I need more from you.

C: I'm not willing to accede to 50 per cent.

D: I'll move to 60:40 if your client is willing to accept that, purely on the grounds that your client is the more vulnerable road user, that should the matter come to court, the sympathy will lie with him.

C: Yes, I feel that really that's still putting too much of the blame for the accident on my client. I don't think we can go quite as far as that. Perhaps you would consider we meet halfway at . . .

D: Well, I've done some figures for you. Would you like to have a look? 50:50; 60:40. I'll make you a final offer, Mr Brown. We will reimburse all special damages to make a flat offer, without any discussion of liability, of £3,500, which will give you a figure of £5,265. Are you prepared to consider that offer? I think it's a fair offer.

C: I'll put it to my client. I'm sorry, I've got to leave now, I'm going to be late for my appointment. I'll be in touch.

D: Goodbye.

C: Goodbye.

QUESTIONS

1. From what you have read, do you think the parties had prepared properly for their meeting? Why/why not?

2. How should you prepare properly for a negotiation? Draw up a checklist of questions you need to answer when planning a negotiation.

3. What strategy was each side using? Did it change? If so, why?

4. How effective was each side's strategy?

5. Was there any risk of deadlock at any point? If so, how was it avoided?

6. What tactics did each side use in pursuit of their strategy? Give examples of behaviour and language which specified any of the following:
   - opening positions;
   - attempts to dictate the agenda;
   - willingness to make offers/concede;

- *bluff and counter-bluff;*
- *stalling;*
- *tactics to put pressure on the opponent;*
- *signals that you are willing to move;*
- *signals that you are not willing to move;*
- *bargain testing ('if you . . . , then I . . . ');*
- *threats.*

7. *Which party set the agenda for the meeting, and at what point?*
8. *How would you describe the relationship between the parties? Is there tension at any point? If so, at what point? What caused it? Do you think the cause was deliberate or accidental?*
9. *Is there anything that you would advise the participants to do differently next time? If so, what, and why?*

## Step 4: Work out your tactics

Up to now we have concentrated on identifying the critical issues and selecting a negotiating strategy. It is your strategy which will determine your choice of tactics. By tactics we mean the techniques you use to put your strategy into operation.

However, you won't be able to make decisions about any of these issues until you have researched your case thoroughly. You must know your facts and law inside out before you enter the negotiation. This means knowing its strong points and weak points, along with those of the other side. Identify any aspects of the case or information which need clarification, and try to clarify them with your opponent before the negotiation.

You are already aware of your own strengths and weaknesses as a negotiator. You will be all the better prepared if you can anticipate those of your opponent. If you don't know her or haven't met her, find out as much as you can about her. For example, is she a shark by reputation? This may help you predict the tactics she is likely to use, so that you can determine in advance how to respond to these.

If you plan to use the win/win strategy, an important preliminary tactic is to establish friendly relations with the opposing lawyer. If you are making the arrangements for the meeting, plan the seating so that you are not confronting each other face to face. When you meet, avoid plunging straight into the issues, as your opponent could think you are trying to dictate the agenda. Instead, agree how you both want the negotiation to proceed and, if necessary, set a time limit on it. Setting a framework before you start makes it easier to agree to return to it if you stray off the beaten track or get bogged down in superfluous detail.

The next stage of the negotiation involves you and the other side exchanging information. This will help you assess or re-assess the strengths and weaknesses of the other side's case. You can start by going through the facts and establishing points of agreement and difference. How open you are about your client's objectives will depend on your choice of strategy. Whatever strategy you have chosen, don't make offers or concede anything at this stage.

The third stage is the bargaining stage, where both of you test the ground with offers and counter-offers. If you are using win/win, your objective is to agree an outcome which benefits both sides. Remember to bargain on objective criteria.

At the fourth stage you should be able to finalise an agreement. Tie up all loose ends, so that no peripheral details are omitted. Recap on what you have agreed and make a record of it.

Bear in mind that these stages of the process are flexible. If, after some coffee and friendly chat, you estimate that your opponent will respond positively, why not get down to the 'nitty gritty'? For example:

> Well, as we're here to talk about money, why don't we ignore liability for the moment? What kind of figure are we looking at?

Do you think that taking this line would have altered the course of the *Rose v Krantz* negotiation for better or worse?

Taking such a direct approach does not necessarily mean you are a win/lose negotiator. It means you are a flexible one. Furthermore, some negotiators are much more comfortable with an approach that puts the cards on the table at the beginning. It establishes early on how far apart the two of you are. If you are far apart, you can then concentrate on the discrepancies. Bear in mind, however, that if you use this method of opening, you should have planned for it in advance.

Plan too for the possibility of having misread your opponent's likely response! For instance, by opening in this way, aren't you effectively conceding liability? A competitive negotiator will almost certainly read it in that way. What would be your response? Would you then become a win/lose player yourself? Or can you sustain a principled position?

Where there are issues that you disagree about, you must decide in advance whether to broach the more serious or less serious disagreements first. Again, this will be dictated by your strategy and whether you prefer to get the big issues dealt with first or later on.[60]

John Rose's lawyer seemed to want to dictate the agenda from the beginning. Rather than discuss together how they should proceed, he did not let his opponent get a word in, so that in the end she had to interrupt him. They also failed to determine any time limit for the meeting, so that D was taken by surprise when C suddenly said he had to leave. She could not know whether he had another

---

60. You need to plan tactics carefully if your opponent is from a different cultural background. If you don't take into account matters like levels of formality, pleasantries, non-verbal signals, and the stages of the process, your behaviour could be misinterpreted. Many Japanese, for example, like a lengthy preliminary phase of informal meetings and social events. According to Ann Halpern, 'it is only when they feel on the same wavelength with you that they will begin to do business with you.' See Halpern, *Negotiating Skills*, pp. 82–7 at p. 85, and J. Mulholland, *The Language of Negotiation: A Handbook of Practical Strategies for Improving Communication*, Routledge, London, 1991, pp. 75–97.

appointment, or whether he was using it as a tactic to force her into making further concessions. His abrupt closure, together with the inconclusive result of the meeting, left D dissatisfied and frustrated.

Whichever strategy you decide to use, you have to be able to give and interpret hidden messages. These messages convey attitudes and responses in an indirect way. As you know, body language, intonation, stress, wordless sounds and pauses signal such messages. There are also messages hidden in the language of the participants. For example, John Rose's lawyer says

> I think we can negotiate on that to a certain extent, but that's my opening gambit.

Indirectly, he is saying that he is prepared to move towards the other side. D picks up the signal and demands a 50:50 split. Signals which indicate a willingness to move towards the opponent are known as 'floppies'. They are signals which an effective negotiator will both recognise and know when to use.

C signals another floppy near the end of the negotiation:

> I don't think we can go quite as far as that. Perhaps you would consider we meet halfway at . . .

D, who is in a great hurry to conclude an agreement at this point, misses this signal, which is indicating C's willingness to settle for halfway between 40 per cent and 20 per cent contributory negligence – i.e. 30 per cent.

Signals which indicate an unwillingness to move and a potential deadlock, are known as 'flinches'. For example:

> Well, there's absolutely no way we can accept 50 per cent liability.

This is C's response to D's demand for a 50:50 share of liability. So his floppy was followed speedily by his flinch. Did you spot any other floppies and flinches?

When C was reflecting on his performance, he pointed out that he had no intention of starting off in the way he did, not allowing his opponent to get a word in. So why did it happen? Perhaps the answer is that the best-laid plans and thorough preparations can go awry when you are in the thick of it.

EXERCISE 9.10 **Staying cool, calm and collected**

*In your groups, discuss:*

(a)   *what you could do in the course of a negotiation if:*
   (i)   *you don't feel in control of things;*
   (ii)  *you feel angry with your opponent;*
   (iii) *you can't concentrate on what your opponent is saying;*
   (iv)  *the opponent won't let you get a word in;*
   (v)   *the other side won't respond to your win/win approach;*
   (vi)  *your opponent threatens to break off negotiations.*
(b)   *Should you take a checklist into the negotiation with you? Why/why not? If yes, what should it contain, and in how much detail? How should you use it?*

## Step 5: Keep your act together during the negotiation

C may have launched in with a monologue because he was nervous and needed to feel in control of the process to increase his confidence. D put up with it for a while, but then felt she had to interrupt, to re-distribute the power relationship and impose her agenda.

When planning, you have to anticipate your opponent's tactics, and deal with them during the negotiation. This is a tall order, when you already have the problem of processing a large amount of information very quickly. You have to use a number of skills simultaneously: active listening, observing non-verbal behaviour, taking notes, thinking out how to respond. To keep on top of things, you want to impose a structure on what is an open-ended interaction, so it is all the more frustrating when you find you are losing concentration, because this signifies to you, rightly or wrongly, that you are losing control.

Your interviewing practice has made you aware of the problems of information overload. In our experience, however, many students find negotiation gives them more anxiety. With a lay client, they say, you are the expert, and that makes you feel secure and more powerful, because you know more than they do – or the client thinks you do. On the other hand, you negotiate with a fellow-expert, so you can't get away so easily with bluff and flannel. In your discussions you will have picked up C's negative response to D:

D:   I would like you to move towards me and accept that there was fault on both sides. If I continue here . . .

C:   Well, um, there are several points that we do have to discuss, can I run through them?

C's stalling may have been a tactic to keep the onus on D to carry on making concessions, or he simply may have needed time to absorb the information and make a more appropriate and conciliatory response.

There are no prescribed techniques to cope with information overload, anxiety and other unwelcome emotions. Separating the people from the problem is not easy, as we have said. However, we can suggest some general guidelines:

1. You will feel more confident when you enter the negotiation if you know your case inside out.
2. Aim to be flexible. When planning, anticipate every possible direction the negotiation could take. For example, if you think the issue in a personal injury claim is quantum, don't assume the other party won't want to discuss liability.
3. Don't rush. Remember you don't have to conclude an agreement until you are quite ready. Pause if you need to, to take information in.
4. Hide nerves, anger, frustration and insecurity by speaking quite slowly, keeping your voice low, asking your opponent to justify her unreasonable position, behaviour, etc.
5. Don't get drawn into pointless arguments. Allow your opponent to let off steam.

6. Don't take a checklist with you unless it is short. Some students like to have lengthy checklists with them as security blankets, but they will increase the amount of information you have to try and absorb and so divert your attention from the important skills of listening actively, responding appropriately and questioning. Remember it is a checklist and not a recipe. Use it only to check you have covered everything, not to determine the agenda.

7. Reflect on your negotiation experiences: make an entry in your learning diary.

The reflections of C and D immediately after their negotiation should give you some useful hints about the difficulties you can encounter during negotiation, despite what you thought was careful planning.[61]

During their reflections, both C and D said they intended to use a co-operative strategy, but felt forced to become adversarial when they got into the negotiation. D had planned to talk about quantum, and was not prepared for the very lengthy discussions on liability. Talking about the first few minutes, she said:

> I'd planned my strategy. C departed from that plan. I didn't know what to do. He flattened me. I had to counter-attack, to re-establish my own agenda.

When the tutors asked what each lawyer had planned as their best possible outcome on quantum, it was revealed that they were only £200 apart!

TUTOR:  So you've spent twenty-five minutes arguing around liability when you were about £200 apart on your best outcome. What does that tell you about your strategy?

C:  I don't quite know how we got so sidetracked on the other issues, because I didn't want to be really discussing those ...

D:  Nor did I, nor did I. I kept on thinking I didn't want to be talking about this, it's not the issue.

and later ...

C:  I felt I wanted to be more friendly and not talking so much.

D:  So did I. We wanted the same things. But if I'd said I didn't want to go to court, instead of hiding that, I'd have felt I'd conceded everything.

and later ...

D:  Last time we practised I was conscious that I had entered the negotiation as myself. For this I wanted to make sure everything was right for the client, but I still wanted to be myself. I could have done that. Instead I felt myself trying to put on a ... I was consciously trying to be someone I wasn't.

C:  I think that was my problem as well. I wasn't quite sure who the hell I was.

---

61. In Chapter 2 you will find an extract from D's learning diary on the subject of this negotiation. See pp. 46–7.

*D:* I could still have been myself.

*C:* Yes, I wanted to ... we got stuck on the nit picking ... not the intention at all ... Every time I said something, you came back and argued. We started winding each other up.

*D:* I'm sorry to think of myself like that, that I did that.

*C:* I kept telling myself to be flexible.

Red–Blue all over again?

## Step 6: Keep a negotiation journal

By now we shouldn't have to remind you to record your learning in your diary. However, we recommend you keep a negotiation journal as well. It is a useful way of recording:

- your preparation for negotiation;
- the course of the negotiation (pattern of offers, counter-offers, etc);
- the details of the agreement;
- the implementation of the agreement.

Earlier we asked you to draft a checklist for preparation. You can build your journal around this. You may find it helpful to compare your checklist with ours below.

## Planning the negotiation

### The critical issues and potential outcomes

| | |
|---|---|
| What are my client's goals? | . . . . |
| What are my client's instructions? | . . . . |
| What are the factual issues? | . . . . |
| What are the legal issues? | . . . . |
| What are the strengths of our case? Fact? Law? | . . . . |
| What are its weaknesses? Fact? Law? | . . . . |
| What are the opponent's strengths? Fact? Law? | . . . . |
| What are the weaknesses? Fact? Law? | . . . . |
| What do I anticipate are the opponent's goals? | . . . . |
| What do I know about the opposing negotiator? | . . . . |
| What are the options? Priorities: | . . . . |
|     What is our best possible outcome? | . . . . |
|     What is the least we will accept? | . . . . |
|     What is unacceptable? | . . . . |
|     What is our BATNA? | . . . . |
|     How would the other side answer these questions? | . . . . |

CHECK:

a.  Present objective criteria to back up each option.
b.  Client's authority for each option.
c.  Test out what is unacceptable to the other side.

## Our strategy and tactics

| | |
|---|---|
| What strategy are we intending to use? Why/why not? | . . . . |
| Am I comfortable with our chosen strategy? | . . . . |
| What tactics will we use? | . . . . |
| What is our agenda? | . . . . |
| What will be our opening position? | . . . . |
| How much information will we share/withhold? | . . . . |
| What information do we want from them? | . . . . |
| What offers are we prepared to make? | . . . . |
| What concessions are we prepared to make? | . . . . |
| What concessions do we want the opponent to make? | . . . . |
| Have we anticipated and resolved the ethical issues? | . . . . |

## Their strategy and tactics

| | |
|---|---|
| Might we need to alter strategy/tactics? Why? How? | . . . . |
| What strategy will they use? Why? | . . . . |
| What tactics should we be prepared for? | . . . . |
| How will we respond to: | . . . . |
|    Threats/intimidation? | . . . . |
|    Stalling? | . . . . |
|    Arrogance? | . . . . |
|    Discourtesy? | . . . . |
|    Anger? | . . . . |
|    Floppies? | . . . . |
|    Flinches? | . . . . |
|    Obstinacy? | . . . . |
|    Silence? | . . . . |
|    Interruptions? | . . . . |

CHECK: Are we thinking of taking this giant checklist into the negotiation with us?

Don't even think of it. When the negotiation is over, you can use the list again to check what you did, at which point, what worked well and what was less effective. Record the details of the settlement, and which of your client's objectives you achieved. If you failed to reach agreement, give reasons and note down what is to happen next.

## Are lawyers poor negotiators?

We have spent some time identifying a few of the possible pitfalls that professional negotiators can fall into. Remember, though, that negotiation is a skill you have been developing since you were a baby, so you have a wealth of successful (and unsuccessful) techniques at your disposal already.

So what do legal negotiators actually do in practice, and how effective are they? The empirical research there is suggests that experienced practitioners are less effective than you might expect. According to Carrie Menkel-Meadow

> ... many negotiators persist in wasteful and counter-productive adversarial or unnecessarily compromising behaviour ... [62]

She observed live negotiations conducted through mediation. Her study confirms the pattern established by other researchers whose data is based on interviews with lawyers: that most negotiation is 'low intensity'. Lawyers spend little time bargaining, preferring to settle quickly, on the basis of first or early offers. Any bargaining there is tends to be positional.[63] There is evidence of co-operative behaviour, but few signs of problem-solving approaches.

She further found that both lawyers and the parties seemed to approach their disputes from a particular orientation or 'mind-set', and that this predetermined how they acted in the negotiation.[64] She concludes:

> ... that there may be an empirical reality to the polarised models of negotiation, but that these behaviours are not limited to lawyers. Parties too may have polarised orientations to the world; seeing in each dispute or encounter with another human being an opportunity to 'get mine' or to 'see what can be done about this problem and work things out'. If, as many researchers report, most people are lazy about negotiation, that is they seek to 'satisfice' with low intensity contacts and expect to compromise in the middle, the two polarised orientations will, in reality, meet in a compromised middle and may not accurately reflect what the parties really need or what they are really entitled to, unless they have made explicit choices about the transaction costs of more involved, higher intensity negotiation processes.[65]

---

62. Menkel-Meadow, 'Lawyer Negotiations; Theories and Realities' (1993) 56 *Modern Law Review* 361 at p. 363. Note, however, that Eekelaar, Maclean and Beinart concluded that family solicitors in their study adopted elements of competitive, co-operative and principled bargaining, but that it was the principled model of negotiating that was most closely reflected in the behaviour of their sample: *Family Lawyers*, pp. 123–5.
63. For example, H. Genn, *Hard Bargaining*; H. Kritzer, *Let's Make A Deal: Understanding the Negotiation Process in Ordinary Litigation*, University of Wisconsin Press, Madison, Wisc, 1990; L. Ross, *Settled Out of Court: The Social Process of Insurance Claims Adjustment*, Aldine Press, Chicago, 1980; C. McEwen, L. Mather and R. Maiman, (1994) 28 *Law and Society Review* 149; A. Boon, 'Co-operation and Competition in Negotiation: The Handling of Civil Disputes and Transactions' (1994) 1 *International Journal of the Legal Profession* 109 at p. 118; A. Boon, 'Ethics and Strategy in Personal Injury Litigation' (1995) 22 *Journal of Law & Society* 353.
64. Cf. the discussion of the relational and rule-orientated mind-sets of litigants and judges in the small claims hearings studied by J. Conley and W. O'Barr in *Rules Versus Relationships: The Ethnography of Legal Discourse*, University of Chicago Press, Chicago, 1990, and in Chapter 10, below.
65. Menkel-Meadow, (1993) *Modern Law Review* 361 at p. 377.

So what are the factors which inhibit – or allow for – creative solutions? Studies suggest that the lawyer-client relationship, the personalities of both lawyer and disputant, the history of relations between the parties to the dispute, and the amount of negotiation experience a lawyer has – both in general and in that specific field of law – all make a difference. The general culture of the firm will also play a part. As one of Boon's respondents observed:

> In litigation over contracts I was required to do some very hard bargaining – not necessarily because I wanted to do it that way but because it was the sort of firm where the solicitor did what the client wanted. Our client profile was 'hard-nosed business-man'. They believed threats would produce results ... If one co-operated with the other side in any way, or suggested they might have a valid point, this was seen as weakness ... [66]

Moreover, the reality of legal practice, with its need to keep costs down and heavy caseloads can also encourage routinisation and standard resolutions; tort disputes are about money, divorce settlements about compromise, etc, which may reduce the potential for creative dispute settlement. At the same time, a number of studies have urged caution. Different lawyers have different styles and the most effective negotiators may be those who can adapt. We should not too readily assume that most lawyers routinely operate within Genn's frame of 'hard bargaining'. As Dingwall et al. observed, negotiation and settlement is embedded in organisations and networks in a way that precludes over-generalisation. Even in Genn's paradigmatic field of personal injury work, marked differences could be observed:

> [While] the 'hard bargainers' characterized the negotiation process in simple terms and regarded it as something of a game with the players occupying fixed roles ... Other experienced informants were concerned to come to 'know the people on the other side, treat them all individually' and develop professional relationships. [67]

So, what kind of negotiator do you want to be?

## Negotiation and mediation advocacy

Before leaving the subject of negotiation we want to make one final link between negotiation and mediation. As a lawyer you could go through your career without training as a mediator or conducting a mediation. However, it is now very unlikely that you could go through a legal career, particularly as a civil or commercial litigator, without advising a client about mediation, or representing a client in mediation.

---

66. Boon, (1994) 1 *International Journal of the Legal Profession* 109 at p. 115.
67. R. Dingwall, T. Durkin, P. Pleasence, W. Felstiner and R. Bowles, 'Firm Handling: The Litigation Strategies of Defence Lawyers in Personal Injury Cases' (2000) 20 *Legal Studies* 1 at p. 13. See also Boon, (1995) 22 *Journal of Law and Society* 353.

Research on mediation has made the point that lawyer attitudes can be one of the biggest hurdles to successful mediation.[68] This does not mean that all lawyers are necessarily a problem, but it is clear that lawyers who *understand* the mediation process are best placed to advise their clients sensibly about mediation, and, where appropriate, to support them effectively in mediation. This is the essence of what we call 'mediation advocacy'.[69] It does not require you to be a complete fan of mediation. Indeed, taking an objective view of the mediation process is probably what is most required if you are to act in the best interests of your client. To understand mediation fully, you need to be aware of three things:

- How mediation fits into the legal process (we have touched on this already in this chapter).
- The structure of a mediation and how it works; of course, this goes beyond our present concerns, but there are plenty of other sources you can refer to.[70]
- The theory that underpins mediation practice.

The key link with negotiation lies in relation to the last of these three areas. Mediation as a practice draws directly from the model of principled negotiation developed by Fisher and Ury. In essence, mediators are trained to be principled negotiators, and hence to achieve an environment in which the parties:

- are prepared to co-operate;
- see their dispute as a common problem;
- have a clear understanding of their own needs and interests;
- understand and value each other's interests.

The parties' legal representatives can thus support their clients in mediation in three ways. First, they can help their clients identify and analyse their (and their opponent's) legitimate needs and interests. Secondly, they can support the process by being open to creative solutions, where possible, and, thirdly, they can assist by providing background legal advice, where necessary. For example, this might involve keeping the client realistic about how their case is likely to fare in court,

---

68. A number of studies have emphasised that at least some lawyers see mediation as, at best, unnecessary and, at worst a threat to their clients' (and perhaps, their own) interests. Studies also stress the lack of understanding of the mediation process displayed by some lawyers, and their tendency to hinder mediation by focusing on legal issues and only distributive bargaining. See, e.g., M. Davies, G. Davis and J. Webb, *Promoting Mediation*, Research Study No. 21, Law Society, London, 1995; H. Genn, *Central London County Court Pilot Mediation Scheme. Evaluation Report*, Research Series No 5/98, Lord Chancellor's Department, London, 1998; D. Golann, (2002) 7 *Harvard Negotiation Law Journal* 301; N. Gould and M. Cohen, 'Appropriate Dispute Resolution in the Construction Industry' (1998) 17 *Civil Justice Quarterly* 103; L. Mulcahy, (2001) 8 *International Journal of the Legal Profession* 203. For evidence of perhaps significant differences between personal injury and commercial lawyers in their attitudes to mediation, cf. Mulcahy, *ibid.* and P. Brooker and A. Lavers, 'Commercial and Construction ADR: Lawyers' Attitudes and Experience' (2001) 20 *Civil Justice Quarterly* 327.
69. See further M. Stone, *Representing Clients in Mediation: A New Professional Skill*, Butterworths, London, 1998; J. Greenstone, S. Leviton and C. Fowler, 'Mediation Advocacy: A New Concept in the Dispute Resolution Arena' (1994) 11 *Mediation Quarterly* 293.
70. See the references on p. 311, n. 14, for some suggestions.

about the cost implications of failing to mediate, or failing to settle, and by protecting clients from agreeing to terms (negotiated or mediated) that really are contrary to their basic interests. Of course, at this point you might wonder, if lawyers can do all that, then why can't they negotiate a principled settlement for themselves? Which really begs the final question: if more lawyers were better at principled negotiation, would we need so much emphasis on mediation?

EXERCISE **9.11** **Concepts**

In this chapter we have discussed a number of concepts. We list the main ones below. The procedure for learning these concepts is as follows:

1. *Divide into pairs.*
2. *Each pair is to:*
   *(a) define each concept, noting the page on which it is defined and discussed; and*
   *(b) make sure that both members of the pair understand the meaning of each concept.*
3. *Combine into groups of four. Compare the answers of the two pairs. If there is disagreement, look up the concept and clarify it until all agree on the definition and understand it.*

| | |
|---|---|
| repeat players | mediation |
| zero sum bargaining | flinch |
| co-operative strategy | lose/lose strategy |
| floppy | negotiation journal |
| BATNA | low intensity negotiation |

EXERCISE **9.12** **Yet another negotiation**

*In pairs:*

1. *From the five cases on pp. 318–20, select one you have not yet negotiated and allocate roles.*
2. *Individually, write a detailed plan for the negotiation and show it to your tutor.*
3. *Role play the negotiation and feed back.*
4. *Individually, write up your negotiation journal. Show it to your tutor. Then make an entry in your learning diary, preferably after you have seen the video recording of your negotiation.*

## Review questions

1. Discuss the following:[71]
   (a) Should mediators be legally qualified? Why/why not?

71. The following reading may be helpful: R. Ingleby, 'Court Sponsored Mediation: The Case Against Mandatory Participation' (1993) 56 *Modern Law Review* 441; S. Roberts, 'Alternative Dispute Resolution and Civil Justice: An Unresolved Relationship' (1993) 56 *Modern Law Review* 452; C. McEwen, N. Rogers and R. Maiman, 'Bring in the Lawyers: Challenging the Dominant Approaches to Ensuring Fairness in Divorce Mediation' (1995) 79 *Minnesota Law Review* 1317; N. Foster and J. Kelly, 'Divorce Mediators: Who Should Be Certified?' (1996) 30 *University of San Francisco Law Review* 665; C. Morris, 'The Trusted Mediator: Ethics and Interaction in

(b) What should be the role of the mediator? Should they comment on the merits of the case/predict trial outcomes? Why/why not?

(c) In what circumstances, if any, should mediation be mandatory? Give reasons.

2.  Which aspects of your negotiation skills and behaviour do you think you need to improve? Give reasons, and indicate how you will go about making improvements.

## Further reading

A. Halpern, *Negotiating Skills*, Blackstone Press, London, 1992.

D. Tribe, *Negotiation*, Cavendish, London, 1993.

R. Fisher and W. Ury, *Getting to Yes: Negotiating an Agreement Without Giving In*, Business Books, London, 1991.

M. Palmer and S. Roberts, *Dispute Processes: ADR and the Primary Forms of Decision-Making*, Butterworths, London, 1998.

Mediation' in J. Macfarlane (ed.), *Rethinking Disputes: The Mediation Alternative*, Cavendish, London, 1997; L. Mulcahy, 'The Possibilities and Desirability of Mediator Neutrality – Towards an Ethic of Partiality (2001) 10 *Social and Legal Studies* 505.

# 10

## Advocacy: case management and preparation

> Advocacy is often seen as the apogee of the lawyer's skills. This chapter aims to set out the basic skills of fact management, problem-solving and pre-trial preparation that support effective advocacy. It shows how evidence and procedure control – or do not control – courtroom strategy and process, and it begins to look critically at the ways in which a kind of reality is reconstructed through the adversarial process.

## Objectives

To:

- Examine the social and institutional context in which advocacy takes place.
- Enable you to appreciate the importance of preparation for advocacy.
- Identify and discuss a range of fact analysis and case preparation skills that will support your advocacy.
- Introduce you to some advanced case management techniques, including the use of outlines and simplified charting.
- Encourage you to think about the experience of appearing in court as a non-lawyer, whether as an accused, a victim, or other witness.

## Supports benchmark statements

Students should be able to:

1. Knowledge:
   - explain the main legal institutions and procedures of [the English Legal] system.
2. Application and problem-solving:
   - demonstrate a basic ability to apply knowledge to a situation of limited complexity in order to provide arguable conclusions for concrete problems.
3. Sources and research:
   - demonstrate a basic ability to identify accurately the issue(s) which require researching;
   - demonstrate a basic ability to identify and retrieve up-to-date legal information, using paper and electronic sources.

4.  Analysis, etc:
    - demonstrate a basic ability to recognise and rank items and issues in terms of relevance and importance;
    - demonstrate a basic ability to bring together information and materials from a variety of different sources;
    - demonstrate a basic ability to make a critical judgment of the merits of particular arguments, and
    - to present and make a reasoned choice between alternative solutions
5.  Communication and literacy:
    - demonstrate a basic ability to understand and use the English language proficiently in relation to legal matters, and
    - to present knowledge or an argument in a way which is comprehensible to others and which is directed at their concerns.

## Advocacy in context

The focus of this chapter is not on advocacy itself, but trial preparation and case management. The skills involved are an essential pre-requisite to effective advocacy. Like negotiation, and most other transactions, you are ultimately only as good as your – or your team's – preparation. Traditionally, we tend to view litigation management as the work of solicitors and advocacy as the work of the Bar. There is some truth in this still, though the distinction is less clear-cut as the functional boundaries between solicitors and barristers begin to blur, for example, by virtue of higher court advocacy rights for solicitors and direct access to barristers for some categories of client. But even where these structural distinctions remain more or less intact, and despite a degree of intra-professional competition, links between particular barristers and solicitors seem to have been strengthened by the growing tendency toward specialisation in both branches of the profession.[1] Lawyers – whether barristers or solicitors – increasingly define themselves as a team that is responsible for managing the litigation for the client.

Now, in this chapter we are not intending to provide you with a guide to the whole process of litigation management. That is too complex for our purposes. Rather, we intend to focus on skills and techniques that will have a direct impact on your preparation for advocacy. But first, let's be clear about the context in which both your preparation and advocacy are set, because it is the context that in many ways determines how you need to prepare for the job.

### The adversarial nature of advocacy

The present style of advocacy reflects the adversarial nature of most English legal proceedings. Sir David Napley encapsulated the essence of English advocacy in the

---

1. See e.g. A. Boon and J. Flood, 'Trials of Strength: The Reconfiguration of Litigation as a Contested Terrain' (1999) 33 *Law and Society Review* 595, *seriatim*.

title of his book – one of the first of the advocacy manuals – *The Technique of Persuasion*.[2]

Within this model, the essence of the advocate's task is to persuade a supposedly neutral third party (judge or jury) that her view of events (or of the law) is more correct than her opponent's. The process is adversarial because it is up to the lawyers themselves to make the running; they choose the territory to fight on (i.e. the legal and factual issues in dispute), and each will choose arguments not so much with a view to establishing an objective 'truth', but (within the limits that ethics allow) in order to advance their client's version of events, or to discredit their opponent's. As one experienced criminal practitioner has put it:

> ... one is really not dealing with a static set of facts at all. It's an area of shifting sand. I have been known to say that, when I go into the criminal courtroom, I don't expect to hear anybody tell the truth at all. That is perhaps again a cynical view, but certainly I don't expect to be able to identify readily who is telling the unvarnished truth, who it is who is varnishing it a bit, who it is who is deliberately lying and perhaps what difference that is going to make in assessing the totality of the evidence being presented. [3]

This is not just a problem in criminal trials. Trials, whether they are civil or criminal, tend to turn on disputed facts. To give a simple anecdotal example, Julian once had the (not unusual) experience in one civil case, involving a road traffic accident, of the parties disagreeing on most issues of fact. For example, though the case showed incontrovertibly that the accident was caused by the defendant driving into the back of the claimant's car, the claimant said the impact pushed the car thirty or forty feet, while the defendant said about ten or twelve feet.[4] Neither was necessarily lying – that may well be how they remembered events, but equally either or both may have been reinventing the details of the accident to their own advantage, as they saw it. The manner in which these contested versions of 'reality' come to be represented in court is central to wider concerns about the ability of the trial process to deliver 'justice'.

## Recreating facts in the courtroom

The basic point we need to bear in mind is that courts are places where decisions are made on the basis of available evidence. This fairly innocuous sounding principle is important for a number of reasons.

First, English courts do not operate on a principle of 'freedom of proof'. As a lawyer or litigant, you cannot just appear before a court and tell your story. The

---

2. Sweet & Maxwell, London, 4th edn, 1991.
3. B. Nash, 'The Psychologist as Expert Witness: a Solicitor's View' in J. Shapland (ed.), *Lawyers and Psychologists – Gathering and Giving Evidence*, Issues in Criminological and Legal Psychology No. 3, British Psychological Society, Leicester 1982, p. 32 at p. 35.
4. Not surprisingly, this was not ultimately at issue; an admission of negligence was obtained by the defendant's insurers and the case proceeded on quantum only.

ability to tell your story will be affected by the complex body of legal rules which determine what evidence may be heard in court, and for what purposes.[5] That means that a good advocate should have a sound grasp of the law of evidence, though anyone watching a busy magistrates' court in action will recognise that there is often a gap between theory and reality here. How good is your knowledge of evidence? The next exercise gives you a flavour of what the law involves.

EXERCISE 10.1 **Evidential quiz**

*Answer all the following questions. A word of warning – unlike most multiple choice tests, do not assume that there is only one right answer listed (there may be more); but equally, do not assume that any of the answers are necessarily correct!*

|  |  | TRUE | FALSE |
|---|---|---|---|
| 1. | The standard of proof in criminal cases is: | | |
| | (a) proof on a balance of probabilities; | [ ] | [ ] |
| | (b) proof so that you are sure; | [ ] | [ ] |
| | (c) proof beyond reasonable doubt; | [ ] | [ ] |
| | (d) proof of a prima facie case. | [ ] | [ ] |
| 2. | A confession is: | | |
| | (a) any inadmissible statement made by a witness in legal proceedings; | [ ] | [ ] |
| | (b) any admission of fact against his own interests made by a party in civil proceedings; | [ ] | [ ] |
| | (c) any admission of fact made by a witness in criminal proceedings; | [ ] | [ ] |
| | (d) an admission of fact against his own interests made by D in criminal proceedings. | [ ] | [ ] |
| 3. | The defence apply for bail. Any statement made by D or his solicitor is: | | |
| | (a) admissible evidence; | [ ] | [ ] |
| | (b) a representation; | [ ] | [ ] |
| | (c) incomprehensible; | [ ] | [ ] |
| | (d) hearsay. | [ ] | [ ] |
| 4. | A prima facie case is: | | |
| | (a) small, red, and carried by the Chancellor of the Exchequer; | [ ] | [ ] |
| | (b) evidence on which a court might convict; | [ ] | [ ] |
| | (c) evidence on which a court must convict; | [ ] | [ ] |
| | (d) evidence on which a court must acquit. | [ ] | [ ] |

5. For a useful introduction to the relationship between evidential rules and the adversary form of justice, see J. McEwan, *Evidence and the Adversarial Process*, Hart Publishing, Oxford, 2nd edn, 1998, ch. 1.

5.  A police officer may refer to his/her notebook
    ('Incident Report Book' – IRB – as it is
    now called) in giving evidence in order to:
    (a)  corroborate his/her testimony;                                    [ ]        [ ]
    (b)  corroborate another witness's testimony;                          [ ]        [ ]
    (c)  refresh his/her memory;                                           [ ]        [ ]
    (d)  contradict defence witnesses.                                     [ ]        [ ]
6.  A witness is 'hostile' if:
    (a)  he attacks the character of another witness;                      [ ]        [ ]
    (b)  he attacks the judge;                                             [ ]        [ ]
    (c)  he gives evidence which is unhelpful
         to his side;                                                      [ ]        [ ]
    (d)  he gives evidence which is unhelpful
         to the other side.                                               [ ]        [ ]
7.  Which of the following is inadmissible
    hearsay evidence:
    (a)  evidence given by a witness stating
         what someone else said;                                          [ ]        [ ]
    (b)  evidence given by a witness of a statement
         he/she made to someone else;                                     [ ]        [ ]
    (c)  a written statement made by a person who is not
         called as a witness in civil proceedings;                        [ ]        [ ]
    (d)  the video-taped evidence of a child who
         is not called as a witness in criminal proceedings.              [ ]        [ ]
8.  Corroborative evidence is required as a matter of law:
    (a)  to confirm the facts in issue in all
         criminal and civil proceedings;                                  [ ]        [ ]
    (b)  to confirm the facts in issue in all
         criminal proceedings;                                            [ ]        [ ]
    (c)  in no criminal or civil proceedings;                             [ ]        [ ]
    (d)  to confirm evidence given in criminal
         proceedings by any person under
         16 years of age;                                                 [ ]        [ ]
    (e)  to ground any conviction otherwise
         based on confession evidence alone.                              [ ]        [ ]

The rules of evidence allow for the exclusion of important evidence because there
are problems with the way in which such evidence would have to be presented
(e.g. because it would offend the hearsay rule[6]) or because a procedural

---

6.  The hearsay rule is intended to limit the use of 'second-hand' testimony. This is not as easy as it
    sounds. One particular consequence of the rule is that evidence in criminal proceedings must be
    produced from the most reliable source – i.e. the originator. Such evidence should be given as oral
    testimony. This means that, in theory, witness statements, confessions, etc. are technically hearsay,
    but they are in fact often admitted under various statutory exceptions. Confessions in particular

requirement, such as the need for an alibi warning, has not been met. These procedures may operate particularly against the interests of an unrepresented party,[7] or those who obtain representation at the last minute. Even where the rules of evidence mean that only part of a person's story would need editing/exclusion, this may paint a dramatically different picture from one that would appear if the courts operated a presumption of freedom of proof. For example, much of the context of a conversation – the communication episode of which it is part – may be lost.[8]

They can also make psychologically dubious assumptions about the (un)reliability of certain categories of evidence, or categories of witnesses. For example, for many years the English legal system treated the evidence of women and children as inherently less reliable than that of adult men, and created many restrictions concerning the reception of and weight attached to such evidence. Most of these restrictions have now been abolished, but the point illustrates the extent to which legal 'truths' are often socially and historically contingent, and may change with the system's changing perception (and reception) of external 'realities'.

Second, your presentation of a case can be affected by gaps in the factual information. For example, the defence may be unable to challenge prosecution forensic evidence, because the forensic material was all used up in the original tests, or because the integrity of that material has been destroyed by testing, or by the passage of time. The court cannot refuse to come to a decision simply because the evidence has gaps in it. It must assess the issues by reference to the burden of proof, and decide whether there is sufficient evidence to discharge that burden. If there is not sufficient evidence, the court must find against the person carrying the burden.[9]

Third, evidence may be subject to a series of distorting influences which will affect the views of those receiving the evidence – e.g. selectivity exercised by the parties (as above); prejudgment or prejudice. The following exercise is a simple example of the way in which we unconsciously make assumptions and filter information.

EXERCISE 10.2 **The surgeon's story**

Read the following:

> A father and son have been out for a day's drive in the country. As they are returning home, their car is hit by an oncoming vehicle which swerves into their path on a

---

may be admitted, subject to the exclusionary rules in the Police and Criminal Evidence Act 1984, ss. 76 and 78. In other contexts, be warned: sometimes the distinction between first-hand evidence and hearsay is extremely fine.

7. See, e.g., the discussion in D. McBarnet, *Conviction: Law, the State and the Construction of Justice*, Macmillan, London and Basingstoke, 1981, pp. 127–8.

8. Cf. the discussion of conversations and communication episodes in Chapter 3, above.

9. *Woolmington v DPP* [1935] AC 462; in civil cases, see, e.g., *Rhesa Shipping Co SA v Edmunds* [1985] 2 All ER 712.

tight bend. The father is killed outright and the son is seriously injured. He is rushed to hospital for emergency treatment. A surgery team, led by one of the hospital's top orthopaedic surgeons, is standing by. As he is wheeled into the operating theatre, the surgeon turns around, sees his face and exclaims: 'It's my son!'

*Who is the surgeon?*

Aside from these sorts of difficulties, the quality of the advocacy itself, and the sometimes partial conduct of the judge can also have an impact.[10] Moreover, research in the US suggests that there is a significant social dimension to the production of evidence. Cooney has attached the label 'the Matthew Effect' to this phenomenon, after the passage from St Matthew's Gospel in the Bible: 'For unto everyone that hath shall be given, and he shall have abundance.'[11] Thus, it is suggested that high-status parties are more effective at obtaining high status advocates; they are therefore more likely to get the respected experts through their own and their advocates' networks; they will find it easier to get influential character witnesses. Indeed witnesses generally seem to be more willing to come forward to assist high status rather than low status associates, and so on.[12] These sorts of distortions will inevitably have an impact on the trial process.

It follows, therefore, that there is always a potential gap between truth and evidence.

---

10. The classic adversary image of the judge as distant umpire is widely doubted, by criminal practitioners as well as academic lawyers. See, e.g., the discussions in J. Morison and P. Leith, *The Barrister's World*, Open University Press, Milton Keynes, 1992, pp. 149–50. There are a number of detailed analyses of individual cases: see, e.g., J. Wood on the summing-up by Bridge J (as he then was) in the original *Birmingham Six* trial in C. Walker and K. Starmer (ed.), *Justice in Error*, Blackstone Press, London, 1993, pp. 159–61; also the Court of Appeal's powerful criticism of Lord Goddard CJ's summing up in the trial of Derek Bentley, for the alleged murder of a policeman. The court described parts of the summing-up as 'highly rhetorical ... The language used was not that of a judge but of an advocate ... such as to deny the appellant [a] fair trial ...' *R v Bentley*, *The Times*, 31 July 1998. The tragedy, of course, was the posthumous nature of Bentley's appeal, as he had been hanged for the original offence in January 1953.

    In civil procedure there has of course been a deliberate move to reduce adversariality, and as part of this judges are increasingly required to 'actively' manage cases – see, e.g., the reforms now contained in the Civil Procedure Rules, notably r. 1.4, which requires judges to use their powers to manage cases in pursuit of the 'overriding objective' of the CPR. See also C. Glasser, 'Civil Procedure and the Lawyers – The Adversary System and the Decline of the Orality Principle' (1993) 56 *Modern Law Review* 307. The increase in judicial intervention in civil cases has not, however, raised the same level of concern about judicial partiality as in criminal cases. Be aware that the criminal court system is also undergoing a period of significant structural and procedural change, with the Criminal Justice Act 2003 and the Courts Act 2003 introducing substantive reforms, including increased disclosure obligations in criminal proceedings, which, in theory at least, are intended to increase the capacity of criminal trials to establish truth, not just proof. The Criminal Justice Act 2003 in particular leaves few parts of the criminal process untouched. See R. Taylor, M. Wasik and R. Leng, *Blackstone's Guide to the Criminal Justice Act 2003*, Oxford University Press, Oxford, 2004.

11. M. Cooney, 'Evidence as Partisanship' (1994) 28 *Law and Society Review* 833 at p. 850. (In fact, as Cooney notes, this label was coined by Robert Merton in his study of the process of recognition of scientific achievement: see 'The Matthew Effect in Science' (1968) 159 *Science* 56.

12. *Ibid.*

Many of the problems go deeper than the evidential, however. As lawyers we tend to forget just how artificial and, indeed, alienating an environment the courtroom is. It is 'blind to the outside like an archive or a bunker, its reality is exclusively within'.[13] This helps create what Rock has termed a form of *anomie* – a sense of displacement which he defines as 'social reality dissolving into meaninglessness'.[14] It is a discursive environment 'free of the conventional sensate world in which an audience could move about independently and probe and ask questions'.[15]

We shall continue to explore these contextual issues, and the techniques of advocacy, through a case study and a range of exercises presented in the course of this and the following chapter. You should read the case study before progressing to the next section of text.

## A case study: the case of William Gardiner[16]

In 1902–3 William Gardiner was tried for the murder of a young unmarried woman, Rose Harsent, who lived near his home in the Suffolk village of Peasenhall. The case was remarkable for the fact that Gardiner was actually tried twice, first in November 1902, then in January 1903. On neither occasion could the jury agree on its verdict. As majority verdicts were not acceptable at the time, Gardiner's case had to be set down for re-trial on each occasion. The case became of national interest even before the second trial, and it is probable that public sympathy for Gardiner was largely behind the authorities' decision to enter a *nolle prosequi* after the second trial, which spared him the ordeal of a third. No other person was ever tried for Rose's murder. William Gardiner died in 1941, at the age of 72, neither formally guilty nor formally innocent of the murder, and still overshadowed by it.

The facts of the case are quite complex, but can be summarised as follows.

Rose Harsent died at some time during the Saturday night/Sunday morning of 31 May–1 June 1902. Gardiner (aged 35) was a married man with six children. He was foreman carpenter at the local drill works and a prominent member of the

---

13. P. Goodrich, *Languages of Law*, Weidenfeld and Nicolson, London, 1990, p. 189.
14. *The Social World of an English Crown Court*, Clarendon Press, Oxford 1993, p. 92.
15. *Ibid.*, p. 93. Even in civil cases many litigants experience the courts as alienating and threatening places – see, e.g., J. Baldwin, 'Litigants' Experience of Adjudication in the County Courts' (1999) 18 *Civil Justice Quarterly* 12 at pp. 37–9.
16. The case has spawned an extensive literature, including at least two novels. The main sources used here are W. Henderson, *The Trial of William Gardiner* (Notable British Trials series) Hodge, London, 1934 (which relied heavily on the contemporary newspaper reports of the case) and M. Fido and K. Skinner, *The Peasenhall Murder*, Alan Sutton, Stroud, 1990, which is probably the most thorough of the modern studies; see also J. Rowland, *The Peasenhall Mystery*, John Long, London, 1962, to which we have not referred. As Phillip Rawlings has observed, unusually among popular criminology, the accounts of the Peasenhall murder have tended to be sympathetic to Gardiner: 'True Crime' in J. Vagg and T. Newburn (eds.), *The British Criminology Conferences: Selected Proceedings, Volume 1* (September 1998) at www.britsoccrim.org/journal.htm (last accessed 18 December 2003).

Methodist congregation. His home in Peasenhall was some 200 yards from Providence House, where Rose Harsent lived and was employed as the servant of Mr and Mrs Crisp. Rose was friendly with both Gardiner and his wife. On the Saturday evening Gardiner had been seen outside his house from between 9.55 and 10.10 p.m., chatting to a friend, Harry Burgess. Soon after 11.00 p.m. a heavy storm broke, which continued until around 1.30 a.m. At about 11.30 p.m. Mrs Gardiner went across the road to visit a friend, Mrs Dickinson, who had recently been widowed and was frightened by the storm. Her husband joined her after checking the children were all right – this was at some time between 11.30 and 12.00. They stayed with Mrs Dickinson until the storm abated and then went home and to bed at about 2.00 a.m. Mrs Gardiner was unable to sleep. After seeing to one of the children who had woken up, she went downstairs to get some brandy to help her sleep (at some time after 2.20 a.m.). The brandy did not help and she was still awake when the Gardiners' twin girls woke about an hour later (the time is uncertain). She put one of the twins in with an older sister, and brought the other one back to her (and her husband's) bed. By about 5.00 a.m. she had finally fallen asleep. Around 7.00 a.m. a neighbour saw what appeared to be a larger than usual fire in the Gardiners' wash-house (where they normally boiled the kettle for their morning tea); he also saw Gardiner coming away from the wash-house half an hour later. Mrs Gardiner got up at about 8.00 a.m.

Rose Harsent's movements are less well documented. Burgess saw a light in her attic bedroom on leaving Gardiner. A few minutes later, Rose said goodnight to Mrs Crisp in the main hall of Providence House, as Mrs Crisp went upstairs to bed. Shortly after the storm broke, the Crisps went downstairs again to check that water was not coming into the house. Rose was not downstairs at the time. They did not check the kitchen itself, which was built on to the west wall of the house, though, as she closed the door between kitchen and dining-room, Mrs Crisp noticed that the kitchen seemed unusually dark. The Crisps then went back to bed. Mrs Crisp was woken, she surmised, at some time between 1.00 and 2.00 a.m. by a thud and a scream that seemed to come from inside the house. The storm was still raging over the village. She woke her husband (who was very deaf) and asked whether they should check on Rose. He thought that unnecessary, as Rose knew she could come into their bedroom if anything was wrong. They went back to sleep.

At 8.00 a.m. the next morning, Rose's father, William Harsent, called round to Providence House to leave his daughter's clean linen for the week. He went round to the back of the house as usual, and noticed the conservatory door, which led to the kitchen, was open. He opened the kitchen door. The kitchen was darker than normal, as a black shawl had been pinned over the only window. Rose lay on her back on the floor, with her feet pointing towards the outside door. Around her was a pool of blood that covered much of the floor in the small kitchen. There was a strong smell of paraffin and burnt flesh. Rose's night clothes were virtually burnt away; her right arm and the right side of her abdomen were charred. Harsent felt her arm; it was quite cold and he covered her body with a rug. He then told a neighbour what had happened and stayed with his daughter until the police and the doctor arrived (at around 8.30 a.m.).

The scene that they discovered did not make the events any easier to reconstruct. The doctor estimated that Rose had been dead some four to six hours. She had died from having her throat cut. There were three wounds in her neck. The deepest had severed the left jugular vein and opened her windpipe – this alone would have proved fatal. A second wound ran from the angle of the right jaw up under the chin; this had missed major blood vessels but had also penetrated the windpipe. A stab wound also ran upwards from the juncture of the left collar bone and breast bone to the throat, where it joined the first, cutting, wound. There was a bruise on her right cheek and a number of cuts to her hands – one across the right forefinger, others to her left thumb and forefinger and the ball of the same thumb. Blood had spurted some 24 inches beyond her feet, and had also splashed the open door and steps to her bedroom, directly behind her head (as she lay). It was clear from the nature of her burns that these occurred after death. It also became apparent that Rose was pregnant – six months pregnant to be exact.

A variety of items surrounded the body. Rose's head lay on a copy of that Friday's *East Anglian Daily Times*. This was burnt at the edges only, and Rose's face and hair were not singed. To the left of her head lay the candlestick she used to light herself to bed. This was upright and the candle had burned out. Between the candlestick and Rose's head was an oil lamp. This was unlit and unbroken, and had been taken apart, though no paraffin had apparently been emptied from its well. Close to the candlestick were the pieces of a broken medicine bottle, which had contained paraffin. The neck of the bottle had rolled away from the body. The cork stopper was still in place, and there was a label around the neck which was covered in blood and paraffin. Only after it had been cleaned by Home Office experts could the inscription be read: 'Two or three teaspoonfuls' and 'Mrs Gardiner's chdn'. Among the fragments of the bottle were found a half-burnt match and a small piece of blue woollen fabric, which was never matched to any other items of clothing. A wooden shelf bracket to Rose's left, which supported a small wooden shelf on the wall next to the staircase door, had been broken, apparently by the door hitting it with some force. Despite all the blood no footprints appear to have been found at the scene. However, a set of impressions (not bloodstained) were seen by one witness at about 5.00 a.m. that Sunday morning. Morris, a local gardener, saw a set of barred imprints on the wet road which seemed to lead from Gardiner's house to Providence House and back. Morris's statement was not made until a week after the murder, and the existence of the footprints was never corroborated.

When the police examined Rose's bedroom, it was clear that her bed had not been slept in. A number of letters were also found. One set, of love letters and indecent poems, were unsigned but later attributed to a young man (Fred

Davis) in the village. There was another unsigned note, in a different hand, which read:

> D R
> I will try to see you tonight at 12 oclock at your Place if you Put a light in your window at 10 oclock for about 10 minutes then you can take it out again. dont have a light in your Room at 12 as I will come round to the back.

This was in a buff envelope which had been posted locally on the Saturday (31 May). Envelopes of the same kind were found in the Gardiners' home, but it was also established that the envelopes were of a common kind that were sold locally.

Two other letters were also of interest. These were signed by William Gardiner and had been sent to Rose a year previously. In them he referred to action he intended to take to clear their names after he and Rose had become linked in a village scandal. The scandal had arisen when Wright and Skinner, two younger men from Gardiner's works, claimed that they had seen Gardiner and Rose – separately – enter the village chapel one evening and that they had subsequently heard them making love there. This Gardiner vehemently denied, and he was cleared by an internal inquiry set up by the Methodist chapel. This did not stop village gossip from suggesting a relationship not only had existed, but was continuing. If true, this might well have given Gardiner a motive for murdering the now pregnant Rose. It was to be a matter of contention at the trials whether Gardiner was the author of the anonymous note which apparently set up Rose's last and fatal assignation.

If Rose's death was the result of a sexual assault, or some lovers' tryst that had gone wrong, was there any evidence that sexual activity had taken place before the murder? Interestingly, the issue appears only to have been raised at the second trial,[17] but the medical evidence on the point proved wholly inconclusive.

The only real evidence against Gardiner was his clasp knife which the Home Office analyst was able to show had recently been scraped clean of mammalian blood.[18] Gardiner's response was to say that he had recently used the knife to gut a rabbit. No bloodstained clothing or footwear was ever found and attributed to him.

So, Gardiner went to trial on the strength of this accumulation of circumstantial evidence. At both trials, his defence was led by a relatively young and inexperienced barrister, Ernest Wild.[19] The prosecution was led by Henry Fielding Dickens, a King's Counsel who was later elevated to the judiciary as Common Serjeant of the City of London.[20]

---

17. This was not generally considered a fit subject for publication by the papers of the day, and only one of them, the *News of the World* noted, very obliquely, that Lawrence J raised the issue himself during the examination of Dr Richardson (who had conducted the postmortem). See Fido and Skinner, *The Peasenhall Murder* pp. 114, 162.
18. Forensic science in 1902 could not distinguish human blood specifically in such circumstances.
19. Later Sir Ernest, and, from 1922, Recorder for the City of London.
20. He was also a son of the novelist Charles Dickens, a pedigree Wild made ironic use of more than once in the subsequent proceedings.

So, having set the scene, we return to the practicalities of advocacy. We shall deal with these under three headings: Preparation, Speeches, and Examination. In each of these sections we have sought to recognise and distinguish between two related dimensions of competent advocacy. The first of these is a strategic dimension. All advocacy is involved in the development and advancement of a strategy for the case. The second dimension is the technical, in that your strategy is chiefly advanced by the use of practical techniques of presenting your case.

## Preparation

Advocacy is the culmination of the litigation process. So, in a sense, everything the lawyer does in a contentious matter, from the moment of taking instructions, is preparation for advocacy, even though it is advocacy that may never happen. It is therefore important to be aware of how the advocate's role fits in with all the other stages and processes in litigation. This is perhaps why some lawyers would argue that the sum of a good litigator is greater than the individual parts. It is the capacity to bring it all together before the trial that really counts:

> Litigation is a creative art form – you need tactical skill, a knowledge of factual background and a good level of academic knowledge. Attention to detail is important and the ability to move quickly and analyse material. You must be able to almost predict what will happen . . . [21]

As this suggests, much of the advocate's preparation is focused on developing an intimate knowledge of the details of the case: the facts alleged; the law; the evidence necessary to establish your claim, etc. In addition, there are a number of specific issues which you need to have considered. We will discuss these various points under the following five headings:

- Developing a working hypothesis
- Constructing your theory of the case
- Organising your material
- Preparing your client and witnesses
- On the day

### Developing a working hypothesis

As an advocate your job is to present your client's explanation of what happened in a way that makes sense of the factual issues in their legal context. This is the essence of what advocacy trainers call 'developing a theory of the case' (which we will consider in more depth in the next section). Before you have a fully-fledged theory of the case, however, you need what we call a working hypothesis, or sometimes a set of

---

21. Solicitor cited by A. Boon, 'Assessing Competence to Conduct Civil Litigation: Key Tasks and Skills' in A. Boon, K. Mackie and A. Halpern, *Skills for Legal Functions II: Representation and Advice*, Institute of Advanced Legal Studies, London, 1992, p. 23.

hypotheses, that is based on the available facts, offers a plausible explanation of those facts, and provides you with a framework for further legal and factual research. A word of warning: in this chapter we often talk of notions like fact and story 'construction'. We do not mean by this that you are 'concocting' or inventing a story for your client. To do so would be unethical: remember that you are under a duty not to mislead the court. Your job is to say for your client what she would say for herself if she had your advocacy skills. It is not your job to put words in your client's mouth or ideas in her head, e.g., by suggesting that if the facts were actually x, y, z, she would have a defence. With that in mind, let's begin, as usual, with an exercise.

EXERCISE 10.3 **Malice aforethought?**[22]

A man and a woman, who are in the living room of the man's house, are heard arguing by a neighbour. Shortly afterwards two shots are heard. The man shouts for help, and the neighbour rushes in to find the man nursing the woman, who has a severe head wound. A doctor is called and the woman is taken to hospital but she later dies.

You have evidence that a handgun was found in the man's pocket shortly after the incident by a policeman investigating what happened. The man admits that he has owned the gun for several years. You also have evidence that the man and woman had been living together for several years, but their relationship had not been happy recently.

*Assuming the man is charged with murder:*

(a)   *In pairs, construct an explanation which might establish the man's innocence of the charge.*

(b)   *Test your theory on another pair. How credible is it? Are there significant gaps you have missed?*

(c)   *What elements of the story require further investigation by the defence?*

If we step back and think about the kinds of *skills and processes* we use to present a potential explanation and hence a kind of resolution to this sort of problem, we can see that we tend to start by analysing the problem on the basis of what we already know about the world: we look to see if the explanation fits the events (and the law) in ways that are 'plausible'. This is both the strength and the weakness of our method; we are very good at dealing with the familiar and routine, but sometimes less effective with the unfamiliar, precisely because we often don't know what we don't know about a problem. So the first step to becoming a more effective problem-solver, is to acknowledge the importance of our *not-knowing*. Jack Ricchiuto emphasises that projects (another way of looking at a bundle of problems, we suggest?) are ambiguous and dynamic creatures. We need to respond

---

22. Taken from Inns of Court School of Law, *Evidence and Casework Skills*, Blackstone Press, London, 1994/95, p. 264 (note this volume was subsequently discontinued from the series).

to them with what he characterises as 'curiosity' – 'the willingness to respect the power of what we don't know … acting with the intellectual honesty to be uncertain when we lack data – to treat assumptions as the humble intuitions they are …'[23] This is absolutely critical to legal problem-solving and decision-making. As an advocate especially, you are ultimately constrained by the need for proof – proof is the advocate's definition of knowing – at the end of the day the court only 'knows' those facts that you can prove. But this is not your starting point; first you need to get as much information as you can about what happened, to identify all those things that you may or may not want (or be able) to prove, and to minimise the risk of being taken by surprise by your opponent's fact investigation. There are a number of things you can do to help ensure that you start investigating and analysing the case with the appropriate degree of 'curiosity'.

### Get clear about what you already know

With factually complex problems, a crucial first task is to be clear about what you do know. There are various techniques you can use to support your analysis:

1. *Identify the problem(s) within the problem*. Many complex problems are only complex because they involve layers of little problems. We can often simplify problems by just unpacking them into their constituent parts. In legal settings the most common problems within problems are:
   - Missing or inaccurate information.
   - A breakdown in communication.
   - A question that no-one has identified yet.
   - A failure to deal with unacknowledged emotional issues (quite often an issue for clients).
   - A client goal that is technically difficult to achieve.
   - Conflicting ideas of how best to achieve a goal (i.e. conflict between lawyer and client, or within the legal team).

   Identifying and categorising these features of a problem can immediately give us access to ways in which we might begin to resolve the larger problem a piece at a time.
2. *Construct a chronology*. Advocates make substantial use of chronologies or 'time-lines', as we shall see in this and the next chapter. By actually writing down the events in a clear chronological order you can begin to get a good grasp not just of the sequence of events, but also of possible gaps in the chronology. The chronology may be a good way of organising the story you actually present in court. It may even be one of the presentation tools you use in your advocacy where the timing of events is in issue in some way (e.g., where your client has an alibi defence which makes it less plausible – though perhaps not impossible – for him to have also been at the scene of the crime). In these circumstances the chronology might be presented in tabular form, or as a line with events marked on it, or even as a computer graphic.[24]

---

23. J. Ricchiuto, *Project Zen*, Designing Life Books, Cleveland, OH, 2003, p. 28.
24. See further P. Leith and A. Hoey, *The Computerised Lawyer*, Springer Verlag, London, 2nd edn, 1998, pp. 228–30.

3. *Visualise the problem and/or make a mind map or other plan of the main issues.* By 'visualising' a problem we mean running a picture of what you think happened 'inside you head'. Some people are very good at visualisation techniques, and use them for a whole range of purposes. If this works for you (or even if you are not sure), try it in this context. Imagine your client's story as a movie; analyse it; keep re-running it until you have a clear sense of the critical elements of the 'plot', and what is missing. Make a note of anything you need to follow up by way of fact investigation. Mind-mapping is another way of doing the same thing. A mind map is a non-linear paper representation of issues and events. Precisely because it avoids the vertical listing of a chronology (though you should always use it in addition to rather than as a substitute for your chronology), it is a powerful way of identifying links between events and ideas. In theory, it is said, mind maps work because they correspond much more closely to the natural way in which the brain processes information. We include a mind map of 'Malice Aforethought' (Figure 10.1), as an example of what is possible. In drafting and reading a mind map, always start at the circle in the centre of the page. From the centre you radiate outwards, setting out the links and associations your key concept/problem has raised. You can use different colour pens, pictograms, or just words to describe the interrelationship between your ideas and information. Because no two people structure information, or make associations in identical ways, no two mind maps of a problem will look exactly the same.

## Use logical and lateral thinking

A lot of both our technical and 'everyday' reasoning works on the back of simple deductive or inductive (logical) reasoning: we match patterns on the basis of what we already know about the world; we create and apply logical and behavioural 'rules'. This, after all, is largely how the law works.[25] But sometimes we need to be a bit more creative. As one solicitor has put it:

> There are two kinds of lawyer: the 'fixed paradigm' type and the creative sort. The former treats the law as a rigid set of 'cans' and 'cannots', while the latter treats it as an art form, skilfully manipulating its rich pattern to evolve a solution.[26]

Often a worthwhile hypothesis can only be developed with the aid of creative thinking. It is important to be able to use lateral as well as *logical* thinking. The idea of lateral thinking has been popularised by Edward de Bono.[27] Its essence is the rejection of standard – what de Bono terms vertical – methods for problem-solving. Lateral thinkers are those who tend to deploy fresh, often visual or spatial, perspectives on a problem. Activists, in Honey and Mumford's terms,[28] are meant

---

25. See, e.g., F. Schauer, *Playing by the Rules – A Philosophical Examination of Rule-Based Decision-Making in Law and in Life*, Oxford, Clarendon Press, 1993.
26. Mark Stephens in *Law Society's Gazette*, 25 November 1992, p. 14. Stephens' particular piece of ingenuity was to rediscover the long-dormant action of malicious falsehood, which enabled his client to sidestep the rules preventing individuals from obtaining legal aid to pursue actions for defamation.
27. *The Five-Day Course in Thinking*, Allen Lane, London, 1968.    28. See Chapter 2, above.

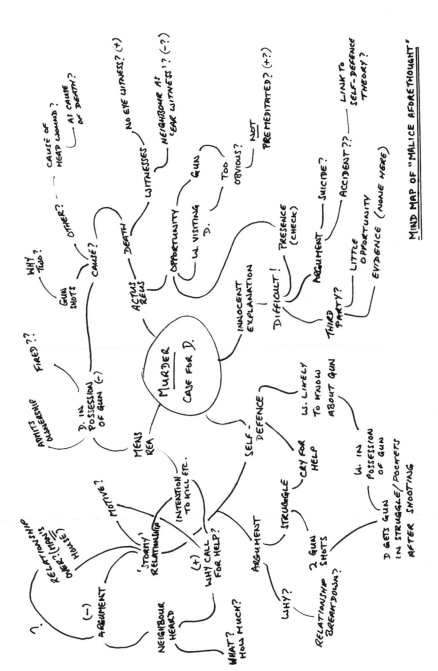

Figure 10.1. Mind map of 'malice aforethought'

to be good lateral thinkers. De Bono identifies four critical attributes associated with effective lateral thinkers:

1.  The capacity to recognise the dominant ideas that polarise perception of a problem.
2.  The tendency to search for different ways of looking at things.
3.  A willingness to relax rigid control of thinking.
4.  The openness to randomness and chance as access to alternative perspectives on a problem (this reflects the fact that lateral thinking involves recognising the possibility of low-probability or uncommon solutions).

Are you a good lateral thinker? Try the next exercise:

EXERCISE 10.4 **The money-lender and the merchant's daughter**[29]

A merchant owed money to an old money-lender. The money-lender proposed a deal to the merchant: he will cancel the debt if the merchant will let him marry the merchant's beautiful daughter. The merchant was horrified at the proposal, so the cunning money-lender proposed a solution that would put the young woman's future – and the debt – in the hands of fate. The outcome would be determined by the choice of two stones (one black, one white) which he would place in a cloth money bag. If the merchant's daughter chose the white stone, the debt would be cancelled; if she picked the black stone, the money-lender would marry her in lieu of repayment. Reluctantly the merchant agreed, for he knew he could never repay the debt. The money-lender bent down to pick two small stones from the pebble-strewn path. To the horror of the young woman he covertly put two black stones in the bag, before asking her to pick one pebble from the bag.
*What would you advise the young woman to do?*

### Look for remote associations

This idea is also a feature of lateral thinking. A defining characteristic of creativity is often said to be the capacity to link ideas that had not previously been associated[30] – e.g., Stephens's success for his client lay in his capacity to see that malicious falsehood might be resurrected, and could be brought within the legal aid eligibility criteria, even though defamation could not. Techniques like mind mapping can help in creating such associations, by giving you an overview of the problem. Another useful technique is 'brainstorming'.

Many of you will be familiar with this method, which is intended to increase the flow of creative ideas around a reasonably well defined problem. The aim in a brainstorming session is to produce as many solutions as possible without regard, initially, to their viability. This suspension of judgment is essential to promoting the free flow of ideas. Only once you have brainstormed the problem, do you begin

29. From E. de Bono, *The Use of Lateral Thinking*, Jonathan Cape, London, 1972, p. 9.
30. A. Koestler, *The Act of Creation*, Hutchinson, London, 1964.

to assess the solutions proposed. Brainstorming can be undertaken as an individual or group task – both are effective. In the legal context, consider the possibility of brainstorming not just with colleagues, but also with your client – as Binder and Bergman point out,[31] although you have the legal expertise, there will be many situations where the client's experience of the actual subject-matter will be greater than yours.

### Go with your intuition

Intuition is not always right, but in today's rational world there is a great temptation to throw this particular baby out with the bathwater. Intuition can be a useful creative tool. Many of us have had what you might call the '*Eureka!* experience', where a solution has come to us in an unexpected way, or where we 'sense' a solution without having worked out how we got there. To be sure, such intuitive conclusions need to be tested and validated subsequently, but they are often worth following up.

### Use expansionary thinking[32]

There are a variety of expansionary techniques. Ones that strike us as particularly useful are the methods of:

- *reversing* – look at the problem from the other side's perspective;
- *rearranging* – choose a different starting point in the chronology of a case – start with your desired outcome and work back to your objectives, etc.

So, let's put some of these techniques into use with another exercise.

### EXERCISE 10.5  Gardiner: chronology and issues

*Imagine you are counsel for Gardiner or for the Crown. Individually or in small groups:*

(a)   *Construct a chronology of the relevant events on the night of the murder.*
(b)   *Make a mind map of the issues as they appear to you from the summary of the case.[33]*
(c)   *Using your chronology and mind map, construct a working hypothesis for the case for the defence or prosecution.*

Of course, having created an initial hypothesis, you do not stop there. Even a working hypothesis has to evolve, and be tested against your objectives, before you are ready for the next stage, which is to develop it into a fully-fledged 'theory

31. D. Binder and P. Bergman, *Fact Investigation: From Hypothesis to Proof*, West Publ., St Paul, Minn, 1984, p. 205.
32. See M. Costanzo, *Problem Solving*, Cavendish, London, 1995, pp. 61–2.
33. You might find it interesting additionally to compare your mind maps with the ones Andy Boon constructs, including one for a closing speech in the Rouse case (discussed briefly below): see *Advocacy*, Cavendish, London, 2nd edn, 1999, pp. 5–6 and 145.

of the case' – our next section. So the next exercise is about testing your hypothesis.

EXERCISE 10.6 'Elementary, my dear Watson ... '

*Now, on the basis of your experience with Exercises 10.4 and 10.5, construct a general checklist of the questions you would ask yourself to test a hypothesis you have constructed.*

As a minimum, we suggest you need to consider the following when constructing a working hypothesis:

- Is it consistent with the facts I have?
- Is it consistent with my client's objectives?
- Is it believable?
- Are there significant gaps in the story?
- Is it an argument, ethically, that I can advance?
- If it is accepted, what will be the legal outcome (e.g. what remedy would I obtain)?

Do not become too wedded to a singly hypothesis early on. It is often important to keep an open mind, and to adapt your hypothesis to later facts that emerge, rather than try to bend the facts to fit your hypothesis. Also, do not worry too much about evidence and proof at this stage, they only really become critical once you start to develop a firm theory of the case.

## Constructing your theory of the case

A good theory of the case is the very heart of advocacy, since it provides a comfortable viewpoint from which the jury can look at all the evidence – and if they look at the evidence from that viewpoint, they will be led ineluctably to decide in your favour. [34]

The idea of a 'theory of the case' sounds much more daunting that it actually is. Your theory of the case is simply the narrative device you use to explain how the law, facts and evidence fit together. For example, if you are representing a female client accused of killing an abusive partner, you might construct a theory of the case that fits with what is sometimes called 'Battered Woman's Syndrome', by showing in evidence how a pattern of long-term abuse led your client to an emotional breaking point, at which point she 'snapped' and killed her abuser. This narrative, of course only matters in law because it fits with the law's own construction of the defence of provocation. It only works as a theory if your evidence establishes a set of facts that together justify a finding of provocation.

Developing a theory of the case not only supports your oral advocacy in civil and criminal matters, it can be useful in providing a structure for presenting a 'skeleton argument' (i.e. a written summary of your case). Skeletons are increasingly required

---

34. J. McElhaney, *Trial Notebook*, Chicago, American Bar Association, 2nd edn, 1987.

in both civil and criminal matters that raise an issue of law that will require argument before the court or tribunal.[35] Developing a theory involves two main elements:

● creating a legal theory of the case;
● creating a factual theory of the case.

### The legal theory of the case[36]

By developing a 'legal theory' we mean the construction of an argument for a specific legal action, i.e. a claim for breach of contract, negligent misrepresentation, etc. The creation of a legal theory requires three things:

● identifying a legal right from the facts;
● identifying the legal source of that right;[37]
● identifying the appropriate cause of action, prosecution, or defence accruing from that right (e.g. an action for damages, an application for an injunction, etc.).

### The factual theory of the case

This is the participants' part of your story. It is your explanation of what happened, why and how, as told through your client and witnesses. It must fit together as a 'story' – a coherent whole, and it must also link into the legal framework, so as to 'activate' your legal theory.

The trick with your factual theory lies in using it to establish clearly and logically the links between law, fact and evidence. This is necessary because the relationship between your legal and factual theories is symbiotic, that is they are mutually dependent on each other. A good of way of seeing if your theory of the case works is to try out how it sounds in a summary form. Think of it as the opening speech in your presentation of the case, or the crux of your skeleton argument.

In developing your factual theory, you need to remember these basic rules:

● Every cause of action is established by proof of the elements that make up that cause, or that criminal offence. For example, a charge of theft is only made out if all the elements of theft (that is, a *taking* of *property belonging to another*, with the intention *permanently to deprive*, etc. ... ) are proved or admitted.
● Every element not admitted requires proof of a fact or set of facts (these are called the 'facts in issue').
● Every fact in issue must be proved, directly or indirectly, by evidence.

In the earliest stages of analysis, as we have said, you should not worry too much about evidential requirements. Your first aim is to try and build up as full a picture

---

35. See, e.g., section II.17, *Practice Direction (Criminal Proceedings: Consolidation)* [2002] 1 WLR 2070, as amended, and the requirements contained in the numerous Practice Directions to the Civil Procedure Rules – notably PD 52 (Appeals) and PD 54 (Judicial Review).
36. See T. Anderson and W. Twining, *Analysis of Evidence*, Butterworths, London, 1991, pp. 124, 165–6.
37. That is, the specific common law or statutory rules.

of what happened as you can – regardless of the relevance or admissibility of that information. However, by the time you are seeking to establish a coherent theory of the case you should begin to process that information more critically, both on logical and, increasingly, on evidential grounds. There are three issues we need to address around the matter of evidence.

First, you need to consider carefully the need for, and availability of, *sources of evidence*, e.g.:

- availability of eye- and expert witnesses;
- the quality of testimony witnesses are likely to provide;
- whether witnesses can, or should, be compelled to testify;
- problems of hearsay in any documentary or oral evidence – which will mean statements may be inadmissible, or only admissible after editing.

Secondly, you need to understand the way in which we *prove* facts. In most academic law courses, this is not something you have to think about. The facts are generally presented as part of the 'problem', and your job is simply to discuss their legal effect. In court, you first have to (try and) prove those facts by calling evidence. Before we look at this as a reasoning process, we need to be clear about our terminology. Please read and make sure you understand the definitions given in Table 10.1 before moving on.

The relationship between facts and inferences is absolutely critical to the process of proof. In reality all legal deliberation requires some degree of inference. Even where we are relying on direct evidence there is some inference that the testimony we accept is accurate. The link between a fact in issue and an evidentiary fact is always made by inference. This is most obvious where we are relying on circumstantial evidence – this always requires us to judge the 'goodness of fit' between the events established by the evidence and the facts the proponent is seeking to prove. What we actually infer from the proof of an evidentiary fact is that the fact in issue *should*[38] be taken as proven. An inference, strictly speaking, is not itself proof because it is based on a premise – a generalisation[39] (often a common-sense assumption) that something is true; and some of these premises are more debatable than others. For example, to quote from Binder and Bergman:

> ... assume a litigant with the words 'rinse cycle' impressed in her head introduces evidence that a washing machine was pushed out of a window. The premise which may support an inference that the washing machine fell toward the ground is something like, 'Objects pushed into the air are affected by gravity'.[40]

---

38. We cannot logically say *is* proven, precisely because inferring involves some degree of value judgment.
39. See further Anderson and Twining, *Analysis of Evidence*, pp. 66–9. On the links between generalisation and story structure in court, see N. Pennington and R. Hastie, 'Explanation-based Decision Making: Effects of Memory Structure on Judgment' (1988) 14 *Journal of Experimental Psychology: Learning, Memory, and Cognition* 521.
40. Binder and Bergman, *Fact Investigation*, p. 83.

Table 10.1 *Know your terms*

- **FACT:** a fact is any act or event, alleged to have taken place, or a situation or condition that allegedly exists. For purposes of proof there are two kinds of fact:
  - ○ *Facts in issue* – the facts which ultimately must be proved or denied for the proponent to win her case
  - ○ *Evidentiary Facts* – those facts which support, or enable us to *infer* the existence of a fact in issue.

- **EVIDENCE:** the specific data used by a court or tribunal to reach a conclusion on the existence or otherwise of a fact. In short, facts are *proved* by evidence. Evidence can also take two forms:
  - ☐ *Direct evidence* – testimony (which enables us to prove the fact in issue by assertion) or other 'real' evidence that enables the tribunal to perceive a fact directly with its senses – e.g. the murder weapon itself, documents, CCTV recordings, and other objects.
  - ☐ *Indirect evidence* – also called *circumstantial* evidence, which requires the tribunal to infer the existence of a fact from surrounding events or circumstances.

- **INFERENCE:** the process by which we reach a conclusion based on evidence; the method of moving from evidence to proof of a fact.
- **PROOF:** 'The persuasive operation of the total mass of evidentiary facts' (J. H. Wigmore, *The Science of Judicial Proof*, Little, Brown, Boston, 1937, p. 9). Proof in law is assessed according to the allocation of both a *burden* (who must prove what) and a *standard* (degree of probability or likelihood) of proof.

As they point out, inferences at this level are virtually indisputable (unless presumably the defence could adduce evidence that the plaintiff was living on the moon at the time) but, most often, facts have to be proved on the back of a whole set of inferences which are themselves drawn on inferences, rather than on a single inference. We refer to these as 'catenate inferences'[41], or, more simply as a 'chain of inferences'.

The challenge in constructing your case, then, is twofold: first you need to identify the evidence you have and the facts you need to prove; then you have to identify and evaluate the inferences that you are asking your trier of fact to draw to connect the two. Distinguishing the kinds of evidence you have is an important part of this process. For example, in the Gardiner trial, the expert testimony on Gardiner's knife provided direct evidence only of the fact that his knife had

---

41. Anderson and Twining, *Analysis of Evidence*, pp. 57–9.

mammalian blood on it. It is thus only circumstantial evidence for the assertion that Gardiner killed Rose – and relatively weak circumstantial evidence at that. It requires two considerable inferential steps from there to assume (i) that the blood was human and (ii) that it was Rose's blood. The challenge for the prosecution, then, would be to see whether there might be additional evidence relating to the knife which could be obtained and which might reduce the inferential 'jump' that was required.

Let's try all this in some less abstract contexts.

EXERCISE 10.7 **Making inferences**[42]

A.   Read the following short story
B.   Then read the 15 statements about the story and, by yourselves, mark EACH one to show whether you think the statement is true, or false, or you can't decide:
  ● 'T' means that the statement is definitely true on the basis of the information provided in the story.
  ● 'F' means that the statement is definitely false on the basis of the information provided in the story.
  ● '?' means that you cannot be sure whether the statement is true or false on the basis of the information provided in the story.
C.   Please answer each statement in turn. Do not go back and change any later, and do not re-read any statements after you have answered them.

*The story:*
A businessman had just turned off the lights in the store when a man appeared and demanded money. The owner opened a cash register. The contents of the cash register were scooped up, and the man sped away. A member of the police force was notified promptly.

*The statements:*

| | | | | |
|---|---|---|---|---|
| 1. | A man appeared after the owner had turned off his store lights. | T | F | ? |
| 2. | The robber was a man. | T | F | ? |
| 3. | The man who appeared did not demand money. | T | F | ? |
| 4. | The man who opened the cash register was the owner. | T | F | ? |
| 5. | The store owner scooped up the contents of the cash register and ran away. | T | F | ? |
| 6. | Someone opened a cash register. | T | F | ? |
| 7. | After the man scooped up the contents of the cash register, he ran away. | T | F | ? |

---

42. This exercise has been adapted by many people over the years. Our source is Phil Race, *Who Learns Wins!*, Penguin/BBC Publications, London, 1995 (now out of print).

8.  While the cash register contained money, the story does not state
    how much.                                                          T    F    ?
9.  The robber demanded money of the owner.                            T    F    ?
10. A businessman had just turned off the lights when a man
    appeared in the store.                                             T    F    ?
11. It was broad daylight when the man appeared.                       T    F    ?
12. The man who appeared opened the cash register.                     T    F    ?
13. No one demanded money.                                             T    F    ?
14. The story concerns a series of events in which only three persons are
    referred to: the owner of the store; a man who demanded money and
    a police officer.                                                  T    F    ?
15. The following events occurred: someone demanded money; a cash
    register was opened; its contents were scooped up, and a man
    dashed out of the store.                                           T    F    ?
D.  *Discuss the results you have each obtained. What does this exercise
    tell us about how we use inferences, and our ability to distinguish fact
    and inference?*

When you have completed Exercise 10.7 (and not before) have a go at Exercise 10.8,
which develops what you have learnt about inferences in a legal problem setting.

### EXERCISE 10.8 **Moriarty's a murderer**

Moriarty is accused of murdering Holmes. The only evidence in the case is as
follows: Holmes was strangled two days ago. Scratches are apparent on Moriarty's
arm; they are no more than three days old. Traces of blood and skin were found
under the deceased's fingernails. Moriarty could not account for his movements at
the time of the killing.

(a)  *Identify:*
     (i)  *the evidentiary facts, and*
     (ii) *the fact(s) in issue they would go to prove.*
(b)  *Construct the necessary chains of inference between the evidentiary facts and the fact
     in issue.*

Suppose your chain of inferences looks something like Figure 10.2 (though
perhaps not as pretty).

In this example the evidentiary facts obviously go to one fact in issue: the *actus
reus* – the killing. You have insufficient evidence of the mental element (though the
scratches could be consistent with an intention to kill, etc. – otherwise why didn't
Moriarty let go at that point?). Note too how the overall chain of inference may
be drawn from an amalgam of evidence. There is absolutely no reason why you
cannot draw a chain of inferences from a single evidentiary fact, but it may be more
speculative than one that is supported at various points. Moreover, as a rule of
thumb, the longer the chain of inferences between an evidentiary fact and the fact

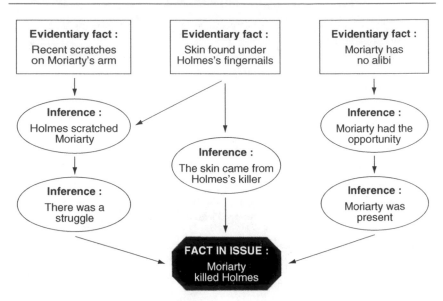

Figure 10.2. Evidentiary flow-chart

in issue, the weaker the probative link between the two. Remember always that your aim is to determine whether your evidence is sufficient, both in terms of its relevance to the legal issues, and in terms of its *weight* – i.e. its sufficiency to persuade the trier of fact that you have satisfied whatever burden of proof you bear. Do remember what we have said: no inference is logically conclusive and may be viewed as more or less strong or weak. Problems can arise because the evidence forces us to make a large number of inferences about the facts, and there is a danger therefore that we lose sight of the distinction between fact and inference in the process.[43]

EXERCISE 10.9  **Moriarty rides again?**

*Look again, critically, at the links in the Moriarty chain and compare them with your own analysis. Does it convince? If so, why? If not, why not? Consider the following questions.*

1.   *Are you satisfied that the inferences logically follow the evidentiary facts, or are any based on a false premise?*
2.   *How convincingly do they lead to the fact in issue? Is this a strong or a weak chain?*
3.   *What evidence would you need to make it stronger?*

43.  For examples from case law, see, e.g., *Morrison v Jenkins* (1949) 80 CLR 626 (extracted in Anderson and Twining, *Analysis of Evidence*, pp. 29–38); also the discussion in *Voelker v Combined Insurance Co of America* (1954) 73 So 2d 403.

We do not guarantee that these are always the only questions you need to ask when assessing the inferences you draw, but they are a start.

Thirdly, do not exclude alternative theories too soon: the Common Law allows you the doubtful luxury of presenting more than one theory, or as it is often called 'arguing in the alternative'. Irving Younger famously illustrated this by his example of the defence an advocate could offer to a charge that his client's goat had eaten the claimant's cabbages:[44]

> You had no cabbages.
> If you did, they were not eaten.
> If they were eaten, it was not by a goat.
> If they were eaten by a goat, it was not my goat.
> And if it was my goat, he was insane.

Now, we would not want to suggest you should ever run the equivalent of a 'mad goat' defence. It is likely to convince the trier of fact of one thing only: that you are desperate. A single theory, or at worst a couple of equally plausible alternatives, are what you ought to aim for. But the 'mad goat' in some ways is not a bad starting point, if only to test your own thinking about the range of options. This is why we started out by suggesting that you think first in terms of some initial hypotheses, rather than a firm theory of the case. For example, imagine you are defending our simple running-down action again. You might well think about preparing your defence, at least initially, along these lines, until you are clear which (if any) of these theories *are* seriously arguable:

- The accident was not my fault.
- If it was my fault, you were contributorily negligent.
- And even if you were not contributorily negligent, you were not badly hurt.

**Fitting the legal and factual theories together: a summary**

As we have shown, constructing a theory of the case involves the following seven steps.

1. Identify and assess any *cause of action, crime, or defence* appropriate to your case. Make sure you have done the library research necessary to be confident that this is the most appropriate basis for your legal theory.
2. Identify the legal issues arising from that cause (etc.) that will require *proof.*
3. Identify and analyse the *facts* you need to prove to make your case and any *contrary facts* alleged by your opponent, in order to determine what facts are likely to be disputed pre-trial and at trial.
4. Identify the *evidence* you will bring to prove any facts in issue, and to counter facts alleged by your opponent. Research any evidentiary problems that may affect the

---

44. Quoted in A. Boon, *Advocacy*, Cavendish, London, 2nd edn, 1999, p. 47.

admissibility of your or your opponent's evidence. Use your knowledge of the facts and evidence to keep the appropriateness of your legal theory under review.

5.   Assess the evidential *strengths and weaknesses* of your own and your opponent's case. Identify *strategies* you may be able – i.e. ethically and legally – to adopt to limit the impact of your weaknesses and to emphasise your opponent's (the 'principle of concentration of fire').

6.   Develop a *theory* of what happened that fits this legal and factual context, and the available evidence. Do not exclude alternative theories too soon – but be careful to avoid the temptation of 'mad goat' defences.

7.   Convert your theory into a narrative *story* that provides a credible explanation of the whole theory (we look at how you do this later in the chapter).

## Organising your material

While there are no equivalent studies in law, studies of medical decision-making indicate that mistakes are made more because of failure to *use* the information in your possession appropriately, rather than as a result of faulty information gathering.[45] This places the onus on your organisational skills. Techniques like mind-mapping may help you to sort out the relationship between various bits of information, and between law and fact, but these are not sufficient by themselves.

Your aim is to get into court in control of your information and therefore confident that you can access any information you are likely to need quickly and easily. The techniques for doing so do not require high-level skills, and you can get into the habit of using them quite quickly. The first two tools are developmental, and draw substantially on what we have already said about developing your theory of the case. The last is a final organisational tool for trial itself.

### Charting a case

Charting techniques are intended to provide a graphic representation of the law and evidence relevant to a case. The basis for our system of simplified charting is material developed originally for the College of Law in Sydney, Australia, though it has now been adopted in much of the Common Law world. The chief strength of this system is its capacity for representing the legal and fact analysis conjunctively.

In litigious work, this system operates by representing the legal and fact analysis of a case on five separate levels:

*Level 1:* the source of the client's/Crown's right;
*Level 2:* the cause of action or charge;
*Level 3:* the ingredients of the cause or charge;
*Level 4:* the propositions of fact;
*Level 5:* items of evidence.

45.  A. Elstein and G. Bordage, 'Psychology of Clinical Reasoning' in J. Dowie and A. Elstein, *Professional Judgment: A Reader in Clinical Decision Making*, Cambridge University Press, Cambridge, 1988, p. 109 at pp. 114–15.

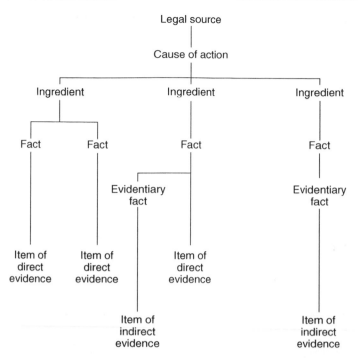

Figure 10.3. The charting structure

Levels one, two and three represent the kind of research you are already well familiar with.

At levels one and two you determine from the facts whether a legal right/remedy exists, identify the formal source of the right (e.g. Common Law negligence, etc.) and translate that into a specific cause of action and jurisdiction (action for damages for negligence in the County Court). At this stage, you will also identify the appropriate claimant/defendant.

At level three you must establish more precisely the particular elements or ingredients of the action or offence (e.g. in negligence, duty, breach, causation and remoteness of damage). This is essential if you are to establish what needs to be proved or admitted.

Levels four and five will probably take most of you into newer territory. At level four you are identifying the necessary facts to prove each ingredient while, at level five, you will identify the specific evidence you will bring to prove each level four fact.

The relationship between these various levels is represented diagrammatically rather like a family tree. This gives you a very clear visual representation of the case, as in Figure 10.3.

As you can see, it is a relatively simple system, though the charting can become more complex if one takes account of the distinction between facts in issue and evidentiary facts discussed above. Proof of evidentiary facts will introduce a new element into the chart between levels four and five, as shown.

Now have a try for yourself.

EXERCISE 10.10 *Maughan v Webb*

Here is another legal 'problem'. Read it and then follow the instructions.

Webb Ltd writes to Maughan Ltd: 'We require 30,000 2mm widgets by Friday week (17/X/0X). Can you provide? Please fax confirmation urgently.'

Maughan Ltd replies: 'Have widgets on our standard terms, can deliver from stock – price £30,000.'

Webb Ltd confirms its acceptance by telephone on 15/X/0X.

Friday arrives and 30,000 widgets are duly delivered to Webb Ltd by one of Maughan Ltd's drivers. The driver checks the load off the lorry, and gets Webb Ltd's Stock Control Manager to sign the delivery note. Maughan Ltd's standard terms appear on the back. Clause 4 states: 'All goods to be paid for in full within 10 working days of delivery or by the end of the calendar month in which the goods are delivered, whichever period shall be the longer.'

The Manager keeps the top copy, the driver takes the carbon.

Webb Ltd does not pay by 30/X/0X. One month later (on 31/X/0X) Maughan Ltd writes to Webb Ltd demanding immediate payment. Webb Ltd does not reply.

Maughan Ltd seeks your advice.

1.   *Identify what legal right and cause of action should Maughan Ltd pursue?*
2.   *In your groups, using the charting technique, construct a diagrammatic representation of the issues, facts and evidence, and compare.*

### Developing evidential outlines

A useful technique, which forms the basis of Binder and Bergman's[46] work, is to summarise your case through a series of interlocking 'outlines'. These can subsequently form the basis of a 'trial notebook' if the case proceeds to court. We only have the space to summarise the system here. If you wish to pursue the technique more fully, you should read Binder and Bergman for yourself.

The purpose of an outline is twofold. First, it is a means of marshalling your existing information into both narrative and evidentially useful forms. Second, it is a mechanism for determining what additional information you require. Binder and Bergman[47] draw a distinction between two types of outline – *story* and *evidentiary outlines*. Their method in fact involves five such outlines:

(a)    the story outline;
(b)    outline of client's existing affirmative evidence;

46. Binder and Bergman, *Fact Investigation*, pp. 39–42 for a summary of their system.    47. *Ibid.*

(c)   outline of opponent's existing affirmative evidence;
(d)   outline of client's potential affirmative evidence;
(e)   outline of client's potential rebuttal evidence.

These should be developed more or less contemporaneously, and together will provide you with a reasonably thorough and complete representation of the case.

The story outline provides you with an overview of the case. In it you should present the events leading up to the case in a chronological order. You should try to represent both sides' versions of events (they will usually agree on more of the story than they dispute) and identify inconsistencies in those versions which need to be explained. Gaps in the facts which are of importance and need to be filled can also be listed separately. The outline thus breaks down into three columns:

GAPS            EVENTS            INCONSISTENCIES

In putting together a story outline, begin with the events column, as this will provide the core of your case. It should focus only on the specific facts which constitute the parties' explanation of what happened. For simplicity's sake, you should save the fine detail for the evidentiary outlines.

The evidentiary outlines each marshal the evidence, according to its proponent and its purpose. Each outline is structured so that the evidence is listed under the substantive legal element it supports. In respect of each outline of existing affirmative evidence, you can also list your opponent's rebutting evidence in a parallel column to its equivalent affirmative evidence. Thus, assuming you are the claimant in a simple contract dispute, your affirmative outline might contain the following:[48]

| AFFIRMATIVE EVIDENCE | EVIDENCE IN REBUTTAL |
| --- | --- |
| *Agreement* | |
| Jack agreed to lend Jill £500, repayable on 1 April 200X. | Jack agreed to lend Jill £500, with no stipulation as to date of repayment. |
| *Performance* | |
| Jack gave £500 to Jill. | Admitted. |
| *Breach* | |
| Jill failed to repay the loan on or before 1 April 200X. | Jill paid £100 on 30 March 200X. |

In addition to the items of evidence, you could also note the source (e.g. 'oral evidence – Jack', etc.) under each respective item. This system can thus provide useful narrative support for the charting method we have just discussed.

---

48. Damage is excluded here because it does not require evidence other than that admitted as proof of performance.

## Creating a trial notebook

One particular method, originally developed in the US but now being used widely in the UK as well, is the 'trial notebook'.[49] This can be constructed out of one or more ring binders, which you can organise systematically into a number of sections. Most of you probably do something similar to this already, with your own coursework and study materials. The precise organising principles may vary somewhat between different methods, but the notebook should contain:

- A 'dramatis personae' – that is a list of the persons involved, the capacity in which they are involved, and their relationship to any other persons involved.
- A chronological summary of events – this helps you to reconstruct the events as they happened. Key elements of the chronology may then be built into it.
- Your theory of the case – this is best done in point form, though some advocates like to flesh it out to a full, narrative story.
- An analysis of the other side's case, and their probable theory of the case.
- A proof checklist. This may be a two- or three-column list detailing (i) the points of law requiring proof and (ii) the relevant facts and the evidence proving those facts (these may be listed together, or in separate columns – it's up to you). For the defence, of course, this would involve itemising evidence in rebuttal, or evidence that supports an affirmative defence. This should be cross-referenced to ...
- The documents and exhibits, which should be copied or recorded in a separate section.
- Research notes, if necessary, can be included on any complex points of law or on technical information required to understand any of the (expert) evidence.

## From organisation to implementation

Once you have a theory you feel reasonably happy with, you must implement it. Implementation is simply *converting theory into action*. You must now take the necessary procedural and practical steps to move your case along.

In these final stages there are various devices you can use to make sure you are on top of the case, and maintain your own risk management:

- Use a *diary* to maintain a record of key dates and *action checklists* to keep track of the tasks to be undertaken – identify who has to do what, by when.[50]
- Maintain a regular system of *case review* to keep a check on progress and to ensure your theory continues to offer the best fit. *This is absolutely critical.*
- Use *Murphy's law analysis*.[51] Murphy's law states that, in any conceivable situation, if something can go wrong, it will. Anticipate Murphy's law by checking for weak points; try and devise alternative courses of action for if, or when, the worst happens.

Now, having worked through all this technical preparation, we can focus again on the people involved.

49. See McElhaney, *Trial Notebook*; also Boon, *Advocacy*, pp. 62–4.
50. See J. Webb et al., *LPC Guide: Lawyers' Skills*, Oxford University Press, Oxford, 2004, para. 6.7.1.
51. M. Costanzo, *Problem Solving*, Cavendish, London, 1995, p. 204.

## Preparing your client and witnesses

### A lay perspective

> I was terrified up there. My legs were quaking.[52]
> I was in shock. It was unreal.[53]

These statements reflect what is a well-known fact: that courts are often alien and unsettling territory for lay people. This is commonly put down to fear, and the inarticulateness of many who appear before the courts. But as both Carlen and McBarnet[54] have emphasised, this is an oversimplification. What most effectively silences the lay person is the trial process itself. This is not a problem unique to the criminal courts. The context could as easily be, for example, a debt or repossession action.[55] Both Carlen and McBarnet's work focused on the silencing of the unrepresented defendant. We would argue that a represented person may also be effectively silenced by the trial process, in even more subtle ways. Worrall, for example, argues that the client becomes what she calls the 'dominated object of legal discourse':

> Solicitors do not talk about making assessments (as for example, do social workers, probation officers and doctors), they talk about 'taking instructions'. The implication is that they as servants articulate with confidence and competence in public that which the defendant has said haltingly and nervously in private. But what in fact happens is that a privileged discourse is constructed from the broken utterances of the powerless.[56]

Clark Cunningham offers a simple yet quite literal illustration of just such a silencing of a client.[57] As a law clinic supervisor he was involved with a client who had been charged with driving with excess alcohol.[58] The client spoke Spanish as a mother tongue, but very little English. The indications from the client were that he wanted to plead guilty, but translation problems generally made it difficult to advise and obtain instructions, even through an interpreter. The client's version of events also suggested that the police had administered the breathalyser test despite the fact that he had indicated that he did not speak English. This created an important issue for his lawyers. The police in this particular jurisdiction were required to obtain the suspect's consent to the test and to read a statement of rights to the suspect to ensure that any such consent was informed. Clearly, if the suspect could not understand English, and no attempt was made at translating his rights

---

52. Female witness, quoted by D. McBarnet in *Conviction: Law, the State and the Construction of Justice*, Macmillan, London and Basingstoke, 1981, p. 90.
53. Witness-victim, cited by P. Rock in *The Social World of an English Crown Court*, Clarendon Press, Oxford, 1993, p. 128.
54. P. Carlen, *Magistrates' Justice*, Martin Robertson, Oxford, 1976; D. McBarnet, *Conviction*.
55. See Baldwin, 18 *Civil Justice Quarterly* 12.
56. A. Worrall, *Offending Women: Female Law Breakers and the Criminal Justice System*, Routledge, London, 1990, p. 22.
57. 'A Tale of Two Clients: Thinking About Law As Language' (1989) 87 *Michigan Law Review* 2459 at pp. 2464–5.
58. For simplicity we have translated the American offence into its nearest English equivalent.

into Spanish, there could be no informed consent. Without that consent, the lawyers felt they had grounds for arguing the test results should be excluded from the hearing. Furthermore, the court file did not contain a police report, or the breathalyser test result. Cunningham takes up the story again on the day of the trial:

> We decided that our lack of necessary information made plea negotiations at the arraignment unwise. We therefore told our client, through the law student interpreter, that we recommended a plea of 'not guilty'. Our client said he did not understand and insisted that he was 'guilty'. At that point our case was called and we advised our client to 'stand mute', which he did. When we told the judge that our client was 'standing mute', he entered a plea of not guilty 'on behalf of' the defendant, as is customary . . .
>
> Even though the client was silent, the judge, in effect, put words into his mouth: according to the record he 'pled' not guilty. The court (with our tacit connivance) 'made up' a defendant who took the proper adversarial position so that the case could proceed. In this sense, the defendant who 'appeared' in court was indeed only a 'representation', an image projected by the institutional needs of the judge and lawyers.[59]

Although the client's literal silence was converted into a figurative utterance, the client remained effectively silenced within the proceedings. His own version of his guilt or innocence was never heard.

We suggest that Worrall's argument rather overstates the case, by disregarding what it is actually possible for practitioners to achieve within the constraints of the existing system. Nevertheless, we accept that 'silencing' happens, both literally (as Cunningham shows) and, more commonly, metaphorically, and it is an underlying theme to which we shall return again. It is most certainly an issue at the preparatory phase. The question is: what can you do as a lawyer to try and prevent the silencing of your clients becoming what a number of legal theorists call an act of (symbolic) violence against them?[60]

For the moment, we will try to answer that question in a very practical fashion.

### Preparing your client and witnesses

While many of the principles are common to both, we will first consider a range of issues relating to preparing your client and then talk about preparing witnesses.

*(a) Preparing your client for trial*

#### EXERCISE 10.11  A crusty in court

Your client, John, is a 22-year-old white male. He is charged with breach of the peace after getting caught up in a disturbance at a protest site against the re-opening

---

59. (1989), 87 *Michigan Law Review* 2459 at p. 2465. Note that, similarly under English law, an accused who is 'mute of malice' will have a not guilty plea entered on their behalf: Criminal Law Act 1967, s.6(1).
60. See, e.g., R. Cover, 'Foreword: Nomos and Narrative' (1983) 97 *Harvard Law Review* 4.

of a quarry in one of the English national parks, which proposes further restrictions on the movement of travellers. Your client is not a traveller: he is normally settled at home with his parents, who live in a very middle-class neighbourhood. He is sympathetic to the traveller lifestyle, however, and has a very 'crusty' appearance. The police have charged a group of eight individuals in total with offences arising out of the same event. Your client's version of events is that he and a friend were part of the demo, but were in fact leaving the scene because they could see things were turning nasty. He was arrested as they tried to push out of the side of the crowd and leave the area. They did not know the other people arrested (who were all travellers from outside the local area) and were not involved with them. Your client's friend, who dresses more 'normally', was behind the group arrested, and did not get picked out by the police. Your client was not individually identified, but with the other seven was collectively identified as part of an aggressive crowd. He wants to plead not guilty.

*Make a note of three or four practical matters of client preparation you need to address as the trial approaches.*

Client preparation is an important part of the total process of trial preparation, and one where you must remember that your behaviour is clearly circumscribed by the Codes of Conduct which proscribe witness rehearsing. These rules are generally wide enough to encompass preparing both the client and any other witness.[61] Nevertheless, there are still a number of tasks you ought to complete before the hearing.

You must *confirm final instructions*. As the hearing approaches, your counselling role becomes more important. You must ensure you are covered by instructions from your client which are given in the light of clear advice from you about possible outcomes (e.g. the range of orders or awards the court might make) and the costs – or legal aid – implications of these various alternatives. This will be particularly important if (as quite often happens in civil cases) your client is not in court on the day.

In criminal cases, negotiating the plea with your client is often the most critical and, perhaps, most difficult preliminary task you have to perform. Defendants often do not receive legal advice until they see the duty solicitor in court. Even if they have received advice beforehand, they can change their plea right up to the last minute, with the result that discussions about the plea may continue until you are literally at the door of the court, or even in court. There is often considerable pressure placed on defendants, particularly in the magistrates' court, to accept the outcomes of plea- or charge-bargaining, not least because of procedural implications such as the need to adjourn for a special court, if a not guilty plea is entered. Consider the following example. This is taken from a real solicitor–client

---

61. See *Law Society Code of Advocacy*, para. 6.5(b); CCB 607.3.

interview which took place in the interview room at a magistrates' court, on the day of the defendant's hearing.[62]

The defendant 'Janet' is a single parent accused of shoplifting with her boyfriend. She is charged with stealing the cassette tapes that were found in her boyfriend, Richard's, possession. She has also been charged with an assault on a police officer arising out of a scuffle in the police station cells. This happened after an officer took her cigarettes away when she complained that no one had heard her calling for a light. She has agreed to plead guilty to that offence. The theft case has been prosecuted as a 'joint enterprise' and there is evidence from a store detective and a shop assistant, alleging that Janet had put the tapes in Richard's bag. Janet denies this. Janet has previous convictions for petty theft, though none since the birth of her children. She states her intention to plead not guilty to the theft, and her solicitor ('Jane Gregson') is about to proceed on that basis, when she seems to change her mind, and starts to question her client again. We come in just after Janet has denied acting as look-out for Richard.

S:    I'll tell you what I think. I think you've been through the mill with this, partly because you've been frightened in the past and you feel you'll lose the children if you're sent to prison ... My view is I think you did know what was going on and you did help.

C:    I didn't take part myself.

S:    Did you put it in his bag?

C:    I didn't.

S:    I don't want to put you through the grief of a trial if you helped him ... But you didn't walk off. You stayed with him. You're not a child ... By staying with someone if they're doing something like that, it can be seen as encouragement. You could have walked out of the shop.

C:    He'd have turned on me. I just stood away from him.

S:    You should have got out of the shop ... You see, if someone's with you when they're doing it and you stay there, that can be viewed as participating. I feel that's what happened and you're frightened to say that because of your fears. Am I right?

C:    No ... You see I had an idea but I didn't know for sure until we got out and he took the tapes out of the bag. I just told him to put them away.

S:    Even telling him to put them away is actually participating. You should have said nothing ... You see, on the basis of what they're saying here, you'll be bound to be convicted anyway. But I think you'll be guilty because you stayed with him and assisted him. If you stay with anyone and assist in committing a crime, this means you're guilty.

C:    But I didn't pinch anything.

62. The case is taken from M. Travers, *Persuading the Client to Plead Guilty: an Ethnographic Examination of a Routine Morning's Work in the Magistrates' Court*, Manchester Sociology Occasional Paper No. 33, University of Manchester, Manchester, 1992.

s:     Technically, I feel you're guilty, but I can present it to the court as if it's only
       a technical offence. Legally, if you assist someone by advising them before or
       after, you're guilty of taking part in crime. Technically you ... So you will
       have to plead guilty to that. But it will be presented to the court as that.
       He's involved you in that against your will ... (Gregson moves towards the
       door) ... I wasn't happy representing you on your story before. Now I'm
       happy I'm at the bottom of it ... [63]

### EXERCISE 10.12 Jane's dilemma (1)

Working in pairs:

(a)    In your view:
       (i)   Does Janet comprehend why her solicitor is advising her to plead guilty?
       (ii)  Why/why not?
       (iii) On the evidence you have, does Janet seem willing to participate in the re-definition
             of her 'innocence' as 'guilt'?
       (iv)  Why/why not?
(b)    Do you feel that Jane (the solicitor) handled the question of Janet's plea appropriately
       in terms of:
       (i)   the law;
       (ii)  her responsibilities to her client;
       (iii) her responsibilities to the court?
       Give reasons for each of your answers.
(c)    Now compare your answers with those of the other pairs in the group. Account for any
       differences you find.

Any differences are likely to depend on whether you take a critical or pragmatic
stance on what Jane should have achieved. Any practitioner's experience would tell
them that Janet would most likely be convicted on the evidence, even if she pleaded
not guilty. It would also be clear that the offences would not justify a custodial
sentence – Janet's greatest fear. In that context, it might be argued that Jane's
strategy was to do the best she could for her client in the circumstances, which
meant get it over and done with, without the stress of a full trial (and the loss of
discount from the sentence for a guilty plea – though that would be fairly marginal
in a case like this). But could she have done more to take her client along with her,
even allowing for the fact that the magistrates were sitting next door waiting for the
case to begin? Was the way she handled the client heavily dependent on her exercise
of superior knowledge and status – and hence power – over that client? Would
you – could you – have handled it any differently? If so, how?

---

63. Ibid., pp. 21–2.

EXERCISE 10.13 **Jane's dilemma (2)**

*Two volunteers should role-play Janet and Jane, to test out any alternative strategies that have emerged from the discussion.*[64]

Another major issue is the question of *whether your client should testify*. This is an issue in both civil and criminal cases, though we will focus chiefly on the criminal side once again, addressing first the defence and then the prosecution perspective.

There are significant tactical implications to a defendant testifying, not the least being that the defendant who testifies leaves herself open to cross-examination on the issues, with generally no protection against self-incrimination. A defendant who testifies similarly may be cross-examined as to her bad character (if any), either if: (i) she asserts her own good character; or (ii) attacks the character of a prosecution witness; or (iii) testifies against a co-accused.[65]

Equally, there are compelling reasons why an accused should testify. In Kalven and Zeisel's classic study of the US jury trial, it was noted that less than a fifth of defendants relied on the presumption of innocence and did not testify.[66] Their study also assumed that, whatever judges may say about the presumption of innocence, it will be difficult to prevent juries from drawing adverse inferences from an accused's failure to give evidence.[67] Later mock jury research in the US appears to support that assumption as generally correct.[68] Further, in both civil and criminal cases, trying to prevent a defendant from testifying can also serve as a form of disempowerment that is inconsistent with the principles of participatory practice. Put simply, the opportunity to have a say can be of great significance to the way a person feels about their case, even if they lose.[69]

For the prosecution, the issue becomes: should the victim testify? The views of the victim of a crime are of some significance throughout the criminal process. The victim's support (or otherwise) for the action will be a factor in determining whether or not to prosecute in the first place. The problem for the prosecution is often a simple one: without the victim's testimony, there would be no case. This

---

64. In fact, we have deliberately distorted events slightly. Jane did not believe that Janet's final admission was the truth either. When challenged about whether she had put the tapes in the bag, Janet had tended to stress how the prosecution had got the description of Richard's bag wrong. This evasion left Jane suspecting, but unable to prove, that Janet had actively participated in the theft. Getting Janet to agree to this less culpable version was therefore ethically less problematic than pursuing those doubts with her, and presented a less damaging 'truth' to the court. See Travers, *Persuading the Client to Plead Guilty*, pp. 30–1.

65. These are the circumstances under s.1(f) of the Criminal Evidence Act 1898 in which an accused can lose the statutory protection of the 'shield' provided by s.1 of the same Act.

66. *The American Jury*, Little, Brown, Boston, 1966.    67. *Ibid.*, p. 144.

68. See, e.g., the studies cited by D. Shaffer, 'The Defendant's Testimony' in S. Kassin and L. Wrightsman, *The Psychology of Evidence and Trial Procedure*, Sage, Beverley Hills, 1985, p. 124 at pp. 140–5.

69. Cf. Cunningham's discussion of his second case: 'A Tale of Two Clients' (1989) 87 *Michigan Law Review* 2459, pp. 2465–9, 2492.

creates difficulties which are widely recognised, though not necessarily widely acted upon.

First, the system itself has been unsympathetic to victims of crime. Victims and other witnesses may experience:

- Lack of awareness of and sensitivity to their needs among criminal justice personnel (police, court services, CPS, prosecuting counsel, etc).

- Insufficient information about the progress of the case against the alleged offender, or sometimes insufficient, or no advance notice of delays or changes to court dates.

- Poor inter-agency co-operation between criminal justice personnel and other services supporting the victim – e.g. social or medical services.

- Intimidation, threats or actual violence from the offender or persons associated with the offender.

- Insufficient opportunities to experience a sense of reparation or 'closure', even after an offender has been found guilty and sentenced.

Despite growing emphasis on victim support services, counselling and increased information on the prosecutorial process,[70] victims can still feel marginalised and intimidated by the process. This is especially true of the trial, and a number of studies have independently shown that victims often feel unsupported by 'their'[71] lawyers at trial.[72]

Second, it can be difficult to assess how much protection victims of crime can be given without destroying the due process of adversary trial and the rights of the accused. In an adversarial system the accused must be entitled to put the prosecution to proof, and that tends to mean that the evidence of witnesses – including the victim – must be subjected to scrutiny, chiefly by cross-examination.[73]

Nevertheless, vulnerable witnesses can be assisted as much as possible to testify. Preparation is important, and you should assess whether the use of special procedures

---

70. See, e.g., Home Office, *A New Deal for Victims and Witnesses: National Strategy to Deliver Improved Services* (July 2003) available at www.homeoffice.gov.uk/docs2/vicwitstrat.pdf (last accessed 12 January 2004).

71. Strictly, of course, the prosecutor is not the victim's lawyer, and arguably this is part of the problem: the victim remains essentially unrepresented and largely invisible when she is not testifying.

72. See, e.g., Rock, *The Social World of an English Crown Court*, pp. 127–8, 305–6. What this certainly indicates is that prosecutors have been very poor at explaining the effect of their ethical obligation not to discuss the case with the victim once she has been called. Prosecutors tend to take the safe course, which is to have no contact with the victim at this point, but the reason for this is not always explained to the victim in advance. The Witness Service (which provides victim support at trial) may ameliorate this problem, though evidence suggests the quality of support and advice remains variable.

73. There is, perhaps, a danger that in seeking to protect the victim, the law can go too far and infringe a defendant's right to a fair trial under Art. 6 of the European Convention on Human Rights: see, e.g., discussion of the 'rape shield' provisions in s. 41 of the Youth and Criminal Justice Act 1999 by D. Birch, 'A Better Deal for Vulnerable Witnesses?' [2000] *Criminal Law Review* 223, and the subsequent creative (re-)interpretation of s. 41 by the House of Lords in *R v A* [2001] UKHL 25, [2001] 2 AC 45.

to help the victims of crime is appropriate – e.g. the use of documentary, or live video-link[74] or (more exceptionally) videotaped testimony.[75] However, a victim, or other vulnerable witness, can rarely be protected entirely from cross-examination, and this has to be taken into account at the initial stages of any prosecution.

So, what would we suggest you should do to prepare your client (including, so far as possible, the victim)? Well, even though direct rehearsing is not allowed, there are four particular strategies available which would not seem to contravene the Codes of Conduct, and yet help prepare the client for the court.

First, build your case with the *co-operation* of your client. If both lawyer and client are committed to the theories and themes you wish to present, your client will feel more confident in the case and is, perhaps, less likely to do anything that will contradict the lines you intend pursuing.

The second of these is pure common sense. You should always send your client a copy of her *witness statement*, and get her to check it and let you know if there is anything she wishes to amend or reconsider. This will at least help refresh the client's memory of what she has said. Also, if anything is changed, you will be able to deal with it in advance, rather than be surprised in the hearing itself. Given the possible need for changes, it is best to do this a couple of weeks (rather than days) before the trial.

Third, you should outline the *basic trial procedure* to the client. Explain what will happen and how long it is likely to take; who the main functionaries are, and the basic order of events. If time allows, some of this can be done in the letter you send out confirming, or reminding her of, the date set down for trial but, regardless of this, you should always try to meet your client on the day and give her the chance to talk through any concerns.

Lastly, there seems to be no ethical difficulty in *role-playing* a client through testimony on facts different from those in their own case. This is not coaching them on their evidence, but it is getting them used to the style of examination and cross-examination that they are likely to face in court. It appears that a number of solicitors' firms have adopted this tactic on occasion.[76] It is certainly preferable to one American advocate's avowed tactic of the 'stress test' he applies to new clients:

---

74. See particularly s. 51 of the Criminal Justice Act 2003 for the circumstances in which a criminal court may use live video-link testimony.
75. This is much more widely used in the US than the UK, particularly in civil trials (some of you, for example, may recall hearing about Bill Gates giving videotaped testimony in the Microsoft anti-trust litigation). In England and Wales videotaped testimony may be allowed for vulnerable witnesses, particularly children, and it has been increasingly common, since changes to procedure were introduced in 1998 to facilitate the reception of videotaped evidence in chief for child witnesses. For discussion of its uses see J. Wilson and G. Davies, 'An Evaluation of the Use of Videotaped Evidence for Juvenile Witnesses in England and Wales' (1999) 7 *European Journal on Criminal Policy and Research* 81. See also more generally J. Swim, E. Borgida and K. McCoy, 'Videotaped Versus In-Court Witness Testimony: Does Protecting the Child Witness Jeopardize Due Process?' (1993) 23(8) *Journal of Applied Social Psychology* 603; and Birch, [2000] *Criminal Law Review* 223.
76. A. Sherr, *Advocacy*, Blackstone Press, London, 1993, p. 42.

... I ask them to tell me everything they can about themselves and their case; then, using that information, I hit them with a barrage of insults and sarcasm.[77]

'Not surprisingly', Pannick adds, 'some break down, go home and never come back'.[78]

*Creating the right impression* may also have appeared, in some form or another, on your list. Your client's physical appearance may be an issue. You are probably aware of the fact that there are a number of 'image consultants' making a handsome living out of high profile (and high value) criminal defence work in the US – cases such as the O. J. Simpson murder trial – where they are employed to make witnesses and, if necessary, the defendant more presentable and, they would argue, more believable. To our knowledge, no-one has yet tested the Legal Services Commission's views of an expenses claim for an image consultant in the UK, and we do not anticipate that English practice is in a hurry to follow this particular American trend. Nevertheless, English lawyers are certainly conscious that appearance could be an issue. Why?

The answer, of course, is stereotyping. Lay magistrates and juries in particular are thought to be judgmental and influenced by extraneous factors, such as appearance. This sort of ideology is supported by media images (think of the bigotry displayed by some of the jurors in the film *Twelve Angry Men*, for example), and certainly by advocates, in print, and otherwise.[79] But is this assumption accurate?

Research does suggest that factors such as ethnicity, mode of dress, and even gender may have some impact,[80] though it is debatable how far appearance factors have an independent effect, or whether they are only significant when taken in conjunction with other negative factors, such as a lack of linguistic skill or confidence,[81] or possibly because appearance is associated with powerful images of guilt – e.g. where an accused appears in handcuffs, or where the jury see an accused pleading guilty to another charge.[82] It is debatable whether any tribunal of fact will routinely allow a person's appearance to outweigh the impact of the evidence itself. However, in the end, most advocates will not take the chance.

So, you might well advise your clients to look neat, tidy and conventional (a particular issue in John's case), and encourage them to speak clearly and to the point. It is not going to do any harm to their case, though all this may not do much for their comfort or self-respect. Similarly, in John's case, you could warn him not

77. From R. Grutman and B. Thomas, *Lawyers and Thieves* (1990), cited in D. Pannick, *Advocates*, Oxford University Press, Oxford, 1992, p. 18.
78. *Ibid.*    79. See, e.g., Clarence Darrow, cited by Shaffer, 'The Defendant's Testimony'.
80. See, e.g., W. O'Barr, *Linguistic Evidence: Language, Power and Strategy in the Courtroom*, Academic Press, New York, 1982; J. Jackson, 'Law's Truth, Lay Truth and Lawyer's Truth: The Representation of Evidence in Adversary Trials' (1992) III *Law and Critique* 29.
81. Cf M. Myers 'Rule Departures and Making Law: Juries and their Verdicts', (1979) 13 *Law and Society Review* 781. We will return to the linguistic dimension in the next section.
82. See Jackson, (1992) III *Law and Critique*, 29 at p. 48.

to let any friends, who might want to disturb the proceedings by suitably anarchic comments or behaviour, come and give him their 'support'. In contrast, maybe you will encourage his parents along (good evidence of a supportive home environment) and any nice middle-class character witnesses as well. And do not stop to ask what any of this has to do with the grander notions of justice that we are supposed to be concerned with!

*(b) Preparing and evaluating witnesses*

It is axiomatic to state that the quality of your case will turn largely on the quality of your witnesses. Indeed, Saks and Hastie[83] suggest that the nature and quality of evidence presented in the trial has greater impact on the fact finder than any other factor – including the composition of the jury.

Determining who you call is largely a matter for your own professional judgment – or luck. In many cases, you may have relatively little choice. You may need everyone you can get! But if you have a choice, what criteria do you use in exercising it? Witness evaluation is an important part of case preparation. You are looking, ideally, for witnesses who will not just come up to proof, but will do so convincingly.

EXERCISE 10.14 **Superwitness**

Imagine you were able to construct the ideal witness: what characteristics would that person have?
*Make a list of no more than four or five things you would look for in a good witness.*
We suggest you need to consider a number of factors which would influence the credibility of your witness:

- Will the witness answer questions immediately, without substantial delay or hesitancy?
- Will they answer questions directly, or will they 'beat about the bush'?
- Can they present their evidence chronologically? (This is difficult for most people to do spontaneously; it is also not that easy for you as the advocate to direct the chronology, especially in chief, when you cannot lead the witness.)

Arguably, these factors all have one thing in common: the need for *narrative coherence* in court. The ability to tell a story well will often make or mar the 'quality' of testimony provided by witnesses. Chronology – a sense of the timing of events – is frequently important in this context. As one advocate has observed:

> Chronology is a very important aspect in producing order. There are very few people who think chronologically ... when you meet them you want to hug them: they do your job for, they are the very best witnesses. [84]

---

83. M. Saks and R. Hastie, *Social Psychology in Court*, Van Nostrand Rheinhold, New York, 1978.
84. Morrison and Leith, *The Barrister's World*, p. 110.

Sometimes it is not just a matter of chronological and narrative coherence, though the time of events may well be at issue. For example, in the Gardiner case, part of Gardiner's defence rested on the alibi evidence provided by his wife and Mrs Dickinson for what, on the evidence, was the most likely time at which the murder was committed. In that sort of context, evidence of time of death, or of possible periods in which the accused's whereabouts could not be accounted for, will be critical, and a witness who has the ability to go through their evidence chronologically can greatly strengthen the case. Even where time is not at issue, a chronological delivery can increase the comprehensibility of a story.

But the problem goes beyond simple chronology. The practice in trials more generally favours those witnesses who are most capable of telling their story in the formal, relatively abstracted way expected in court. What do we mean by this?

First, we would stress that legal discourse makes assumptions about what is the appropriate subject for legal argumentation. If someone fails to meet the expected criteria for a legal argument, we tend to ignore or silence their different voice. To illustrate this, we draw on the work of Conley and O'Barr, who distinguish between 'relational' and 'rule-oriented' discourse about law:

> Many litigants speak of their place in a network of social relations and emphasise the social context of their legal problems ...
>
> By contrast, the official discourse of the law is oriented to rules. This orientation is typical of all forms of official legal discourse, including both discourse among legal professionals and the talk that characterises the interaction of lawyers and judges with lay people. This dominant discourse of the law treats rules as transcending the social particulars of individual cases. It thus rejects the fundamental premise of the relational orientation ...
>
> The distribution of these orientations is not random, but is socially patterned. The discourse of relationships is the discourse of those who have not been socialised into the centres of power in our society. Gender, class and race are deeply entangled with the knowledge of and ability to use the rule-oriented discourse that is the official approach of the law. Thus, it is no surprise that the agenda of relational speakers is often at variance with the agenda of the law.
>
> ... the relational orientation and the powerless style are two components of a pattern of thinking and speaking that typifies those on the fringes of power. [85]

Let us illustrate this with an extract from one of Conley and O'Barr's small claims court cases. These are relatively informal tribunals yet, even here, the litigants who structure their arguments relationally are at a disadvantage. The case we will consider was brought against the parents of a minor who had borrowed a friend's car and then collided with the claimant's car. The judge clearly took the view that

85. J. M. Conley and W. M. O'Barr, *Rules versus Relationships: The Ethnography of Legal Discourse*, University of Chicago Press, Chicago, 1990, pp. 172–3.

the parents' liability, as a matter of law, was beyond dispute, and that the only real issue was one of quantum. His discussion with the parents proceeds as follows:

JUDGE:        Have you any questions as to the liability of parents for minors under ordinary circumstances?

MR FLOYD:     Uh, in some cases because, uh, what chance do we have when he doesn't mind us, you know?

JUDGE:        Well, sir, that's, that's nothing I can decide here today. There's a case has been filed ... against two parents for the operation of a motor vehicle owned by the parents and in the possession of the minor, uh, son of the party. An accident arose and there was damage.

MR FLOYD:     Well ...

JUDGE:        Basically the question is this, and I understand your concerns that the driver should pay, but that's, he's not a party to this and cannot be a party, uh, because of his age. He may have obligations to you. That's not before the court today. But are you concerned only with the dollar amount of what this is going to conclude to us?

MRS FLOYD:    No. We're concerned with that also, but we don't feel that we're responsible. We feel that he should have to be responsible for it.

JUDGE:        All right, well you're bypassing the question now. Are you saying that it, the accident was not the fault of your son?

MRS FLOYD:    No, we're not saying that. We don't know whose fault it was.

JUDGE:        All right. We don't know. Then maybe that answers the next question, which is how this all got started. Uh, do you deny that it was your son's fault?

MR FLOYD:     Could be. His friend loaned him the car.

JUDGE:        Well, at the accident when this thing happened, are you admitting, let's phrase it that way, are you admitting that it was your son's fault?

MR FLOYD:     Yeah, I admit that.[86]

The parents' answers clearly show their different, relational, agenda. They are concerned with the rightness of their being held responsible for a son over whom they feel they have little control. They thus insist on raising a problem that is non-legal, which the judge feels he cannot address, let alone solve. Through their responses to the judge's questioning, they then display their incapacity to adapt their story to the judge's theory of the case. Similar problems will arise in formal trials.

Second, a number of studies point (albeit in different ways) to the conclusion that the court is a place where both some degree of standard language ideology[87]

---

86. *Ibid.*, pp. 53–4.    87. See the discussion of this term in Chapter 3, above.

and certain narrative assumptions rule. For example, where witnesses use vocabulary incorrectly (malapropisms again), or try to overcorrect their speech styles, or where their narratives are fragmented by lots of short answers, or are full of qualification and hedging, their competence is likely to be underrated.[88] Counsel may even rely more powerfully and explicitly on standard language ideology to create inferences about a witness; the aim here is to pander to the view, to put it simplistically, that only 'bad people' know 'bad language'. Consider the following interchange. In this case the lawyer is cross-examining a woman who is jointly charged with possessing heroin with her daughter. She has just disclosed that her daughter has been in trouble with the police previously:

COUNSEL:    What kind of trouble?
WITNESS:    She was just found with some works in her pocket.
COUNSEL:    Works eh? Now where did you pick up the slang expression works?
WITNESS:    I've heard it used quite frequently.
COUNSEL:    What's meant by the term works?
WITNESS:    It means, uh, a needle.
COUNSEL:    A syringe?
WITNESS:    Yes, sir.
COUNSEL:    And cooker?
WITNESS:    Ye– I don' know about the cooker.
COUNSEL:    Pardon?
WITNESS:    I don't know about the cooker.[89]

The effect of this interchange is to show not just the witness's familiarity with the drug user's tools but also her familiarity with the slang ('works', 'cooker') used to describe them. The implication counsel is trying to plant in our minds is pretty obvious. People who are not involved in the drugs culture would not be so familiar with such terms.

As Bennet and Feldman point out, when witnesses fail to meet the story-telling expectations of judge or juror:

the presumption is not that the speaker merely uses a different language code or structures accounts differently. The presumption is that the speaker's version of an incident is suspect.[90]

88. See generally W. M. O'Barr, *Linguistic Evidence: Language, Power and Strategy in the Courtroom*, Academic Press, New York, 1982.
89. Taken from P. Drew, 'Strategies in the Contest Between Lawyer and Witness in Cross-Examination' in J. N. Levi and A. G. Walker, *Language in the Judicial Process*, Plenum Press, New York and London, 1990, p. 39 at p. 52.
90. W. Bennet and M. Feldman, *Reconstructing Reality in the Courtroom*, Tavistock, London and New York, 1981, p. 174. For a case study of where problems of linguistic register have actually led to perjury charges being brought against a witness, see R. Shuy, *Language Crimes*, Blackwell, Oxford and Cambridge, Mass., 1993, pp. 136–48.

Would you expect witness credibility to be dependent solely on their *verbal* behaviours, or would you suspect that the process of building credibility is more complex than that? What else might play a part?

You will, of course, have made the connection with our earlier work on the communication process and recognised that credibility also turns on other factors. Consider for a moment what you think these might be, and make a note to yourself before reading on. (We have grouped our factors into two specific categories, which may not exactly correspond to how you have done it.)

First, there are important *non-verbal behaviours* which will also have an impact on testimony. O'Barr[91] describes actors in the courtroom (whether as witnesses or advocates) as being either powerful or powerless. His research suggests that the credibility of these actors is intrinsically connected to their style of delivery. NVC will often reinforce the signals that are sent out verbally. 'Limited' vocabulary, a hesitant speech style and a lack of audibility will combine to produce indications of powerlessness.

Secondly, as we noted in the context of client preparation, *physical appearance* almost invariably plays some part in the evaluation of evidence. These same factors could also influence the way witnesses are perceived.

If necessary you may need to decide that a case cannot run simply because the evidence – as presented in court, rather than as presented on paper, or in conference – will not convince. This is difficult to assess. You cannot easily mimic the atmosphere of a courtroom to test how individuals will react, and sometimes it is the most unexpected witnesses who fail to come up to proof: 'I've known a bomb disposal officer faint in the witness box because he can defuse bombs but he couldn't give evidence.'[92] Really good witnesses are rare, so you are often trying to assess not so much whether witnesses are good, but whether they are not so bad as to make a real difference to your chances.

The principles governing witness preparation are essentially the same as those governing preparation of the client. Coaching witnesses on what to say is unethical, as, of course, is any attempt to put pressure on a witness to change their testimony (except of course under cross-examination). In practice, of course, in many criminal cases there will be insufficient time to undertake effective rehearsal (even to the very limited extent that such is allowed), or even to give much advice on presentation and delivery.

## On the day – a final checklist

The first time you appear in court 'for real' is a nerve-wracking experience for any advocate. Make sure you reduce the stress on yourself by being well prepared and allowing yourself time to get to the court or tribunal and deal with any last minute

91. *Linguistic Evidence.*
92. Detective Constable at Wood Green Crown Court, London, quoted in Rock, *The Social World of an English Crown Court*, p. 27.

problems. The following checklist probably sounds terribly obvious, but every-thing on it reflects a mistake that most advocates have made at an early point in their career!

1.  Do you know your destination and how long it will take to get there? Watch out that you don't confuse different courts with similar sounding names; watch out for last minute transfers from one local court to another (this often happens to facilitate listing); or for proceedings that have been moved to allow video testimony.[93] Be aware that some tribunal suites are hidden in some very anonymous office buildings and are not always well signposted; also that some courts can sit in a number of locations. If in doubt, contact the listing officer.

2.  It follows from this, you should always carry the telephone number of the court or tribunal at which you are due to appear, just in case. Most advocates regard a mobile phone as indispensable – keep it charged, but remember to switch it off before you go into court!

3.  If you are meeting a client at the court, make sure your client is clear about the time and location, and any consequences if she is late or does not attend. You should allow sufficient time for a final conference, to confirm instructions and/or deal with any last minute questions or concerns.

4.  Check you have working pens and writing paper; your case papers (the 'bundle'), any precedents you need and an appropriate guide to the law and procedure – e.g., *Blackstone's Criminal Practice*, or Antony and Berryman's *Magistrates' Court Guide*, or the *Green Book*, etc.

Now you are ready to engage with the skills of advocacy itself.

EXERCISE 10.15  **Concepts**

The procedure for learning these concepts is as follows:

1.  *Divide into pairs.*
2.  *Each pair is to:*
    (a) *define each concept, noting the page(s) on which it is discussed, and undertaking any additional research that is necessary; then*
    (b) *make sure that you both understand the meaning of each concept.*
3.  *Combine into groups of four. Compare the answers of the two pairs. If there is disagreement, look up the concept and clarify it. Make sure you are all agreed on the definition and understand it.*

| | |
|---|---|
| facts in issue | proof checklist |
| powerful/powerless speech | dramatis personae |
| hearsay evidence | relational discourse |
| rule-orientated discourse | silencing |

---

93. Section 53 of the Criminal Justice Act 2003 permits a magistrates' court to sit at other locations when this is necessary (or likely to be necessary) to receive evidence by live video-link under s. 51.

| catenate inferences | lateral thinking |
|---|---|
| reversing | indirect evidence |

EXERCISE 10.16 **Review question**

**Peace train coming**

Read the newspaper story in Anderson and Twining, pp. 285–7, as if it were an opening statement by counsel for the claimant (still called a plaintiff in the US). Then answer the following questions.[94]

(a)  Assume that an action is brought by the family of Donna Ulrich against the Ford Motor Co. From the standpoint of the claimant's counsel:

  i.  who are the witnesses and what other evidence would you call to support this statement of facts?

  ii.  Are there any assertions in the statement that are insupportable by evidentiary facts? Identify them.

(b)  Assume that you also have expert testimony which supports the assertion that Ford's engineers knew that, for an additional $25 on the manufacturing cost per vehicle, the company could have reduced the probability that the fuel tank would explode in such a collision from 1 in 10 to 1 in 50. National regulatory standards did not require the design features that would have had that effect. Invent additional facts that seem plausible inferences accordingly.

(c)  Assuming the following legal principles govern liability, chart the case using five-level analysis.

  *Manufacturer's liability requires that:*

i.  The vehicle or its components were defectively designed, manufactured or assembled, and

  (a)  the manufacturer knew or should have known of the defect, and

  (b)  the defect was correctable at reasonable cost, and

  (c)  correction of the defect would have significantly reduced the probability that injury or death would occur.

ii.  But for the specific defect in design (etc.), injury or death would not have occurred.

## Further reading

T. Anderson and W. Twining, *Analysis of Evidence*, Butterworth, London, 1991.

D. Binder and P. Bergman, *Fact Investigation: From Hypothesis to Proof*, West Publ., St Paul, Minn., 1984,

A. Boon, *Advocacy*, Cavendish Publishing, London, 2nd edn, 1999.

J. McEwan, *Evidence and the Adversarial Process*, Hart Publishing, Oxford, 2nd edn, 1998.

94.  Adapted from T. Anderson and W. Twining, *Analysis of Evidence*, Butterworths, London, 1991, pp. 287–8.

# 11

---

# Into court: the deepest swamp?

This chapter aims to explore the basic skills of the advocate, through a range of exercises and examples from real cases. It gives you the opportunity to practise those skills within the context of a 'narrative' or 'story' model of advocacy. And it furthers our critical reflection on the ways in which 'reality' is reconstructed in the courtroom.

## Objectives

To:

- Introduce you to the social and institutional context in which advocacy takes place.
- Explore a range of techniques applicable to narrative and interrogatory styles of advocacy.
- Enable you to develop your advocacy skills in a range of settings.
- Facilitate your reflection on the relationship between advocacy and ethics.

## Supports benchmark statements

Students should demonstrate a basic ability:

2.  Application and problem-solving:
    - to apply knowledge to a situation of limited complexity in order to provide arguable conclusions for concrete problems.
4.  Analysis, etc.:
    - to recognise and rank items and issues in terms of relevance and importance;
    - to bring together information and materials from a variety of different sources;
    - to make a critical judgment of the merits of particular arguments;
    - to present and make a reasoned choice between alternative solutions.
6.  Communication, etc.:
    - to understand and use the English language proficiently in relation to legal matters;
    - to present knowledge or an argument in a way which is comprehensible to others and which is directed at their concerns.

## The art of advocacy

In this final chapter we begin to look at the process of advocacy itself. We say 'begin' deliberately. For reasons that will become apparent, we cannot pretend – and do not attempt – to offer more than an introduction in a book of this kind.[1] We also intend to focus only on trial advocacy. John Mortimer may feel that

> no one has felt the full glory of a barrister's life who has not, in wig and gown, been called to the podium in the committee room of the House of Lords by an official in full evening dress and, on a wet Monday morning, lectured five elderly Law Lords in lounge suits on the virtues of masturbation . . .[2]

but appellate advocacy is too specialised an art form to incorporate here.

Advocacy is probably the most obviously 'artistic' (in Schön's sense) of the DRAIN skills. It is certainly the most complex to master, because it is a composite skill involving some highly specialised processes and techniques. To see what we mean, think back to your answers to Exercise 1.2. You will see that we identified quite a number of attributes that a good advocate needs. But is advocacy difficult only because of the *range* of skills it involves?

EXERCISE 11.1 **Advocacy as communication**

On the face of it, advocacy may seem to be just another application of our communication skills, but is that right?

1.  *In pairs, consider what factors, if any, distinguish advocacy from the other oral communication processes in this book.*
2.  *Briefly discuss your conclusions with the whole group.*

The key point is that, even though all the basic communication skills are there – talking, active listening, appropriate use of NVCs – they have to be put together in a very artificial environment and for highly specialised purposes. Advocacy as communicative action is far removed from our 'everyday' experience of communication, because:

● the context is relatively formalised, ritualistic even;
● you are often trying to communicate effectively to very different constituencies (e.g. judge, jury, opponent, client) at more or less the same time;

---

1. In so doing we must admit to a bias towards criminal advocacy. We would explain this on three bases: first, it remains the context where the problems of adversarialism and lay adjudication are most interwoven; second, it is the area where there is the greatest volume of research into the processes involved; third, in the context of our own teaching programme, advocacy is explored largely through a criminal case study.
2. *Clinging to the Wreckage*, Penguin, Harmondsworth, 1982, p. 12. We should point out that he was talking about an obscenity case in which he was counsel at the time!

- the scope for interaction is often limited: there is a far greater emphasis on one-way communication than in interviewing or negotiating;
- the style of your communication may be very different from the more participatory techniques recommended for interviewing or negotiating, e.g., where you are deliberately trying to control or coerce the person you are communicating with.

Most advocates, and advocacy trainers, acknowledge that advocacy is crucially a process of storytelling,[3] of constructing a narrative. This is an idea we have already touched on at a number of points in this chapter. But very few of the guides to advocacy go on to develop this idea into a coherent structure and method for learning to be an advocate. This is what we set out to do in the next section.

## Theme and method: advocacy as storytelling

In trial advocacy there are two specific modes of advocacy: what we call the *narrative* and *interrogatory* modes. The narrative mode refers to those points of a trial at which the advocate is free to make some form of speech – e.g. when opening or closing the case. The interrogatory mode operates at those points where the narrative is fractured into the classic question and answer style of examination or cross-examination. Any trial is likely to involve some use of both modes. Each mode requires often very different skills, but underpinning both there should be a common aim: *to tell your side's story.*

### The story model

The notion of a trial as a process of story reconstruction is by no means a novel idea. It builds on a variety of approaches which encompass the experimental, linguistic, jurisprudential and experiential.[4] The idea of a trial as a story emphasises the point we made in the last chapter, that 'reality' is something that has to be reconstructed in the courtroom. In fact Hale and Gibbons argue that courts are places in which there are two, intersecting functioning realities: the *primary reality* of the courtroom itself, with all its players and participants, and the *secondary reality* of the events that are the subject of the case.[5] This secondary reality has to be 'projected' through the primary reality of the curtroom, and of course that primary reality acts as a filter, not least by imposing constraints (ethical and procedural) on what can be said, and how. The question for us here, then, is how do we project that

3. See, e.g., A. Boon, *Advocacy*, Cavendish, London, 2nd edn, 1999, pp. 22–5, 64–7.
4. Relevant studies include W. Bennet and M. Feldman, *Reconstructing Reality in the Courtroom*, Tavistock, London and New York, 1981; B. Jackson, *Law, Fact and Narrative Coherence*, Deborah Charles, Roby, 1988; J. Conley and W. O'Barr, *Rules versus Relationships: The Ethnography of Legal Discourse*, University of Chicago Press, Chicago, 1990; W. Twining, 'Lawyers' Stories' in W. Twining, *Rethinking Evidence*, Basil Blackwell, Oxford, 1990; J. Gibbons, *Forensic Linguistics*, Blackwell, Oxford, 2003, ch. 4.
5. S. Hale and J. Gibbons, 'Varying Realities: Patterned Changes in the Interpreter's Representation of Courtroom and External Realities' (1999) 20 *Applied Linguistics* 203.

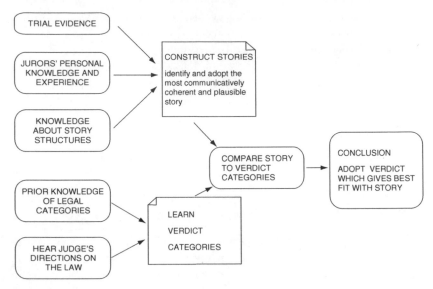

Figure 11.1. Pennington and Hastie's story model

secondary reality strongly to the key actors – namely the jury, or other trier of fact? The answer, we suggest, lies in effectively constructing and telling a story that will be meaningful to that trier of fact. The strongest experimental support for this assertion comes from the lengthy researches of Pennington and Hastie and their associates.[6]

Pennington and Hastie argue that jurors[7] use three techniques to construct trial stories. These they term 'story construction', 'learning verdict definitions' and 'making a decision'. In summary, the story model they propose suggests that juries construct stories from their available knowledge; they obtain instructions on the *legally* permissible verdict categories from the judge, and then reach a decision by matching their story to the best-fitting verdict category (see Figure 11.1).

*Story construction*, Pennington and Hastie argue, determines the juror's decision. Trial stories are not constructed in a vacuum. Jurors bring 'outside' knowledge into the process, often inferentially, as a way of making sense of the evidence in court.[8] Such knowledge includes their understanding of ordinary practices in constructing discourse, and expectations about what makes a complete story; their knowledge of (and biases about) the world, perhaps of how people have behaved in

6. Most of this work is summarised in N. Pennington and R. Hastie, 'The Story Model for Juror Decision Making' in R. Hastie (ed.), *Inside the Juror: The Psychology of Juror Decision Making*, Cambridge University Press, Cambridge, 1993, p. 193.
7. Note that, strictly, their research and model apply only to jury decisions. Intuitively, we suspect that other processes of lay adjudication are not, structurally, that dissimilar. The learning and matching of verdict categories to stories may be less problematic in the sense that the verdict categories are more familiar to, say, lay magistrates. This remains pure speculation, of course.
8. Pennington and Hastie, 'The Story Model for Juror Decision Making', pp. 194–5.

similar situations, and so on. As trials normally involve the construction of two or more competing stories, individual jurors will tend to take the one which seems to them to be the most coherent as a communicative episode [9] and the most plausible as *their* story. Note that, as advocates, we therefore need to be sensitive to the ways in which 'ordinary' discursive practices and expectations may be disrupted by the primary reality of the courtroom, especially by the formal requirements of legal discourse.

The *verdict definition* describes the legal information on the crime itself which the jury must absorb, chiefly from the judge's summing-up at the end of the trial. This is a difficult area for the jury. It often involves a relatively complex, one-off, learning task in which the jurors are expected to understand abstract information and then to apply it to a concrete situation. As Pennington and Hastie note, prior knowledge and experience will often interfere with this task, because a juror's exposure to the legal categories may be informed by media misrepresentations of the law.[10]

*Making a decision* involves matching the accepted story with the verdict definition or definitions (e.g. where alternative counts exist, such as wounding or wounding with intent). Although they recognise that this process of matching is also difficult, Pennington and Hastie point out that there is a cognitive link between the way in which we (all) represent human action as communication episodes and the way in which we (lawyers) describe the attributes of a crime.

Thus, as we have seen,[11] episodes have initiating *Events*[12] which cause psychological *Responses* that are translated into *Actions* with particular *Consequences* (ERAC). Similarly, crimes generally arise in circumstances in which a person in a prescribed mental state commits an unlawful act. (We will try this matching exercise for ourselves later). This is not coincidental, but:

> a reflection of the fact that both stories and crimes are culturally determined generic descriptions of human action sequences.[13]

Moreover, Pennington and Hastie argue that the closer the fit between the episode schema and the verdict category, the greater the confidence the jurors will have in the rightness of their decision.[14] Obviously, as an advocate, you can use this model to shape the way you present your evidence to construct your story for the jury.

---

9. Cf. the discussion of communication episodes in Chapter 3.
10. Pennington and Hastie, 'The Story Model for Juror Decision Making', p. 200.
11. At p. 70, above.
12. Gibbons, *Forensic Linguistics*, p. 152 makes the point that, strictly, not all cases are about events as such. Many may involve what he calls 'the description of a state of affairs', e.g. where a company is being prosecuted for releasing industrial effluent into a river or lake, and this is a continuing state of affairs rather than a (past) sequence of events. Nevertheless the narrative structure of such stories is very similar.
13. Pennington and Hastie, 'The Story Model for Juror Decision Making', p. 201.   14. *Ibid.*

EXERCISE 11.2  **Let me tell you a story**

(a)    *Prepare a brief story of no more than five minutes' duration on each of the following scenarios. Prepare your story in advance and commit it to memory, so that you can tell your story without reference to notes.*

   (i)    *You have been on a day out with some friends. Relate the day's events as you would to another friend who was not there.*

   (ii)   *You are a trainee solicitor. Yesterday you were late for work for the third time in two weeks. Your principal has called you in to her office and asked you to explain your continuing lateness.*

(b)    *In small groups:*

   (i)    *present both stories (one presentation of each is adequate, but you can do more if everyone wants a turn);*

   (ii)   *reflect on the style of delivery and content, and particularly*
          *– on whether each story involved all the ERAC elements;*
          *– on the significance of context for the style of the story.*

Now, let's take this a step further, and develop our storytelling skills with some more legalistic material:

EXERCISE 11.3  **Making a case into a story**[15]

Take a well-known legal case, that you are familiar with: for example *R v Collins*, *The Wagon Mound* or *Donoghue v Stevenson*. Consider what you need to do to convert the rather 'dry' information you find in the Law Reports into a living story, told from the perspective of one of the main protagonists. To help you to do this we have identified a number of steps:

(a)    *Identify the main characters who are important in telling your story (you may have to invent some names or other details, as the factual information in the Law Reports can sometimes be insufficient for this kind of exercise).*

(b)    *Identify your standpoint and perspective on the case: whose story are you proposing to tell?*

(c)    *Identify the key facts and their legal significance – you may find it helpful to use mind-mapping or charting techniques here.*

(d)    *Don't worry too much at this stage about factual accuracy – concentrate on making the story interesting and 'real' for those who are listening.*

(e)    *Present your story to your group. Afterwards, discuss what features of your story were most memorable, and why?*

With this model in mind, we can now begin to consider the specific courtroom skills of the advocate.

---

15. Exercise adapted from Boon, *Advocacy*, pp. 23–5.

## Speeches

We use the term speeches here as a shorthand for those situations where you can use a narrative as opposed to interrogatory style of advocacy. These will include not just the formal stages of opening and closing before a jury, or addressing the magistrates in a criminal trial, but other specific procedures such as bail applications, pleas in mitigation, or, in civil matters, a variety of chambers applications. These other events are often circumscribed by a lot more formal rules (the limits set by the primary reality again!) than opening or closing speeches, but they are still essentially narrative events, and we will explore one or two examples in this part of the chapter.

### Opening and closing speeches

Opening and/or closing speeches in a case are the main, often the only, opportunity that the advocate has to address the court at any length. There are skills the advocate must use here which are therefore significantly different from the skills used in examination or cross-examination. Opening and closing speeches also have particular formal functions which distinguish them from other occasions when an advocate may be expected to deliver some form of 'speech' (e.g. when arguing a point of law in a voir dire, or before an appellate court), though in other respects the latter situations have some similarities in terms of the skills used.

The formal requirements for opening and closing speeches differ between civil and criminal cases and between different courts within each of those systems. It is therefore essential first to know whether you have the right to open and/or close in a particular case, and then to decide whether to exercise that right.

**Opening speeches**

A competent opening speech should achieve the following aims:

- It should introduce the advocates to the court.
- It should tell your story.
- It should address the court on the relevant law.

Do not think that the order indicated here needs to be followed absolutely slavishly – it does not, though we shall follow that order in our analysis of these stages. Now, we can build on the last exercise to practice storytelling in the more formalised, advocacy, context.

EXERCISE 11.4 **Gardiner: opening for the prosecution**

We need two volunteers for this exercise, preferably from among those who have prepared a prosecution theory of the case in Exercise 10.5.

(a)   Re-read the Gardiner 'case' if necessary. Prepare an opening speech for the prosecution. Try to commit as many of the facts as possible to memory, and minimise the need to refer to a written note.

(b)   Those listening to the speeches should make notes on both content and style of the opening.

(c)   Reflect on performance, and give feedback as usual.

(d)   From this produce your own set of guidelines for an effective opening speech.

We suggest the following points are of note. We will also use some additional exercises to break opening down into its component parts and thereby help you to build on the above reflection.

First, the prosecution/claimant should always introduce themselves and the advocate appearing for the other side. In so doing it is important to bear in mind the need to maintain (a) a style of introduction appropriate to your court and (b) the correct modes of address for your judge(s) and your opponent.[16]

Secondly, we have already said that the chief function of an advocate is to tell their client's story to the court. In court, your story should be as brief as the facts allow; it should be plausible, and presented in language that is clear. Do not forget your basic oral communication skills: use eye contact, body language etc. to your advantage. Consider also who you have to persuade. How does that affect your sense of audience and the style of what you have to say? Try the following exercise.

### EXERCISE 11.5   The road map[17]

*Divide into pairs. In each pair one person should be designated the 'guide', the other the 'driver'. The 'driver' must select a road journey that is known to both participants. The 'guide' has one minute to describe the route. The 'driver' should then judge how well the 'guide' has performed the task.*

*After the first run-through 'driver' and 'guide' should exchange roles and repeat the exercise with a different start and finish point.*

It is important we do not forget the purpose of an opening (or closing) speech. It is to provide the advocate with an opportunity to present the story in a coherent narrative form. This is invaluable. In telling your story in an opening speech, however, you should not just set out to present 'the facts' as you see them; you should aim to:

- summarise your version of what has happened;
- identify the issues between the parties;[18]
- outline what your witnesses will say.

---

16. The formalities are outlined in most of the advocacy guides – see, e.g., J. Welsh, *Advocacy in the Magistrates' Court*, Cavendish, London, 2003, pp. 14–17.

17. Adapted from A. Sherr, *Advocacy*, Blackstone Press, London, 1993, p. 74.

18. This may be of less significance in a defence opening, if the territory has been covered objectively enough by the prosecution.

By so doing you are telling the tribunal of fact precisely what you are setting out to do and how you will do it. As in Exercise 11.5, the opening speech enables you to identify your route via the key landmarks along the way. In Pennington and Hastie's terms it provides you with an opportunity to establish 'goodness-of-fit' of your story with the verdict category you seek. To establish goodness-of-fit you normally need to focus on two themes:

- *Who is responsible for the relevant events*: remember that both the criminal and civil law, in most situations, are primarily concerned with allocating blame or finding fault. This is nearly always a key element of the facts in issue.
- What Gibbons calls *the complication*, that is the thing that goes wrong, or the causal or unforeseen event that is at the heart of your story.[19]

It is also worth noting that there is a line of psychological research[20] which suggests that if you misjudge the theme you pursue, so that there is a serious lack of fit between some parts of your story and the evidence, it is this mismatch that may be remembered better than the parts that fit!

While this warning is quite important, it is probably impossible wholly to guard against inconsistency. If things were that clear cut, there would be little need for a trial in the first place. But the fit should be as good as you can make it. If possible, you should try to find favourable explanations for such inconsistencies as arise in the course of the trial. Whether you should address such inconsistencies in your own opening is rather more debatable. What do you think are the pros and cons?

It might be useful to consider a real example here. Look how, in the second Gardiner trial, Wild sought to explain away the medicine bottle (of paraffin), which he seems to have regarded as the most critical piece of evidence against his client:

> But for [the bottle] Gardiner would never have been accused in this case. But the police in Peasenhall had got the bottle, and they said to themselves: 'Gardiner did this murder, and he has left his card. Out of consideration for us, in order not to tax our brains too heavily, Gardiner has considerately brought a labelled bottle with his name on it – and, of course, he did the murder.' If this were not a murder case, it would make us laugh ...
>
> In all probability the bottle was on that shelf which was broken, because you remember the shelf was standing above the side of the door and the bottle fell down, and the pieces were found just on the left of the girl's head. It would be exactly where they would be found if they fell off the shelf. The very fact of this paraffin falling in the scuffle that must have ensued made the [murderer] suddenly think: 'I will try to burn the body.' So he at once went to get the paraffin out of the lamp, and in his hurry neglected to hide the bottle.[21]

19. Gibbons, *Forensic Linguistics*, pp. 153–5.
20. See, e.g., R. Hastie, 'Memory for Behavioral Information that Confirms or Contradicts a Personality Impression' in R. Hastie, T. Ostrom, E. Ebbesen, R. Wyer, D. Hamilton and D. Carlston (eds.), *Person Memory: the Cognitive Basis of Social Perception*, Lawrence J Erlbaum, Hillsdale, NJ, 1980, p. 155.
21. Quoted in M. Fido and K. Skinner, *The Peasenhall Murder*, Alan Sutton, Stroud, 1990, p. 118.

What do you think of this extract? What is there about it that works for you? Is there anything that does not fit?

Lastly, you should always address the court on the law. In a criminal case before a jury the prosecution must explain the nature of the offence and the burden and standard of proof and also indicate the division of functions between judge and jury. Whether the defence wishes to go over this territory again is for the defence to decide. If the prosecutor has been wholly scrupulous and fair, it may be unnecessary to dwell on the same issues at length. However, it is usual to stress points such as the presumption of innocence together with any major procedural points affecting the prosecution case, e.g. the dangers (in a case such as Gardiner's) of convicting on circumstantial evidence.

In a civil case, the claimant's lawyer should open by stating the obvious – what the case is about, e.g.: 'May it please your Honour, this is a claim for damages for breach of contract.' This is really a standard ritualistic opening, but it is an easy way of getting started. It leads you into summarising the facts and reading through the statements of case (or giving the judge the opportunity to read through them). You should then briefly refer to any rule of law relevant to your case, and state why, on the law and facts, the claimant should succeed.

The defence may open as a matter of course before the High Court, but need not do so. In county court procedure, the practice tends to vary, but neither claimant nor defendant has an absolute entitlement to a second speech, so the common practice is for the claimant to open and defence to close.

### Closing speeches

The closing speech is the one aspect of the (criminal) trial which gives the advocate the occasional opportunity to indulge in Perry Mason fantasies! Most advocates regard the closing speech as potentially critical.[22] It gives both sides the opportunity to try and make a last impression on the bench or jury. The closing speech should contain the following:

- a reminder of your themes/theories;
- a recapitulation of the evidence;
- some reiteration of the relevant law;
- reference to burdens/standards of proof.

Again, this is not in any given order of tasks. In closing, it is often best (certainly for the defence) to stress first the onus on the jury, and then to consider the evidence. Once again, the best advice is to go for quality, not quantity. Keep it short and to the point. In recapping the evidence, try to follow the order in which it

---

22. Whether this intuitive view is wholly supportable on psychological grounds is doubtful – the complexity of the trial process as a whole makes it harder to predict in general which phase, if any, has the greatest potential impact on the tribunal of fact – see the discussion by E. Allan Lind and G. Ke, 'Opening and Closing Statements' in Kassin and Wrightsman, *The Psychology of Evidence and Trial Procedure*, Sage, Beverley Hills, 1985, p. 229 at pp. 242–3.

was presented and concentrate on the evidence critical to your themes/theories. In the closing speech concentrate on the evidence which best supports your case. In the first Gardiner trial, for example, Wild did this by stressing three key points in his client's favour:

> The first was – struggle and moving of the body, yet no sign of blood or paraffin on the clothes, boots or shoes of the accused man; the second, the agreement of independent explanations given by both husband and wife to the police before they had the opportunity of consulting; the third, that piece of cloth on the bottle, which was undoubtedly hacked in some way from the clothes of the murderer, but which was certainly not hacked from any clothes that the prisoner possessed.[23]

It is debatable whether some of its impact would have been lost on the jury as much else of Wild's speech was taken up with defensive work (some, perhaps, not wholly necessary) on his own evidence and some rather risky theorising, as we shall see in a moment.

If there is admissible evidence which damages your case, deal with it if you can by challenging its weight or interpretation. Try to make your challenge as reasoned and as objective as possible – do not be seen simply to dismiss it out of hand. If you have to make limited concessions, do so, and make it clear that this is what you are doing: it will make you seem reasonable. It should also heighten the impact of your challenge of other aspects of the evidence. There are two particular techniques that are widely used to challenge the opponent's case.

First, advocates often say that the best advice is always to concentrate on an opponent's weakest points – the principle of concentration of fire. This applies to cross-examination, to arguments about legal principles, and certainly to the closing speech. As we noted a moment ago, possibly the weakness of Wild as an advocate was his tendency to extemporise theories to explain away the prosecution case. One example of this was his attempt to divert attention by showing someone else had committed the killing: possibly a reasonable tactic, where the evidence supports it. But Wild had little reliable positive evidence to lay the blame elsewhere. When it came to the closing speeches, Dickens was able to dent Wild's case by taking up his suggestion and seeming to sink it, almost without trace:

> What conditions must be fulfilled in order to make the unknown man fit in with the circumstances of the case? He must have been the man who wrote the letter 'A' [the assignation note], who, according to the defence, wrote in a handwriting extraordinarily like the prisoner at the bar;[24] who on that night wore indiarubber

23. Fido and Skinner, *The Peasenhall Murder*, p. 94. Counsel for the Crown was never really able to explain these points away convincingly.
24. The dispute over handwriting was highly problematic at both trials. Forensic graphology was in its infancy. The prosecution had called one of very few 'professional' experts in the field, who had found few similarities between the note and Gardiner's handwriting, and indeed was contradictory in his own evidence. Though he did conclude that the authors of a letter written by Gardiner and the assignation note were the same, it was not a strong performance. See Fido and

shoes and walked to and fro between the prisoner's house and Providence House; a man who had a knife similar to the kind of knife found in the possession of the prisoner; who was curiously brought into connection with a medicine bottle bearing the words, 'Mrs Gardiner's children'; who got hold of those buff envelopes in order to write that letter making the assignation; who had the same reason to get rid of the woman as we have been able to prove the prisoner had; who must have been on the look-out for the light in the window at ten o'clock, in the way that the prisoner was; he must have been a man of such position that it was imperative for him to conceal his shame, as we say the prisoner's position was. It is my painful duty to point out these facts. Are all these coincidences? Is it probable that this unknown man who committed the murder must fulfil all the conditions which in every case point to the prisoner at the bar?[25]

What makes this an impressive piece of argument? Does it really matter that it had been countered in many particulars by defence evidence?

Second, it is often better if you can contradict evidence in an innocent rather than hostile fashion, for example, by finding a plausible explanation that a witness was mistaken rather than suggesting they were lying.

In assessing how much you need to say in a closing speech, you should rely heavily on your powers of observation. All through the trial you need to observe closely the reactions of participants: when is the judge writing (especially in examination/cross-examination)? When do jurors take notes/look bored/fidget/pay close attention? Use these elements to assess how aspects of the case have been received, and use that information to inform your approach to your closing speech. You should also use it generally for more pragmatic purposes – to gauge a jury's understanding of your points, your speed of delivery, etc.

We have so far provided a basic structure for opening and closing speeches and addressed some of the specific tactics that apply to each. However there are also a number of common threads that are worth exploring before we move on to consider interrogatory techniques.

**Techniques common to opening and closing**

First we wish to stress again that the ultimate purpose of a speech is to persuade. This engages the *rhetorical* dimension of advocacy. The great advocates of history are the orators who possess the ability to persuade by both the force of their arguments and their use of language. The grand style of rhetorical advocacy, personified in the great Victorian and Edwardian barristers like Marshall Hall, has passed out of fashion. But effective use of language and style has not. While it cannot wholly overcome poor logic and even less, poor preparation, it can help to sway the jury in your favour. Your syntax, the careful use of pace, metaphor,

---

Skinner, *The Peasenhall Murder*, pp. 83–4. The amateurs engaged by the defence fared even worse, with one suggesting that the writer of the assignation note was actually trying to imitate Gardiner's hand – hence Dickens's comment in this passage!

25. Ibid., p. 95.

repetition and the adoption of powerful imagery can all increase the rhetorical effect of your speech. Consider, for example, the next exercise.

### EXERCISE 11.6  Done to death?

*Assess the impact each of the following statements has as a plea against the imposition of the death penalty. What is it about them that is effective or ineffective?*[26]

### Reflections on the guillotine
*Albert Camus*

Instead of saying, 'If you kill someone you will pay for it on the scaffold', would it not be more politic – if we are interested in setting an example – to say instead: 'If you kill someone, you will be thrown into prison for months or even years, torn between an impossible despair and a constantly renewed fear, until one morning we will sneak into your cell, having taken off our shoes in order to surprise you in your sleep, which has at last overcome you after the night's anguish. We will throw ourselves upon you, tie your wrists behind your back, and with a pair of scissors cut away your shirt collar and your hair, if it should be in the way. Because we are perfectionists we will lash your arms together with a strap so that your body will be arched to offer unhampered access to the back of your neck. Then we will carry you, one man holding you up under each arm, your feet dragging behind you, down the long corridors, until, under the night sky, one of the executioners will at last take hold of the back of your trousers and throw you down on a board, another will make sure your head is in the lunette, and a third one will drop, from a height of two metres twenty centimetres, a blade weighing sixty kilograms that will slice through your neck like a razor.'

### Furman v Georgia
(1972) 408 US 238, 405

BLACKMAN J:    Cases such as these provide for me an excruciating agony of the spirit. I yield to no one in the depth of my distaste, antipathy, and, indeed, abhorrence for the death penalty, with all its aspects of physical distress and fear and of moral judgment exercised by finite minds. That distaste is buttressed by a belief that capital punishment serves no useful purpose that can be demonstrated. For me, it violates childhood's training and life's experiences, and is not compatible with the philosophical convictions I have been able to develop. It is antagonistic to any sense of 'reverence for life' . . .

It is comforting to relax in the thoughts – perhaps the rationalisations – that this is the compassionate decision for a maturing society; that this is the moral and the 'right'

26. Both passages are taken from J. White, *The Legal Imagination*, Little, Brown, Boston, 1973, pp. 131–2; 137–9.

thing to do; that thereby we convince ourselves that we are moving down the road toward human decency; that we value life even though that life has taken another or others or has grievously scarred another or others and their families; and that we are less barbaric than we were in 1879, or in 1890, or in 1910, or in 1947, or in 1958, or in 1963, or a year ago, in 1971, when *Wilkerson, Kemmler, Weems, Francis, Trop, Rudolph* and *McGautha* were respectively decided.

The focus on rhetoric emphasises the extent to which lawyers need to influence the tribunal of fact, to use the psychological jargon, 'affectively' (meaning through their feelings and emotions) as well as cognitively. Boon stresses the importance of using issues of fact as 'psychological anchors'[27] to achieve this end. 'Psychological anchors' are points of fact that are so significant the jury will not only remember them, but may use them to organise and make sense of the conflicting stories in the trial. Boon takes as an example of the use of an anchor, the opening speech of Sir Norman Birkett in his prosecution of Alfred Rouse for murder.[28] The passage opens with the report of a conversation between Rouse and two strangers he passed on the road shortly after setting fire to the car:

> ... one of them said 'What is the blaze up there?' pointing to a glare up the lane, and then, having gone 15 or 20 yards beyond the men, the accused said these very remarkable words: 'It looks as if someone is having a bonfire up there'. Members of the jury, you will hear what was found up that lane. You will hear the accused's part in it, and you will bear in mind at every stage of this case the fact that, right at the outset, when the accused met these two young men, he passed without a word. No appeal for help! No call for assistance! Nothing. And then 'it looks as though someone is having a bonfire up there'. You will hear what he called a bonfire was the burning of his own car; and that there was the body of that unknown man being steadily burned beyond all recognition. The significance of the remark 'It looks as though someone is having a bonfire up there' cannot be over-emphasised in view of the fact that 400 yards away there was that terrible fire. The car had shortly before been drawn up by the side of the road by the prisoner himself; he had shut off the engine and put on the brake ... and yet, at that moment, his observation to these two young men was 'It looks as if someone is having a bonfire' ...[29]

What is it in this speech that makes the psychological anchor so effective? You might want to look back at the work you did in Exercise 11.2 – to what extent was the memorability of your story shaped by your ability to create such anchors?

---

27. Boon, *Advocacy*, p. 75ff.
28. Rouse was convicted of killing a man to whom he had given a lift in his car. It transpired that he had strangled the man and then set fire to the car in an attempt to destroy the body sufficiently to prevent its identification. His aim thereby was to fake his own death, so that he could disappear with his mistress. Rouse confessed after the trial, and was executed in March 1931. His victim was never identified. The text of the trial has been republished in the Penguin *Famous Trials* series.
29. Cited in Boon, *Advocacy*, p. 78.

Second, we suggest that *focus* is also essential. In a jury trial, it is the jury that you have to persuade. You ignore your jury at your peril – particularly at the opening and final stages. Focus on the jury: you want to make eye contact and to observe their reactions, though not to the extent that you are entering into an individual staring match, or constantly shifting your gaze to one or other of twelve pairs of eyes – try this and you will probably end up appearing nervous, shifty, cross-eyed or some permutation of the three! Talk to the jury, not to the judge, or some point on the floor, or half way up the wall. Try to make them feel that they are your exclusive audience, and that they want to hear what you have to say.

Third, you should use your speeches to try to establish and maintain an organising *frame* that helps give coherence to your story. That frame may be technical, causal or chronological: each has its own particular uses. For example, a technical frame is one which adopts some technical organising principle – based upon a scientific or legal concept that is central to the case. It will often serve in cases, especially civil cases before a professional judge, where you can afford to organise your factual information around the legally relevant categories, such as duty, breach, and damage. A causal frame seeks to describe circumstances according to some recognisable behavioural explanation – e.g. where the defence might try to argue that the situation was such that the accused acted under extreme provocation. A chronological frame is one that is commonly adopted. In this you establish an order of events that makes sense of what happened. The advantage of a chronological approach for new advocates is that it will usually fit easily with any theory of the case you wish to pursue. Both causal and chronological explanations fit particularly neatly with conventional story structures.

Whichever type of frame you adopt, there are two things you need to be aware of. First, you are, to an extent, prioritising one aspect of the communication episode that is your story. This is fine, so long as you recognise that the frame forms part of a wider story which the tribunal of fact needs to understand. To take the chronological example, it is one thing to stress what happened and when, but the court will often need to understand how and why as well. The frame is only an organising principle, not an end in itself. Second, for much the same reason, it needs to connect logically to your theory of the case.

## Summary

*WHEN OPENING:*
- INTRODUCE THE ADVOCATES.
- ESTABLISH YOUR FACTUAL THEORY AND THEMES.
- IDENTIFY WHAT YOUR WITNESSES WILL SAY.
- DON'T FORGET TO EXPLAIN THE LEGAL ISSUES AND BURDEN/STANDARD OF PROOF.
- REMEMBER THE POWER OF RHETORIC.

*WHEN CLOSING:*
- IDENTIFY WHAT HAS TO BE PROVED AND BY WHOM.
- REITERATE THEORY/THEMES.

- SHOW THE LINKS BETWEEN LAW AND EVIDENCE.
- IDENTIFY WEAKNESSES IN OPPONENT'S CASE.
- TELL THE TRIER OF FACT WHAT YOU WANT.
- REMEMBER THE POWER OF RHETORIC.

## Other narrative contexts

As we have said, we don't just use narrative styles of advocacy for opening and closing speeches. Many of the common forms of advocacy that you might come across as a new advocate also involve primarily presentational and narrative skills, notably when:

- making or opposing a bail application;
- offering a plea in mitigation (before sentencing);
- representing a defendant at a 'plea before venue' (PBV);[30]
- making or opposing interlocutory applications (in civil proceedings).

Before leaving this section we will give you an opportunity to practise your skills in one of these contexts – making and opposing a bail application. Bail is an important part of criminal procedure for more serious offences, where a court would have the power to remand an accused in custody pending trial. Under the Bail Act 1976, as amended, [31] there is a general presumption in favour of granting an accused bail, as an alternative to custody. When the issue of bail comes up for consideration both prosecution and defence can make submissions to the court on whether or not bail should be granted. Many students get confused on the law here. Bail can only be refused where there are valid objections to bail being granted, except where an accused has already absconded on bail, in which case the presumption is now reversed – it becomes a presumption against bail. We are not going to do all the work for you – this is part of your preparation, but you should be aware that an objection to bail can only be based on one or more of the statutory 'objections' laid down in the Act (e.g. that there are substantial grounds for believing that, if granted bail, the accused would fail to surrender to custody, or that the defendant has already absconded). Having specified an objection, the prosecution must also identify the *grounds* on which that objection is based. The grounds are, if you like, the particular facts on which an objection is based. There are thus numerous grounds that can be relied on. For example, if the prosecution object to bail on the basis that the accused is likely to abscond, the grounds for

---

30. The plea before venue is a relatively new procedure when deciding whether an 'either way' offence is to be tried summarily or in the Crown Court. This procedure enables the justices to know what the plea is likely to be before deciding on venue. This helps them assess which cases are going to the Crown Court on a guilty plea, and thus will be disposed of quickly without any further investigation. For further information on the PBV procedure, see *Blackstone's Criminal Practice*, Oxford University Press, Oxford (published annually), or Welsh, *Advocacy in the Magistrates Court*, ch. 9.
31. You need to be aware when researching this area that the 1976 Act has been substantially amended by Part 2 of the Criminal Justice Act 2003.

the objection may be that the accused is a single, unemployed man with few connections to the locality, and that the gravity of the offence is such that the court may wish to impose a custodial sentence; i.e. the prosecution is thus making out a case, based on these grounds, that it is likely that he will abscond.

The defence are entitled to make a submission opposing refusal, e.g. by seeking to explain away the prosecutor's grounds for objecting. The defence can also try to offer conditions (e.g. residence or curfew conditions) which may seem to meet the fears of the prosecution, as a way of staving off a refusal of bail. Consequently, bail applications can be looked upon as both quite technical and tactical procedures.

EXERCISE 11.7  **Bailing out?**

Using the case papers distributed by your tutor, prepare and make applications:

    (a)    for the prosecution, opposing the granting of bail;
    (b)    for the defence, opposing objections to bail.

At the end of the exercise, review your performance, reflecting:

    (i)    on the quality of your presentation skills;
    (ii)    on your technical understanding of the law and procedure;
    (iii)    on the tactics you adopted.

## Examining witnesses

The skills required for the examination of witnesses differ substantially from those used in other forms of advocacy. There are also significant stylistic and tactical differences between the different forms of examination. Accordingly, we have divided this section of the chapter into three parts, to consider examination in chief, cross-examination and re-examination respectively.

### Examination in chief

Surprising though it may sound, examining your own witness is probably the most difficult of the advocacy skills to develop. Why might that be?

We think it is difficult for three reasons:

- You are seeking to present a witness's story in a non-narrative form.
- You are constrained in the type of questions you may ask.
- At the same time, you are attempting to protect that testimony from effective cross-examination.

Let us now look at how these difficulties arise, and how they are best dealt with.

We have already said that the structure of the examination is interrogatory. That is, it works by the process of question and answer, thus:

EXERCISE 11.8  **Twenty questions?**

Read the following extract from a fictitious examination in chief:

Q:    Mrs Smith, can you please tell the court where you were on the evening of 3 February 1995? (*This question assumes that, broadly speaking, the time and date are not in dispute*).

A:    I was at home.

Q:    Did you stay at home all evening, or did you go out?

A:    Well, I went out once, to get some cigarettes.

Q:    Can you recall what time that was?

A:    It must have been about 8 o'clock.

Q:    And did anything in particular happen while you were out?

A:    Yes, it was just before I got to the newsagent's on the corner. I saw this young couple arguing.

Q:    Can you tell the court more precisely what you saw?

A:    Well, they were really having a go at each other, shouting and screaming . . .

Consider the following questions.

(a)    *What type of questions is the advocate using here?*

(b)    *What effects does this form of question and answer process have on the narrative? Note down three or four points before you continue reading.*

Although this is a simple illustration, you have probably come up with a number of both positive and negative aspects to the process. We have noted some of our own ideas below.

On the positive side, it has a number of practical advantages. The use of clear, focused, questions gives you, the advocate, substantial control over the direction in which the testimony is going by making sure you just get small chunks of very specific information. It helps make your witnesses cross-examination proof by limiting the risk of them introducing inconsistencies in their evidence. Such questions should also help make the information clear to the jury. However, it thus puts the onus on you to maintain narrative coherence.

On the negative side, it potentially makes the storytelling process far more drawn out than in everyday talk – it can easily take half a dozen questions to establish who the witness is, and what their connection with events is – before you actually get into the details of the story. Listening to evidence elicited in this way can become very tedious for judge or jury. As we have seen, it can serve to fragment the narrative and may present the witness as 'powerless'.[32] This might appear to create difficulties for all sides in the criminal process, but research in fact suggests it creates a particular bias against defence witnesses, often precisely because of their lack of courtroom experience:

32. See p. 394, above.

... we were struck by the fact that a whole lineup of witnesses for certain defendants produced testimony that was hard to reconstruct in story form, while prosecution witnesses (particularly police officers and experts) delivered accounts that fit easily into coherent stories.[33]

A neat example of the effect courtroom experience can have is offered by the cross-examination of Wright in the second Gardiner trial. Wright had been seriously embarrassed by Wild's cross-examination of his version of the chapel incident in the first trial. However, he was rather more ready the second time around, and even won one exchange against his sharp-tongued cross-examiner:

WILD: Did you leave out [in the magistrates' court] about hearing Rose Harsent say 'Oh, oh!' and hearing the rustling noise?

WRIGHT: Yes, I left that out.

WILD: Why?

WRIGHT: Because it did not come into my mind; there was a long time between.

WILD: But there is a longer time between [then and] now?

WRIGHT: I have been over it since.

WILD: Oh! Who have you been over it with?

WRIGHT: I have with you.[34]

So, how do we limit the fragmentation and anomie caused by interrogatory advocacy? Think about this and then try the next exercise.

### EXERCISE 11.9 *R v Wainwright*

Garry Wainwright has been charged with assault occasioning actual bodily harm to Terry Kline. Wainwright has claimed he acted in self-defence. Your tutor will give you a witness statement from an eyewitness to the incident, Jenny Lee, who has been called as a witness for the prosecution.

Select a pair of volunteers: one to act as advocate, the other to act as witness. They should both take some time to familiarise themselves with the witness statement and prepare for the examination (10 minutes should suffice). The rest of the group should pretend to be the jury. Jurors should not look at the witness statement.

*Tasks:*

- Student A: examine Jenny in chief;
- Student B: answer questions put by counsel;
- Group: take notes.

---

33. Bennet and Feldman, *Reconstructing Reality in the Courtroom*, p. 174. This overlooks the extent to which victim-witnesses may themselves often be subject to the same disadvantages – cf. the case analysis in P. Rock, *The Social World of an English Crown Court*, Clarendon Press, Oxford, 1993, pp. 95–129, especially at pp. 127–9.
34. See Fido and Skinner, *The Peasenhall Murder*, p. 106.

So how easy or difficult did you find that? In our experience, most student advocates find it rather easier than expected. In some respects, it should not be that difficult, as the statement is short and reasonably chronological in its order. But is that intuition right?

### EXERCISE 11.10 You, the jury

Now, ask at least two members of the jury to repeat the evidence they have heard.

(a)    *Did they get the date and time the events took place?*
(b)    *Did they get an identification of the accused?*
(c)    *Are they clear that, on Jenny's evidence, it was not Terry's fault?*
(d)    *What was the advocate's organising frame?*
(e)    *What do they think was the advocate's theory of the case?*

So, let's use the Wainwright case to reflect more generally on the examination in chief.

First, in preparing the case, get a clear sense of how each witness's testimony relates to the whole story you are trying to tell. Part of the difficulty in the Wainwright exercise is that there is not a complete case history to provide that context. It is a bit like going into court when you have not had time to go through all the case papers.

Second, it is critical, if you can, to maintain 'story order'[35] – i.e. a sequence of testimony that matches the temporal or causal sequence of the events (which you have already emphasised by your choice of frame in opening, or will emphasise in closing). Pennington and Hastie indicate that significant differences between story and witness order make it far harder for the jury to construct the story for themselves.[36] As we have noted, there are few procedural constraints on witness order, so it should normally be possible to set up the appropriate witness order for yourself.[37]

Next, you need to think about the way you phrase your questions. Closed questioning gives you a lot of control and direction, but it reduces the witness's freedom. In some situations, the last thing you will want to do is give the witness freedom, but in others it is more effective to let the jury hear the story in the witness's words, with little interruption from you. The use of open questions (i.e. of the 'what happened next?'/'what did you do then?' variety) will certainly help. If your witness is a good story teller, do not interrupt the flow. The jury will find the

---

35. N. Pennington and R. Hastie, 'The Story Model for Juror Decision Making' in R. Hastie (ed.), *Inside the Juror: The Psychology of Juror Decision Making*, Cambridge University Press, Cambridge, 1993, p. 210.
36. *Ibid.*, pp. 210–12.
37. Note, however, that if an accused testifies, she must do so before any other witnesses to the facts, unless the court in its discretion decides otherwise: Police and Criminal Evidence Act 1984, s. 79. The parties in civil cases normally testify first also, but this is customary rather than required by law.

witness's story far more memorable if it is not consistently interrupted. But, do remember that a great deal of your tactics will depend on your perception of the witness's quality. If you are uncertain about how your witness will come across, of what she will say, or of your own ability to redirect a narrative that has gone off in the wrong direction, then keep the witness under close control. On balance, the best examinations are generally those which use a mixture of questioning styles. Try using a technique like the funnel or 'T' technique[38] in your questioning in court.

You can also use the style and direction of questioning to help sustain your storyline. Two particular techniques are useful here: these are the use of *transitional questions* and of *points of reference*.

A transitional question is a means of moving a witness from one topic to another. It is permissible, though not necessary, to signal that change by some kind of short statement, such as 'I would like to turn now to the circumstances of your meeting with Mr Jones'. You can also use such statements to help highlight the key issues in the testimony.

Points of reference can be helpful in adding emphasis or detail to the testimony. It is a method of including in a further question reference to a fact already stated by the witness. Thus:

Q:   Did the defendant have anything in his possession?
A:   Yes, he was holding a gun.
Q:   Can you describe the gun that he was holding?

emphasises the importance of the gun and gives the witness the cue to provide more detailed testimony about the weapon.

Lastly (within the context of each examination), you should also think about the order of the questions you ask. How did you start the examination of Jenny Lee? What did you allow the jury to find out about her as a person? Did you establish her connection to the victim? It is a good idea for a number of reasons to start with the testimony that is most familiar to the witness, and least contentious. This usually means you start by asking about *them* rather than the incident. It helps get your witnesses used to testifying. For example, if you are examining a witness about an accident at work you might begin by asking them about the job they do, how long they have been employed etc., before getting into the details of the accident. Most judges and opposing counsel understand the need to build up the witness in this way, and will not usually challenge the relevance of such early questions, provided you keep the process brief, and reasonably relevant. These contextual questions can also help 'personalise' your witness and make them and their evidence more memorable, perhaps even more believable.

It makes sense to rough out a plan of your questions, based on each witness's proof of evidence. This helps you keep track of the issues and, so long as the proofs have been ordered chronologically, it helps you sustain the chronology too.

38. See Chapter 5, above.

However, even with a plan of the examination, witnesses can wander off course. How do you bring them back? The answer lies in your ability to link the issues coherently, so as to move the witness from where she is now to where you want her to be. Try it with the next exercise.

### EXERCISE 11.11 The gestatory period of the African elephant[39]

Divide the group into pairs – one advocate and one witness. The witness must think of a topic as far away from the gestatory period of the African elephant as possible. Tell your advocate what the subject is.

*The advocate must begin the examination by asking this question: 'Do you know what is the gestatory period of the African elephant?' Using the witness's answer, the advocate must link in the next question and following questions until the advocate can get to a question on the witness's chosen topic.*

One reason why linking can be difficult in trial contexts is that you are normally not allowed to lead your own witness. So all of you who got through Exercise 11.9 by leading Jenny through her evidence should consider yourselves disbarred!

It is not always easy to spot, never mind avoid, leading questions. Leading questions are those which are phrased so as to assume facts which are yet to be proven. The effect of leading questions is to diminish the testimony – the facts come from the advocate, not the witness. For example, a question phrased: 'Did you see Smith driving down the road?' would be a leading question if it had not been established already by that witness that Smith was present at the time and place referred to, and that he was driving, rather than walking, riding a unicycle or any other form of transport. Try and work the next one out for yourselves.

### EXERCISE 11.12 You lead and I'll follow

*Read the following extract. Which question(s) if any are leading and in what circumstances?*

> Note: Assume the following exchange takes place in the examination in chief of a witness to the facts who will testify that he saw the accused punch the victim in a pub brawl. We come in just after the witness has identified himself . . .

Q:    Mr Birks, please tell the court your occupation.
A:    I'm a barman.
Q:    And where do you work?
A:    At the Frog and Frigate in Dilchester High Street.
Q:    Have you ever seen the accused before?
A:    Yes, I know him.

39. From Sherr, *Advocacy*, p. 87.

Q:   How do you know him?

A:   Because he is a regular at the Frog and Frigate.

Q:   Did you see the accused on the evening of 12 April 200X?

A:   Yes.

Q:   In the Frog and Frigate?

A:   That's right.

Q:   Did anything happen in the pub that night?

A:   Yeah, there was a punch-up.

Leading a witness leaves you open to challenge by your opponent, and to rebuke by the judge.[40] In either case it can damage your witness's credibility by giving the impression that you cannot trust the witness to tell her own story.

A useful guide to avoiding leading questions is what Murphy and Barnard term the 'two-for-one rule'.[41] They point out that most leading questions are asked because the advocate is trying to be too specific. You should try asking two questions instead of one. If you take a step back, and ask a more general or open question first (e.g. 'what happened?', 'where did you go?', 'what did you do then?') you can use that to lead into the specifics. Try this on the text in Exercise 11.12.

The best practice is to avoid leading the witness whenever possible. However, there are times when leading is permissible, and sometimes necessary.

*It is permissible to lead on facts which are not in issue.* This is a right which should be used judiciously, as it is easy to get into the habit of leading the witness. It is vital to keep in mind the boundaries of what is or is not in dispute when framing leading questions. For example, in Exercise 11.12, if it is not disputed that the defendant was in the pub, the question 'In the Frog and Frigate?' is unobjectionable. If the accused claims misidentification, the question would be leading.

*You can lead in situations where you have obtained the agreement of the other side.* This tends to happen only where the evidence is not in dispute, or at least not really crucial, or where the distress caused to the witness by giving testimony in the ordinary way would be so counter-productive that the other side are happy to agree.[42] If you get agreement to lead, you should tell the judge of this before you begin the examination.

*If a witness is hostile,[43] you are entitled to lead that witness.* In effect the rules allow you, within certain parameters, to cross-examine a witness you have called. You can only treat a witness as hostile with the leave of the judge.

---

40. Evidence obtained in chief by leading questions carries little evidential weight: *Moor v Moor* [1954] 1 WLR 927.

41. P. Murphy and D. Barnard, *Evidence and Advocacy*, Blackstone Press, London, 4th edn, 1994, p. 143.

42. In the second Gardiner trial, for example, Dickens and Wild agreed that Dickens could lead Rose's father through his testimony, to save him the distress of having to describe in his own words, for the fourth time, how he found his murdered daughter.

43. See Criminal Procedure Act 1865, s. 3; Civil Evidence Act 1968, s. 3(1). A witness is hostile if they testify against your interests through malice or bad faith: see *R v Prefas and Pryce* (1988) 86 Cr App R 111.

Sometimes it will be worth taking the risk and deliberately leading the witness on a particular point, especially if failure to lead may mean that your witness does not come up to proof on a key part of her testimony. An objection from the other side will be of limited use at this stage. The question has been asked, and even if you are required to re-phrase it, it has served its purpose: the witness has been reminded of the critical event.

EXERCISE 11.13 **There are more questions than answers**...

Assume the following is the transcript of an examination by the prosecutor (P) in an assault case where accused and complainant are husband and wife. The witness is a neighbour. P is seeking to establish where she was when the events happened, and the fact that she heard the husband threaten his wife at a time consistent with the latter's complaint.

*Consider:*
(a)   *The nature of each question asked – what sort of question is it?*
(b)   *How effective is each question at carrying the story along?*
(c)   *Are there other questions you might want to ask, or questions you would ask differently?*

Q:   May it please your Honour, I call Mrs Sally Sings.(*Witness enters and takes the oath.*)
Q:   Please give the court your full name and address.
A:   Sally Margaret Sings, and I live at Flat 143, Bevan Tower, Summerhayes Lane, Bristol.
Q:   So you are a resident of the same flats as the defendant and his wife?
A:   Yes, they live just opposite me.
Q:   Have you lived there long?
A:   About six years.
Q:   And have you got to know Mr and Mrs Jackson in that time?
A:   Oh yes, they moved in shortly after me, and Janice and me, well, neither of us work, so we've got to know each other pretty well.
Q:   Would you say that you know the defendant, Mr Jackson, well?
A:   Mike? Not really well; he doesn't much like me going across to their flat. He says Jan and me spend too much time gossiping.
Q:   I see. Let me now turn to the real issue here. Do you recall anything particular happening on the evening of 15 June 2004?
A:   Yes, there was a fight between Mike and Janice.
Q:   How do you know this?
A:   I heard them.
Q:   How did you come to hear them?
A:   I had just got back from Tesco's with my shopping. I put the bags down outside my door while I got the keys from my handbag. I could hear them

shouting at each other through the wall. You can hear a mouse sneeze through those walls, they're that thin. Anyway, I could hear him really shouting at Jan, going mad he was – then she screamed . . .

Q: Could you hear anything that was said?

A: A lot, I reckon, there was certainly enough f–ing and blinding.

Q: Could you hear what Mr Jackson said?

A: Yes. I heard him say something like 'I'll get you for that, you bitch'.

Q: You are quite sure that was what he said?

A: Yes.

Q: So you have no doubt that it was the defendant who attacked Mrs Jackson?

A: No, none.

Q: What happened after that?

A: That was when she screamed. And I got my keys, ran into the flat and phoned the police.

Q: And then?

A: Well, after I put the phone down, I just sat and waited for a bit. I hardly dared go out. I heard their door slam after a minute or two. I went out into the corridor. I couldn't hear anything from their flat. I knocked on the door. Jan came to the door, and said 'Who is it?' I said it was me, and she opened the door. She was in a bad way. She had a bloody nose – I think it was broken – and she had been crying. I think I said something like 'Oh Jan', and we both had a bit of a weep, then the police arrived.

Q: Thank you, Mrs Sings. Please wait there.

## Summary

*WHEN EXAMINING IN CHIEF*:

- NEVER LEAD, UNLESS YOU REALLY HAVE TO.
- PLAN THOROUGHLY, BOTH FRAME AND QUESTIONS.
- MAKE THE LINKS TO YOUR THEORY AS EXPLICIT AS YOU CAN.
- KEEP TO STORY ORDER.

## Cross-examination

Imagine you are representing Mike Jackson in court. You now have the chance to cross-examine Mrs Sings. Your client maintains that his wife started the argument, and struck him two or three times. He will testify that her injury was caused unintentionally when he slammed the bedroom door shut, just as his wife launched herself at him. The Jackson's next-door neighbour will testify that he heard a door slam just before Mrs Jackson screamed. Mr Jackson has a low opinion of Mrs Sings, whom he regards as a busybody. As he puts it: 'Jan tells her all sorts, which she then spreads around her mates in the flats – all sorts of rubbish about us. I had it out with her once – was none too polite about it. She's had it in for me ever since.'

EXERCISE 11.14 **The worm turns?**

*You have two minutes in which to decide:*

(a)    *Do you cross-examine Mrs Sings at all? Why/why not?*
(b)    *If you do, what will you want to achieve by that cross-examination?*

This exercise is intended to establish two very basic points. One, that you should not assume that you need to cross-examine every witness the other side presents, and, two, that you need to identify quickly, but carefully, your aims in cross-examining.

So, first, how do you decide whether or not to cross-examine? It is likely that several factors will influence your decision.

You need to consider how close to the 'truth' of the events the witness's testimony is. You might assess this by virtue of the evidence's consistency or inconsistency with other testimony in your possession, or by its internal coherence, and its vividness – i.e. the depth and detail of the description.[44] If the evidence scores highly on such criteria there may be little to gain from cross-examination. A cross-examination which merely reinforces the other side's case clearly does you little good.

Equally, you may feel that not to cross-examine the witness (especially if this is the only witness you do not intend to cross-examine) will itself have a damaging effect on your case. Arguably, you will be seen by the jury to be giving absolute credence to that testimony, or in some way avoiding a confrontation with the witness or her evidence. Moreover, if there is a direct conflict between your client's version of events and this witness's, you have some responsibility to your client to put the case, even if this means you end up with a string of denials. In such a situation, it is advisable to keep the cross-examination low key, and you should not try too hard to test the witness.

Assessing which is the right decision is terribly hard. It is one aspect of advocacy where, trite though it sounds, experience really does tell.

If you decide to cross-examine, you need to have a clear idea of what you want to achieve. Any cross-examination has two basic aims:

- To advance your own case.
- To undermine the case for the opposition.

These aims can be achieved by a number of tactics, some of which can serve both ends.

---

44. Whether or not such vivid descriptions are true, they tend to be seen as convincing – a view shared by advocacy texts and psychologists – see, e.g., E. Loftus and J. Goodman, 'Questioning Witnesses' in Kassin and Wrightsman (eds.), *The Psychology of Evidence and Trial Procedure*, Sage, Beverley Hills, 1985, pp. 265–6; M. Stone, *Proof of Fact in Criminal Trials*, W. Green & Son, Edinburgh, 1984, pp. 181–5.

**Try to obtain favourable testimony**

Do not make the mistake of assuming that a witness called by the other side is inevitably hostile towards your case. Most witnesses can be led into giving testimony that will support your case in some detail or other.

In seeking favourable testimony an obvious approach is to look for possible points of consensus – e.g. on a point of identification evidence, will this witness support your client's contention about the lighting conditions/distance apart at the time of the sighting/length of the sighting, etc.? Such an admission may provide valuable corroboration.

Equally, you may try to obtain favourable testimony by other means. Consider, for example, Sir Edward Carson's cross-examination of Oscar Wilde,[45] which is often thought of as a copybook example. Carson's defence was one of justification, which had the effect of putting Wilde's character in issue. Carson therefore set out, first, to build a picture of Wilde as an immoral person before adducing direct evidence of his homosexuality.[46] In the following extract, Wilde is being cross-examined on the significance of his novel, *A Portrait of Dorian Gray*. Carson began by reading a short extract from the book:

CARSON: 'There is no such thing as a moral or immoral book. Books are well written or badly written.' That expresses your view?

WILDE: My view on art, yes.

CARSON: Then I take it, no matter how immoral a book may be, if it is well written, it is, in your opinion, a good book?

WILDE: Yes, if it were well written so as to produce a sense of beauty, which is the highest sense of which a human being can be capable. If it were badly written, it would produce a sense of disgust.

CARSON: Then a well-written book putting forward perverted moral views may be a good book?

WILDE: No work of art ever puts forward views. Views belong to people who are not artists.

CARSON: A perverted novel might be a good book?

WILDE: I don't know what you mean by a 'perverted' novel.

CARSON: Then I will suggest *Dorian Gray* is open to the interpretation of being such a novel?

WILDE: That could only be to brutes and illiterates. The views of philistines on art are unaccountable...

CARSON: The majority of persons come under your definition of Philistines and illiterates?

---

45. This is taken from Wilde's action against Lord Queensberry in 1895, for the alleged criminal libel of calling Wilde a 'sodomite'.
46. The direct evidence was never adduced in this trial; the threat was sufficient for Wilde, on legal advice, to withdraw the action. It did come out in the later prosecutions of Wilde himself for indecency.

WILDE: I have found wonderful exceptions.

CARSON: Do you think the majority of people live up to the position you are giving us?

WILDE: I am afraid they are not cultivated enough.

CARSON: Not cultivated enough to draw the distinction between a good book and a bad book?

WILDE: Certainly not.

CARSON: The affection and love of the artist of *Dorian Gray* might lead an ordinary individual to believe that it might have a certain tendency?

WILDE: I have no knowledge of the views of ordinary individuals.

CARSON: You did not prevent the ordinary individual from buying your book?

WILDE: I have never discouraged him![47]

What devices does Carson use to get Wilde to damn himself by his testimony?

### Always be seen to 'put your case'

In cross-examination you should put to the witness every fact disputed by your client to which that witness is competent to speak. This is called putting your case. It is a vital part of any good cross-examination and is a central means of advancing your theory of the case. In its simplest form, putting your case can involve questioning by confrontation – traditionally lawyers have used a ritualised form of question to signal this, thus: 'I put it to you that (X happened)', but this style has fallen out of favour. Putting your case can be achieved by a number of more subtle means.

In the Gardiner trials, for example, Wild recognised that the time of the murder was at issue. The key witness here was Mrs Crisp, who heard Rose's scream in the night. Mrs Crisp had been uncertain about the time when she testified, both before the Coroner at the inquest, and before the magistrates. The prosecution theory of the case was undoubtedly weak on this point. They did not challenge Gardiner's alibi and thus, implicitly, left it to the jury to determine whether Gardiner could have committed the killing after leaving Mrs Dickinson's, and before going to bed at about 2.00 a.m. Wild's cross-examination of Mrs Crisp pressed home the advantage. He obtained two vital admissions: first, that it could have been after midnight when she and Mr Crisp first came downstairs; second, that the storm was still raging when she heard Rose scream. This placed the time of the murder squarely within the period for which Gardiner had an alibi.

### Insinuation

Questioning by insinuation is an important means of putting your case to the witness. It is a technique in which you present your theory of the case as a

---

47. Adapted from H. Montgomery Hyde (ed.), *Famous Trials 7: Oscar Wilde*, Penguin Books, Harmondsworth, 1962, pp. 109–10.

counterpoint to the theory which opposing counsel had initially tried to establish through the same witness. The effect of insinuating cross-examination is to give force and momentum to your version of the facts. Wild used insinuation against Wright in the second Gardiner trial, to suggest malice against Gardiner as a motive behnd his evidence:

WILD: Were you found fault with in your work?
WRIGHT: No; not by Mr Smyth.
WILD: Mr Gardiner?
WRIGHT: No, I don't think I was.
WILD: You don't know one way or the other?
WRIGHT: I feel perfectly sure.
WILD: You feel a little surer as you go on? (*Laughter*)[48]

What impact does Wild's questioning have, do you think? How does he achieve that effect?

Various techniques of insinuation can be used. Accusations are routinely made against opponent's witnesses, and these are most effective because they are treated as routine. The advocate can, by tone of voice and choice of phrase, signal to the jury that a witness's mendacity is to be expected. It is not a subject for histrionics, but, rather, so self-evident as to require no especial comment:

> Accusations would be slipped in and proved by fiat: in one ordinary instance, a defence counsel asked a police officer, 'Having been abusive to him, did you . . .' as if the abusiveness itself was not in doubt.[49]

Witnesses' partiality is similarly to be signalled by phrase and tone – 'According to your version of events'; 'yet you insist that . . .' and so on. In its most powerful form insinuation can operate by the use of false leads[50] and what the American literature calls 'tag questions' – where the question is presented in the form 'You did x, didn't you'. Thus, instead of saying: 'Did you see the accused?' you could ask: 'You saw the accused, didn't you?' Research suggests that, where people are under pressure, tag questions are more likely to receive a positive response than less loaded questions.[51]

It is not usually necessary to put the same challenges to successive witnesses, unless you anticipate getting inconsistent responses, or particularly wish to emphasise some aspect of your case to the jury.

48. Fido and Skinner, *The Peasenhall Murder*, p. 105.
49. Loftus and Goodman, 'Questioning Witnesses', p. 261.
50. For example, where you might ask, 'Could you describe the colour of the defendant's coat?' knowing full well the defendant was not wearing one at the time. Unless the witness spots the trap and answers accordingly, you have got them – even the answer 'No' is potentially damaging to a question of this sort.
51. E. Loftus, 'Language and memories in the judicial system' in R. Shuy and A. Shnukal (eds.), *Language Use and the Uses of Language*, Georgetown Unversity Press, Washington, 1980, p. 257.

**Look for ways to discredit the witness's testimony**

This is probably the most common form of cross-examination. It does not mean that you are challenging every witness and proclaiming them to be liars. The tactic of saying to a witness 'I suggest that you are lying' is risky. You may use this technique to plant doubts about the veracity of the witness, but as it is most likely to get the response 'No I'm not', you need to be reasonably sure that your jury are going to be more persuaded by your accusation than the witness's denial. Unless you have a previous inconsistent statement which you intend to prove, you are stuck with that answer![52] Moreover, you are on ethically shaky ground if you cannot substantiate your accusation: an advocate must not make an allegation which is 'intended only to insult, vilify or annoy either a witness or some other person'.[53] Discrediting can be achieved legitimately and more effectively by either attacking the witness's recollection itself, or the reliability of that witness more generally – provided the evidence supports your attack.

There are a number of techniques that can work here, in particular:

- *Leading questions*, which are the stock in trade of cross-examination, can be used to force a witness into an admission against their own interests. For example, in Birkett's cross-examination of Rouse, Birkett uses three steps to obtain a damaging admission from Rouse. First, he adopts a line of questioning which shows that Rouse had a 'fair working knowledge of cars', including knowledge of the petrol supply system. He then shifts focus onto one of the key elements of the prosecution case – that Rouse had the specific knowledge to set a fire like the one he was alleged to have set. He achieved this by using a series of leading questions to obtain admissions from Rouse: (i) that he knew the location of the leaking union joint; (ii) that he had experienced a leaking union joint before (though not in that car), and (iii) that he knew such a leak would, in a Morris Minor car, result in petrol coming onto the floor of the car. Finally, Birkett uses another leading question to obtain the damaging admission from Rouse that he knew that a very loose union joint would result in a steady flow of petrol on to the floor of the car.[54] This admission was consistent with evidence the prosecution expert had already given in chief; that same expert had also testified that it was unlikely that the fire had started accidentally.

- *Probing* questions – use our old friends 5WH (Who? What? When? Where? Why? or How?) to concentrate on inconsistencies or points where, from proofs of evidence, or from their performance in chief, you suspect the witness's recollection may be unreliable. (Though you need to be very careful in asking 'why' questions; they might be challenged on grounds of relevance, and even more critically, they can often produce unexpected responses.) You can also use probing questions in an attempt to get more detail out of a witness, or to handle evasion or prevarication by the witness, or simply to get the admission 'I don't remember' or 'I am not really sure', which is well worth having. Loftus and Goodman cite a simple example of how this operates:

---

52. For an example of this kind of cross-examination in action, see P. Rock, *The Social World of an English Crown Court*, Clarendon Press, Oxford, 1993, pp. 104–8.
53. CCB 708(g); LSG 21.08.    54. See Boon, *Advocacy*, pp. 123–4.

Q: ... and ... you rolled down the window of your car ...
A: [It] was rolled down.
Q: ... [it] was a warm evening?
A: Yeah
Q: ...'bout how warm was it? [Do you] remember?
A: No, I don't.
Q: Seventies? Eighties?
A: I don't remember![55]

Arguably, the witness in this situation is caught in a trap by the lawyer's questions about the temperature. If she finally answers, e.g. 'seventies' she risks being seen as inconsistent. But, by continuing to say she does not know she may lose credibility, or be perceived as hedging, especially if such responses become commonplace. Having said that, the extent to which her credibility is, or is not, damaged may well depend on the evidential importance of the issue on which she hedges.[56]

**Confrontation**
Confronting the witness can also work well, if the evidence allows it. This may be done directly by, e.g. confronting the witness with a document which contradicts her evidence, or by a tag question on some aspect of the testimony. In the right context, it hardly matters if your question receives a denial. The point is that the momentum and style of questioning carries its own impression of the 'truth'. Often, confrontation may be achieved by building up to a trap by a process of insinuation, possibly by encouraging the witness to embellish evidence by fabricating some detail which she thinks she should have known. This technique indicates clearly the importance of your thinking about what a witness should or should not know about an event.

Attacking the character of a witness is risky. Attacks on the character of a prosecution witness leave the defence open to the prosecutor adducing evidence of the accused's bad character (if any). Unless character is at issue, or the defence has already lost its 'shield' protecting the character of the accused,[57] attacks on the character of an accused by the prosecutor are a serious breach of procedure and would normally warrant a re-trial. If character is 'fair game', then use it. Cross-examination on character can leave a very powerful impression.

In pursuing these strategies, you need to think carefully about the style of questioning you adopt. As a general guide, you should:[58]

---

55. Loftus and Goodman, 'Questioning Witnesses', at p. 275.    56. See *ibid.*, pp. 275–6.
57. See Criminal Evidence Act 1898, s. 1(f).
58. Many of these points are repeated as folk wisdom in the advocacy manuals: however, there is a certain amount of psychological support as well: see Loftus and Goodman, 'Questioning Witnesses'.

- rely heavily on closed and leading questions;
- prevent the witness from qualifying her answers in a way that limits the impact of your question;[59]
- adopt a fairly fast pace of questioning, which can force the witness into hurrying her evidence;
- never misquote the witness's evidence in chief – this will do your credibility no good;
- listen carefully to the answers you get – be prepared to change your line of questioning, or to ask supplementary questions where necessary;
- resist the temptation to ask one question too many – only television advocates always get to deliver the one question that totally demolishes the witness.

Style of delivery is another factor. As a rule, ask your questions politely and confidently. In certain circumstances, do you think there is any place for lawyers to display anger in a trial? We certainly get used to media images of counsel haranguing a reluctant witness. Is that appropriate behaviour, do you think?

EXERCISE 11.15 **Anger**

*For this exercise, follow your tutor's instructions.*

Generally, haranguing a witness may lose you the support of judge and/or jury, and the court is no place for 'genuine' anger to be displayed by the lawyers involved. This does not mean that some simulated anger cannot be directed at the situation or even a particular witness. As one practitioner explains:

> The amount of acting you do is almost directly proportional to how much is required. A lot of cases are very laid-back and there is no acting involved at all. A fraud case, for example, which is just document after document. Apart from some humour, to keep the thing alive, there is no acting. But if you have police officers who are accused of lying or civilians who are accused of lying or bad conduct, an element of artificial heat is generated by counsel in parts of cross-examination. Not all of it. But those parts that it's important to emphasise or to express the rage of your client's case. But it's simulated rage, or ought to be.[60]

The principle most commonly expressed is, reserve such tactics for those few witnesses who deserve it. If a witness is obviously messing you about, you can go into the attack and still seem a perfectly reasonable character. If you have an aggressive witness, stay calm: the last thing you want is for cross-examination to degenerate into a slanging match.

---

59. This is best achieved by a focused style of questioning, rather than asking the witness, in true movie style, to 'please confine yourself to answering my question', which can come across as discourteous.
60. From Rock, *The Social World of an English Crown Court*, p. 56.

## Summary

ALWAYS START BY ASKING, WHY CROSS-EXAMINE?

*WHEN CROSS-EXAMINING:*

- KEEP IN CONTROL OF THE WITNESS.
- ALWAYS PUT YOUR CASE.
- LOOK FOR POINTS OF AGREEMENT WITH YOUR CASE.
- FOCUS ON THEIR WEAKEST POINT.
- KEEP CALM.
- RESIST THE ONE QUESTION TOO MANY.

EXERCISE 11.16  **Driven to distraction?**[61]

This exercise may be run in pairs or as a demonstration. Each performance requires one lawyer and one witness (Forsythe). The basic facts are as follows, though 'Forsythe' may need to be prepared to invent some explanations for the testimony given in chief:

> James/Jane Forsythe is being prosecuted on a charge of dangerous driving. S/he has given sworn evidence that s/he has been driving for 10 years and has never had a conviction. In fact s/he has held a licence for eight years (s/he is 26 years old) and has had convictions in 1999, 2000 and 2001, all in the Oakleigh Magistrates' Court, for speeding, driving with excess alcohol and driving without due consideration for other road users.

*(a)    Cross-examine Mr/Ms Forsythe.*
*(b)    Feedback as usual.*

## Re-examination

The skills involved in re-examination are not very different from those involved in examining in chief. For that reason we will deal with this phase of the trial very briefly.

The purpose of re-examination is to give the advocate an opportunity to repair damage caused in cross-examination. The basic principle to remember about re-examining is: don't do it unless you have to! At its worst re-examination is merely a damage limitation exercise, and will be seen as such. It can be better not to admt that the damage has been done in the first place!

Evans[62] suggests that re-examination should only be undertaken with at least one of three aims in mind:

---

61. Adapted from Leo Cussen Institute 'Introduction to advocacy' in N. Gold, K. Mackie and W. Twining, *Learning Lawyers' Skills*, Butterworths, London and Edinburgh, 1989, p. 255 at p. 301.
62. *Advocacy at the Bar: A Beginner's Guide*, Blackstone Press, London, 1983, pp. 169–73.

**Clarification and clearing up**

Cross-examination may only have elicited a partial answer. Often it will have got the answer the cross-examiner wants, but not the explanation that you want. Re-examination, therefore, can be used to clarify the standpoint or position of your witness, or to try and clear up any muddled testimony created by the cross-examination.

**Crucifixion**

This term (Evans's, not ours) describes the very rare situation where the re-examining advocate has knowledge of a piece of testimony (arising out of facts already before the court) that did not emerge either in chief or under cross-examination. Now is the chance to deliver it as the *coup de grâce*.

**Taking advantage of the open door**

This is rather more common. It describes the situation where, typically, the cross-examiner has inadvertently raised inadmissible evidence, or evidence of character. This evidence thus becomes available to the opponent to raise at re-examination. If you have substantial evidence of good character on your side, this can sometimes be tantamount to being given the verdict on a plate.

So far as tactics are concerned:

- You should not seek to raise fresh evidence by re-examination.[63]
- You should not lead the witness.
- You should keep it short and to the point.

## Conclusion: advocacy, ethics and adversarialism

In the title of this chapter we suggested that through advocacy we enter the deepest and murkiest area of the legal swamp. We hope that you can now begin to see why we made that suggestion.

At anything above the most basic level, advocacy becomes a highly complex activity, dependent upon your ability to use a matrix of practical skills and technical knowledge. The capacities to think on your feet and to learn quickly from mistakes are central to the art of the advocate.

But advocacy is not just about technical artistry. The courtroom is an important site for both relational and ethical problems. The participatory principles of practice can be difficult to sustain. Clients are easily silenced (as we have seen in this and the previous chapter), often by good intentions, such as the desire to protect their legal interests:[64] perhaps sometimes by the simple desire to win the case. Themes and theories may thus be constructed around the client, rather than

---

63. *Prince v Samo* (1838) 7 Ad. & E 627.
64. Cf. C. Cunningham, 'A Tale of Two Clients' (1989) 87 *Michigan Law Review* 2459.

with her.[65] The adversarialism of the court can also bring into stark relief the ethical problems surrounding 'hired gun' approaches to lawyering.[66] The court is the obvious place for both zealous advocacy, and paradoxically almost, the failure of zeal too.

Either way, the advocate in court wields an immense amount of power; it is power that can be easily abused, especially given the adversary system's insistence on proof, not truth. As the novelist Terry Pratchet observes, 'stories are a parasitical life form, warping lives in the service only of the story itself'.[67] As lawyers we exercise control over how individual lives are 'warped' into the stories we tell in the courtroom. Conventional legal ethics takes only limited cognisance of the damage we can cause in performing this role.

As a defence advocate you must be vigilant that you do not breach your duties to the court, whilst also remaining loyal to your client. As a prosecutor, you must remember that you are not just there to secure a guilty verdict.[68] At the same time, many of the practical pressures that advocates face, particularly in the lower courts, such as insufficient time for adequate preparation, late or missing case papers, institutional pressures to plea-bargain, and the de-personalising experience of 'processing' so many cases,[69] can result in standards of defence, and perhaps prosecution too, that are significantly less than zealous.[70] Moreover, the adversary ethic does not easily admit to the demands of community which are stressed in many of the revisionist versions of ethics currently being debated. It is these dimensions which also serve to create a 'swampy' environment, and one which ultimately you must learn to negotiate by yourselves.

EXERCISE 11.17　**Concepts**

The procedure for learning these concepts is as follows:

1. *Divide into pairs.*
2. *Each pair is to:*

---

65. Cf. L. E. White, 'Goldberg v Kelly on the Paradox of Lawyering for the Poor' (1990) 56 *Brooklyn Law Review* 861.
66. Cf. Chapter 6, above.
67. *Witches Abroad*, Victor Gollancz, London, 1988, cited in Gibbons, *Forensic Linguistics*, p. 129.
68. It has long been argued, with judicial *dicta* in support, that the prosecutor must be a 'minister of justice' rather than a zealous advocate – see, e.g., S. Rogers, 'The Ethics of Advocacy' (1899) 15 *Law Quarterly Review* 259 at p. 261, and both professional written standards and the *Code for Crown Prosecutors* (published by the Crown Prosecution Service) emphasise the importance of prosecuting cases fairly and objectively: see R. Young and A. Sanders, 'The Ethics of Prosecution Lawyers' (2004) *Legal Ethics* 190 at 195–6.
69. See, e.g., M. McConville, J. Hodgson, L. Bridges and A. Pavlovic, *Standing Accused: The Organisation and Practices of Defence Lawyers in Britain*, Clarendon Press, Oxford, 1994.
70. See Chapter 6, above; also D. Nicolson and J. Webb, *Professional Legal Ethics: Critical Interrogations*, Oxford University Press, Oxford, 1999, pp. 178–80, 194–7 and R. O'Dair, *Legal Ethics: Text and Materials*, Butterworths, London, 2001, pp. 188–92 on 'overprotection' and under-representation of client interests.

(a)  *define each concept, noting the page(s) on which it is discussed, and undertaking any additional research that is necessary; then*

(b)  *make sure that you both understand the meaning of each concept.*

3.    *Combine into groups of four. Compare the answers of the two pairs. If there is disagreement, look up the concept and clarify it. Make sure you are all agreed on the definition and understand it.*

| | |
|---|---|
| leading question | bail |
| putting the case | under-representation of clients |
| psychological anchor | primary and secondary realities |
| rhetoric | hostile witness |
| the complication | tag questions |
| transitional questions | verdict definition |

### EXERCISE 11.18  Review questions

1.    *Review your experience of advocacy so far. What aspects do you most need to improve? Identify the steps you will take to make those improvements.*

2.    *In this chapter we have done two things. We have set out to present advocacy as it is in the reality of an adversary system, and we have also offered a number of insights that are consistent with the participatory approach to lawyering that has informed the rest of this book. Do you consider:*

(a)  *that there is a contradiction between the zealous advocacy traditionally implicit in the adversary system and a client-centred approach to lawyering? If so, why; if not, why not?*

(b)  *If there is a contradiction, how might you resolve it?*

## Further reading

A. Boon, *Advocacy*, Cavendish Publishing, London, 2nd edn, 1999.

A. Sherr, *Advocacy*, Blackstone Press, London, 1992.

J. Welsh, *Advocacy in the Magistrates Court*, Cavendish Publishing, London, 2003.

# Index